Advanced Strategies in Financial Risk Management

Robert J. Schwartz

Clifford W. Smith, Jr.

Editors

NEW YORK INSTITUTE OF FINANCE

New York London Toronto Sydney Tokyo Singapore

Library of Congress Cataloging-in-Publication Data

Advanced strategies in financial risk management / Robert J.
Schwartz and Clifford W. Smith, Jr., editors.
    p.   cm.
    Includes bibliographical references and index.
    ISBN 0–13–068883–5
    1. Financial futures. 2. Interest rate futures. 3. Options
(Finance) 4. Swaps (Finance) 5. Hedging (Finance)
I. Schwartz, Robert J. II. Smith, Clifford W.
HG6024.3.A38 1993
332.64'5—dc20   92–47036
                                         CIP

This publication is designed to provide accurate and authoritative information in regard to the subject matter covered. It is sold with the understanding that the publisher is not engaged in rendering legal, accounting, or other professional service. If legal advice or other expert assistance is required, the services of a competent professional person should be sought.

From a Declaration of Principles Jointly Adopted by
a Committee of the American Bar Association
and a Committee of Publishers and Associations

Printed in the United States of America

10 9 8 7 6 5 4 3 2 1

ISBN 0-13-068883-5

NEW YORK INSTITUTE OF FINANCE
Englewood Cliffs, NJ 07632

Simon & Schuster, A Paramount Communications Company

TO OUR CHILDREN:

**MATTHEW, MICHAEL, ALEXANDRA,
ALEXANDER, TAYLOR, AND MORGAN**

CONTENTS

CONTRIBUTORS

Vipul Bansal is Assistant Professor of Finance in the Graduate School of Business at St. John's University, New York. He is an author or coauthor of two books dealing with financial engineering. As a financial engineer, professor Bansal has contributed to the development of both new types of swaps and new uses for swaps. He is serving as a Director of the International Association of Financial Engineers. He holds the M.B.A. and Ph.D. degrees and is a Chartered Financial Analyst (CFA).

Rod A. Beckström is founder and Chief Executive Officer of C•ATS Software, Inc., in Palo Alto, California. Mr. Beckström was previously with Morgan Stanley International in London where he traded interest rate currency swaps during the early and mid 1980's. He has published numerous articles on swaps and international securities markets. A Fulbright scholar, he also received a B.A. in Economics with Honors and Distinction and an M.B.A. from Stanford University.

Tanya Styblo Beder is the President of SB Consulting Corp., which provides derivatives and other specialized consulting services to financial institutions worldwide. Prior to founding SB Consulting in 1987, Ms. Beder was a Vice President of The First Boston Corporation, where she worked over a 10-year period in a variety of areas, including Mergers & Acquisitions, Capital Markets, Derivative Products and Fixed Income Research. Ms. Beder is currently a Management Fellow on the faculty of the Columbia University Business School. Her articles on derivatives have been published in books and professional magazines, including the *Harvard Business Review* and *The Journal of Financial Engineering*. She received a B.S. in Mathematics from Yale University and an M.B.A. from the Harvard Business School.

Richard M. Bookstaber is a principal at Morgan Stanley & Company, a New York-based investment banking firm. His experience at the firm has included research and product development both for clients and for proprietary trading. He is currently responsible for proprietary computer-assisted trading. Mr. Bookstaber is an authority in the field of options; he has written several books and dozens of articles, both academic and professional, on this topic. Prior to joining Morgan Stanley in 1984, he was a professor in the Graduate School of Management at Brigham Young University. He was also a Senior Fulbright Fellow and Visiting Professor at the Hebrew University at Jerusalem. Mr. Bookstaber holds a Ph.D. from the Massachusetts Institute of Technology.

Rupert Brotherton-Ratcliffe is a vice president of research at General Re Financial Products. His responsibilities cover quantitative analysis of fixed income and foreign exchange derivatives, new product development, and also credit risk measurement. He previously worked at Manufacturers Hanover. He has a Ph.D. in mathematics from London University and a B.A. in mathematics from Cambridge University.

John B. Caouette has been CEO of Capital Markets Assurance Corporation, or CapMAC, since its inception in 1987. Prior to his affiliation with CapMAC, Mr. Caouette was a Senior Vice President of Citicorp Insurance Group, Inc. where he developed the strategic plan for Citicorp's financial guarantee insurance business. Previous responsibilities at Citicorp included global management of swaps and Eurosecurities, loan syndication and project finance in the Asia Pacific region, and corporate lending and operations management within the International Division. Mr. Caouette also served as Senior Vice President-General Manager of the Foreign Exchange and Money Market Division of Continental Grain Company.

Donald Chew is Editor-in-Chief of the *Journal of Applied Corporate Finance,* and was a founding partner of Stern Stewart & Co. He has published a number of books, including *The Revolution in Corporate Finance* (Basil Blackwell, 1986, with Joel Stern), and *The New Corporate Finance: Where Theory Meets Practice* (McGraw-Hill, 1992). Mr. Chew holds a Ph.D. in English and an M.B.A. in finance from the University of Rochester.

Ian A. Cooper is Associate Professor of Finance and Baring Brothers Research Fellow at London Business School. He has also taught at the University of Chicago and the Australian Graduate School of Management. He holds an M.A. (Economics) from Cambridge University and an M.B.A. and Ph.D. (Finance) from the University of North Carolina at Chapel Hill.

Georges R. Courtadon is a Vice President in charge of quantitative research for the Equity Derivatives area of Bankers Trust. He was formerly Vice President in charge of quantitative research for the Capital Markets Group of The First National Bank of Chicago. Prior to joining First Chicago, Mr. Courtadon was Vice President in charge of Derivative Products Research at Citibank. He has published several articles on the pricing of options and other derivative products. His research interests include pricing and hedging of interest rate, foreign currency and equity derivative products and their use in rebalancing portfolios. He is a graduate of ESSEC in France and holds a Ph.D. in Finance from Northwestern University.

Paul DeRosa is Managing Director of Eastbridge Capital. He is the head of Eastbridge's money management operation and helped define that division's unique quantitative investment style, which emphasizes mortgage-based securities and stresses risk control. DeRosa is also responsible for Eastbridge's proprietary trading portfolio. Before Eastbridge, he was Senior Vice President at E. F. Hutton in charge of all trading and sales for mortgage-backed securities, fixed-income options, and fixed-income research. He also spent a decade at Citibank, where he ran the bank's global interest rate swap and fixed-income derivative business and authored the bank's interest rate risk management system. Mr. DeRosa received a B.A. from Hobart College and a Ph.D. in Economics from Columbia University.

Jennifer Francis is a member of the accounting faculty at the Graduate School of Business, University of Chicago. She has published several articles on firms' hedging decisions, and the effects accounting rules have on these decisions. Prior to joining the academic ranks, Professor Francis was a certified public accountant with Price Waterhouse. She holds a B.S. degree from Bucknell University, and a Master's degree and a Ph.D in Philosophy (Accounting) from Cornell University.

Dean Furbush is Senior Economist at Economists Incorporated, in Washington, D.C., where he works on securities and derivative market issues for new markets and products, and in support of litigation. Mr. Furbush has served as Economic Advisor to the Chairman of the Commodity Futures Trading Commission, as a research economist at the Securities and Exchange Commission, and has served on the staff of the President's Council of Economic Advisers. He received the Ph.D. and the M.A. in economics from the University of Maryland and the B.A. from the University of Washington.

Don Goldman is Vice President and Manager of Interest Rate Analytics for the New York, Tokyo and London Offices of Bankers Trust. He is responsible for designing models and assessing risk for emerging Derivative Products Markets. His interests include the applications of Stochastic Calculus, Differential Equations, Probability Theory and Numerical Analysis to Financial Structuring, Risk Management and Proprietary Trading. Prior to joining Bankers Trust, Mr. Goldman was President of Sophisticated Software, a firm specializing both in option pricing software for business applications and animation software designed for the emerging home market. Previously, as a member of Mocatta Metals Research

Department, he gained wide experience with exotic options, proprietary trading and risk management technique.

Anthony C. Gooch is a partner in the New York office of Cleary, Gottlieb, Steen & Hamilton. He is a frequent speaker at seminars and has written and co-authored books and articles on loan documentation and documentation for derivative products. He holds J.D. and LL.M. degrees from New York University Law School, where he was Articles Editor of the *Law Review*.

Laurie S. Goodman is a first vice president and fixed income strategist at Merrill Lynch & Co., responsible for assessing cross sector relative value with emphasis on derivatives (futures, options, swaps) and mortgages. Prior to joining Merrill Lynch, Ms. Goodman was a Vice President and Senior Portfolio Manager at Eastbridge Capital, a small quantitatively oriented money management firm. Prior to that she developed and applied financial models for the capital markets trading desks at Goldman Sachs & Co. and Citicorp Investment Bank. Ms. Goodman received a B.A. in Mathematics and a B.S. in Economics from the University of Pennsylvania, and an M.A. and Ph.D. in Economics from Stanford University.

Anthony F. Herbst is Professor of Finance in the University of Texas at El Paso where he holds the Carter Chair in Business Administration and is actively engaged in research, writing and consulting in the areas of futures markets and capital investment management, and in computerized decision support and market forecasting. He has written *Handbook of Capital Investing* (Harper Business, 1990) and *Analyzing and Forecasting Futures Prices* (Wiley, 1992). Mr. Herbst has also held teaching posts in Canada and Saudi Arabia, and is a member of the board of directors of the Foundation for the Study of Cycles. Prior to his academic career he was operations research manager at the National Bank of Detroit. He has a Ph.D. from Purdue University's Krannert Graduate School.

John Hull is currently Professor of Finance in the Faculty of Management at the University of Toronto. He has written widely in the area of derivative securities. Recently his research has focused on the valuation and hedging of interest rate options. He was with Alan White one of the winners of the Nikko-LOR 1989 research competition. He has acted as consultant to many North American financial institutions. He has written two books *Options, Futures, and Other Derivative Securities* and *Introduction to Options and Futures Markets,* both published by Prentice Hall and widely used by practitioners. Dr. Hull is a principal in A-J Financial Systems Inc., a corporation which produces specialized option pricing and risk management software.

Ben Iben is a vice president at General Re Financial Products where he is responsible for risk management and new product development. Formerly he was vice president for swaps and foreign exchange research at Manufacturer's Hanover Trust Company. Prior to that he was a Research Associate at the San Francisco Federal Reserve Bank. He holds a B.A. in economics from the University of California, Berkeley and an M.B.A. from the University of Chicago.

James V. Jordan is Associate Professor of Finance at the Northern Virginia Graduate Center. He is research associate at the Center for Study of Futures and Options Markets (CSFOM). Mr. Jordan has served in government as financial economist, special assistant to a Commissioner, and consultant to the Chairman at the Commodity Futures Trading Commission. Through CSFOM he is active in seminars and study groups bringing together government regulators, market professionals and academicians to examine current issues in financial markets. His business consulting includes projects on the design of new financial instruments and risk management by financial institutions. He holds a Ph.D. from the University of North Carolina, Chapel Hill.

Linda B. Klein is a partner in the New York office of Whitman & Ransom. She is a frequent speaker at seminars and has written and co-authored books and articles on loan documentation and documentation for derivative products. She holds a J.D. degree from Columbia University School of Law, where she was Editor-in-Chief of the *Columbia Journal of Transnational Law*. She holds a Ph.D. degree from Columbia University.

Edward D. Kleinbard is a partner at Cleary, Gottlieb, Steen & Hamilton, resident in the New York office. His practice focuses on federal income tax matters, including specialties in taxation of new financial products, financial instruments and mergers and acquisitions. Mr. Kleinbard received a J.D. degree from Yale Law School, where he was an articles editor of the Law Journal. He received M.A. and B.A. degrees in history and medieval and renaissance studies respectively from Brown University. He is a member of the Bar in New York and is admitted to practice before the United States District Court, Southern District of New York, and the United States Claims Court.

James C. Lam is a senior consultant of First Manhattan Consulting Group and a member of its Risk Management Practice. He specializes in derivative products, credit risk management, treasury and A/L management, line-of-business MIS, and M&A strategy. Prior to joining First Manhattan Consulting Group, Mr. Lam was a Vice President and Director of the Strategic Risk Management Group of Glendale Federal Bank. He has lectured and published extensively on risk management topics, and is a contributing editor of *Bank Asset/Liability Management*. He holds a B.B.A. from

Baruch College and an M.B.A. from UCLA Graduate School of Business.

Robert J. Mackay is Professor of Finance and Director of the Center for Study of Futures and Options Markets at Virginia Tech. He has also taught at the University of California-Berkeley, the University of Maryland, and Tulane University and was a Visiting Scholar at the Hoover Institution at Stanford University. Mr. Mackay has extensive experience in the government, having served most recently as Chief of Staff of the Commodity Futures Trading Commission, during which time he also served as a member of the senior staff of the President's Working Group on Financial Markets. He holds a Ph.D. from University of North Carolina, Chapel Hill.

John F. Marshall is Professor of Finance in the Graduate School of Business at St. John's University. He is also a senior partner with Marshall & Associates, a New York based financial engineering/consulting firm, and Executive Director of the International Association of Financial Engineers. He has authored or coauthored seven books on risk management, derivative products, and financial engineering. He is a frequent contributor to the financial literature and a regular speaker at financial conferences and symposia.

Peter C. McDonald is a Client Services Executive with C•ATS Software Inc. in California. Previously he was Chief Dealer, Swaps with Australia & New Zealand Banking Group (ANZ) in Melbourne, Australia. He was a Visiting Fellow at Macquarie University in Sydney, Australia where he lectured on Swaps & OTC Debt Options. In London with ANZ Merchant Bank he was a dealer in equity derivatives. Mr. McDonald holds a B.Sc. (Honors) from Monash University, Australia and an M.B.A. from Melbourne University.

Joanne T. Medero was appointed General Counsel of the Commodity Futures Trading Commission in March 1989. Previously she had been Associate Director for Legal and Financial Affairs in the Office of Presidential Personnel. Prior to joining The White House staff in 1986, Mrs. Medero was a partner in private law practice specializing in corporate, banking, and securities law. Mrs. Medero was graduated from St. Lawrence University, *magna cum laude* in 1975, where she was elected to Phi Beta Kappa. She received her J.D., with honors, in 1978 from the National Law Center of George Washington University.

Antonio S. Mello is at the Research and Statistics Department of the Central Bank of Portugal. Prior to this he has been an Assistant Professor of Finance at MIT. He holds a Ph.D. from University of London and both a M.A. (Economics) and M.B.A. from Columbia University. His research interests are in Corporate Finance and Capital Markets.

James C. F. MeVay is a Managing Director of Chase Securities, Inc. in New York where he heads the corporate Derivatives Origination and Structuring Group. Prior to joining Chase, he held a variety of domestic and international treasury positions at General Foods Corp. Mr. MeVay holds a B.A. from Transylvania University and an M.B.A. from the University of Connecticut.

Phoebe A. Mix is currently Of Counsel at Coffield Ungaretti & Harris. Ms. Mix specializes in the taxation of financial products including futures, forwards, options, notional principal contracts and other derivative products, and hybrid and derivative financial products and their use in hedging transactions. She is co-founder of the Financial Innovation Study Committee, an interdisciplinary forum for leading lawyers, economists, accountants, regulators and market participants to discuss issues relating to new financial products. She received her A.B. degree from Bryn Mawr College and a J.D. (cum laude) from Vermont Law School.

Eugene Moriarty is president of Evergreen Financial Management, Inc., Arlington, VA and is an Associate of the Futures Industry Institute. Previously, he was Director of Research, Division of Economic Analysis, Commodity Futures Trading Commission. He holds a B.S. in mathematics from St. John's University and an M.B.A. in finance and investment management from New York University.

Ronald D. Reading is a Managing Vice President of First Manhattan Consulting Group and co-head of its Financial Risk Management Practice, serving clients in the areas of credit, market and capital risk management. Prior to joining First Manhattan Consulting Group in 1988, Mr. Reading was a Senior Vice President at the Chase Manhattan Bank, where, over a 15 year period, he managed a variety of financial markets businesses including Foreign Exchange and Securities Trading in London and Worldwide Funding in New York. Mr. Reading has an M.B.A. from the Stanford Graduate School of Business and a B.S. from Harvey Mudd College.

Thomas A. Russo was a partner with the law firm Cadwalader, Wickersham & Taft from 1977–1992 specializing in U.S. securities and commodities law. He served on the staff of the Securities and Exchange Commission and was the first Director of the Commodities Futures Trading Commission's Division of Trading and Markets. Mr. Russo received his M.B.A. and J.D. degrees from Cornell University. As of January 1, 1993, Mr. Russo became a Managing Director and member of the Operating Committee at Lehman Brothers.

Michael S. Sackheim is Counsel to the international law firm of Brown & Wood and is a member of the Bar in New York. He concentrates in the regulation of derivative financial products and related litigation. Mr. Sackheim has written numerous articles on commodities regulation and is a member of the Board of Editors of *Futures International Law Letter*. He holds a B.A. from Queens College, an M.A. from the New School for Social Research, a J.D. from Brooklyn Law School and an LL.M. from New York University School of Law.

Richard L. Sandor is Executive Managing Director of Derivative Products and New Ventures with Kidder, Peabody & Co., Incorporated. He was formerly President and Chief Executive Officer of Indosuez International Capital Markets Corporation and Chairman of Indosuez Carr Futures. Previously, he held positions with Drexel Burnham Lambert and the Chicago Board of Trade, and faculty positions at the University of California, Berkeley, Stanford University and Northwestern University. In 1991 Mr. Sandor was elected as a Nonresident Director of the Chicago Board of Trade where he is chairperson of the Clean Air Committee developing the first spot and futures markets in environmental contracts. He received his Bachelor of Arts degree from City University of New York and his Ph.D. in Economics from the University of Minnesota.

Matt Singleton is the partner in charge of Arthur Andersen's Audit and Business Advisory practice in New York and serves on his firm's Chairman's Advisory Council. Previously, he had responsibility for the New York Financial Services audit practice. In addition to his management responsibilities, he continues to spend a significant portion of his time consulting with bankers and investment bankers on the accounting implications of their activities, both in the U.S. and abroad. Mr. Singleton also leads the Arthur Andersen team that serves as technical advisor to the International Swap Dealers Association on swaps and other derivative products. Between 1981 and 1983, Mr. Singleton served as a Practice Fellow at the Financial Accounting Standards Board. He attended Princeton University (A.B.-Economics) and New York University (M.B.A.).

Charles W. Smithson is a Managing Director in the Global Risk Management sector of the Chase Manhattan Bank. In addition to articles in academic journals, he is the co-author of a well-known economics textbook, *Managerial Economics* (with S. C. Maurice), an economic perspective on commodity "crises," *The Doomsday Myth* (with S. C. Maurice), and a description of the emerging financial risk management market, *Managing Financial Risk* (with C. W. Smith and D. S. Wilford). With C. W. Smith, he edited the *Handbook of Financial Engineering*.

Jens A. Stephan is an Assistant Professor of Accounting at the University of Cincinnati. He earned a Ph.D. from Cornell University in 1985.

Professor Stephan teaches financial accounting and financial statement analysis to M.B.A. students. His research interests are in the area of accounting information and stock prices and he has several publications in journals such as the *Accounting Review*, the *Journal of Accounting Research*, and the *Journal of Finance*.

Alan L. Tucker is Assistant Professor of Finance in the College of Business of Temple University. He has authored dozens of articles and two books, and is also an Associate of Marshall & Associates.

Stuart M. Turnbull is the Bank of Montreal Professor of Banking and Finance, Queen's University, Canada. He is author of *Option Valuation*, and has published many academic articles on options and risk management. He has recently published papers on pricing interest rate options, interest rate risk management, the pricing of credit options, and hedging long-term foreign currency options. He is an associate editor of *Mathematical Finance* and has been an associate editor of the *Journal of Finance*. He has been a consultant to many financial institutions in America, Australia, Canada, and Britain. Mr. Turnbull holds a B.Sc. in Physics, and a M.Sc. in statistics from Imperial College (London), and a Ph.D. in Financial Economics from University of British Columbia.

Marlisa Vinciguerra was an associate at Cadwalader, Wickersham & Taft, New York from 1989–1992. B.S. 1986, Cornell University; J.D. 1989, Yale Law School. As of January 1, 1993, Ms. Vinciguerra became a Vice President and Counsel to Lehman Brothers.

Lee M. Wakeman is currently president of Risk Analysis and Control, Inc. Previously he was Managing Director and Head of Risk Management at Sakura Global Capital, Inc., New York. He started Chemical Bank's Interest Rate Options Desk, and headed the bond research and risk evaluation units at Citicorp London. He earned a B.A. from Cambridge University and a Ph.D. in Finance and Economics from MIT.

Michael J. Walsh is Advisory Economist for the Chicago Board of Trade where he currently works on development of new environmental and energy markets. Prior to joining the Chicago Board of Trade, he was a Financial Economist in the Office of Tax Policy in the U.S. Department of the Treasury, and taught Economics in the College of Business at the University of Notre Dame. Mr. Walsh received his M.S. and Ph.D. in Economics from Michigan State University, and his Bachelors Degree in Economics and Political Science from Illinois State University.

Alan White is currently Associate Professor of Finance in the Faculty of Management at the University of Toronto. He has been involved with the financial community for the last 7 years. His research is principally in the area of derivative securities: their pricing and their use by financial institutions for risk management. Prior to joining the University of Toronto he taught at York University and at the University of New Brunswick. Earlier in his career he worked as a research engineer at Canadian Marconi Ltd. Mr. White is also a principal in A-J Financial Systems Inc., a corporation which produces specialized option pricing and risk management software.

INTRODUCTION

In the years since the publication of our first volume, *The Handbook of Currency and Interest Rate Risk Management,* markets have been volatile. For example, over this three-year period, U.S. interest rates have fallen by several hundred basis points; during the Middle East crisis in 1990–91, oil markets experienced very large price moves (implied volatilities at times exceeded 100 percent); approaching the French vote on the Maastricht Treaty in 1992, currency markets fluctuated widely. In response to this sustained volatility, financial markets have responded with continuing advances in the development of new risk management instruments. Sophisticated risk management techniques employing the new instruments are being widely adopted. These developments are the result of a productive interaction between the Wall Street and academic communities. In the *Handbook* we sought to provide a broad practical and theoretical foundation for the currency and derivative markets. In this volume we bring together contributions from leaders in this continuing development. Since the central focus on this book is current practice, the contributors have extensive experience in these markets.

The papers in Part One analyze interest rate risk, offering models of interest rates and developing their implications for valuing derivatives. Courtadon provides an overview and a survey of bond option pricing models. Goldman analyzes the implications of mean reversion in interest rates and how such a process might be tractably modeled. Hull and White's first paper discusses criteria for choosing among interest rate models; their second discusses the pricing of options on caps and floors.

In Part Two, the papers focus on foreign exchange rate markets. Turnbull and Wakeman provide an algorithm for pricing options on the average foreign exchange rate over a period. MeVay discusses currency derivatives for investors.

The papers in Part Three discuss innovative applications of risk management techniques. Goodman discusses the use of swaps in managing corporate liabilities. Chew and Smithson analyze hybrid investments as packages of financially engineered cash flows and their uses in managing corporate risk exposures. Smith discusses risk management implications for banks. Bookstaber discusses sophisticated option replication, going beyond simple delta hedging techniques. DeRosa and Goodman examine techniques for managing a LIBOR Plus Fund.

In Part Four the papers discuss innovative applications of financial engineering to new products. Sandor and Walsh examine the new futures market in pollution rights. Marshall, Bansal, Herbst, and Tucker focus on how instruments might be structured to hedge business cycle risk. Tanya Styblo Beder examines equity derivatives for investors. Finally, Brotherton-Ratcliffe and Iben analyze yield curve application of swaps.

The papers in Part Five examine systems and credit issues. Beckström and McDonald suggest a set of techniques to graph facets of derivatives so that their risks can be visualized more easily. Cooper and Mello analyze the default risk of swaps.

The remainder of the book focuses on important institutional considerations. In Part Six, the Kleinbard and Mackay and Mix papers examine the tax treatment of derivatives. The focus on Part Seven is legal and regulatory issues. Gooch and Klein review case law affecting derivatives. Russo and Vinciguerra discuss the impact of regulation, and especially regulatory uncertainty, on the development of new financial products. Furbush and Sackheim examine the evolving legal standards for hybrids. The Medero and Jordan, Mackay and Moriarity papers discuss the regulation of new hybrid securities. Reading and Lam discuss the impact of the new risk based capital rules. Part Eight is devoted to accounting issues. Singleton reviews hedge accounting rules. Francis analyzes the impact on earnings of the rules for accounting for futures. Finally, Francis and Stephan examine the hedging practices of firms. The book ends with a glossary by Tanya Styblo Beder, Schwartz and Smith to help the reader keep up with the ever expanding list of terms employed in risk management.

Robert J. Schwartz
Clifford W. Smith, Jr.

Part One

INTEREST RATES

A SURVEY OF BOND OPTION PRICING MODELS

Georges Courtadon

1

1. Introduction

The area of debt option pricing has received academic and professional interest. However, the complexity of the subject is such that a commonly agreed upon pricing methodology does not yet exist. Many authors have proposed approaches which have been used to price interest rate options, starting with Merton (1973), Black (1976), Vasicek (1977), Brennan and Schwartz (1982), Courtadon (1982), Ball and Torous (1983), Cox, Ingersoll, and Ross (1985) and, more recently, in the papers written by Ho and Lee (1986), Schaefer and Schwartz (1987), Black, Derman, and Toy (1990), Heath, Jarrow, and Morton (1988), Jamshidian (1989) and Hull and White (1990). These models belong to two broad categories of pricing methodologies. The first category attempts to model the option on an interest bearing security as an option on a stock by assuming that the underlying source of risk is the price of the underlying security, while the second category prices interest rate options on fixed income securities, and the securities themselves, as functions of the term structure of interest rates. A minor distinction should be made across the papers belonging to the second category. The first group of papers, including Vasicek, Brennan and Schwartz, and Courtadon, does not explicitly propose a methodology to ensure that the model prices the underlying securities consistently with their observed market prices. The second group, on the other hand, including the papers of Cox, Ingersoll, and Ross, Jamshidian, Hull, and White, Black, Derman, and Toy, Ho, and Lee, and Heath, Jarrow, and Morton, explicitly proposes solutions to this consistency issue.

The purpose of this paper is to present an introduction to these debt option pricing methodologies. The best way to introduce the debt option pricing literature is to start with the first category of models, which attempts to extend the stock option pricing literature to debt option pricing. The obvious shortcomings of this methodology will help the reader understand the reasons which have pushed most debt option pricing theorists to incorporate the modeling of the term structure of interest rates in the pricing of debt options.

The organization of this paper is as follows. Section 2 of this paper presents the modifications which are currently made to the standard stock option pricing model to make it applicable to the pricing of debt options. We conclude section 2 by presenting the shortcomings of this approach. Section 3 reviews the category of option pricing models which are based on a modeling of the term structure of interest rates. In section 4, we compare the pricing of several of these models for European and American options. The conclusion is presented in section 5.

2. Price Based Approaches to Debt Option Pricing

The extent to which stock option pricing models are applicable to bond option valuation depends on how realistic the assumptions made by these models are when they are applied to bonds and bond options rather than stocks and stock options. The first part of this section will therefore point out the differences between the assumptions which should underlie a reasonable bond option pricing model and those which underlie the model proposed by Black and Scholes. We will then examine how these differences can be incorporated into the standard stock option valuation model. Finally, we will point out the differences which cannot be resolved by modifying the standard stock option pricing methodology.

There are four main differences which must be addressed when applying the Black–Scholes pricing methodology to bond option pricing. These differences are:

a) The underlying bond usually pays a coupon.

b) The underlying bond ages because of the fact that it has a stated maturity.

c) It is inconsistent to assume a constant financing rate (or cost of carry) and stochastic bond prices (or, equivalently, yields).

d) The bond option may be American.

It is not difficult to understand why the coupon payment made on the bond has a significant effect on the value of a bond option. The effect is similar to the effect of a dividend on the value of a stock option. A greater coupon rate will decrease the value of a call option and increase the value of a put option.

The aging problem is also quite simple to grasp once one understands that assuming that the price of the underlying security follows a lognormal process implies that the distribution of the instantaneous rate of return remains the same through time. This assumption may be reasonable in the case of a stock but is certainly not appropriate in the case of a bond which has a known and finite maturity. The aging process of the bond implies that the instantaneous rate of return on the bond is distributed with a variance which decreases through time, since ultimately the bond price must converge to par at maturity. The aging of the bond will clearly be a very important factor in the valuation of a bond option when the option has a long maturity and when the maturity of the underlying bond is short.

Concerning the applicability of the constant financing rate assumption to the pricing of bond options, it is important to note that uncertainty about the behavior of the rate of interest through time is the cause of stochastic bond prices. Applying the Black–Scholes model to the pricing of a bond option is equivalent to assuming that the behavior of the rate of interest is known for the life of the option. This is equivalent to assuming that the price of any default free bond which has a maturity shorter than the maturity of the option is constant. This assumption is not unrealistic when the maturity of the option is short relative to the maturity of the underlying bond. However, it becomes quickly untenable as the maturity of the option increases for a given maturity of the underlying bond.

Finally, the fact that a bond option is an American option is significant when there is a significant probability that the option will be exercised before its expiration date. This will be the case if the option is a call option and the underlying bond pays a coupon, or if the option is an in-the-money put option in an environment where rates are expected to decrease, i.e., in an environment where the term structure of interest rates is decreasing. Finally, the importance of early exercise is increased by the aging of the underlying bond as the maturity of the option increases.

In the remainder of this section, we present the modifications which can be made to the standard stock option pricing model to resolve these differences. It will become apparent from the analysis that the most difficult difference to resolve is to account for the early exercise privilege of an American bond option.

In the case of a European option, the simplest way to solve the differences that we have mentioned is to value the option with respect to the forward price of the bond for delivery on the option maturity date. Suppose that F is the forward price of this bond on that date and that v represents the volatility of the forward price, the value of the call option is given by the formula derived by Black (1976):

$$U(F,t) = \left[FN(d_1) - EN\left(d_1 - v\sqrt{T-t}\right) \right] P \tag{1}$$

$$\text{where} \quad d_1 = \frac{\ln\frac{F}{E} + .5v^2(T-t)}{v\sqrt{T-t}},$$

where P is the value of a zero coupon security paying one on the option maturity date and where E, T, and t are, respectively, the exercise price, the maturity date, and the pricing date of the option. The value of the otherwise equivalent put option, $W(F,t)$, can be easily computed from the call option value by using the put-call parity relationship with respect to the forward price:

$$W(F,t) = U(F,t) + (E-F)P \tag{2}$$

This approach will clearly account for the fact that the bond pays a coupon stream during the life of the option which is not captured by the exercise of a European call option or will not be delivered through the exercise of a European put option. The forward price is indeed the correct underlying source of risk since it only represents the value of the payments to be made on the bond after the maturity date of the option.

Valuing the option with respect to the forward price of the bond is also a solution to the aging of the bond. For example, a one-year European option on a three-year bond can be viewed as a one-year option on a one-year forward contract to buy this bond. This forward commitment will never age since its value will depend on the value on the option maturity date of two years of remaining interest payments and principal repayment. Other methods have been proposed to account for the aging of the bond and its convergence to par. Ball and Torous (1983) derive a model to value an option on a zero coupon bond which incorporates the aging of the bond by assuming that the stochastic component of the instantaneous rate of return on the bond follows a process similar to a Brownian bridge process. This process modifies the drift of the logarithm of the bond price to account for the convergence of the bond price to par but assumes a constant variance for the instantaneous rate of return on the bond. Therefore, this model is not a realistic representation of the aging process, since the aging of the bond will affect the instantaneous variance of the rate of return process.[1] Schaefer and Schwartz (1987) present an

---

[1] It is interesting to note that their formula is exactly the same as Merton (1973) with stochastic interest rates. This is due to the fact that both models assume exactly the same behavior for the stochastic component of the instantaneous rate of return on the bond and that both models use an approach based on continuous arbitrage where the drift of the bond price, the instantaneous expected rate of return on the bond, does not affect the option value since it is hedged continuously.

approach which is more realistic to the extent that they make the instantaneous variance a function of the duration of the underlying bond. Their method is more costly, however, since it requires the use of numerical methods.

The issue of a stochastic short rate of interest is also addressed by using the forward price of the bond as the underlying source of risk. This can be verified by comparing the model given by equation (1) with the model derived by Merton (1973). Merton derives a model analogous to Black and Scholes for a stochastic financing rate by assuming that the price P, of the zero coupon security maturing at the same time as the option follows a geometric Wiener process. This model gives option values identical to those given in equation (1) and (2) if we express the volatility of the forward price in terms of the volatility of the price of the underlying bond tail, the volatility of the zero coupon bond price and the correlation coefficient between unanticipated changes in these two prices. The bond tail is defined as the stream of cashflows to be received on the bond after the option maturity date. If σ represents the volatility of the underlying bond tail value β, the volatility of the price of the zero coupon bond and ρ the correlation coefficient, we have:

$$v = \sqrt{\sigma^2 + \beta^2 - 2\rho\sigma\beta}.$$

It is worth noting that Merton's result is consistent with a model of the term structure of interest rates only for options on zero coupon bonds.[2] This is due to the fact that the price of a coupon paying bond cannot be lognormal if the prices of zero coupon bonds are lognormally distributed.

Up to this point in our analysis, we have shown how European options on bonds can be valued within a price based option pricing model. In the remainder of this section, we will find that it is not possible to follow the same approach for American options. American options differ from European options in that the holder of the option has the right to exercise not only at maturity but at any time before maturity. We must therefore solve simultaneously for the value of the option and the optimal early exercise boundary. In the stock option pricing literature, the optimal early exercise boundary is a function of the time to maturity of the option and gives, for a given time to maturity, the value of the stock at which it becomes optimal to exercise the option early. In the case of a call option, the holder of the option will exercise prematurely for any stock price above the price given by the boundary. Put options will be exercised

---

[2] The implicit term structure model is a model where the short rate is normally distributed. This model may be unrealistic since it assumes that the short rate can take negative values.

prematurely for any stock price below the price given by the boundary.

In some instances, the valuation of an American option collapses to the valuation of a European option if it can be shown that it will never be optimal to exercise the option early. This is the case for call options on nondividend paying stocks as shown by Merton (1973). However, in most cases the early exercise privilege of the American option is valuable and a valuation model different from the European option valuation model must be used. Several such models have been derived in the stock option pricing literature. The most important models among them are those derived by Brennan and Schwartz (1977a), Parkinson (1977), Roll (1977), Schwartz (1977), Geske (1979), Geske and Johnson (1984), Cox, Ross, and Rubinstein (1979), Whaley (1981), and Cox and Rubinstein (1985). All of these models solve the basic valuation model with an additional boundary condition to account for the possibility of early exercise. Most of these models account for dividend payments on the underlying stock.

A straight application of these models to bond option pricing implies that the option must be valued with respect to the spot price of the bond since the American option is directly exercisable against the bond itself. Because of this, the aging of the bond as well as the issue of a stochastic financing rate become the critical issues which must be addressed. Schaefer and Schwartz (1987) propose a methodology which incorporates the aging of the bond into the model by assuming that the volatility parameter is a function of the bond duration. Their methodology, however, does not address the issue of a stochastic financing rate. In fact, they have to assume that the financing rate is constant to apply the standard American stock option pricing methodology. This assumption is clearly unrealistic and will have an effect on the value of early exercise, by artificially keeping the cost of carry at a high level when bond prices go up and at a low level when bond prices decrease. In other words, it will not give an accurate picture of what is happening to the future expected prices of the bond, its forward prices, as the spot price evolves through time.

Therefore, if we want to preserve a price based approach to the valuation of American bond options, we need to introduce additional sources of price risk in addition to spot price risk. For example, a three-year American option on a ten-year bond depends on a continuum of forward bond prices from the price of a one day forward contract to the price of a two year forward contract. The exercise decision after one year will not only depend on the value of the bond at that time but also on the forward prices of the bond for delivery between one year from now and three years from now. We can no longer assume, as in the case of the European option, that the option can be valued as a function of the forward price of the bond for delivery on the option maturity date. The only way to take all these possible forward prices into account in the pricing of debt options is to abandon the price based approach and to find a new methodology. This new methodology is based on finding a common denominator which explains the pricing of this continuum of forward prices. This common denominator is the term structure of interest rates.

The models, which we present in the next section of this paper, derive the value of the bond option as a function of a few state variables which represent the behavior of the term structure of interest rates.

3. Bond Option Pricing Models Based on a Modeling of the Term Structure of Interest Rates

These models can be classified in two groups. The first group prices the option and the underlying bond as functions of the term structure of interest rates, and do not explicitly show how to make the models consistent with the observed market prices of zero coupon bonds. The second group prices the option as a function of the term structure of interest rates and restricts its behavior to ensure that the observed market prices of zero coupon bonds are respected by the model. Models belonging to the second group are often referred to as arbitrage free models since they price interest rate options consistently with the observed market prices of fixed income securities. We will see below that this qualifier can also be applied to the models of the first group, once a methodology is implemented to force these models to respect the observed zero coupon yield curve.

The models which belong to the first group can be differentiated by the number of state variables used to describe the evolution of the term structure of interest rates over time. Brennan and Schwartz (1977b), Vasicek (1977), Dothan (1978) and Courtadon (1982) have derived pricing models for default free bonds or options on default free bonds which depend on one state variable, the short term rate of interest. In the one state variable model, the entire term structure of interest rates is known once the short rate is known. Several authors found that this approach tends to oversimplify the real behavior of the curve through time. Consequently, several authors have derived other models of the curve which depend on more than the short-term rate of interest. These authors include Brennan and Schwartz (1979), (1982) and Schaefer and Schwartz (1984), who have used a two state variable model to value default free securities as well as Brennan and Schwartz (1983) and Dietrich-Campbell and Schwartz (1986), who have used this approach to value options on default free bonds. Finally, the arbitrage free debt option pricing literature which constitutes the second group of models based on the modeling of the term structure of interest rates is more recent and includes papers by Cox, Ingersoll, and Ross (1985), Ho and Lee (1986),

Heath, Jarrow, and Morton (1988), Jamshidian (1989), Black, Derman, and Toy (1990) and Hull and White (1990).[3]

3.1 Models Based on One State Variable

These models assume that the term structure of interest rates can be derived from the behavior of the instantaneous rate of interest r, also referred to as the short rate, and from a set of assumptions regarding investors' aversion to risk on the default free bond markets. Though different stochastic processes have been used to represent the short rate, most of these processes are of the form:

$$dr = \mu(r,t)\,dt + \sigma r^a dz \tag{3}$$

where dz is a Brownian motion. The case where a is equal to 0 and $\mu(r,t)$ is equal to c, a constant, has been proposed by Merton (1973) and lately by Ho and Lee (1986), Heath, Jarrow, and Morton (1988) and Jamshidian (1989). The case where a is equal to zero and $\mu(r,t)$ is of the form $K(c-r)$ has been proposed by Vasicek (1977). The case where a is equal to one half and $\mu(r,t)$ is of the form $K(c-r)$ has been proposed by Cox, Ingersoll, and Ross (1985). These last two cases are often referred to as mean reverting processes since the non-random component of the change in the short rate, $K(c-r)\,dt$, always tends to bring the short rate back to its long run level c. Finally, the case where a is equal to one and $\mu(r,t)$ is equal to cr, where c is a constant, has been investigated by Black, Derman, and Toy (1990).[4]

In these models the value of any bond or any bond option is a function of the short rate and of time. Suppose that $U(r,t)$ represents the value of the bond option, then we know from Ito's lemma that:

$$dU = \left[\frac{\partial U}{\partial t} + \frac{1}{2}\sigma^2 r^{2a}\frac{\partial^2 U}{\partial r^2} + \mu(r,t)\frac{\partial U}{\partial r} \right]dt + \sigma r^a \frac{\partial U}{\partial r}dz \tag{4}$$

$$= \mu_u U dt + \sigma r^a \frac{\partial U}{\partial r}dz$$

---

[3] The papers by Cox, Ingersoll, and Ross, Jamshidian, and Hull and White are particularly interesting since they propose closed form solutions for zero coupon bonds as well as European options on zero coupon securities. These formulas can be easily extended to coupon bonds and options on coupon bonds.

[4] Black, Derman, and Toy also assume that the volatility of the short rate can be a function of time. This assumption has been made by other authors. For simplicity's sake, we have not allowed the volatility to be a function of time in this paper.

The value of the underlying bond at time t will be known if we can compute the value at time t of a zero coupon bond, $P(r,t;s)$, which pays \$1 at any time s in the future since any coupon paying bond is simply the sum of several zero coupon bonds. $P(r,t;s)$ will be such that:

$$dP = \left[\frac{\partial U}{\partial r} + \frac{1}{2}\sigma^2 r^{2a}\frac{\partial^2 P}{\partial r^2} + \mu(r,t)\frac{\partial P}{\partial r}\right]dt + \sigma r^a \frac{\partial P}{\partial r}dz \qquad (5)$$
$$= \mu_p P dt + \sigma r^a \frac{\partial P}{\partial r}dz$$

Given equations (4) and (5), it is clear that it is possible to create a portfolio which is insensitive to any unanticipated change in the rate of interest by buying the option and by selling against it $\frac{\partial U}{\partial r} / \frac{\partial P}{\partial r}$ of the zero coupon bond. Given that this portfolio is instantaneously riskless, this portfolio must earn the short rate r over the next instant of time, therefore:

$$\mu_u U - \left(\frac{\partial U}{\partial r} / \frac{\partial P}{\partial r}\right)\mu_p P = \left[U - \left(\frac{\partial U}{\partial r} / \frac{\partial P}{\partial r}\right)P\right]r \qquad (6)$$

Equation (6) implies that:

$$\frac{\mu_u - r}{\dfrac{1}{U}\dfrac{\partial U}{\partial r}} = \frac{\mu_p - r}{\dfrac{1}{P}\dfrac{\partial P}{\partial r}} = \lambda(r,t)^5 \qquad (7)$$

The quantity $\lambda(r,t)/\sigma r^a$ represents the market price of risk on the default free bond market at time t given that the short rate is r. If we substitute into equation (7) the values of the expected rate of return on the option and the expected rate of return on the bond given by equations (4) and (5), we obtain the following valuation equations for $U(r,t)$ and $P(r,t)$:

$$\frac{1}{2}\sigma^2 r^{2a}\frac{\partial^2 U}{\partial r^2} + \left[\mu(r,t) - \lambda(r,t)\right]\frac{\partial U}{\partial r} - rU + \frac{\partial U}{\partial t} = 0 \qquad (8)$$

$$\frac{1}{2}\sigma^2 r^{2a}\frac{\partial^2 P}{\partial r^2} + \left[\mu(r,t) - \lambda(r,t)\right]\frac{\partial P}{\partial r} - rP + \frac{\partial P}{\partial t} = 0 \qquad (9)$$

---

[5] This quantity cannot be a function of the maturity date of the discount bond or of the option since the equality must hold for all bonds and all options of any maturity.

If the maturity date of the option is time T, equation (8) must be solved subject to the following boundary condition:

$$U(r,T) = \text{Max}\left[0, B(r,T) - E\right] \tag{8a}$$

where $B(r,T)$ is the value of the underlying bond at time T and E is the exercise price of the option. If, in addition, the option is an American option, an additional boundary condition must be added to the valuation problem:

$$U(r,y) = \text{Max}\left[U^*(r,y), B(r,y) - E\right] \tag{8b}$$

where $t \leq y \leq T$ and $U^*(r,y)$ is the value of the option if kept alive at time y. As far as the value of the zero coupon bond is concerned, for any time s with $t < s$, the value of the bond will be solved for by solving equation (9) subject to the following boundary condition:

$$P(r,s) = 1 \tag{9a}$$

If these two systems of equations do not have a closed form solution, the value of the bond and the value of the option must be solved for by a numerical method. The valuation problem for a put option will be similar to the valuation problem for a call option except that boundary conditions (8a) and (8b) will now account for the fact that the option is a put option.

3.2 Models Based on Two State Variables

Instead of using one state variable to represent the behavior of the term structure of interest rates over time, these models use two state variables. Most models, for example Brennan and Schwartz (1979), (1982), (1983), use as underlying state variables the short rate of interest r, and the yield of a consol, or long rate y.[6] We will assume in this paper that the two rates follow the following diffusion processes:

$$dr = K(c-r)\,dt + \sigma r\,dz \tag{10}$$

$$dy = \alpha y\,dt + \beta y\,dz^* \tag{11}$$

---

[6] This is not always the case. Schaefer and Schwartz (1984) use the short rate and the difference between the yield on a consol and the short rate. They are able to derive an approximate analytical solution for the value of a discount bond.

where dz and dz^* are two Brownian motions such that $(dz)\,(dz^*) = \rho dt$. The coefficient ρ is the correlation coefficient between unanticipated changes in the short rate and unanticipated changes in the long rate.

It is clear that this approach to modeling the term structure is more realistic than the previous one since it gives more degrees of freedom to represent the behavior of the term structure of interest rates over time. However, the cost of this added realism is a greater computational burden in terms of solving the valuation model for the value of the option. The principle behind the derivation model is similar to the principle used to derive valuation equations (8) and (9). The idea is that the expected instantaneous rate of return on a portfolio should be equal to the short rate if over the next interval of time this portfolio is immunized against an unanticipated change in the short rate and an unanticipated change in the long rate. This portfolio will have to take positions in two bonds in addition to the option since there are two sources of risk to immunize against. As in the one state variable case, the valuation equation will be derived from the restriction put on the instantaneous expected rate of return on the option by this no arbitrage opportunity condition. The derivation of the valuation equation for the value of the option $U(r,y,t)$ is derived in detail in Brennan and Schwartz (1982). We simply state it in this paper:

$$\frac{1}{2}\sigma^2 r^2 \frac{\partial^2 U}{\partial r^2} + \frac{1}{2}\beta^2 y^2 \frac{\partial^2 U}{\partial y^2} + \rho\sigma r\beta y \frac{\partial^2 U}{\partial r\partial y} + \left[K(c-r) - \lambda(r,y,t)\right]\frac{\partial U}{\partial r} \qquad (12)$$

$$+\left(\beta^2 + y - r\right)y\frac{\partial U}{\partial y} - rU + \frac{\partial U}{\partial t} = 0$$

where λ is defined as in section 3.1. This equation must be solved subject to the following boundary condition:

$$U(r,y,T) = \text{Max}\left(0, B(r,y,T) - E\right) \qquad (12a)$$

where B and E are defined as in section 3.1. If the option is an American option, we must add to the valuation problem the following boundary condition:

$$U(r,y,s) = \text{Max}\left[U^*(r,y,s), B(r,y,s) - E\right] \qquad (12b)$$

for $t \le s \le T$ and where U^* is defined as in section 3.1.

This valuation problem cannot be solved analytically and one must use a numerical solution technique.

3.3 Strengths and Shortcomings of These Models

The strength of these models is the fact that the value of the option and the value of the underlying bond are determined in a consistent manner from a set of assumptions governing the term structure of interest rates. Therefore, if these assumptions are sufficiently realistic, these models should be able to determine accurately the value of the early exercise privilege of the American bond option.

Unfortunately, the answer is not quite this straightforward. As shown in equations (8), (9), and (12), the valuation equation depends on a crucial unknown function: the market price of risk. More importantly, as pointed out by Cox, Ingersoll, and Ross (1985), assuming a specific functional form for the market price of risk can lead to internal inconsistencies in the model. A sufficient condition to maintain internal consistency and to prevent arbitrage opportunities with respect to today's spot or forward curve is to assume that the function $\lambda(r,t)$ is a function of time $\lambda(t)$, and estimate it piecemeal by sequentially matching the price of zero coupon securities of increasing maturities through standard backward induction. This estimation procedure is cumbersome and requires a fair amount of computer time even for one state variable models. Recently, Jamshidian (1991) has shown that this procedure can be greatly simplified by deriving the market price of risk through forward induction along a binomial lattice. This methodology can also be implemented on more complex lattices for models of the curve involving two state variables. However, the time required to derive the market price of risk still remains prohibitive for models of the curve with two state variables.

Several authors have therefore proposed models where the market price of risk can be easily estimated. These models have often been referred to as arbitrage free models. Most of these models are one state variable models. The solution technique is either numerical or closed form, or a mix of the two. Black, Derman, and Toy (1990) assume a lognormally distributed short rate without mean reversion. They solve for the option value by using a binomial approach, rather than by solving the corresponding partial differential equation, and determine the market price of risk numerically. Cox, Ingersoll, and Ross present a simple closed form methodology to fit their model to the observed zero coupon curve.[7] Jamshidian (1989) and Heath, Jarrow, and Morton (1988) take the one

---

[7] Equation (29) on page 395 of their paper. The function which is fitted to the zero coupon curve is the long-term value of the rate of interest. However, this methodology is equivalent to fitting the market price of risk to the observed zero coupon curve.

state variable originally proposed by Merton and show that in this case the function $\lambda(r,t)$ in equations (8) and (9) is such:

$$\lambda(r,t) = \mu(r,t) - \left(\partial f(0,t) / \partial t + \sigma^2 t \right)$$

where $f(0,t)$ is today's instantaneous forward rate curve for delivery at time t. Similarly, Jamshidian (1989) examines the model originally proposed by Vasicek (1977) and shows that in this case:

$$\lambda(r,t) = \mu(r,t) - \left(\partial f(0,t) / \partial t + K\left(f(0,t) - r \right) + \sigma^2 \left(1 - e^{-2Kt} \right) / 2K \right).$$

Hull and White (1990) have generalized this model to the case where the volatility of the rate of interest is a function of time. They also present a simple procedure to fit model prices to observed prices for zero coupon securities.

There are no two state arbitrage free models of the curve except for Heath, Jarrow, and Morton (1988). While the arbitrage-free one state variable models are direct extensions of the pricing methodology presented in section 3.1, the Heath, Jarrow, and Morton arbitrage-free model cannot be derived from the models presented in section 3.2. This model uses the behavior of the instantaneous forward rate to represent interest rate uncertainty. This assumption simplifies their analysis since today's curve is automatically explained by their model. However, this assumption limits the kinds of processes which can represent the evolution of forward rates by imposing intertemporal constraints on the behavior of the forward rate. If $f(t,T)$ represents the instantaneous forward rate at time t for delivery at time T, Heath, Jarrow, and Morton characterize the behavior of the curve by the following set of equations:

$$df(t,T) = \mu(t,T)\, dt + s_1 dz_1 + s_2 \exp\left(-\alpha(T-t)/2 \right) dz_2 \qquad (13)$$

where s_1 can be considered as long term volatility and s_2 can be considered as short term volatility which decays at the rate and where $\mu(t,T)$ is the arbitrage-free drift.[8] The two processes dz_1 and dz_2 are independent brownian motions.[9]

---

[8] It is important to note that specifying the model in terms of forward rates has its costs. Even though the market price of risk does not have to be determined, the behavior of the different forward rates must be made consistent with the behavior of the short term rate $f(t,t)$, at any point in time to prevent arbitrage opportunities.

[9] Hull and White (1990) have also proposed an arbitrage-free two state model which generalized the process of Vasicek to two sources of risk. They find in their paper that the differences between the two state and one state Vasicek models are negligible.

In the next section, we will investigate the pricing biases of these models. In particular, we will address the following questions:

—What is the relative bias of assuming a normally distributed interest rate instead of assuming a lognormally distributed interest rate?

—Are there any substantial pricing differences between the Vasicek/Hull and White model and the Cox, Ingersoll and Ross model?

—What is the effect of mean reversion on the pricing of debt options?

—Is there any substantial difference in option values when we use a two state pricing model?

The interest rate processes used in the comparison will be the arbitrage free versions of the following processes:

Normal Model / Ho and Lee: $dr = cdt + s_n dz$ (14)

Lognormal Model / Black, Derman and Toy: $d\ln r = cdt + sdz$ (15)

Vasicek / Hull and White: $dr = K_v \left(c - r \right) dt + s_v dz$ (16)

C.I.R. Model: $dr = K_{cir} \left(c - r \right) dt + s_{cir} r^{1/2} dz$ (17)

while the two state model of Heath, Jarrow, and Morton will be represented by equation (13).

4. Comparison of the Pricing Biases of the Different Arbitrage-Free Debt Option Valuation Models

The first set of data needed to run our comparisons is the form of the observed term structure of interest rates. To simplify our analysis, we choose to approximate the existing forward rate curve at the time of pricing by the following functional relationship:

$$f(0,T) = b_0 + b_1 \exp\left(-T/b_3\right) + \left(1 - T/b_4\right) b_2 \exp\left(-T/b_4\right) \quad (18)$$

The equivalent zero coupon yield curve $y(T)$ is given by:

$$y(T) = b_0 + b_1 \left(1 - \exp\left(-T/b_3\right)\right) / \left(T/b_3\right) + b_2 \exp\left(-T/b_4\right) \quad (19)$$

We choose $b_0 = .08028$, $b_1 = -.00601$, $b_2 = .00378$, $b_3 = 4.99686$, $b_4 = 4.97594$ as the base case. This corresponds to a relatively flat yield curve with an instantaneous rate today equal to .07805 ($b_0+b_1+b_2$) and a limit for the yield on a zero coupon bond of .08028 (b_0) as the maturity of the zero goes to infinity. In addition, since the shape of the curve may be important in the case of American options, we also run some of our tests for a decreasing curve by changing b_0 to .06028 and b_1 to .01399 and for an increasing curve by changing b_0 to .10028 and b_1 to –.02601.

The comparisons also require the estimation of the parameters in equations (13) to (17). In the case of the normal/Ho and Lee and lognormal/Black, Derman, and Toy models, one must estimate s_n and s. Concerning the Vasicek/Hull and White and Cox, Ingersoll, and Ross models, we must respectively estimate s_v and K_v, and s_{cir} and K_{cir}. Finally, for the Heath, Jarrow, and Morton model, α, s_1 and s_2 must be estimated. Though all of these parameters can be interpreted as speeds of adjustment in the case of K_v and K_{cir}, or as volatilities in the case of s_n, s, s_v, s_{cir}, s_1, and s_2, their values will differ since they correspond to different models. For example, s_n is the volatility of the change in rate while s is the volatility of the proportional change in rate.

To make the comparisons more relevant, we decided to imply the values of these parameters from existing option prices. The market information that we attempt to match is the price of a three-month European call option on a two-year note paying a coupon of 7.875% and the price of a three-month European call option on a ten-year note paying a coupon of 8%. Both options are assumed to be struck at the money forward. The two options are assumed to be worth, respectively, $.55 and $1.44 per $100 of underlying face value.

In the case of the Vasicek/Hull and White and Cox, Ingersoll, and Ross models, we are able to exactly match the two observed option prices since we have two parameters to imply. Similarly, for the Heath, Jarrow, and Morton models, we are able to exactly match the observed option prices. In fact, we must first assume a value of α and then imply the two volatility parameters, s_1 and s_2, from the two observed option prices.[10] However, we do not have enough degrees of freedom in the case of the normal and lognormal models to explain both observed option prices. In this case, we chose to explain the price of the three-month option on the ten-year note when comparing the two models to each other. However, when we compare these models to mean reverting models, we used two different values of interest rate volatility to price the option on the two-year note and the option on the ten-year note.

Tables 1.1 to 1.4 present paired comparisons of the different pricing models. Each table reports pricing results for put and call options for different option maturities (three months, one year, and two years), for dif-

---

[10] We chose $\alpha = .4$ as our base case. Changing the value of α to .8 substantially changes the estimate of the two volatilities, but barely changes the option values.

ferent maturities of the underlying notes (two years and ten years) and for different degrees of out-of-the money or in-the-moneyness. Some of the tables report the results of the comparison only for European options, while others report the results of the comparisons for European and American options.

Table 1.1 shows a comparison of the normal/Ho and Lee and lognormal/Black, Derman, and Toy models. This comparison only involves European options. Table 1.1 indicates that the lognormal model underprices out-of-money call options and overprices out-of-the-money put options relative to the normal model. This is clearly due to the fact that the

Table 1.1: Normal/Ho and Lee vs. Lognormal/Black, Derman, and Toy Models, $s_n = .0106$, $s = .136$

Call Option Values

Option Maturity	.25 yr		1.0 yr		2.0 yr	
Note Maturity	2 yr	10 yr	2 yr	10 yr	2 yr	10 yr
Out of the Money						
Strike	100.881	103.206	100.946	103.196	—	103.143
Normal	.06	.45	.09	1.48	—	2.05
Lognormal	.05	.42	.07	1.39		1.94
At the Money						
Strike	99.881	100.206	99.946	100.196	—	100.143
Normal	.34	1.44	.38	2.58	—	3.11
Lognormal	.34	1.44	.38	2.56		3.09
In the Money						
Strike	98.881	97.206	98.946	97.196	—	97.143
Normal	1.03	3.35	1.01	4.15	—	4.49
Lognormal	1.04	3.38	1.03	4.23		4.59

Put Option Values

Option Maturity	.25 yr		1.0 yr		2.0 yr	
Note Maturity	2 yr	10 yr	2 yr	10 yr	2 yr	10 yr
Out of the Money						
Strike	98.881	97.206	98.946	97.196	—	97.143
Normal	.05	.41	.09	1.37	—	1.93
Lognormal	.06	.44	.10	1.45		2.02
At the Money						
Strike	99.881	100.206	99.946	100.196	—	100.143
Normal	.34	1.44	.38	2.58	—	3.11
Lognormal	.34	1.44	.38	2.56		3.09
In the Money						
Strike	100.881	103.206	100.946	103.196	—	103.143
Normal	1.04	3.39	1.01	4.25	—	4.62
Lognormal	1.03	3.36	1.00	4.17		4.50

normal model is not a realistic representation of interest rate behavior since it allows for negative rates. Because of this, the normal model will bias the probability distribution of bond prices toward large unrealistic values, thus overpricing out-of-the-money call options relative to at-the-money call options and underpricing out-of-the-money put options relative to at-the-money put options. The result could easily be extended to caps and floors. Caps would suffer from the same type of mispricing as puts, while floors would suffer from the same type of mispricing as calls. The mispricing biases also tend to increase with the maturity of the option when we assume a constant maturity for the tail of the underlying bond. It is also interesting to note that both models have an equal pricing bias on the price of the at-the-money three-month option on the two-year note; both models price this option at $.34 instead of $.55. This is due to the fact that we have implied the volatilities by using the price of the three-month option on the ten-year note and that the observed option price of the three-month option on the two-year bond implies more volatility on the short end of the curve than on the long end of the curve. Clearly, a realistic implementation of these two models requires a volatility curve.

In Table 1.2, we compare the two mean reverting models with respect to the pricing of European options. These two models give very similar results. The results are nearly identical except for longer dated options on the ten-year note. The Vasicek/Hull and White model tends to slightly overprice out-of-the-money call options and underprice out-of-the-money put options when compared to the Cox, Ingersoll, and Ross model. This result should be anticipated since the Vasicek/Hull and White model still assumes a normal distribution of future interest rates. Consequently, it still gives some positive probability to negative rates and to very high bond prices, thus implying an overpricing bias on out-of-the-money call options and an underpricing bias on out-of-the-money puts. These biases are quite minimal, however, and could be further reduced by allowing the volatility to be a function of time.

Since the Vasicek/Hull and White model appears to be a reasonable way to incorporate mean reversion in the behavior of the rate of interest, we will use this model to examine the effect of mean reversion on the value of debt options. We will therefore compare the normal/Ho and Lee model to the Vasicek/Hull and White model. In addition, since this issue is important for European and American options, we will make this comparison for both types of options. Given that we are now running this comparison for American options, we also have to examine different term structures of interest rates. Tables 1.3a to 1.3c present the results of this comparison for the three possible curves that we presented above. These tables show that the two models price options on the two-year note similarly, once we use two different volatilities to price the options on the two-

Table 1.2: Cox, Ingersoll, and Ross vs. Vasicek/Hull and White Models, $K_{cir}=.15$, $s_{cir}=.07$, $K_v=.1625$, $s_v=.01972$

Call Option Values

Option Maturity	.25 yr		1.0 yr		2.0 yr	
Note Maturity	2 yr	10 yr	2 yr	10 yr	2 yr	10 yr
Out of the Money						
Strike	100.881	103.206	100.946	103.196	—	103.143
C.I.R.	.19	.42	.24	1.34	—	1.79
Vas./H.W.	.20	.45	.26	1.41		1.89
At the Money						
Strike	99.881	100.206	99.946	100.196	—	100.143
C.I.R.	.55	1.44	.61	2.51	—	2.93
Vas./H.W.	.55	1.44	.61	2.52		2.95
In the Money						
Strike	98.881	97.206	98.946	97.196	—	97.143
C.I.R.	1.18	3.38	1.19	4.16	—	4.42
Vas./H.W.	1.17	3.36	1.18	4.11		4.36

Put Option Values

Option Maturity	.25 yr		1.0 yr		2.0 yr	
Note Maturity	2 yr	10 yr	2 yr	10 yr	2 yr	10 yr
Out of the Money						
Strike	98.881	97.206	98.946	97.196	—	97.143
C.I.R.	.20	.44	.27	1.38	—	1.86
Vas./H.W.	.19	.42	.25	1.33		1.80
At the Money						
Strike	99.881	100.206	99.946	100.196	—	100.143
C.I.R.	.55	1.44	.61	2.51	—	2.93
Vas./H.W.	.55	1.44	.61	2.52		2.95
In the Money						
Strike	100.881	103.206	100.946	103.196	—	103.143
C.I.R.	1.17	3.36	1.16	4.12	—	4.36
Vas./H.W.	1.18	3.39	1.18	4.19		4.46

year note and the options on the ten-year note in the normal model. The pricing differences become greater for the case of the option on the ten-year note. Most noticeable is the fact that the normal model tends to systematically undervalue the early exercise privilege of American put and call options. This is due in part to the fact that the normal model tends to overvalue the time value of European options.

Finally, it is very interesting to note that the Heath, Jarrow, and Morton model gives option prices which are very close to those given by the Vasicek/Hull and White model. This result is quite apparent when examining Tables 1.4a to 1.4c. The result holds for the three-term structure

Table 1.3a: Normal vs. Mean Reverting Normal (Vasicek/Hull and White) Model, $s_n=.0168$ for two-year note, $s_n=.0106$ for ten-year note, $K_v=.1625$, $s_v=.01972$
Flat Curve

Call Option Values

Option Maturity	.25 yr		1.0 yr		2.0 yr	
Note Maturity	2 yr	10 yr	2 yr	10 yr	2 yr	10 yr
Out of the Money						
Strike	100.881	103.206	100.946	103.196	101	103.143
Normal Eur.	.20	.44	.26	1.47	—	2.04
Vas/HW Eur.	.20	.47	.26	1.41	—	1.89
Normal Am.	.20	.45	.42	1.53	.42	2.28
Vas/HW Am.	.21	.47	.44	1.53	.44	2.32
At the Money						
Strike	99.881	100.206	99.946	100.196	100	100.143
Normal Eur.	.55	1.44	.61	2.57	—	3.11
Vas/HW Eur.	.55	1.44	.61	2.52	—	2.95
Normal Am.	.57	1.45	.86	2.69	.88	3.48
Vas/HW Am.	.57	1.46	.88	2.73	.92	3.58
In the Money						
Strike	98.881	97.206	98.946	97.196	99	97.143
Normal Eur.	1.17	3.36	1.18	4.16	—	4.51
Vas/HW Eur.	1.17	3.36	1.18	4.11	—	4.36
Normal Am.	1.21	3.39	1.49	4.36	1.79	5.06
Vas/HW Am.	1.21	3.41	1.52	4.44	1.82	5.23

Put Option Values

Option Maturity	.25 yr		1.0 yr		2.0 yr	
Note Maturity	2 yr	10 yr	2 yr	10 yr	2 yr	10 yr
Out of the Money						
Strike	98.881	97.206	98.946	97.196	99	97.143
Normal Eur.	.19	.41	.25	1.38	—	1.93
Vas/HW Eur.	.19	.42	.25	1.33	—	1.80
Normal Am.	.20	.42	.44	1.44	.48	2.16
Vas/HW Am.	.20	.42	.46	1.45	.50	2.21
At the Money						
Strike	99.881	100.206	99.946	100.196	100	100.143
Normal Eur.	.55	1.44	.61	2.57	—	3.10
Vas/HW Eur.	.55	1.44	.61	2.52	—	2.95
Normal Am.	.57	1.45	.90	2.69	.99	3.47
Vas/HW Am.	.57	1.46	.93	2.74	1.03	3.59
In the Money						
Strike	100.881	103.206	100.946	103.196	101	103.143
Normal Eur.	1.18	3.38	1.18	4.24	—	4.60
Vas/HW Eur.	1.18	3.39	1.18	4.19	—	4.46
Normal Am.	1.22	3.43	1.57	4.45	1.92	5.17
Vas/HW Am.	1.22	3.43	1.60	4.54	1.96	5.36

Table 1.3b: Normal vs. Mean Reverting Normal (Vasicek/Hull and White) Model, $s_n=.0168$ for two-year note, $s_n=.0106$ for ten-year note, $K_v=.1625$, $s_v=.01972$
Increasing Curve

Call Option Values

Option Maturity	.25 yr		1.0 yr		2.0 yr	
Note Maturity	2 yr	10 yr	2 yr	10 yr	2 yr	10 yr
Out of the Money						
Strike	100.234	96.150	100.443	95.887	101	95.749
Normal Eur.	.19	.36	.25	1.26	—	1.77
Vas/HW Eur.	.19	.36	.25	1.21	—	1.64
Normal Am.	.20	.37	.39	1.32	.25	1.99
Vas/HW Am.	.20	.37	.40	1.34	.27	2.04
At the Money						
Strike	99.234	93.150	99.443	92.887	100	92.749
Normal Eur.	.55	1.33	.60	2.35	—	2.81
Vas/HW Eur.	.55	1.33	.60	2.30	—	2.68
Normal Am.	.56	1.35	.80	2.49	.60	3.19
Vas/HW Am.	.57	1.36	.83	2.54	.63	3.31
In the Money						
Strike	98.234	90.150	98.443	89.887	99	89.749
Normal Eur.	1.17	3.29	1.17	3.95	—	4.22
Vas/HW Eur.	1.17	3.27	1.17	3.91	—	4.10
Normal Am.	1.20	3.36	1.42	4.23	1.48	4.83
Vas/HW Am.	1.21	3.36	1.45	4.32	1.51	5.02

Put Option Values

Option Maturity	.25 yr		1.0 yr		2.0 yr	
Note Maturity	2 yr	10 yr	2 yr	10 yr	2 yr	10 yr
Out of the Money						
Strike	98.234	90.150	98.443	89.887	99	89.749
Normal Eur.	.19	.35	.25	1.18	—	1.67
Vas/HW Eur.	.19	.33	.25	1.14	—	1.55
Normal Am.	.20	.35	.48	1.22	.74	1.86
Vas/HW Am.	.20	.33	.49	1.22	.77	1.90
At the Money						
Strike	99.234	93.150	99.443	92.887	100	92.749
Normal Eur.	.55	1.33	.60	2.34	—	2.81
Vas/HW Eur.	.55	1.33	.60	2.30	—	2.68
Normal Am.	.57	1.33	.96	2.42	1.37	3.13
Vas/HW Am.	.57	1.33	.99	2.46	1.41	3.23
In the Money						
Strike	100.234	96.150	100.443	95.887	101	95.749
Normal Eur.	1.17	3.30	1.18	4.02	—	4.31
Vas/HW Eur.	1.18	3.30	1.18	3.98	—	4.19
Normal Am.	1.21	3.31	1.64	4.17	2.31	4.81
Vas/HW Am.	1.22	3.32	1.67	4.24	2.35	4.99

Table 1.3c: Normal vs. Mean Reverting Normal (Vasicek/Hull and White) Model, $s_n=.0168$ for two-year note, $s_n=.0106$ for ten-year note, $K_v=.1625$, $s_v=.01972$
Decreasing Curve

Call Option Values

Option Maturity	.25 yr		1.0 yr		2.0 yr	
Note Maturity	2 yr	10 yr	2 yr	10 yr	2 yr	10 yr
Out of the Money						
Strike	101.533	111.01	101.452	111.271	101	111.28
Normal Eur.	.20	.58	.26	1.72	—	2.36
Vas/HW Eur.	.20	.55	.26	1.64	—	2.17
Normal Am.	.21	.59	.47	1.78	.67	2.63
Vas/HW Am.	.21	.56	.48	1.76	.69	2.64
At the Money						
Strike	100.533	108.01	100.452	108.271	100	108.28
Normal Eur.	.55	1.60	.61	2.86	—	3.44
Vas/HW Eur.	.55	1.58	.61	2.77	—	3.25
Normal Am.	.57	1.61	.92	2.95	1.25	3.82
Vas/HW Am.	.58	1.60	.95	2.96	1.28	3.90
In the Money						
Strike	99.533	105.01	99.452	105.271	99	105.28
Normal Eur.	1.17	3.47	1.18	4.41	—	4.83
Vas/HW Eur.	1.18	3.46	1.18	4.34	—	4.66
Normal Am.	1.21	3.48	1.57	4.55	2.16	5.36
Vas/HW Am.	1.22	3.48	1.60	4.61	2.20	5.51

Put Option Values

Option Maturity	.25 yr		1.0 yr		2.0 yr	
Note Maturity	2 yr	10 yr	2 yr	10 yr	2 yr	10 yr
Out of the Money						
Strike	99.533	105.01	99.452	105.271	99	105.28
Normal Eur.	.19	.52	.25	1.62	—	2.23
Vas/HW Eur.	.19	.51	.25	1.56	—	2.08
Normal Am.	.20	.53	.41	1.71	.29	2.51
Vas/HW Am.	.21	.52	.43	1.72	.31	2.56
At the Money						
Strike	100.533	108.01	100.452	108.271	100	108.28
Normal Eur.	.55	1.60	.61	2.85	—	3.43
Vas/HW Eur.	.55	1.58	.61	2.77	—	3.25
Normal Am.	.58	1.62	.86	3.02	.68	3.86
Vas/HW Am.	.57	1.61	.88	3.06	.72	3.98
In the Money						
Strike	101.533	111.01	101.452	111.271	101	111.28
Normal Eur.	1.17	3.52	1.19	4.50	—	4.94
Vas/HW Eur.	1.18	3.49	1.19	4.42	—	4.76
Normal Am.	1.22	3.57	1.50	4.79	1.60	5.58
Vas/HW Am.	1.22	3.57	1.53	4.87	1.63	5.76

Table 1.4a: Heath, Jarrow and Morton vs. Vasicek/Hull and White Models, $\alpha = .4$, $s = .00507$, $s_2 = .0193$, $K_v = .1625$, $s_y = .01972$
Flat Curve

Call Option Values

Option Maturity	.25 yr		1.0 yr		2.0 yr	
Note Maturity	2 yr	10 yr	2 yr	10 yr	2 yr	10 yr
Out of the Money						
Strike	100.881	103.206	100.946	103.196	101	103.143
H.J.M. Eur.	.19	.44	.25	1.40	—	1.87
Vas/HW Eur.	.20	.45	.26	1.41	—	1.89
H.J.M. Am.	.20	.45	.43	1.52	.43	2.28
Vas/HW Am.	.21	.45	.44	1.53	.44	2.32
At the Money						
Strike	99.881	100.206	99.946	100.196	100	100.143
H.J.M. Eur.	.55	1.44	.61	2.51	—	2.94
Vas/HW Eur.	.55	1.44	.61	2.52	—	2.95
H.J.M. Am.	.57	1.46	.88	2.71	.90	3.54
Vas/HW Am.	.57	1.46	.88	2.73	.92	3.58
In the Money						
Strike	98.881	97.206	98.946	97.196	99	97.143
H.J.M. Eur.	1.17	3.35	1.17	4.10	—	4.35
Vas/HW Eur.	1.17	3.36	1.18	4.11	—	4.36
H.J.M. Am.	1.22	3.40	1.52	4.42	1.81	5.19
Vas/HW Am.	1.21	3.41	1.52	4.44	1.82	5.23

Put Option Values

Option Maturity	.25 yr		1.0 yr		2.0 yr	
Note Maturity	2 yr	10 yr	2 yr	10 yr	2 yr	10 yr
Out of the Money						
Strike	98.881	97.206	98.946	97.196	99	97.143
H.J.M. Eur.	.19	.41	.25	1.32	—	1.79
Vas/HW Eur.	.19	.42	.25	1.33	—	1.80
H.J.M. Am.	.20	.41	.45	1.44	.49	2.18
Vas/HW Am.	.20	.42	.46	1.45	.50	2.21
At the Money						
Strike	99.881	100.206	99.946	100.196	100	100.143
H.J.M. Eur.	.55	1.44	.61	2.51	—	2.94
Vas/HW Eur.	.55	1.44	.61	2.52	—	2.95
H.J.M. Am.	.58	1.46	.93	2.73	1.01	3.56
Vas/HW Am.	.57	1.46	.93	2.74	1.03	3.59
In the Money						
Strike	100.881	103.206	100.946	103.196	101	103.143
H.J.M. Eur.	1.17	3.38	1.18	4.18	—	4.45
Vas/HW Eur.	1.18	3.39	1.18	4.19	—	4.46
H.J.M. Am.	1.22	3.43	1.59	4.52	1.94	5.33
Vas/HW Am.	1.22	3.43	1.60	4.54	1.96	5.36

Table 1.4b: Heath, Jarrow and Morton vs. Vasicek/Hull and White Models, $\alpha = .4$, $s = .00507$, $s_2 = .0193$, $K_v = .1625$, $s_v = .01972$
Increasing Curve

Call Option Values

Option Maturity	.25 yr		1.0 yr		2.0 yr	
Note Maturity	2 yr	10 yr	2 yr	10 yr	2 yr	10 yr
Out of the Money						
Strike	100.234	96.150	100.443	95.887	101	95.749
H.J.M. Eur.	.19	.35	.25	1.19	—	1.62
Vas/HW Eur.	.19	.36	.25	1.21	—	1.64
H.J.M. Am.	.20	.36	.39	1.31	.25	2.00
Vas/HW Am.	.20	.37	.40	1.34	.27	2.04
At the Money						
Strike	99.234	93.150	99.443	92.887	100	92.749
H.J.M. Eur.	.54	1.31	.60	2.28	—	2.66
Vas/HW Eur.	.55	1.33	.60	2.30	—	2.68
H.J.M. Am.	.57	1.35	.82	2.52	.61	3.26
Vas/HW Am.	.57	1.36	.83	2.54	.63	3.31
In the Money						
Strike	98.234	90.150	98.443	89.887	99	89.749
H.J.M. Eur.	1.16	3.25	1.17	3.89	—	4.08
Vas/HW Eur.	1.17	3.27	1.17	3.91	—	4.10
H.J.M. Am.	1.21	3.35	1.46	4.30	1.50	4.97
Vas/HW Am.	1.21	3.36	1.45	4.32	1.51	5.02

Put Option Values

Option Maturity	.25 yr		1.0 yr		2.0 yr	
Note Maturity	2 yr	10 yr	2 yr	10 yr	2 yr	10 yr
Out of the Money						
Strike	98.234	90.150	98.443	89.887	99	89.749
H.J.M. Eur.	.19	.32	.25	1.13	—	1.54
Vas/HW Eur.	.19	.33	.25	1.14	—	1.55
H.J.M. Am.	.20	.33	.48	1.21	.75	1.87
Vas/HW Am.	.20	.33	.49	1.22	.77	1.90
At the Money						
Strike	99.234	93.150	99.443	92.887	100	92.749
H.J.M. Eur.	.55	1.32	.60	2.29	—	2.67
Vas/HW Eur.	.55	1.33	.60	2.30	—	2.68
H.J.M. Am.	.58	1.33	.98	2.45	1.40	3.21
Vas/HW Am.	.57	1.33	.99	2.46	1.41	3.23
In the Money						
Strike	100.234	96.150	100.443	95.887	101	95.749
H.J.M. Eur.	1.17	3.31	1.18	3.97	—	4.19
Vas/HW Eur.	1.18	3.30	1.18	3.98	—	4.19
H.J.M. Am.	1.23	3.33	1.67	4.24	2.34	4.96
Vas/HW Am.	1.22	3.32	1.67	4.24	2.35	4.99

Table 1.4c: Heath, Jarrow and Morton vs. Vasicek/Hull and White Models, $\alpha = .4$, $s = .00507$, $s_2 = .0193$, $K_v = .1625$, $s_v = .01972$
Decreasing Curve

Call Option Values

Option Maturity	.25 yr		1.0 yr		2.0 yr	
Note Maturity	2 yr	10 yr	2 yr	10 yr	2 yr	10 yr
Out of the Money						
Strike	101.533	111.01	101.452	111.271	101	111.28
H.J.M. Eur.	.20	.55	.26	1.63	—	2.15
Vas/HW Eur.	.20	.55	.26	1.64	—	2.17
H.J.M. Am.	.21	.55	.47	1.74	.67	2.59
Vas/HW Am.	.21	.56	.48	1.76	.69	2.64
At the Money						
Strike	100.533	108.01	100.452	108.271	100	108.28
H.J.M. Eur.	.55	1.58	.61	2.76	—	3.24
Vas/HW Eur.	.55	1.58	.61	2.77	—	3.25
H.J.M. Am.	.58	1.60	.94	2.94	1.27	3.86
Vas/HW Am.	.58	1.60	9.5	2.96	1.28	3.90
In the Money						
Strike	99.533	105.01	99.452	105.271	99	105.28
H.J.M. Eur.	1.18	3.46	1.18	4.33	—	4.65
Vas/HW Eur.	1.18	3.46	1.18	4.34	—	4.66
H.J.M. Am.	1.22	3.49	1.60	4.60	2.19	5.48
Vas/HW Am.	1.22	3.48	1.60	4.61	2.20	5.51

Put Option Values

Option Maturity	.25 yr		1.0 yr		2.0 yr	
Note Maturity	2 yr	10 yr	2 yr	10 yr	2 yr	10 yr
Out of the Money						
Strike	99.533	105.01	99.452	105.271	99	105.28
H.J.M. Eur.	.19	.50	.25	1.54	—	2.06
Vas/HW Eur.	.19	.51	.25	1.56	—	2.08
H.J.M. Am.	.20	.51	.42	1.70	.29	2.53
Vas/HW Am.	.21	.52	.43	1.72	.31	2.56
At the Money						
Strike	100.533	108.01	100.452	108.271	100	108.28
H.J.M. Eur.	.55	1.57	.61	2.75	—	3.24
Vas/HW Eur.	.55	1.58	.61	2.77	—	3.25
H.J.M. Am.	.58	1.61	.87	3.03	.70	3.94
Vas/HW Am.	.57	1.61	.88	3.06	.72	3.98
In the Money						
Strike	101.533	111.01	101.452	111.271	101	111.28
H.J.M. Eur.	1.17	3.48	1.18	4.40	—	4.73
Vas/HW Eur.	1.18	3.49	1.19	4.42	—	4.76
H.J.M. Am.	1.22	3.56	1.52	4.85	1.62	5.72
Vas/HW Am.	1.22	3.57	1.53	4.87	1.63	5.76

scenarios and for European options as well as American options. This result is especially interesting given that the Heath, Jarrow, and Morton model is substantially more cumbersome to implement than the Vasicek/Hull and White model. It should also be mentioned that changing the value of α in the Heath, Jarrow, and Morton model does not modify the results of the model once we have adjusted the volatility parameters to reflect the value of our two benchmark options.

5. Conclusions

In this paper we have examined the problems linked to the derivation of a "good" bond option pricing model. The analysis has shown that the problem of valuing bond options is more complicated than the problem of valuing stock options. Nevertheless, one can derive two important results from our analysis.

The first result deals with the pricing of European options. A modification of the Black-Scholes model which accounts for the coupon paid on the bond, the aging of the bond, and the uncertain cost of carry of the underlying bond during the life of the option will be adequate to value a European bond option.

The second result concerns the valuation of American options on bonds. We have shown that there is no reason for the standard American stock option valuation model to be applicable to the pricing of American options on bonds. The main reason for this result is that the optimal early exercise of bond options will depend on the term structure of interest rates and on its evolution over time. Therefore, the only way to compute the value of this early exercise privilege correctly is to develop a bond option valuation model which is based on a set of realistic assumptions regarding the term structure of interest rates and its evolution through time. Several models along these lines have been described in this paper. However, as we pointed out, these models still have characteristics which make them delicate to apply. In particular, it is of the utmost importance that the model is arbitrage free. Most of these models are one state variable models which use the instantaneous rate of interest as the source of risk. We have presented several of these models above. These models are the models proposed by Ho and Lee (normal model), Black, Derman, and Toy (lognormal model), Jamshidian and Hull and White (Vasicek model) and the model proposed by Cox, Ingersoll, and Ross.

The results derived for the normal and lognormal models are similar except for the pricing of out-of-the-money call options, which are overpriced by the normal model, and out-of-the-money put options, which are underpriced by the normal model when compared to the lognormal model results. As was intuitively expected, mean reverting models like the Vasicek or Cox, Ingersoll and Ross models are superior to constant volatility implementations of the normal or lognormal models in situations where the short end of the forward curve is more volatile than the long end of the curve. It is clear, however, that this comparison is somewhat unfair to the normal or lognormal models. A more accurate comparison would allow for a rate volatility curve in the normal and lognormal models. Another interesting result derived from this comparison is the systematic underpricing of the value of the early exercise privilege of American options by the normal model when compared to the Vasicek model. This underpricing may also be significantly reduced once we allow for a volatility curve in the normal model.

It is also interesting to note that the more complicated two state option pricing model proposed by Heath, Jarrow, and Morton does not appear to add much to the pricing of European options when compared to the simpler mean reverting model proposed by Vasicek. Consequently, a simple one state mean reverting model, or the normal or lognormal model with an appropriate volatility curve, appears to be the most rational model to use in the pricing of European note and bond options when the tradeoff between accuracy in pricing and difficulty of implementation is taken into account.

It still remains, however, that a two state option pricing methodology is a must when one attempts to value more complex derivative instruments which derive significant value from changes in the shape of the term structure of interest rates. This would be the case for options on yield spreads and for index amortizing swaps where the amortization of principal is a function of the level of a given rate.

REFERENCES

Ball, C. and W. Torous. 1983. "Bond Price Dynamics and Options," *Journal of Financial and Quantitative Analysis,* 18, No. 4, December, 517–32.

Black, F. 1976. "The Pricing of Commodity Contracts," *Journal of Financial Economics,* 3, No. 1, January-March.

Black, F., E. Derman, and W. Toy. 1990. "A One Factor Model of Interest Rates and its Application to Treasury Bond Options," *Financial Analysts Journal,* January-February, 33–39.

Black, F. and M. Scholes. 1973. "The Pricing of Options and Corporate Liabilities," *Journal of Political Economy,* 81, 637–659.

Brennan, M. J. and E. Schwartz. 1977a. "The Valuation of American Put Options," *Journal of Finance,* 32, May, 449–462.

Brennan, M. J. and E. Schwartz. 1977b. "Savings Bonds, Retractable Bonds and Callable Bonds," *Journal of Financial Economics,* 5, December, 67–88.

Brennan, M. J. and E. Schwartz. 1979. "Savings Bonds: Theory and Empirical Evidence," Monograph Series in Finance and Economics, Monograph 1979–4, Graduate School of Business, New York University.

Brennan, M. J. and E. Schwartz. 1980. "Analyzing Convertible Bonds," *Journal of Financial and Quantitative Analysis,* 15, No. 4, November.

Brennan, M. J. and E. Schwartz. 1982. "An Equilibrium Model of Bond Pricing and a Test of Market Efficiency," *Journal of Financial and Quantitative Analysis,* 17, No. 3, September, 301–329.

Brennan, M. J. and E. Schwartz. 1983. "Alternative Methods for Valuing Debt Options," *Finance,* 4, No. 2, October, 119–137.

Courtadon, G. 1982. "The Pricing of Options on Default Free Bonds," *Journal of Financial and Quantitative Analysis,* 17, March, 75–100.

Cox, J., J. Ingersoll and S. Ross. 1985. "A Theory of the Term Structure of Interest Rates," *Econometrica,* 53, No. 2, March, 385–407.

Cox, J., S. Ross and M. Rubinstein. 1979. "Option Pricing: A Simplified Approach," *Journal of Financial Economics,* 7, No. 3, September.

Cox, J. and M. Rubinstein. 1985. *Options Markets,* Prentice-Hall, New York.

Dietrich-Campbell, B. and E. Schwartz. 1986. "Valuing Debt Options: Empirical Evidence," *Journal of Financial Economics,* 16, 3, 321–343.

Dothan, U. 1978. "On the Term Structure of Interest Rates," *Journal of Financial Economics,* 6, No. 1, March, 59–70.

Geske, R. 1979. "A Note on an Analytical Valuation Formula for Unprotected American Call Options on Stocks with Known Dividends," *Journal of Financial Economics,* 7, December, 375–380.

Geske, R., and H. Johnson. 1984. "The American Put Option Valued Analytically," *Journal of Finance,* 39, December, 1511–1524.

Heath, D., R. Jarrow and A. Morton. 1988. "Bond Pricing and the Term Structure of Interest Rates: A New Methodology," Working Paper, Cornell University, August.

Ho, T. and S. Lee. 1986. "Term Structure Movements and Pricing Interest Rate Contingent Claims," *Journal of Finance,* 41, No. 5, December, 1011–1030.

Hull, J. and A. White. 1990. "Pricing Interest-Rate Derivative Securities," *The Review of Financial Studies,* 3, No. 4.

Jamshidian, F. 1989. "The Preference-Free Determination of Bond Prices from the Spot Interest Rate," Working Paper, Merrill Lynch Capital Markets, World Financial Center, New York.

Jamshidian, F. 1991. "Forward Induction and Construction of Yield Curve Diffusion Models," Working Paper, Merrill Lynch Capital Markets, World Financial Center, New York.

Merton, R. C. 1973. "Theory of Rational Option Pricing," *Bell Journal of Economics and Management Science*, 4, 141–183.

Parkinson, M. 1977. "Option Pricing: The American Put," *Journal of Business*, 50, January.

Roll, R. 1977. "An Analytic Valuation Formula for Unprotected American Call Options on Stocks with Known Dividends," *Journal of Financial Economics*, 5, No. 2, November, 251–58.

Schaefer, S. and E. Schwartz. 1984. "A Two Factor Model of the Term Structure: An Approximate Analytical Solution," *Journal of Financial and Quantitative Analysis*, 19, No. 4, December.

Schaefer, S. and E. Schwartz. 1987. "Time-Dependent Variance and the Pricing of Bond Options," *Journal of Finance*, 42, 5, 1113–1128.

Schwartz, E. 1977. "The Valuation of Warrants: Implementing a New Approach," *Journal of Financial Economics*, 4, No. 1, January.

Vasicek, O. 1977. "An Equilibrium Characterization of the Term Structure," *Journal of Financial Economics*, 5, November, 177–178.

Whaley, R. E. 1981. "On the Valuation of American Call Options on Stocks with Known Dividends," *Journal of Financial Economics*, 9, June, 207–211.

MEAN REVERSION INTEREST RATE MODELING

Don Goldman

2

Overview

This article begins with a discussion of intuitive approaches that have been used historically by practitioners for the valuation of options on bonds. These basic models and extensions of them may still represent a basis for the only pragmatic and flexible approaches available in some circumstances. These models are not presented for accuracy or content but rather as a means for developing a logical pathway to the modeling of short rate, interest rate processes.

We then discuss the Hull–White extended Vasicek one-factor, mean reverting approach. Equations (15 through 18) are developed that enhance the Hull–White technique by expressing the reversion parameters directly as a function of observable market quantities in continuous time. These equations are then used to develop intuition about the mean reversion parameters.

Intuition is an important ingredient when introducing a new modeling approach. Many book runners will not use a new modeling approach if it does not appear to be in line with their intuition. Book runners can expose themselves and their businesses to risk by using a model which they do not fully understand. Because of this, simple models are often used in practice over complex models under the astute observation that there may be an inherent risk in using a model based on assumptions and mechanisms that are not clearly understood. This risk cannot be hedged.

The price paid by using less accurate underlying modeling assumptions when managing risk with a simple, transparent model may buy a clearer understanding of the results and may result in a risk tradeoff. This article attempts to build some of the required intuition for the extended

Vasicek model by relating mean reversion parameters directly to the market and interpreting the resulting equations.

We do not claim one factor models are the ultimate answer to all situations. There are structures that cannot be modeled with a one-factor approach. One-factor models imply perfect correlation along the yield curve and thus cannot be used to value, for example, an option on the spread between two yields. There are many instances in which multifactor modeling is required.

There are, however, a large number of cases that either lend themselves to one factor modeling or in which intelligent modeling can reduce the problem to one that can be handled satisfactorily by a one factor approach. If it is possible to pose a derivatives valuation and risk management problem in a one-factor framework, one need not estimate correlations for which there may not exist a natural hedge. It often is easier to manage risk when that risk is a function of fewer parameters rather than when it is a function of many parameters.

We do not claim that the Hull–White extended Vasicek approach is the only viable approach to one factor modeling. We do believe that the approach is a significant advance which is pragmatic and can be used to cover many interesting applications.

The article is divided as follows:

Section 1: A discussion of intuitive approaches to bond option modeling

Section 2: A brief review of the Hull–White approach

Section 3: The derivation of the equations which express the reversion parameters as a function of market observable quantities in continuous time

Section 4: A discussion of mean reversion parameters using the equations derived in Section 3 as a basis

Section 1: A Discussion of Intuitive Approaches to Bond Option Modeling

A Commodity Like Approach

If one is asked to price a short dated European-style call option on a coupon-bearing bond and the only model available is Black–Scholes, one possible intuitive approach is as follows. One can think of the option as being on a forward contract on the bond. The forward contract "delivers" a moment after the option expires. The value of the call depends on two quantities associated with the forward bond contract, the forward price and the volatility of the forward price. This approach is reasonable if one can hedge directly with the forward bond and if the expiration of the option is short with respect to the maturity of the bond.

Commodity Approach—Forward Price Diffusion

Suppose the forward quote price of the bond at expiration is q_f. This is the no arbitrage break even future quote price given coupon payments and refinancing. Suppose the volatility of q_f is σ_p (standard deviation of returns or 'log normal volatility'). Assume time to expiration is T_e, the strike on the quote is K and assume the discount to present value is $d = e^{-rT_e}$, where r is the continuously compounded risk-free rate. We assume log normality of q_f. This is often referred to as *forward price diffusion*. We treat the option on the forward contract like a simple option on a commodity.

A simple application of Black–Scholes provides an expression for the value of the option:

$$C = \left(q_f * N(y_1) - K * N(y_2)\right) * d \tag{1}$$

Where

$$y_1 = Ln\left(\frac{q_f}{K}\right) / \left(\sigma_p \sqrt{T_e}\right) + \left(\sigma_p \sqrt{T_e}\right)/2$$

$$y_2 = y_1 - \left(\sigma_p \sqrt{T_e}\right)$$

and,

$$N(z) \equiv \int_{-\infty}^{z} \frac{e^{-\frac{1}{2}\zeta^2}}{\sqrt{2\pi}} d\zeta$$

A simple American model can be had by generalizing the above to a binomial or a differential equation with finite differencing while holding r constant. This would be a rough approximation for the reasons outlined below.

The above procedure is what we mean by "taking a commodity like approach" to value the bond option. Here we use the term commodity loosely. It refers not only to true commodity assets like gold and silver but also to equity and currency. It refers to any asset whose basic financial structure does not change with time and whose pricing is not directly related to interest rates. We are interested in using an analogy to simple structures under simple stochastic assumptions which will allow us to shed light on the pricing and hedging of more complex structures.

A bond's basic financial structure can change with time. If a bond matures at some fixed time, the price of the bond converges at maturity to par. Thus, the price varies less as maturity approaches—the price volatility decreases. This is known as the *par* effect.

Given a world in which complete information on interest rates is known—including all information of a stochastic nature—does not determine what the price of gold must be. However, complete information on interest rates does determine the value of all bonds and their stochastic propagation.

It is easier to rationalize the separation of the effects of interest rate propagation from the effects of the propagation of the price of gold than it is to rationalize the analogous separation of the rate process from the bond process.

The commodity approach is what allows us to hold the risk free rate r, constant through the option's term. It allows us to separate the discounting of the option premium from the stochastic nature of the market which imparts time value on the option's payoff function. The ability to separate these two effects can be the difference between a simple, analytically manageable situation from a complex and possibly difficult to manage situation.

As a consequence of the par effect, the price volatility σ_p, decreases as the maturity of the bond approaches. Different bonds in the same portfolio can have very different price volatility levels, thus complicating the task of risk management. For this reason, traders tend to trade on yield volatility (the standard deviation of the percent changes of the bond's yield to maturity), σ_y. One might choose to assume the yield volatility to be constant while the price volatility varies. Trading on yield volatility tends to make it easier to manage bond portfolio risk since yield volatilities are easier to relate across bonds in an intuitive manner than are price volatilities.

The assumption of a constant price volatility when pricing bond options is usually referred to as *price diffusion*. Assuming yield volatility to be constant when pricing bond options is usually referred to as *yield diffusion*. Of course, if the restriction that the respective volatilities are constant is lifted—if the volatilities are allowed to vary with time, then there is no difference between the two approaches. Though few market participants realize this and the notion of price diffusion versus yield diffusion persists.

Using Ito's lemma, the relation between the two types of volatility on an instantaneous basis may be expressed as

$$\sigma_q = \sigma_y \cdot \frac{dq}{dy} \cdot y / q \tag{2}$$

Where $\frac{dq}{dy}$ is the derivative of the quote price of the bond with respect to the yield to maturity of the bond.

Given the assumption of constant forward yield volatility, the par effect issue may be partly addressed as follows.

Commodity Analog Under a Forward Yield Volatility Assumption

Suppose the forward quote price of the bond at expiration is q_f. Suppose the volatility of the forward yield to maturity of the bond is σ_y. The term forward yield to maturity means the yield associated with the forward bond whose forward quote price is q_f at time of delivery (T_e). Assume time to expiration is T_e, the strike on the quote is K and assume the discount to present value is d. We assume log normality of the forward yield, this is sometimes referred to as forward yield diffusion.

The approximate value of the option in Black–Scholes terms:

$$C = \left(q_f * N(y_1) - K * N(y_2) \right) * d \tag{3}$$

Where

$$y_1 = Ln\left(\frac{q_f}{K}\right) / \left(\sigma_p \sqrt{T_e}\right) + \left(\sigma_p \sqrt{T_e}\right)/2$$

$$y_2 = y_1 - \left(\sigma_p \sqrt{T_e}\right)$$

Where,

$$\sigma_q = \sigma_y * \frac{dq_f}{dy} * y / q_f$$

We have mapped a constant forward yield volatility into a constant forward quote price volatility. The equation derives from Ito's lemma and is only true at a given yield, price level, and for a given derivative. At a different yield, price level, the same yield volatility will map into a different price volatility. Still, the above approximation is widely used and is a fairly good approximation if nothing else is available for short-dated options.

An improvement over the above method might be numerical integration: One could integrate the option payoff over the forward yield diffusion process. This would allow you to keep the yield volatility constant and not have to use the yield to price volatility conversion as a link to Black–Scholes. But these methods still fall short.

For example, American-style Options cannot be properly valued by the yield diffusion technique discussed so far. This is because we only discussed forward processes. To value an American Option, we need a spot process.

We may express a log normal spot yield to maturity diffusion process with a constant yield volatility, σ_y, as:

$$\frac{dy}{y} = \mu_y(t)dt + \sigma_y dz \qquad\qquad\qquad (4)$$

A Partial Differential Equation may be derived based on a standard arbitrage argument. That is, we assume a continuously hedged portfolio which contains a position in the option and a position in the bond. The portfolio returns the risk-free rate because it is risk neutral. The risk-free rate is assumed to be constant throughout the life of the option. The solution leads to a partial differential equation which can be solved by finite differencing.

Spot Yield Diffusion may be used to value American Options as well as Europeans. The par effect will be better handled by yield diffusion than it will by price diffusion.

An option valued under spot yield diffusion will tend to be priced higher than when it is valued under forward yield diffusion when the reinvestment rate is fixed. The reason is that since the reinvestment rate is fixed to the expiration date of the option, all the variability in the bond—which is a function of yield curve movements—must take place between the expiration date of the option and the maturity date of the bond. Thus, the second section of the yield curve must be more volatile than σ_y to make up for the fact that the front end of the yield curve cannot move at all. Hence, a higher forward yield volatility and a resulting higher option price results. For distant expirations, this effect will be especially severe.

By assuming a constant reinvestment rate through expiration, the model will not correctly pick up the value of the American premium because of the distortion of this assumption on carry. There will be cases in which the model picks up no extra American premium when there should be a premium.

Some practitioners may use more than one value for r. They may use one value for repo, another for the general collateral rate, or they may use a deterministic function of time for these two quantities. But the problematic effects associated with a nonstochastic short rate remain and will continue to suffer from the implications discussed above.

Section 2: A Brief Review of the Hull–White Approach

The term *short rate* refers to the instantaneous reinvestment rate or the risk-free rate. We require a model that addresses the issues raised in Section 1. These models must necessarily take into account the stochastic nature of the short rate r, whereas the models discussed in Section 1 all assume r is deterministic. This class of models is sometimes referred to as term structure models or short rate models.

The first issue is to decide on the form of the Ito process for r, i.e., How should the Stochastic process be described?

$$dr = \mu_r(t)dt + \sigma_r(t)dz...$$

Interest rates tend to mean revert. That is they tend to drift away from a middle level and then drift back. The further they drift away, the harder they are pulled back. A process known as the Ornstein–Uhlenbeck process describes this type of behavior. Oldrich Vasicek proposed the Ornstein–Uhlenbeck process for the short rate in his 1977 paper. In our own version of notation, we have

$$dr = \left(\frac{L_r - r}{T_r}\right)dt + \sigma \, dz \tag{5}$$

Where L_r is the reversion level and T_r is the reversion time. r tends to be drawn to the reversion level L_r. T_r determines how fast or slow that happens. Usually the reciprocal of T_r is used and is referred to as the reversion rate. We prefer the notation T_r since it is easier to develop an intuitive feel for it than for its reciprocal.

One of the weaknesses of this specification is that it only contains three degrees of freedom. Three degrees of freedom is not, in general, enough to allow the practitioner to fit the market. Usually the market consists of at least one volatility parameter and several yields associated with securities which go into defining the yield curve.

Unless a model can be made to fit the existing market, it may be subject to arbitrage. This is not to say there is no value in models which do not fit the market. There is value in this but the value is primarily speculative in nature instead of value as a risk management tool. Even if there is a desire to develop speculative models, it pays to first develop models that conform to the market in order to have a point of reference.

Hull and White generalized the Vasicek model

$$dr = \left(\frac{L_r(t) - r}{T_r(t)}\right)dt + \sigma(t)dz \tag{6}$$

by using functions for the parameters which drive the model instead of scalers. This adds enough degrees of freedom to match observed term structure information.

Notice where the complexity comes in with this model specification.

When we used a commodity like approach, we were able to specify the stochastic process in the same terms as we specified the value of the asset to be optioned. That is, we assume the equity price is both the way to describe the stochastic process that drives the market and the way to describe the value of the optioned security which enters directly into the payoff function on the option.

When we went to yield diffusion, the stochastic process was defined by the bond's yield and the bond's value was defined by the bond's price—a simple functional relation—but enough to complicate the analysis. Now we are in a situation where the stochastic process is defined by a risk free rate and we do not, *a priori*, even have a functional *relation* between the optioned asset's value and the risk free rate which drives the stochastic process!

Furthermore, we cannot ignore the relations between bonds along the yield curve now. With the commodity approach, we could value an option on a bond in isolation. That is no longer the case because the process on the risk-free rate provides information about the entire yield curve. All bonds and all derivative yield curve securities must be a function of this one process and are therefore intimately related.

These models can only be useful to the practitioner if the mean reversion functions can be expressed in terms of quantities which are directly observable and commonly used. Hull and White show that an interest rate term structure and a volatility term structure are sufficient to determine the mean reversion functions. We need the relations derived by Hull and White expressed in a somewhat different way in order to develop intuition about the functions $T_r(t)$ and $L_r(t)$.

Section 3: The Derivation of the Equations Which Express the Reversion Parameters as a Function of Market Observable Quantities in Continuous Time

Hull and White show that with the proper choice for the form of the price of risk function, the resulting differential equations for the extended Vasicek and the extended CIR models can be satisfied by a function similar to this:

$$P(r,t,T) = e^{A(t,T)-B(t,T)^* r}$$

for some functions $A(t,T)$ and $B(t,T)$. Where $P(r,t,T)$ may be interpreted as the price of a discount bond at time t which matures at time T and pays $1.

We also have

$$P(r,t,T) = e^{-R(r,t,T)^*(T,-t)}$$

Where $R(r,t,T)$ is the continuously compounded interest rate at time t corresponding to $P(r,t,T)$.

We may relate the functions $A(t,T)$ and $B(t,T)$ to the observed term structures of rates and volatilities.

We have,

$$(T-t)^* R(r,t,T) = r^* B(t,T) - A(t,T)$$

Differentiating both sides with respect to T gives,

$$F(r,t,T) = r^* \frac{\partial B}{\partial T} - \frac{\partial A}{\partial T}$$

Where $F(r,t,T) =$ Instantaneous forward reinvestment rate observed at time t forward to time T.

Differentiating both sides with respect to r yields,

$$\frac{\partial F(r,t,T)}{\partial r} = \frac{\partial B(t,T)}{\partial T}$$

From Ito's lemma,

$$\frac{\partial F(r,t,T)}{\partial r} = \frac{\sigma_f(r,t,T)}{\sigma_r(r,t)}$$

Where

$\sigma_f(r,t,T)$ is the normal volatility of $F(r,t,T)$ and $\sigma_r(r,t)$ is the normal volatility of r at time t.

We therefore have,

$$\frac{\partial B(t,T)}{\partial T} = \frac{\sigma_f(r,t,T)}{\sigma_r(r,t)}$$

and,

$$F(r,t,T) = r * \frac{\sigma_f(r,t,T)}{\sigma_r(r,t)} - \frac{\partial A(t,T)}{\partial T}$$

Rearranging . . .

$$\frac{\partial A(t,T)}{\partial T} = r * \frac{\sigma_f(r,t,T)}{\sigma_r(r,t)} - F(r,t,T) \tag{7}$$

Set $t = 0$, $T = t$, drop the explicit dependence on r, let $\sigma_f(t) = \sigma_f(0,t)$ ($\sigma_f(t)$ is the forward standard deviation to forward time t viewed at time 0), $F(t) = F(0,t)$, ($F(t)$ is the forward rate to forward time t viewed at time 0). From equation (6), the normal volatility of r, $\sigma_r(r,t)$ can be written $\sigma_r(t)$, i.e., it is independent of r.

The equations at time 0

$$\frac{\partial B(0,t)}{\partial t} = \frac{\sigma_f(t)}{\sigma_r(0)} \tag{8}$$

$$\frac{\partial^2 B(0,t)}{\partial t^2} = \frac{\sigma_f{}'(t)}{\sigma_r(0)}$$

$$\frac{\partial A(0,t)}{\partial t} = r * \frac{\sigma_f(t)}{\sigma_r(0)} - F(t)$$

$$\frac{\partial^2 A(0,t)}{\partial t^2} = r * \frac{\sigma_f{}'(t)}{\sigma_r(0)} - F'(t)$$

The primes on the σ and F functions indicate time derivatives. The Extended Vasicek term structure equation becomes

$$\frac{\partial P}{\partial t} + \left(\left(\frac{L_r(t) - r}{T_r(t)} \right) - \sigma_r(t) * \lambda(t) \right) \frac{\partial P}{\partial r} + \frac{1}{2} \frac{\partial^2 P}{\partial r^2} \sigma_r^2(t) - r * P = 0 \tag{9}$$

We may write:

$$\left(\frac{L_r^o(t) - r}{T_r(t)} \right) = \left(\frac{L_r(t) - r}{T_r(t)} \right) - \sigma_r(t) * \lambda(t) \tag{10}$$

Where

$$L_r^a(t) \equiv L_r(t) - \sigma_r(t) * \lambda(t) * T_r(t)$$

We define $L^a_r(t)$ as the risk adjusted mean reversion level as a function of time.

Furthermore, we assume, as do Hull and White, that the price of risk function, $\lambda(t)$, is only a function of time and is bounded on any finite interval.

The Term Structure equation and the Ito process for the modified Vasicek model:

$$L_r^a(t) \equiv L_r(t) - \sigma_r(t) * \lambda(t) * T_r(t) \tag{11}$$

The term structure equation becomes

$$\frac{\partial P}{\partial t} + \left(\frac{L_r^a(t) - r}{T_r(t)} \right) * \frac{\partial P}{\partial r} + \frac{1}{2} \frac{\partial^2 P}{\partial r^2} * \sigma_r^2(t) - r * P = 0$$

Where $L^a_r(t)$ and $T_r(t)$ have been expressed in terms of known quantities, the PDE above can be solved through finite differencing for flexible contingent cash flow structures, including European and American option contingent cash flows.

The Ito process can be written as

$$dr = \left(\left(\frac{L_r^a(t) - r}{T_r(t)} \right) + \sigma_r(t) * \lambda(t) \right) dt + \sigma_r(t) dz \tag{12}$$

The method used to determine $L^a_r(t)$ and $T_r(t)$ is to solve the PDE in (11) for a particular case, discount bonds: $P(r,t,T) = e^{A(t,T) - B(t,T)*r}$ which imposes functional constraints (see Hull and White) on $A(t,T)$ and $B(t,T)$. $A(t,T)$ and $B(t,T)$ can then be related to the entered term structures through the boundary conditions in (8). Once $A(t,T)$ and $B(t,T)$ are known, $L^a_r(t)$ and $T_r(t)$ can be determined. The coefficients in the PDE are then known and the PDE can be solved for arbitrary boundary conditions, yielding a general evaluation technique.

Hull and White show, albeit with a somewhat different notation:

$$T_r(t) = -\frac{\partial B(0,t)/\partial t}{\partial^2 B(0,t)/\partial t^2} \tag{13}$$

and,

$$L_r^a(t) = -\frac{\partial A(0,t)}{\partial t} - \frac{\partial^2 A(0,t)}{\partial t^2} \cdot T_r(t) \tag{14}$$

$$+ \left(\frac{\partial B(0,t)}{\partial t}\right)^2 \cdot \int_0^t \left(\sigma_r(\tau)/\frac{\partial B(0,\tau)}{\partial \tau}\right)^2 d\tau \cdot T_r(t)$$

Algebraic manipulation of equations (8), (13) and (14) leads to mean reversion parameters in terms of rate and volatility term structures:

$$T_r(t) = \frac{-\sigma_f(t)}{\sigma_f'(t)} \tag{15}$$

$$L_r^a(t) = F(t) + \left\{ \frac{\partial F(t)}{\partial(t)} + \sigma_f(t)^2 \cdot \int_0^t \left[\frac{\sigma_r(\tau)}{\sigma_f(\tau)}\right]^2 d\tau \right\} \cdot T_r(t) \tag{16}$$

$T_r(t)$ (mean reversion time as a function of time) and $L_r^a(t)$ (risk adjusted mean reversion level as a function of time) have been expressed directly in terms of the functions $F(t)$ (forward rates at time 0 as a function of maturity), $\sigma_f(t)$ (forward normal volatilities at time 0 as a function of maturity) and $\sigma_r(t)$ (the normal volatility of r as a function of time). The functions $F(t)$, $\sigma_f(t)$ and $\sigma_r(0)$ represent the observable market.

Equations (15) and (16) may be inverted. Thus one may ask the question, Given mean reversion parameters and a short rate volatility, what characteristics will the resulting market exhibit? Consider the case in which reversion parameters (T_r, L_r^a) and spot volatility (σ_r) of the short rate are constant. Simple manipulation of equations (15) and (16) yields:

The *state of the market* corresponding to constant reversion parameters and spot volatility of the short rate:

$$\sigma_f(t) = e^{-t/T_r}\sigma_r \tag{17}$$

$$F(t) = L_r^a + \left(r - L_r^a\right)e^{-t/T_r} + \left(e^{-t/T_r} - \frac{1}{2}e^{-2t/T_r} - \frac{1}{2}\right) \cdot \sigma_r^2 T_r^2 \tag{18}$$

The term state of the market here means the interest rate term structure and associated volatilities. These can be used to generate swaps, swaptions, caps and floors, and so on and thus are equivalent to the market in terms of these financial structures.

Section 4: A Discussion of Mean Reversion Parameters Using the Equations Derived in Section 3 as a Basis

Mean Reversion Time

The expression (15) for $T_r(t)$ is analogous to a basic equation from physics: distance divided by velocity equals time to cover the distance. To see the analogy, consider that mean reversion implies lower forward volatilities. Consider a fixed reversion time. The more time the short rate evolves over, the greater chance it has to be drawn to the reversion level. The rate may start off with high volatility but as time passes, the mean reversion process will reduce the volatility of the rate because of the constant reversion pull. Thus forward volatilities decrease, and the derivative, $\sigma_f'(t)$ is negative. So an interpretation of T_r is: all things held constant, T_r is the time it would take for the volatility, $\sigma_f(t)$, to decrease to zero when observed at time t. Of course, in the next moment, we could make the same statement, i.e., at $t = t + \Delta t$, it would still seem like it would take T_r years to bring $\sigma_f(t+\Delta t)$ to zero.

Mean Explosion Time

Unfortunately, the real world is not so well behaved. In fact, it is possible to have negative mean reversion times! This can happen whenever $\sigma_f'(t)$ is positive. Since mean reversion implies decreasing forward volatilities, increasing forward volatilities imply no mean reversion. If we examine the equation for $T_r(t)$ again, we see that a negative time to reversion can be interpreted as: all things held constant, $T_r(t)$ is the time it would take for the volatility, $\sigma_f(t)$ to double. In a sense, the rate diffusion process is exploding around the mean reversion level.

Another interesting point is this. The market tends to look at standard deviation in terms of returns or percentual changes—log normality. This has become a standard because of the history of Black–Scholes and because log normality is an easy way to keep a process from becoming negative. Often, interest rate standard deviations are specified in log normal terms. Suppose we have a situation where these log normal volatilities are either flat or decreasing with forward time, i.e., $_{logn}\sigma_f(t)$ = a constant or $_{logn}\sigma_f(t)$ is decreasing, where $_{logn}\sigma_f(t)$ corresponds to the log normal volatility on a forward rate at forward time t. Forward and volatility term structures are observed at time 0.

We may write: $\sigma_f(t) = F(t)*_{logn}\sigma_f(t)$. Suppose the forward curve is steep. Suppose it is steep enough so that $\sigma_f(t)$ is an increasing function. If this is the case, we end up with negative reversion times and no mean reversion—as defined above—mean explosion, because of the increasing forward normal volatilities. All this, even though the log normal volatilities were flat or even decreasing. A steeply increasing yield curve may end up implying that the process is mean exploding. There is actually no contradiction here. The argument may seem counter intuitive. But if mean reversion as defined by equation (6) is actually the state of the market, then the situation described above will not happen.

Inadmissible Functions $\sigma_r(t)$

An issue related to the discussion of forward volatilities is the issue of how to specify the function that defines the standard deviation of the short rate as time passes. Though the mean reversion parameters themselves have been shown to be a function of the term structure of interest rates and the term structure of interest rate volatilities, the same cannot be said of $\sigma_r(t)$. This function can be 'freely' specified. There are two intuitive ways to specify $\sigma_r(t)$. We can specify the normal volatility of the short rate as a constant or we might choose to take $\sigma_r(t)$ equal to the forward volatilities observed at time 0. Suppose we take the latter approach.

We take $\sigma_r(t) = \sigma_f(t)$. This is an intuitive approach in the sense that today's forward volatility at a maturity of time t is the expectation of the spot volatility at that future time. It seems to fall in line with other common market assumptions. However, this assumption does not derive from an arbitrage argument.

We show that this assumption, in fact, is not admissible in the sense that it contradicts a reasonable state of the world. Consider the state of the world in which reversion parameters and spot volatility are constant. Thus T_r, L_r and σ_r are constant.

From Equation (17), $\sigma_f(t) = e^{-t/T_r}\sigma_r$. Yet we have assumed $\sigma_f(t) = \sigma_r$. Thus the assumption $\sigma_r(t) = \sigma_f(t)$ is not allowed in at least one reasonable state of the world.

Another interesting observation comes directly from equation

$$L_r^a(t) = F(t) + \left\{ \frac{\partial F(t)}{\partial t} + \sigma_f(t)^2 * \int_0^t \left[\frac{\sigma_r(\tau)}{\sigma_f(\tau)} \right]^2 d\tau \right\} * T_r(t) \tag{16}$$

One might ask the question, How much does the risk adjusted reversion level—not the actual reversion level (we would need to know the price of risk function to make a statement about the actual reversion level)—deviate from the forward rate curve? From equation (16), the deviation is:

$$\left\{ \frac{\partial F(t)}{\partial(t)} + \sigma_f(t)^2 * \int_0^t \left[\frac{\sigma_r(\tau)}{\sigma_f(\tau)} \right]^2 d\tau \right\} * T_r(t).$$

Thus if $T_r(t) \neq 0$, we have that $L_r^a(t) = F(t)$ if and only if

$$\frac{\partial F(t)}{\partial t} = -\sigma_f(t)^2 * \int_0^t \left[\frac{\sigma_r(\tau)}{\sigma_f(\tau)} \right]^2 d\tau.$$

We observe, in this case, the forward rate curve is a decreasing function of time. Therefore, if we observe a nondecreasing rate curve, we would not expect risk adjusted reversion levels to equal forward rates.

In an increasing forward rate environment, we would have:

$$\frac{\partial F(t)}{\partial t} > -\sigma_f(t)^2 * \int_0^t \left[\frac{\sigma_r(\tau)}{\sigma_f(\tau)} \right]^2 d\tau.$$

We observe, in this case, if

$$T_r(t) > 0, \text{ then}$$

$$\left\{ \frac{\partial F(t)}{\partial t} + \sigma_f(t)^2 * \int_0^t \left[\frac{\sigma_r(\tau)}{\sigma_f(\tau)} \right]^2 d\tau \right\} * T_r(t) > 0$$

Hence in a mean reverting environment with an increasing forward curve, we must have

$$L_r^a(t) > F(t).$$

We graphically illustrate the relation between mean reversion parameters and the market in Figures 2.1 and 2.2. By 'the market' we mean a term structure of interest rates and a term structure of volatilities. The term structure of interest rates is expressed as a curve of continuously compounded, instantaneous rates. The term structure of volatilities is expressed in log normal form and corresponds to the volatilities associated with the forward rates.

Both graphs are based on constant risk adjusted mean reversion levels of eight percent, constant short rate log normal volatilities of twenty-five percent and a starting short rate of five percent. The graph in Figure 2.1 is based on a constant mean reversion time of one year. The graph in Figure 2.2 is based on a constant mean reversion time of ten years.

By comparing these graphs we see that the forward rates converge asymptotically to the risk adjusted mean reversion levels more quickly

Figure 2.1

Volatilities of Forward Rates

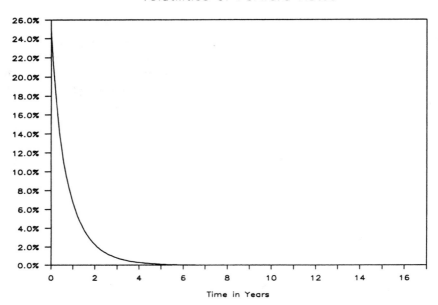

Continuously Compounded Forward Rates

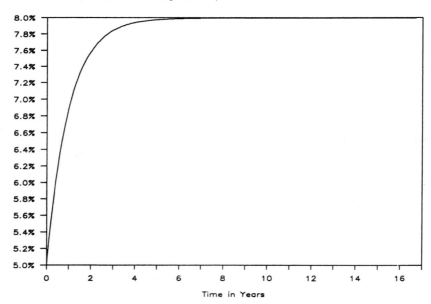

Figure 2.2

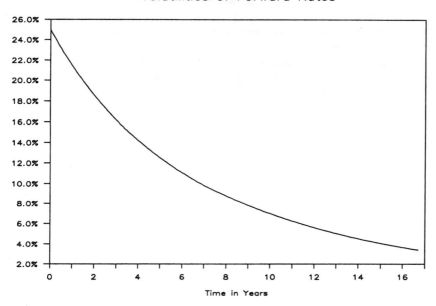

Volatilities of Forward Rates

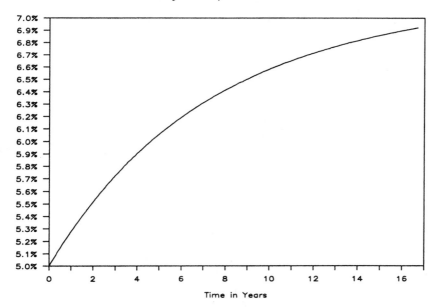

Continuously Compounded Forward Rates

when the time to reversion is less. The forward volatilities converge more quickly to zero when the time to reversion is less. Conversely, we see that in a market environment with forward volatilities that become smaller, faster, we expect a smaller reversion time. This is a graphical demonstration of why the reversion time is inversely related to the derivative of the forward volatility curve.

We also note the equation derived above, $L^a_r(t) > F(t)$, is satisfied in both graphs. In words: the risk adjusted reversion level is an upper bound for the forward rates in a mean reverting environment with an upwardly sloping yield curve.

INTEREST-RATE OPTIONS: CHOOSING A MODEL FOR TRADING*

John Hull and Alan White

3

The Black–Scholes model and its extensions are now widely accepted throughout the world as tools for pricing European options on stocks, currencies, indices, and commodity futures. Numerical procedures based on the models are used to price American options and wide range of exotics. The models are not perfect, but they do provide important benchmarks for traders. At present there is a need for a similar generally accepted benchmark model for trading interest-rate options.

The most common interest-rate options are caps, European bond options and European swap options. Practitioners have tended to value these using an extension of the Black–Scholes model, proposed by Fischer Black in 1976, for valuing options on commodity futures. Under the model, a cap is treated as a portfolio of options on forward interest rates. A bond option or a swap option is similarly treated as an option on a forward bond price or its yield.

If a financial institution wishes to trade only caps, European bond options, and European options on plain vanilla swaps, there may be no need to change from Black's model. Market prices can be used to provide implied volatilities for a range of options similar to those being traded. These implied volatilities can then be used to price deals as they arise.

The limitation of a Black or Black–Scholes type of model as a tool in interest rate options markets becomes apparent when nonstandard deals are being priced. Consider, for example, the valuation of a long-dated American bond option. It is tempting to treat the bond like a stock and

---

* This article originally appeared in *Risk Magazine,* vol. 5 no. 3, March 1992 under the title, "In the Common Interest." Reprinted with permission.

represent the possible evolution of its price in the form of a binomial tree. As it turns out, this does not work well because of two fundamental differences between bonds and stocks:

1. A bond's price volatility naturally declines with the passage of time; and

2. A bond's price converges to its face value at maturity

Figure 3.1 shows how our uncertainty about the price of a stock and a bond changes as we look further into the future. In the case of a stock our uncertainty (as measured by standard deviation) increases as we look further ahead. In the case of a bond it first increases and then decreases. There is no uncertainty at all about the bond's price when it matures, since its price must equal its face value at this time. It is not surprising that a model like Black or Black–Scholes which captures the evolution of a stock's price uncertainty is inappropriate for a bond. By choosing the volatility appropriately a Black or Black–Scholes model can be made to reflect our uncertainty about the price of a bond at one particular time in the future. However, it cannot do so at all future times. This means that the model cannot be used for American options.

An alternative is to work in terms of bond yields rather than bond

Figure 3.1: Evolution of Uncertainty for Stock and Bond Prices

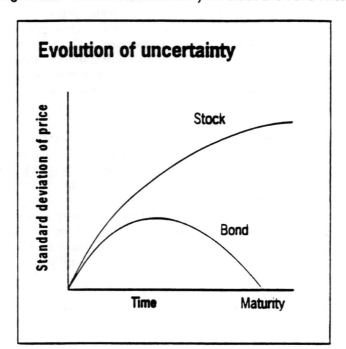

prices. Unfortunately, this is also less than ideal. A bond's yield volatility tends to increase as the bond's maturity is approached. Also, a model which values options by converting prices into yields is not consistent with the put-call parity no-arbitrage relationship for European options.

The real problem with Black's model is that it provides no way of relating the price of one type of interest-rate option to the price of another. Once a financial institution starts to trade nonstandard products, it is essential that it switch to a yield-curve-based model. This is a model of the way in which the whole yield curve can evolve. It provides a consistent framework for pricing and hedging all interest-rate derivatives.

Properties of a Good Trading Model

Many yield-curve-based models have been proposed in the last few years. Which is the best candidate for being the standard model for trading? To answer this we first review the properties of the Black–Scholes stock option pricing model and discuss why it is so popular in the trading room.

The first point to note is that the Black–Scholes model is not perfect. In practice the implied volatilities calculated from Black–Scholes often vary markedly with both strike price and time to maturity. Also, although Black–Scholes assumes that volatility is constant over time, traders find it necessary to change the volatilities used in the model regularly to reflect market conditions. Why then has Black–Scholes been so successful?

One reason is that it is simple. It involves only one variable that is not directly observable in the market, the volatility. An option price can be unambiguously translated into a volatility and vice-versa. An experienced trader can interpolate between, and extrapolate from, the volatilities calculated from actively traded options to price other options. What is more, the model gives the options trader a straightforward target: buy when volatility is low and sell when volatility is high.

The model has one important advantage over more sophisticated models such as those where the volatility is a random variable or where there are jumps. This is that traders can easily develop some intuition for how the model works. They can understand the underlying assumptions, recognize situations where they do not apply, and make appropriate adjustments. More complicated models are useful for research purposes, but tend to be black boxes in the sense that it is difficult for a trader to know how the parameters should be adjusted to cope with changing market conditions.

Another important advantage of the Black–Scholes model is that it presents no computational problems. European options can be valued analytically; the Cox, Ross, Rubinstein binomial tree can be used for American options and exotics; large portfolios can be revalued quickly;

hedge ratios can be calculated easily; scenario analyses present no problems; and so on.

Interest Rate Models

Models describing the behavior of interest rates are in general much more complicated than those describing the behavior of stock prices. This is because, instead of describing the statistical behavior of a single number (the stock price), an interest rate model must somehow capture the way in which a complete yield curve can move around over time.

One requirement of an interest rate model is that it should be consistent with the current term structure of interest rates so that all bonds are priced correctly. Many practitioners are surprised to learn that prior to 1986 the models discussed in the academic literature did not have this basic property. Most practitioners would argue (quite rightly) that they can have little confidence in the price of a bond option if the model being used does not value the underlying bond correctly!

What additional features must an interest rate model have if it is to be widely used for trading? Ideally the model should be the interest rate analogue of Black–Scholes. It must be sufficiently simple that a trader can easily develop an intuitive feel for how it works; it must enable option prices to be unambiguously translated into a measure of market volatility and vice versa; and it must be computationally very fast.

One candidate for the benchmark trading model is the Ho and Lee model. Since it was first published in 1986 analysts have shown that this model is as analytically tractable as Black–Scholes. Formulas exist for valuing European bond options and, when a tree for the short rate is constructed, all bond prices can be calculated analytically at each node. Also, the model involves a single volatility parameter so that option prices can be unambiguously converted into implied volatilities and vice-versa.

The Hull–White Model

The Ho and Lee model has the disadvantage that it assumes that all interest rates have the same variability. We prefer an extension of the model, the Hull–White model, which we discuss in an article in the Review of Financial Studies in 1990 and in the December 1989 issue of RISK. This model incorporates a constant parameter, the reversion rate, which controls the relationship between long- and short-rate volatilities. The model is every bit as analytically tractable as Ho and Lee. Once the reversion rate has been set, option prices can easily be translated into volatilities and vice-versa. (See Appendix 3.1 at end of chapter for presentation of the Hull–White model.)

The Hull–White model is a one-factor model. This means that there is only one underlying source of uncertainty. Why choose Hull–White for trading over more sophisticated two- and three-factor models? The main reason is that it is analytically tractable and is easy to use. The other models are useful as research tools but have the disadvantage that they rely entirely on numerical procedures for the calculation of prices and hedge ratios. This makes them sufficiently slow computationally that there are serious limits to what a trader can do with them.

It is often assumed that, in this age of fast computers and parallel processing, computation time is no longer an issue. This is not true. Unfortunately, computation time is still a very real consideration. Imagine a financial institution with 200 deals in its book. All deals must be valued once each day for marking to market purposes. They must then be revalued perhaps 10 times to calculate deltas with respect to each segment of the yield curve. Twenty different scenarios might have to be investigated to ascertain the effect of different shifts in the term structure/volatility environment on the value of the portfolio. Further calculations are necessary to calculate gamma and vega measures. This means that in total as many as 10,000 option valuations may be needed each day. If it becomes necessary monitor the exposures during the day so that hedges can be rebalanced, even more may be required. If each valuation takes one second, 10,000 valuations take close to three hours. By the time the output is produced it may be too late to adjust the overnight exposure!

Another disadvantage of models that rely entirely on numerical procedures is that the numbers produced are less accurate. Hedge ratios, for example, are calculated by computing the option price, perturbing one of the input parameters and recomputing the option price so as to determine the change. If both option prices are calculated with small errors, the error in the difference between the two may be unacceptably large. In the case of American options we cannot avoid the use of numerical procedures. Luckily, it turns out that the accuracy of hedge ratios for an American option can be improved significantly when the underlying model has some analytic tractability.

Are There Advantages to Being Sophisticated?

Computational considerations aside, should one choose the most sophisticated multifactor interest rate model available for trading and marking to market? We believe that the answer is no. A highly sophisticated model may be useful for R and D purposes, but it can be counter-productive when used for routine trading.

When choosing a model it is important to bear in mind how it will actually be used in the trading room. An option pricing model is, to a large extent, a tool to ensure that nonstandard options are priced consistently with actively traded options. A set of implied volatilities are backed out of the prices of the actively traded options and these are used as a basis for pricing other deals. The model enables a trader to structure his or her thinking about the market and to understand the volatility environment. Models with many parameters can be cumbersome to use in a fast-moving market.

The Black–Scholes model has stood the test of time not because it is the most sophisticated model available, but because it meets the needs of traders. The Hull–White model is designed to meet the needs of traders in a similar way to Black–Scholes, but in the interest-rate options market.

One criticism levelled at both the Hull–White and Ho–Lee models is that they allow negative interest rates. This is not as serious a problem with Hull–White as it is with Ho–Lee since the mean reversion in Hull–White significantly reduces the chance of negative rates. We believe that the advantages of analytic tractability outweigh the disadvantages of negative interest rates. From a theoretical viewpoint there is no question that a model which has some chance, however small, of leading to negative nominal interest rates is less than perfect. However, this is not a serious problem when the model is used for option pricing. As mentioned above, the main purpose of an option-pricing model is to price nonstandard deals correctly relative to standard deals. Research has shown that all models tend to produce much the same results when used for this purpose. As a practical matter, the Hull–White is very robust and consistent with the commonly made assumption of lognormal bond prices (which incidentally also allows negative interest rates).

Implementation

In implementing a model such as Hull–White it is important to be able to relate the model parameters to market data. Consider the use of the model to value swap options. Our approach starts with the user inputting market data for actively traded swap options. This data can consist of prices, price volatilities or yield volatilities. The data is used in conjunction with the model to imply a matrix of short-rate volatilities appropriate for different option maturities and different swap maturities. These are then used to price deals as they arise. The short-rate volatilities can also be inferred from cap volatility data or from cap prices. This allows integration across markets.

The reversion rate parameter is under the control of the user. As mentioned earlier, it governs the relationship between long- and short-rate volatilities. At any given time it is the same for all options. However, it is liable to change over time. During some periods (for example, 1981–82) long rates are much less volatile than short rates. During other periods the volatilities of the two are roughly equal. As a general rule it should be chosen so that it minimizes the variations in the short rate volatilities implied from actively traded options. The user can then have confidence in extrapolating from and interpolating between these volatilities.

This "matrix of volatilities" implementation of our option pricing model will be familiar to all traders who have used Black–Scholes for FX or equity options. It enables the model to be calibrated to the market for both trading and marking to market purposes. The model itself is very robust and can cope with any initial term structure, however bizarre its shape may be. Using the trinomial tree technology, described in our JFQA paper, our working paper, and the September/October 1990 issues of RISK, American bond options and exotics can be priced consistently with European options.

Hedging

Proponents of two- and three-factor models sometimes argue that the real advantages offered by these models over a one-factor model is in the area of hedging. This argument is usually based on a misunderstanding of the way in which hedging is done. The general approach we recommend is outlined in our article in the December, 1990 issue of RISK. If we were to hedge on the basis that there really is only one source of uncertainty, we might end up hedging an exposure to the 10-year rate with a T-bill. This would clearly be totally inadequate. But hedging on the basis that there are only two or three sources of uncertainty would also be inadequate.

In practice the yield curve is divided into a number of segments or buckets and, regardless of the model used, financial institutions calculate a delta for every segment and hedge each of these deltas separately. This means that they are hedging against all possible yield curve movements, both those that are consistent with the model and those that are not consistent with the model. There is a subtle point here. The assumptions made when an option model is used for pricing are usually different from those made when it is used for hedging. To illustrate this, consider how Black–Scholes is used in practice. When pricing, analysts assume that volatility is constant; when hedging, they recognize that the model is imperfect and hedge against volatility changes by calculating vega measures.

Trading Models versus R and D Models

We would like to emphasize the importance of distinguishing between the models appropriate for R and D purposes and the models appropriate for real-time trading. We recommend the Hull–White model for real-time trading and marking to market for the reasons mentioned above. However, we believe that it makes sense to experiment with a variety of models for R and D purposes and for the development of long-term trading strategies.

Again, it is useful to draw an analogy between interest rate option models and other option models. Many financial institutions have developed multi-factor models involving jumps or a random volatility for R and D purposes in the stock option and currency option markets. But when it comes to routine trading and marking to market, they almost invariably revert to the market's benchmark: Black–Scholes.

REFERENCES

Black, F. "The pricing of commodity contracts," *Journal of Financial Economics*, Vol. 3 (1976), pp. 167–179.

Black, F. and M. Scholes. "The pricing of options and corporate liabilities," *Journal of Political Economy*, Vol. 81 (May-June 1973), pp. 637–659.

Cox, J., S. Ross, and M. Rubinstein. "Option pricing: a simplified approach," *Journal of Financial Economics*, Vol. 7 (1979), pp. 229–264.

Ho, T. S. and S. Lee. "Term structure movements and pricing interest rate contingent claims," *Journal of Finance*, Vol. 41 (1986), pp. 1011–1029.

Hull, J. and A. White. "Coming to Terms," *RISK*, December 1989–January 1990, pp. 21–25.

Hull, J. and A. White. "Root and Branch," *RISK*, September 1990, pp. 69–72.

Hull, J. and A. White. "New ways with the yield curve," *RISK*, October 1990, pp. 13–17.

Hull, J. and A. White. "Modern Greek," *RISK*, December 1990, pp. 65–67.

Hull, J. and A. White. "Valuing derivative securities using the explicit finite difference method," *Journal of Financial and Quantitative Analysis*, Vol. 25, No. 1, March 1990, pp. 87–100.

Hull, J. and A. White. "Pricing interest-rate-derivative securities," *The Review of Financial Studies*, Vol. 3, No. 4 (1990), pp. 573–592.

Hull, J. and A. White. "One-factor interest rate models and the valuation of interest rate derivative securities," Working Paper, University of Toronto, latest version: September, 1991, forthcoming: *Journal of Financial and Quantitative Analysis*, June 1993.

Appendix 3.1: The Hull–White Model

r: the short-term interest rate

$\theta(t)$: a function of time determining the average direction in which r moves; it is chosen so that r-movements are consistent with today's term structure of interest rates.

a: the reversion rate; governs the relationship between long- and short-rate volatilities; $a = 0$ corresponds to the Ho and Lee model where all rates are equally variable; as a increases long rates become less volatile.

σ: the standard deviation of the short rate; σ/r is the volatility of the short rate; σ is a measure of the overall level of interest-rate volatility.

In the implementation of the model, σ may vary according to the option being valued, while a is constant across all options. As market conditions change, both a and σ may change.

Bond Prices

The price at time t of a discount bond maturing at time T is $P(t,T)$ where

$$P(t,T) = A(t,T)e^{-B(t,T)},$$

$$B(t,T) = \left[1 - e^{-a(T-t)}\right]/a$$

$$\log A(t,T) = \log \frac{P(0,T)}{P(0,t)} - B(t,T)\frac{\partial \log P(0,t)}{\partial t} - \frac{v(t,T)^2}{2}$$

$$v(t,T)^2 = \frac{1}{2a^3}\sigma^2 \left(e^{-aT} - e^{-at}\right)^2 \left(e^{2at} - 1\right)$$

European Options

The price at time 0 of a European call option maturing at time T on a discount bond maturing at time s is

$$P(0,s)N(h_1) - XP(0,T)N(h_2)$$

where,

$$h_1 = \frac{1}{v(T,s)}\log\left[\frac{P(0,s)}{P(0,T)X}\right] + \frac{v(T,s)}{2}$$

$$h_2 = h_1 - v(T,s)$$

and N is the cumulative normal distribution function.

A cap can be decomposed into a portfolio of European put options on discount bonds. Since this is a one-factor model and future bond prices are known analytically as a function of r, a European option on a coupon-bearing bond can also be decomposed into a portfolio of European options on discount bonds.

American Options

The process for r can be efficiently represented in the form of a trinomial tree. Bond prices are known analytically as a function of r and do not have to be calculated from the tree. The prices of American options are obtained by rolling back through the tree in the usual way.

||

THE PRICING OF OPTIONS ON INTEREST-RATE CAPS AND FLOORS USING THE HULL–WHITE MODEL

John Hull and Alan White

4

In the last several years a very active market in interest-rate caps and floors has developed. In conjunction with this a number of institutions have offered their customers the option to buy or sell a cap or a floor at a future date. One problem with dealing with these complex securities is that there has been no satisfactory way of determining a reasonable price for them. In this article we show how these options can be priced using the no-arbitrage Hull–White term structure model.

The basic properties of the Hull–White model are summarized in the first section. The second section describes how interest-rate caps and floors are priced under the model as options on discount bonds. The procedure for valuing a call or a put on an option on a discount bond is developed in the third section. This is extended in section 4 to cover the pricing of a call option on a cap which is a call on a portfolio of options.

1. The Hull–White Interest Rate Model

The Hull and White interest rate model (1990) extends the model of Vasicek (1977) so that it can exactly replicate any term structure of interest rates and volatilities. This model provides analytic solutions for European-style options on discount and coupon bonds. In this section the principal results of the Hull–White model are summarized.

In the most general version of the Hull–White extended Vasicek model the risk-neutral process for the short-term interest rate is assumed to be

$$dr = \left[\phi(t) - a(t)r\right]dt + \sigma(t)dz$$

where

$$a(t) = -\frac{\partial^2 B(0,t)/\partial t^2}{\partial B(0,t)/\partial t}$$

$$\phi(t) = -a(t)\frac{\partial \hat{A}(0,t)}{\partial t} - \frac{\partial^2 \hat{A}(0,t)}{\partial t^2} + \left[\frac{\partial B(0,t)}{\partial t}\right]^2 \int_0^t \left[\frac{\sigma(\tau)}{\partial B(0,\tau)/\partial \tau}\right]^2 d\tau$$

The risk-neutral process for the interest rate is thus defined by the functions $\hat{A}(0,t)$, $B(0,t)$, and $\sigma(t)$. These three functions are the fundamental determinants of all interest-rate security prices. As explained in Chapter 3, the particular version of the model that we favor is one where $a(t)$ and $\sigma(t)$ are constant. In this paper we present results for the general model.

Consider the price of a discount bond that pays \$1 at time T. Define

- t: The time at which the bond price is to be determined. The current time is 0.
- r: The short rate prevailing at t. The current short rate is r_0.
- $P(r_t,t,T)$: The price at time t of a bond paying \$1 at time T if the short rate is r_t. $P(r_0,0,T)$ is the current price, also written as $P(T)$.

Under the extended Vasicek model the bond price at time t when the interest rate is r_t is

$$P(r_t,t,T) = e^{\left[\hat{A}(t,T) - r_t B(t,T)\right]} \tag{1}$$

where

$$\hat{A}(t,T) = \hat{A}(0,T) - \hat{A}(0,t) - B(t,T)\left[\frac{\partial \hat{A}(0,t)}{\partial t}\right] - \frac{1}{2}\left[B(0,T) - B(0,t)\right]^2$$

$$\int_0^t \left[\frac{\sigma(\tau)}{\partial B(0,\tau)/\partial \tau}\right]^2 d\tau$$

$$B(t,T) = \frac{B(0,T) - B(0,t)}{\partial B(0,t)/\partial t}$$

Now consider a European option on a discount bond. Define

t: The time at which the option price is to be determined.

r_t: The short rate prevailing at t.

T_1: Option maturity time, measured in years.

T_2: Bond maturity time, measured in years.

X: Option exercise price.

The option prices are then

$$\text{Call}\left(r_t,t,T_1,T_2\right)=P\left(r_t,t,T_2\right)N\left(d_1\right)-XP\left(r_t,t,T_1\right)N\left(d_2\right) \tag{2}$$

$$\text{Put}\left(r_t,t,T_1,T_2\right)=XP\left(r_t,t,T_1\right)N\left(-d_2\right)-P\left(r_t,t,T_2\right)N\left(-d_1\right) \tag{3}$$

where

$$d_1=\frac{\log\left(\dfrac{P\left(r_t,t,T_2\right)}{XP\left(r_t,t,T_1\right)}\right)}{\sigma_P}+\frac{\sigma_P}{2}$$

$$d_2=d_1-\sigma_P$$

$$\sigma_P^2=\left[B\left(0,T_2\right)-B\left(0,T_1\right)\right]^2\int_t^{T_1}\left[\frac{\sigma(\tau)}{\left(\partial B\left(0,\tau\right)/\partial\tau\right)}\right]^2 d\tau$$

Using equations (1), (2), and (3) the functions $\hat{A}(0,t)$, $B(0,t)$, and $\sigma(t)$ can be inferred from the prices of a variety of options and the current term structure of interest rates. In the rest of this paper it will be assumed that these functions have been determined.

2. Interest Rate Caps

An interest rate caplet (one leg of a cap) is equivalent to a put option which matures at the caplet start date on a discount bond which matures at the caplet end date. The strike price for the option is one per dollar of principal and the face value of the discount bond is $1 + R_x\tau$ per dollar of principal where τ is the length of the caplet measured in years and R_x is the cap rate. For more details on this see Hull (1989) pages 254–255.

Using equation (3) the price of the ith caplet in a cap is then

$$\text{Caplet}_i\left(r_t,t\right)=\left[P\left(r_t,t,T_i\right)N\left(-d_{2i}\right)-\text{Face}_iP\left(r_t,t,T_{i+1}\right)N\left(-d_{1i}\right)\right]\text{Prin}_i \tag{4}$$

where

$$d_{1i} = \frac{\log\left(\frac{Face_i\, P(r_t,t,T_{i+1})}{P(r_t,t,T_i)}\right)}{\sigma_{Pi}} + \frac{\sigma_{Pi}}{2}$$

$$d_{2i} = d_{1i} - \sigma_{Pi}$$

$$\sigma_{Pi} = \left[B(0,T_{i+1}) - B(0,T_i)\right]^2 \int_t^{T_i}\left[\frac{\sigma(\tau)}{(\partial B(0,\tau)/\partial\tau)}\right]^2 d\tau$$

$$Face_i = 1 + R_{Xi}\frac{DAYS}{YEAR}$$

and

T_i: Time at which the ith caplet starts, measured in years.
T_{i+1}: Time at which the ith caplet ends, measured in years.
R_{Xi}: Cap rate for ith caplet.
DAYS: Number of days in the period covered by the cap.
YEAR: Number of days in a year.
$Prin_i$: Principal underlying the ith caplet.

The price of a cap with n elements is

$$Cap\, Price = \sum_{i=1}^{n} Caplet_i$$

3. A Call Option on a Put Option

In this section we consider a call option which allows the holder to buy a put option on a discount bond. This is equivalent to a call on one element of an interest rate cap.

Consider a European call option expiring at time T_1 on a European put option maturing at T_2 on a discount bond which matures at T_3. The strike price for the put option is X and the exercise price for the call option is K. The current price of the call option on the put option is

$$\hat{E}\left\{max\left[Put(r_{T1},T_1,T_2,T_3) - K, 0\right]e^{-\int_0^{T_1} r_s}\right\}$$

where $\hat{E}$ is a risk-neutral expectation over all possible r_t paths for $0 \le t \le T_1$ and the put price is given by equation (3). It can be shown that this expectation is equivalent to

$$P(r_0,0,T_1)\int_{r^*}^{\infty}\left[\text{Put}(r,T_1,T_2,T_3)-K\right]\hat{g}(r)\,dr \tag{5}$$

where r^* is the rate such that Put $(r^*,T_1,T_2,T_3) = K$, and $\hat{g}(r)$ is the risk-neutral forward-adjusted density function for the interest rate. This density function for r_t is a normal density function with

$E(r_t) = f(t)$, the forward rate,

$$\text{Var}(r_t) = \sigma_r^2(t) = \left[\frac{\partial B(0,t)}{\partial t}\right]^2 \int_0^t \left[\frac{\sigma(\tau)}{(\partial B(0,\tau)/\partial \tau)}\right]^2 d\tau$$

The solution to equation (5) is

$$\text{Call on Put} = P(T_2)XM(-d_2,\alpha-\sigma_2,\rho) \\ -P(T_3)M(-d_1,\alpha-\sigma_3,\rho)-P(T_1)KN(\alpha) \tag{6}$$

where

$$d_1 = \frac{\log\left(\dfrac{P(T_3)}{XP(T_2)}\right)}{\sigma_1} + \frac{\sigma_1}{2}$$

$$d_2 = d_1 - \sigma_1$$

$$\sigma_1^2 = \left[B(0,T_3)-B(0,T_2)\right]^2 \int_0^{T_2}\left[\frac{\sigma(\tau)}{(\partial B(0,\tau)/\partial\tau)}\right]^2 d\tau$$

$$\sigma_2^2 = \left[B(0,T_2)-B(0,T_1)\right]^2 \int_0^{T_1}\left[\frac{\sigma(\tau)}{\partial B(0,\tau)/\partial\tau}\right]^2 d\tau$$

$$\sigma_3^2 = \left[B(0,T_3)-B(0,T_1)\right]^2 \int_0^{T_1}\left[\frac{\sigma(\tau)}{(\partial B(0,\tau)/\partial\tau)}\right]^2 d\tau$$

$$\alpha = \frac{f(T_1)-r^*}{\sigma_r}$$

$$\rho = \sqrt{\frac{\int_0^{T_1}\left[\dfrac{\sigma(\tau)}{(\partial B(0,\tau)/\partial \tau)}\right]^2 d\tau}{\int_0^{T_2}\left[\dfrac{\sigma(\tau)}{(\partial B(0,\tau)/\partial \tau)}\right]^2 d\tau}}$$

and $M(.\,,.\,,\rho)$ is the cumulative bivariate normal with correlation ρ. Using put-call parity the value of a put on a put is

$$\text{Put on Put} = \text{Call on Put} - \text{Put}(r_0, 0, T_2, T_3) + P(T_1)K$$

By analogy the value of a call on a call is

$$\text{Call on Call} = P(T_3)M(d1, -\alpha + \sigma_3, \rho) - \qquad (7)$$
$$P(T_2)X\, M(d2, -\alpha + \sigma_2, \rho) - P(T_1)K\, N(-\alpha)$$

and a put on a call is

$$\text{Put on Call} = \text{Call on Call} - \text{Call}(r_0\, 0, T_2, T_3) + P(T_1)K$$

4. A Call Option on an Interest Rate Cap

An interest rate cap is a portfolio of put options on a series of discount bonds. Thus, a call on a cap (or caption) is a call on a portfolio of put options. This can be transformed into a portfolio of call options each on a single put option by using the technique that Jamshidian (1989) developed to compute the price of an option on a coupon bond.

Consider a European call option which allows the holder to buy the cap described in section 2. Define

T_X: Time at which the option expires.

X: Option exercise price. The payoff on the option is the greater of the cap price at time T_X less X or zero.

First it is necessary to compute the short rate at time T_X for which the cap price equals the strike price X. This is called the critical interest rate, r^*, and is found by solving

$$\sum_{i=1}^{n} \text{Caplet}_i(r^*, T_X) = X$$

where $\text{Caplet}_i(r^*,t)$ is given by equation (4). For all rates greater than r^* the option will be exercised; for all rates less than r^* it will not be exercised.

The critical interest rate is used to allocate the strike price X to each of the elements of the cap underlying the option. Let x_i be the portion of X which is allocated to the ith caplet.

$$x_i = \text{Caplet}_i\left(r^*,T_X\right)$$

Note that $\sum_{i=1}^{n} x_i = X$.

From equations (4) and (6) the value of the call on the ith caplet is then

$$\text{Call}_i = P(T_i)M\left(-d_{2i},\alpha_i - \sigma_{2i},\rho_i\right) - \text{Face}_i P(T_{i+1})M\left(-d_{1i},\alpha_i - \sigma_{3i},\rho_i\right) \\ -x_i P(T_X)N(\alpha_i) \tag{8}$$

where

$$d_{1i} = \frac{\log\left(\dfrac{\text{Face}_i P(T_{i+1})}{P(T_i)}\right)}{\sigma_{1i}} + \frac{\sigma_{1i}}{2}$$

$$d_{2i} = d_{1i} - \sigma_{1i}$$

$$\sigma_{1i}^2 = \left[B(0,T_{i+1}) - B(0,T_i)\right]^2 \int_0^{T_i} \left[\frac{\sigma(\tau)}{\left(\partial B(0,\tau)/\partial\tau\right)}\right]^2 d\tau$$

$$\sigma_{2i}^2 = \left[B(0,T_i) - B(0,T_X)\right]^2 \int_0^{T_X} \left[\frac{\sigma(\tau)}{\left(\partial B(0,\tau)/\partial\tau\right)}\right]^2 d\tau$$

$$\sigma_{3i}^2 = \left[B(0,T_{i+1}) - B(0,T_X)\right]^2 \int_0^{T_X} \left[\frac{\sigma(\tau)}{\left(\partial B(0,\tau)/\partial\tau\right)}\right]^2 d\tau$$

$$\alpha_i = \frac{f(T_X) - r^*}{\sigma_\tau}$$

$$\rho_i = \sqrt{\frac{\int_0^{T_X}\left[\dfrac{\sigma(\tau)}{\left(\partial B(0,\tau)/\partial\tau\right)}\right]^2 d\tau}{\int_0^{T_i}\left[\dfrac{\sigma(\tau)}{\left(\partial B(0,\tau)/\partial\tau\right)}\right]^2 d\tau}}$$

and the value of the call option on the cap is

$$\text{Call on Cap} = \sum_{i=1}^{n} \text{Call}_i \tag{9}$$

The prices of puts on caps and puts and calls on floors are computed in a similar way.

The prices of a number of captions are given below to give the reader some sense of the value of a call on a cap. The term structure of interest rates is flat at 10% with quarterly compounding. The term structure of volatilities is defined by setting $\sigma(t) = 0.014$ and $a(t) = 0.10$ for all t so that $B(t,T) = \frac{1}{a}[1 - e^{-a(T-t)}]$. Under this environment, the implied forward rate volatilities (using Black's (1976) model) for quarterly at-the-money caps of varying maturities are:

Term (years)	1	2	3	4	5	7	10
Implied Vol.	13.80	13.43	13.09	12.77	12.48	11.95	11.31

Table 4.1 gives the prices of call options of various terms on 5-year forward start caps which commence at the maturity of the call. In each case the cap rate is 10 percent and the exercise price on the call is set equal to the forward cap price so that the option is approximately at-the-money.

Table 4.1: Call Option Prices on 5-Year Forward Start Caps

T_X (years)	X = Forward Cap Price	Call Price
0.25	2.76	0.45
0.50	2.85	0.64
0.75	2.90	0.78
1.00	2.94	0.89
2.00	2.97	1.18
3.00	2.90	1.33
4.00	2.77	1.41
5.00	2.60	1.44

REFERENCES

Black, F., 1976. "The pricing of commodity contracts," *Journal of Financial Economics*, 3, 167–179.

Hull, J., 1989. "Options futures and other derivative securities," Prentice Hall, 1989.

Hull, J. and A. White, 1990. "Pricing interest rate derivative securities," *Review of Financial Studies*, 3, 573-592.

Jamshidian, F., 1989. "An exact bond option formula," *Journal of Finance*, 44, 205–209.

Vasicek, O. A., 1977. "An equilibrium characterization of the term structure," *Journal of Financial Economics*, 5, 177–188.

Part Two

EXCHANGE RATES

A QUICK ALGORITHM FOR PRICING
EUROPEAN AVERAGE OPTIONS*

Stuart M. Turnbull and
Lee Macdonald Wakeman**

5

1. Introduction

In the over-the-counter market, many options are written on average prices. For example, the payoff at maturity for a one-year average sterling call option is the maximum of zero and the difference between the arithmetic daily exchange rate, averaged over some prespecified period and the exercise price. Thus, the value of the option depends upon the average price and not the spot price.

There are many possible uses for such options. For corporations that receive or pay foreign currency claims on a regular basis, a foreign currency option based on the average of the exchange rate represents one way to reduce its average foreign currency exposure. Similar comments also apply to interest rate instruments. Average options, by their design, reduce the significance of the closing price at the maturity of the option. This reduces the effects of any possible abnormal price movements at the maturity of the option. Thus, average options provide a way to ameliorate any possible price distortions that might arise because of a lack of depth in the market of the underlying asset.

The pricing and hedging of these options raises some interesting issues. First, the value of the option depends upon the history of the asset

* This article originally appeared in the *Journal of Financial and Quantitative Analysis*, vol. 26, no. 3, September 1991. Reprinted with permission.
** The paper was first written while Turnbull was visiting at the Australian Graduate School of Management. Helpful discussions with Ian Cooper, David Emanuel (of Emanuel and Macbeth Associates), Robert Kohn, Angelo Melino, and especially Edmond Levy are gratefully acknowledged. The authors also thank *JFQA* Managing Editor Jonathan Karpoff.

price movements over the averaging period. Thus, if the binomial tree approach is used to price the option, it is necessary to keep track of 2^n possible paths, where n is the number of nodes. This becomes infeasible for large values of n unless some approximation method is used. Second, if the asset price follows a log-normal distribution, the arithmetic average will not be log-normally distributed. Standard option models, such as Black–Scholes, rely upon the assumption of log-normality. Third, once the maturity of the option is less than the averaging period, the hedging properties of the option can change quite dramatically. There is a practical need for a model that can quickly and accurately price such options and determine the required hedge ratios such as delta, gamma, vega, and theta. Monte Carlo methods offer an obvious solution possibility, yet these methods are relatively slow.

The objective of this paper is to describe a quick way to price European average options. While it is very difficult to determine the probability distribution for the average, all of its moments can be readily determined. Thus, an Edgeworth series expansion can be used to approximate the distribution.

The basic model is described in Section II. The first part of this section prices average options when the maturity of the option is greater than the averaging period. The accuracy of the approximation is tested against Monte Carlo estimates. The second part of this section addresses the case in which the maturity of the option is less than or equal to the averaging period. Again, the accuracy of the approximation is tested against Monte Carlo estimates. It is demonstrated that when the maturity of the option is less than the averaging period, the price of an average value option can be greater than that of a standard European option, contrary to what Kemna and Vorst (1990) assert. Some of the characteristics of the delta ratio also are examined. A closed form solution for European options written on the geometric average is described in Section III, and a comparison of arithmetic and geometric option prices is presented. It is shown that, for some cases, the two sets of prices can be relatively close while, for other cases, there can be substantial differences. A summary is given in Section IV.

II. The Option Model

Consider a call option of maturity T, written on the average of the past n stock prices.[1] It is initially assumed that the maturity of the option is greater than the averaging period $(T > n)$.

---

[1] The average is defined using stock prices at $T - n + 1, \ldots, T$.

Assumptions

A1. No transaction costs, no differential taxes, no borrowing or lending restrictions, and trading takes place continuously;

A2. The term structure of interest rates is flat and nonstochastic;

A3. It is assumed that the stock price S is described by a log-normal probability distribution,

$$dS = S\alpha dt + S\theta dZ \tag{1}$$

where dZ is a standard Wiener process whose increments are uncorrelated; α is the constant instantaneous mean; and θ^2 is the constant variance of the instantaneous rate of return.

Let $A(t)$ denote the average at time t, which is defined by

$$A(t) \equiv \left[S(t) + S(t-1) + ... + S(t-(n-1)) \right] / n, \tag{2}$$

where $S(t)$ is the stock price at time t, and it is assumed that the averaging is done with daily stock prices. Weekends and holidays are ignored, though these complications could easily be incorporated at the cost of additional notation. Assumption A3 implies that the stock price is log-normally distributed, so that

$$S(t) = S(t-1)\exp\left[\alpha - \theta^2 / 2 + \theta Y \right], \tag{3}$$

where $Y \sim N(0, 1)$. Thus, the average is the sum of log-normally distributed random variables. Given that the log-normal distribution is not stable, the distribution of the average is not log-normal.

Let $C(A(t); T, K, n)$ denote the value of a European call option written on the average. The option matures at time T; K is the exercise price; and n is the number of prices included in the average. At maturity, the value of the option is

$$C(A(T), T, K, n) = \max\left\{ A(T) - K, 0 \right\}$$

To value this option, the risk-neutral argument of Cox and Ross (1976) is used. Under the equivalent distribution, relative prices follow a martingale and the expected returns on the stock will be the risk-free rate of interest r, implying that $\alpha = r$ in Equation (1).[2] Given such an adjustment, the value of the option is

$$C\big(A(t);T,K,n\big) = \exp\big[-r(T-t)\big]E_t\big[A(T)-K\,\big|\,A(T)\geq K\big], \tag{4}$$

where E_t is the expectation operator with respect to the equivalent probability distribution, given the stock price at time t.

To evaluate the above expression, it is necessary to determine the probability density function for the average $A(T)$. In general, this is difficult to do, given that $A(T)$ is the sum of correlated log-normally distributed random variables. To circumvent this difficulty, an Edgeworth series expansion will be used. The true distribution will be approximated with an alternative distribution. Given the work of Mitchell (1968), the alternative distribution will be assumed to be log-normal.[3] If $f(y)$ denotes the true probability function and $a(y)$ the approximating distribution, where $a(y)$ is a log-normal probability density function, then

$$f(y) = a(y) + \frac{c_2}{2!}\frac{d^2 a(y)}{dy^2} - \frac{c_3}{3!}\frac{d^3 a(y)}{dy3} + \frac{c^4}{4!}\frac{d^4 a(y)}{dy^4} + e(y), \tag{5}$$

where $c_2 = \chi_2(F) - \chi_2(A); c_3 \equiv \chi_3(F) - \chi_3(A); c_4 \equiv \chi_4(F) - \chi_4(A) + 3c^2_2; \chi_j(F)\,[\chi_j(A)]$ is the jth cumulant of the exact [approximating] distribution; and $e(y)$ is a residual error term. If a random variable Y has a cumulative distribution function F, the first four cumulants are

$$\chi_1(F) = E(Y), \qquad\qquad \chi_2(F) = E\big[Y-E(Y)\big]^2,$$

$$\chi_3(F) = E\big[Y-E(Y)^3\big], \quad \chi_4(F) = E\big[Y-E(Y)\big]^4 - 3\Big[E\big[Y-E(Y)\big]^2\Big]^2,$$

where all expectations are with respect to the distribution F. (See Kendall and Stuart, 1977, pp. 67–73). The first two moments of the approximating distribution have been set equal to the first two moments of the exact distribution. The moments of a random variable Y with respect to the $a(y)$ distribution are given by

$$E\big(Y^m\big) = \exp\left(\mu m + \frac{\sigma^2}{2}m^2\right), m = 1,2,\ldots.$$

---

[2] For foreign exchange options, the mean would be set such that $\alpha = r - rf$, where rf is the foreign exchange rate.
[3] The question of convergence is discussed in detail in Mitchell (1968).

To apply an Edgeworth expansion, it is necessary to determine the cumulants of the distribution for the average, $A(T)$. While it is difficult to determine the probability density function for $A(T)$, all of its moments can easily be determined using a recursive relationship. Given the stock price at time $t-1$, the stock price at time t can be written in the form,

$$S(t) = S(t-1)R_t, \tag{6}$$

where R_t is the price relative, and from (3), it is log-normally distributed. Repeated use of (6) in Equation (2) implies that the average can be written in the form,

$$A(T) = S[T - (n-1)][1 + R_{i+1} + R_{i+1}R_{i+2} + \cdots + R_{i+1}R_{i+2} \cdots R_{i+n-1}]/n, \tag{7}$$

where $i \equiv T - (n-1)$. Let $L_{i+n} \equiv 1$; and $L_{i+j} = 1 + R_{i+j}L_{i+j+1}, j = 1, ..., n-1$, so that

$$A(T) = S(i)L_{i+1}/n. \tag{8}$$

But to value the option at $t = 0$, the stock $S(i)$ is random. Let R_i denote the price relative from $t = 0$ to $t = i$, so that

$$A(T) = S(0)R_iL_{i+1}/n. \tag{9}$$

From (9), the option will be exercised if

$$Y \equiv R_iL_{i+1} > k, \tag{10}$$

where $k \equiv nK/S(0)$. The mth moment of Y is given by

$$E(Y^m) = E(R_i^m)E(L_{i+1}^m), \tag{11}$$

given the Assumption A3 of independence. (See Boyle, 1976). The value of $E(L^m_{i+j})$ can be determined from

$$E(L_{i+j}^m) = E\left[(1 + R_{i+j}L_{i+j+1})^m\right],$$

$j = 1, ..., n-1$. Thus, all the cumulants of the exact distribution can be calculated.

The Edgeworth series expansion is applied to (10), so that if $\psi \equiv E(Y-k)[Y \geq k]$, then

$$\psi = \int_k^\infty (y-k)f(y)dy \tag{12}$$

$$= \int_k^\infty (y-k)a(y)dy + \frac{c_2}{2!}a(k) - \frac{c_3}{3!}\frac{da(k)}{dy} + \frac{c^4}{4!}\frac{d^2a(k)}{dy^2} + e(k),$$

(see Jarrow and Rudd, 1982, Equation 12). The first term on the right-hand side of (12) can be written in the form

$$\int_k^\infty (y-k)a(y)dy = \exp\left(\mu + \sigma^2/2\right)N(d_1) - kN(d_2),$$

where $d_1 \equiv [-\ln(k) + \mu + \sigma^2]/\sigma; d_2 \equiv d_1 - \sigma$. While this is similar to the expression for Black–Scholes, it differs in an important way. In applying the risk-neutral argument, the expected rate of return for the stock is set equal to the risk-free rate of interest. However, this is not the case for the expected value of the arithmetic averaging process, implying that the mean μ is not the risk-free rate, due to the discrete nature of the average.

B. Accuracy

The accuracy of the approximation can be tested by pricing the option using the antithetic Monte Carlo method, as described by Boyle (1977) and Rubinstein (1981). The accuracy of the approximation is examined in Table 5.1. In Part A, the instantaneous standard deviation of the rate of return is 20 percent per year and, in Part B, 30 percent per year. The maturity of the option is assumed to be 120 days and the averaging period is 30 days. The reported Black–Scholes values are derived using the standard deviation of the rate of return on the stock and provide a measure of the effects of averaging. It is seen that, in all cases, the error from using the approximation is very small. Similar results (not reported) are obtained using different averaging periods.

C. Pricing in the Averaging Period

Up to the present point, it has been assumed that the maturity of the option is greater than the averaging period. This assumption is now relaxed and it is assumed that $T \leq n$. Given that the average is defined over n days, then $(n - T)$ prices have been observed where, for convenience, T is treated as an integer. Three important implications follow. First, the effect of averaging is to reduce the variance of the terminal distribution, which will lower option prices. Second, the effective exercise price is al-

Table 5.1: Accuracy: Maturity Greater than Averaging Period. The Approximation Is Calculated Using Equation (12).

Exercise Price	Call Option			Put Option		
	Monte Carlo	Approxi- mation	Black– Scholes	Monte Carlo	Approxi- mation	Black– Scholes
Part A. Standard Deviation 0.20 per year						
90	12.68 (0.01)	12.67	13.16	0.50 (0.01)	0.50	0.64
95	8.68 (0.01)	8.69	9.24	1.37 (0.01)	1.38	1.59
100	5.47 (0.01)	5.46	6.04	3.01 (0.01)	3.01	3.25
105	3.12 (0.01)	3.13	3.66	5.53 (0.01)	5.53	5.73
110	1.61 (0.01)	1.62	2.05	8.89 (0.01)	8.89	8.98
Part B. Standard Deviation 0.30 per year						
90	13.84 (0.01)	13.85	14.52	1.67 (0.01)	1.68	2.01
95	10.35 (0.02)	10.37	11.11	3.06 (0.01)	3.06	3.46
100	7.46 (0.02)	7.48	8.25	5.01 (0.01)	5.03	5.45
105	5.18 (0.02)	5.20	5.94	7.59 (0.01)	7.60	8.01
110	3.46 (0.02)	3.48	4.16	10.74 (0.01)	10.75	11.08

Spot Price	100
Maturity	120 days
Interest Rate	9 percent
Averaging Period	30 days

(Figures in parentheses are the standard errors for the Monte Carlo estimates)

---

tered as maturity decreases. Consider a call option, which will be exercised if

$$A(T) = \left[\tilde{F} + P\right] / n > K,$$

where $\tilde{F}$ denotes the sum of future prices; and P denotes the sum of observed prices. This can be written in the form,

$$\tilde{F}/n > K - P/n \equiv EK,$$

where EK is defined to be the effective exercise price. The effective exercise price changes as maturity decreases. The expected payoff at the maturity of a call option is

$$E\left[\tilde{A}(T) - K \middle| \tilde{A}(T) \geq K\right] = E\left[\tilde{F}/n - EK \middle| \tilde{F}/n \geq EK\right].$$

The Edgeworth series expansion can be applied to evaluate the above term.

The third implication is that the effective exercise price can be negative. If this happens, then it implies that a call option will be exercised for certain at maturity. When the effective exercise price becomes negative, then even if all future prices are zero, the average at maturity will still be greater than the true exercise price. This also implies that a put option will be worthless.[4] It should be noted that this contradicts a result in Kemna and Vorst (1990) who argue that the price of an average-value option will always be lower than that of a standard European option. This is not correct if the maturity of the option is less than the averaging period.

D. Accuracy

The accuracy of the algorithm is tested against Monte Carlo estimates. To calculate the average, it is assumed that all past prices have remained constant at 100. The averaging period is assumed to be 120 days. Thus, if the maturity is 90 days, the first 30 past prices are assumed to be 100. The results are shown in Table 5.2. In Part A, the volatility of the rate of return on the stock is 0.20 per year. It is seen that the approximation does an excellent job. In Part B, the volatility of the rate of return is 0.30 per year. Similar results are obtained, though for deep in-the-money call options, the accuracy slightly deteriorates.

An interesting result is obtained for put options when the exercise price is 105. The put option price decreases and then increases as matu-

---

[4] Suppose that at some point before maturity the effective exercise price becomes negative, so that $EK \equiv K - P/n < 0$. At maturity, the value of a call option is $[\tilde{F} + P]/n - K > 0$, for all values of F, given that $\tilde{F} \geq 0$. Thus, a call option will be exercised for certain at maturity if the effective exercise price becomes negative. This is not the case, of course, for a standard European option. At maturity, the value of a put option is $K - [\tilde{F} + P]/n = [K - P/n] - \tilde{F}/n < 0$, as $K - P/n < 0$ and $\tilde{F} \geq 0$. The option is worthless.

Table 5.2: Accuracy: Pricing in the Averaging Period. The Approximation Is Calculated Using Equation (12)

Maturity	95 Monte Carlo	95 Approxi-mation	100 Monte Carlo	100 Approxi-mation	105 Monte Carlo	105 Approxi-mation
Part A. Standard Deviation 0.20 per year						
Call Option						
120	6.80	6.82	3.36	3.37	1.31	1.29
90	5.84	5.86	2.13	2.13	0.43	0.42
60	5.29	5.29	1.12	1.13	0.03	0.03
30	5.06	5.06	0.38	0.38	0	0
1	5.00	5.00	0	0	0	0
Put Option						
120	0.54	0.56	1.96	1.97	4.76	4.74
90	0.15	0.17	1.33	1.34	4.53	4.52
60	0.01	0.01	0.77	0.77	4.61	4.60
30	0	0	0.29	0.29	4.87	4.87
1	0	0	0	0	5.00	5.00
Part B. Standard Deviation 0.30 per year						
Call Option						
120	7.71	7.75	4.65	4.65	2.54	2.50
90	6.28	6.31	2.97	2.97	1.10	1.07
60	5.36	5.37	1.59	1.59	0.20	0.19
30	5.06	5.06	0.55	0.55	0	0
1	5.00	5.00	0.01	0.01	0	0
Put Option						
120	1.45	1.49	3.25	3.25	5.99	5.96
90	0.59	0.62	2.18	2.18	5.20	5.17
60	0.08	0.09	1.23	1.23	4.77	4.76
30	0	0	0.46	0.46	4.87	4.87
1	0	0	0.01	0.01	5.00	5.00

Spot	100
Averaging Period	120 days
All Past Prices	100
Interest Rate	9 percent
Standard Error of Monte Carlo Estimate	0.01

rity decreases, and finishes in-the-money. Consider the option with one day left to maturity. The option will be exercised if

$$K - \left[\tilde{S}(1) + 119*100 \right] / 120 > 0,$$

where $\tilde{S}(1)$ is the stock price at maturity. If K is 105, then the above can be written

$$5.83 - \tilde{S}(1)/120 > 0.$$

Given the spot price of the stock is 100, the probability of exercise is almost unity. When the maturity is 120 days, no stock prices have been observed that contribute to the average. Thus, the option is like an ordinary option and its price declines as the variance of the terminal distribution declines, given that maturity is decreasing. When the maturity is 90 days, however, the probability of the option being in-the-money at maturity has increased, given that the first 30 prices are 100. This effect will increase the price of the option. A priori, no statement can be made about which effect will dominate.

The hedging properties of these options depend in part upon whether the maturity of the option is greater or less than the averaging period. If the maturity of the option is less than the averaging period, then the properties of the option will depend upon the path of stock prices inside the averaging period, as demonstrated in the last section.

In Table 5.3, the effects upon the option price and hedge ratio are examined as the number of daily observations used to calculate the average is changed. The maturity of the option is 15 days. First, consider the case of 28 observations used to calculate the average. For this case, the maturity of the option is clearly less than the averaging period. It is assumed that past prices have remained at the spot rate when calculating the effective exercise price. For the call option with an exercise price of 100, there is a dramatic difference in the price and hedge ratio when 28 observations are used for the average, compared to the other two cases. The reason for this difference is that when 28 observations are used to calculate the average, given the maturity is 15 days, 13 observations that contribute to the average have already been observed. When 14 observations are used to calculate the average, the maturity of the option is still greater than the averaging period. For the call option with exercise price 95, there is very little change in the price, as the option is deep in-the-money. However, the hedge ratio is reduced by nearly a half when 28 observations are used to calculate the average. Thirteen observations that

Table 5.3: Increasing the Number of Observations
in the Average. Price and Hedge Ratios.

Maturity 15 Days

Number of Observations in Average		Call Option Exercise Price			Pull Option Exercise Price		
		95	100	105	95	100	105
1	Price	5.496	1.797	0.276	0.160	1.444	4.904
	Hedge Ratio	0.915	0.543	0.136	−0.085	−0.457	−0.864
14	Price	5.202	1.139	0.038	0.019	0.939	4.819
	Hedge Ratio	0.979	0.536	0.037	−0.020	−0.463	−0.463
28	Price	5.083	0.576	0	0	0.475	4.881
	Hedge Ratio	0.535	0.287	0	0	−0.249	−0.535

Spot Price	100
Interest Rate	9 percent
Standard Deviation	0.20 per year

contribute to the average have already been observed and, thus, the option is less sensitive to changes in the spot price.

III. Geometric Average

Consider a call option of maturity T written on the geometric average of the past n stock prices. It is initially assumed that the maturity of the option is greater than or equal to the averaging period $(T \geq n)$. The geometric average is defined by

$$G(T) \equiv \left[S(T-n+1) \cdot S(T-n+2) \ldots \cdot S(T) \right]^{1/n}. \tag{13}$$

Substituting (6) into the above expression gives, after simplification,

$$G(T) = S(T-n) \left[R_{T-n+1}^{n} \cdot R_{T-n+2}^{n-1} \cdots \cdot R_{T} \right]^{1/n}. \tag{14}$$

Given Assumption (A3), $G(T)$ is log-normally distributed. Let $\exp(x) \equiv G(T)$, where $x \sim N(m_x, \sigma^2_x)$. Using (6) and (3) then, under the risk-neutral distribution,

$$m_x = \ln\left[S(0)\right] + \left(r - \theta^2/2\right)(T-n) + \left(r - \theta^2/2\right)\sum_{j=1}^{n} j/n \qquad (15a)$$

and

$$\sigma_x^2 = \theta^2(T-n) + \theta^2\sum_{j=1}^{n} j^2/n^2.$$

It is now assumed that the maturity of the option is less than the averaging period $(T < n)$. Suppose that n_0 prices have been observed, while the remaining $n_1 (\equiv n - n_0)$ prices are random, where n_1 is also the maturity of the option. The geometric average can be written in the form,

$$G(n_1) = \left[S(-n_0+1)\cdot S(-n_0+2)\ldots S(0)\cdot S(1)\ldots S(n_1)\right]^{1/n}$$

$$= G\cdot S(0)^{n_1/n}\left[R_1^{n_1} R_2^{n_1-1}\ldots R_{n1}\right]^{1/n},$$

where $G \equiv [S(-n_0+1)S(-n_0+2)\ldots S(0)]^{1/n}$. For this case, Equation (15a) becomes

$$m_x = \ln(G) + (n_1/n)\ln\left[S(0)\right] + \left(r - \theta^2/2\right)\sum_{j=1}^{n_1} j/n \qquad (15b)$$

and

$$\sigma_x^2 = \theta^2\sum_{j=1}^{n_1} j^2/n^2.$$

Theorem: European Geometric Average Options

a) The price of a European call option is given by

$$C(0) = B(T)\left[\exp\left(m_x \sigma_x^2/2\right)N(d) - K\,N(d-\sigma_x)\right],$$

where K is the exercise price; $\sigma_x d = -\ln(K) + m_x + \sigma_x^2; m_x$ and σ_x^2 are defined by (15); and $B(T) \equiv \exp(-rT)$.

b) The price of a European put option is given by

$$P(0) = B(T)\left[K\,N(-d+\sigma_x) - \exp\left(m_x + \sigma_n^2/2\right)N(-d)\right].$$

Proof. The proof follows from using (4) and the theorem given in Smith (1976).

For the case of the maturity being greater than or equal to the averaging period, the above expression can be written in a more familiar form. For a call option,

$$C(0) = S(0)\exp(\eta)N(d) - KB(T)N(d - \sigma_x),$$

where $\eta \equiv -T\theta^2/2 - (r - \theta^2/2)(n-1)/2 + \sigma_x^2/2$; and $\sigma_x d \equiv \ln[S(0)/KB(T)] + \eta + \sigma_x^2$. If $n = 1$, the above expression becomes the Black–Scholes formula for a call option.

It is instructive to compare the prices of options written on arithmetic and geometric averages. In Table 5.4, prices are compared for options that have a maturity of 120 days and an averaging period of 60 days. In Part A, the standard deviation is 0.20 per year. The results are very similar. In Part B, the standard deviation is 0.30 per year. The increase in the standard deviation drives a wedge between the two sets of prices, with the

Table 5.4: Comparison of Arithmetic and Geometric Average Option Prices.

	Call Option		Put Option	
Exercise Price	**Arithmetic Average**	**Geometric Average**	**Arithmetic Average**	**Geometric Average**
Part A. Standard Deviation 0.20 per year				
90	12.18	12.13	0.36	0.36
95	8.09	8.05	1.13	1.14
100	4.83	4.79	2.73	2.74
105	2.55	2.53	5.31	5.34
110	1.19	1.18	8.81	8.85
Part B. Standard Deviation 0.30 per year				
90	13.14	13.04	1.32	1.34
95	9.56	9.47	2.60	2.63
100	6.63	6.56	4.53	4.58
105	4.38	4.33	7.14	7.21
110	2.76	2.72	10.38	10.46

Spot Price	100
Maturity	120 days
Interest Rate	9 percent
Averaging Period	60 days

Table 5.5: Pricing in the Averaging Period. Arithmetic Price / Geometric Price

Exercise Price

Maturity	90		100		110	
	AP	GP	AP	GP	AP	GP

Part A. Standard Deviation 0.20 per year

Call Option

120	11.22	11.10	3.37	3.30	0.37	0.36
90	10.59	10.50	2.13	2.07	0.04	0.03
60	10.22	10.16	1.13	1.09	0	0
30	10.02	10.00	0.38	0.37	0	0

Put Option

120	0.10	0.09	1.97	2.01	8.69	8.79
90	0.01	0.01	1.34	1.37	9.04	9.12
60	0	0	0.77	0.79	9.50	9.56
30	0	0	0.29	0.30	9.84	9.86

Part B. Standard Deviation 0.30 per year

Call Option

120	11.68	11.43	4.65	4.50	1.20	1.16
90	10.69	10.48	2.97	2.85	0.29	0.26
60	10.22	10.09	1.59	1.52	0.01	0.01
30	10.02	9.98	0.55	0.50	0	0

Put Option

120	0.56	0.55	3.25	3.35	9.52	9.72
90	0.11	0.11	2.18	2.27	9.29	9.46
60	0	0	1.23	1.29	9.51	9.63
30	0	0	0.46	0.48	9.84	9.88

Spot Price	100
Averaging Period	120 days
All Past Prices	100
Interest Rate	9 percent
AP	Arithmetic Price
GP	Geometric Price

geometric average consistently underpricing call options and overpricing puts. A similar result is seen in Table 5.5. The averaging period is set at 120 days and, when the maturity of the option is less than the averaging period, all past prices are assumed to be 100. It is seen that, as the maturity of the option increases, the differences between the two sets of prices increase.

It might be concluded from Tables 5.4 and 5.5 that, for "short" maturities and "low" variance of return, the geometric average option provides a good estimate for the price of an arithmetic option. If the maturity of the option is less than the averaging period, however, then care must be exercised as these options are path dependent.

Consider an option of 60-days maturity and an averaging period of 120 days, implying that 60 prices have been observed. Instead of assuming that all past prices are fixed at 100, as was assumed in Table 5.2, it is assumed in Table 5.6 that, over the first 60-day period, prices go through a complete cycle, so that the arithmetic average over the 60-day period is 100. It is seen that, even for a standard deviation of 0.20 per year, substantial pricing differences can arise.

Table 5.6: Path Dependence

	Call Option		Put Option	
Exercise Price	Arithmetic Average	Geometric Average	Arithmetic Average	Geometric Average
Part A. Standard Deviation 0.20 per year				
90	10.22	10.00	0	0
95	5.29	5.07	0.01	0
100	1.13	1.00	0.77	0.87
105	0.03	0.02	4.60	4.82
110	0	0	9.50	9.73
Part B. Standard Deviation 0.30 per year				
90	10.22	9.92	0	0
95	5.37	5.10	0.08	0.11
100	1.59	1.43	1.23	1.37
105	0.19	0.15	4.76	5.00
110	0.01	0	9.51	9.80

Averaging Period	120 days
Maturity of Option	60 days
Interest Rate	9 percent

IV. Summary

An algorithm has been developed for pricing European arithmetic options. The algorithm was tested against Monte Carlo estimates and was found to be accurate. The speed of the algorithm is similar to that of the Black–Scholes algorithm. The algorithm can easily be extended to price average options when nonconsecutive prices are used, and to price foreign currency average options. A closed form solution was derived for pricing European geometric options. From a comparison of arithmetic average and geometric average option prices, two conclusions can be drawn. First, if the maturity of the option is greater than the averaging period and if the standard deviation of the rate of return is "small" and the option's maturity "short," then the results are similar.[5] Second, if the maturity of the option is less than the averaging period, then there can be substantial differences in the prices of the two types of options.

REFERENCES

Boyle, P. P. "Rates of Return as Random Variables." *Journal of Risk and Insurance,* 43 (Dec. 1976), 694–711.

———. "Options: A Monte Carlo Approach." *Journal of Financial Economics,* 4 (May 1977), 323–338.

Boyle, P. P., and D. Emanuel. "Options and the General Mean." Working Paper, Accounting Group, Univ. of Waterloo (July 1982).

Cox, J., and S. Ross. "The Valuation of Options for Alternative Stochastic Processes." *Journal of Financial Economics,* 3 (Jan./March 1976), 145–166.

Jarrow, R., and A. Rudd. "Approximate Option Valuation for Arbitrary Stochastic Processes." *Journal of Financial Economics,* 10 (Nov. 1982), 346–369.

Kemna, A. G. Z., and A. C. F. Vorst. "A Pricing Method for Options Based on Average Asset Values." *Journal of Banking and Finance,* 14 (March 1990), 113–129.

Kendall, M., and A. Stuart. *The Advanced Theory of Statistics,* Vol. 1, 4th ed. New York: Macmillan (1977).

Mitchell, R. L. "Permanence of the Log-Normal Distribution." *Journal of the Optical Society of America,* 58 (Sept. 1968), 1267–1272.

---

[5] This does suggest the geometric average option model could be used as a control variate in a Monte Carlo simulation to estimate arithmetic average option prices. See Kemna and Vorst (1990). However, such an approach would be a lot slower than using the algorithm described in this paper.

Rubinstein, R. Y. *Simulation and the Monte Carlo Method.* New York: John Wiley & Sons (1981).

Smith, C. "Option Pricing: A Review." *Journal of Financial Economics,* 3 (Jan./March 1976), 3–52.

CURRENCY DERIVATIVES FOR THE INVESTOR

James C. F. MeVay

6

A New World of Opportunity

The decade of the 1980s represents a watershed period for participants in the capital markets whether they were investors or issuers of securities. The key development was unquestionably the advent of the interest rate swap. This event also had the effect of stimulating further development of interest rate option products as well as the continued evolution of currency products from their genesis in the underlying forward markets.

Prior to the development of the swap market, issuers and investors were locked into a bilateral relationship fraught with significant compromise. In making the investment decision, the fixed income investor had to consider the following characteristics of the issuer:

country	industry
credit quality	maturity
currency of issue	coupon type
yield and spread	option features

The obvious dilemma was to achieve yield targets without incurring undesirable exposures to other characteristics. The nature of this condition is shown in Figure 6.1. The fundamental observation is that *both* issuer and investor are constrained by the need to create a security that exactly matches each other's preferences.

The emergence of the swap market radically altered the traditional relationship between issuer and investor for all time. Figure 6.2 shows the tremendous increase in alternatives to the capital markets players afforded by derivative products. No longer was the investor held hostage to the available supply of securities to meet his objectives. Through deriva-

Figure 6.1

Debt Markets <u>Before</u> Derivatives

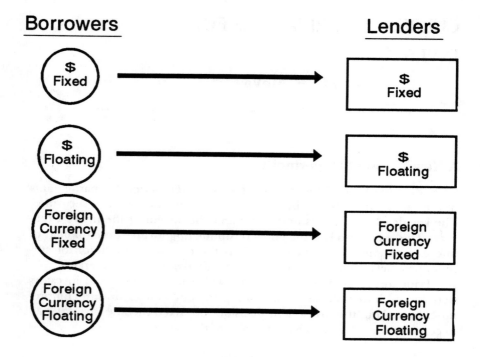

<u>Borrowers</u>   <u>Lenders</u>

tives, it now became possible to separate the liquidity/issuer characteristics from the economic components of currency and coupon repricing characteristics that drive total return. Through derivatives, the investor could easily change the currency exposure or coupon repricing and even add or subtract option features at will to meet his economic preferences.

One Risk/Return Dilemma: Solved

While this turn of events vastly improved the efficiency of the global capital markets, many investors in the mid to late 1980s sought to diversify their portfolios to gain more international exposure either through asset reallocation, derivative structuring, or both. Not coincidentally, extensive discussions were also taking place in corporate boardrooms over the tradeoff of reducing debt coupons by borrowing in foreign currencies,

Figure 6.2

Debt Markets <u>After</u> Derivatives

Borrowers

Lenders

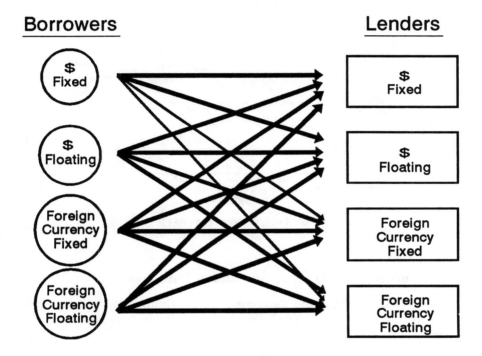

most notably Swiss francs and yen that, in fact, more than a few borrowers issued on an unhedged basis much to their future consternation. In the end, much energy was expended on both sides agonizing over the question of improved coupons weighed against the unavoidable currency risk.

Increased sophistication on the part of derivative product specialists resulted in the very recent innovation of a product to precisely address these concerns of both issuers and investors. The revolutionary aspect of the product, called a *cross index basis swap,* was the separation of coupon returns from currency exposure risk. In essence, this refinement has a similar effect as the first swaps did by segregating specific risks and permitting their independent management. The effect of this swap is to allow the user to swap from an interest rate in one currency to another *without* incurring any outright foreign exchange risk.

Figure 6.3

Comparison of 6M US LIBOR vs 6M DM LIBOR
1984 - April 1992

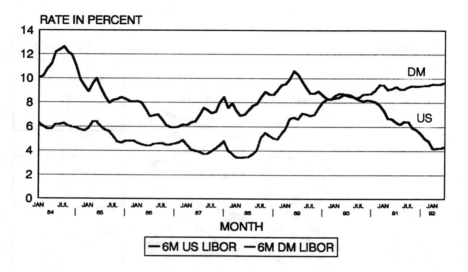

The Market in 1991: Investor Yields Plummet

Throughout 1991, the difference between eurodollar interest rates and those of other major international currencies continued to diverge to historically high levels as the Federal Reserve Bank sought to stimulate economic growth through very aggressive reductions in short-term interest rates. An example of this is shown in Figure 6.3 which shows the movement in dollar and deutschemark LIBOR over the period 1984 through 1991. As can be seen, dollar rates moved to record low levels for the period (levels that, in fact, had not been experienced since 1963) while deutsche mark (DM) interest rates moved to record high levels for the period. The movement of the differential in rates from 1984 through 1991 is shown in Figure 6.4. For the majority of this period, the spread of dollar rates over DM rates was positive and tended to be between 200 and 400 basis points. During 1990, the differential reached essential parity in rates and then turned negative as DM rates edged higher and US rates plunged, descending to a record negative spread which is currently 538 basis points. The result is that a dollar investor saw his yield on short-term money market investments shrink by over 400 basis points or essentially *in half.*

Figure 6.4

Spread of 6M US LIBOR vs 6M DM LIBOR
1984 - 1991

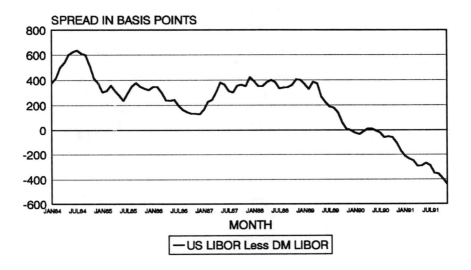

A Synthetic Higher Yield Alternative

Unlike the prior dilemma of seeking higher returns in foreign currencies at the expense of incurring foreign exchange risk, the investor now had available to him the alternative of the cross-index basis swap to increase yield without the risk of foreign exchange fluctuations. Figure 6.5 shows an example of a five-year cross-index basis swap in which dollar returns are exchanged for deutschemark returns, but are applied against a dollar notional principal amount. In this example, the investor has an investment horizon of five years and, for liquidity reasons, has a preference to maintain funds in money market investments and also wants to avoid exposure to financial risk by preserving the floating rate character of the investment. The swap would be structured so that the notional principal amount, which is denominated in dollars, matches the dollar principal amount of the money market investment. Under the swap, the investor is obligated to pay the counterparty the six-month eurodollar rate which is match funded with the interest payments received on the underlying dollar deposit. In exchange for paying the eurodollar return, the investor receives the eurodeutschemark return minus a spread, which, in this example, is 163 basis points, calculated on the dollar notional prin-

Figure 6.5

5 YEAR CROSS INDEX BASIS SWAP

375 basis point pickup in 1st period with all settlements made in USD

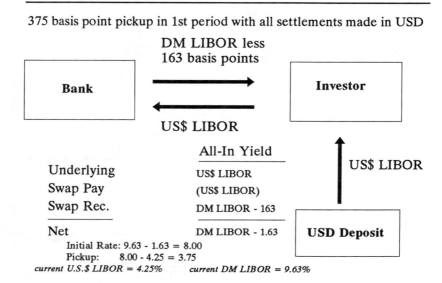

cipal amount of the swap. With six-month eurodeutschemarks currently yielding 9.63 percent, the first period payment due to the investor, less the spread of 163 basis points, would be 8.00 percent. The investor's obligation to the counterparty would be the eurodollar yield which is currently 4.25 percent. Therefore, the net payment under the swap to the investor would be 3.75 percent. When the swap receipt is added to the interest income on the deposit of 4.25 percent, the total return to the investor would be 8.00 percent for a yield pickup of 375 basis points versus a straight eurodollar deposit investment. The actual payment settlements would be as shown in Table 6.1.

Dynamics of the Deal

While the investor is obviously very pleased with an immediate cash pickup in his investment yield, the thought has probably crossed his mind that there is some risk involved in this structure. The risk, in fact, is in having exchanged one floating rate index for another much like the risk that would be involved if he had exchanged one dollar index, such as eurodollars, for another, such as the prime rate. In this latter example, the risk to the investor would be a convergence or tightening of the prime

Table 6.1: Cross-Index Basis Swap Settlement Payments

Deposit Amount: $100,000,000
Notional Principal Amount of Swap: $100,000,000
Initial Interest Period: April 16, 1992–October 16, 1992
Days in Interest Period: 183
Swap Dollar Rate: 4.25%
Swap Deutschemark Rate: 9.63%
Deutschemark Basis Spread: –1.63%
Dollar Deposit Rate: 4.25%

A. *Swap Payments*

Receivable:
$100,000,000 × (9.63% – 1.63%) × (183/360) = $4,066,666.67

LESS

Payable:
$100,000,000 × (4.25%) × (183/360) = $2,160,416.67
           Net Receipt from Swap Counterparty $1,906,250.00

PLUS

B. *Deposit Interest Income*

$100,000,000 × (4.25%) × (183/360) = $2,160,416.67

C. *Combined Interest Income*

Net Swap Receipt Plus Deposit Interest Income $4,066,666.67

D. *Yield Equivalency at 8.00%*

$100,000,000 × (8.00%) × (183/360) = $4,066,666,67

versus LIBOR spread. A similar risk exists in the cross-index basis swap in that should the DM versus dollar interest rate spread drop below the basis spread adjustment incorporated in the swap, i.e. 163 basis points, the investor will have suffered an opportunity loss for as long as that condition persists for not having remained in a straight dollar interest rate investment structure.

A floating rate index basis swap in the same currency, such as eurodollars and the prime rate, involves an assessment of the sector spread between an administered domestic bank lending rate and an international interbank money market rate. In the case of the example here of DM and eurodollars, the rates are from the same sector, i.e., the international interbank money market, but denominated in different currencies. Assessment of the spread in this case is, perhaps, a little more straightforward than in the case of sector spread analysis since each currency has its own term structure of interest rates which can give insight into the expected future movement of each interest rate.

The swap yield curves for DM and dollars from spot six months out to five years is shown in Figure 6.6. Since the swap fixed rate in both currencies is paid or received against eurodollars or eurodeutschemarks flat, by inference each yield curve represents the term LIBOR rate for each respective currency. At the time these yield curves were prepared, there existed some interesting features of both. In the case of DM, the yield curve exhibited an inverted condition with longer rates less than short rates. This difference was about 150 basis points and suggested that the market expected German rates to decline over the period. By way of contrast, the dollar yield curve exhibited a very steeply upwardly sloping pattern with the difference in long rates over short rates of about 275 basis points suggesting that dollar rates would rise significantly in the future. In all cases, the DM rates were in excess of the dollar rates. At a six-month maturity the excess of DM rates over dollars was about 540 basis points which narrowed to around 120 basis points at the five-year maturity.

Taken at face value, these curves may suggest that DM rates will be

Figure 6.6

Interest Rate Swap Curves
6 Month to 5 Year Maturities
Semiannual, actual/360 basis.

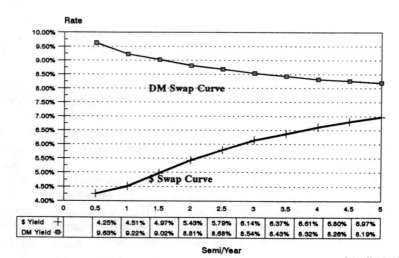

		0.5	1	1.5	2	2.5	3	3.5	4	4.5	5
$ Yield +		4.25%	4.51%	4.97%	5.43%	5.79%	6.14%	6.37%	6.61%	6.80%	6.97%
DM Yield ▣		9.63%	9.22%	9.02%	8.81%	8.68%	8.54%	8.43%	8.32%	8.26%	8.19%

Semi/Year

as of April 14, 1992

higher than dollar rates throughout the period and by huge margins in the earlier periods. However, the relevant analysis to make is to ascertain the expected future rates for the maturity of the indices under consideration, i.e., six months, as opposed to rates for the term of the structure, in this case five years. Using the rates in the respective yield curves, it is possible to extract the market's expectation for future six-month DM and dollar interest rates as of the point in time the yield curves were constructed. The first step is to convert the coupon rates in the yield curve to the equivalent zero coupon rate. Given the zero coupon rates for adjacent maturities, e.g., six months apart, it is possible to calculate the forward six-month rate that is implied by the yield curve for the six-month period between the two points on the curve. Table 6.2 shows the calculation of the implied six-month dollar rate between the six-month and one-year maturity, i.e., the six-month rate six months forward:

Table 6.2: Derivation of Implied Forward Six Month Dollar Rate

Maturity	Coupon Rate	Zero Coupon Rate	F. V. Factor	Implied Forward
Six Months	4.2500%	4.3090%	1.021545	
One Year	4.5100%	4.5726%	1.045726	4.6693%

A plot of the implied forward interest rates for both DM and dollars is shown in Figure 6.7. This chart shows a significantly different view of the future than is suggested by the raw coupon yield curves. Here we not only have convergence of the forward rates, but an outright inversion in spreads. This analysis shows that although the spread on a spot basis begins at 540 basis points, the implied forward six month spread is *negative* by 150 basis points in the last period of the five year horizon. Just as the fixed rate of a floating for fixed interest rate swap represents a uniform rate that is the economic equivalent of the implied forward floating rate over the horizon involved, the pricing of the cross-index swap reflects the economics of these expected interest rate differentials as embodied in the spread adjustment of 163 basis points. A path-dependent break-even analysis of the DM LIBOR rate required to equal the effective yield of a dollar investment at the implied forward dollar rates is shown in Table 6.3. While there is essentially an infinite number of scenarios of DM rate assumptions that will generate a break-even condition over the five-year horizon, a simplistic assumption was applied in this example. This scenario assumes a constant periodic change in DM rates that will produce a break-even condition. This is far more realistic than the assumption of an

Figure 6.7

Implied Forward 6 Month LIBOR Rates
5 Year Horizon
Semiannual, actual/360 basis.

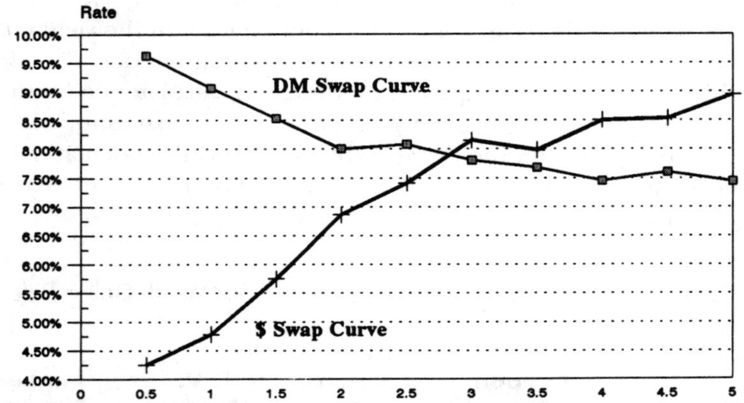

	0	0.5	1	1.5	2	2.5	3	3.5	4	4.5	5
USD L(6) +		4.25%	4.67%	5.75%	6.86%	7.41%	8.15%	7.98%	8.50%	8.53%	8.94%
DEM L(6) ⊟		9.63%	9.06%	8.53%	8.00%	8.08%	7.80%	7.68%	7.45%	7.60%	7.44%

Semi/Year

as of April 14, 1992

instantaneous change to an equilibrium rate that holds constant over the whole horizon period in that it recognizes that rates must pass through successive levels to reach future values. The outcome of the analysis shows that DM rates must decline by 25 basis points *each* six month period for five years. Taken in conjunction with the average implied forward dollar change of 52 basis points per period, the resulting break-even spread is a *decline* of 77 basis points per period for a total decline in spread over five years of 695 basis points. In examining the resulting DM rates, it will be discovered that they approximate the implied forward DM rate curve, but, in fact, are somewhat lower. This difference represents the residual cost to the dealer of offsetting the remaining cross currency foreign exchange risk.

The Value is in the View

At this point, the investor may have come to the conclusion that what at first seemed like found money in terms of an immediate cash investment yield return pickup seems closer to a fairly priced proposition taking into account the respective yield curve expectations as well as the re-

Table 6.3

DM/US FIVE YEAR CROSS INDEX BASIS SWAP RETURN ANALYSIS

SCENARIO: PATH-DEPENDENT BREAKEVEN DM LIBOR GIVEN US LIBOR IMPLIED FORWARDS

BASIS ADJ.: 1.630%

	S/360		S/360		B.P.
INITIAL DM L(6):	9.630%	INITIAL US L(6):	4.250%	INITIAL SPREAD:	538.0
FINAL DM L(6):	7.369%	FINAL US L(6):	8.940%	FINAL SPREAD:	-157.1
TOTAL DM L(6) CHANGE:	-226 B.P.	TOTAL US L(6) CHANGE:	469 B.P.	TOTAL CHANGE:	-695.1
PERIOD DM L(6) CHANGE:	-25.1 B.P.	PERIOD US L(6) CHANGE:	52.1 B.P.	PERIOD CHANGE:	-77.2

EFFECTIVE DM YIELD: 7.098%
EFFECTIVE US YIELD: 7.098%
YIELD (+/-): 0.0 B.P.

USD LIBOR RATE ASSUMPTIONS			USD LIBOR RETURNS			DEM LIBOR RETURNS				
RESET DATE	S.A. PERIOD	LIBOR RATE	FLOATING US RATE	FLOATING US RETURN	CUM. US RETURN	FLOATING DM RATE	DM BASIS SPREAD	NET DM RATE	FLOATING DM RETURN	CUM. DM RETURN
Apr-92	0.0	4.250%	4.250%			9.630%	1.630%	8.000%		
Oct-92	0.5	4.670%	4.670%	2.125	2.125	9.379%	1.630%	7.749%	4.000	4.000
Apr-93	1.0	5.750%	5.750%	2.335	4.510	9.128%	1.630%	7.498%	3.874	7.968
Oct-93	1.5	6.860%	6.860%	2.875	7.514	8.876%	1.630%	7.246%	3.749	11.946
Apr-94	2.0	7.410%	7.410%	3.430	11.202	8.625%	1.630%	6.995%	3.623	15.979
Oct-94	2.5	8.150%	8.150%	3.705	15.322	8.374%	1.630%	6.744%	3.498	20.068
Apr-95	3.0	7.980%	7.980%	4.075	20.021	8.123%	1.630%	6.493%	3.372	24.258
Oct-95	3.5	8.500%	8.500%	3.990	24.810	7.872%	1.630%	6.242%	3.246	28.472
Apr-96	4.0	8.530%	8.530%	4.250	30.115	7.620%	1.630%	5.990%	3.121	32.803
Oct-96	4.5	8.940%	8.940%	4.265	35.664	7.369%	1.630%	5.739%	2.995	37.197
Apr-97	5.0			4.470	41.728				2.870	41.730
TOTAL				35.520	41.728	TOTAL			34.348	41.730
EFFECTIVE YIELD					7.098%	EFFECTIVE YIELD				7.098%

quired currency risk management. That conclusion is the correct one for, if it weren't, arbitrage opportunities would exist which would be removed from the market by the activities of market professionals until market equilibrium was restored.

The key to understanding the value of this, or any other instrument for that matter, whether it be a cash or derivative, lies in the degree of agreement that the user has with the market's expectations. The conditions that gave rise to this market valuation were a U.S. market with an extremely steep yield curve reflecting a significant inflation premium and a German market with an inverted yield curve that expected lower future rates that would be necessary to generate an economic rebirth of the severely stunted East German economy.

The reason why this structure has been so enormously popular with investors, more so than with virtually any other currency, is because there is what amounts to a widespread disagreement with the implied future rate scenarios. The feeling is that the economic recovery in the U.S. is anemic and that the inflation premium in the yield curve is substantially overestimating the rate of growth that will be seen. The view on the German situation is that there will not be a wholesale abandonment of the strict historical behavior of fighting inflation at virtually any cost. The view here is that rates will probably remain higher than implied as a monetary policy is pursued to ruthlessly control inflation. The result is that the opportunity offered by this swap structure represents a prudent risk to assume given the perceived price value to the investor.

The emergence of this specific product structure, while simple in concept, has had enormous power in that it has been able to provide investors the potential for investment yield improvement by synthetically creating returns based on foreign currency interest rates but absent the significant risk of foreign exchange exposure that was previously unavoidable. As a result, this product has served as the introduction as well as the stimulus for many investment managers to evaluate the many advantages and flexibility that derivative instruments affords in managing their investment activities in a manner that can precisely tailor risk and return characteristics to their preferences at any point in time.

Part Three

RISK MANAGEMENT TECHNIQUES

THE USE OF INTEREST RATE SWAPS IN MANAGING CORPORATE LIABILITIES*

Laurie S. Goodman

7

$\mathbf{A}$s a result of the high and volatile interest rates of the early 1980s, companies began to emphasize active management of their liabilities as well as their assets. Issuers started to realize that the type of debt used and its maturity could make a considerable difference in their funding costs. At the same time, a number of new risk management products—futures, options, swaps, and caps—made it possible for corporate treasurers to manage their liabilities more actively. They began to understand that debt could be readily transformed to take advantage of changing market conditions. Rates on floating-rate debt could be fixed by using futures or swaps, floating debt could be capped, fixed rates could be transformed into floating rates, and issuers could hedge the cost of a new issue by fixing or capping the rate. Corporate treasurers also discovered that the cheapest way to issue a given variety of debt was not always the most straightforward. Issuers have sometimes found opportunities to make initial debt offerings in one form and then, with the use of risk management products, to convert that debt into the desired form, thereby producing a lower all-in cost of funds.

In this article, I discuss the corporate uses of one of the most widely used risk management products: interest rate swaps. The principal roles that swaps have assumed in corporate liability management can be summed up in the following three:

1. reducing the cost of current issuance,
2. locking in the cost or spread on an expected future issue, and

---

*This article originally appeared in the *Journal of Applied Corporate Finance*, vol. 2, no. 4, Winter 1990. Reprinted with permission.

3. hedging the corporate exposure to interest rates by altering the cash flows on an existing liability.

In the process of allowing corporations to manage interest rate exposures and reduce funding costs, the growth of the interest rate swap market has contributed significantly to the further integration of the fixed-rate and floating-rate debt markets. As a result of corporate attempts to exploit pricing differences between these markets, many of the financing "arbitrage" opportunities described below are no longer available. For example, while the combination of floating debt with a swap has at times been considerably cheaper than issuing fixed debt, the disparities are not nearly as great as they were reported to be five years ago. Thus, while some of the funding techniques presented here may still be used on a fairly regular basis, most should be probably be regarded as "window-of-opportunity" arbitrages that appear only from time to time—and are thus available to only the most opportunistic corporate treasurers.[1]

Reducing the Cost of a Current Issue

By using the swap market, companies have obtained their desired financing at a lower cost than issuing the desired debt directly. For example, if a firm wants to issue fixed-rate noncallable debt, it has at least five choices:

1. issue the fixed-rate debt directly;

2. issue floating-rate debt and swap the floating-rate debt into fixed-rate debt;

3. issue callable fixed-rate debt and enter into a callable swap or write an option on a swap;

4. issue putable fixed-rate debt and enter into a putable swap; or

5. issue an unconventional instrument and enter into a swap to obtain the equivalent of a fixed-rate bond.

Figure 7.1 illustrates each of these funding strategies, as well as a number of others. For example, to obtain fixed-rate noncallable debt (row 2), any of the original debt issues listed in the top row can be transformed by adding the features of the cell that intersects the applicable column and row 2. Thus, an issue of callable fixed-rate debt (column 3) can be transformed into noncallable fixed-rate debt (column 3, row 2) by entering into a callable swap or writing an option on a swap (also known as a "swaption").

---

[1] This article considers the economics of various swap transactions, but does not address tax and accounting issues. An issuer would want to take these into account before making a final decision as to what form the debt will take.

Figure 7.1: Using Swaps and Swaptions to Transform Debt

	Original Debt				
	(1)	**(2)**	**(3)**	**(4)**	**(5)**
Transformed Debt	**Floating Rate**	**Fixed Rate Non-callable Non-putable**	**Callable Fixed Rate Debt**	**Putable Fixed Rate Debt**	**Non-Conven-tional**
(1)					
Floating rate debt	X	Vanilla Swap	Callable Swap	Putable Swap	FROG + yield Curve Swap
(2)					
Fixed rate non-callable non-putable debt	Vanilla Swap	X	Callable Swap + Vanilla Swap or Swaption	Putable Swap + Vanilla Swap	Inverse Floater + Vanilla or FROG + yield curve swap + vanilla swap
(3)					
Callable fixed rate debt	Swaption + vanilla swap	Swaption	X	not economical	not economical
(4)					
Putable fixed rate debt swaption + vanilla swap	swaption	two swaptions	X	not economical	

Figure 7.1: *Continued*

Original Debt

	(1)	(2)	(3)	(4)	(5)
Transformed Debt	**Floating Rate**	**Fixed Rate Non-callable Non-putable**	**Callable Fixed Rate Debt**	**Putable Fixed Rate Debt**	**Non-Conven-tional**
5)					
Non-conventional debt	not economical	not economical	not economical	not economical	X

This figure shows how swaps can transform one type of debt to another. The original form of the debt is given in the columns, the transformed debt in the rows. The entry in the cell shows the swap requirements that are necessary to accomplish the transformation. Thus, callable fixed rate debt (Column 3) can be transformed into floating rate debt (Row 1) via a callable swap (Column 3, Row 1). An "X" indicates no transformation is necessary. "Not economical" means the transformation has never made sense economically—the transformed debt has never been cheaper than the original.

The choice among the five alternatives outlined above will depend primarily on which is cheapest for the issuer. Although the development of competitive markets over time should limit the cost differences among such financing alternatives, issuers should nonetheless consider all possibilities to ensure their achieving the lowest cost of funds in fixed-rate *non-callable* debt. That is, pricing inefficiencies arise from time to time, and thus issuers should examine all of the alternatives across row 2 to be sure of gaining the lowest-cost means to this method of funding.

In addition, many issuers will want to investigate the other funding opportunities that are available, while bearing in mind the necessary trade-offs. For example, issuers should weigh the cost of issuing fixed-rate noncallable debt against the cost of issuing callable fixed-rate debt in order to evaluate the cost of purchasing the right to call the debt. They might also want to see how much issuing a put bond might lower the required coupon on an issue. In terms of Figure 7.1, after finding the lowest-cost funding method in each row, issuers may also want to compare the various rows as alternative financing strategies. Thus, an issuer interested in ending up with some form of fixed-rate debt should compare the low-cost entry into row 2 with those in rows 3, 4, and 5.

As we proceed in this article, we will first look at the various ways of creating straight fixed-rate debt with no embedded options. Then we will consider ways of creating floating-rate debt, callable fixed-rate debt, and putable fixed-rate debt. All the techniques discussed in these pages, I should point out, have been used in the market. Some, though, have been used only sparingly, and thus seem to have been appropriate only for a special set of market conditions. The "arbitrage" financial techniques in the first part of this article are all premised on some kind of market mispricing. As the swap market further integrates the fixed and floating debt markets, the cost reductions achieved by issuing synthetic debt should become increasingly hard to find.

Creating Synthetic Optionless Fixed-Rate Debt

The interest rate swap market provides a variety of ways to create noncallable fixed-rate debt using original debt of another form. Such synthetic fixed-rate debt is most often created in one of two ways: (1) if the original bond is a floater, it can be combined with a conventional (or "plain vanilla") swap to convert floating payments to fixed; or (2) if the original bond is callable, it can be combined with the sale of a callable swaption. Less frequent variations use putable bonds and unconventional bonds as the original underlying instrument.

Transforming Floating-Rate Debt into Synthetic Fixed-Rate Debt. Companies with credit ratings lower than AA have taken advantage of opportunities to achieve cheaper fixed-rate financing by using floating-rate debt plus swaps instead of conventional fixed-rate issues. These opportunities arise from sizeable differences in the relative credit spreads between the fixed-rate market and the floating-rate market. Firms with a lower credit rating often pay a smaller spread over a more highly rated borrower in the floating market than in the fixed market.

To illustrate how swaps have been used to take advantage of this disparity, assume that an issuing firm would have to pay a fixed rate of 200 basis points over a 10-year Treasure (T_{10}). Alternatively, it could issue a floating-rate note (FRN) at LIBOR + 50 bp. Assume also that the swap rate it faces is T_{10} + 70 bp. The firm could arrange LIBOR-based financing and swap the proceeds for fixed at an interest rate equal to the 10-year Treasury + 70 bp. By so doing, the firm would obtain "synthetic" fixed financing of T_{10} + 120 bp, calculated as shown in Table 7.1:

Table 7.1

Instrument	Action	Cash Flow
FRN	Firm pays	LIBOR + 50 bp
Swap	Firm receives	(LIBOR)
	Firm pays	T_{10} + 70bp
Synthetic Fixed	Net payment	T_{10} + 120 bp

When this net payment is compared with an original fixed-rate issue of T_{10} + 200 bp, the net saving is 80 bp.[2]

If the firm issues a floating-rate note as illustrated above, the payment of the synthetic fixed-rate instrument is locked in. Typically, however, the firm chooses to issue floating-rate debt in which the credit spread is reset each period. Examples of this include short-term issues in the Euromarket and commercial paper market. In these instances, the firm has not actually locked in a rate beyond the first period. The borrowing rate can be decomposed into two parts—a base interest rate and a credit spread. As the base interest rate rises, the rate received on the swap (and paid on the commercial paper) will also rise. Changes in the firm's credit standing are unhedged. Thus, if the firm-specific credit spread narrows (the firm's credit quality improves), then the firm will achieve a lower cost for subsequent periods. If a firm expects its credit spread to remain constant or to narrow, a series of short-term borrowings will be preferable to a floating-rate note. In choosing that option, however, the firm is bearing the risk that its credit spread will widen.

Corporate treasurers should be aware that short-term borrowings usually have a lower credit spread than floating-rate notes, as credit spreads generally increase with maturity. Thus, when a corporate treasurer is comparing the cost of a commercial paper issue plus a swap to a fixed-rate financing, the cost savings will appear to be misleadingly large, as he has not locked in the credit spread. The cost of doing so is the cost differential between a floating-rate note and short-term borrowings.[3]

Transforming Callable Debt into Noncallable Debt Using Callable Swaps. Callable swaps have often been used together with callable bonds

---

[2] For a much more detailed and precise attempt to calculate the cost savings from this kind of financing "arbitrage," see the next article in this issue ("Swaps at Transamerica: Analysis and Applications," by Robert Einzig and Bruce Lange). Among other important points made by Einzig and Lange, this article demonstrates that creating synthetic fixed-rate debt with swaps sometimes imposes considerable refunding and basis risk that is often ignored in popular accounts of the benefits of swaps.

[3] Actually, many firms may make a deliberate decision to use short-term financing rather than a floating-rate note. There are two possible reasons for this. First, short-term financing plus a swap allows a firm to achieve a fixed base interest rate plus a floating credit spread. There is no other combination of instruments available which can achieve this result. (See Marcelle Arak, Arturo Estrello, Laurie Goodman, and Andrew Silver, "Interest Rate Swaps: An Explanation," *Financial Management*, Summer 1987 for a complete explanation.) Second, short term paper plus a swap fixes an interest rate while avoiding agency costs. If a firm has only long-term debt (either fixed rate or floating rate notes), the firm would have an incentive to shift toward more risky projects because bondholders share the downside, but not the upside. Short-term debt requires the firm to go to the markets each period to be re-evaluated and hence saves these agency costs. This argument is developed by Larry R. Wall, "Interest Rate Swaps, an Agency Theoretic Model with Uncertain Interest Rates," *Journal of Banking and Finance* (in press).

to create synthetic noncallable debt. The reason: Bond investors may demand less for the call option inherent in a callable bond than such an option will bring in the swap market.[4] An issuer generally pays a premium to investors (in terms of a higher interest rate than otherwise) for the right to call the original bond after a stated period of time, say, 10 years. In essence, the issuer has purchased a call option. Having purchased this call option, the issuer is thus in a position to *sell* an equivalent call option— but in the form of an option to call (or terminate) an interest rate swap. In this way, some issuers have been able to obtain noncallable debt at lower cost.

The mechanics of this transaction, which can best be illustrated by means of a simple example, actually involve entering into two swaps. Say that a firm issues a 10-year note that can be called at par after five years. The note is sold to yield 10.20 percent. This option may add 20 bp to the cost of the debt. In other words, if the firm issued a non-callable bond, it would pay only 10.00 percent. But as we shall see, the issuer will ultimately be better off by issuing the callable debt.

Along with the callable issue, the firm executes two transactions in the swap market. It enters into a callable swap—a swap with an option to-call or terminate the swap after five years. The firm pays the floating rate and receives a fixed rate of 10.40 percent. For illustrative purposes, we further assume that the fixed rate on a vanilla swap is 10.00 percent, which means that the counterparty to the callable swap is willing to pay 40 bp per annum for the right to terminate the swap after five years. Because the swap counterparty will terminate the swap only if rates decline—that is, if it can enter into a new swap and pay less than 10.40 percent—the counterparty has effectively purchased a call on the debt.

The net effect is that the issuing firm pays a net floating rate of interest of LIBOR minus 20 bp. In order to transform the debt into fixed rate, the issuer can then enter into a plain vanilla swap in which it agrees to receive floating and pay fixed. Assuming the fixed interest rate is 10.00 per-

---

[4] There is considerable anecdotal support, as well as some academic evidence, that corporate bond investors have "underpriced" the option they give corporations on the typical bond. Investors might, however, rationally change less than "fair value" for granting such an option. A failure by corporate management to exercise the option efficiently (by exercising as soon as the bond price exceeds the call price by an acceptable margin) would cause investors to underestimate its true value. (For a discussion of the optimal bond refunding strategy, see Alan Kraus, "An Analysis of Call Provisions and the Corporate Refunding Decision," *Midland Corporate Finance Journal,* Vol. 1 No. 1 (Spring 1983).

The amount of refunding activity in the last 7–8 years would suggest underpricings of the call option by bond market investors should become increasingly scarce over time. Moreover, the growth of markets for callable swaps and swaptions (those with surrogate call provisions) should further act to erase large call pricing disparities between the swaps and bond markets.

Figure 7.2: Using Callable Swaps to Create Synthetic
Non-callable Debt

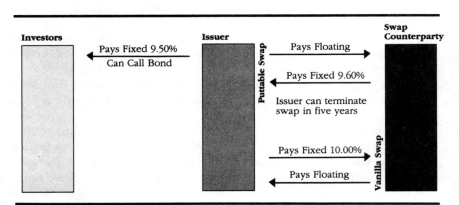

cent, the firm ends up with a net interest cost of 9.80 percent (10.20 per–
cent on the bond less 10.40 percent on the swaption plus 10.00 percent
on the vanilla swap), which is 20 bp less than it would have cost to issue
the noncallable debt directly. (This series of transactions is illustrated in
Figure 7.2.)

Let's also look at the transactions from the perspective of the issuer
and the swap counterparty under different interest rate scenarios shown
in Table 7.2:

Table 7.2

Scenario	Issuer	Swap Counterparty	Result
Interest rates are higher after five years.	No action on bond.	No action. Both swaps remain outstanding.	Issuer has ended up with 10-year fixed rate money.
Interest rates are lower after five years.	Bond is called. Issuer funds floating.	Swap in which issuer pays floating and receives fixed is called. Swap in which issuer pays fixed and receives floating remains outstanding.	Issuer has ended up with 10-year fixed rate money.

Thus, a callable swap is simply a swap in which the fixed payer (the counterparty) has the right of early termination without penalty. In either scenario, the issuer has achieved 10-year fixed rate financing.

Other variants of this structure are, of course, possible. For example, rather than receiving 10.40 percent per annum on the callable swap, the bond issuer could receive 10 percent plus 2.00 percent–2.25 percent of the var value of the bond as an upfront fee. In this case, the firm is paying the same 10.20 percent to issue debt as initially, but has traded away its call option for a fee of 2.00 percent–2.25 percent.

Transforming Callable Debt into Noncallable Debt Using Swaptions. Thus far we have discussed how to achieve fixed-rate financing by transforming callable debt into noncallable debt using callable swaps. The same result can be achieved using "swaptions." A swaption is an option providing a counterparty the right, but not the obligation, to enter into an interest rate swap at a future date. A callable bond and a swaption can be used to create fixed-rate funding to the call date and synthetic fixed-rate financing from the call date to the maturity date. As with the use of callable swaps described above, the use of swaptions to convert callable into noncallable debt is likely to be undertaken only if and when the call feature is priced more cheaply by the bond market than by the swap market.

In order to create five-year noncallable debt, one funding technique uses callable debt with a final maturity of five years and a "back-end fixed" swaption—that is, an option to enter into a swap to pay fixed and receive floating extending from the call date to the maturity date on the notional amount of debt. If the call can be exercised after year 3, the swaption would allow the issuer to pay fixed from year 3 to year 5. Alternatively, an issuer could achieve the same result by issuing longer maturity (10-year) debt with a call in five years and a "back-end floating" swaption to enter into a swap to pay floating and receive fixed for the balance of the 10-year maturity. A "back-end fixed" swaption simply means that the issuer pays fixed and receives floating if the swaption is exercised. With a "back-end floating" swaption, the issuer pays floating and receives fixed.

Let's look at an example of callable debt and a "back-end fixed" swaption. Assume an issuer wants five-year fixed-rate funding. He can create it by issuing a five-year bond, callable at par after three years, and selling a back-end fixed swaption. This swaption provides the buyer with the option to enter into a two-year interest rate swap commencing in three years. The back-end fixed swaption would commit the issuer to pay fixed and receive floating if desired by the counterparty. We show the results in Table 7.3:

Table 7.3

Scenario	Swap	Issuer	Result
Interest rates are higher after three years.	The swaption is not exercised.	The issuer does not call the bond.	Issuer has five-year fixed rate money.
Interest rates are lower after three years.	The swaption is exercised. The issuer pays fixed and receives floating for years four and five.	The issuer calls the bond and funds loating for years four and five.	Issuer has five-year fixed rate money.

Note that, under either scenario, the issuer has obtained five-year fixed-rate money.

An issuer could also obtain noncallable debt by issuing a 10-year note callable at par after five years and selling a "back-end floating" swaption. This swaption would allow the buyer the option to enter into a five-year swap, commencing in five years. The back-end floating swaption would commit the issuer to pay floating and receive fixed. Here are the results under the two interest rate scenarios:

Table 7.4

Scenario	Swap	Issuer	Result
Interest rates are higher after three years.	The swaption is exercised. Issuer pays floating and receives fixed from years 6-10.	The issuer does not call the bond.	Issuer has five-year fixed rate money. Over years 6-10 the issuer has floating money.
Interest rates are lower after five years.	The swaption is not exercised.	The issuer calls the bond.	Issuer has five-year fixed-rate money.

Again, the issuer has achieved fixed-rate funding for five years under either interest rate scenario.

One advantage of this structure is that if the swaption is exercised, and the issuer does not call the bond, he still has the call option. That is, the swaption does not extinguish the call on the bond. This option can be exercised if rates move down in the future.

In all of these alternatives, the issuer obtains synthetic noncallable debt. The choice among these alternatives will depend on how costly the embedded call option is relative to the back-end fixed swaption, the back-end floating swaption, and the callable swap.

Transforming Putable Debt into Optionless Debt

Putable swaps paired with put bonds have occasionally been used by issuers wanting to issue noncallable debt as cheaply as possible. They are used less frequently than callable swaps. With a put bond the investor purchases the right to put the bond back to the issuing firm—an option which becomes more valuable to the investor as interest rates rise. For example, assume a firm issues a 10 percent 10-year bond with a put that can be exercised after five years. If after five years rates had risen to 12 percent, the investor would put the bond back to the issuer and reinvest at the 12 percent rate. Naturally, from an investor's perspective, a 12 percent reinvestment rate is preferable to the 10 percent rate implicit in the bond. If rates fall, the put bond remains outstanding.

To the extent investors are willing to pay more for the put feature than the price of the put in the swap market, a put bond can be combined with a putable swap to create inexpensive noncallable debt. With a put bond, as suggested above, the issuer writes an option. He can then buy a putable swap to offset the exposure created by the put in the bond. But, once again, this would make sense only if the issuer can realize more by selling the put option on the bond than he must pay for the put on the swap he purchases.

This funding strategy, as illustrated in Figure 7.3, is achieved by using two swaps. In the putable swap, the issuer receives a fixed rate and pays a floating rate. The fixed rate the issuer receives is lower than the rate on a vanilla swap, reflecting the fact that the issuer can terminate the swap if

Figure 7.3: Using Puttable Swaps to Create Synthetic Non-callable Debt

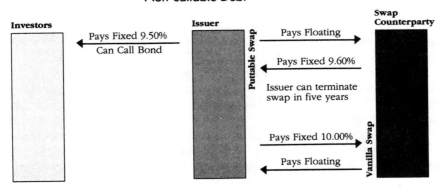

rates rise. The issuer will terminate the swap if rates rise. The issuer will terminate the swap if he can receive a higher rate than 9.60 percent at the expiration of the option—in other words, if interest rates have risen. The vanilla swap converts the then-floating rate payments of LIBOR less 10 bp into fixed payments. The issuer pays an effective interest rate on the non-callable, nonputable debt of 9.90 percent—9.50 percent on the bond less 9.60 percent on the swaption plus 10.00 percent on the vanilla swap. This is 10 bp cheaper than optionless debt with the same characteristics.

Table 7.5 shows our alternative interest rate scenarios:

Table 7.5

Scenario	Issuer	Swap Counterparty	Result
Interest rates are higher after five years.	Bond is put to issuer.	Swap for issuer to pay floating and receive fixed is terminated. Swap for issuer to pay fixed and receive floating remains standing.	Issuer has 10-year fixed rate money.
Interest rates are lowest after five-years.	No action.	Both swaps remain outstanding.	Issuer has 10-year fixed rate money.

Note that a putable swap is a swap in which the fixed-rate receiver (in this case, the issuer) has the option to walk away from the swap.

Creating optionless debt from put bonds is an arbitrage-driven transaction—that is, it is done only if the optionless debt can be created synthetically more cheaply than it can be issued directly.

Transforming Unconventional Debt

Inverse Floaters into Fixed-Rate Debt. Another, less frequently used method of obtaining fixed-rate financing is through the use of an inverse floating rate security. An inverse floater is an instrument that pays a pre-specified interest rate minus LIBOR. This is generally coupled with a swap in which the issuer receives fixed and pays floating.

We can illustrate this transaction with an example viewed from the issuer's perspective (see Figure 7.4). We assume the floater pays 19.50 percent minus LIBOR. The swap spread in this example would be $T_{10} + 70$ bp or 10.00 percent.

Using an inverse floater plus a vanilla swap, the issuer has locked in a coupon payment of 9.5 percent. The coupon payments on a new fixed-rate issue would be 10.00 percent. Thus, the borrower has saved 50 bp over a traditional bond. (See Table 7.6.)

Figure 7.4: Synthetic Fixed Financing Using Inverse Floaters

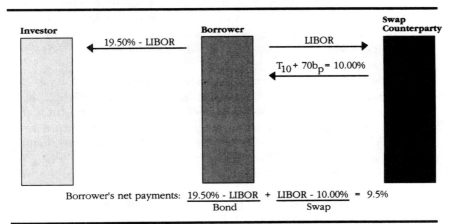

Borrower's net payments: $\underline{\text{19.50\% - LIBOR}}$ + $\underline{\text{LIBOR - 10.00\%}}$ = 9.5%
                                         Bond   Swap

    With this sort of funding strategy, a cap is necessary to protect against very high rates. Without a cap, if LIBOR happened to rise above 19.5 percent, the investor would owe the issuer money. Obviously, the issuer could not logistically collect from the investor. Thus, the issuer can buy a cap that will enable him to be paid if rates go above 19.50 percent. This cap is far out of the money, and the protection is very inexpensive.

    This structure attracted a great deal of interest when introduced in 1986. Investors initially did not realize that it was equivalent to holding a long position in *two* fixed-rate bonds and a short position in a floating-rate instrument. They could easily recreate this position by purchasing a fixed-rate bond and entering into a swap in which the investor received fixed and paid floating. Investors showed interest in the security because they were convinced short rates would drop. When LIBOR rates fell, the coupon on an inverse floater increased. But once investors realized how easily this strategy could be replicated, it was priced fairly and there were no new issues.

    Transforming FROGS into Fixed-Rate Debt. There is one other kind of unconventional debt that has been transformed into fixed-rate debt.

Table 7.6

Instrument	Action	Cash Flow
FRN	Firm pays	19.50% – LIBOR
Swap	Firm receives	(10.00%)
	Firm pays	LIBOR
Synthetic Fixed	Net payment	9.50%

FROGS are floating-rate notes with coupons based on the 30-year treasury rate that are reset quarterly or semi-annually. They have typically been combined with "yield curve" swaps in order to produce floating-rate debt. In a yield curve swap, floating payments are exchanged at two different points of the yield curve. This debt can then be transformed into fixed-rate debt with a vanilla swap.

To see how this works, assume that a firm issues a FROG that pays the 30-year Treasury rate, reset every six months (UST), minus 115 bp. The issuer enters into a yield curve swap in which he pays six-month LIBOR and receives the 30-year Treasury rate, reset every six months, less a fixed spread (say 105 bp). (This is called a "yield curve" swap because floating-rate payments indexed to the short end of the market are being exchanged for floating rate payments indexed to the long end of the yield curve.)

As shown below, the issuer has essentially locked in floating-rate financing:

Table 7.7

Instrument	Action	Cash Flow
FROG	Firm pays	UST – 115 bp
Swap	Firm receives	(UST – 105 bp)
	Firm pays	LIBOR
Synthetic Floating	Net payment	LIBOR – 10 bp

This synthetic floating-rate instrument can be converted to fixed-rate payments by means of a vanilla swap in which the issuer pays the three-year Treasury rate (T_3) + 70 in exchange for LIBOR (as shown below).

Table 7.8

Instrument	Action	Cash Flow
Synthetic Floating	See above	LIBOR – 10 bp
Vanilla Swap	Firm receives	(LIBOR)
	Firm pays	T_3 + 70 bp
Synthetic Fixed	Net payment	T_3 + 60 bp

FROGs, in fact, were initially created out of the desire to locate counterparties for yield curve swaps. Firms were enticed to issue FROGs and swap for LIBOR funding—a transaction that generated sub-LIBOR financing for the issuer.

FROGs were very popular investments in mid-1988 as a yield curve strategy, in large part because the average spread between 30-year Treasuries and LIBOR during 1983–87 was 125 bp. At 115 basis points (which was 10 basis points less than historical levels), these notes became very attractive. Moreover, investors who preferred (or were required) to purchase only short-term securities were able to obtain a short-term instrument reset off a longer-term rate—a combination not previously available.

Ex-post, however, FROGs have turned out not to be attractive investments. If the yield curve had steepened, FROGs would have performed well. With the yield curve flattening and inverting in 1989, FROGs have performed poorly and no new issues have come to market since late 1988.

Creating Floating-Rate Debt

We now consider funding alternatives that have enabled issuers to create synthetic floating-rate debt. The two most common alternatives are as follows: (1) a fixed rate optionless bond plus a vanilla swap and (2) a callable bond plus a callable swap. Less commonly used alternatives include put bonds combined with putable swaps and FROGs combined with yield curve swaps. We examine each of these in turn.

Synthetic Floating Using Vanilla Swaps

Companies with well-known names and high credit ratings have taken advantage of very inexpensive fixed-rate financing in the Eurobond market.[5] In fact, many of these entities have been foreign banks that actually prefer floating-rate financing because their loan portfolio is primarily floating rate. To see how an issuer might create synthetic floating-rate assets, we start by assuming that the firm can raise 10-year fixed-rate funds at only 50 bp over the 10-year Treasury (T_{10}) bond rate. The swap rate is LIBOR against T_{10} + 70 bp. Using the swap market, the firm can create synthetic floating-rate debt directly, it would issue at LIBOR. This is illustrated below:

Table 7.9

Instrument	Action	Cash Flow
Fixed Rate Bond	Firm pays	T_{10} + 50 bp
Swap	Firm receives	T_{10} + 70 bp
	Firm pays	LIBOR
Synthetic Fixed	Net payment	LIBOR − 20 bp

---

[5] For a discussion of the cost savings from Eurobond financing, see Wayne Marr and John Trimble, "The Persistence Borrowing Advantage in Eurodollars: A Plausible Explanation," which appeared in the Summer 1988 issue of this journal.

Thus, the firm ends up paying LIBOR minus 20 bp for its funds, 20 bp less than the cost of issuing new floating rate debt at LIBOR flat.

Transforming Callable Debt into Floating-Rate Debt. Issuers can create synthetic floating-rate financing by using a callable bond and a callable swap. The rate on this financing will be less than on a straight floating-rate issue whenever the issuer is able to purchase a call option from investors (the call option that is embedded in the debt) for substantially less than the swap market is willing to pay for the call option.

The mechanics of this transaction are similar to those described in the previous section for transforming callable debt into noncallable debt. The firm issues callable debt and enters into a callable swap (as illustrated earlier in Figure 7.2). The difference in this case is that there is no vanilla swap.

Let us consider the payoffs from this combination under different scenarios. If rates are higher at the call date than they were at the time of issue, neither the bond nor the swap will be called, and the issuer will obtain floating funding until maturity. If rates are lower at the call date than at issue, the issuer will call the bond. The counterparty will terminate the swap. Thus, if rates go down, the issuer will have floating money until the call date.

The issuer, then, has issued floating-rate funding for a period either to call or to maturity. If interest rates are lower, the issuer has locked in floating rate debt for only the time until the call. If interest rates go up, he locks in floating-rate money until maturity—a desirable situation.

Transforming Putable Debt into Floating-Rate Debt. Putable debt can be transformed into floating-rate debt by pairing a put bond with a putable swap. This is similar to transforming putable debt into optionless fixed-rate debt (as illustrated in Figure 7.3). In this case there is no need for the vanilla swap.

Let us now consider the payoffs from this combination under different scenarios. Assume a firm issues 10-year money, putable at the investor's option after year 5. If rates turn out to be higher at the put date than at the issue date, the bond will be put and the swap in which the issuer pays floating and receives fixed will be terminated. The issuer can raise new floating rate money during years 6–10 at par. Thus, the issuer has floating money over the 10-year period. If rates decline, the bond remains outstanding and the swap remains outstanding. The net result here is also floating-rate money over the 10-year period.

Transforming FROGs into Floating-Rate Debt FROGs are frequently transformed into floating-rate rather than fixed-rate debt. This is done by pairing a FROG with a yield curve swap. The issuer pays the long-term

Treasury rate less a spread on the FROG. Again, the long-term rate is re-set every six months. The issuer then enters into a yield curve swap in which he pays six-month LIBOR and receives the long-term Treasury rate, reset every six months, less a spread.

Creating Callable Debt

Issuers with access to the U.S. long-term fixed-rate debt markets have generally not found it economical to replicate callable debt. However, there are certain issuers, such as U.S. savings and loan associations, that have been unable to borrow economically in these markets. These issuers have occasionally used the swap market to transform fixed- and floating-rate debt into long-term callable debt. In other instances, issuers that do have access to the corporate market prefer instead to issue debt using a medium-term note strategy, with which they can bring a small issue or an odd amount to market. Medium-term notes are noncallable.

Long-term callable debt can be created from long-term noncallable fixed-rate debt by purchasing a back-end floating swaption. If rates decline, the swap will be activated and the issuer will pay floating and receive fixed. Consider an issuer of five-year noncallable debt who has purchased a back-end floating swaption for years four and five. If rates remain high, the issuer will have five-year debt. If rates decline, the issuer will have three-year fixed-rate debt.

A floating-rate issue can be transformed into fixed-rate debt through combination with a vanilla swap and then be made callable by purchasing a back-end floating swaption.

Creating Putable Debt

We now consider a synthetic alternative to a put bond issued in the marketplace. The most common synthetic put bond is constructed by combining a callable bond issue with the sale of both a back-end fixed swaption and a back-end floating swaption. By holding both these options, the swap counterparty has a one-time right either (1) to make the issuer pay the fixed-rate versus receiving floating (by exercising the back-end fixed swaption) or (2) to make the issuer receive fixed (by exercising the back-end floating swaption) and pay floating.

The swap counterparty, to repeat, purchases two options. The effect of one (the back-end fixed swaption) is to cancel the embedded option on the call, and the effect of the other (the floating swaption) is to create the put that is inherent in a putable bond.

Let us use the example of a five-year issue, callable in three years. At the end of three years, the results under alternative interest rate scenarios are shown on the next page.

Table 7.10

Scenario	Swap	Issuer	Result
Interest rates rise higher after three years.	Issuer caused to receive fixed and pay floating for years four and five.	No action.	Issuer has ended up with three-year fixed rate followed by two-year floating-rate money.
Interest rates are lower after three years.	Issuer caused to pay fixed and receive floating for two years.	Issuer calls issue, funds floating rate.	Issuer has ended up with five-year fixed rate money.

As with a regular put bond, if rates fall the issuer has ended up with five-year fixed-rate money. If rates rise the issuer has ended up with three years of fixed funding and two years of floating funding.

The major difference between a synthetic put bond and a real put bond is that, with a synthetic put bond, the issuer has to raise funds in the floating-rate market if rates fall. With a real put bond, the issuer has to borrow in the floating rate market if rates rise. This is important to some issuers, such as banks and finance companies, that are more concerned about funding in a higher-rate than in a lower-rate environment.

Note that whatever cost savings can be achieved by using a synthetic rather than a straightforward put bond depend upon investors' pricing the call option for less than the swap market. By contrast, swap counterparties will pay full value for that call and a further significant premium for the right to buy the put.

A less commonly used variation on the synthetic put bond has been accomplished by issuing fixed-rate noncallable debt and selling a back-end fixed swaption. This eliminates the arbitrage opportunity in the call option. Assume the debt is issued for a five-year period, and the back-end fixed swaption can be exercised at the end of year three. The swaption will be exercised and the issuer will have received fixed and paid floating for years four and five if rates are lower.

This transaction could also be done by using floating-rate debt as the initial issue. Such debt could then be transformed into fixed debt by means of a five-year swap. It could then be further transformed into a synthetic put bond with a back-end fixed option.

Locking in the Cost of a Future Issuance

While the major use of swaps centers on altering the character of a current bond issue, issuers also apply strategies involving the swap market to expected future issuances. For example, a company that expects rates to rise may want to lock in a fixed cost on a future issuance by using a forward swap (also known as a "delayed start" swap). A corporate treasurer who expects interest rates to remain steady or decline while credit spreads widen may wish to lock in a generic credit spread by means of a "spread lock." We examine each of these in turn.

Forward Swaps

A forward swap is exactly like a regular interest rate swap transaction, except that the accruals begin on a future date—normally the expected date of the bond issuance. A forward swap is usually combined with a floating-rate issue in order to lock in a fixed rate.

Consider the following example. A firm enters into a three-month forward swap agreeing to pay the current five-year Treasury rate plus 75 bp. In return, the firm will receive six-month LIBOR. The notional amount of the swap will be the same as that of the anticipated debt issue. In three months the firm issues floating-rate debt. Six months after the issuance, the first payments are exchanged. The firm pays the fixed rate available at the time the swap was entered into and receives six-month LIBOR. The LIBOR payment is used to pay the interest on the floating-rate debt.

The net cost of the issuance will be the fixed rate on the swap plus the difference between six-month LIBOR and the floating rate at which the firm issues its debt. If the firm issues floating-rate debt at six-month LIBOR + 25 bp, its all-in funding cost will be the five-year Treasury yield plus the 75 bp swap spread plus the 25 bp margin on the floating-rate debt. Note that the only component not locked in is the margin on the floating-rate debt.

If the firm later issues floating-rate debt off a different index from LIBOR, it can realize cost savings but will incur basis risk. If, for example, the firm issues floating-rate debt at the commercial paper rate, the cost of funds to the firm will be less than the five-year Treasury yield plus 75 bp, reflecting the fact that the commercial paper rate is below LIBOR.

Forward swaps are most attractive for issuers that like the current level of interest rates and expect a rate increase in the future, but do not currently need funding. Entering into a forward swap locks in the rate without forcing the issuer to fund immediately.

Spread Locks

A spread lock allows an issuer to fix the credit spread without fixing the base rate. Thus, a spread lock can be viewed as a tool to hedge the general level of corporate spreads. A spread lock is most effective when a firm knows it will have to come to market within a relatively short time—two or three months.

In a spread lock, the issuer agrees to enter into a swap deal at a specified spread to Treasuries but delays fixing the base Treasury rate for a period ranging up to two or three months. In other words, the issuer must fix the base interest rate by the end of the period, but may choose to fix the rate anytime within that period. When the base rate is eventually fixed, the pre-specified swap spread is added to arrive at the fixed rate payable on the swap. If Treasury rates fall over near term, the firm is able to take advantage of the decline.

To see how a spread lock would work, assume that a firm wants a spread lock for the next two months. At the end of the two-month period—or earlier if Treasury rates look attractive in the interim—the firm issues floating-rate debt and takes down the swap (in which it pays fixed and receives floating). Assume that the fixed swap spread is 80 bp and its issuing rate is LIBOR + 25bp. The firm will, on net, pay the Treasury rate prevailing at the time the swap is taken down plus 105 bp (80 + 25).[6]

A spread lock will be used if the firm does not expect rates to rise, but is concerned that credit spreads may widen. Issuers should note, however, that the spread lock does not hedge their firm-specific credit spread, but rather a general credit market spread.

Managing Corporate Interest Rate Exposures by Altering the Cash Flows on an Existing Liability

Companies can also use swaps to alter the cash flow on an existing liability, in a variety of ways: (1) by entering into a swap in order to fix the payment on an existing floating liability; (2) by entering into a swap in order to turn an existing fixed payment security into a floating-rate liability, and (3) by entering into a forward swap to lock in attractive interest rates after the call date on existing debt with in-the-money call options.

Fixing a Payment on a Floating-Rate Issue

A firm can convert a floating rate issue into a fixed-rate instrument by using a swap in which the issuer receives floating and pays fixed. The fixed rate is the then-prevailing fixed rate. Thus, when interest levels look attractive and a firm feels vulnerable to higher rates, it can lock its floating debt into a fixed rate through the use of the swap market.

Converting an Existing Fixed-Rate Bond

Similarly, a firm that has initially issued fixed-rate debt can also convert that debt to floating rate through the swap market. In this instance,

---

[6] A spread lock is typically offered at a 2–4 bp premium over the straight swap. The premium exists because of the swap counterparty's hedging cost. The swap counterparty will short Treasury securities and invest the proceeds in short-term instruments until the swap is taken down. The negative carry during the hedge period is figured into the quoted spread. Thus, 150 bp of negative carry for two months is $0.25 per $100 par, or 2.5 bp for a seven-year issue.

the firm pays floating and receives fixed. If market rates have changed, the fixed rate at which the firm issued the debt is different from the prevailing fixed rate. The firm can either receive the fixed rate prevailing in the swap market, or match its own funding cost with an upfront payment if rates have declined or with an upfront receipt if rates have risen.

This is not, it is important to note, a means of escaping high-coupon debt in a declining rate environment. It does, however, provide a way for the firm to benefit from a further future reduction in rates.

To give an example, we assume that three years ago a firm issued fixed-rate 10-year noncallable debt at 11 percent. The firm now wishes to convert this debt to floating-rate debt. The swap market is such that the firm currently would have to pay LIBOR to receive 70 bp over the rate on seven-year Treasury notes (T_7+ 70bp, or 9.70 percent). If the firm entered into a market swap, its cash flows would be as follows:

Table 7.11

Instrument	Action	Cash Flow
Bond	Firm pays	11.00%
Swap	Firm receives	(9.70%)
	Firm pays	LIBOR
Synthetic Floater	Net payment	LIBOR + 130 bp

Note that the firm is paying LIBOR + 130 bp. The large increment over LIBOR reflects the fact that the firm has above-market (11%) noncallable debt outstanding. It cannot escape this obligation. If rates decline further, however, the LIBOR financing will prove more attractive than the fixed rate financing. If rates increase, the reverse will be true.

Alternatively, the firm could enter into an off-market swap in which it pays an upfront amount in order to pay LIBOR and receive 11 percent on the swap. The upfront payment would reflect the 130 bp per annum, capitalized into an upfront sum, as shown below.

Table 7.12

Instrument	Action	All-in Cost per Annum
Bond	Firm pays	11.00%
Swap	Firm receives	(11.00%)
	Firm pays	LIBOR
	Firm pays upfront $6.50	130 bp
Synthetic Floater	Net payment	LIBOR + 130 bp

Note the present value of the all-in costs is roughly the same if the firm accepts a market swap or an off-market swap.

If rates have risen and the issuer is convinced they have peaked, it may want to swap an outstanding fixed-rate issue into a floating-rate obligation. This allows the issuer to benefit from lower rates in the future. The issuer could opt for a swap at market rates, or for an off-market swap in which it accepts a below-market rate on the swap plus an upfront payment.

To give an example, let's assume that three years ago a firm had issued 8.00 percent debt for 10 years. In the swap market, this firm could pay LIBOR and receive $T_7 + 70$ bp, or 9.7 percent. If the firm agreed to a swap at now-current rates, its cash flows would be as follows:

Table 7.13

Instrument	Action	Cash Flow
Bond	Firm pays	8.00%
Swap	Firm receives	(9.70%)
	Firm pays	LIBOR
Synthetic Floater	Net payment	LIBOR – 170 bp

The net payment of LIBOR minus 170 bp reflects the fact that the firm had below-market debt on its books.

If the firm wanted an off-market swap, the all-in cost would be as follows:

Table 7.14

Instrument	Action	All-in Cost
Bond	Firm pays	8.00%
Swap	Firm receives	(9.70%)
	Firm pays	LIBOR
	Firm receives $8.50 upfront	(170 bp)
Synthetic Floater	Net payment	LIBOR – 170 bp

In both cases, the firm's all-in cost is the same. With an off-the-market swap, the firm is compensated for accepting a below-market rate on the swap.

Thus, if converting fixed-rate debt to floating-rate debt is designed only to take advantage of an expected fall in rates, any fall or rise that has already occurred will be built into the price of the swap. Nonetheless, if further changes in rates are anticipated, a review of outstanding liabilities is in order.

Locking in Attractive Interest Rates on Existing High-Coupon Debt

Forward swaps can be used to lock in future rates on outstanding callable debt. To see how this can be done, assume that a firm has 14.00 percent debt oustanding, originally issued in 1984. The debt matures in 10 years, or 1994. It is callable in 1991. If the notes were currently callable, the issuer would call the bond and refinance with lower-cost debt. However, since the notes are not callable for some years, the company must leave the bonds outstanding until the call date and continue to pay the 14.00 percent coupon.

If the company feels that interest rates will rise by 1991 and eliminate some or all of the benefits of today's relatively low interest rates, the issuer can execute a forward swap. Essentially, this would lock in current forward rates. In other words, the firm can enter into a three-year swap effective two years from now in which it agrees to pay fixed and received floating. We will assume here that the firm can lock in a 10 percent fixed rate on this swap.

This strategy leaves the company with a great deal of flexibility on the call date. If interest rates turn out to be lower than 14 percent on the call date, the firm could refinance on a floating-rate basis. The floating payments on the debt would be offset by payments on the swap. The firm's all-in cost would be the 10 percent fixed rate plus (minus) its issuing cost above (below) LIBOR.

If the firm wanted to refinance at a fixed rate, the forward swap could be sold. The cash settlement to (or by) the issuer will be equal to the present value of the difference between the forward rate swap and the market rate for new swaps with a three-year maturity. If rates turn out to be higher than 10 percent, the issuer will receive a payment. If rates prove to be lower than 10.0 percent, the issuer will pay the cash settlement from the sale of the swap.

There is a third alternative, as well. Say the firm wants to refinance with a fixed rate, but rates are lower and the issuer is reluctant to buy out the forward swap. As an alternative, it could enter into an offsetting spot transaction. To see how this might work, assume the fixed rate is 9 percent, and the firm has locked in a 10 percent forward swap. The forward swap can be offset on the call date as shown in Table 7.15 on the next page. Note that the firm has locked in the 10 percent rate. The rate on the new bond is 9.00 percent, and the 1 percent per annum loss on the forward swap takes the form of a higher net payment.

So far we have assumed that the interest rates on the call date are below 14 percent and that the issue will be called. The forward swap does

Table 7.15

Instrument	Action	Cash Flow
Original Bond	Called	
New Bond	Firm pays	9.00%
Forward Swap	Firm receives	(LIBOR)
	Firm pays	10.00%
New Swap	Firm receives	(9.00%)
	Firm pays	LIBOR
Fixed + Swap	Net payment	10.00%

not affect the company's ability to leave the issue outstanding if rates are above 14 percent on the call date. In this instance, if the issuer chooses to leave the issue outstanding, it could sell the forward swap. The windfall profit on the forward swap would be the difference between the then-current market rates for a three-year period. Thus, the forward swap locks in the "intrinsic value" of the call option.[7] It does not, however, extinguish the option. And it can gain further value in the future if rates rise sufficiently.

Conclusion

The primary corporate uses of interest rate swaps are to reduce corporate exposures to interest rate movements by altering the cash flow pattern of outstanding debt, to reduce the cost of a current issuance by "arbitraging" disparities between debt and swap markets, and to lock in the cost or spread of an expected future issue. Historically, much of the corporate use of swaps has centered on reducing the cost of a current issue. Prior to the introduction of swaps, companies had to issue debt into the ultimately desired form. For example, companies wanting long-term fixed-rate noncallable debt had to include all the desired features in the issue itself. There was no way to transform callable debt into noncallable or putable debt.

With swaps, however, debt can be easily and inexpensively transformed from one form into another. Issuers have sometimes been able to obtain the desired form of debt synthetically at a lower cost than by a direct issuance. This arises, in part, because the swap market allowed issuers to take advantage of differential pricing between the new issue bond market and the swap market. Call options, for example, appear to be cheaper in the bond market than in the swap market. Floating-rate issues can be

---

[7] The "intrinsic value" is the value of the option if exercised immediately.

less expensive than fixed-rate issues for lower-rated issuers. In addition, certain new structures can give investors their desired risk-return tradeoff while allowing the issuer to end up with what looks like conventional debt.

Issuers can also lock in the cost of a future issue through a forward swap. Spread locks can be used to lock in generic credit spreads. Finally, the swap market allows issuers to transform floating rates into floating (although off-market swaps are generally necessary to equate cash flows on a new swap with those on the old debt).

Swaps, in short, are highly versatile and cost-effective instruments for managing corporate liabilities. They have transformed liability management into a more active undertaking, one that involves not only evaluating what is desirable for current issuances, but also re-evaluating past issues and anticipating those of the future.

THE USES OF HYBRID DEBT IN
MANAGING CORPORATE RISK*

**Charles W. Smithson and
Donald H. Chew, Jr.**

8

The corporate use of hybrid debt securities—those that combine a conventional debt issue with a "derivative" such as a forward, swap, or option—increased significantly during the 1980s. And, while many of the more esoteric or tax-driven securities introduced in the last decade have disappeared, corporate hybrids now seem to be flourishing. In so doing, they are helping U.S. companies raise capital despite the restrictive financing climate of the 1990s.

Hybrid debt, to be sure, is not a new concept. Convertible bonds, first issued by the Erie Railroad in the 1850s, are hybrid securities that combine straight debt and options on the value of the issuer's equity.[1] What is distinctive about the hybrid debt instruments of the 1980s is that their payoffs, instead of being tied to the issuing company's stock price, are linked to a growing variety of *general* economic variables. As illustrated in Figure 8.1, corporate hybrids have appeared that index investor returns to exchange rates, interest rates, stock market indices, and the prices of commodities such as oil, copper, and natural gas.

The recent wave of corporate hybrids began in 1973, when PEMEX, the state-owned Mexican oil producer, issued bonds that incorporated a *forward contract* on a commodity (in this case, oil). In 1980, Sunshine Mining Co. went a step further by issuing bonds incorporating a commod-

---

*This article originally appeared in the Continental Bank *Journal of Applied Corporate Finance,* vol. 4, no. 4, Winter 1992. Reprinted with permission.
[1] The date for the introduction of convertible bonds is reported by Peter Tufano in "Financial Innovation and First-Mover Advantages," *Journal of Financial Economics,* 25, pp. 213–240.

Figure 8.1: Development of Hybrid Securities: 1973–1991

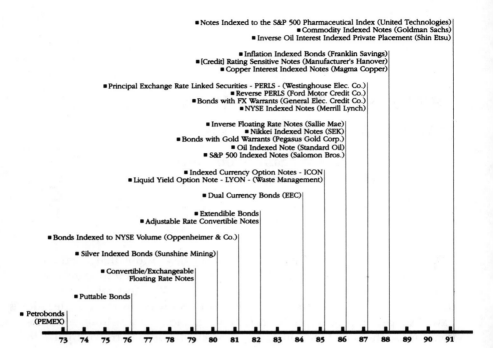

ity *option* (on silver). In 1988, Magma Copper made yet another advance by issuing a bond giving investors a *series of commodity options* (on copper)—in effect, one for every coupon payment.

Other new hybrids, as mentioned, have had their payoffs tied to interest rates, foreign exchange rates, and the behavior of the stock market. In 1981, Oppenheimer & Co., a securities brokerage firm, issued a security whose principal repayment is indexed to the volume of trading on the New York Stock Exchange. Notes indexed to the value of equity indexes appeared in 1986, and inflation-indexed notes (tied to the CPI) were introduced in 1988.

The 1980s also saw new hybrids with payoffs that, like those of convertibles, are tied to company-specific performance. For example, the Rating Sensitive Notes issued by Manufacturer's Hanover in 1988 provide for increased payments to investors if Manny Hanny's creditworthiness declines. And the LYON´ pioneered and underwritten by Merrill Lynch in 1985 grants investors not only the option to convert the debt into equity, but also the right to "put" the security back to the firm.

The pace of hybrid innovation peaked around 1987. But hybrids are now staging a comeback. As the title of a recent *Wall Street Journal* article put it, 1991 was "A Boom Year for Newfangled Trading Vehicles."[2] The past year witnessed the introduction of notes indexed to a subset of a general equity index, Goldman Sachs' notes indexed to a commodity index, private placements incorporating options on commodities, and a boom in convertible debt.

Why do companies issue, and investors buy, such complex securities? Before the development of derivative products in the 1970s, investors may have been attracted by the prospect of purchasing a "bundle" of securities—say, debt plus warrants—that they could not duplicate themselves by purchasing both of the components separately. And this "scarce security" or "market completion" argument also holds for some of today's debt hybrids (especially those that provide longer-dated forwards and options than those available on organized exchanges).

But, because active exchanges now provide low-cost futures and options with payoffs tied to all variety of interest rates, exchange rates, and commodity prices, markets are becoming increasingly "complete," if you will. Given the existence of well-functioning, low-cost markets for many of the components making up the hybrid debt instruments, we have to ask the following question: Is there any reason investors should be willing to pay more for these securities sold *in combination* rather than separately?

In this article, we argue that hybrid debt offers corporate treasurers an efficient means of managing a variety of financial and operating risks—risks that, in many cases, cannot be managed if the firm issues straight debt and then purchases derivatives. By hedging such risks and thereby increasing the expected stability of corporate cash flows, hybrids may lower the issuer's overall funding costs.[3] At the same time, though, part of the present corporate preference for managing price risks with hybrids rather than derivative products stems from current restrictions on the use of hedge accounting for derivatives, as well as tax and regulatory arbitrage opportunities afforded by hybrids.

Price Volatility: The Necessary Condition for Hybrids

The stability of the economic and financial environment is a key determinant of the kinds of debt instruments that dominate the marketplace. When prices are stable and predictable, investors will demand—and the capital markets will produce—relatively simple instruments.

---

[2] December 26, 1991, p. C1. The *Journal* article dealt more with exchange-traded products than with hybrids.

LYON™ is a trademark of Merrill Lynch & Co.

[3] For preliminary evidence of the impact of issuing hybrid debt on the firm's cost of capital, see Charles Smithson and Leah Schraudenbach, "Reflection of Financial Price Risk in the Firm's Share Price," Chase Manhattan Bank, 1992.

In the late 1800s, for example, the dominant financial instrument in Great Britain was the *consol:* a bond with a fixed interest rate and no maturity—it lasted forever. Investors were content to hold infinite-lived British government bonds because British sovereign credit was good and because inflation was virtually unknown. General confidence in price level stability led to stable interest rates, which in turn dictated the use of long-lived, fixed-rate bonds.

But consider what happens to financing practices when confidence is replaced by turbulence and uncertainty. As one of us pointed out in an earlier issue of this journal, in 1863 the Confederate States of America issued a 20-year bond denominated not in Confederate dollars, but in French Francs and Pounds Sterling. To allay the concern of its overseas investors that the Confederacy would not be around to service its debt with hard currency, the issue was also convertible at the option of the holder into cotton at the rate of six pence per pound. In the parlance of today's investment banker, the Confederate States issued a *dual-currency, cotton-indexed* bond.[4]

The Breakdown of Bretton Woods and the New Era of Volatility

Throughout the 1950s and most of the 1960s, economic and price stability prevailed in the U.S., and in the developed nations generally. Investment-grade U.S. corporations responded predictably by raising capital in the form of 30-year, fixed-rate bonds (yielding around 3–4 percent). But, toward the end of the 1960s, rates of inflation in the U.S. and U.K. began to increase. There was also considerable divergence among developed countries in monetary and fiscal policy, and thus in rates of inflation. Such pressures led inevitably to the abandonment, in 1973, of the Bretton Woods agreement to maintain relatively fixed exchange rates. And, during the early 1970s and thereafter, the general economic environment saw higher and more volatile rates of inflation along with unprecedented volatility in exchange rates, interest rates, and commodity prices. (For evidence of such general price volatility, see Figure 8.2.)

In response to this heightened price volatility, capital markets created new financial instruments to help investors and issuers manage their exposures. Indeed, the last 20 years has seen the introduction of (1) futures on foreign exchange, interest rates, metals, and oil; (2) currency, interest rate, and commodity swaps; (3) options on exchange rates, interest rates, and oil; and (4) options on the above futures and options. Flourishing markets for these products in turn helped give rise to corporate hybrid debt securities that effectively incorporate these derivative products.

---

[4] Waite Rawls and Charles Smithson, "The Evolution of Risk Management Products," *Journal of Applied Corporate Finance,* Vol. 1 No. 4 (1989).

Figure 8.2: General Price Volatility

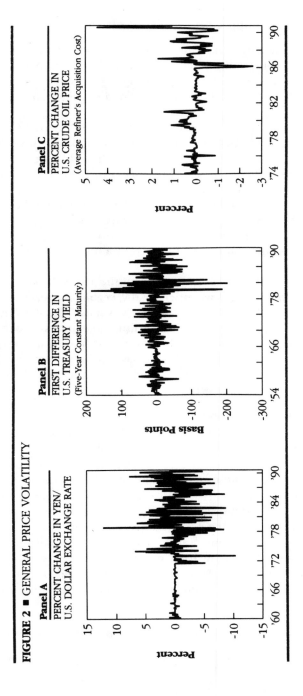

FIGURE 2 ■ GENERAL PRICE VOLATILITY

Panel A

PERCENT CHANGE IN YEN/
U.S. DOLLAR EXCHANGE RATE

Panel B

FIRST DIFFERENCE IN
U.S. TREASURY YIELD
(Five-Year Constant Maturity)

Panel C

PERCENT CHANGE IN
U.S. CRUDE OIL PRICE
(Average Refiner's Acquisition Cost)

Using Hybrids to Manage Commodity Risk

Unlike foreign exchange and interest rates, which were relatively stable until the 1970s, commodity prices have a long history of volatility. Thus, it is no surprise that hybrid securities designed to hedge commodity price risks came well before hybrids with embedded currency and interest rate derivatives.

As mentioned earlier, the Confederacy issued a debt instrument convertible into cotton in 1863. By the 1920s, commodity-linked hybrids were available in U.S. capital markets. A case in point is the gold-indexed bond issued by Irving Fisher's Rand Kardex Corporation in 1925. Similar to the PEMEX issue described earlier, the principal repayment of this gold-indexed bond was tied directly to gold prices.[5] Fisher realized that he could significantly lower his firm's funding costs by furnishing a scarce security desired by investors—in this case, a long-dated forward on gold prices. And Fisher's successful innovation was imitated by a number of other U.S. companies during the 1920s.

Like so many of the financial innovations of the 1920s, however, that wave of hybrid debt financings was ended by the regulatory reaction that set in during the 1930s.[6] Specifically, the "Gold Clause" Joint Congressional Resolution of June 5, 1933 virtually eliminated indexed debt by prohibiting "a lender to require of a borrower a different quantity or number of dollars from that loaned." And it was not until October 1977, when Congress passed the Helms Amendment, that the legal basis for commodity-indexed debt was restored.

Hybrids with Option Features

The hybrids issued by Rand Kardex and PEMEX represent combinations of debt securities with forward contracts; that is, the promised principal repayments were designed to rise or fall directly with changes in the prices, respectively, of gold and oil. In the case of PEMEX, moreover, this forward-like feature reduced the risk to investors that the issuer wouldn't be able to repay principal; it did so by making the *amount* of the principal vary as directly as possible with the company's oil revenues.

Unlike the PEMEX and Rand Kardex issues, Sunshine Mining's 15-year silver-linked bond issued in 1980 combined a debt issue with a *European option*[7] on silver prices. In this case, the promised principal repayment could not fall below a certain level (the face value), but would

---

[5] See J. Huston McCulloch. "The Ban on Indexed Bonds," *American Economic Review* 70 (December 1980), pp. 1018–21.

[6] See Merton Miller's account of financial innovation in the 1920s and 1930s in the first article of this issue.

[7] European options can be exercised only at maturity, as distinguished from American options, which can be exercised any time before expiration.

increase proportionally with increases in the price of silver price above $20 per ounce at maturity.[8] Because most of the commodity-linked hybrids that followed the Sunshine Mining issue in the 1980s contain embedded options rather than forwards, let's consider briefly how the embedding of options within debt issues manages risk and lowers the issuer's cost of capital.

How Hybrids with Options Manage Risk. Corporate bondholders bear "downside" risk while typically being limited to a fixed interest rate as their reward. (In the jargon of options, the bondholder is "short a put" on the value of the firm's assets.) Because of this limited upside, they charge a higher "risk premium" when asked to fund companies with more volatile earnings streams. Like the forward contract embedded in the PEMEX issue, options also provide bondholders with an equity-like, "upside" participation. In return for this upside participation, bondholders will reduce the risk premium they charge. Indeed, the greater the expected volatility of the commodity price in question, the more valuable is that embedded option to the bondholders.[9]

Unlike hybrids with forwards, hybrids with embedded options provide investors with a "floor"—that is, a minimum principal repayment or set of coupons. And, though options therefore effect a less complete transfer of risk than in the case of forwards (in the sense that the firm's financing costs don't fall below the floor in the event of an extreme decline in commodity prices), investors should be willing to pay for the floor in the form of a reduced base rate of interest. To the extent they lower the rate of interest, option-like hybrids reduce the probability of default, thus reassuring bondholders and the rating agencies.

A good example of corporate risk management with options was a 1986 issue of Eurobonds with detachable gold warrants by Pegasus Gold Corporation, a Canadian gold mining firm. In effect, this issue gave investors two separable claims: (1) a straight debt issue with a series of fixed interest payments and a fixed principal repayment; and (2) European options on the price of gold. By giving bondholders a participation in the firm's gold revenues, the inclusion of such warrants reduced the coupon rate on the bond—which in turn lowered the issuer's financial risk.

Probably the most newsworthy hybrid in 1986, however, was Standard Oil's *Oil-Indexed Note.* This hybrid combines a zero-coupon bond with a

---

[8] From the perspective of 1991, during which the silver price has averaged $4.00 per ounce, this exercise price of $20 per ounce may seem bizarre. But keep in mind that this bond was issued in early 1980. During the period October 1979-January 1980, the price of silver averaged $23 per ounce.

[9] For a discussion of how the equity option embedded in convertibles could make convertible bondholders indifferent to increases in the volatility of corporate cash flow, see Michael Brennan and Eduardo Schwartz, "The Case for Convertibles," *Chase Financial Quarterly* (Fall 1981). Reprinted in *Journal of Applied Corporate Finance* (Summer 1988).

European option on oil with the same maturity. The issue not only aroused the interest of the IRS, but also succeeded in rekindling regulatory concerns about the potential for "speculative abuse" built into hybrid securities.[10]

Commodity Interest-Indexed Bonds. The commodity hybrids mentioned thus far are all combinations of debt with forwards or options with a single maturity. In effect, they link only the principal repayment to commodity prices, but not the interim interest payments. But, in recent years, hybrids have also emerged that combine debt with a *series of options* of different maturities—maturities that are typically designed to correspond to the coupon dates of the underlying bond.

In 1988, for example, Magma Copper Company issued *Copper Interest-Indexed Senior Subordinated Notes.* This 10-year debenture has embedded within it 40 option positions on the price of copper—one maturing in 3 months, one in 6 months, . . . , and one in 10 years. The effect of this series of embedded option positions is to make the company's quarterly interest payments vary with the prevailing price of copper, as shown in Table 8.1:

Table 8.1: Relation of Interest Rate to Copper Price

Average Copper Price	Indexed Interest Rate
$2.00 or above	21 %
1.80	20
1.60	19
1.40	18
1.30	17
1.20	16
1.10	15
1.00	14
0.90	13
0.80 or below	12

In 1989, Presidio Oil Company issued an oil-indexed note with a similar structure, but with the coupons linked to the price of natural gas. And, in 1991, Shin Etsu, a Japanese chemical manufacturer, issued a hybrid with a similar structure; however, the issue was a private placement and the coupon payment floated *inversely* with the price of oil.

---

[10] See James Jordan, Robert Mackay, and Eugene Moriarty, "The New Regulation of Hybrid Debt Instruments," *Journal of Applied Corporate Finance*, Vol. 2, No. 4 (Winter 1990).

The Case of Forest Oil: The Consequences of Not Managing Risk

It was Forest Oil, however, and not Presidio, that first considered issuing natural gas-linked debt. But Forest's management was confident that natural gas prices would go higher in the near future and thus decided that the price of the natural gas-linked debt would turn out to be too high. Unfortunately, the company's bet on natural gas prices ended up going against them. Natural gas prices since the issue was contemplated have fallen dramatically, and the company has been squeezed between high current interest costs and reduced revenues. Indeed, the squeeze has been so tight that Forest has been forced to restructure its debt.

Using Hybrids to Manage Foreign Exchange Risk

As Figure 8.2 suggests, exchange rates became more volatile following the abandonment of the Bretton Woods agreement in 1973. As a result, many companies have experienced foreign exchange risk arising from transaction, translation, and economic exposures.

The simplest way to manage an exposure to foreign exchange risk is by using a forward foreign exchange contract. If the firm is long foreign currency, it can cover this exposure by selling forward contracts. Or if it has a short position, it can buy forwards.

Dual Currency Bonds. Similar to PEMEX's oil-indexed issue, the simplest FX hybrid debt structure is a *Dual Currency Bond*. Such a bond combines a fixed-rate, "bullet" (that is, single) repayment bond and a long-dated forward contract on foreign exchange. For example, in 1985, Philip Morris Credit issued a dual-currency bond in which coupon payments are made in Swiss Francs while principal will be repaid US Dollars.

PERLs. A variant of the dual currency structure is the *Principal Exchange Rate Linked Security*. In 1987, Westinghouse Electric Company issued *PERLs* wherein the bondholder received at maturity the principal the USD value of 70.13 million New Zealand dollars. The issuer's motive in this case was likely to reduce its funding costs by taking advantage of an unusual investor demand for long-dated currency forwards. Earlier in the same year, and presumably with similar motive, Ford Motor Credit Company issued *Reverse PERLs*. In this case, the principal repayment varied inversely with the value of the yen.[11]

Creating a Hybrid By Adding Options

As in the case of commodity-linked hybrids, forward-like FX hybrids seemed to have given way to structures containing warrants or other option-like features. In 1987, for example, General Electric Credit Corpor-

---

[11] See Michael G. Capatides, *A Guide to the Capital Markets Activities of Banks and Bank Holding Companies*, (Browne & Co.), 1988, p. 132.

ation made a public offering made up of debt and yen-USD currency exchange warrants.

Bonds with Principal Indexed (Convertible) to FX. Like bonds with warrants, convertible bonds are made up of bonds and equity options. But there is one important difference: In the case of bonds with warrants, the bondholder can exercise the option embodied in a warrant and still keep the underlying bond. With convertibles, the holder must surrender the bond to exercise the option. Sunshine Mining's Silver-Indexed Bonds and Standard Oil's Oil Indexed Notes are similar constructions. The bondholder can receive either the value of the bond or the value of the option, but not both.

When this debt structure appeared with an embedded foreign currency option, the hybrid was called an *Indexed Currency Option Note* (or *ICON*). This security, which was first underwritten by First Boston in 1985, combines a fixed rate, bullet repayment bond and a European option on foreign exchange.[12]

Using Hybrids to Manage Interest Rate Risk

Some companies have significant exposures to interest rates. Take the case of firms that supply inputs to the housing market. When interest rates rise, the revenues of such firms tend to fall. The use of standard, floating-rate bank debt in such cases would likely increase the probability of default.

Creating a Hybrid with Embedded Swaps

To manage interest rate risk, such companies may be best served by a debt instrument wherein the coupon payment actually declines when interest rates rise. Such an *Inverse Floating Rate Note*—or a *Yield-Curve Note*, as it was called when first issued by the Student Loan Marketing Association (Sallie Mae) in the public debt market in 1986—can be decomposed into a floating-rate, bullet repayment note and a plain vanilla interest rate swap for twice the principal of the loan.

Creating a Hybrid by Adding Options

Just as bondholders can be provided options to exchange their bonds for a specified amount of a commodity or foreign currency, hybrid securities have been issued that give bondholders the option to exchange a bond (typically at maturity) for another bond (typically with the same coupon and maturity).

Convertible/Exchangeable Floating Rate Notes. These hybrids, which give the holder the right to convert to (or exchange for) a fixed-

---

[12] In his article in this issue, "Securities Innovation: An Overview," John Finnerty notes that ICONs "were introduced and disappeared quickly."

rate bond at a pre-specified interest rate, first appeared in 1979. Such notes contain embedded "put" options on interest rates; that is, investors are likely to exercise their conversion or exchange rights only if interest rates fall below a certain level.

Extendible Notes. The same, moreover, is true of extendible notes, which give the holder the right to exchange the underlying bond for a bond of longer maturity. Such bonds first appeared in 1982.

Using Hybrids to Reduce Conflicts Between Bondholders and Shareholders

In "normal" circumstances—that is, when operations are profitable and the firm can comfortably meet its debt service payments and investment schedule—the interests of bondholders and shareholders are united. Both groups of investors benefit from managerial decisions that increase the total value of the firm.

In certain cases, however, corporate managements find themselves in the position of being able to increase shareholder value *at the expense of bondholders*.[13] For example, as happened in a number of leveraged recapitalizations, management could reduce the value of outstanding bonds by increasing debt or adding debt senior to that in question. (In professional circles, this is known as *event risk*; in academic parlance it is the *claims dilution problem*.) Or, if the firm were in danger of insolvency, management could choose—as did some S&L executives—to invest in ever riskier projects in desperate attempts to save the firm (the *asset substitution problem*). Finally, a management squeezed between falling revenues and high interest payments could choose to pass up value-adding projects such as R&D or, if things are bad enough, basic maintenance and safety procedures (the *underinvestment problem*).[14]

Corporate debtholders are well aware that such problems can arise, and they accordingly protect themselves by lowering the price they are willing to pay for the debt. For corporate management, such lower prices translate into higher interest payments, which in turn further raise the probability of financial trouble.

Hybrids reduce these shareholder-bondholder conflicts by reducing current interest rates, shifting debt service payments to periods when

---

[13] For the seminal discussion of the effect of conflicts between shareholders and debtholders (and between management and shareholders as well) on the behavior of the firm, see Michael C. Jensen and William H. Meckling, "Theory of the Firm: Managerial Behavior, Agency Costs, and Capital Structure," *Journal of Financial Economics* (1976), pp. 305–360.

[14] For an account of the underinvestment problem, see Stewart Myers, "The Determinants of Corporate Borrowing," *Journal of Financial Economics* (1977). For a more detailed examination of these sources of shareholder/debtholder conflict, see Clifford W. Smith and Jerold B. Warner, "On Financial Contracting: An Analysis of Bond Covenants," *Journal of Financial Economics*, 7 (1979), pp. 117–161.

firms are better able to pay, stabilizing cash flow, and thereby reducing the likelihood of financial distress. In so doing, they also raise the price of the corporate debt to investors and lower the overall corporate cost of capital.

Using Hybrids to Reduce the Claims Dilution Problem (or Protect Against "Event Risk")

Puttable Bonds. Introduced in 1976, these bonds give their holders the option to "put" the bond back to the issuer. Such an option would be exercised only if interest rates rise or the issuer's credit standing falls. In this sense, puttable bonds give bondholders both a call option on interest rates and an option on the credit spread of the issuer.[15] Such put options thus protect bondholders not only against increases in interest rates, but also against the possibility of losses from deteriorating operating performance or leveraged recapitalizations. In the wake of the widely publicized bondholder losses accompanying the KKR buyout of RJR Nabisco in 1989, the use of put options to protect against such "event risk" enjoyed a new vogue.

Floating Rate, Rating Sensitive Notes. These notes, issued by Manufacturer Hanover in 1988, contain explicit options on the issuer's credit standing. In this security, Manufacturer's Hanover agreed to pay investors a spread above LIBOR that increased with each incremental decline in the bank's senior debt rating.

From the standpoint of risk management, however, there is an obvious flaw in the design of this security. Although it may partially compensate investors for increases in risk, it actually increases the probability of default instead of reducing it. The security increases the corporate debt service burden precisely when the issuing firm can least afford it—when its credit rating has fallen and, presumably, its operating cash flow declined.

A hybrid structure designed to overcome this problem was a syndication of oil-indexed bonds created by Chase Manhattan for Sonatrach (the state hydrocarbons company of Algeria) in 1990. As illustrated in Figure 8.3, the transaction was structured so that Chase accepted two-year call options on oil from Sonatrach and then transformed those two-year calls into seven-year calls and puts that were passed on to the syndicate members. Investors were compensated for a below-market interest by a payoff

---

[15] Extendible notes also provide bondholders with an option on the firm's credit standing. But, unlike puttable debt, it represents the opportunity to benefit from increases in the firm's credit standing, or decreases in the spread. In the case of extendible notes, if the credit spread of the issuer decreases, the right to extend the maturity of the note (as the old credit spread) has value.

Figure 8.3: Oil-Linked Credit-Sensitive Syndicate

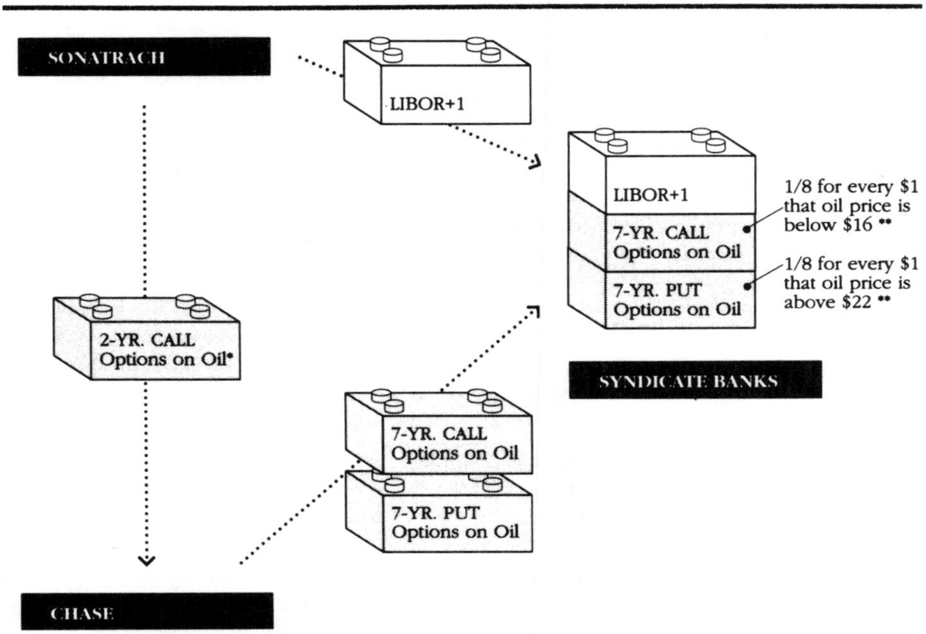

structure that would provide them with higher payoffs in the event of significantly *higher or lower* oil prices.

For the issuer, however, the security requires higher payments to Chase *only in the event of higher oil prices.* If the price of oil declines, although the syndicate members receive a higher yield, the increase comes from Chase, not Sonatrach.

Using Hybrids to Reduce the Asset Substitution and Underinvestment Problems

Convertibles. At the outset, we noted that convertible bonds contain embedded options on the company's equity. By providing bondholders with the right to convert their claims into equity, management provides bondholders with the assurance that they will participate in any increase in shareholder value that results from increasing the risk of the company's activities—whether by leveraging up or undertaking riskier investments. By lowering current interest rates and thus reducing the likelihood of financial trouble, convertibles also reduce the probability that financially strapped companies will be forced to forgo valuable investment opportunities.[16]

Convertibles (and debt with warrants, their close substitutes) are also potentially useful in resolving disagreements between bondholders and shareholders about just how risky the firm's activities are. The value of convertibles are risk-neutral in the following sense: Unexpected increases in company risk reduce the value of the bond portion of a convertible, but at the same time increase the value of the embedded option (by increasing volatility). It is largely because of this risk-neutralizing effect—and for their role in reducing the "underinvestment problem" mentioned below—that convertible issuers tend to be smaller, newer, riskier firms characterized by high growth and earnings volatility.[17]

The Case of LYONs

While a number of bonds are puttable or convertible, the Liquid Yield Option Note (LYON) introduced by Merrill Lynch in 1985 is both puttable and convertible. The combination of the put and conversion features are especially useful in controlling the asset substitution, or risk-shifting, problem just described.[18] For this reason, the LYONs structure should be particularly attractive to issuers with substantial capital investment opportunities and a wide range of alternative investment projects (with varying degrees of risk).

It is thus interesting to note that the LYON structure was first used to fund companies where the asset substitution problem was acute. Take the case of Waste Management, the first issuer of LYONs. Although Waste Management is today a household name among even small investors, in 1985 the company could best be viewed as a collection of "growth options." As such it posed considerable uncertainty for investors.

The Economic Rationale for Issuing a Hybrid Security

We are still left with a fundamental question: Given the well-functioning, low-cost markets for derivative products available today, why should a corporate issuer ever prefer the "bundled" hybrid to simply issuing

---

[16] More technically, the underinvestment problem arises from the fact that, in financially troubled firms, an outsized portion of the returns from new investments must go to help restore the value of the bondholders' claims before the shareholders receive any payoff at all. This has also been dubbed the "debt overhang" problem.

[17] For an exposition of this argument, see Michael Brennan and Eduardo Schwartz, "The Case for Convertibles," *Chase Financial Quarterly* (Fall 1981). Reprinted in *Journal of Applied Corporate Finance* (Summer 1988).

[18] As described at length in the next article in this issue, the put feature also enabled Merrill Lynch to tailor the security for its network of retail investors.

standard debt and buying or selling the derivatives. We now discuss the following three reasons why corporate management might choose hybrids:

(1) If the firm issuing the hybrid can provide investors with a "play" not available otherwise—that is, a derivative instrument not available in the traded derivatives markets—the issuing firm will consequently be paid a premium for "completing the market."

(2) The hybrid may enable the issuer to take advantage of tax or regulatory arbitrages that would lower the cost of borrowing.

(3) By embedding a risk management product into a hybrid, the issuer may be able to obtain hedge accounting treatment, which may not be allowed if the derivative was bought or sold separately.

Using Hybrids to Provide Investors with a "Play"

The most straightforward reason for issuing a hybrid is to provide investors with a means of taking a position on a financial price. If the issuer provides a "play" not otherwise available, the investor will be willing to pay a premium, thereby reducing the issuer's cost of funding. (And, if the hybrid provides investors with a "scarce security" not otherwise obtainable, it may also provide corporate issuers with a hedge they can't duplicate with derivative products.)

The "play" can be in the form of a forward contract. Perhaps the best example of such is dual currency bonds, which provided investors with foreign exchange forward contracts with longer maturities than those available in the standard market. The forward contracts embedded in dual currency bonds have maturities running to 10 years, whereas liquidity in the standard foreign exchange forward market declines for maturities greater than one year, and falls very significantly beyond five years.

The "play," however, has more commonly been in the form of an option embedded in the bond—generally an option of longer maturity than those available in the standard option market. Sunshine Mining's Silver Indexed Bond fits this category, as do Standard Oil's Oil Indexed Note and the gold warrants issued by Pegasus Gold Corporation. In 1986 long-dated options on stock market indices were introduced with the development of hybrid debt in which the principal was indexed to an equity index. While the first such debt issues were indexed to the Nikkei, Salomon Brothers' "S&P 500 Index Subordinated Notes (SPINs)" have probably received more public attention. A SPIN is convertible into the value of the S&P 500 Index, rather than into an individual equity. Since then, debt has been issued that is indexed to other equity indices (for example, the NYSE index) or subsets of indices. For example, in 1991, United Technologies issued a zero-coupon bond indexed to the S&P Pharmaceutical Index.

Using Hybrids to "Arbitrage" Tax and/or Regulatory Authorities

Hybrid debt has also been used to take advantage of asymmetries in tax treatment or regulations in different countries or markets. One classic example is a case of "arbitrage" reported in *Business Week* under the provocative title, "A Way for US Firms to Make 'Free Money.' " The "free money" came from two sources:

(1) A difference in tax treatment between the U.S. and Japan—the Japanese tax authorities ruled that income earned from holding a zero-coupon bond would be treated as a capital gain, thereby making interest income on the zero nontaxable for Japanese investors. In contrast, U.S. tax authorities permitted any U.S. firm issuing a zero coupon bond to deduct from current income the imputed interest payments.

(2) A regulatory arbitrage—The Ministry of Finance limited Japanese pension funds' investments in non-yen-dominated bonds issued by foreign corporations to at most 10 percent of their portfolios. The Ministry of Finance also ruled that dual currency bonds qualified as a yen issue, thus allowing dual currency bonds to command a premium from Japanese investors.

Consequently, U.S. firms issued zero-coupon yen bonds (to realize the interest rate savings from the tax arbitrage), and then issued a dual currency bond to hedge the residual yen exposure from the yen zero, while realizing a further interest savings from the regulatory arbitrage.

Tax-Deductible Equity. Perhaps the most thinly disguised attempt to issue tax-deductible equity was the *Adjustable Rate Convertible Debt* introduced in 1982.[19] Such convertibles paid a coupon determined by the dividend rate on the firm's common stock; moreover, the debt could be converted to common stock at the current price at any time (i.e., there was no conversion premium). Not surprisingly, once the IRS ruled that this was equity for tax purposes, this structure disappeared.

On a less aggressive level, hybrid structures like Merrill Lynch's LYON take advantage of the treatment of zero coupon instruments by U.S. tax authorities—that is, zero coupon bonds allow the issuer to deduct deferred interest payments from current income (although the holder of the bond must declare them as income). Given the impact of the IRS ruling on adjustable rate convertible debt, it is not surprising that a great deal of attention has been given to the tax status of the LYON.

Using Hybrids to Obtain Accrual Accounting Treatment for Risk Management

If a U.S. company uses a forward, futures, swap, or option to hedge a specific transaction (for example, a loan or a purchase or a receipt), it is relatively simple to obtain accrual accounting treatment for the hedge.

---

[19] This point is made by John Finnerty in his article in this issue.

(Changes in the market value of the hedging instrument offset changes in the value of the asset being hedged, so there is no need to mark the hedging instrument to market.)

If, however, the firm wishes to use one of the risk management instruments to hedge expected net income or an even longer-term economic exposure, the current position of the accounting profession is that the hedge position must be marked to market. Some companies have been reluctant to use derivatives to manage such risks because this accounting treatment would increase the volatility of their reported income—*even while such a risk management strategy would stabilize their longer-run operating cash flow.*

With the use of hybrids, by contrast, which contain embedded derivatives, the firm may be able to obtain accrual accounting treatment for the entire package. Accountants are accustomed to valuing convertible debt at historical cost; and, given this precedent, they can extend the same treatment to hybrids.[20]

Concluding Remarks

Beginning in 1980 with Sunshine Mining's issue of silver-linked bonds, U.S. corporations have increasingly chosen to raise debt capital by embedding derivatives such as forwards or options into their notes and bonds. In the early 1980s, such hybrids typically provided investors with payoffs (at first only principal, but later interest payments as well) indexed to commodity prices, interest rates, and exchange rates. But, in recent years, companies have begun to issue debt indexed to general stock market indices and even subsets of such indices.

Critics of such newfangled securities view them as the offspring of "supply-driven" fads. According to this view, profit-hungry investment banks set their highly-paid "rocket scientists" to designing new securities that can then be foisted on unsuspecting corporate treasurers and investors.

As economists, however, we begin with the assumption that capital market innovations succeed only to the extent they do a better job than existing products in meeting the demands of issuers and investors. The evidence presented in these pages, albeit anecdotal, suggests that hybrid debt is a capital market response to corporate treasurers' desire to manage pricing risks and otherwise tailor their securities to investor demands. In some cases, especially those in which hybrids feature long-dated forwards or options, hybrids are furnishing investors with securities they cannot obtain elsewhere.

---

[20] See J. Matthew Singleton, "Hedge Accounting: A State-of-the-Art Review," *Journal of Banking and Finance*, 5 (Fall 1991), pp. 26–32. [This article appears as Chapter 25 in this volume.]

Like the remarkable growth of futures, swaps, and options markets beginning in the late 1970s, the proliferation of corporate hybrids during the 1980s is fundamentally an attempt to cope with increased price volatility. The sharp increase in the volatility of exchange rates, interest rates, and oil prices—to name just the most important—during the 1970s provided the "necessary condition" for the rise of hybrids.

But another important stimulant to hybrids has come from other constraints on companies' ability to raise debt. In the early 1980s, for example, when interest rates were high, hybrid debt was used by riskier firms to reduce their interest costs to manageable levels. Given the current level of interest rates today, most companies would likely choose to borrow as much straight debt as possible. But except for the highest-rated companies, many firms also now face *non-price* credit restrictions that have greatly enlarged credit spreads. In some such cases, companies are using hybrid debt to lower their risk profile and thus avoid the higher funding costs now associated with being a riskier corporate borrower. In other cases, hybrids are providing access to debt capital that would otherwise be denied on any terms.

RISK MANAGEMENT IN BANKING

Clifford W. Smith Jr.*

9

1. Introduction

Corporate risk management is important for firms in the banking industry for at least two reasons. First, the asset risk in a bank's loan portfolio depends on its customers' risk-management policies. Second, a bank's value depends directly on its risk-management policy. In this paper, I analyze these implications of corporate risk-management for banks.

In section 2, I array corporate risks along a spectrum. Firm-specific risks are at one extreme while market-wide risks are at the other. I note that derivatives such as forwards, futures, options, and swaps are specialized off-balance-sheet risk-management tools that allow the firm to hedge many sources of market-wide financial risk. In addition, financially engineered instruments, such as dual-currency bonds, provide on-balance-sheet hedging alternatives. In section 3, I examine motives for value-maximizing firms to use risk-management instruments. This section thus identifies the implications of customer hedging for a bank's asset-portfolio risk. Section 4 applies these principles to derive the implications for bank risk-management policies. In section 5, I present my conclusions.

2. Risk Exposures and Hedging Instruments

Of the numerous risks to which firms are exposed, some are firm-specific while others are market-wide. In Figure 9.1 I array these risks along a risk spectrum. At one end are firm-specific risks; examples include fires, lawsuits, outcomes of research and development projects, and outcomes

* I would like to thank David Mayers and Charles W. Smithson for many stimulating conversations in the process of working on related questions. Financial support was provided by the John M. Olin Foundation and the Bradley Research Center of the University of Rochester.

147

Figure 9.1: Risk Management Spectrum

Risk Exposures	Risk Management Tools		
	Off-Balance-Sheet	On-Balance-Sheet	
		Financial	Production
Firm Specific — Fire			Loss Prevention and Control
Lawsuit	Insurance		
Payoffs to R&D Projects	Warrants	Convertible Bonds	Joint Ventures
Commodity Prices	Forwards	Hybrids (Dual Currency Oil Indexed Notes, etc.)	Technology Choice
Interest Rates	Futures Swaps		Plant Siting
Market Wide — Foreign Exchange Rates	Options		Vertical Integration

of exploration and development activities. At the other are market-wide risks; examples include the impact of unexpected changes in interest rates, foreign exchange rates, oil prices and GNP.

Corporate Risk Exposures. To analyze firms' hedging incentives, it is important to understand how their exposures are related to value. For some risks, this relation is straightforward. For example, an uninsured casualty loss directly reduces firm value. However other exposures are more complex. In Figure 9.2 I illustrate the risk profile for an oil producer. This firm is long oil, thus higher oil prices raise revenues and increase firm value (see Smith/Smithson/Wilford, 1990). Therefore, the risk profile has a positive slope. For simplicity, I illustrate this relation with a straight line. But, for an oil user, the firm is short oil; thus higher oil prices raise costs and reduce firm value. In Figure 9.2(b), this firm's risk profile has a negative slope. With the firm's risk exposure identified, we now can examine the impact of hedging on firm value. To hedge its exposure to oil prices, the oil user in Figure 9.2(b) must employ a hedging instrument that with higher oil prices will appreciate in value. Because gains on the hedge offset losses in the firm's core business, hedging reduces

Figure 9.2: Relation Between the Change in Firm Value and Change in Oil Prices for an Oil Producer and an Oil User.

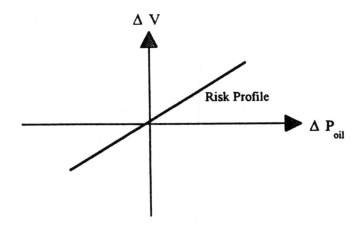

For an oil Producer, rising oil prices ($\Delta P_{oil} > 0$) and rising revenues lead to an increase in the value of the firm ($\Delta V > 0$).

(a)

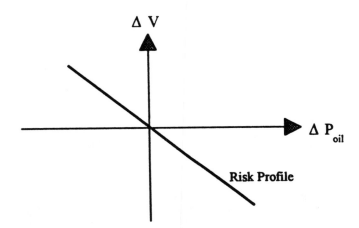

For an oil user, rising oil prices ($\Delta P_{oil} > 0$) mean increasing costs: so the value of the firm declines ($\Delta V < 0$).

(b)

this firm's exposure to oil-price changes. Therefore the variance of firm-value is reduced through risk management.

Off-Balance-Sheet Hedging Instruments. A major advantage of arraying the sources of risks as in Figure 9.1 is that it clearly illustrates that different risks are managed with different hedging instruments. In the second column, I note that insurance policies are employed to hedge firm-specific risks like fires or lawsuits. Market-wide risks such as exposures to interest rates, foreign-exchange rates, and commodity prices can be managed with the use of off-balance-sheet derivative instruments, such as forward, futures, swap, and option contracts.

The forward contract is the simplest of these four basic instruments. A forward contract obligates its owner to buy a stipulated asset on a stipulated date at a stipulated price. These provisions are all specified at contract origination. At the maturity date, the buyer has a contract whose value is equal to the difference between the market value of the asset and the exercise price. If the spot price of the asset is higher than the exercise price, the buyer has a gain; however, if the market price is lower than the exercise price, the buyer has suffered a loss. In Figure 9.3 the payoff profiles from buying and writing a forward contract are illustrated. Buying a forward contract hedges the firm's exposure if its core-business cash flows are a negative function of the asset value; writing a forward hedges the exposure if core-business cash flows are a positive function of the asset value.

Figure 9.3: Payoff Profile from (a) Buying a Forward and (b) Selling a Forward Contract.

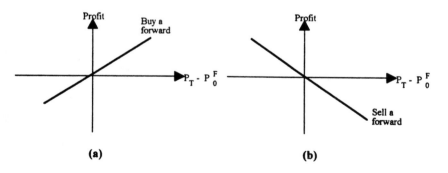

At contract maturity (time=T), the profit to the buyer of a forward contract is equal to the difference between the spot price at T and the exercise price agreed to at contract origination ($P_T - P_0^P$) times the size of the forward contract. The profit to the seller of the contract is the reverse.

In form, a futures contract is quite similar to a forward contract. Buying futures also obligates the purchaser to buy a stipulated asset at a stipulated price on a stipulated date. Aspects of the contract administration such as marking to market with daily settlement, margin accounts, exchange trading, and contract standardization are the primary differences between forwards and futures. However, their impact on hedging firm value is similar; Figure 9.4 can thus be employed to illustrate the payoff profiles for futures.

A swap obligates two parties to exchange cash flows at specified intervals. For example, in a simple interest rate swap, parties exchange specified cash flows determined by two different interest rates. At each settlement date, this interest rate swap provides an imbedded forward contract on interest rates. Therefore a swap is in essence a strip of forward contracts, each with a different maturity date (see Smith/Smithson/Wakeman (1986, 1988)); and thus Figure 9.3 also can be employed to illustrate the basic payoff profile for a swap.

An option gives the owner of the contract the right, but not the obligation, to transact (see Black/Scholes (1973) or Smith (1976)). Options come in two basic forms: puts and calls. A call is an option to buy a stipulated asset at a stipulated price on or before a stipulated date; a put is an option to sell. Buying a call plus writing a put on the same asset with the same exercise price and the same expiration date creates payoffs that are equivalent to those of buying a forward. This equivalence among puts, calls, and forwards is referred to as put-call parity.

On-Balance-Sheet-Hedging. The previous decade has produced a substantial increase in financially engineered securities to provide customized solutions to corporate financing problems. Financial engineers operate much like General Motors. GM produces automobiles to meet specific customer demands by offering different models with different wheel bases, different engines, different exteriors, different interior appointments, different sound systems, and so on. By exploiting the myriad opportunities to mix different off-the-shelf options, GM produces many different cars. Similarly, financially engineered instruments are customized securities, but the components that make up the securities are themselves fairly basic off-the-shelf loans, forwards, swaps, and options. (See Smith/Smithson 1990.)

For example, Phillip Morris Credit Corporation issued over $50 million of dual-currency bonds. While the principal amount of the bonds is stated in U.S. dollars, the interest payments are denominated in Swiss francs. Therefore, the cash flows of this dual-currency bond are equivalent to those of a financial package containing a level-coupon Swiss franc bond plus a long-term forward-exchange forward contract to exchange the Swiss franc principal repayment into dollars.

Sallie Mae, the Student Loan Marketing Association, issued yield-curve notes. The coupon payments on the yield-curve notes are equal to twice the fixed rate minus the floating rate times the principal; hence, if the floating rate rises, the net coupon payment falls. Thus, the cash flows of this reverse floating-rate note are equivalent to those of a package containing a traditional fixed rate bond plus a swap where the party pays fixed and receives floating.

As a last illustration, the Standard Oil Company issued oil indexed notes. At maturity, the holder of each note receives $1000 plus the excess of the crude oil price over $25 multiplied by 170 barrels ($1000 + 170 × $(P_{crude\ oil} - \$25)$). The cash flows of these notes are equivalent to those of a 48-month maturity zero-coupon bond with a face value of $1000 plus a 4-year call option on 170 barrels of crude oil with an exercise price of $25.

As illustrated in Figure 9.1, these risks can also be managed by the firm's choice of real production activities. For example, foreign-exchange risk can be reduced by moving production overseas. Yet it is difficult to believe that plant-siting decisions would be made primarily to manage foreign-exchange exposures. Producing in a new market with new suppliers, new workers, different labor laws, and so on is not a decision to be taken lightly. Moreover, if market conditions change and exposures change; financial contracts are more flexible and thus can be modified at lower cost than real production decisions.

3. Risk Management Benefits

Financial markets have experienced a dramatic increase in volatility over the past two decades. Given a firm's risk exposure, increased volatility of foreign-exchange rates, interest rates or commodity prices translates into increased volatility of firm value. Since risk management reduces firm-value volatility, one might presume that all firms would want to engage in hedging. Yet there is wide variation in the use of risk-management instruments across firms. Thus, I now focus on identifying firm characteristics that provide strong economic incentives to hedge.

Company Ownership Structure. To examine economic risk-management incentives, I assume that the firm's objective is to maximize the expected present value of its net cash flows. Hence, a company should manage its financial price risk if that risk management strategy increases the expected present value of its cash flows. In their individual affairs, risk-averse people have incentives to hedge because reducing risk lowers the rate of return they require to engage in a risky activity. However, for a widely-held corporation, this logic fails. Portfolio theory tells us that a corporation's required rate of return doesn't depend on total risk but only on systematic risk. A hedging instrument that works primarily on diversifiable risk does not provide a lower discount rate for firms with well-diversified owners. Yet, for organizations in which the owners do not hold well-diversified portfolios, such as partnerships, proprietorships, and closely-held firms, risk aversion can be an important risk-management incentive (see Mayers/Smith 1982).

If hedging does not reduce the required rate of return for widely-held firms, then to increase value, hedging must increase the firm's expected net cash flows. To analyze how this might occur, recall the Modigliani-Miller proposition. It states that the firm's financial decisions, including its risk management decisions, will not affect firm value if there are no taxes, no transactions costs, and if the firm's real investment activities are fixed. Although this is the emphasis Modigliani/Miller gave the proposition in their original paper, it is useful to restate it. If financial decisions affect firm value, the decisions must do so through their impact on taxes, transactions costs, or investment decisions. The Modigliani/Miller proposition thus can be employed to identify firms that have strong economic incentives to hedge.

Taxes. If the firm faces some form of effective tax progressivity (the firm's effective tax function is convex) then hedging taxable income by reducing the volatility of pretax income, reduces the firm's expected tax liability. As long as the tax function is linear—the firm faces a constant effective tax rate—hedging doesn't affect the expected tax liability of the firm. This implication is quite general, it follows from Jensen's Inequality (see Smith/Stulz 1985). Convexity in the tax schedule can arise from three general considerations: First, although its range is limited, the tax code specifies statutory progressivity. Second, tax-preference items such as tax-loss carry forwards, foreign tax credits, and investment tax credits generally have limitation on use. If taxable income falls below some level, the tax-preference item's value is reduced either by the loss of the tax shield or by the postponement of its use (see DeAngelo/Masulis 1980). Finally, the alternate minimum tax specifies tax liabilities linked to the difference between reported income and taxable income. These tax provisions imply that firms with stronger tax-related incentives to hedge are: firms with a higher probability of income in the progressive region of the tax schedule (e.g., smaller firms, start-up firms), firms with more tax-preference items, and firms with greater volatility of the difference between taxable and financial income.

Financial Distress Costs. Risk management reduces the expected costs of financial distress the firm faces by reducing the variance of firm value, thereby reducing the probability of encountering financial distress. The size of this expected cost reduction depends both on the change in probability of distress from hedging and the level of costs associated with financial distress.

There are two major components of the cost of financial distress. The first is the direct expense of dealing with a default, bankruptcy, reorganization, or liquidation. The second is the indirect costs arising from the changes in incentives of the firm's various claimholders. For example, if the firm files for bankruptcy and attempts to reorganize its business, the bankruptcy court judge overseeing the case is unlikely to approve nonroutine expenditures. The judge receives little credit if the activities turn out well, but is criticized by creditors with impaired claims if they turn out badly. Thus firms undergoing reorganization are likely to systematically pass up positive net present value projects due to the nature of the oversight by the bankruptcy court.

Incentives to turn down positive net present value project also can arise in firms that avoid bankruptcy. For a firm with fixed claims in its capital structure, enough of the benefits of taking a positive net present value project can accrue to the debtholders that the stockholders are not provided a normal expected return. Myers (1977) calls this the underinvestment problem. The greater the firm's leverage, the greater is this underinvestment incentive. I illustrate this incentive to engage in risk management in Figure 9.4. The risk profile of this oil user indicates that if oil prices increase, firm value falls. Given the fixed claims in the firm's capital structure, leverage increases. Higher leverage exacerbates the underinvestment problem causing the firm to turn down additional positive net present value projects. Thus, the underinvestment costs are graphically depicted by the shaded area in Figure 9.4. For this firm to hedge its oil

Figure 9.4: Illustration of the Underinvestment Costs for an Oil User.

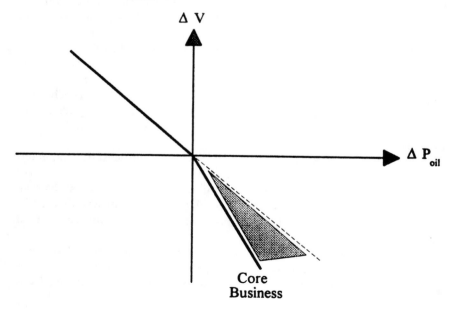

price exposure, it must add hedging instruments with payoffs that increase with higher oil prices (see Figure 9.5). By acquiring forwards, futures, or swaps, the firm reduces its net exposure to oil price changes. With such a hedge, a given increase in oil prices results in a smaller fall in firm value, a smaller induced change in leverage, a smaller exacerbation of the underinvestment problem, and a reduction in the frequency of rejected positive net present value projects (see Mayers/Smith 1987). Thus, the impact of hedging on the control of the underinvestment problem is graphically illustrated by the reduction in the shaded area between the firms core business exposure and its net exposure in Figure 9.5.

Riskshifting Within the Corporation. Although thus far, I have focused on corporate bondholders and stockholders, the firm is really a vast network of contracts among parties with common as well as conflicting interests. Managers, employees, and certain customers and suppliers are frequently less able to diversify their claims on the firm than stockholders and bondholders; in this respect, they are materially different. Thus, like the owners of a closely-held firm, the risk aversion of these corporate claimholders can provide an important incentive for the firm to engage in risk-management activities.

The magnitude of the incentive provided the managers to adopt risk-management policies is directly related to the terms of their compensa-

Figure 9.5: Impact of Hedging for Oil User in Figure 9.4.

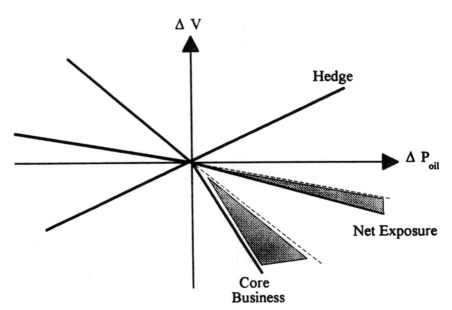

tion package and the specification of the payoff structure of their claims. A manager's risk aversion will motivate lobbying for extensive risk-management activities if compensation is primarily through fixed claims such as salary. But managers compensated through stock options or bonus plans have incentives to increase the volatility of stock prices or reported earnings because of the option-like payoffs of the compensation provisions (see Smith/Watts 1982). The magnitude of these incentives depends both on the relative importance of the components of the compensation package as well as on the specific terms of the particular plan. For example, incentives with respect to increasing volatility are greatest when the stock option is at the money.

Firms that produce goods or services where quality is difficult to ascertain prior to purchase (e.g., airlines) can bear large financial-distress costs. If such firms' operating results deteriorate, their customers' expectation of product quality can suffer and thus the price they are willing to pay for their product can fall. This problem is ultimately another facet of the underinvestment problem discussed above. For example, if an airline experiences financial distress, the benefits of an investment in maintaining its equipment disproportionately accrue to the bondholders. Customers thus rationally expect that the firm will reduce its maintenance activities. Such firms therefore have incentives to establish policies that reduce their exposure to these risks. They should employ less leverage and engage in more hedging.

The more important are product warranties or guarantees offered to the customers, the larger are the costs of financial distress. Product warranties are product-specific insurance policies. If the firm experiences financial distress, the price customers are willing to pay for the firm's product falls, in part because the value of this insurance policy falls. Moreover, if there is an important continuing stream of firm-provided customer services, similar revenue deterioration occurs. For example, expectations about continuing software development by a computer manufacturer or replacement parts for automobiles are important considerations in the purchase decision. If financial distress reduces the probability of the continuation of these activities then customers lower their valuation of the firm's product.

A complimentary set of problems arises between the firm and its suppliers. When the supplier provides specialized inputs to the firm, these problems are most severe. The problem is exacerbated if there is a relatively long time between incurring production costs and the ultimate receipt of the revenue. In such circumstances financial distress disrupts normal supply relationships. The supplier typically responds by demanding either cash in advance or cash on delivery. This exacerbates the firm's liquidity problems. Such changes in effective supply prices are additional costs of financial distress.

4. Implications for Banks

Customer Risk Management. The benefits of risk management are important for the bank to recognize. While risk management makes the client firm more valuable, it also allows the bank to profit in at least three ways. First, a bank whose calling officers are well versed in risk management are likely to provide more effective advice to customers, more effectively differentiate their products, and thus are likely to book more profitable business. Second, fees associated with supplying derivatives and financially engineered transactions can be an important source of revenue for the bank. Third, these transactions make the bank's customers better, more profitable customers. By lowering their customers' probability of financial distress, these transactions lower that bank's loss exposure. In sum, hedging by the bank is not a substitute for hedging by the bank's customers.

Bank Exposure Management. Banking is an industry where product quality is an important concern of potential customers. This concern is primarily focused on whether the financial commitments of the bank under its contracts will be met. Thus, risk management by banks affects the probability of financial distress and therefore the willingness of potential customers to enter into contracts. For specific banks interest-rate risk, foreign-exchange-rate risk and commodity-price risk can each be important, depending on the product mix of the bank. For example, a bank with oil producers as major loan customers will have an oil exposure. However, in this analysis I will focus primarily on interest-rate exposure management.

If the effective maturity of a bank's asset portfolio is greater than the effective maturity of its liabilities, then the bank has a duration imbalance and is exposed to interest-rate risk. Figure 9.6 illustrates the effect of interest rate changes on the value of a bank that books short-term deposits and long-term fixed-rate mortgage loans. If interest rates rise unexpectedly, the market value of its asset portfolio will experience larger capital losses than that of its liabilities, thus bank value falls. Conversely, if interest rates fall unexpectedly, firm value rises. Without imbedded options in its financial contracts, the response of the value of the bank to unexpected changes in interest rates is generally symmetric. Line aa in Figure 9.6 illustrates the interest-rate exposure for such a bank. If the duration imbalance is reduced, the response of bank value to a change in interest rates falls and the line becomes flatter. Conversely, if the duration imbalance increases, line aa becomes steeper.

Effect of Imbedded Options. Bank loan contracts historically have provided customers the option to prepay the loan prior to maturity. Early-withdrawal options also are included in certificates of deposit. Thus, if market interest rates change, these imbedded loan and deposit options change in value. These imbedded interest-rate options present an impor-

Figure 9.6: Line aa represents the interest rate exposure for a bank with a duration imbalance but no imbedded interest rate options. Line bb represents the interest rate exposure of a bank with imbedded interest rate options sold to its deposit and loan customers.

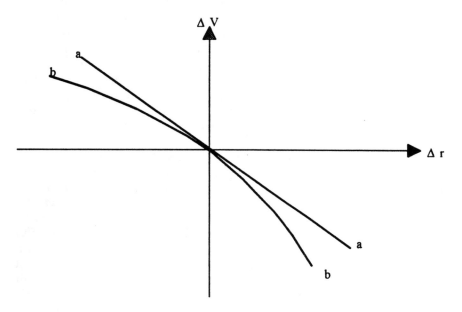

tant complication to the analysis of the effects of interest-rate changes on bank value. Since the bank has written the imbedded options to the depositors and the borrowers, line aa in Figure 9.6 is not appropriate. If interest rates fall, borrowers have incentives to prepay existing mortgages. They refinance the property at the new prevailing rate. Mortgage prepayments lower the value of a short-funded bank because the prepayment eliminates a capital gain equal to the difference between the market and face value of the mortgage. With prepayment options in its loan portfolio, the mortgage lender receives capital gains only on the mortgages which are not prepaid. Prepayments thus reduce the increase in bank value in response to lower interest rates. Line bb to the left of the origin in Figure 9.6 reflects these reduced capital gains. Since early-withdrawal options in CDs are more valuable at higher rates, line aa also overstates the change in bank value if interest rates rise. The value of this option is reflected in line bb to the right of the origin. Bank value changes produced by interest-rate changes are not symmetric because of these imbedded options offered to both loan and deposit customers. Rate increases lead to reductions in loan prepayments and a lengthening of the effective maturity of the loan portfolio. This increases the fall in the value of a bank from a rate increase. Depositors simultaneously increase their demand for early withdrawal of funds from CDs, again increasing the fall in the value of the bank.

The gains from declines in interest rates are less than the losses associated with rate increases because of these imbedded financial options. As a result bank value is reduced by increases in interest-rate volatility. The bank is short interest-rate volatility because it has written a set of imbedded interest-rate options to its customers. Unexpected increases in volatility therefore reduce the firm value while unexpected reductions in volatility increase firm value.

Hedging Bank Interest-Rate Exposure. Through a simple static portfolio strategies involving forwards, futures or swaps, a bank can change the slope of its exposure. Figure 9.7 illustrates the firm's net exposure to interest-rate changes after hedging by entering an interest-rate swap where the bank pays fixed and receives floating. While its exposure to interest-rate changes is reduced, the firm is still exposed to changes in interest-rate volatility. To hedge this risk the bank must buy interest-rate options. The options either can be purchased by themselves or imbedded in other financial packages, for example, CMO residuals.

A strategy of buying a matching portfolio of options to hedge the

Figure 9.7: Illustration of the Impact of Hedging Interest Rate Risk with a Swap for the Bank in Figure 9.6.

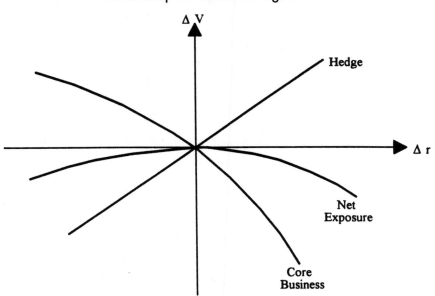

portfolio of imbedded interest-rate options written is an unwieldy and expensive proposition. It is more efficient to manage this risk through a dynamic hedging strategy. In general, one cannot hedge both the interest-rate risk and the volatility risk through the simple dynamic trading strategy pioneered by Black/Scholes. Given the Black/Scholes assumptions of constant volatility of the underlying asset, no jumps in the value of the underlying asset, and continuous costless trading, the only risk that must be hedged is that of unexpected changes in the underlying asset value. (The delta of the option measures the sensitivity of the value of an option to changes in the value of its underlying asset.) Their delta-hedging strategy replicates the option payoffs by acquiring rate-sensitive assets as the option goes in the money. While this dynamic delta-hedging strategy can hedge the bank's interest-rate risk, given the volatility of rates, it cannot simultaneously hedge volatility risk. This basic dynamic-hedging strategy must be extended to hedge additional option parameters.

A sophisticated dynamic-hedging strategy must consider the options gamma and vega in addition to the options delta. (Gamma is the second derivative of the option value with respect to a change in the underlying asset value; it is the change in delta associated with a change in the underlying asset value. Vega is the sensitivity of the option value to changes in the underlying asset's volatility.) To hedge the option's delta, gamma, and vega generally requires at least three assets; appropriate portfolio weights for the hedging portfolio can be derived with three linearly independent rate-sensitive assets (see Bookstaber 1993). Use of such a generalized hedging strategy reduces the valuation errors from periodic rather than continuous rebalancing, jumps in the underlying asset value, and volatility changes.

Programming techniques can be employed to identify the minimum-cost hedging strategy with more than three assets. Yet, there are potential problems associated with such a technique. Estimation of relevant parameters inevitably involves measurement error. The impact of measurement-error-induced selection bias can be reduced by employing more assets than identified by the program as "optimal." If the program identifies out-of-the-money options, one must be especially careful since such options are typically illiquid.

5. Conclusions:

In this paper, two major implications of risk-management theory for banks are explored: (1) The direct impact of interest-rate risk-management policy on the value of a bank, and (2) the risk-management policies of loan customers for the risk of the bank's asset portfolio. With respect to the first issue, I argue that in the traditional method of structuring this business, the bank sells imbedded interest-rate options and thus creates a significant exposure to interest-rate volatility. This exposure can be managed only by buying options. The second issue is important specifically because banks have not aggressively pressed their loan customers about their hedging policies. The hedging motives I identify in this paper change corporate activities, cash-flow distributions, and firm value. These benefits cannot be generated without borrower participation, therefore, hedging by lenders is not a substitute for hedging by borrowers.

Banks have long exploited certain risk-management activities; the industry pioneered the use of duration as an interest-rate risk-management technique. However, the control of financial risks via derivative securities has been less extensively pursued. Surveys suggest that especially among smaller banks there is a problem with hiring and retaining management with the requisite skills to manage a financial risk-management program (see Booth/Smith/Stolz 1984).

However, if financial prices remain volatile, the implications of not hedging can prove disastrous. With the increased awareness of the financial distress problems on the part of both regulatory bodies and customers as a result of the Savings and Loan crisis, the pressure for banks to adopt effective risk-management policies is likely to mount.

REFERENCES

Black, Fischer and Myron Scholes. 1973. "The Pricing of Options and Corporate Liabilities," *Journal of Political Economy* 81, 637–659.

Booth, J. R., R. L. Smith, and R. W. Stolz. 1984. The Use of Interest Rate Futures by Financial Institutions, *Journal of Bank Research*, 15, 15–20.

Mayers, David and Clifford W. Smith. 1982. "On the Corporate Demand for Insurance," *Journal of Business* 55, No. 2, 281–296.

Mayers, David and Clifford W. Smith. 1987. "Corporate Insurance and the Underinvestment Problem." *Journal of Risk and Insurance*, Vol. LIV, No. 1, 45–54.

Myers, Stewart. 1977. "Determinants of Corporate Borrowing," *Journal of Financial Economics* 5, No. 2, 147–175.

Nance, Deana R., Clifford W. Smith, and Charles W. Smithson. "On The Determinants of Corporate Hedging," *Journal of Finance* (forthcoming).

Smith, Clifford W. 1976. "Option Pricing: A Review," *Journal of Financial Economics* Vol. 3, 3–52.

Smith, Clifford W., and Charles W. Smithson. 1990. *"Handbook of Financial Engineering,"* Harper and Row: New York.

Smith, Clifford W., Charles W. Smithson, and Lee M. Wakeman. "The

Market for Interest Rate Swaps," *Financial Management* Vol. 17, No. 4, 34–44 (Winter 1988).

Smith, Clifford W. and René Stulz. 1985. "The Determinants of Firm's Hedging Policies," *Journal of Financial and Quantitative Analysis* 20, No. 4, 391–405.

Smith, Clifford W. and Ross Watts. 1982. "Incentive and Tax Effects of U.S. Executive Compensation Plans," *Australian Journal of Management* 7, 139–157.

Smith, Clifford W., Charles W. Smithson, and Sykes D. Wilford. 1990. "Financial Risk Management" Ballinger/Institutional Investor: New York.

Smith, Michael. 1982. "Life Insurance Policy as an Options Package," *Journal of Risk and Insurance* 49 (4), 583–601.

OPTION REPLICATION TECHNOLOGY*

Richard M. Bookstaber

10

In this chapter we will sketch out the mechanics of option replication, based on the use of delta, gamma, and the other exposure methods. The applications of option replication extend beyond direct application to option positions in option trading, arbitrage houses and hedging to cover a wide variety of strategies in areas as diverse as asset/liability management and mortgage-backed security analysis. The methods of option replication also can be applied to create and hedge more exotic options, such as lookback options and options on the better of two payoffs.

The objective of option replication is to create a payoff that is the same as the payoff of the target option. For example, if we wish to replicate a call option with an exercise price of $100 and one year to expiration, then our objective is to follow a trading strategy which will pay off the maximum of zero or the asset price minus $100 in one year.

How Option Replication Works

Suppose our option model tells us the price of a call option today will change 60 percent as much as the price of the underlying asset, i.e., the option's delta is .60. If the asset goes up by $1.00 the call option will increase in price by $.60, and if the asset price drops by $1.00 the call option's price will drop by $.60. To mirror the price characteristics of the target option, we will then take a 60 percent position in the underlying asset.

If tomorrow the asset has risen by $2.00, our position will have risen by $1.20. An observer looking at the way our portfolio is moving will not be able to distinguish our position's performance from the performance

---

*This chapter is from the book, *Option Pricing and Investment Strategies*, Probus Publishing, Chicago, IL, 1991. Reprinted with permission.

we would have had if we had actually purchased the target option in the market place.

The option replication proceeds by asking the same question of the option model each day, "If I had actually bought the target option, how would its price change with a change in the price of the underlying asset?" The hedge is then adjusted to make the position of the replicating strategy have the same movement as the option itself would have. Since day by day we have mirrored the price movement of the option, we will match the option price as the time to expiration arrives. At the end of the program we will have the same payoff as if we had purchased the option.

Delta-Neutral Hedging

This hedging process is illustrated in Figure 10.1. It shows the value of the target call option as a function of the price of the underlying asset. Since the target option is a call option, its price increases at an increasing rate with a change in the price of the underlying asset. The slope of this curve at the current asset price is its delta. In our example, the slope is .60.

It is this payoff diagram that the hedging strategy must reproduce. At its current price, this can be done by buying 60 percent of the underlying asset. As the tangent line illustrates, doing so will mimic the price movements of the option around the current price level. Since we are attempt-

Figure 10.1: Creating an Option with an Asset

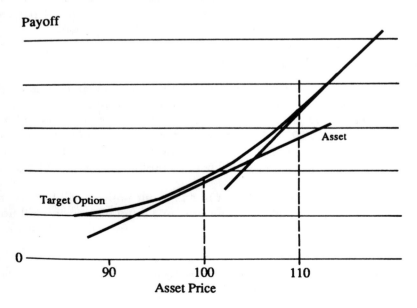

Payoff

Asset

Target Option

0

90   100   110

Asset Price

ing to match the slope, or delta, of the underlying payoff, this hedge is called a *delta-neutral hedge.*

It is readily apparent that this hedge will fail to match the target option if there is a significant price movement. The option payoff has positive curvature—its delta increases as the asset price increases—while the underlying asset has constant exposure. This curvature reflects the gamma of the option. Because of the curvature, the hedge must be adjusted as the asset price changes.

For example, if the asset increases from 100 to 110, the delta might increase from .60 to .80. The asset position held in the hedge needs to increase from a .60 to a .80 position, as illustrated by the second tangent line in the exhibit. The hedge must be adjusted frequently with asset price changes so that the tangent lines trace out facets of the curvature. The more frequently the hedge is adjusted, the smoother the facets will be, and the better the match of the curvature of the target option.

It should be noted that the payoff curve itself shifts from day to day as the option moves closer to expiration. The change in the option price with the passage of time, measured by the option's theta, will require a periodic recalculation of the option price and all the option's exposure measures, even if no other variables change.

Delta-Gamma Neutral Hedging

The fact that the option price has curvature while the underlying asset has no curvature will lead to errors in the hedge. Since in practice the hedge cannot be adjusted every instant the asset price changes, the delta-neutral hedge will only approximate the actual option payoff. The hedge can be improved by introducing a hedging instrument that itself has curvature.

One method of doing this is illustrated in Figure 10.2, which presents the payoff of both the target option and of a second call option that is available to use in the hedge. The second call option has a shorter time to expiration than the target option, and because of this has a greater gamma. By combining the higher-gamma option and the zero-gamma underlying asset in the hedge, we can form a hedging portfolio that will match both the slope and the curvature of the target option. Just as the delta-neutral hedge can match the slope of the target option only at the current asset price, the delta-gamma neutral hedge can match both the slope and curvature only at the current asset price. A sufficient change in price or simply the passage of time will still lead to inaccuracies in the hedge. However, as is clear from the figure, this hedge leads to smaller hedging errors than does the delta-neutral hedge.

There are variables other than the price of the underlying asset that affect the option price, such as interest rates and volatility. The option replication question can therefore be made more complete by generaliz-

Figure 10.2: Using Options in the Option Replication

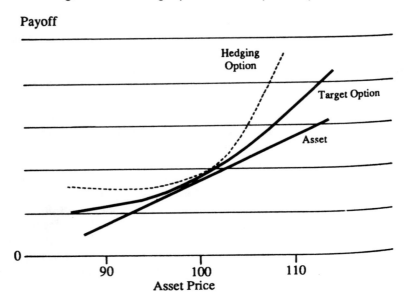

Payoff

ing it to ask; "If I had actually bought the target option, how would its price change with a change in the underlying asset price, interest rates, volatility and other variables?"

It is the function of the option pricing model to provide the answer to this question. If the model is wrong, following its prescriptions day by day will lead to a payoff different from what is intended. Indeed, the best measure of an option model is how closely it matches the specified payoff when its day to day hedging prescription is followed. Since so much has been written about option models elsewhere, we will take the model as a given, and assume that its pricing and exposure measures are correct.

A Day in the Life of a Dynamic Hedge

To illustrate the use of dynamic hedging, we will go through the mechanics of a single dynamic hedging adjustment in replicating a one-year call option on the OEX index of 100 stocks, traded on the CBOE. OEX options are the most widely traded options in the U.S. equity market. The index is assumed to be initially priced at 300. The target option we are replicating is a one-year call option with an exercise price of 300. We assume the carrying cost for the option position (the interest rate at which the asset used in the hedge can be borrowed or the proceeds of the hedge can be loaned out) is 8 percent, and the price volatility of the underlying index is 18 percent.

The specifications of the index, and its critical exposure measures, are presented in Table 10.1. The option price and the associated "Greeks" are derived from the dividend-adjusted Black-Scholes option pricing model, assuming a dividend rate of 3 percent. The option formula and the related exposure measures are presented in the chapter appendix.

This example is quite straightforward, but nonetheless contains the essentials for applying dynamic hedging and option replication in many settings. For example, since both the prices and the exposure measures of a portfolio of options can be aggregated, we can treat a portfolio of options in the same manner as we treat the single option position in the cases in this chapter. If we wish to hedge a portfolio of options, we can apply an option model to solve for the exposure of measures of each of the options individually, and then add up the individual measures to obtain an aggregate delta, gamma, kappa, and rho. We can then treat the resulting aggregates as if they represented the exposure of a single option.

Thus, while the particular numbers will differ, all of the analysis of the one-year call option is immediately applicable to other strategies. Indeed, once a computer has done the aggregation and computed the total exposures, it is no harder to hedge a position with many options than it is to hedge a single option.

Case 1: Delta Hedging

As Table 10.1 shows, the delta of the one-year option is .6245. To mimic the behavior of the delta of the option, we take a position in .6245 units of the index. The result of this hedge is illustrated in part A of Table 10.2. According to the option model, if the underlying index increases from 300 to 301, the price of the target call should move from $28.25 to

Table 10.1: Target Option Specifications

Underlying index:	OEX 100
Index value:	300
Exercise price:	$300
Interest rate:	8.00%
Time to maturity:	1 year
Price volatility of the underlying portfolio:	18%
Dividend rate:	3%

Exposure Measurements:	
Call price	$28.25
Delta	.6245
Gamma	.0067
Kappa	.0109
Rho	.0159

$28.87. Our delta position moves from $187.34 to $187.96, for a change in price of $.62. We have tracked our target option to within $.01.

The $.01 error occurs because, like all the exposure measures of the option model, the delta is a local measure. That is, it only provides the relative price change between the option and the underlying asset only for very small changes in price. Even a one point move in the underlying index is sufficient to change the delta of the option from .6245 to .6311. So while the hedge position we use is correct for the first small movement in the option, it is slightly off over the remainder of the one point move. To get things exactly correct, we would have needed to increase the hedge continuously as the index moved from 300 to 301. While the error here is insignificant, it points to the potential for far greater errors.

This potential is illustrated in part B of Table 10.2. Here we maintain the same .6245 hedge while the index moves from $300 to $310. Over the course of this 10-point move, the delta changes from .6245 to .6879. Since our hedge is maintained at the initial level, we end up with a error of $.32. This is a direct manifestation of the hedging errors illustrated in Figure 10.1. We have maintained the same tangent exposure to the option payoff, while the option price has moved up the curve. The $.32 error is the difference between the tangent line and the option curve once we have moved 10 points from the tangent point.

Case 2: Delta-Gamma Hedging

The mistracking of the delta hedge is symptomatic of violations in the continuous hedging assumption that underlies the option pricing model. It results from the failure to adjust the hedge because of gap moves, or from the accumulated impact of repeatedly adjusting the hedge after a number of relatively small moves.

Recalling the discussion of Figure 10.2, when we hedge with the underlying asset an error occurs because of the failure of the tangent line to match the curvature of the option being replicated. The curvature is measured by the gamma of the option. For example, the gamma of the one-year option is .0067. This means that the delta of the option will change by .0067 per one-point change in the underlying index. As with the delta, the gamma changes with changes in the price of the underlying asset, and is therefore a precise measure only for very small incremental changes in the asset price. Even a one-point change in the asset will lead to a small change in the value of gamma.

To hedge against the curvature or gamma risk, we must employ an asset that has gamma exposure—that is, one which itself has a delta that will change as the index changes. The underlying index has zero gamma—it always changes one-for-one with itself—so we must look elsewhere if we are to hedge against the gamma risk. The natural place to look is to other options. One way to see why it makes sense to use other

Table 10.2: Delta Hedging

A: Index moves from 300 to 301

	Initial Value	New Value	Change in Value
Target call	28.25	28.88	.63
Delta hedge for index	187.34	187.96	.62
Error			−.01

B: Index moves from 300 to 310

	Initial Value	New Value	Change in Value
Target call	28.25	34.81	6.56
Δ of index	187.34	193.58	6.24
Error			−.32

options in the hedge is to go back to the objective we stated earlier of matching the price changes of the target option that are induced by changes in other variables. The more similar a hedging instrument is to the target option and the more these other variables impact its price, the better it will do at mirroring the target option's sensitivity.

Table 10.3 presents the characteristics of an option we will use to address the gamma exposure: a call option with three-months to expiration and with a 305 exercise price. Because this option has a shorter time to expiration, its payoff curvature, and hence its gamma, is greater than that of the one-year option, .0148 versus .0067.

We follow a two-step process to use this option in the hedge. First, we purchase enough of the short-term options to match the gamma of the

Table 10.3: Hedge Option Specification

Underlying index:	Same as target call
Index value:	300
Exercise price:	305
Interest rate:	8.00%
Time to maturity:	3 months
Price volatility of the underlying index:	
Dividend rate:	3%
Exposure Measurements:	
Call price	$10.02
Delta	.4952
Gamma	.0148
Kappa	.0059
Rho	.0034

Table 10.4: Steps in Delta-Gamma Hedge

Step 1: Eliminate Gamma Exposure

	Delta	Gamma	Kappa	Rho
Target call option	.6245	.0067	.0109	.0159
.453 3-month call Options	.2245	.0067	.0027	.0015
Remaining exposure	.400	0	.0082	.0144

Step 2: Eliminate Delta Exposure

	Delta	Gamma	Kappa	Rho
.400 of index	.400	0	0	0
Remaining exposure	0	0	.0082	.0144

target option. This can be done by buying $.0067/.0148 = .453$ of the three-month option. Second, we use the index portfolio itself to hedge the net delta of these two option positions. The net delta is equal to the delta of the target option minus the delta of the three-month option we have already purchased. This process is illustrated in Table 10.4.

The result is a position that is both delta and gamma neutral—that is, a position that matches both the slope and the curvature of the target option payoff at the current index price.

Parts A and B of Table 10.5 illustrate the performance of this hedge in matching the target payoff for the two cases considered in the delta hedging strategy. For a one-point move in the index, the hedge performs to an accuracy of better than $.01. For a ten-point move, the hedge has just a $.01 tracking error—compared to the $.32 error of the delta-neutral hedge. However, it is important to note that even the delta-gamma neutral hedge does not perform perfectly for large moves in the index, since the curvature is matched precisely only at the current index price of 300. The performance can be enhanced by proper selection of the option used in the hedge. The closer the characteristics of the hedging option are to the target option (the closer the gamma of the two options, for example), the wider the range of asset prices and parameter variations where the hedge will be secure. The hedge can also be improved by combining two options, one with a shorter and one with a longer time to expiration than the option to be replicated.

It is easy to imagine tightening the hedge further by not only matching the slope and the change in the slope, or curvature, of the target option, but also using more options to match the change in the curvature, the change in the change in the curvature, and so on. Alternatively, we could use additional instruments to match the delta and gamma along the curve, not just at the current asset price. We are limited only by the

Table 10.5: Delta-Gamma Hedging

A: Index moves from 300 to 301

	Initial Value	New Value	Change in Value
Target call	28.25	28.88	.63
.453 of 3-month call	4.54	4.77	.23
.400 of index	120.00	120.40	.40
Error			0

B: Index moves from 300 to 310

	Initial Value	New Value	Change in Value
Target call	28.25	34.81	6.56
.453 of 3-month call	4.54	7.11	2.57
.400 of index	120.00	124.00	4.00
Error			.01

C. Index price moves from 300 to 310 and the carrying cost of the options drops by 100 basis points

	Initial Value	New Value	Change in Value
Target call	28.25	33.05	4.80
.453 of 3-month call	4.54	6.91	2.37
.400 of index	120.00	124.00	4.00
Error			1.57

number of options there are in the marketplace. The tradeoff is between the frequency of hedge adjustments and the number of options that must be purchased and managed, since the better the match, the less frequently hedge adjustments will be needed.

As a practical matter, adding too many options to the arsenal will give hedge improvements that look better on paper than when actually executed. First, option models are imperfect, and those imperfections become more manifest the greater the number of disparate options the model combines. If five or 10 different options with widely varying times to expiration and exercise prices are aggregated, the cumulative error in the model may exceed the theoretical improvement in the hedging fit. Second, generally only the near-the-money options with a short time to expiration are liquid. Adding options to the arsenal gives a tighter fit, but may end up doing so at an upfront cost that exceeds the potential cost of mistracking. Part B of Table 10.5 gives some idea of what this mistracking potential is, since a 10 point price gap leads to only a $.01 mistracking for even the simplest delta-gamma neutral hedge.

Case 3: Delta-Gamma-Rho Hedging

Part C of Table 10.5 illustrates the impact of interest rate changes on hedging performance. It shows the same delta-gamma neutral hedge of part B, but now under the assumption that the carrying cost of the option drops by 100 basis points, from 8 percent to 7 percent. The differing times to expiration of the three-month and one-year call cause them to be affected differently by the drop in the carrying cost. While the target call drops $1.76 in price, the three-month call drops by only $.20. This differential is apparent by comparing the rhos of the respective options: .0034 for the three-month and .0159 for the one-year option. The net result of the interest rate drop is to cause the hedging error to increase from $.01 to $1.57.

As we see in part C of Table 10.5, the delta-gamma neutral hedge has a shortcoming in not controlling for changes in the carrying cost of the option position. The option pricing model requires an interest rate assumption that measures the cost of financing the hedge position. For a call option, an increase in interest rates will increase the carrying cost, and cause the option price to increase. For many hedging applications, we need an instrument to explicitly address this interest rate risk.

Just as we hedged the gamma error by introducing a hedging vehicle that contained gamma exposure, we can hedge the interest rate error by introducing a hedging vehicle that has interest rate exposure. The hedging instrument we chose for this example is a Eurodollar futures contract, although since all options have some degree of exposure to carrying cost, the rho can be addressed by adding a second option into the hedge as well. The specifications for the Eurodollar future are presented in Table 10.6.

The most interesting characteristic of using the Eurodollar futures from a hedging perspective is that it focuses on interest rate risk without

Table 10.6: Hedge Futures Specification

Eurodollar Futures Specifications:
Interest rate:	8.00%

Exposure Measurements
Price	92.00
Delta	0
Gamma	0
Kappa	0
Rho	−.01*

* Assumes a $1.00 change in futures value per 100 basis point change in rates.

Table 10.7: Steps in Delta-Gamma-Rho Hedge

Step 1: Eliminate Gamma Exposure

	Delta	Gamma	Kappa	Rho
Target call option	.6245	.0067	.0109	.0159
.453 3-month call options	.2245	.0067	.0027	.0015
Remaining exposure	.400	0	.0082	.0144

Step 2: Eliminate Delta Exposure

	Delta	Gamma	Kappa	Rho
.400 of index	.400	0	0	0
Remaining exposure	0	0	.0082	.0144

Step 3: Eliminate Rho Exposure

	Delta	Gamma	Kappa	Rho
−1.44 of Eurodollar futures	0	0	0	−.0144
Remaining exposure	0	0	0.0082	0

affecting the delta, gamma, or kappa. This exposure-specific feature means that to hedge the interest rate risk, we can proceed with the hedge as we did above for the delta-gamma hedge, and then add a third step of matching the aggregate rho with an appropriate Eurobond futures position. The sequence of steps is presented in Table 10.7.

The result of including the Eurodollar futures in the hedge is shown in Table 10.8. The hedging error is cut more than ten-fold, to only $.13 error. This is remarkable given the specter of a ten point gap in price and a 100 basis point drop in rates.

Table 10.8: Delta-Gamma-Rho Hedging

Index price moves from 300 to 310 and the carrying costs of the options drops 100 bp.

	Initial Value	New Value	Change in Value
Target call	28.25	33.05	4.80
.453 of 3-month call	4.54	6.91	2.37
.400 of index	120.00	124.00	4.00
−1.44 of Eurofuture	−132.48	−133.92	−1.44
Error			.13

Kappa Hedging

So far, we have covered exposure from sudden gaps and from interest rate shifts. The next area is exposure to volatility changes: kappa hedging.

By widening the set of options we use in the hedge, it is possible at any point in the hedging process to construct a kappa hedge in a manner similar to the way we hedge delta or gamma. Just as it took one hedging instrument to hedge delta, two instruments to hedge delta and gamma, and three instruments to hedge delta, gamma, and rho, it takes four instruments to add kappa to the hedging targets. Also, since both gamma and kappa are option-specific characteristics, at least two of the hedging instruments must be options. If we use the underlying asset and three options as the hedging vehicles, we have a four-equation system to relate the hedging vehicles to the target option we are seeking to replicate, one equation for each exposure measure we seek to hedge. Table 10.9 shows these equations. In this table, W_0 is the hedging weight given to the underlying asset—note that it only appears in the delta hedge equation, since it has no gamma, kappa, or rho exposure—and W_1, W_2 and W_3 are the weights given to the three options used in the hedge. The target option is denoted by a subscript T. Kappa and rho do not appear explicitly in the equation; functional relationships are used to re-express these measures in terms of delta, gamma, the option price C, and the value of the underlying asset S, with the other terms. Once the values of the terms are entered into the equations, the hedging weights come out as the solution to this simultaneous equation system. (While this may appear to be a

Table 10.9

Hedge delta

$$W_0 + W_{1\Delta 1} + W_2 + \Delta_2 + W_{3\Delta 3} = \Delta_T$$

Hedge gamma

$$W_{1\Gamma} + W_{2\Gamma 2} + W_{3\Gamma 3} = \Gamma_T$$

Hedge kappa

$$W_{1\Gamma 1}(t_1 - t_T) + W_{2\Gamma 2}(t_2 - t_T) + W_{3\Gamma 3}(t_3 - t_T) = 0$$

Hedge rho

$$W_1(\Delta_1 - C_1/S)(t_1 - t_T) + W_2(\Delta_2 - C_2/S)(t_2 - t_T) + W_3(\Delta_3 - C_3/S)(t_3 - t_T) = 0$$

Note: For a solution to exist, the three options in the hedge cannot all have the same time to expiration. That is, t_1, t_2, and t_3 cannot all be equal.

daunting job, many computer packages—including some spreadsheets—contain simultaneous equation solution methods.)

The result of one solution is presented in Table 10.10. Here we hedged the target call option with the underlying index and three options: 3-month calls with 295 and 305 exercise prices, and a 6-month call with a 300 exercise price. (The prices and exposure measures for these options are listed in Table 10.11.) As Table 10.10 shows, the hedge leads to a tracking error of only $.09 when the target call option price increases 50 percent, as induced by a ten-point index gap, 100 basis point interest rate move and 6 percent volatility increase. By contrast, the simple delta hedge only increases by $6.25, leading to $8.31 of tracking error.

The key difference between delta or gamma hedges and volatility hedges is that there is an incremental cost to hedging volatility. The cost of hedging delta and gamma, by contrast, is already part of the theoretical option price. Furthermore, there is no instrument available to directly address volatility risk for a predetermined cost over the life of the option. Since the cost of the volatility hedge at any point is a function of the asset price, time to expiration and volatility that exists at that time, the total

Table 10.10: Delta-Gamma-Kappa-Rho Hedging

Index price moves from 300 to 310, the carrying cost of the option rises 100 basis points, and volatility rises to 24%.

A. Delta-Gamma-Kappa-Rho Hedging

	Initial Value	New Value	Change in Value
Target call	28.25	42.81	14.56
.212 of index	63.60	65.72	2.12
−1.900 of 90-day, 295 call	−29.05	−48.97	−19.92
.838 of 90-day, 305 call	8.40	16.42	8.02
2.042 of 180-day, 300 call	37.97	62.22	24.25
Error			−.09

B: Delta Hedge

	Initial Value	New Value	Change in Value
Target call	28.25	42.81	14.56
Delta hedge for index	187.34	193.60	6.25
Error			−8.31

Table 10.11: Hedge Option Specification

	Call Option 1	Call Option 2	Call Option 3
Underlying Index:	Same as target call	Same as target call	Same as target call
Exercise price	295	305	300
Time to maturity	3 months	3 months	6 months
Interest rate	8%	8%	8%
Price volatility of the underlying bond	18%	18%	18%
Dividend rate	3%	3%	3%
Exposure Measurements:			
Price	15.29	10.02	18.59
Delta	.6398	.4954	.5931
Gamma	.0138	.0148	.0100
Kappa	.0055	.0059	.0080
Rho	.0044	.0034	.0079

volatility hedging cost cannot be known at the outset of the hedge. Since the cumulative cost of a volatility hedge is uncertain, the risk imposed by variations in volatility cannot be eliminated.

The distinction between hedging delta and gamma and hedging volatility should not be surprising. Since the model we are employing was developed explicitly assuming that volatility is known, any application of the model to a market with stochastic volatility is asking more of the model that it was designed to do.

What About Theta Hedging?

Those who are familiar with the option lexicon may be wondering why we have ignored theta—the time decay of an option position—in our treatment of the members of that Greek family. The reason is that theta exposure is closely related to gamma exposure, and in hedging the delta and gamma risk, theta exposure is hedged as well. That is, a delta-gamma neutral position will automatically also be theta neutral, so we do not have to discuss theta hedging explicitly. The relationship between delta-gamma and theta neutrality means that, even though we are forming these hedges on the basis of the current instantaneous exposures, barring market gaps, a well-conceived hedge will retain its effectiveness over a period of time.

Exposure Measurement

It is clear from the case study presented in the previous section that any hedging strategy will face a number of sources of error. We can use the exposure measures to disaggregate the total error of the hedging strategy. In particular, we can disaggregate the error into four categories:

1. Error due to directional price movements (Delta Error).
2. Error due to price gaps (Gamma Error).
3. Error due to changes in the option carrying cost (Rho Error).
4. Error due to changes in volatility (Kappa Error).

For example, in the case presented in Table 10.10, where the index moved from 300 to 310, the option carrying cost dropped by 100 basis points, and the volatility increased from 18 percent to 24 percent, the delta-neutral hedge generated a total tracking error of $8.31.

By using the exposure measures for the target option listed in Table 10.1, we can decompose this tracking error according to the specific impacts of the interest rates, volatility, and change in delta:

- *Delta Error:* The delta error is zero by construction, since we are employing a delta-neutral hedge.

- *Gamma Error:* Since only the underlying asset is used in the delta-neutral hedge, there will be some gamma error. The curvature of the option exposure will lead to a change in the size of the correct hedge as the asset price changes. The change in the delta to use in the hedge will be approximated by multiplying the gamma by the ten-point price move: $.0067 \times 10 = .067$. Over the course of the ten-point move, the hedge will be off on average by half this total delta change, or .034. Multiplying the average mishedging by the total change in the asset price gives us an estimate of the gamma impact: $.34.

- *Rho Error:* To estimate the impact of the 100 basis point interest rate drop on the hedge, we multiply the rho by the interest rate change (in basis points): $.0159 \times 100 = \$1.59$.

- Kappa Error: The kappa of the position is .0109. The kappa of the position is .0109. This means a 100 basis point (one percent) change in volatility will change the option price by $1.09. Since volatility incraesed by six percent, the volatility impact is $6.54.

- *Total Error:* We can sum up these effects to get a measure of the total error: $8.47.

The exposure analysis thus shows a total error of $8.47 compared with an actual error of $8.31, leaving an unexplained error of just $.16. Since this example is based completely on the model for both the hedging and the error analysis, the unexplained cannot be attributed to model misspecification. In this example, the $.16 error comes about because we use the exposure measures from Table 10.1 as if those measures are constant, when in fact they change slightly with the changes in the interest rates, volatility, and asset price. In practice, however, the hedge will mis-perform both because of identifiable changes in the parameters such as those we have just calculated, and because of inaccuracies in the model design and the parameter estimates. Thus, in practice, the unexplained error may be attributable to the approximation methods, errors in volatil-ity or interest rate estimation, or model misspecification. Pinpointing the residual error requires analysis beyond the exposure measures discussed here.

For risk management purposes, the disaggregation of risks and a knowledge of the level of residual or unexplainable risk is important. Knowing that the errors are attributable to shifts in a certain parameter might lead more attention to be placed on addressing that particular source of risk. For example, we may be able to live with a certain amount of risk from parameter shifts if we have a good sense of their long-term behavior and variability. However, if the hedging error cannot be identi-fied, we are at a loss to know just how bad things might become.

The time series characteristics of the error can provide insight into hedging performance. Ideally, the unexplained residual should have a zero mean. Improvements in hedging expertise will be manifest by the standard deviation of each of the sources of error decreasing over time. Improvements in the option model will be manifest by decreases in the standard error of the unexplained residual.

Table 10.12: Exposure Matrix; Delta Hedging

Index Value	Realized Volatility		
	Error in Cents (Initial Volatility = 18%)		
	12%	*18%*	*24%*
270	2.73	−3.26	−9.45
275	4.05	−2.24	−8.61
280	5.08	−1.42	−7.92
285	5.82	−0.79	−7.38
290	6.29	−0.35	−6.97
295	6.47	−0.08	−6.70
300	6.40	0.00	−6.56
305	6.09	−0.08	−6.56
310	5.57	−0.32	−6.67
315	4.84	−0.71	−6.89
320	3.94	−1.24	−7.24
325	2.89	−1.90	−7.69
330	1.72	−2.67	−8.22

Table 10.13: Exposure Matrix; Delta-Gamma Hedging

Index Value	Realized Volatility		
	Error in Cents (Initial Volatility = 18%)		
	12%	*18%*	*24%*
270	5.54	−0.45	−6.64
275	6.04	−0.25	−6.62
280	6.38	−0.12	−6.62
285	6.57	−0.04	−6.63
290	6.62	−0.01	−6.63
295	6.55	0.00	−6.62
300	6.40	−0.00	−6.56
305	6.17	0.00	−6.48
310	5.89	0.01	−6.34
315	5.56	0.01	−6.17
320	5.19	0.01	−5.99
325	4.80	0.01	−5.78
330	4.38	−0.01	−5.56

Assessing Disaster Scenarios

Since the greatest risk in option replication strategies comes from price gaps and volatility changes, a useful "what-if" exercise is to look at the potential losses should price gaps or volatility changes occur. Tables 10.12 and 10.13 present exposure measurement matrices for the delta-neutral hedge and the delta-gamma neutral hedge in the previous section. These tables measure the exposure for index values ranging from $270 to $330, and for volatility values of 12 percent, 18 percent, and 24 percent. The matrix form of the table is especially useful, since gaps in price will generally be accompanied by at least short-term changes in volatility.

By looking at these tables, we can assess the risk of various size gaps and changes in volatility. For example, if the underlying index were to gap up 10 percent to $330, and volatility were to simultaneously increase from 18 percent to 24 percent, the delta hedge would realize a mistracking of $8.22. Under the same circumstances, the delta-gamma neutral hedge would realize a loss of $5.56. The error potential is not all one-sided; a drop in volatility would lead to unexpected gains in the hedges.

Conclusion

The purpose of this chapter has been to sketch out and explain the mechanics of dynamic hedging and option replication. We started with the most rudimentary method, delta-neutral hedging, and then showed how more sophisticated hedging methods can lead to more accurate replication strategies by bringing in a wider array of hedging instruments. The presentation of strategies was simplified in a number of respects.

First, we looked at only one adjustment in the hedging process. In reality, the hedge needs to be continually revised with the passage of time, changes in the price of the underlying asset and changes in the parameter values. The decision of when to make the hedging adjustments is an important one. Too infrequent adjustments will cause the hedge to move out of line, while hedging too frequently will lead to higher transaction costs.

Second, we ignored the difficulties of properly estimating model parameters, particularly market volatility and interest rates.

Finally, we assumed at the outset that the option model we employed gave the correct hedging prescription, that the option prices and the exposure measures provided by the model are correct. Thus we assumed that if we followed the model precisely we would obtain the desired terminal payoff at expiration. We did not address the question of which model is best at replicating options in practice. The chapter does, however, point out the critical criterion for the validity of an option model: the measure of an option model is its ability to replicate an option payoff. The best option pricing model is the one whose dynamic hedging prescription provides the target payoff with the smallest hedging error.

APPENDIX: FORMULAS FOR EXPOSURE MEASUREMENT

variables

$$S = \text{security price}$$
$$T = \text{time to expiration}$$
$$E = \text{exercise price}$$
$$r = \text{risk free interest rate}$$
$$\delta = \text{cashflow from security}$$
$$\sigma = \text{volatility}$$
$$N(\cdot) = \text{cumulative normal distribution}$$
$$N'(\cdot) = \text{normal density function; } N'(x) = \frac{1}{\sqrt{2\pi}} e^{-x^2/2}$$

$$C = e^{-\delta T} S N(d_1) - e^{-rT} E N(d_2)$$

where

$$d_1 = [\ln(S/E) + (r - \delta + \tfrac{1}{2}\sigma^2)T]\sigma\sqrt{T}$$

and

$$d_2 = d_1 - \sigma\sqrt{T}$$

Call Options

$$Gamma \quad \Gamma = \frac{\partial \Delta}{\partial S} = e^{-rT} N'(d_1)/S\sigma\sqrt{T}$$

$$Kappa \quad K = \frac{\partial C}{\partial \sigma} = e^{-rT} S \sqrt{TN'(d_1)}$$

$$Delta \quad \Delta = \frac{\partial C}{\partial S} = e^{-rT} N(d_1)$$

TECHNIQUES FOR MANAGING A LIBOR-PLUS FUND*

Paul DeRosa and Laurie Goodman

11

Techniques for Managing a LIBOR-Plus Fund

Over the past several years, a number of offshore funds which pay 3-month LIBOR-plus a spread of 60–75 basis points have been brought to market. The LIBOR rate is reset every three months, but the spread remains constant over the life of the fund. In addition to the spread paid to noteholders, the funds generally have expenses of about 50–60 basis points; thus the funds accrue at the rate of 3-month LIBOR-plus 120–135 basis points. If the fund makes more than the accrual rate, the additional profit is added to the net asset value of the fund. If there is a shortfall, the amount of the shortfall is subtracted from the net asset value of the fund. Thus neither the spread on these funds nor the total return is guaranteed.

Most of these funds rely on U.S. mortgage securities in order to meet the return target. There are a number of different securities that can be used to deliver the promised return, each of which has its unique set of risks. Investors should be aware of what types of securities are used by each fund, the risks they entail and how the risks are hedged.

There are four potential risks inherent in a LIBOR-plus fund: duration risk, convexity risk, LIBOR-Treasury spread risk, and mortgage-Treasury spread risk. Duration risk is simply interest rate risk. With the interest rate on the LIBOR-plus funds resetting every three months, the duration of the fund should theoretically be the time to reset of the liabilities. Thus, if there were only one month until the reset, the duration of the liability would also be one month. A fund with a longer or shorter du-

---

* An earlier version of this article appeared in *Risk Magazine,* vol. 5 no. 1, December 1991/January 1992, under the title, "LIBOR-Plus Lifelines." Reprinted with permission.

ration is incurring interest rate risk. The danger in this is that if rates were to rise substantially, the fixed rate mortgages would decline in value, and the net asset value of the fund would fall. If a fund had a 15-month duration on its assets and a 3-month duration on its liabilities, the duration gap would be one year. For this gap, a 1 percent rise in interest rates would cause a 1 percent fall in net asset value.

Most LIBOR-plus fund managers are quite sophisticated and take great pains to control their interest rate risk. Fund managers tend, however, to have longer durations than the time to reset on the liabilities. There are two reasons for this. First, hedging is costly in an upward sloping yield curve environment. If it is believed that the forward rates embedded in the yield curve are too high relative to one's market expectations of future interest rates, a manager would want to be a bit longer than one's bogey. Second, mortgages tend to lag the Treasury market; they tend to perform well when the Treasury market falters (spreads tighten), and tend to underperform during market rallies (spreads widen). This interaction between spread risk and interest rate risk suggests that it is prudent to run a portfolio slightly longer than would otherwise be indicated.

Convexity refers to how quickly the duration of a portfolio changes as interest rates change. On mortgage securities, as rates decline prepayments increase and hence the durations of the securities shorten. This reduces the potential for price appreciation on mortgages. Conversely, as rates rise, prepayments slow, lengthening the security and increasing its potential for price depreciation. This property, in which one loses no matter which way interest rates move, is called negative convexity and is the greatest source of unsatisfactory results in mortgage investing.

There is a great disparity in the amount of convexity risk different fund managers are willing to absorb. Negatively convex securities tend to have the highest yield. If a fund has a portfolio with substantial negative convexity, and interest rates do not change, that fund will perform superbly. It will underperform, however, if rates move sharply in either direction. Many fund managers have a great deal of negative convexity in their portfolios because of either a forecast that volatility will remain low or a decision to reach for yield. Other fund managers, such as ourselves, have very little negative convexity. Hedging convexity is expensive if rates remain unchanged, but it is rewarding if rates move in either direction.

LIBOR-Treasury spread risk is the risk of LIBOR rates rising dramatically relative to Treasury rates while all fund holdings are held in Treasury and mortgage issues. In November 1990, for example, 3-month LIBOR rates were more than 135 basis points above 1-year bill rates. If one invests in bill based assets, with liabilities set over LIBOR, this differential must be made up out of the earnings of the portfolio, resulting in a decrease in net asset value.

All mortgage securities encounter Mortgage-Treasury spread risk.

This is the risk that mortgage securities will underperform equal duration Treasury securities. Mortgage-Treasury spreads have narrowed dramatically from early 1990, the inception date for most LIBOR-plus funds, to the present. Many funds have registered increases in net asset value because of this narrowing, and would give it back if spreads were to widen. For a fixed rate mortgage portfolio with a 5-year duration, every narrowing (widening) of 20 basis points will cause a 1 percent increase (decrease) in net asset value. Spreads on the current coupon mortgage have narrowed roughly 28 basis points (measured relative to the 7-year Treasury) from April 1990 to October 1991.

Controlling Portfolio Duration

The decision to rely primarily on mortgage securities in a LIBOR-plus fund is almost a necessity; other government and agency securities do not provide the yield necessary to meet the fund's obligations. Even with mortgage securities, most LIBOR-plus funds rely on leverage in order to deliver the needed return. Deciding which mortgage to use is more difficult. Some LIBOR-plus portfolio managers use fixed rate mortgages, and others use adjustable rate mortgages.

In order to make a comparison between fixed and floating rate securities, it is necessary to hedge the fixed rate mortgages down to the appropriate duration. Adjustable rate mortgages have durations very close to the target duration of LIBOR-plus funds, so no hedging is required.

Hedging Fixed Rate Mortgages

To illustrate how we hedge a 30-year pass-through position, assume we purchase a portfolio consisting half of FNMA 8.5 percent 30-year pass-throughs and half of GNMA 9.0 percent 30-year mortgage pass-throughs. Portfolio yields and durations are as follows (as of November 25, 1991):

Security	Price	Market Value Weight	Yield	Duration
FNMA 8.5	101–15	50%	8.23	4.8
GNMA 9.0	104–08	50%	8.29	4.5
Portfolio		100%	8.26	4.65

These durations are based on estimates of how much the market prices would change for a small change in interest rates. This, in turn, is dependent on a model of how prepayments change as interest rates change. The average duration for the portfolio shown above is 4.65 years. With no hedging, this portfolio would entail far too much interest rate risk.

In order to shorten the duration of this portfolio to .75 years, the fund manager must shorten duration by 3.90 years (4.65–.75). If one were to shorten duration by selling short the U.S. Treasury 7.875 Treasury notes of 8/2000, $.59 market value of notes must be shorted for each $1.00 market value of the portfolio. This number is obtained by dividing the amount of duration to be shortened (3.70 years) by the duration of the security to be used as a hedge (6.62 years).

In order to sell short a security that a fund does not own, the security must be borrowed. This is done via a repurchase agreement (repo). The cash obtained from shorting the security is taken and loaned simultaneously at the repo rate, with the security that is being shorted used as collateral on the loan. Since the fund is short the security, it must pay the coupon. The fund receives the repo rate; the yield on the security is 7.44. The repo rate is expected to be 4.75 over the next six months, producing negative carry of 269 basis points. The cost of shorting the security is 159 basis points, which is the negative carry of 269 basis points times the size of the short (.59). Thus the yield on the hedged portfolio is the yield on the mortgage securities (8.26) less the hedging cost (1.59), or 6.67 percent. At the present time, this is equal to 3-month LIBOR + 167 basis points. This hedged yield is the relevant number to a LIBOR-plus fund manager comparing fixed and floating rate securities.

In addition to shorting securities in the cash market, there are two other commonly used methods to shorten the duration of a fixed rate mortgage portfolio: selling futures and using swaps. A short position in a futures contract is roughly comparable to a short position in the underlying instrument. Consider a position in the 10-year note contract rather than a position in the 7 7/8 of 8/2001, a cash security in the 10-year sector. The December 1991 and March 1992 futures contracts are trading 24/32 apart. If rates remain constant over the next three months and there are no changes in the relative value of the futures contract, the March contract will converge to the current price on the December contract. Calculating carry very crudely, this is a pick up of 24/32 over three months, or 3.00 percent per year. This is very similar to the carry of 269 basis points on the 7.875 of 8/2001.

Swaps have two disadvantages and one advantage as compared to short Treasury positions. The first disadvantage to a swap is the lack of flexibility once the initial position is selected. Swaps are less liquid than Treasury securities or note futures—10-year swaps trade in 5 basis point markets. This is equivalent to 10/32, 5–10 times the average transactions costs of the alternatives. Thus, swap positions are much more expensive to adjust as warranted by changes in the underlying portfolio.

Moreover, swaps lock a manager into a short position on a particular point on the yield curve. Most LIBOR-plus fund managers swap for the life of the fund, generally seven years. By using futures and short positions in cash instruments, the short position can be actively managed, adding an extra dimension that can be used to increase return. A fund manager can short whichever sector of the Treasury yield curve regarded as the most expensive. Since the inception of the ECI Fund, we have hedged with 3-year notes, 5-year notes, current and off-the-run 7-year notes, current and off-the-run 10-year notes, the long bond, and note futures. Our turnover on our short position has far exceeded the turnover on our long mortgage position.

The extent to which it is advantageous to manage the short position depends on the volatility of the Treasury yield curve. If all shifts in the Treasury yield curve were parallel, it would make little difference which security we were short. In an environment with a great deal of yield curve volatility, however, choosing the correct coupon to be short makes a big difference. Between April 30, 1990 and November 29, 1991, an unusually volatile period for the yield curve, the spread between the 2-year note and 30-year bond increased from 5 basis points to 256 basis points. One would ordinarily hedge mortgages no shorter than the 5-year Treasury and no longer than the 10-year Treasury. The spread between the 5- and 10-year Treasury has increased from 1 basis point to 90 basis points. Thus, one would have been 89 basis points worse off hedging with the current 5-year rather than the duration equivalent amount of the current 10 year. If one expects a steepening of the yield curve, it is reasonable to hedge with a security longer than the mortgages to be hedged. If one expects a flattening the reverse is true. If one has no strong view, it is reasonable to hedge Treasury of the same duration on the long mortgage position. In a swap, one is implicitly hedged with a note equal to the swap's term to maturity, without the flexibility to adjust the hedge.

The second disadvantage is that swap spreads introduce an element of uncertainty into the hedge. Many LIBOR-plus portfolio managers hedge mortgages with swaps in which they pay the fixed coupon and receive LIBOR. Swap spreads have narrowed a great deal, eliminating some of the profit they otherwise would have realized from the narrowing in mortgage spreads. For example, at the end of December 1990, the spread on the 7-year swap was bid at 75 basis points over the 7-year and offered at 81 over. In November 1991, the swap spread was bid at 46 basis points and offered at 53. On a mark to market basis, this change in the swap spread would have caused a 1.45 percent change in the value of the swap. The advantage of using swaps is that it hedges the LIBOR-Treasury spread risk. By creating a LIBOR based source of income, the LIBOR spread is essentially "locked in" over the life of the swap.

The alternative to using hedged positions in fixed rate mortgages is using adjustable rate mortgages (ARMs). These generally reset at a margin above the 1-year constant maturity Treasury (CMT) index. One year CMT ARMs have, on average, six months to the next reset. The duration on these instruments is the time to the next reset plus the duration created by the annual and lifetime caps, so a typical Treasury ARM would have a duration of approximately 120 basis points above 1-year CMT (4.78). Thus the yield is 5.98, rather than the 6.67 from our hedged fixed rate portfolio. While we firmly believe that these securities, after hedging out the negative convexity from the caps, are substantially more expensive than fixed rate mortgages, other managers of LIBOR-plus funds disagree. They argue that with mortgage rates the lowest in 14 years, homeowners would prefer a fixed rate product leading to low ARM production. Meanwhile, demand is high for products with low interest rate risk. This creates an imbalance and, going forward, spreads on adjustable rate mortgages could narrow more than those on fixed rate instruments. The anticipated tightening on ARMs more than offsets the more favorable carry on a hedged fixed rate position. We would argue that an expected acceleration in prepayments would inhibit any tightening. Investors should be aware that ARMs would be affected almost as much as fixed rate securities by a change in the mortgage-Treasury spread.

Managing Convexity Risk

Instruments with a great deal of negative convexity have the highest yield. Holding a position in a negatively convex security is equivalent to holding a position in a security with zero convexity and writing options against the position. Thus, the yield on the negatively convex security represents the base yield plus the yield that would be received from writing options. One can reduce the convexity risk only by reducing the yield; one way to do this is by purchasing mortgages with less negative convexity and accepting lower yields. Alternatively, one can reduce the risk by purchasing instruments with positive convexity such as options or long-term zero coupon bonds. Adding these instruments to the portfolio will reduce portfolio yield, but will create a more symmetric return profile. In order to determine whether one would be better off holding the negatively convex securities and hedging them, or avoiding the securities altogether, the investor must price convexity. This requires a reliance on quantitative techniques.

Many portfolio managers rely on binomial option pricing. In order to make a comparison of relative value across securities with the binomial option pricing model, an investor can evaluate the cost of the call features of mortgage backed securities by computing the equivalent yield on the security if it had no options. This is done by valuing the option under hundreds of different interest rate scenarios and compressing the results of many interest rate paths into one number.

This is too concise for portfolio construction. Two securities with the same option adjusted yield may be equivalent from a probabilistic point of view; their actual returns, however, will differ greatly, depending on how interest rates change. To avoid this difficulty, it is necessary to supplement option-adjusted pricing with simulation analysis to see how different securities perform under different scenarios.

Table 11.1 shows how simulation analysis might be applied to a GNMA 10, a security with a great deal of negative convexity. As rates go up, the rate of return goes down dramatically as the security lengthens. As rates go down, the rate of return goes up, but not as much as would otherwise occur because prepayments increase and the security shortens. Assume we wish to create a symmetric profile at +100 basis points and −100 basis points and see what yield can be achieved in the base case. If interest rates go up 100 basis points, the rate of return on the security declines by 3.00 percent. If interest rates go down 100 basis points, the security will appreciate by only .50 percent. We can increase the return if interest rates decline by purchasing at-the-money call options on a 10 year note, at a cost of 58 basis points per annum. This would make the rate of return symmetric at +100 and −100 basis points, as shown in Table 11.1. If we were to try to hedge the −200 case completely, more options would be necessary, contributing to an even lower yield in the base case.

It is important to realize that the appropriate rate-of-return profile is not that on individual securities, but rather that on the overall portfolio. Table 11.1 is an example of selected securities that complement each other and produce a portfolio with stable returns under different interest rate scenarios.

Portfolio managers differ dramatically in their attitudes toward convexity risk. Some, such as ourselves, do not wish to take convexity risk. Those mortgage portfolios that consistently outperform Treasury issues do so because of the managers' ability to maintain a stable duration under a variety of market conditions. Other portfolio managers maximize yield regardless of the consequences, believing that, on average, it is not cost effective to hedge convexity risk. Still other portfolio managers view convexity risk or volatility as another vehicle to enhance yield. When they believe volatility will decline, convexity risk is not hedged. Convexity risk is hedged when the fund managers believe volatility will increase.

Table 11.1: Scenario Return Profile—GNMA 10 (1-year horizon)

	Interest Rate Scenario				
	−200	**−100**	**0**	**+100**	**200**
GNMA 10 return	6.21	8.42	7.92	4.92	.35
Change from base case (unhedged)	−1.71	.50	0	−3.00	−7.57
Return on options position	5.53	2.44	−.32	−.58	−.58
Hedged return	11.74	10.86	7.60	4.34	−.23
Change from base case (hedged)	4.14	3.26	0	−3.26	−7.83

Managing the LIBOR Treasury Spread Risk

LIBOR-plus funds pay out spreads over 3- and 6-month LIBOR, but have mortgage and Treasury based assets. If the spread were unhedged, investors would be concerned that exogenous increases in LIBOR-Treasury spreads would substantially reduce their returns. That is, with the asset side of the portfolio unchanged, the LIBOR reset on the portfolio would be considerably higher because of these credit concerns.

LIBOR-plus portfolio managers are cognizant of this risk and try either to purchase or convert a substantial amount of assets to a LIBOR basis. One way to do this is to use the swap market. By swapping a fixed cash flow (derived from a fixed rate mortgage security) for a LIBOR-based income stream, the assets and liabilities are now on the same basis. The swap can be tailored such that the reset dates coincide with the reset dates on the liability.

Another way to do this is to finance basic mortgage positions and use the proceeds to purchase LIBOR based assets. Most LIBOR-plus funds may use up to 50 percent leverage; in other words, borrowed money may not exceed 50 percent of total assets. Thus a $100 million fund could hold up to $200 million in assets. If 100 percent of the basic mortgage positions were financed, money could be placed in LIBOR-based securities, eliminating virtually all the LIBOR-Treasury spread risk. As a practical matter, 100 percent of the mortgage positions cannot be financed, because it is uneconomical to finance mortgage derivatives. Moreover, basic mortgage positions cannot be 100 percent financed, as some haircut is required. We estimate that most LIBOR-plus portfolio managers hedge 50–80 percent of the LIBOR-Treasury spread risk, either by using the swap market or by purchasing LIBOR based assets.

Financing considerations affect our decision to use agency mortgages rather than AA or AAA products. These private label mortgages yield 25–45 basis points more than their agency counterparts. They are, however, much less liquid and trade with bid ask spreads of five basis points. In addition, they finance at much higher rates than agency mortgages, and opportunities to roll these securities are unavailable. Taking into account the financing considerations, the true yield advantage of these securities is a more modest 0–10 basis points.

Managing the Mortgage-Treasury Spread Risk

The major risk in most LIBOR-plus funds is that mortgage-Treasury spreads may widen. The spread between the current coupon GNMA and the 7-year Treasury is shown in Figure 11.1. As one can see mortgages have been significantly wider in the past than they are now. Structural changes in the market would preclude a widening to 1986 levels, but some further widening is possible. If one anticipated a widening, mort-

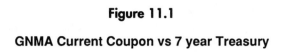

Figure 11.1

GNMA Current Coupon vs 7 year Treasury

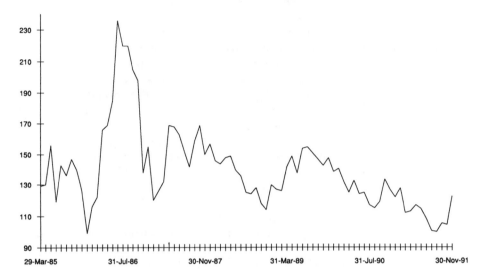

gage holdings could be reduced and substituted with Treasury securities. Alternatively, mortgage positions could be hedged with other mortgage positions. It is important to realize that either switching into Treasury securities or moving the short position into mortgages involves forfeiting the mortgage Treasury spread.

In order to determine if it is worthwhile to give up the additional carry provided by mortgages, one can analyze the sacrifice in yield versus the likelihood that spreads will widen. If mortgage-Treasury spreads were 100 basis points on a security with duration 5.0 (such as a GNMA), spreads can widen 20 basis points over the course of a year before the mortgage underperforms the Treasury. In a six-month horizon, spreads can widen only 10 basis points, and can widen only five basis points in the course of the quarter. If spreads were 80 basis points, they could widen only 16 basis points over the course of the year and proportionally less over shorter time periods. In general, the amount of permissible widening can be calculated as follows:

$$\text{Permissible Spread widening} = \frac{\left(\text{mortgage} - \text{Treasury spread} \times \text{fraction of a year}\right)}{\text{Duration of the mortgage}}$$

Using this formula, one may have an idea how much wider mortgage-Treasury spreads are likely to be at the end of a horizon and how quickly they will widen. The wider current spreads and the longer the period over which they are expected to occur, the more attractive it is to hold mortgages. This analysis assumes that a mortgage security is of the same duration as the Treasury. Calculations would be slightly more complicated if mortgages were compared with Treasury securities of a longer or shorter duration, as financing considerations would enter into the calculation.

It is important to realize that the mortgage-Treasury spread cannot be summarized in one number. Many investors take the spread between current coupon mortgages and the 10-year Treasury as the benchmark for spreads, but this is very misleading in the current environment; the yield curve is very steep and the current coupon GNMA has the duration of a 7-year Treasury. While still infrequent, it is becoming increasingly common to make the comparison between the current coupon GNMA and the 7-year Treasury. Moreover, the current coupon is not necessarily representative of the mortgage market. Currently, the GNMA 8 is the current coupon; it is also the lowest coupon mortgage that is actively traded. The rest of the mortgage market is at a premium, has shorter durations and may trade somewhat differently. GNMAs may also trade differently from conventional mortgages (FNMA and FHLMC). When making mortgage-Treasury spread comparisons, it is important to compare the mortgage one plans to buy with the Treasury to be used as a benchmark, rather than generalizing about the mortgage market as a whole.

Fund managers disagree about whether mortgage-Treasury spread risk should be managed. Most portfolio managers consider this risk a given, and do not believe it should be managed; other fund managers are constantly evaluating the attractiveness of mortgage securities versus Treasury securities. Most fund managers who try to manage the risk are inclined to hold their mortgage positions until they believe a widening is imminent as this minimizes the yield sacrifice. The more liquid the portfolio, the easier it is to move between Treasury securities and mortgages as mortgage-Treasury spreads change. Thus a portfolio of agency securities is easier to maneuver than a portfolio of private pass-throughs; a portfolio of fixed rate securities is easier to maneuver than a portfolio of Treasury ARMs, each of which has its own coupon and margin.

Management of the mortgage-Treasury spread risk may become more common if we go through a period of sustained spread widening. Spreads are tighter now than they were at the inception of most LIBOR-plus funds in late 1989 and early 1990; consequently, many fund managers may not have focused on this risk. Spreads have fluctuated significantly over the period, and managers could eliminate periods of underperformance by being in Treasury securities rather than mortgages.

Conclusion

There is a wide disparity in risk management techniques among managers of LIBOR-plus funds. Virtually all portfolio managers control their duration risk. All portfolio managers are aware of convexity risk; some control it and others choose to enjoy a higher base case return in exchange for a less attractive profile if rates move in either direction. Most LIBOR-plus fund managers hedge the LIBOR-Treasury spread risk either through swaps or by purchasing LIBOR-based instruments. Some portfolio managers try to manage the mortgage-Treasury spread risk; others do not. The more liquid the mortgage securities, the easier it is to move between mortgages and Treasuries, and the more readily this risk can be managed. In the future, the mortgage-Treasury spread risk will merit more attention as fund managers begin to realize that they can eliminate significant periods of underperformance.

Part Four

INNOVATIVE APPLICATIONS

ENVIRONMENTAL FUTURES: PRELIMINARY THOUGHTS ON THE MARKET FOR SULFUR DIOXIDE EMISSION ALLOWANCES*

Richard L. Sandor and
Michael J. Walsh

12

Introduction

The 1990 Clean Air Act Amendments (CAAA) created the largest attempt ever to use a tradeable permits approach for limiting pollution. The market approach is intended to lower the cost of achieving the mandated reductions in total emission levels. The purpose of this paper is to examine the implementation of an organized market for sulfur dioxide (SO_2) emission allowances and the feasibility of a successful futures market in allowances.

After providing some background on the emission allowance market created by the 1990 Clean Air Act Amendments, we discuss the development and expansion of futures markets. We then discuss the function of futures markets and the preconditions typically associated with successful new futures markets. Subsequent sections address the prospects for the SO_2 emission allowance futures market and the patterns of market development often observed in other markets.

---

*Portions of this paper are based on and directly quoted from "Feasibility of a Futures Market for SO_2 Allowances" submitted by Richard L. Sandor to the Coalition for Acid Rain Equity, 1989, and "An Inquiry into the Feasibility of a Reinsurance Futures Market" by Robert C. Goshay and Richard L. Sandor. The views expressed here are those of the authors only and do not necessarily reflect those of Kidder Peabody and Company or the Chicago Board of Trade.

I. Background on the Emission Allowance Market

The CAAA mandated a 50 percent cut in aggregate annual emissions of SO_2 from electric power plants in the continental United States, the primary source of the emissions thought to cause acid precipitation.[1] The CAAA also established tradable SO_2 emission "allowances" (EAs), each of which allows its holder to emit one ton of SO_2 in a designated year or later years. The program is phased in; Phase 1 (1995–1999) covers 110 large power plants with 265 generation units (owned by roughly 40 utilities) in the eastern United States, while Phase 2 (starting in the year 2000) covers 800 power plants with 2200 generating units scattered across country. In Phase 2 the total number of allowances (and hence emissions) is generally limited to 8.9 million tons per year. Because allowances can be carried forward, actual annual emissions can vary from this level. Continuous emission monitors must be installed on each smokestack, and units that do not hold enough EA's to cover SO_2 emissions during a year face a $2000 fine and confiscation of a next-year allowance for each excess ton emitted.

The CAAA provides for annual auctions of "spot" allowances which are usable in current year or later years, and "advance" allowances usable seven years later or later. The CAAA allowed EPA to delegate the auction administration responsibilities to outside entities, and several entities have applied to be the delegate. Allowances will exist only as entries in an EPA computer file, and transfers will be recorded in the book entry accounts on that system.

To encourage early installation of certain scrubbers that remove 90 percent of emissions from coal-fired plants, the Act provides for distribution of 3.5 million allowances usable in 1995 and 1996 to utilities that install such equipment. Another small pool of allowances can be distributed to utilities that show their emissions declined due to electricity conservation programs or use of renewable or alternative fuels.

Affected utilities have two basic choices for complying with the law. Since they will be issued fewer EAs than would cover past emission levels, they must either cut emissions or buy more EAs. Emissions can be cut by switching to lower-sulfur coal (or to other "clean" fuels), "scrubbing"—by either cleaning fuel before combustion or cleansing gases resulting from combustion—or changing the economic dispatch order used to determine when the various generating plants are utilized.

If utilities overcontrol—that is, cut emissions below the number of EAs held—then the freed-up EAs can be sold or banked for future use. If a utility undercontrols it must buy EAs or face stiff fines. Firm-level cost

---

[1] See Endnotes on page 210.

savings due to the EA market occur if the utilities that overcontrol sell freed-up EAs and use the revenues to offset emission reduction costs (some of which may have been borne by ratepayers) and those that undercontrol purchase EAs at a cost below that of reducing their own emissions.

Thus, utilities that can cut emissions for less than the market price of EAs are encouraged to do so, while those facing high emission abatement costs will find it less costly to buy EAs instead of cutting emissions. If effective, these incentives result in efficient achievement of emission reductions by causing them to be undertaken in a way that uses fewer resources than a command-and-control emission reduction requirement. Publicly visible EA prices will also reveal the marginal value placed on further emission reductions. This signal offers a guide for determining economically efficient emission reduction actions, and also indicates the costs of the policy and the price of achieving additional emission reductions.

Lowering the total costs of complying with the SO_2 restrictions in the CAAA would mean smaller electricity rate increases for consumers. One estimate finds the CAAA emission market provisions can cut compliance costs 25 percent ($2 billion per year) (ICF Inc., 1990). While much of this savings will come from intra-firm changes in electricity production and company-wide emission control strategies, much would also come from inter-firm trading. Anything that impedes active, low-cost EA trading would mean those seeking to sell would receive lower net revenues, while those seeking to buy would pay more. Such a barrier would impair least-cost attainment of the aggregate emission reductions, since the incentive to cut emissions is reduced for potential sellers, and the incentive to use allowances instead of taking costlier emission abatement steps is reduced as the net advantage of buying allowances goes down.

For the emission allowance market an organized public exchange can play the important role of providing public price signals, open price discovery process, and a low-cost mechanism for transacting. Futures contracts can be used to manage the emission allowance price risk that will be inherent in the market and will help utilities and others manage the transition to a market-oriented pollution control environment. Trading in futures contracts also generates market prices for future exchange that can be used in determining the least-cost method of complying with tightened emission rules.

State Public Utility Commissions (PUCs) play a critical role in assuring this market works. If regulators focus on achievement of least-cost compliance, and if utilities consider all compliance options—including purchase or sale of emission allowances—trading in allowances will occur naturally. PUCs have a natural interest in helping the market develop since use of the market can help limit electricity rate increases that might result from the tighter emission standards.

II. Growth and Expansion of Futures Markets

Application of futures contracts to the SO_2 emission allowance market will help to continue the trend of expanding the range of commodities subject to futures trading and will probably contribute to the long-trend of growth in the use of these markets.

From 1960 to 1970 the volume of futures trading in the United States increased from 3,878,151 contracts to 13,662,607. The dollar value of commodities traded on U.S. futures markets was $29.3 billion in fiscal 1960 and reached $135.6 billion in fiscal 1970. In 1960, trading was generally limited to primary agricultural commodities. Soybeans and their products accounted for nearly 40 percent of the trading on all commodities exchanges. Since 1960 a significant portion of the total growth in

Figure 12.1: Total Volume (in millions) of Futures and Futures-options Contracts Traded on U.S. Exchanges, 1960–1991

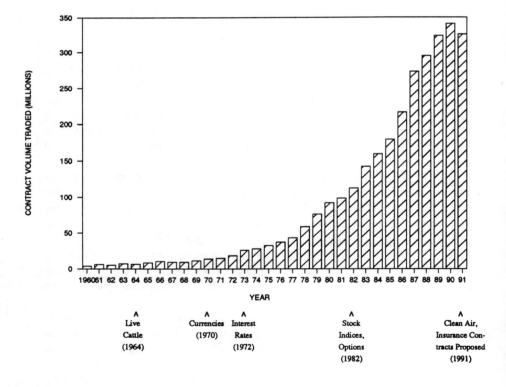

trading volume is attributable to the development of new markets. The success of the cattle, frozen pork belly, and plywood contracts indicated that the feasible set of tradeable commodities on organized exchanges could be expanded to include live animals as well as semi-and fully-processed commodities. The next two decades witnessed an even more dramatic growth in trading activity. In 1991 the total U.S. futures industry volume reached 325,096,928 contracts with a total dollar volume of over $63 trillion.

Figure 12.1 shows the remarkable growth of trading in futures and futures-options contracts on U.S. exchanges over the past 30 years. Years during which several important new markets are launched are also indicated.

The application of futures contracts to financial instruments, stock and commodity indices clearly demonstrates that the conditions traditionally thought to be prerequisites for a futures contract have undergone major revision. Application of futures contracts to emission allowances represents another breakthrough by applying the technology to a property right for the first time.

III. The Functions and Benefits of Futures Markets

The purchase (sale) of a futures contract is tantamount to entering into an agreement to buy (sell) a particular grade and quantity of a commodity, financial instrument, or index at some point in the future for a specified price; traditionally this is termed a long (short) position. Industrial users minimize the associated price risk of the underlying commodity by "hedging," which is the initiation of a position in the futures market equal and opposite to their position in the cash market. (More recently, the U.S. Commodity Futures Trading Commission—which regulates the futures industry and has approved trading in Clean Air futures—has broadened the definition of a hedge so as to include modern risk management tools in financial markets). Others assume risk by "speculating," which is simply the establishment of a position in an attempt to make a profit. Liquidation of a contract can occur by initiating a position equal and opposite to the original position or by making or taking delivery. With respect to the former, there is a possible concomitant profit or loss associated with transactions occurring at different prices as well as transactions costs.

An exchange-traded futures contract can be considered a standardized forward contract. It specifies several factors that often vary when forward contracts are used, including: quantity to be bought or sold, the future date of the exchange, the procedures for delivery, minimum standards for the deliverable commodity. Because futures markets are anonymous, the intentions and positions of buyers and sellers are not revealed when transactions occur. Another critical feature of exchange-traded futures contracts is the guarantee provided when the clearing-house interposes itself as the buyer to every seller and the seller to every buyer. Even if one party to a trade defaults on his commitment, the clearinghouse guarantees the other party will be able to buy or sell in fulfill-ment of the original transaction agreement.

Because a futures contract fixes other relevant transaction terms, price is the only variable to be negotiated. Since all participants deal in the same underlying agreement, markets in futures contracts generally become more liquid than forward markets. Liquidity means there is fre-quent trading and trading is inexpensive; it implies there are generally buyers or sellers present in the market, and prices at a given point in time do not differ much from the last transaction price observed in the mar-ket. In an illiquid market sellers (or buyers) may face a long wait before finding a willing buyer (or seller), and thus buyers must often raise their bid prices to induce a seller, while sellers may have to lower their offer price to induce a buyer.

A clearinghouse is the guarantor of the contract and serves as the in-termediary between buyers and sellers by being on the opposite side of the agreement for each of the parties. Trading is conducted by a limited number of individuals, i.e., members of the exchange. Only clearing members can assume the financial responsibility associated with initiating and maintaining a position in the market, so all exchange members must clear their trades through a clearing member. The prerequisite financial requirements imposed on these members help to ensure the integrity of the market. The clearinghouse also facilitates the delivery procedure for markets that are not indexed or cash settled. Delivery instruments, such as warehouse receipts or shipping certificates, are presented in lieu of the physical commodity and vary according to the commodity traded. The clearinghouse maintains surveillance and control over the eligibility of de-livery facilities. The clearinghouse also guarantees that the delivered com-modity is consistent with the specifications of the contract.

Economists ascribe three major economic benefits to the existence of organized futures markets. They provide a mechanism for the efficient re-distribution of risk through the mechanism of hedging; they help to dis-seminate price and industrial or financial information; and they provide alternate sources of supply in markets where delivery mechanisms exist. Market participants, academicians and regulators traditionally have attrib-uted these benefits to futures markets ranging from soybeans to U.S. Treasury bonds.

Futures Market Development

There have been numerous attempts to identify the complete list of prerequisites for a successful futures contract; there is no definitive evidence, however, that a particular set of prerequisites is either necessary or sufficient for success. The prerequisites discussed here and frequently mentioned by economists do not violate the characteristics of commodities or financial instruments currently being traded and are consistent with the sparse attempts at theory, but they should be considered tentative.

The following six prerequisites represent market conditions which should be satisfied if a futures contract is to be successfully traded:

1. product homogeneity or the close movement of the prices of the different grades of the commodity;
2. price variability;
3. competitive determination of prices;
4. viable cash market (transactions in a commodity for immediate delivery at a specific place) in order to facilitate delivery procedures;
5. inefficient or ineffective alternatives for hedging price risk; examples of the latter include a break down in forward contracting or contracts not being executed or requiring renegotiation;
6. a futures contract design that adequately reflects cash market conditions and practices.

Adaptability of Emission Allowances to Futures Markets

We now consider the various features of successful futures contracts in the context of the emission allowance market.

1. Homogeneity. As noted above, product homogeneity is provided by the legislation. A unit in this market is one ton of SO_2 emissions. By definition, this is a standardized commodity.

2. Price Variability. Because futures contracts are risk transfer instruments, the presence of price risk in the underlying commodity is a critical condition for success of a futures contract. Regulatory policies that allow a utility to easily transfer price risk to consumers would reduce the need to use other risk management tools. An automatic fuel price adjustment clause sometimes transfers price risk to ratepayers, and use of such a clause for emission allowances would unnecessarily expose rate-payers to risk.

Many experts on pollution abatement suggest that the cost differentials for cleaning up one ton of emissions might range from \$200 to \$600. This suggests that it might be possible for prices to fluctuate within this range. It is important to emphasize that a futures market can be successful with volatility as low as 20 percent per annum. Alternatively stated, fluctuations of $40 to $120 per ton would provide enough volatility to attract hedgers.

The following events could be expected to cause price volatility by causing unexpected changes in electricity production and emission rates:

- hotter or colder weather than expected
- unexpected variation in the level or mix of economic activity of electricity consumers
- unexpected power plant outages at "dirty" or "clean" plants
- unexpected purchases or sales of wholesale electricity
- unexpected use of higher- or lower-sulfur coal (due to price incentives, shipping, or quality problems)
- unexpected deviations in scrubber system performance
- technological improvements in emission abatement equipment.

While this list is clearly not exhaustive, it does give a sense that a good number of external factors could cause prices to be fairly volatile and thus increase the price risk faced by emission allowance buyers, sellers and owners.

3. Competitive Determination of Prices. In perfect competition, participants view prices parametrically, that is individuals or firms are "price takers" and cannot influence prices. The emission allowance market is characterized by large supplies and numerous participants. Around 40 utility companies are involved in Phase 1 and many more in Phase 2. Furthermore, industrial emissions sources can participate in the market, as can any other interested party.

If we assume a price of $400 per ton, then the dollar value of the emission allowance market be approximately $2.4 billion to $3.0 billion in Phase 1, and $3.6 billion in Phase 2. This would provide a "crop" equivalent to around 70 percent of the annual wheat crop, on which a very important and successful agricultural futures market is based.

4. A Viable Cash Market in the Underlying Commodity. An exchange-based cash market is planned and will help fulfill this condition. In fact, the existence of a futures market may attract a significant number of commodity dealers and or investment banks into the cash market. This alone may be an important by-product which would enable the market to perform the function desired by the Clean Air Act.

5. Patterns of Forward Contracting. Since the market is entirely new, almost no hedging alternatives are now available. One example of the utility industry's interest in managing risk is the attempt to coordinate an arrangement for sharing the "bonus" allowance pool that will be distributed to utilities that install certain scrubbing equipment.

It is also interesting to note that a futures market with no alternative forward contracting mechanism may provide for the simultaneous development of forward and cash markets.

6. Futures Contract Design. The Commodity Futures Trading Commission has approved an emission allowance futures contract for trading at the Chicago Board of Trade. In reference to the goal of the enabling legislation, the CBOT calls the contract "Clean Air" futures. The salient features of the contract are listed in Table 12.1.

Generally the contract terms are designed to be consistent with cash market provisions, and some terms are specifically designed to attract trading participation of exchange members. Such trading will be critical to supporting market liquidity. These terms are aimed at mimicking specifications of other contracts that are currently successful. For example, the contract size of 25 allowances is chosen because it would have a total value similar to that of the CBOT Corn futures contract (worth around $12,000 per 5,000 bushel contract) if, as might be the case, emission allowances

Table 12.1: Salient Features of the Chicago Board of Trade Clean Air (SO_2 Emission Allowance) Futures Contract

Unit of Trading:	The contract unit shall be 25 1-ton sulfur dioxide emission allowances.
Standards:	Deliverable emission allowances are those issued by the U.S. Environmental Protection Agency. Deliverable allowances must be applicable against emissions in the year of the delivery month.
Months Traded In:	Trading in Clean Air Futures may be conducted in the current month and any subsequent months.
Price Basis:	All prices in Clean Air futures shall be in multiples of one dollar ($1.00) per allowance.
Hours of Trading:	Daytime hours for trading shall be 8:50 A.M. to 2:10 P.M. central time. The evening hours of trading shall be determined by the Board.
Trading Limits:	Daily trading limits shall be $100 per allowance or $2500 per contract. Variable limits shall be $150 per allowance or $3750 per contract. No limits shall be in effect for the current contract month.
Last Day of Trading:	No Trades in Clean Air futures deliverable in the current month shall be made in the last three business days of that month.
Delivery:	Delivery shall be made by book entry transfer between accounts on the book entry system designated by the U.S. Environmental Protection Agency.
Position Limits:	Speculative position limits shall be 2,000 contracts in the current month and 5,000 contracts overall.

are worth \$400 to \$500 each. Trading hours for Clean Air futures are intentionally set so that CBOT agricultural product traders can trade Clean Air futures before agriculture futures markets open (at 9:30 A.M.) and those who trade CBOT financial products can trade after their markets close at 2:00 P.M.

IV. Patterns of Market Development

Let us first consider whether the conditions associated with successful emissions or property rights market are present in the sulfur dioxide emission allowance program. Several attempts at emission offset markets have been tried, but most had very little trading due to regulatory hurdles and other impediments to trading, ill-defined rights, and a potential participant base that was either too small or not clearly identified.[2]

Most of the conditions thought to be associated with a successful emissions market appear to be present in the SO_2 emission allowance market. The item traded is clearly defined (one ton of SO_2 emissions in a year indicated by the allowance number, or later years), potential market participants are numerous and well-known (including non-utility emission sources that can "opt-in" the program and vendors of fuel and emission control equipment that can package emission allowances with their product), and many utility regulators have acknowledged the need to avoid imposing unneeded administrative constraints. In addition, the incentive to trade is present since there are significant opportunities for gains from trade due to differing emission abatement costs.

Given that the market appears to be well-designed, we now consider some patterns of market development that are sometimes seen in other markets. The following describes the progressive stages of market development that are often observed:

1. bilateral (search) or over-the-counter (brokered) markets
2. an active spot market, sometimes having auction market characteristics
3. organized or exchange-administered cash market
4. futures and options contract markets

In early 1992 the over-the-counter market in SO_2 allowances began developing, as evidenced by the brokered and bilateral sales announced by Wisconsin Power and Light to the Tennessee Valley Authority and Duquesne Light Company in May, 1992. While these trades were not large relative to the size of the annual "crop" of allowances, they do indicate a real belief in the benefits of trading on the part of utilities. Such

---

[2] See Endnotes on page 210.

trading can be expected to continue as utilities more seriously consider the desirability of transacting at prices in the $250–$400 per ton range reported for the publicized trades, and as the first year of emission limits (1995) approaches.

An active spot market may develop after the first emission allowance auction is held in March, 1993. Sponsorship of an organized spot market by an organized exchange will help increase cash market liquidity, lower transaction costs and increase price visibility. As with futures markets, cash market liquidity is self-perpetuating; each additional trade raises market activity and increases execution speed and liquidity for all participants.

Utilities will be more inclined to use fluid, strategic inventory management if it becomes clear allowances can be readily obtained in the market. Some utilities have indicated they would like to use the emission allowance market each time they commit to increasing or decreasing emissions when a bulk power transaction is done. Such frequent inventory management would mirror that used by large grain processors and bond and stock dealers, and would improve the prospects for an active market in futures contracts.

The appendix discusses the rationale for use of emission allowance futures contracts by electric utilities, and provides some examples demonstrating the benefits of hedging.

Conclusion

The movement away from command-and-control social and environmental regulation is intended to use the amazing power of market incentives to produce desired results at a lower cost to society. The Clean Air emission allowance market will, for the first time, put a market determined price on what economists have long recognized is a scarce but unpriced and misallocated resource—clean air. Both industrial competitiveness and consumers can benefit from a market-oriented approach to limiting pollution because the cost of achieving an improvement in national environmental quality is lowered. Environmentalists benefit because their goals can be furthered at lower cost, thus making it more likely that pollution restrictions can pass the cost-benefit test that is implicitly conducted through the legislative process.

The success of the sulfur dioxide emission allowance market may lead the way to more widespread adoption of a marketable permits approach for limiting pollution. Another area where this approach would be sound is limiting greenhouse gas emissions. The emissions thought to contribute to global warming are measurable, subject to varying control costs, and have the same effect on the global environment regardless of where emitted.

It appears that the necessary conditions for the development of successful futures contracts in emission allowances are satisfied. An active futures market will help utilities and others adjust to and benefit from the new market, and thus would be a critical component for the success of this socially important legislation.

Appendix

Examples of Hedging SO$_2$ Emission Allowances Using Futures Contracts

As noted earlier, allowance prices may show considerable variation over time. This will introduce more uncertainty to the utility planning processes and reduce the accuracy of dividend, budget and rate-making plans. Planning needs, especially for pollution control expenditures, also mean utilities will be interested in securing allowances well before the year for which they are needed, or may wish to sell and monetize unneeded allowances. When a commodity price varies over time and sellers or buyers of a commodity wish to secure prices ahead of time, interested parties often enter forward contracts. This arrangement, widely used by electric utilities to secure future coal supplies, fixes prices and quantities for specific dates and time periods (although renegotiation of contracts is common). The terms of forward contracts addressing delivery location, commodity grade, payment terms and guarantees are typically customized for each agreement. Utilities may find that forward contracting is useful in solving some of the uncertainty problems faced by allowance suppliers and demanders.

Hedging is the use of futures contracts to protect against the risk of price increases (for buyers) or decreases (for sellers or owners). When futures contracts are combined with positions in the underlying commodity, the net effect is to lock-in the purchase or sales price in advance of the transaction date. Futures-based hedging strategies are an inexpensive tool often used to:

- lock-in the purchase price of acquisitions expected to occur in the future
- protect against the decline in value of items in inventory
- improve accuracy of revenue and cost stream projections
- guarantee profitability of an enterprise by securing input or output prices
- isolate some risks faced by the firm and allow the business to focus on its main business functions.

Futures contracts are widely used because use of the markets is inexpensive and rapid. Futures provide agreements that can be easily reversed if events warrant, and are often superior to alternative risk management tools. By any reasonable definition, utilities that hedge emission allowance prices—or any other significant price exposure they face, such as interest rate risk—are taking prudent steps to control expenses or revenues.

Consider the following examples for the emission allowance market.

Long Hedging: Locking-in a Purchase Price for Allowances. We assume utilities must hold enough allowances to cover current-year emissions on January 31 of the subsequent year, and emission allowance futures contracts provide for December delivery of 25 allowances applicable to current-year emissions. To simplify the examples, we ignore brokerage commissions and other transaction costs. (Of course, these costs will have to be taken into account when considering whether to trade, and they should be compared with the cost of trading outside an organized exchange.) These assumptions do not change the nature of the examples.

All prices used in the examples are strictly hypothetical and do not reflect any expectations regarding actual market price levels.

Suppose during February 1995 a utility holds 100,000 allowances but expects to need 50,000 more allowances to cover emissions for the current year. The firm can, in effect, use futures contracts to lock in the future price of allowances. In reality, the fact that the relationship between futures prices and cash prices—the basis—is close but not perfect, hedging through use futures allows the hedger to sharply narrow (but not exactly fix) the ultimate range of net purchase or sale prices (i.e., hedgers essentially remove price risk but accept basis risk).

Assume the February 1995 "cash" (immediate delivery and payment market) price for emission allowances is $300, but prices have varied between $200 and $400 per allowance. This variation means the total cost of needed allowances might be expected to range from $10,000,000 to $20,000,000, i.e., a $10,000,000 range. Assuming this uncertainty can significantly affect utility plans and profits, the utility might want to "lock-in" its costs at a known level rather than face the risk that prices will rise. To do so, the firm could buy 2,000 emission allowance futures contracts (corresponding to 50,000 allowances) for December 1995 delivery at the current futures price of, say, $315 per allowance. Thus the buying firm is "long"; it holds a contract that entitles it to acquire allowances for $315 each in December. If the "long" chooses to take delivery, it would ultimately pay $15,750,000 for its allowances. (The party selling the futures contract—the short—requires a price above the current cash price because, in effect, he foregoes the opportunity to sell the commodity now and earn interest on the revenues).

Table 12.2 summarizes the example:

Table 12.2: Long Hedging Strategy: Lock-in Acquisition Price
for Emission Allowances

Cash Market		Futures Market	
February 1995 Cash Price:	$300/ton	Buy December 1995 Futures:	$315/ton
November 1995 Cash Price:	$400/ton	Sell December 1995 Futures:	$405/ton
Effects of Price changes:	($100)/ton		+$90/ton
Net Price Paid with hedging:	$310/ton, or $15.5 million total		
Price paid without hedging:	$400/ton, or $20 million total		

In November the hedger has two choices: wait to take delivery of the emission allowances, or offset his obligation to take delivery by taking a futures position opposite to his original position. Most hedgers in existing markets find it best to offset their obligation to take delivery by selling futures to offset and terminate their original commitment to take delivery.

Suppose the long hedger chooses to take delivery of the 50,000 EAs in December 1995 and cash market prices remain the same as they were in November ($400/ton). In this case the hedger will receive 50,000 allowances and will pay $315 per ton. By locking-in prices, the hedger avoided paying $100 per ton increase in cash market prices.

Alternatively, suppose in November the hedger chooses to offset his obligation to take delivery, perhaps because he chooses to purchase allowances in the cash market. To offset his long position, the hedger sells 2,000 futures contracts at, we assume, $405/ton. This represents an increase in the value of the futures position equal to $90 per ton. However, to acquire the allowances in the cash market the hedger must pay $400 per ton; subtracting from this the $90 gain on the futures position, the net price paid for allowances is $310 per ton.

Why not just pay $300 per ton back in February? There are several reasons. First, by using futures contracts the long hedger secures prices and supplies but does so with minimum up-front cash outlays, and thus he frees up funds for alternative uses in the interim. Hedging using futures also lets the buyer secure prices even if enough funds to pay for the total acquisition are not yet available. Another reason for using futures is reversibility; if emission rates are below expected levels, the utility can terminate his obligation to take delivery, and does not incur the major cash flow opportunity loss that a full cash purchase would imply.

Short Hedging: Fixing Sales Prices, Protecting Inventory Values. Suppose in March 1996 a utility finds its scrubber systems allow it to cut SO_2 emissions for approximately $150 per ton, and the December 1996 futures contract price is $310 per ton. If the utility's post-scrubbing emission rates remain at 1995 levels, the utility will have 20,000 1996 allowances it can sell. In effect, the utility will be building up an inventory of allowances during the year; a short hedge allows the utility to protect the value of that inventory from declines in value.

Table 12.3 summarizes an example where a short hedge of 800 contracts (to cover 20,000 allowances) helps the utility avoid a loss due to a price decline.

Suppose by November cash market prices fell to $250. If the utility finds its emissions rose unexpectedly during the year, and it needed the 20,000 allowances to cover its own emissions, it can offset its commitment to sell by buying back 800 futures contracts, in this case at a price of $255 per ton. Because he sold for $310 per ton and bought for $255 per ton, the short hedge earns the utility $55 per ton or a total of $1.1 million. The reversible nature of futures contracts gave the flexibility needed in case expectations regarding emission levels that were incorrect.

Alternatively, suppose the utility decides to sell in the cash market in November (at $250 per ton) and terminate its commitment to deliver on the short futures position. In this case the net price received is $250 plus $55 per ton, since the cash price of $250 per ton is supplemented by the $55 gain in the futures position. In effect, the utility achieved its goal of locking-in a sales price of approximately $300 per ton (in fact changed conditions helped the utility net $305 per ton).

In both these examples the hedger benefitted because prices moved against an unhedged position. Had prices moved in the opposite direction (the price paid by the buyer fell, the price received by the seller rose), the hedger would felt some regret. Some ask, "Don't the gains and losses all even out?" Over enough time they may, but many businesses find that increasing control over some of the many (often uncontrol-

Table 12.3: Short Hedging Strategy: Lock-in Allowance Sales Price, Protect Inventory Value

March 1996 Cash Price:	$300/ton	Sell December 1996 Futures:	$310/ton
November 1996 Cash Price:	$250/ton	Buy December 1996 Futures:	$255/ton
Effects of Price changes:	($50)/ton		+ $55/ton
Net Price Received with hedging:	$305/ton, or $6.1 million total		
Price received without hedging:	$250/ton, or $5.0 million total		
Price received without hedging:	$250/ton, or $5.0 million total		

lable) risks they face helps them improve their planning accuracy and allows them to focus on their primary business lines. The alternative to hedging against price risk is to implicitly extend a business into an area that some prefer to avoid: speculating on commodity prices.

Endnotes

1. While the scientific debate on the effects of acid precipitation continues, many have concluded it damages lakes, forests and structures, reduces visibility in some notably scenic areas, and may directly threaten human health.

   The acid rain problem is considered a regional one, not a local one. Because sulfur dioxide is transported long distances (several hundred miles) by upper air currents, the CAAA mandated a nationwide cut in aggregate emissions. The transferability of allowances means the location of the emission cuts will be determined in part by the market for allowances. Regardless of where the emission cuts occur, all power plants must continue to comply with the National Ambient Air Quality Standards that require maintenance of local air quality.

2. The most successful offsets program to date in the U.S. is the market used to allocate lead content in gasoline as the allowable content level was phased down from 1983 through 1987. Anderson et. al. offer a good description of that program and other attempt to implement offset markets.

REFERENCES

Anderson, Robert C., Hofman, Lisa A., and Rusin, Michael. "The Use of Economic Incentive Mechanisms in Environmental Management," Research Paper #051, American Petroleum Institute, (June 1990).

Bohi, Douglas R., and Burtraw, Dallas. 1991. "Avoiding Regulatory Gridlock In The Acid Rain Program," *Journal of Policy Analysis and Management*, Vol. 10, No. 4, 676–684.

Goshay, Robert C., and Sandor, Richard L. 1973. "An Inquiry into the Feasibility of a Reinsurance Futures Market," *Journal of Business Finance*, No. 3, 56–66.

ICF Resources Incorporated. *Comparisons of the Economic Impacts of the Acid Rain Provisions of the Senate Bill (S.1630) and the House Bill (S.1630)*, (July, 1990).

Rose, Kenneth, and Burns, Robert E. "Overview and Discussion of the Key Regulatory Issues in Implementing the Electric Utility Provisions of the Clean Air Act Amendments of 1990," The National Regulatory Research Institute, (June 1991).

Sandor, Richard L. "Innovation by an Exchange: A Case Study of the Development of the Plywood Futures Contract," *Journal of Law and Economics,* Vol. 16, No. 1, April 1973, 119–136.

Sandor, Richard L. and Sosin, Howard. "Inventive Activity in Futures Markets: A Case Study of the Development of the First Interest Rate Futures Market," *Futures Markets: Modelling, Managing and Monitoring Futures Trading,* ed. Manfred E. Streit, Basil Blackwell, Cambridge MA, 1985, 255–272.

Sandor, Richard L. 1989. "Feasibility of a Futures Market for SO_2 Allowances," submitted to the Coalition for Acid Rain Equity.

HEDGING BUSINESS CYCLE RISK WITH

MACRO SWAPS AND OPTIONS*

John F. Marshall, Vipul K. Bansal, Anthony F. Herbst, and Alan L. Tucker

13

The 1980s witnessed the birth and explosive growth of currency swaps and interest rate swaps, and, more recently, commodity swaps and equity swaps. These instruments have revolutionized modern risk management, completed markets, opened new avenues for arbitrage, and otherwise served to make existing markets more efficient.

Currency swaps allow multinational corporations, banks, and central governments to hedge exchange rate risk. In so doing, they have helped speed the integration of the world's formerly segregated capital markets. Interest rate swaps, in the process of allowing corporations and institutional investors to hedge interest rate risk, have erased the traditional distinction between the money and capital markets. Commodity swaps have made it possible to achieve long-term fixed pricing in a volatile real asset market environment. And equity swaps allow equity fund managers to hedge systematic market risk, which in turn has brought about further integration of the debt and equity markets.[1]

In this article, we present the outline of a new kind of swap now under development: the macroeconomic swap (or macro swap) and its associated macroeconomic options (macro options).[2] Unlike previous swaps,

---

* This article originally appeared in the *Journal of Applied Corporate Finance*, vol. 4, no. 4, Winter 1992. Reprinted with permission.

[1] The swaps literature is thoroughly reviewed by Kenneth R. Kapner and John F. Marshall in *The Swaps Handbook, 1991* and *The Swaps Handbook, 1991–1992 Supplement*, both published by the New York Institute of Finance.

[2] Macroeconomic swaps are currently under development at one leading swap dealer bank. The authors developed the concept of the macro swap independently but are now collaborating on development of these instruments.

which exist principally to hedge *price* risk, macro swaps hold the promise of becoming effective tools for hedging *quantity,* or business cycle risk—a form of risk that has never been readily managed with financial instruments. Macro swaps achieve the hedging of quantity risk by tying the floating leg of the swap to a macroeconomic variable (or index) such as growth rates in GNP, durable goods orders, wholesale price indices, housing starts, or measures of consumer confidence. Similarly, macroeconomic options are options on which the underlying asset "price," sometimes called a reference rate, is the value of a macroeconomic index or a function of a macroeconomic index. These options can be single-period calls, single-period puts, or a series of puts or calls that amount to a multi-period "cap" or "floor." For companies whose sales and profits are highly correlated with such variables, macro swaps and options can be used to hedge the quantity risk associated with unanticipated fluctuations in these measures.

In the remainder of this article, we begin by describing the potential role of macro swaps and options in managing risks associated with the business cycle. Next, we describe the proposed structures of macro swaps and options in more detail. Finally, we discuss the role of the macro swap dealer in the development of markets for such innovative securities, and how such a dealer may lay off its macro swap risk.

Macroeconomic or Quantity Risk

Most hedging is designed to offset a price volatility to which a producer, consumer, or investor is exposed. By engaging in a swap or other form of derivative security, the party is hedging fluctuations in price on the assumption that quantity is fixed. Quantity, however, may not be fixed, and such quantity risk has always proven to be a difficult risk to hedge.

Quantity risk is most often portrayed in the context of agricultural production. A farmer might use a commodity swap or an agricultural futures contract to fix the price for which his product may be sold in the future. But, in so doing, the farmer has done nothing to hedge the quantity risk associated with the vagaries of the weather and other sources of uncertainty. Quantity risk also exists in the industrial sector. For instance, automobile manufacturers can use wage contracts and commodity swaps to control the costs of input factors of production. They can also use currency swaps to hedge exchange rate risk and interest rate swaps to manage financial costs. But the manufacturer can do little to hedge against a decline in unit sales resulting from a general economic slowdown. That is, the firm has a cyclical exposure that can be described as a "macroeconomic" risk. It is thus also, of course, a quantity risk.

Many other services and industries have an exposure to the business cycle that is similar to auto producers'. These include vacation and tour operators, durable goods manufacturers, residential and commercial builders, credit card franchisers whose revenue is based on transactional card volume, and so on. What all of these industries have in common is that unit sales and profit are highly correlated with measures of consumer confidence, a macroeconomic variable.

To some degree, a firm can manage its quantity risk by massaging its production process—for example, by employing or laying-off evening-shift assembly workers. The essence of such a strategy is to pass on much of the risk to others, principally the firm's workers and vendors. However, such a strategy has obvious drawbacks, and it may be costly as well (resulting, for example, in considerable training costs). Also, a firm's ability to pass its quantity risk to others may be limited by the nature of its contracts with its workers and vendors, and by the degree of leverage employed in its operating and financial structures. Because of these costs and constraints, the firm may have few means to control quantity risk.

It is this source of revenue and profit volatility that macro swaps are designed to hedge. Provided the firm can identify a macroeconomic variable highly correlated with its own unit sales, management can hedge its quantity risk by engaging in a swap in which the firm pays a fixed rate and receives a payment that varies inversely with changes in that variable. Such a swap would be designed to produce payoffs when the firm's sales are expected to be down, thus allowing the firm to outperform its unhedged competitors.

Macro Swaps

As stated earlier, a macro swap is a fixed-for-floating swap in which the floating leg is tied to a macroeconomic variable or index. As in the case of any swap contract, a macro swap contract would specify the notional principal, the coupon rate (fixed or otherwise), payment dates, and swap tenor (i.e., maturity). The contract would also specify the macroeconomic variable or index that would determine the "floating" payments. The end user and the macro swap dealer would simply exchange periodic payments based on the prevailing value of the floating macroeconomic variable, given the fixed coupon rate and the notional principal.[3]

To provide just one illustration, consider a fixed-for-floating swap in which the floating leg is tied to an index of consumer confidence (ICC), such as the University of Michigan's Consumer Sentiment Index or the Conference Board's Index of Consumer Confidence. Our concocted ICC

---

[3] In practice, these cash flows would be netted. That is, one party simply makes a payment covering the difference between the fixed and the floating payments to the other party. Also, such net payments would be made in-arrears: that is based on the previous quarter's prevailing macroeconomic index.

Table 13.1: Hypothetical Cash Flows on an ICC Swap

Calendar Quarter	Average ICC	Dealer Pays (million)	Firm Pays (millions)	Net Flow (millions)
1st 1991	80.00	$0.500	$0.500	$0.000
2nd 1991	78.00	0.550	0.500	0.050
3rd 1991	74.00	0.650	0.500	0.150
4th 1991	70.00	0.750	0.500	0.250
1st 1992	70.00	0.750	0.500	0.250
2nd 1992	78.00	0.550	0.500	0.050
3rd 1992	84.00	0.400	0.500	-0.100
4th 1992	92.00	0.200	0.500	-0.300

is based on a scale of 0 (absolutely no confidence) to 100 (perfect confidence), and we will assume it currently stands at 80. Assume further that the notional principal of the macro swap is $10 million, the coupon rate is 20 percent,[4] and the payments are scheduled to occur quarterly.

In such a case, the floating and fixed rate legs would be calculated as follows:

$$\text{Dealer Pays (Floaing)} = \left(\left(100 - \text{ICC}\right)/100\right) \times \left(\$10\text{mm}\right) \times \left(0.25\right)$$

$$\text{End User Pays (Fixed)} = 20.0\% \times \left(\$10\text{mm}\right) \times \left(0.25\right)$$

Table 13.1 shows the first eight quarterly payments that would result from such a swap assuming our hypothetical ICC declined steadily during the first year and then recovered in the next.[5] (The inverse relationship between the net cash flows and the ICC is illustrated in Figure 13.1.) In this case, the net cash flow to the firm from the macro swap over the entire two-year period would be a positive $350,000.

As long as the firm's profits exhibit the expected cyclical behavior and the ICC proves to be an accurate gauge of general economic conditions, the swap illustrated above would offset most, if not all, of the firm's losses due to a weak economy and reduced sales. But, if the firm's profits instead decline far more sharply than the index, then the hedge would be only partly effective. And such a hedge would actually penalize the

---

[4] Determining how the coupon rate is established is beyond the scope of this article.
[5] The ICC values reported can be assumed to be the average values that prevailed during the three months spanned by each calendar quarter.

Figure 13.1: Net Cash Flows on ICC Swap

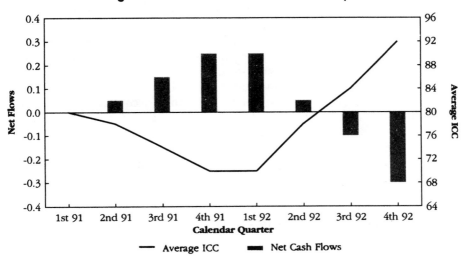

firm in the opposite set of circumstances—that is, if the index rose sharply instead of falling, and the firm's profits failed to increase as expected.

Thus, as this example illustrates, the effectiveness of a macro swap in reducing a firm's quantity risk depends ultimately on the degree of correlation between the swap's underlying macroeconomic variable and the firm's sales and profitability. Given a reasonably strong and predictable correlation, though, the macro swap should enhance the firm's profits in a soft market.

As with any swap or derivative security, the end user can enter into a macro swap to hedge during a period of expected market downturn or temporarily heightened market uncertainty. But it is also important to recognize that swap dealers will price general market expectations into the swap to make it a "fair game." That is, the expected payoff (net of the dealer's commission) to both parties, dealer and user, should be zero at the outset of the contract. For end users, this means that, at any given time, a macro swap will be priced to yield payoffs only to the extent the actual decline in the economy exceeds the decline *currently anticipated* by the consensus of market participants.

Macro Options

Macro options are similar in structure to interest rate caps and floors, except that the reference rate is defined as the macroeconomic variable of choice rather than an interest rate or rate index. Novel strategies for hedging quantity risk can also be created by combining different macro options or by combining macro options with macro swaps. For example, the sale of a macro floor and the purchase of a macro cap would produce a macro collar.

To consider a simple case, imagine a firm that wants to hedge against a possible decline in consumer confidence. The firm would purchase an *ICC floor*. Having purchased such an option, the firm would receive payments from the swap dealer during any period that the average ICC (reference rate) turns out to be below the option's contract rate (strike price). But when the ICC is equal to or above the contract rate, the dealer would pay nothing. This procedure would be repeated at each settlement period over the life of the option.

The payoff to the hedging firm in this case is given by the following equation:

$$\text{Dealer Pays} = \text{Maximum}\left[(CR-RR)/100,0\right] \times NP \times LPP.$$

where NP is the notional principal, LPP is the length of the payment period, CR is the contract rate (80 in this case), and RR is the reference rate, which is the average value of the ICC during the relevant calendar quarter. Table 13.2 shows the payoffs from this ICC floor under the same scenario as presented for the macro swap in Table 13.1 (except that the notional principal is assumed to be $5 million instead of $10 million).

The Cost of Hedging. As with all options, an ICC option would be purchased for an upfront fee or premium. But since the option provides, in effect, a macroeconomic insurance policy that extends over multiple periods, the proper way to interpret the cost of this multiperiod option is to amortize the premium over the number of periods covered by the option. This amortization procedure yields a per-period premium equiva-

Table 13.2: Hypothetical Cash Flows on an ICC-Based Floor

Calendar Quarter	Average ICC	Dealer Pays (million)
1st 1991	80.00	$0.000
2nd 1991	78.00	0.025
3rd 1991	74.00	0.075
4th 1991	70.00	0.125
1st 1992	70.00	0.125
2nd 1992	78.00	0.025
3rd 1992	84.00	0.000
4th 1992	92.00	0.000

Figure 13.2: Payoff Profile on ICC Floor (After Deduction of Amortized Premium)

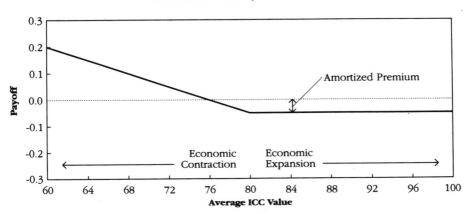

lent.[6] Using such an amortization procedure, the payoff profile for the ICC floor would be similar to that shown in Figure 13.2.

Using standard option valuation principles, the premium on the macro option will depend heavily, but not exclusively, on (1) the contract rate (or strike price), (2) the volatility of the ICC, (3) the value of the ICC at the time the option is written, and (4) the tenor, or maturity of the option. As in the case of macro swap coupons, the option premium will also reflect current trends in the ICC index or, more precisely, the consensus among market participants about the probability of that trend continuing.

Macro Collars Can Lower Costs. The option premium paid by the user for the ICC floor can be reduced by the sale of an ICC cap. That is, the firm could sell the option dealer an ICC cap, and the proceeds be used to offset at least part of the cost of the floor. This particular combination might best be described as an *ICC collar.* Moreover, the strike price of the cap can be chosen to generate a premium received exactly equal to the premium paid on the floor, thus producing a *zero-cost ICC collar.* The payoff profile for a zero-cost ICC collar is presented in Figure 13.3.

Hedging the Dealer's Book

As in all market-making activity, it is essential for the dealer to have a means of laying off its own risk from a given swap until a counterparty to that swap can be found. The futures markets are by far the preferred vehicle for swap dealers seeking such a transitional hedge for their swap books. While some macro futures have been attempted (for example, CPI

[6] For suggestions as to how this amortization might be carried out, see K. Kapner and J. Marshall, *The Swaps Handbook,* New York Institute of Finance, 1991, Chapter 6.

Figure 13.3: Payoff Profile on Short Macro Collar (Zero Cost Dollar)

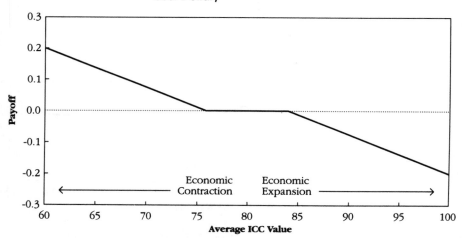

futures were once traded on the NYFE), none has ever been introduced in conjunction with a swap. The trading of swaps would add considerable liquidity to such a macro futures market.

Suppose, then, that we introduce a cash-settled ICC futures contract with settlement dates that correspond to the release of the monthly ICC value. With such a futures available, swap dealers would likely be readily willing to write ICC swaps. This suggests a logical next step in the evolution of the derivative securities markets—namely, a coordination of contract design efforts between futures exchanges and swap dealers. Indeed, evidence of such coordinated efforts already exists. For example, the FINEX introduced a cash-settled, five-year Treasury note futures contract for the expressed purpose of helping interest rate swap dealers hedge their swap books. The CBOT has introduced swap futures for the same purpose.

But, given the current absence of such macro futures, macro swap dealers would likely employ existing futures, or combinations of such futures, to "cross hedge" their swap risk until they could lay it off with an appropriate counterparty. In constructing such a cross hedge,[7] swap dealers

---

[7] Indeed, one of the present writers has demonstrated the potential for hedging the CPI with combinations of physical and financial futures contracts. See Anthony Herbst, "Hedging Against Price Index Inflation with Futures Contracts," *Journal of Futures Markets* (Winter 1985).

We should, however, point out two remaining difficulties associated with writing macro swaps and options. First, the observations on the "cash value" of the underlying index on a macro swap are discontinuous. That is, observations are made at discrete intervals. Second, the discontinuous observations on most macroeconomic indexes are themselves subject to revisions. Although we believe that these difficulties are surmountable, we make no effort to offer solutions here except to say that macro futures prices may serve as a good proxy for cash values.

(or, more likely, their financial advisers) would employ a technique known as "factor analysis" to determine if there exists some combination of futures that would produce payoffs highly correlated with the macroeconomic index employed in the swap.[8] Having identified such a combination, swap dealers could then hedge their books with sufficient confidence to sustain a reasonably liquid market in macro swaps and options.

Conclusions

Macro swaps and options are derivative securities now under development that have the potential to hedge corporate quantity or macroeconomic risk. They do so by linking the payoff to changes in a specific macroeconomic variable or index—for example, growth rates in GNP or changes in consumer confidence indices.

Macro swaps and options would allow companies exhibiting cyclical (or countercyclical) sales to exchange a series of fixed payments (or an upfront option premium) for a series of "floating" payments tied to a key macroeconomic variable. Provided the correlation between the chosen macro variable and the firm's operating cash flows were reasonably high and predictable, such companies could hedge their quantity risk over the life of the swap or option.

We hope that our analysis motivates continued research into the role of macro swaps in quantity risk management, and into the creation and uses of new swap forms. As just one possibility, a swap written on a comprehensive weather index might prove popular for farmers and citrus producers seeking to hedge their quantity risk.

---

[8] Unfortunately, the precise combination of futures is not identified by the factor analysis itself. However, by employing factor rotation or, alternatively, a series of multiple regressions, the proper combination can be identified.

EQUITY DERIVATIVES FOR INVESTORS

Tanya Styblo Beder

14

I. Overview

Opportunities abound for investors to use derivatives in the 1990s. Derivative markets, largely driven by the borrower's fixed income needs in the 1980s, have expanded to include equity markets around the world. And in many cases, it is the *investor's* needs that are driving the structure of the transactions. Rounding out interest rate-related, currency-related and commodity-related derivatives are an estimated two hundred billion in equity-related derivatives (1). As with their predecessors, equity derivatives offer both longer maturities as well as customized structures which are not available in exchange-traded products. A full line of equity derivatives is available:

- Options and warrants on one or more equity **indices;**
- Forwards and futures on one or more equity **indices;**
- Equity **index** swaps;
- Interest rate (fixed or floating) versus equity **index** swaps;
- Synthetic equity **index** linked investments;
- All of the above, linked to one or more **specific** domestic or foreign equities; and,
- Hybrid transactions.

For those who already invest in equities, custom-tailored and previously unavailable yield-enhancement and/or hedging vehicles are offered via equity derivatives. Investors may create customized strike levels, maturities or amounts, and may even design an index crossing multiple stock markets to suit specific needs. In addition, existing investors can transform the return on an underlying investment, say in Stock A, to a return based on Stock B, without selling Stock A and buying Stock B. The results are potent: a fund manager can retain ownership, and therefore down-side risk, in a core credit holding while participating in the upside of a riskier domestic or foreign stock. Variations on the theme are seemingly endless, with fund managers able to pick and choose between differing degrees of downside protection versus upside participation.

New equity investors (or those who wish to increase their equity ex-posure) benefit as well. Derivatives can provide a vehicle to obtain equity-linked returns without making or managing investments in *any* stocks. In this structure, the investor maintains a fixed income holding (and there-fore its downside risk) while participating in the upside of a foreign or do-mestic stock, or group of stocks, or stock index. For example, a fund man-ager may own Treasury bills or other AAA investments, while creating international exposure to the German and Japanese stock markets. Again, the degree of tradeoff between downside protection of the fixed income return versus upside participation in the stock(s) is up to the investor.

For restricted investors (many pension funds), equity derivatives can offer access to foreign markets and exchanges yet to be approved by regu-latory bodies. Derivatives may also help fund managers to side-step certain foreign basket limitations or overly restrictive investment policies. Syn-thetic short positions may be created, for example, to lock in portfolio gains and/or to protect against future portfolio losses. This can be partic-ularly attractive to fund managers who have significant unrealized gains and fear that the market is overvalued, thereby putting gains at risk prior to the end of the valuation period. If desired, fund managers may choose to protect such gains via a "zero cost collar" whereby upside beyond an agreed level is exchanged for downside protection at no cost.

In summary, equity derivatives "complete" capital markets by en-abling investors to:

- Fill-in gaps between and beyond alternatives offered by exchange-traded equity futures and options;
- Participate in the returns of foreign or domestic stock markets without purchasing any equities;
- Participate in the returns of foreign stock markets without cur-rency exchange risk;
- Diversify into foreign stock markets without taxation and/or regu-latory risk;
- Benefit in the upside of domestic or foreign equity markets while being protected from stock market declines;
- Achieve guaranteed outperformance of a given equity index;
- Remove commissions and/or management expenses associated with trading the underlying portfolio;

- Eliminate tracking error for index-measured portfolios;
- Create otherwise unavailable domestic and foreign equity-linked investments; and
- Obtain higher-yielding domestic and foreign equity-linked investments.

Participants include domestic and foreign banks, insurance companies, money managers, pension funds, corporations, sovereigns, and others.

II. Evolution of Equity Derivatives

The first domestic, exchange-traded equity options were introduced on 16 *specific* stocks in 1973 (Chicago Board Options Exchange). Equity *index* futures followed a decade later, with the introduction of the Value Line Index futures contract (February, 1982 on the Kansas City Board of Trade), the Standard & Poor's 500 futures contract (January, 1983 on the Chicago Mercantile Exchange) and the Standard & Poor's 100 futures contract (March, 1983 on the Chicago Mercantile Exchange). Today, a combination of equity index futures, equity index options and options on

Table 14.1

Major Stock Index Markets

Country	Stock Index	Futures	Options	Options on Futures
Australia	Ordinaries 250	✓		✓
Canada	Toronto-35/300	✓	✓	
Denmark	KFX 25, All-Share	✓	✓	
Finland	FOX 25	✓	✓	✓
France	CAC-40/240	✓	✓	
Germany	DAX 30; FAZ 100	✓	✓	
Hong Kong	Hang Seng (33)	✓		
Japan	Nikkei 225, Topix 1222	✓	✓	✓
Netherlands	EOE 25; OP-5		✓	
N.Zealand	Barclay 40	✓		
S. Africa	ALSI 138; INDI	✓	✓	
Spain	MSE-70; IBEX 35	✓	✓	
Sweden	SBC-all; OMX 30; SPI	✓	✓	
Switzerland	SMI 24; SBC-all	✓	✓	
U.K.	FTSE; FT-30/500	✓	✓	
U.S.	S&P 500, Midcap 400, NYSE 1750;Value Line 1600	✓✓	✓✓	✓✓

Source: Exchanges of Sydney, Toronto, Copenhagen, Helsinki,   Paris, Frankfurt, Hong Kong, Tokyo, Amsterdam, Aukland, Madrid, Stockholm, Zurich,   London, Chicago, New York.

equity index futures are available on the world's major stock exchanges (see Table 14.1).

In addition, emerging markets seem to be creating a stock index at the outset, with futures and/or options contracts on the indices following in due course. Also playing a role in the equity index market are several multicountry indices launched in the past few years. As shown in Table 14.2, although equity indices provide the basis for many equity derivatives, others are linked to particular stocks or groups of stocks rather than to specific, exchange-traded indices.

The evolution of equity derivatives is tied closely to investors' interest in foreign equities. Over the past decade, investors increasingly looked to foreign equity markets to diversify their risk and obtain otherwise unavailable investment opportunities. As demonstrated in Figure 14.1, many foreign equity markets posted significantly superior returns to the U.S. equity markets during the 1985 to 1991 period.

During the same period, U.S. investors placed an increasing amount of funds in foreign stocks. According to the U.S Treasury Bulletin, purchases of foreign stocks by U.S. investors increased eight-fold from 1985 to 1991 (see Figure 14.2).

Recently, the interest in foreign stocks has continued as investors focus on the apparent undervaluation of European equities relative to the

Table 14.2

Other Stock Indices

Country	Stock Index	Comment
Austria	WBK, ATX	Futures/options started 3/92
Belgium	BEL-20	Futures/options to start late 92
Italy	COMIT, MIB-all FT-A 77	Individual stock options only
Norway	OBX 50	Options only
Multi-Country	Euro-FTSE (Eurotrack) European Index FTA World Europe	} Typically largest stocks of several countries traded on the host exchange
Germany	GEMx 30	Traded in London
Sweden	OMx 30	Traded in London
Japan	TOPIX, Nikkei	Traded in Chicago

Source: Exchanges of Vienna, Brussels, Milan, Oslo, London, New York, Chicago.

Figure 14.1

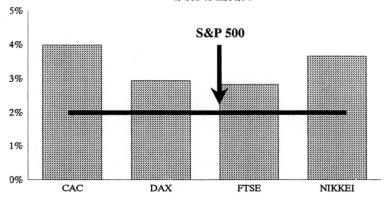

Foreign Equity Markets
Outperformance*vs. S&P 500
1/4/85 to 12/31/91

* Indices normalized in US dollars
Sources: Financial Times, The Wall Street   Journal.

U.S. and Japanese markets. Figure 14.3 demonstrates that on both a price-to-earnings basis as well as on a price-to-cashflow basis, European stocks appear attractive to investors.

Investment in foreign markets, however, is tempered for many by a host of considerations and potential problems:

- Currency and exchange rate risk
- Differing accounting practices
- Differing regulatory environments
- Differing taxation for profits and losses
- Differing liquidity and trading practices
- Potential withholding and/or stamp tax
- Potential custodial fees and higher transactions costs

Although equity derivatives manage many of the risks of foreign markets, this was not enough to launch the equity derivatives market. Playing a significant role were the market crashes in 1987 and the high volatility expe-

Figure 14.2

U.S. Foreign Stock Purchases Rise
Period: 1985-1991*

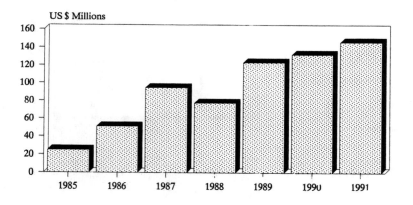

* 1991 represents the first three quarters annualized.

rienced during the Iraqi invasion of Kuwait, which encouraged investors to focus on ways to alter the equity portfolio risk/reward relationship. This focus, combined with investor fear over deteriorating credit quality and increased regulatory attention on the activities of financial institutions, resulted in a decreased pool of funds available to borrowers. Finding a way to increase this pool of funds led financial engineers to design products that satisfied the revised risk/reward demands of institutional investors. This provided the impetus for the international equity-derivatives market to take hold.

III. Common Equity Derivatives

As discussed in the introduction, there are many types of equity derivatives. The majority fall into three categories:

- Customized equity options or futures;
- Equity-related swaps; and
- Equity-linked fixed income instruments.

Figure 14.3

Price Lure of European Stocks*

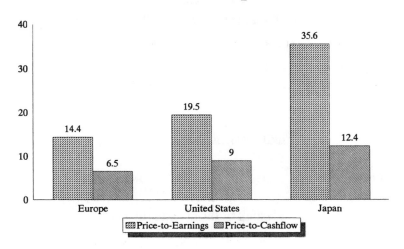

*Figures as of December, 1991.
Source: Euromoney, MSCI.

To create these, financial engineers have duplicated structures found in more established derivatives markets and have designed new structures as well. A partial listing of some of the more common equity derivatives in the market may be found in Table 14.3.

Each type of equity derivative can be designed to suit the particular needs of an investor or portfolio.

IV. Customized Equity Options and Futures

These private market (over-the-counter) equity derivatives, augment the spectrum from exchange-traded options and futures. Typically, one or more features vary from those offered by the exchanges:

- The underlying equity, basket of equities, or customized equity index may not be available in exchange-traded futures or options contracts;

- The maturity of the customized contract may be significantly longer, or fall between dates offered, by exchange-traded futures or options contracts;

Table 14.3

Common Equity Derivatives

Customized Equity Options & Futures

Long-dated forwards & options   Upside forwards
Knock-out options   All-or-nothing options
Knock-in options   Lookback options
Outperformance options   Multi-feature options
Difference options   Collars/Reverse collars
Hi-Lo options   Zero cost collars

Equity-related Swaps

Fixed equity swap   Index plus swap
Floating equity swap   Index percentage swap
Two-way equity swap   Optional equity swap

Equity-linked Fixed Income Instruments

Equity participation notes (EPNs)
Equity-linked income notes   Synthetic convertible bonds
Market index notes   "You-choose" EPN
Protected-equity notes (PENs)   Equity embeddos
                                     Index plus notes

- The size may be large, or may not be able to be created as a multiple of the standard, round-lot sizes offered by exchange-traded futures or options contracts;
- The transaction may be struck outside of the hours that exchange-traded futures or options contracts may be executed;
- Credit support and margin, if any, may be customized. Alternately, documentation may be tailored to suit each party's needs. Note that such transactions may involve futures or options contracts otherwise identical to those traded on exchanges;
- The currency of denomination may vary from exchange-traded futures or options, or may differ from the currency of denomination for the underlying equity, basket of equities, or equity index; and
- Strike levels for options may vary from those available in exchange-traded contracts, or may have unique trigger features.

Specialty Equity Options

Standard options provide the holder with the right, but not obligation, to buy or sell a stated amount of stock, group of stocks or stock index at a fixed price for a fixed period of time. Such options may be exercisable at any time until maturity (American style), on multiple dates prior to maturity (modified American style) or only at maturity (European style). *Specialty* options differ from standard options in that one or more of the option's features is calculated or triggered in a unique fashion. There are many popular specialty equity options:

- **Knock-out options** provide for the purchase or sale of a stock, group of stocks or stock index at a fixed price but *expire if the price moves beyond a stated level* (the knock-out level) over the life of the option.

- **Knock-in options** provide for the purchase or sale of a stock, group of stocks or stock index at a fixed price but *do not commence until the price moves beyond a stated level* (the knock-in level) over the life of the option.

- **Lookback options** provide for the purchase or sale of a stock, group of stocks or stock index *at the best price/strike achieved over the life of the option.* For example, at the option's maturity the owner of a lookback call on IBM stock has the right to buy IBM stock at the lowest price that occurred during the life of the option.

- **Outperformance options** provide for the purchase or sale of *the best performing of two* stocks, groups of stock, or stock indices over the life of the option.

- **Difference options** provide for the purchase or sale of *the difference between the prices of two* stocks, groups of stock, or stock indices relative to a fixed spread for a fixed period of time.

- **Hi-Lo options** provide for the purchase or sale of *the difference between the high and low price* of a stock, group of stock, or stock index relative to a fixed spread for a fixed period of time.

- **All-or-Nothing options** provide for payment of a fixed amount for a fixed period of time, only if the purchase or sale price of a stock, group of stocks or stock index is *at or beyond a stated level* over the life of the option.

A knock-out call option on the S&P 500, and sample outcomes, are illustrated in Table 14.4 and Figure 14.4.

In the event that the knock-out option is triggered, the payout would be similar to that of a plain vanilla call option on the S&P 500, with the exception that the knock-out call option premium is typically lower than the premium for a standard call option with otherwise identical features.

Specialty options may have maturities up to 10 years, although most transactions mature within three years. Common equity indices are the S&P 500, the Nikkei 225, the DAX, the CAC 40, the FTSE 100, the SMI,

Table 14.4

Knock-out Option
Terms

Type:	Call Option on S&P 500
Maturity:	2 Years
Strike:	S&P 500 at 375
Knock-out:	S&P 500 at 350

Results

PATH 1: Triggered; S&P does not fall below knock-out.

PATH 2: Not Triggered; S&P falls below knock-out level but matures above strike at maturity.

PATH 3: Triggered; S&P does not fall below knock-out level and rises above strike at maturity.

PATH 4: Not Triggered; S&P falls below knock-out level

and individual country indices. Specialty options may be executed in the currency of the investor's choice; for example, S&P index options may be denominated in German marks, Swiss francs, Japanese yen, and so on.

Equity Collars

Equity collars are similar to interest rate collars. In essence, an equity collar bands the return on an individual stock, portfolio, or index between a minimum and a maximum rate. The minimum return (or downside floor) as well as the maximum return (or upside cap) may be tailored to suit the needs of the investor. The most common form of collar for investors consists of two components: (i) the purchase of a put option customized to match the target portfolio; and (ii) the sale of a call option in the same amount, and for the same maturity, on the target portfolio. The strike level for the put is such that erosion of the target portfolio is prevented beyond the desired point. The strike level for the call may vary, and is selected to suit the goals and market outlook of the investor.

In many cases, the strike level for the call is selected such that the premium received for the sale of the call exactly offsets the premium paid for the put. In this case, the collar is termed a *zero-cost collar*. A U.S. dollar-denominated, zero-cost collar based on the S&P 500 stock index is illustrated in Table 14.5 and Figure 14.5.

Figure 14.4

Knock-out Option
S&P 500

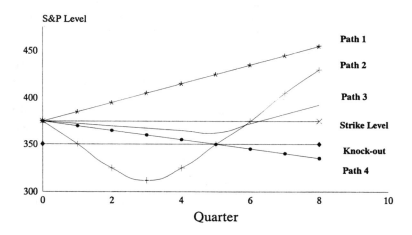

Equity collars may be executed for maturities similar to interest rate collars, with most maturing in less than five years. Common stock indices are the S&P 500, the Nikkei 225, the DAX, the CAC 40, the FTSE 100, the SMI, and specialized country indices. In addition, investors may select combinations of stock indices, an individual stock, or a customized basket of stock. Equity collars may be further tailored to the needs of the investor; for example, the call option may expire prior to the maturity of the put option. Such a strategy allows greater upside potential for investors who are neutral to bearish in the short run but bullish over the longer period. Alternately, equity collars may be constructed with specialty options such as knock-out puts, to achieve custom risk/reward payoffs.

Pension fund managers are frequent users of collars. One common application is the use of a zero cost collar to lock in the surplus subsequent to a stock market rally in a pension fund portfolio. Another common application is to lock in portfolio profits, or to prevent potential losses, prior to the end of a valuation period.

Customized Futures

Customized equity futures are generally one or two basic types:

- Standard, long-term, over-the-counter equity futures contracts; or
- Upside equity forwards.

Standard OTC futures contracts are agreements to buy or sell a specific stock, group of stocks or stock index at a fixed price for a specific time. Settlement may be by physical delivery, or if delivery is difficult or impossible, by cash payment. OTC futures may have maturities up to ten years, although most transactions mature within five years. Common equity indices are the S&P 500, the Nikkei 225, the DAX, the CAC 40, the FTSE 100, the SMI, and individual country indices. OTC futures may be executed in the currency of the investor's choice; for example, IBM futures may be denominated in German marks, Swiss francs, Japanese yen, and so on.

Upside equity forwards are a futures hybrid with an optional twist. The upside equity forward states (i) a minimum price for the stock, group of stocks or stock index; and (ii) a participation rate (typically less than 100 percent) for any price appreciation for the stock, group of stocks or stock index. The investor is thus able to hedge the downside risk of the target stock or portfolio, while maintaining some upside appreciation. In many cases, the participation rate is selected at a rate less than 100 percent such that no hedging fee is required for the downside protection.

Table 14.5

Zero-Cost Collar

Terms

Index:	S&P 500
Maturity:	Two Years
Minimum:	S&P 500 at 380
Maximum:	S&P 500 at 440
Starting Level:	S&P 500 at 350
Notional Amount:	$100 Million

Figure 14.5

Zero Cost Collar
S&P 500

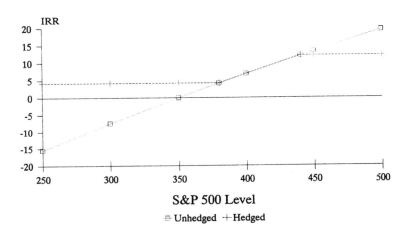

S&P 500 Level
⊟ Unhedged ＋Hedged

To illustrate an upside equity forward, assume a portfolio manager wishes to retain upside exposure to the Japanese stock market while ensuring a maximum downside loss of 10 percent. Further assume that the portfolio manager does not wish to incur upfront hedging costs. A zero-cost, one-year upside forward on the Nikkei 225 is executed, which protects the portfolio beyond 10 percent erosion and provides 80 percent of any appreciation in the index. The result is compared in Figure 14.6, which compares the IRR to that of a standard one-year forward. For illustrative purposes, it is assumed that the portfolio manager had a 3 percent gain in the portfolio at the time of execution.

V. Equity-Related Swaps

Equity-related swaps are similar in structure to standard interest rate swaps. Four basic varieties are available:

- Fixed equity swaps;
- Floating equity swaps;
- Two-way equity swaps; and
- Equity swaps with optional features.

Figure 14.6

Forward and Upside Forward
Nikkei 225

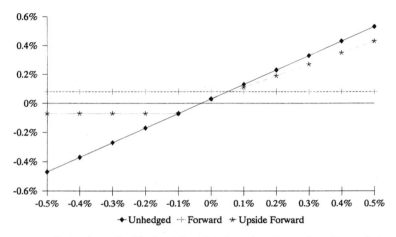

-●- Unhedged -+- Forward -*- Upside Forward

Assumes investor has 3% gain on index at time of execution.   One year forward investor is at spot
Nikkei 225 plus 5%. One year upside forward protects below   10% loss and gives 80% upside.

Fixed Equity Swaps

In a fixed equity swap, the investor owns or purchases a fixed rate security. Under the terms of the swap, a fixed rate payment is exchanged
for the dividend flows plus appreciation/depreciation of the desired equity index. The swap is based on an agreed notional principal amount. A
fixed swap involving the Standard & Poor's 500 equity index and denominated in U.S. dollars is illustrated in Figure 14.7.

The fixed equity swap offers key advantages to money managers.
Depending on market conditions and the yield of the underlying fixed
rate asset, the investor is often able to achieve an all-in return of the given
index *plus* a spread. Such guaranteed outperformance may be superior to
the returns achieved by most passive and many active money managers on
an historical basis. In addition, the fixed equity asset swap removes traditional management expenses and/or the need to trade any equities during the life of the swap. From an asset-allocation perspective, this translates into the opportunity to transform exposure from the fixed income
market to the equity market without incurring the transactions costs normally affiliated with such a change-over.

Figure 14.7

Fixed Equity Swap

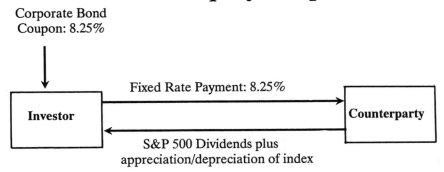

Corporate Bond
Coupon: 8.25%

Fixed Rate Payment: 8.25%

Investor

Counterparty

S&P 500 Dividends plus
appreciation/depreciation of index

- Investor's return is transformed from a fixed rate to a return based on the S&P 500.
- No direct investment in equity market.
- Index appreciation/depreciation may he paid periodically or at maturity.

The fixed equity swap may be executed for maturities similar to those in the interest rate and currency swap markets, although the most common transactions are under three years. Other stock indices commonly used are the Nikkei 225, the DAX, the CAC 40, the FTSE 100, and the SMI. In addition, fixed equity swaps may be transacted which involve a combination of stock indices. The specifics of the transaction may be further tailored to the needs of the investor; for example, the degree of principal and income protection of the fixed rate asset may be altered in exchange for a greater or lesser participation in the equity index. Substituting for the role of the index may also be an individual stock or group of stocks.

Floating Equity Swaps

A second version of the equity swap involves floating rate payments. As illustrated in Figure 14.8, this transaction involves the ownership or purchase of a floating rate money market instrument. As with the fixed equity swap, the investor passes on all or a portion of the yield in exchange for the dividends plus appreciation/depreciation of an index. To date, this has been the most common form of equity swap.

As with the fixed rate equity swap, any major stock index, individual stock, or group of stocks, may be selected. The transaction may also be

Figure 14.8

Floating Equity Swap

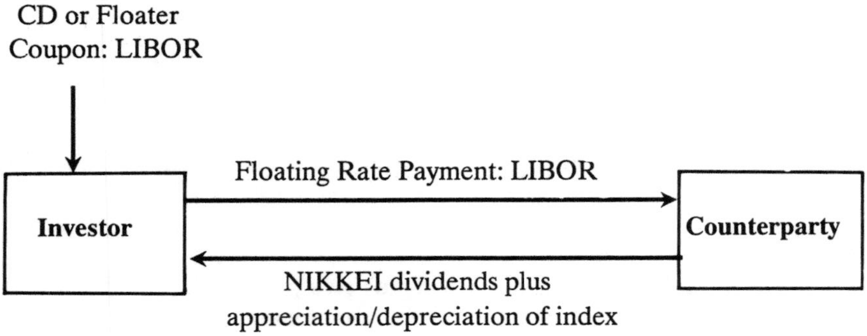

CD or Floater
Coupon: LIBOR

```
   │
   ▼
┌──────────┐   Floating Rate Payment: LIBOR   ┌──────────────┐
│          │ ───────────────────────────────▶ │              │
│ Investor │                                    │ Counterparty │
│          │ ◀───────────────────────────────  │              │
└──────────┘   NIKKEI dividends plus           └──────────────┘
               appreciation/depreciation of index
```

- Investor's return is transformed from a floating rate to a return based on the NIKKEI.

- Upside participation and degree of principal protection may be adjusted to reflect the market view of investor (bearish, moderate, bullish, etc.).

structured to accommodate investors who wish to roll over short-term investments such as Treasury bills or commercial paper. Note that investors may change their floating rate investments and floating rate index during the life of the swap via the interest rate swap market to avoid potential basis risk. In both the fixed and floating equity swaps, the investor effectively creates equity exposure without investing in the equity market(s) directly. An implicit advantage is that principal may be invested in the underlying asset to the swap at a less subordinated level than equity.

Two-Way Equity Swaps

In the two-way equity swap, neither swap payment is linked to a fixed or floating payment. Rather, each swap payment is linked to a stock, group of stocks, or stock index. Typically, one equity's appreciation (or *group* of equities' appreciation or equity *index's* appreciation) is exchanged for a second equity's appreciation. This structure can be particularly attractive to investors who wish to retain one or more specific equities in their portfolio to satisfy asset quality guidelines, base index component requirements, currency guidelines, and so on, but who wish to benefit from the potential appreciation in riskier or foreign stocks that they do not wish to hold, or are unable to hold, directly. A sample two-way equity swap is illustrated in Figure 14.9.

The **index plus asset swap** is the combination of a fixed (floating)

Figure 14.9

Two-way Equity Swap

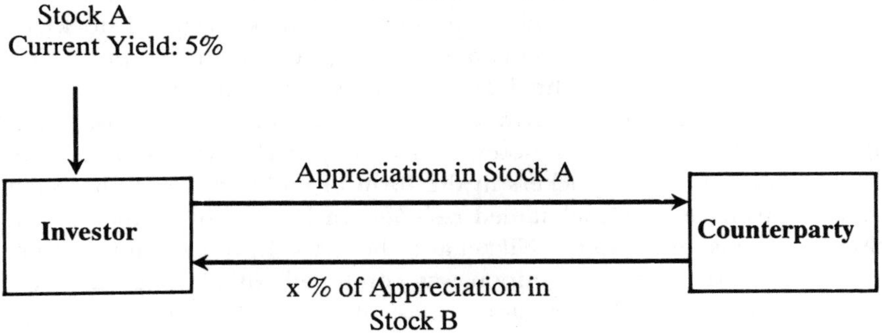

Stock A
Current Yield: 5%

- Investor retains core holding, including dividend yield (5%) on Stock A, but can take a position in a foreign, high-risk and/or growth Stock B.

- Investor exchanges any appreciation in Stock A for any appreciation in Stock B at maturity.

rate bond plus a fixed (floating) equity swap based upon a major stock market index. The bond and swap are customized to suit an investor's specific needs in terms of credit quality, size, maturity, currency, and so on. Typically, as the credit of the bond decreases, the all-in spread achieved over the index (e.g., S&P 500 *plus* 1 percent) increases. Markets such as the Medium Term Note (MTN) market, the Certificates of Deposit (CD) market, the Euro-MTN market, the Euro-CD market, and the Private Placement market are frequent providers of custom-tailored assets for index plus asset swaps.

Optional equity swaps are similar to optional interest rate swaps. For example, the swap may have a put or call feature such as that found in swaptions. Alternately, the swap may have an embedded cap or floor with respect to one or more of the swap payments.

The **index percentage swap** is a fixed, floating, or two-way equity swap in which one of the swap flows is calculated based upon a percentage of the performance of a stock market index. The percentage may be less than 100 percent or greater than 100 percent to provide a leveraged or deleveraged rate of equity return.

VI. Equity-Linked Fixed Income Investments

This class of equity derivative is, in essence, a combination of a principal-guaranteed bond with some type of equity kicker. It is often tailored to suit the exact needs of the investor, although several are pre-packaged transactions have been launched in the market. For example, an investor may select the currency, maturity, desired credit quality (i.e., issuer name) for the principal, the fixed income coupon (it may be a zero-coupon), and the desired equity exposure (to a stock, group of stocks, or index). The investor may then choose the degree of principal protection desired (downside) versus the degree of equity participation (upside).

A sizable number of private placements, domestic MTNs, Euro-MTNs, bonds, floating rate notes, and money-market instruments have been issued with equity kickers in the form of embedded options. Such transactions have been nicknamed *embeddos*. In 1991, many embeddos included options linked to the Nikkei and the DAX. In one common structure, a lower-than market coupon was combined with a long call on a stock or index from the investor's point of view. In a second common structure, a higher-than market coupon compensated the investor for writing a put on a stock or index.

To see how option-linked debt can be customized, assume a fund manager wishes to obtain upside exposure to the German stock market while retaining principal protection in U.S. dollars. Three of many possible versions of a DAX-linked zero-coupon bond are described in Table

Table 14.6

DAX-Linked Bond

Terms

Credit:	AA Financial Institution
Coupon:	Zero
Maturity:	Five Years
DAX Payout:	At maturity, the greater of (1) and (2) is paid:

(1) downside principal amount (dpa)

(2) $dpa\left[+ \dfrac{DAX(end) - DAX(beg)}{DAX(beg)} \times udp \times principal\right]$

	Bond 1	Bond 2	Bond 3
DOWNSIDE PRINCIPAL PROTECTION	100%	75%	125%
UPSIDE DAX PARTICIPATION (udp)	98%	110%	80%

14.6. Note that other structures are available which include a nominal fixed income coupon for the investor.

The investor's return varies according to the selection of downside principal protection and upside DAX participation. This tradeoff is demonstrated in Figure 14.10, which provides the IRR for each option plus the unhedged DAX return as a bench-mark.

In the case of bond #1, the investor retains 100 percent principal protection, and is able to benefit from almost all of any potential appreciation in the DAX (98 percent). In the case of bond #2, the investor retains only 75 percent principal protection, but gains a leveraged share of any potential appreciation in the DAX (110 percent). Such leveraged upside would be attractive to investors who have a bullish outlook. In the case of bond #3, the investor locks in a guaranteed return by protecting 120 percent of the principal invested, and benefits from a lesser portion of any potential appreciation in the DAX (80 percent). Such deleveraged upside would be attractive to investors who have a bearish outlook.

Common versions of such equity-linked fixed income assets are **"Equity Participation Notes," "Protected Index Notes," "Index Plus**

Figure 14.10

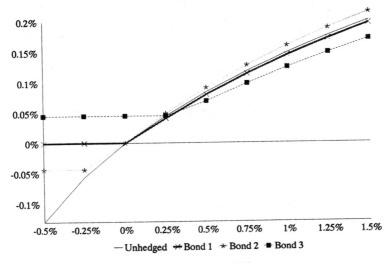

Comparison of Return

Note: Assumes constant DM/US $ exchange rate.

Notes," and **"Synthetic Convertible Bonds."** Each allows the investor to select the equity exposure (an individual stock, group of stocks or stock index), the maturity (up to 10 years), the degree of principal protection (downside protection), the dividend level (typically 0 percent to 10 percent), the degree of currency protection, and the degree of upside participation (this may be leveraged).

Also offered in the equity derivatives market is the **"You Choose"** version of such securities. In this version, the investor selects a list of individual stocks or stock indices which may be chosen over the life of the transaction. At any time (24 hours notice may be required), the investor may alter equity exposure to any desired weighting of the initial list. Thus the investor may transfer exposure completely from one market to another, or allot exposure in any possible combination.

VII. Conclusion

Equity-related derivatives have the potential to fundamentally alter the business of investment and funds management. Facing related potential metamorphosis is the way in which financial intermediaries profit from the investor's choice of markets both at the outset and at asset reallocation. Significant market changes hinge on the ultimate relationship between equity derivatives and their underlying instruments as well as on regulation both intra- and inter-market.

As most derivatives are traded off of the established exchanges, this is likely to impact the historical market predominance of the exchanges. The failed attempt to launch an interest rate swap futures contract despite the trillions of dollars outstanding in interest rate swap contracts, widely accepted ISDA (International Swap Dealers Association) standards, and near-commodity like pricing, illustrates the difficulty that the exchanges face in entering important aspects of the derivatives business. As derivatives grow in volume, their impact in the market grows relative to the volume of the underlying securities on exchanges. This may, in turn, influence the price movement of underlying securities in unexpected ways.

By crossing markets via derivatives—or combinations of derivatives—investors are likely to augment yield beyond direct market opportunities as well as beyond the more common derivative-driven opportunities. Utilizing over-the-counter and exchange-traded derivatives which are introduced to fill-in previous product and/or maturity gaps further enhances such opportunities.

Along with the numerous benefits offered to investors by equity derivatives, come new credit considerations and cross-border uncertainties. Although the credit risk in many transactions resembles that in interest rate and currency derivatives, the complex nature of transactions involving multiple currencies, optional structures, and foreign equity markets makes pricing opaque. In addition, it is difficult to forecast the maximum potential exposure between counterparties over the life of a transaction. As indirect access of foreign equity markets increases, regulators are likely to place increased focus on equity-related derivatives. In summary, the documentation, accounting, taxation, and regulatory status of equity derivatives has yet to evolve.

Footnote

The International Swap Dealers Association, the traditional source for volume in the derivatives market, does not include "equity-related derivatives" as a separate reporting category for members. Regulatory bodies do not require sufficiently detailed reporting to utilize as a source: for example, bank call reports need only disclose *combined* volume of equity and commodity derivatives. Furthermore, if such transactions are booked in off-shore entities, they are not included in the combined totals. *Global Finance Magazine* estimated equity derivatives market size between $100 billion and $200 billion in September, 1991. *Institutional Investor* estimated the size of the equity derivatives market at $125 billion in December, 1991. The $200 billion estimate is derived by adding up (i) worldwide equity option/warrant linked debt $150–175 billion [as reported by Euromoney (March, July 1991)], and (ii) the average of the estimates by three major derivatives dealers for customized equity options or futures and equity-related swaps (average = $30 billion).

YIELD CURVE APPLICATIONS OF SWAP PRODUCTS

**Rupert Brotherton-Ratcliffe
and Ben Iben**

15

Introduction

One area of recent focus in the swaps market is the development of yield curve applications of swaps. The intent has been to develop products which enhance the ability of asset/liability managers to alter their yield curve exposures. That is, to either increase the profit potential from a change in the spread between two yields or to lock in a current spread. Most of the attention to date has been focused on (a) spreads between short-term and long-term yields in the same currency, and (b) spreads between yields available in different currencies. As a result of these efforts, a number of products have been developed.

In this chapter we will analyze three products which include much of the innovation in yield curve applications of swaps: yield curve swaps, differential swaps, and interest rate difference options. The first product, yield curve swaps, involves the exchange of two series of floating rate cash flows in the same currency, one being based on a short-term rate index and the other on a longer-term rate index. The second product, differential swaps, also involves the exchange of two series of floating-rate cash flows; however, one of the floating rate indexes is generally dollar-based while the other is nondollar based. The innovative feature of differential swaps is that although one of the rate indexes is nondollar, all payments are made in dollars. The third product, interest rate difference options (difference options), is linked to the difference between two yields in the same currency or yields available in two different currencies.

We divide analysis of each product into three sections. First we describe the product structure. Second we illustrate specific applications of the structure. The descriptive analysis in the first two sections provides necessary background to the third section: production valuation. Here, we follow standard derivative product valuation methodology which consists of the dynamic replication of the derivative's cash flows with fundamental instruments. We use the principle that if a self-financing portfolio of instruments (possibly continually adjusted) yields the same cash flows as the derivative, then the derivative has the same value as this replicating portfolio. This is the same methodology that underlies option pricing theory, as expounded by Black and Scholes (1973).[1]

In general, replication of derivative products does require a dynamically adjusted portfolio, and as a result, derivative product values depend not only on initial market prices, but also on the distribution of future market prices. Since this distribution depends most crucially on the volatility of the market rates, we will use the term volatility to refer to the effect of any market rate variation. We shall see that in many applications, volatility has only a small effect on swap values and can be ignored. However, we show that in certain cases, ignoring volatility can result in significant biases in valuation.

Yield Curve Swaps

Yield Curve Swap Structures

In the basic yield curve swap two series of floating rate payments are exchanged. One series of payments is generally based on a short-term rate index (or reference rate) such as LIBOR while the other side is set against a longer-term index, such as a constant maturity treasury note (CMT) yield. The relevant details of a yield curve swap include the reference rates, reset frequencies, payment frequencies, rate bases, notional principal, and tenor. Figure 15.1 illustrates a typical yield curve swap. In this swap, counterparty A pays B U.S. dollar LIBOR semiannually and receives the yield on the 10-year CMT minus a spread of 50 basis points also semiannually. The notional principal of the swap is $100 MM.

In this hypothetical swap, counterparty A's net receipts (payments)

Figure 15.1 Basic Yield Curve Swap

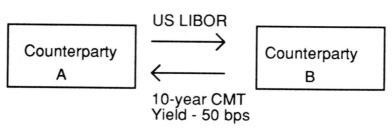

---

[1] Black, F. and M. J. Scholes, 1973, "The pricing of options and corporate liabilities," *Journal of Political Economy* 81.

1 line long

each period are determined by the difference between the 10-year CMT yield and six-month LIBOR on the rate set date. The exact payments are determined by the settlement formula. The general settlement formula for yield curve swaps is

$$CF = N^* (r + s)^* (d/b)$$ (1)

where

CF = cash flow (positive when receiving and negative when paying)
N = notional principal of trade
r = reference rate at rate set date
s = spread
d = number of days in interest rate period
b = rate basis

Using this formula and the example in Figure 15.1, and assuming that the 10-year CMT yield and 6-month LIBOR at the first rate set are 8 percent and 6 percent, respectively, then the net payment from A to B at the end of the first period is

$$\$100\,MM * 0.06 * (180/360) - \$100\,MM * (0.08 - 0.005)$$
$$* (180/360) = -\$750\,M.$$

Here, we are assuming the interest period has 180 days, and that interest is paid on an actual/360 basis.

There are several variants on this basic yield curve swap structure. One alternative is to swap floating payments based on a CMT yield for fixed payments, rather than LIBOR-based floating-rate payments. Another is to swap floating rate payments based on a swap rate for LIBOR-based payments.

Yield Curve Swap Applications

The swap in Figure 15.1 is an example of a typical yield curve swap and we can use this swap to illustrate several applications of the product. First, this swap could be used by counterparty A to lock in a spread between fixed rate assets and liabilities repriced off CMT yields. For example, if A were an insurance company that offers a variable rate annuity promising returns linked to the CMT yield, it could purchase a floating rate note and enter the swap in Figure 15.1. Counterparty A could use the income from the floating rate note to make the LIBOR payments on the swap and its CMT receipts would meet the requirements of the annuity. The yield curve swap could be tailored to enable the insurance company to base its annuity off any portion of the Treasury yield curve. It could also be structured to fit a wide range of annuity structures. For example, the swap could be structured so that A receives the total return of the CMT which would be useful in the event that the annuity payments were to be based off CMT returns, rather than CMT yields.

A second use of this swap is to position a portfolio to take advantage of anticipated changes in yield spreads. For example, when the spread between short-term and medium-term yields is unusually high, an investor may want to position his portfolio to take advantage of any flattening in the curve. Counterparty B could achieve this position with the swap in Figure 15.1. In this swap counterparty B pays the yield of the 10-year CMT and receives LIBOR, and would therefore gain if the CMT yield were initially higher than LIBOR, and the yield curve subsequently flattens.

If counterparty B is only interested in profiting from movements in the treasury yield curve, the swap could easily be structured so that it involves the exchange of the 10-year CMT yield for the 1-year CMT yield instead of LIBOR. Of course, this same position could be achieved with a long 10-year T Note position and a short 1-year T Bill position; however, both positions would be recorded on the investor's balance sheet whereas the swap is not.

A third important use of this yield curve swap is as a temporary hedge of (or an alternative to) a long-term swap position, one which generates a significantly lower credit risk than a long-term swap. A yield curve swap can be structured so that its tenor is very short relative to the maturity of one of the reference rates. This fact enables yield curve swaps to be used as temporary hedges of long-term swaps and is particularly useful for credit sensitive counterparties, since the short tenor of the yield curve swap greatly reduces its credit exposure.

Yield Curve Swap Valuation

As we described earlier, yield curve swaps generally involve the exchange of one series of floating rate payments indexed off LIBOR for another indexed offer a longer-term yield. A standard approach used to value floating payments is to construct a forward rate curve from observed market rates. This forward rate curve is then used to calculate the expected cash flows which are then discounted using a zero-coupon curve, again derived from market rates. In this section we will show that the convexity of the longer-term instruments such as CMTs is not incorporated by the standard forward rate method and that it can lead to the mispricing of yield curve swaps.

Let us consider one cash flow on the CMT side of our earlier yield curve swap example. Suppose that this cash flow is determined by the yield on 9/10/92 of the 8 percent coupon bond of 3/10/02. Suppose that the yield on the bond on 3/10/92 is 8.5 percent, and that the initial six-month rate is 6 percent. Then the forward yield on the bond, for delivery on 9/10/92, is 8.6824 percent. This forward yield is determined by the value of the following simple strategy which is equivalent to the forward purchase of the bond:

On 3/10/92: Buy the bond, $1000 face, at 96.719% (yielding 8.5%);
Borrow $967.19 for 6 months @ 6%

On 9/10/92: Pay back loan of $967.19* (1 + 0.06/2) = $996.21

Effectively, the bond will be purchased at a price of 99.621 percent on 9/10/92, which implies a yield of 8.6824 percent.

Since the bond can be purchased on 3/10/92 for delivery on 9/10/92 at a forward yield of 8.6824 percent, it seems reasonable to suppose that the yield-indexed cash flow can also be purchased at a yield of 8.6824 percent, so that this cash flow can be locked in at $86.824 per $1000 notional. (Here, we are neglecting the 50bp offset shown in Figure 15.1, which can be valued separately.) The present value of this flow is then $86.824/(1 + 0.06/2) = $84.295. It turns out that this valuation, based on the initial forward yield of the bond, is a very good approximation of its true value. However, it is not possible to lock in this cash flow using a static hedge with the bond, and consequently this valuation is not correct.

When we consider how we might hedge this single cash flow, we see why the valuation based solely on the forward yield of the bond is incorrect. We wish to determine the effect of volatility of the forward yield on the value of the cash flow, and we shall therefore assume, for now, that the short term lending/borrowing rate is constant (this assumption enables us to obtain a simple formula quantifying the effect of volatility and as we will see later this formula is a very good approximation of the true effect of volatility, incorporating a varying lending/borrowing rate, but which can only be measured numerically). Now, a long position in the cash flow will increase in value as the forward yield increases. Since an increase in the forward yield will decrease the value of the bond, a long position in the cash flow can be hedged by a long position in the bond. Suppose that the value of the cash flow were equal to the discounted forward yield (as assumed above). Its value as a function of the forward yield is plotted in Figure 15.2(a), along with the value of the bond, and its sensitivity to small changes in the forward yield is plotted in Figure 15.2(b) together with the sensitivity of the bond. The required long position in the bond is given by the ratio of the sensitivity of the cash flow to the sensitivity of the bond. In Figure 15.2(c) we plot the combined value of the cash flow and the bond, given the hedge ratio needed when the forward yield is 8 percent. We see that both positive and negative changes in the

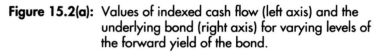

Figure 15.2(a): Values of indexed cash flow (left axis) and the underlying bond (right axis) for varying levels of the forward yield of the bond.

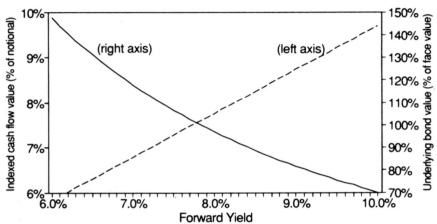

yield increase the value of this portfolio, which suggests that this hedging strategy will generate a riskless profit. It is also clear from the graph that larger movements in the yield (due to a greater yield volatility) will generate higher profits. We conclude that the value of the cash flow is greater than that implied solely by the initial forward yield, and that the greater the volatility of the forward yield the higher the value of the cash flow. We may also expect the value to increase as the time to the maturity of the cash flow increases. Also, as the convexity of the bond price increases, the value of the cash flow must increase.

By analyzing the shape of the graph in Figure 15.2(c) we can quantify the degree to which these factors affect the value of the cash flow. Let us introduce some notation. Suppose D is the discount factor to the cash flow date, and suppose the forward yield on the bond is f. If the forward price of the bond is given by the function $P(y)$ when its yield is y, then the hedge ratio used in Figure 15.2(c) is $-P(f)$ (where the prime denotes a differentiation with respect to the forward yield). The value of the portfolio is then

$$D\{y - P(y) / P'(f)\}. \tag{2}$$

We can approximate this value near $y = f$ by a Taylor expansion, using the fact that

$$P(y) = P(f) + (y - f)P'(f) + \frac{1}{2}(y - f)^2 P''(f) + \dots \tag{3}$$

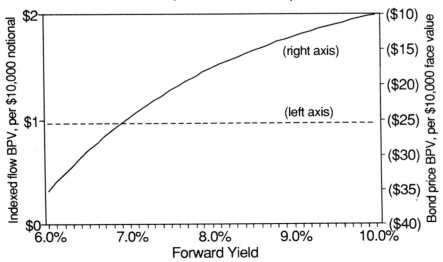

Figure 15.2(b): Sensitivities of the indexed cash flow (left axis) and the underlying bond (right axis) to a one basis point increase in the yield of the bond.

giving the value of the portfolio as

$$D\left\{f - P(f)/P'(f) - \frac{1}{2}(y-f)^2 P''(f)/P'(f)\right\} \tag{4}$$

approximately. The long position in the bond can be funded by borrowing at the short rate. Including the funding in the portfolio then gives a total portfolio value of

$$D\left\{f - \frac{1}{2}(y-f)^2 P''(f)/P'(f)\right\} \tag{5}$$

If we now make the common assumption that the yield is lognormally distributed, with an annualized volatility σ, then on an expected value basis, we get

$$(y-f)^2 \approx f^2\sigma^2 T \tag{6}$$

over a time interval T. (Strictly speaking, this formula for $(y-f)^2$ is correct only for infinitesimally short time intervals.) Using this, we find that the value of the cash flow alone must be

$$D\left\{f - \frac{1}{2}\sigma^2 T f^2 P''(f)/P'(f)\right\} \tag{7}$$

A precise valuation is complex, and depends on further terms in the expansion of $P(y)$ as well as on changes in the discount rate (which we have assumed is constant). An arbitrage-free valuation approach, such as the Black-Derman-Toy model of interest rates (Black et al., 1990),[2] can be used, but this alternative generally requires a numerical solution. In practice, however, a bond's convexity is so small that its contribution to the value of the indexed cash flow is often small relative to the value due solely to the forward yield, and the above analytic approximation to the value of an indexed cash flow is very close to its true value. In Figure 15.3 we give a comparison of the Black-Derman-Toy model valuation of yield curve swaps (for which no analytic solution is available) with valuation based on the above analytic approximation. We consider floating-floating yield curve swaps, with one side indexed to LIBOR, the other indexed to the 10-year swap rate, and compute the required offset to the LIBOR side so that the swap has a zero net present value. For the purposes of comparison, we suppose that the yield curve is initially flat at 8 percent, and the Black-Derman-Toy model is constructed so that the initial term structure of volatility is flat at 10 percent. In this case, the required offset is due entirely to the interaction of the volatility of interest rates with the convexity

Figure 15.2(c): Value of portfolio of indexed cash flow hedged with the underlying bond. The hedge ratio corresponds to an initial forward bond yield of 8 percent.

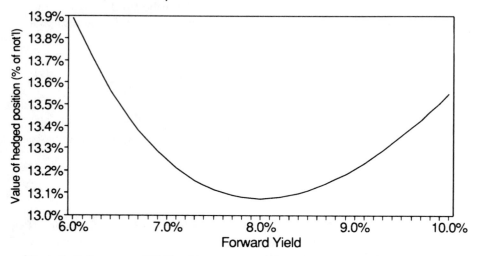

[2]Black, F., E. Derman and W. Toy, "A one-factor model of interest rates and its application to Treasury bond options," Financial Analysts Journal, Jan-Feb 1990.

Figure 15.3: Required offset to LIBOR for zero NPV yield curve swaps indexed to 10-year swap rate. *–Black Derman Toy; + Approx based on eq. (7). Initially flat yield curve (8%) and volatility structure (10%).

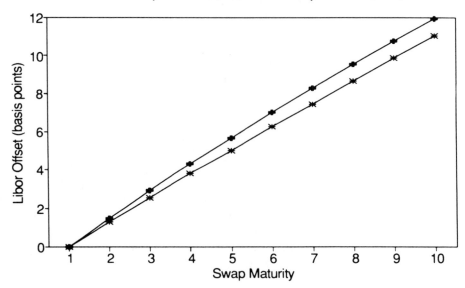

of the price/yield relationship of the 10-year swap, since the initial yield curve is flat. LIBOR offsets are graphed for swap maturities up to 10 years. Note that the required offsets are all very low, the largest being only 12 basis points.

It is interesting to note that the above analytic approximation provides yield curve swap values are very close to those obtained by the more complicated arbitrage-free yield curve model. This strongly suggests that yield curve values are determined primarily by the forward rate curve and the convexity of the price/yield relationship, and that other features of the arbitrage-free yield curve model play a much less important role in valuation. In particular, in the Black-Derman-Toy model, future cash flows are discounted at a stochastic interest rate (whereas, in our approximation, future cash flows are discounted at initial zero coupon rates), but this does not seem to have a significant impact on the value of these yield curve swaps. It is reasonable to conclude, therefore, that a more complicated valuation methodology (such as a two-factor model for interest rates) would be superfluous. This is a significant conclusion, since, as a practical matter, it is important that a valuation procedure for any derivative product is as simple as possible to both understand and use, while at the same time being sufficiently rich in structure that it captures the dynamics of those variables that most affect its value.

Differential Swaps

Differential Swap Structures

Differential swaps involve the exchange of two series of floating payments, both of which are denominated in the same currency. However, the index rates are LIBOR rates in two different currencies. No principal payments are exchanged. Figure 15.4 displays the structure of a typical differential swap in which one series of payments is based on U.S. dollar LIBOR and the other is based on DM LIBOR. All payments are made in dollars and are based on a notional principal of $50 million. As we will show later, there is often a spread associated with differential swaps to compensate for the fact the level of rates in the two currencies are different. In this hypothetical swap we assume that the interest payments are exchanged semiannually and that DM interest rates are higher than U.S. interest rates. Consequently, there is a spread of 100 bps on the U.S. LIBOR side of the swap. That is, at the end of each six-month period counterparty A pays B based on the level of six-month U.S. LIBOR at the beginning of the period plus 100 bps, and B pays A based on the level of six-month DM LIBOR at that time. The calculation of the actual spread on a differential swap is discussed in the section on valuation.

Formula (1) is also appropriate for determining settlement payments on differential swaps. Using the example in Figure 15.4 and assuming that 6-month U.S. and DM LIBOR were 6 percent and 8 percent, respectively, at the start of the first period of this hypothetical swap, then the first payment from B to A would be

$$\$50\,MM * 0.08 * (180/360) - \$50\,MM * (0.06 + 0.01) * (180/360) = \$250\,M$$

Here, it is assumed that the period has 180 days, and that both rates are paid on an actual/360 basis.

A variant on this basic structure is the ratio differential swap. A ratio differential swap involves the exchange of two series of floating rates;

Figure 15.4: Basic Differential Swap

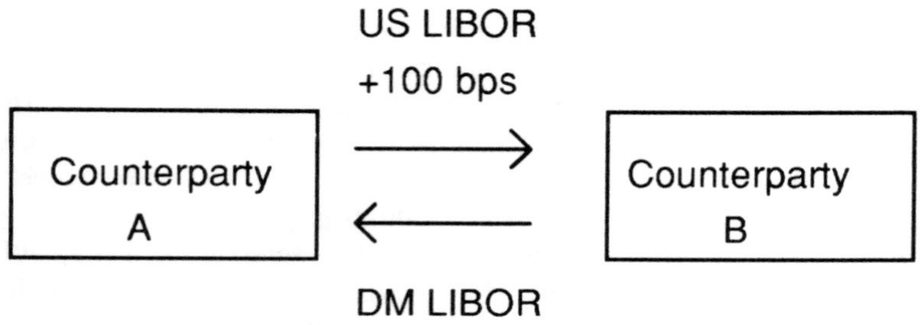

US LIBOR

+100 bps

DM LIBOR

Figure 15.5: Ratio Differential Swap

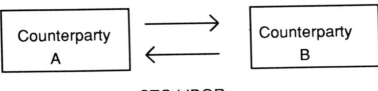

2.2 x USD LIBOR

STG LIBOR

however, the payments are determined based on the ratio of two rates as opposed to the absolute spread. Figure 15.5 displays a typical ratio differential swap. The counterparties in this swap exchange 2.2 × six-month USD LIBOR for six-month STG LIBOR. The ratio here is used to compensate for the fact that STG LIBOR is much higher than USD LIBOR. All flows in this swap are in USD.

With slight modification we can use formula (1) to calculate the payments on ratio differential swaps. We can illustrate this with our example in Figure 15.5. Suppose that the notional principal of this swap is $100 million and that on the first rate set date USD LIBOR is 5.25 percent and STG LIBOR is 11 percent, then A's net payment to B is:

$$\$100\,MM*2.2*(0.0525)*(180/360) - \$100\,MM*(0.11)*(180/360)$$
$$= \$275,000$$

Differential Swap Applications

As the examples above show, the cash flows of a differential swap are determined by either the spread between or the ratio of interest rates in two different currencies, but the payments are denominated in a single currency. Thus, differential swaps provide a mechanism for achieving a payoff based on the differential of yields available in two different currencies which is not directly affected by movements in exchange rates. This is the major use of differential swaps which we will illustrate with the examples in Figure 15.4 and 15.5.

The basic differential swap in Figure 15.4, which provides payoffs linked to nondollar LIBOR that are not directly affected by exchange rate movements, would be useful to U.S.-based investors interested in earning a return based on nondollar LIBOR without taking on any foreign exchange (FX) exposure. For example, counterparty A could buy a $50MM U.S. LIBOR-based floating rate note and enter into the differential swap in Figure 15.1 in order to achieve returns based on DM LIBOR without direct FX risk.

One potential drawback of this strategy from the perspective of an investor is that it may be mandatory to recognize differential swap income on a market-to-market basis while note income is recognized on an accrual basis. The investor can get around this problem (with the assistance of a swap intermediary) by investing in a product called a cross-rate note. The principal and variable interest rate on a cross-rate note are dollar denominated; however, the interest rate on the note is set against a nondollar floating rate index, such as DM LIBOR. For example, a borrower could issue a 10-year cross-rate none with $50 million principal, but the semiannual interest is paid based on six-month DM LIBOR. The investor who purchases the notes is able to earn DM yields without taking FX risk. However, the note issuer may actually wish to make payments based on U.S. LIBOR rather than DM LIBOR. This can be achieved through the use of a differential swap. Figure 15.6 shows an example of a synthetic U.S. LIBOR floating rate note created by combining a cross-rate note with a differential swap.

As Figure 15.6 indicates, the issuer is left with a floating USD LIBOR debt and the investor obtains dollar denominated DM LIBOR-based returns that can be recorded on an accrual basis. Although the investor is not directly involved in the differential swap, the swap is key to the creation of the cross-rate note. In the above example, the borrower ends up with funding at LIBOR flat since we assume that the cross-rate note and the swap have the same spreads. In practice this is not always true and the borrower will generally enter into the synthetic floating rate note only when his funding rate is lower than it would be on a straight USD floating rate note.

The ratio differential swap has basically the same applications as differential swaps; however, it introduces the element of leverage. In short, by adjusting the ratios of a differential swap the counterparties can obtain any desired leverage. The swap in Figure 15.5 contains a leverage factor of 2.2 on USD LIBOR. Therefore, counterparty B will gain 2.2 bps for each basis point USD LIBOR increases relative to STG LIBOR. This position would be interesting to an investor who believes USD LIBOR will increase

Figure 15.6: Interest Rate Flows on Synthetic Floating Dollar LIBOR Note

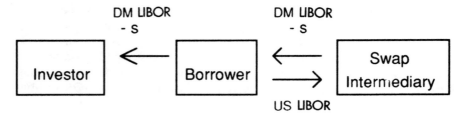

Figure 15.7: 6-Month LIBOR Yield Spread STG LIBOR-USD LIBOR (1980–1992)

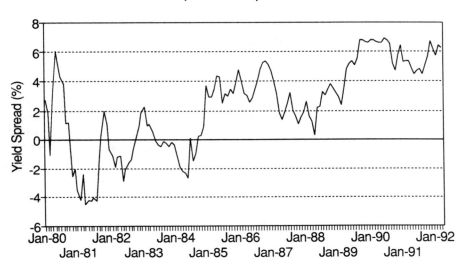

relative to STG LIBOR. Figure 15.7 displays six-month USD and STG LIBOR from January 1980 to April 1992. As this graph indicates, in April 1992, the spread between STG and USD LIBOR was very high relative to the historical data. An investor could take advantage of this by taking counterparty A's position in this swap.

Differential Swap Valuation

Since differential swaps generate cash flows which depend on foreign currency interest rates (or, more generally, foreign currency security prices) but are denominated in the domestic currency, it seems reasonable to expect that differential swap values should not depend on the exchange rate of the two currencies, or for that matter on the volatility of the exchange rate. However, this is not the case since it is necessary to take a position in a foreign currency security in order to hedge this swap and in terms of the domestic currency, the value of such a position changes when the exchange rate changes. Therefore, exchange rate volatility may have an effect on the value of the derivative. We show that this is the case whenever changes in the exchange rate and in the foreign currency security are correlated.

Consider the swap between counterparties A and B shown in Figure 15.4. In particular, consider the risks to which A is exposed due to those cash flows which are linked to DM LIBOR. Although these flows are determined by the level of DM LIBOR, they are paid in dollars, so as U.S. interest rates fall, the present value of these cash flows rises. A may hedge this by paying fixed on a U.S. dollar interest rate swap. Next, as DM interest rates fall, the present value of the DM-linked cash flows falls. Thus, it would seem reasonable for A to hedge this exposure by receiving fixed on a DM interest rate swap. However, if A does hedge its DM exposure with a DM interest rate swap then any gain on this hedge position due to falling DM rates is in DM, and consequently is subject to exchange rate risk. That is, if the \$/DM exchange rate also falls (so that DM depreciates relative to the dollar) then the gain on the hedge is diminished.

The net result of the FX risk on the hedge is that if there is positive correlation of changes in DM rates and the \$/DM exchange rate, then counterparty A will generally lose both when DM LIBOR rises (i.e., he will lose more on his swap than he will make on his hedge) and when DM LIBOR falls (i.e., he will lose more on his hedge than he makes on his swap). Conversely, if there is negative correlation of changes in DM rates and the \$/DM exchange rate then counterparty A will generally make money. In addition, the more volatile either the exchange rate or the DM interest rates, the more he would tend to make or lose. This effect should be reflected in the valuation of a difference swap contract. In the swap in Figure 15.4 it would result in an increase in the spread over U.S. LIBOR that B is willing to pay A, since the correlation between DM rates and the \$/DM exchange rate is actually negative.

Let us analyze this effect in more detail. Consider a cash flow which occurs at time T, and which is equal to the spot price of a foreign currency security at that time, $S(T)$, the cash flow itself being denominated in the domestic currency. If the exchange rate at time t is $E(t)$, then the value of the security at time t in units of the domestic currency is $E(t)S(t)$. The following position:

$$\text{Long } 1/E(t) \text{ units of the underlying security}$$

will replicate the value of the cash flow at time T. Also, this position will not cost anything, over and above its initial cost, *provided the exchange rate $E(t)$ remains constant*. Since the cost of setting up this position is $S(t)$, this is the value of the cash flow, in this case.

Now consider the case when the exchange rate is also variable. Our concern is that a gain in the hedge position due to an increase in the foreign security price S will be offset by a fall in the exchange rate E. The net effect of simultaneous changes dS and dE in S and E over a short time interval dt due to this possible interaction is a gain of

$$dE\,dS / E(t). \tag{8}$$

If we now make the usual Black-Scholes assumptions that S and E are lognormally distributed, with volatilities σ_S and σ_E respectively, and also that the correlation between changes in S and E is ρ, then the change in the value of the hedge due to the interaction of changes in S with changes in E is

$$\rho\sigma_E\sigma_S S(t)dt \tag{9}$$

over the time interval dt. Thus, in effect, the hedge position yields a cash flow which is entirely analogous to a dividend paid by the security at a rate of

$$\rho\sigma_E\sigma_S \tag{10}$$

per unit time and per unit of stock value. Thus if the security actually pays a dividend at a constant proportional rate of d in its own currency, then the derivative can be valued as if it were a security which has a dividend yield of $(d + \rho\sigma_E\sigma_S)$ rather than d in the local currency.

We can apply the above analysis to a cash flow equal to a foreign currency interest rate, but paid in the domestic currency. If the forward currency interest rate is F, and the borrowing/lending rate in the domestic currency is r_d (which we shall assume is non-random) the above argument implies that the value of the derivative in the domestic currency is equal to

$$F \exp\left[-\rho\sigma_E\sigma_S T\right]\exp\left[-r_d T\right] \tag{11}$$

We see that an increase in the covariance, $\rho\sigma_E\sigma_S$ between changes in the foreign security price and changes in the exchange rate decreases the value of the cash flow, and that this decrease is greater the longer the life of the cashflow.

Historically, the covariance between changes in DM LIBOR and the $/DM exchange rate has been about −0.8 percent. Consequently, the effect of volatility on swaps with DM LIBOR paid in dollars is generally small. For example, if the swap in Figure 15.4 had a maturity of one year, the spread that A would be willing to pay B would only increase by about 3 basis points because of volatility, while if the maturity were five years the spread would increase about 15 basis points. Figure 15.8 shows the total offset required to the U.S. LIBOR flows for one-, three- and five-year swaps as a function of the correlation coefficient, given a DM LIBOR

Figure 15.8: Required offsets to U.S. LIBOR flows as a function of the correlation between $/DM exchange rate and DM LIBOR. Here, we assume U.S. and DM term structures flat at 6 percent and 7 percent respectively; volatility of DM LIBOR is 20 percent, and volatility of exchange rate is 12 percent.

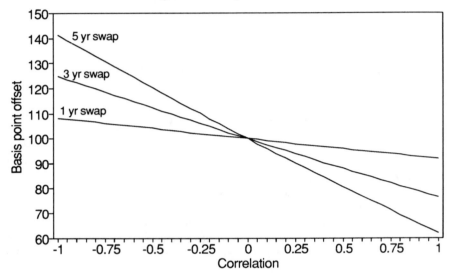

volatility 20 percent, an exchange rate volatility of 12 percent, and flat term structures in the two currencies: 6 percent in dollars, and 7 percent in DM.

Interest Rate Difference Options

Interest Rate Difference Option Structures

Interest rate difference options (difference options) are options written on the difference between two yields expressed either as an absolute spread or a ratio. The relationship chosen can be between two yields in one currency, or between yields available in two different currencies. To simplify the discussion, we will focus on options on the ratio of short-term rates in two different currencies, although the discussion is applicable to other types of difference options.

There are two basic types of difference options: puts and calls. Call options give the holder the right to receive a constant K times a domestic LIBOR rate if that product exceeds the foreign interest rate whereas put options give the holder the right to pay K times the domestic rate if that product is less than the foreign interest rate. All payments are made in the domestic currency. The payoffs to these options are given by the following formulae:

$$\text{Payoff of Call Option} = C = N*\max\left(KR_d - R_f, 0\right)*\left(d/b\right) \qquad (12)$$

$$\text{Payoff of Put Option} = P = N*\max\left(R_f - KR_d, 0\right)*\left(d/b\right) \qquad (13)$$

where

N = Notional principal of the contract, in units of domestic currency
K = Strike Ratio
R_d = Domestic currency LIBOR rate at option expiration
R_f = Foreign currency LIBOR rate at option expiration
d = Number of days in interest rate period
b = Rate basis

Normally, if the option is linked to the ratio of foreign and domestic short-term rates, the length of the interest rate period d, will coincide with the term of the short-term rates, and the rate basis b, will be determined by the basis of the domestic currency short-term rate. Also, although the option payoff may occur at the beginning of the interest rate period (i.e., as soon as the rates R_d and R_f are determined), it more commonly occurs at the end of the interest rate period.

If we assume that the notional principal of these options is the same as our earlier ratio difference swap example, $100 MM, we notice that the payoffs to a combined long call, short put position each with a strike ratio of 2.2 exactly equal those of the differential swap. For example, when the STG and USD LIBOR rates are 11 percent and 5.25 percent, respectively, the payoffs to each option are as follows:

$$C = \$100,000,000*\max\left(0.0525*2.2 - 0.11, 0\right)*\left(180/360\right) = \$275,000$$

$$P = \$100,000,000*\max\left(0.11 - 0.0525*2.2, 0\right)*\left(180/360\right) = \$0.$$

Thus, the net payoff to the long call, short put combination is the same as the difference swap, $275M. Figure 15.9 shows the payoffs to put and call options on the USD/STG LIBOR spread for different levels of USD LIBOR, when STG LIBOR is assumed to be 11 percent. Note that the payoffs to a long call and short put position form a straight line and are, in fact, equal to those of the difference swap for all levels of USD LIBOR. This is an example of a form of put/call parity which holds for all

Figure 15.9: Payoff to STG LIBOR/USD LIBOR Ratio Options with Strike Ratio = 1.8 In this graph STG LIBOR is held constant at 11percent and payoffs are displayed for different levels of USD LIBOR.

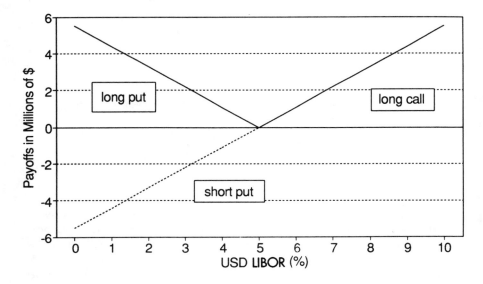

difference options. Namely, the value of a long call/short put is equal to that of a difference swap with the same strike ratio.

Difference Option Applications

The example above demonstrates that payoffs to difference swaps can be replicated with difference options and, as one would expect, the applications of difference options are similar to those of difference swaps. The major advantage of difference options is that they can be used to fit a very specific strategy since they can be tailored to provide payoffs that depend on whether the ratio of two rates is above or below a specified level, or within or outside a specified range on a specific date in the future.

Consider again the difference swap shown in Figure 15.5. The structure shown enables counterparty B to profit should the ratio of STG LIBOR to USD LIBOR return to rates more consistent with the historical data. A ratio put option can be used to fine tune this strategy. Counterparty B could, for example, purchase a ratio put on the STG/USD ratio at any desired strike. Since historically the ratio has generally been below 1.8, counterparty B might purchase a six-month put option with a strike ratio of 1.8. Figure 15.10 displays the payoff to this position. The payoff includes the option premium which, assuming STG LIBOR and USD LIBOR forward rates of 11 percent and 5 percent, respectively, when the

Figure 15.10: Payoffs (net of premium) on STG LIBOR/USD LIBOR Ratio Call Options with Strike Ratio = 1.8 percent. In this Graph STG LIBOR is held constant at 11 percent and payoffs are displayed for different levels of USD LIBOR.

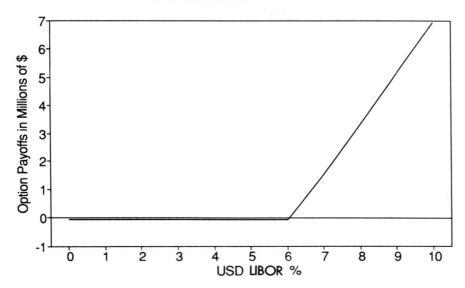

option is purchased would be about 8 bps. The premium is relatively low because the option is out of the money. More precisely, if STG LIBOR remains at 11 percent then USD LIBOR would have to increase to 6.19 percent for the option to have a positive payoff.

Difference options are also used to provide added precision to a strategy involving difference swaps in much the same way that interest rate swaps and cross currency swaps are combined with option products. For example, a portfolio manager might use a difference swap to capitalize on anticipated yield curve movements while also purchasing an option on the spread in order to limit his downside risk.

Valuation of Difference Options

The value of a difference option depends crucially on the volatility of the spread between the two rates. This volatility depends partly on the separate volatilities of the two rates, and partly on the degree to which the two rates move together, i.e., on the correlation of changes in the two rates. Also, we have identified a relationship between difference options and differential swaps. Since differential swap values depend on the covariance of movements in the foreign currency exchange rate with movements in the foreign interest rate, it must also be the case that the difference option depends on this covariance.

We shall concentrate on the valuation of a relatively simple structure, one which has a payoff in the domestic currency equal to

$$\max\left(KR_d(T) - R_f(T), 0\right) \text{ at time } T \tag{14}$$

where $R_d(t)$ and $R_f(t)$ are domestic and foreign short-term interest rates at time t. This is a call option on the spread of the domestic interest rate over the foreign interest rate, with a strike ratio of K. A structure of this type can be used by a borrower to effectively limit interest rate payments to the lower of the domestic and foreign currency interest rates, without the need to borrow in the foreign currency, and thus without the concurrent exchange rate risk. A purchaser of the above option would be reimbursed if the foreign currency interest rate R_f were less than the domestic currency interest rate R_d at time T when an interest payment were due. In this case the strike ratio K, would be 1.

We can identify this type of option with an option to exchange one asset for another (Margrabe, 1978)[3]: we can associate the domestic interest rate with one asset and the foreign interest rate with the other. Margrabe considered the exchange of two assets, both of which were denominated in the same currency. In our case, the second asset is denominated in a foreign currency. From our earlier discussion on differential swap valuation, we know that we can view this second asset as a domestic currency asset which has a dividend yield adjustment of $\rho\sigma_E\sigma_f$, where, as before, σ_E is the volatility of the exchange rate, σ_f the volatility of the foreign currency forward interest rate, and ρ the correlation between changes in these two rates. This effective dividend yield adjustment is due to the interaction of simultaneous changes in the value of the foreign asset with the exchange rate. Assuming changes in the foreign and domestic currency interest rates are lognormally distributed, the value of this differential option at time $t < T$ is

$$C = D\left\{F_d K N(h_1) - F_f \exp\left[-\rho\sigma_E\sigma_f(T-t)\right]N(h_2)\right\} \tag{15}$$

where

$$h_1 = \left(\log(F_d K / F_f) + \rho\sigma_E\sigma_f(T-t)\right) / \sigma\sqrt{(T-t)} + \sigma\sqrt{(T-t)} / 2,$$

$$h_2 = h_1 - \sigma\sqrt{(T-t)}$$

---

[3] Margrabe, W., "The value of an option to exchange one asset for another," *Journal of Finance*, March 1978.

and

F_d = domestic currency forward LIBOR rate

F_f = foreign currency forward LIBOR rate

D = Domestic currency discount factor from option expiration date

T = time to option expiration

K = strike ratio

and σ is the volatility of the ratio of the foreign currency forward LIBOR rate to the domestic currency forward LIBOR rate:

$$\sigma^2 = \sigma_d^2 - 2\rho_{df}\sigma_d\sigma_f + \sigma_f^2 \qquad (16)$$

where σ_d and σ_f are the volatilities of the domestic and foreign forward rates, and ρ_{df} is the correlation between changes in these two rates. The value of a put option can be found from the value of a call using put/call parity.

Of the many parameters that affect the value of the option, the most difficult to estimate in practice are the two correlation coefficients ρ and

Figure 15.11: At-the-money 1-year USD/STG differential call values, given LIBOR volatilities of 20 percent and exchange, rate volatility of 12 percent.

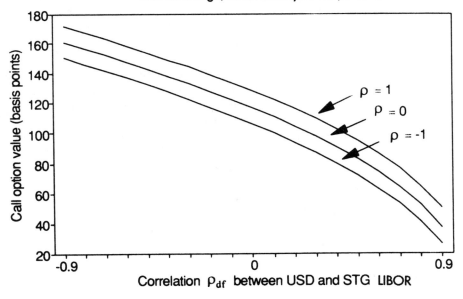

ρ_{df} In the derivation of the option pricing formula, it is assumed that these two correlations are constant. However, these correlations generally vary considerably from one period to another, and it is therefore difficult to estimate future correlations over the life of an option. Of the two correlations, ρ_{df} has a much greater impact on the value of the option than ρ. The dependence of an option's value on these correlations is illustrated in Figure 15.11, where we display the value of an at-the-money USD/STG call option with one year to maturity for the full range of correlations ρ_{df} and ρ. We suppose the term structures in both currencies are flat, 5.5 percent in USD and 11 percent in STG, that the volatilities of both U.S. and STG LIBOR, σ_d and σ_f are 20 percent, and that the exchange rate volatility σ_E is 12 percent. The at-the-money option has a strike of $K = 2$. The reason why the coefficient ρ_{df} has a greater impact on the option value is that it directly effects the volatility σ of the interest rate differential: when $\rho_{df} = -1$, $\sigma = 40$ percent, and when $\rho_{df} = 1$, $\sigma = 0$ percent. However, the correlation ρ only enters through the factor $\rho \sigma_E \sigma_f (T-t)$, which is small even for extreme values of ρ for most option maturities.

Conclusion

The innovations in yield curve applications of swaps represented by the three derivative products described in this chapter are part of the continual extension of the swap product line. As is apparent from our discussion of the various structures and applications of these three products, product development is more evolutionary than revolutionary. This evolutionary process is towards the development of products that address very specific portfolio management needs. For the three products described here, yield curve swaps, differential swaps, and difference options, the focus is on yield spreads, and they are primary examples of the trend towards ever more specialized structures.

In spite of the apparent complexity and specificity of the structures, all three products are essentially merely combinations of simpler instruments. In our descriptive analysis, we focus on both the decomposition of these products into their component parts, and on their combination with other financial instruments to create structured financial products such as cross-rate notes. The decomposition of derivative products into their basic components is an essential step in their valuation. In general, derivative product payoffs can be replicated using dynamically adjusted portfolios of simpler instruments, and as a result their valuation depends on both initial market prices and the future distribution of market prices, or volatility. We show that, in many cases, the effect of volatility is small and that its effect can be quantified with straightforward adjustments to simple valuation formulas.

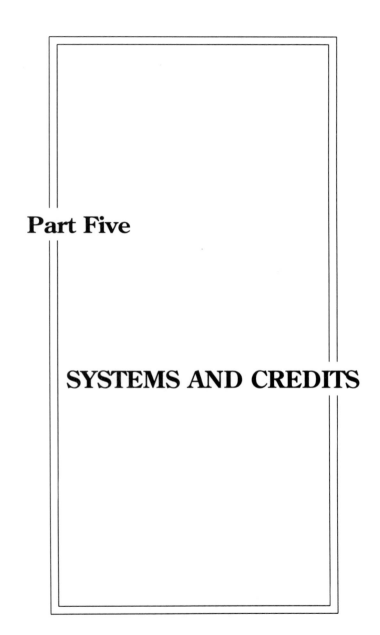

Part Five

SYSTEMS AND CREDITS

VISUALIZATION OF DERIVATIVES RISK*

Rod A. Beckström and
Peter C. McDonald

16

Graphics to View Interest Rate Risk

In the Japanese folk tale "Rashomon," the witnesses to a murder give widely conflicting accounts. They see it in ways that reflect their personal prejudices and the limited information at their disposal. There are irresistible parallels between this story and traditional methods of capital markets risk analysis. Often, market information is sketchy or the technology to interpret it outdated. Sometimes the only strategy is an educated guess—a hunch based on inconclusive data melded with subjective assumptions.

Previous technological advances saved labor and increased precision but had limitations. In the 1970s pocket calculators ousted slide rules but could only deliver one number at a time. From the 1980s PCs were able to offer entire screens of data fields via spreadsheets such as VisiCalc and Lotus 1–2–3, and through text-based third-party applications software.

But this limited and therefore risky approach to decision-making may be rapidly on the way out. Powerful workstations with large, high-resolution monitors, such as the Sun SparcStations and IBM RISC System/6000, can guarantee extremely precise graphic representations of all pertinent risk profiles.

These enable market participants to analyze risk more effectively, to devise multiple risk-reduction strategies, and to engineer instruments customized to their clients' needs. The following examples illustrate some of

* Portions of this article originally appeared in *Risk Magazine*, vol. 4, no. 9, October 1991, under the title, "Visual Magnitude." Reprinted with permission.

the ways in which traders can use graphics to look at derivatives interest rate risk.[1] They cover cash flow based risk analyses on the "greek letters" for various instruments and portfolios as well as partial differential hedge calculations which expose differences apparent between different interest rate option valuation algorithms.

Cash Flow Based Risk Analyses

A derivatives portfolio can be considered as comprising a collection of bilateral transactions[2] where one party or side to each of the transactions is the legal entity which is the owner of the portfolio. A majority of the open or currently active transactions in a derivatives portfolio are likely to be derivatives transactions, but generally a derivatives portfolio will also contain some cash or physicals transactions. Examples of derivatives transactions are trades in swaps, FRAs, caps, and interest rate futures. Examples of cash or physicals transactions are trades in bonds, and bills.

The instruments in the portfolio can be classified into fungibles[3] and non-fungibles. Fungible instruments are those which have equivalent terms. Examples of fungibles are exchange-traded debt options (a given contract in a given maturity at a given strike price), and a particular bond issue. Examples of non-fungibles are FRAs and non-exchange traded interest rate swaps or swaps executed on an "over-the-counter" basis.

With most interest rate swap markets quoting prices out of "spot" start for various maturities (from 2 to between 5 and 10 years typically), swap trading portfolios tend to contain swap transactions with a multiplicity of different start dates, roll dates, and maturity dates (to name just a few of the variables). The larger of the trading debt derivatives portfolios in the global derivatives market, typically contain many thousands of derivatives transactions of a non-fungible nature. Management of market price risk[4] for these large and complex portfolios of debt derivatives, can present the trader with a bewilderingly large amount of information to digest in a short space of time.

The management of the risks in the portfolio can involve decisions where there are trade-offs such as liquidity versus hedge quality[5] versus

---

[1] The graphics presented here are bar charts which have been produced by Lotus 1–2–3 running on a Sun SparcStation.

[2] The term "transaction" is used here to refer to the actual trade which has been entered into by the two particular parties, while the term "instrument" is used here to refer to the type of transaction executed between the parties.

[3] J. Downes and J. E. Goodman, "Dictionary of Finance and Investment Terms," 2nd Ed., (1987) p. 151.

[4] The market price risk in a derivatives portfolio is defined as the impact on the capital value of the portfolio due to changes in market rates.

[5] Hedge quality is defined here as being inversely related to the variance in the expected total return on the hedged portfolio for a given period of time over which market prices may move.

price amongst the various hedge instrument(s) available. Liquidity requirements in particular can and do drive the derivatives traders to make active use of fungible instruments such as cash (or bonds) and futures. Rapid graphical analysis of the projected outcomes of adopting different hedging strategies can facilitate the trader's decisions on choice of hedge instrument(s) and extent of cover.

There are many different ways in which to present the different classes of risk in a derivatives portfolio. In this section a cash flow based method is used. The method is applied to a number of different instrument types and small portfolios.

The cash flow based risk analysis used here takes all known fixed cashflows[6] and performs separate risk analysis on each cashflow. The portfolio of known fixed cash flows can be thought of as a portfolio of zero coupon bonds, with each zero coupon bond being subject to separate risk analysis.

Where the last floating rate set of a deal has been set, then the cash flow arising from that rate set is regarded as a known fixed cash flow. The cash flows which arise from floating rate sets where the rate set has yet to occur, are ignored in this methodology[7] with certain exceptions. Where there are fixed margins applied to the floating side, such as LIBOR + 0.125%, then those fixed margins are counted for risk assessment.

Debt options such as caps[8] are incorporated in the methodology by viewing the various risk classes at each exercise point in the cap. Debt options such as swaptions[9] are incorporated by viewing the various risk classes at each exercise point[10] in the swaption.

The classes of risk which are viewed graphically at each point along the time line are delta, gamma, theta, and vega (the so called "greek letters" of risk management). The ways in which these risk classes are derived are described below.

0.01 Sensitivity/Delta

The 0.01 sensitivity/delta figures show the changes in net present value (NPV) of known fixed cashflows in a deal or portfolio of deals. The changes calculated are the result of a one basis point (one hundredth of

---

[6] Known fixed cash flows include notional exchanges of principal.

[7] This methodology is drawn from the Floating Rate Note (FRN) approach (see footnote 11 below). It is subject to limitations for non-LIBOR transactions and complex reset structures such as "implied forwards."

[8] See "The Handbook of Currency and Interest Rate Risk Management" R. J. Schwartz & C. W. Smith, Jr., (1990), Chapter 11 "Option-Based Rate Risk Management Tools," L. Macdonald Wakeman.

[9] *See supra*, Chapter 12 "Swaptions: Tailoring Interest Rate Swaps," B. J. Crowe.

[10] For American style swaptions use the end of each exercise period.

one percentage point) shift upwards in the master zero curve[11] rate (expressed on an annualized basis) applicable to the date of each cash flow.

The use of a master zero curve assumes there is one master swap yield curve per currency. This implies there is a consensus amongst the banks on the appropriate net present value or price for any future cash flow. If one bank could borrow funds on a zero coupon basis at a lower rate than that implied by the master swap yield curve, then it would be possible for that bank to arbitrage the market. If it is assumed arbitrage is not possible, then it follows that the existence of only one swap yield curve per currency means that all banks must be considered as carrying identical credit ratings. This is clearly not the case, but for the sake of simplicity the existence of one master swap yield curve per currency is assumed.

The swap market in each currency quotes interest rates on a yield to maturity (YTM) basis. That is, a single yield is assumed to be valid over the entire life of a transaction. It is assumed that re-investment of coupons received over the life of the transaction will be at the same yield as used for calculating the coupon payments themselves. From the YTM curve it is possible to construct the zero coupon yield curve which would give, without offering arbitrage opportunities, the yield at which any given zero coupon bond would trade.

Once the master swap zero curve is known, it is possible to price correctly a portfolio consisting of irregular cash flows, or a portfolio consisting of zero coupon bonds.

The delta derived for caps and swaptions is provided from the closed form solution for delta for the instrument in each case, expressed in NPV terms.

Convexity or Gamma

The convexity/gamma figures show the changes in delta (as defined above) as a result of a one basis point shift upwards in the master zero curve rate applicable to the date of each cashflow.

The gamma derived for caps and swaptions is provided from the closed form solution for gamma for the instrument in each case, expressed in NPV terms.

Change in Value with Time (Theta)

The theta figures show the changes in NPV of the same cashflows used as input to the delta analysis above, as a result of the reduction by

---

[11] See "The Handbook of Currency and Interest Rate Risk Management" R. J. Schwartz & C. W. Smith, Jr., (1990), Chapter 7, "Fundamental Models for Pricing Swaps," R. A. Beckstrœdm.

one day of the day count used for discounting the cash flows in each use. The theta for the options instruments is derived from the closed form solutions.

Volatility (Vega)

The vega figures show the changes in NPV of the same cashflows used as input to the delta analysis above, as a result of a 100-basis point increase in the implied volatility (expressed on an annualized yield basis) of the underlying forward[12] zero curve rates used for each of the transactions contributing to the net cash flow for a given date. Vega for the options instruments is derived from the closed form solutions and applied on a consistent basis.[13]

Examples Involving Swaps, FRAs, Swaptions, and Caps

Figure 16.1.1 (delta) shows sensitivity to rate changes for this swap from the fixed payer's perspective. The duration of the fixed side coupon flows becomes greater with time and therefore the sensitivity of each of the cashflows (to a change in discount factor) increases with time. At the far right of the delta window (ref 1997) the notional principal repayment can be seen, and at the far left of the delta window (ref 1992) the notional principal payment (net of the last floating rate set coupon which has received its LIBOR setting) can be seen. The delta sensitivity to the initial notional principal payment for this forward start swap is only a small fraction of the delta sensitivity of the notional principal repayment at the end of the swap because the duration of the final payment is greater than the duration of the initial payment. The reason the overall swap has a net positive delta is because the delta is being measured for a shift up in interest rates from the perspective of the fixed payer.

The gammas for this transaction (see Figure 16.1.2) are negative overall because gamma is being measured for a shift up in rates and the rate of increase in delta decreases as interest rates increase. Notice that the overall gamma exposure (measured in dollars) is some three orders of magnitude smaller than the delta exposure.

Theta (Figure 16.1.3) diminishes over time since the NPV of each payment also decreases, and the final principal theta is the largest negative theta. Since there are no option-related payments, there is no vega.

Figure 16.2 covers the case of a single FRA. To model this transaction properly, an implied one-period-forward swap beginning on the effective date must be created. When viewed from the perspective of the fixed payer, this transation has a negative up-front delta (Figure 16.2.1) at the

---

[12] *See supra*, Chapter 7, "Fundamental Models for Pricing Swaps," R. A. Beckstrœdm.

[13] Vega results from different closed form solutions are not necessarily additive.

Figure 16.1.1: 5-Year Bullet Swap Par Semi-annual Coupons

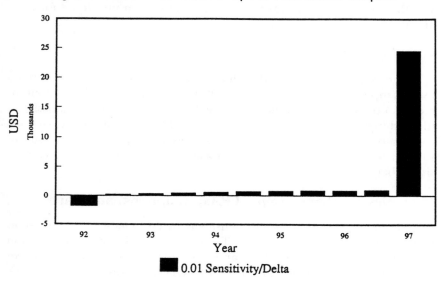

implied maturity date, when principal and interest are theoretically paid. The gamma (Figure 16.2.2) has a sign opposite to the delta, resulting at maturity in a positive up-front gamma and a negative implied repayment gamma. The time decay (Figure 16.2.3) is positive for the up-front principal withdrawal and negative for the implied repayment.

Figure 16.1.2: 5-Year Bullet Swap Par Semi-annual Coupons

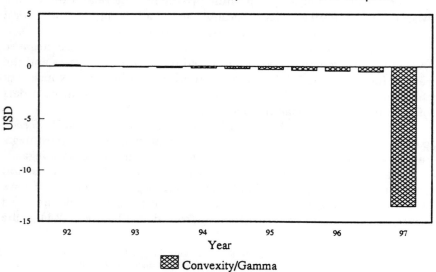

Figure 16.1.3: 5-Year Bullet Swap Par Semi-annual Coupons

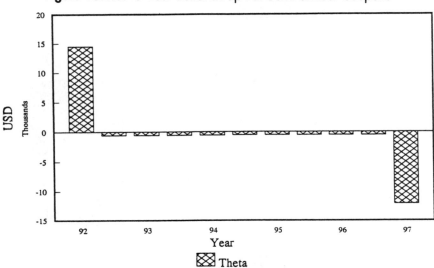

In Figure 16.3, involving a 5 year bullet monthly cap, delta (Figure 16.3.1) increases in magnitude—while remaining positive—steeply at first and then more gradually. The gamma (Figure 16.3.2) increases until the fourth year and then decreases slightly. Notice that the overall gamma ex-

Figure 16.2.1: 3-Month FRA Effective After 3 Months

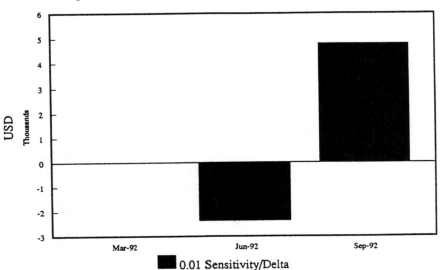

Figure 16.2.2: 3-Month FRA Effective After 3 Months

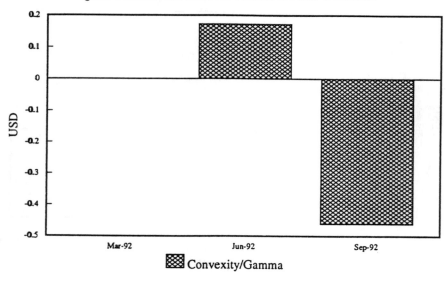

posure (measured in dollars) is some two orders of magnitude smaller than the delta exposure. Theta (Figure 16.3.3) follows a curve similar to gamma except that it starts to decline in the third year. Vega (Figure 16.3.4) follows a curve similar to delta.

Figure 16.2.3: 3-Month FRA Effective After 3 Months

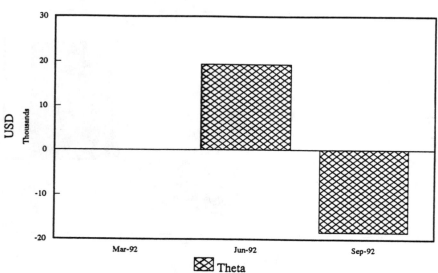

Figure 16.3.1: 5-Year Bullet Monthly Cap (Buyer's Perspective)

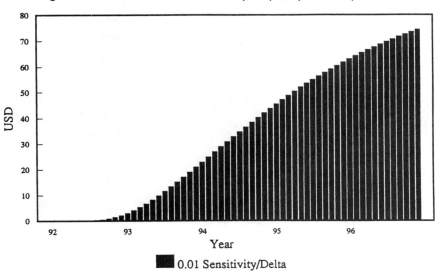

Figure 16.4 shows a portfolio consisting of 10 annual options, each into a five-year swap. When viewed from the perspective of the buyer of the options, delta (Figure 16.4.1) and gamma (Figure 16.4.2) follow a positive declining pattern while theta (Figure 16.4.3) follows a negative

Figure 16.3.2: 5-Year Bullet Monthly Cap (Buyer's Perspective)

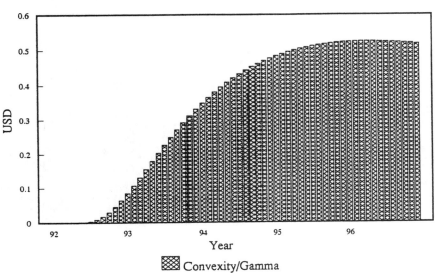

Figure 16.3.3: 5-Year Bullet Monthly Cap (Buyer's Perspective)

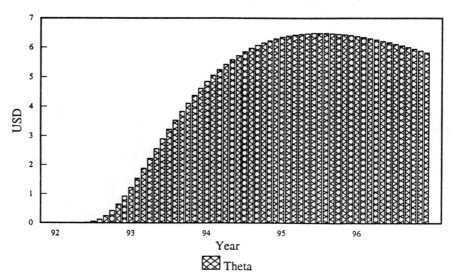

declining pattern. As expected, vega (Figure 16.4.4) is positive and increasing with time to expiration.

Figure 16.5 is viewed from the perspective of the cap buyer. As the decreasing principal balance counterbalances the normally increasing

Figure 16.3.4: 5-Year Bullet Monthly Cap (Buyer's Perspective)

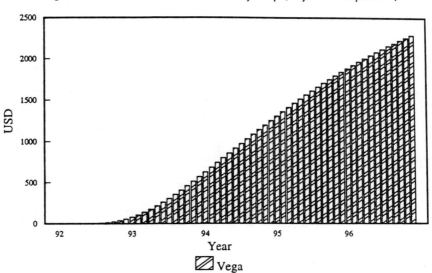

Figure 16.4.1: Portfolio of 10 European Style Swaptions

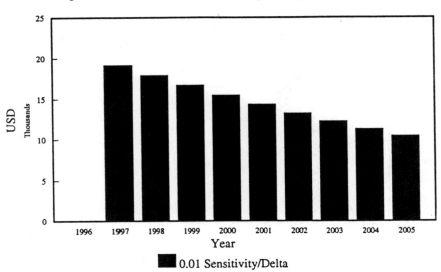

Figure 16.4.1: Portfolio of 10 European Style Swaptions

functions over time, delta, gamma, theta, and vega are visualized as convex structures.

Figure 16.6 is a no-cost collar viewed from the buyer's perspective. The implied value of the cap is equal to the value of the floor. While the

Figure 16.4.2: Portfolio of 10 European Style Swaptions

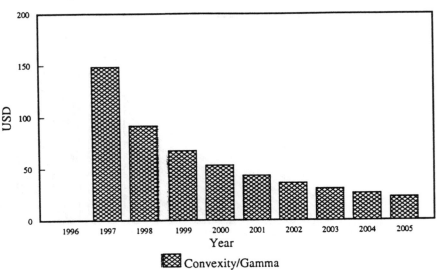

Figure 16.4.3: Portfolio of 10 European Style Swaptions

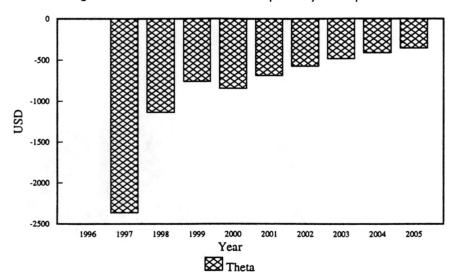

delta (Figure 16.6.1) is a positive increasing function similar to a cap, the gamma (Figure 16.6.2) is more reminiscent of a sine function. The nearby options produce a negative gamma and the later options a positive gamma. The same is true for the theta and the vega (Figures 16.6.3 and 16.6.4, respectively).

Figure 16.4.4: Portfolio of 10 European Style Swaptions

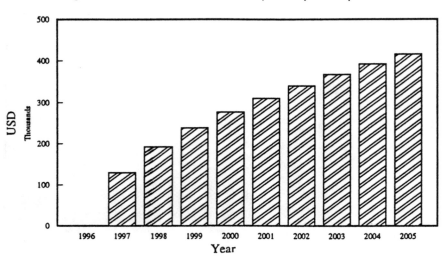

Figure 16.5.1: 3-Year Cap with Equal Principal Amortization

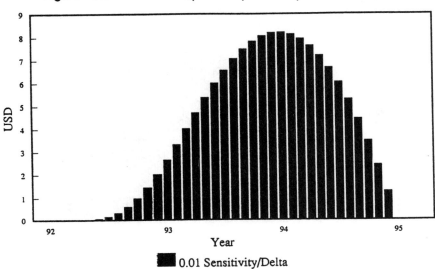

■ 0.01 Sensitivity/Delta

Figure 16.7 is a simple delta hedge with a net value of zero, where a swap is hedging a cap. It is viewed from the perspective of the fixed receiver in the swap and the buyer of the cap. The delta profile (Figure 16.7.1) clearly shows the coupon flows of the swap offsetting the cap

Figure 16.5.2: 3-Year Cap with Equal Principal Amortization

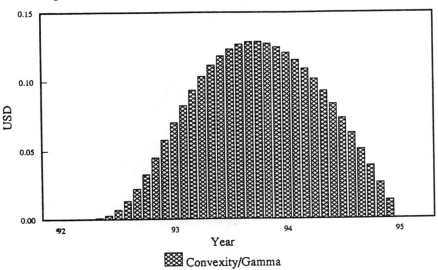

▨ Convexity/Gamma

Figure 16.5.3: 3-Year Cap with Equal Principal Amortization

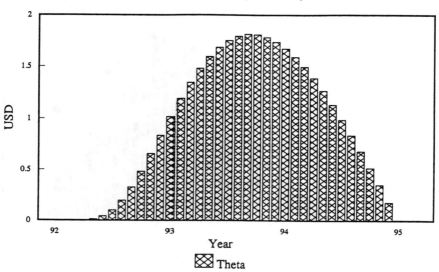

deltas, and the final principal repayment balances the remainder. Convexity, on the other hand, has increased. The positive gamma (Figure 16.7.2) on the cap is further exacerbated by the positive gamma of the swap cash flows and the bumps along the gamma curve are caused by the

Figure 16.5.4: 3-Year Cap with Equal Principal Amortization

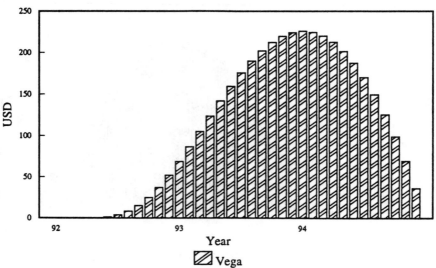

Figure 16.6.1: 5-Year Monthly Collar

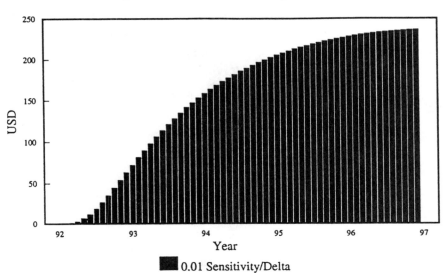

0.01 Sensitivity/Delta

contributions from the positive semi-annual gammas from the swap coupon flows. The theta (Figure 16.7.3) of the swap dominates this hedge set. Vega (Figure 16.7.4) remains unchanged. This transaction is hedged for simple parallel shifts and is not robust with respect to non-parallel

Figure 16.6.2: 5-Year Monthly Collar

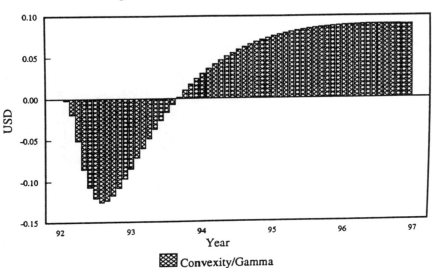

Convexity/Gamma

Figure 16.6.3: 5-Year Monthly Collar

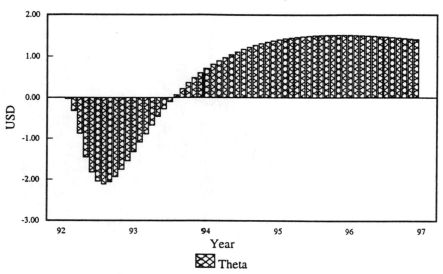

movements. Simply put, it shows the inherent risk in hedging a cap with a bond or swap.

Figure 16.8 shows a 3-year cap identical to the one presented in Figure 16.5, which is being hedged by 3 bullet caps. The 3-year cap is

Figure 16.6.4: 5-Year Monthly Collar

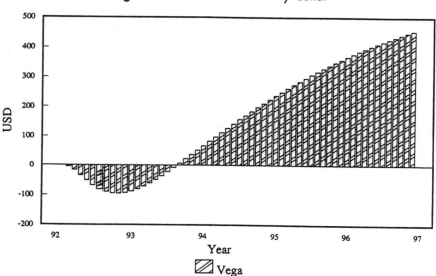

Figure 16.7.1: 5-Year Par Swap Hedging 5-Year Monthly Cap

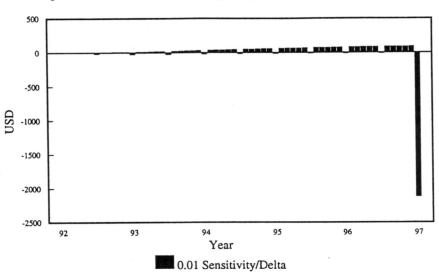

viewed from the buyer's perspective. The hedge caps, which are viewed from the seller's perspective, are bullet transactions maturing at one, two and three years. The bullet caps have semi-annual option exercises, while the amortizing cap has monthly exercises. The teardrop pattern is caused

Figure 16.7.2: 5-Year Par Swap Hedging 5-Year Monthly Cap

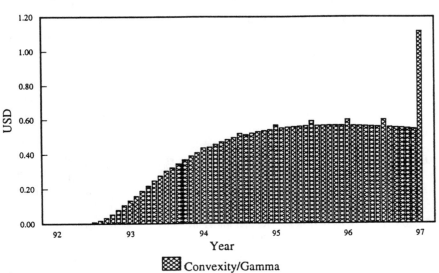

Figure 16.7.3: 5-Year Par Swap Hedging 5-Year Monthly Cap

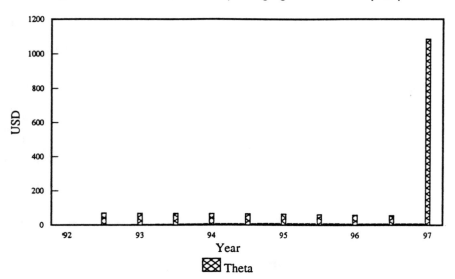

by the longer option exercises of the hedge transactions intersecting the smooth curve of the underlying cap. While the pattern appears irregular, the risks are actually minimal.

Delta Hedging against Non-Parallel Curve Shifts

The cash flow based risk analyses shown above are good at representing graphically the various risks in a portfolio at each point in time, but for hedging purposes traders will often prefer to see their exposures in terms of a particular set of hedging transactions which are needed to "square the book" for a given class of risk. The hedge instruments used to express the risk in the book will not necessarily be the same as those which have created the exposure. For example, a swaps trader may wish to see the exposure in a swaps book in terms of equivalent treasury notes or eurodollar futures, regardless of the basis[14] and gap[15] risks inherent in such a hedging strategy.

The graphical views of risk given below relate to delta risk only. They show the risk in the portfolio in terms of the most appropriate hedge which can be taken out in order to minimize delta risk within the constraints of the set of instruments defined as being available for hedging.

---

[14] Basis risk is defined here as the risk that the yields implied by swap market prices will not move in tandem with the yields implied by other debt instruments in the same currency (such as the futures for example).

[15] Gap risk is defined here as the risks arising from non-parallel shifts in the yield curve.

Figure 16.7.4: 5-Year Par Swap Hedging 5-Year Monthly Cap

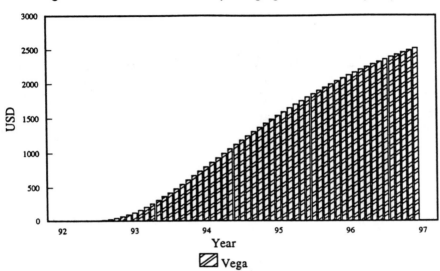

Graphics for simple delta hedge sets for single transactions such as swaps and caps are shown in order to explain the methodology. Then the methodology is used to expose the level of variance which can potentially arise from the use of different published swaption valuation models for delta hedge calculations.

Figure 16.8.1: 3-Year Cap Amortizing Hedging 3 Bullet Caps

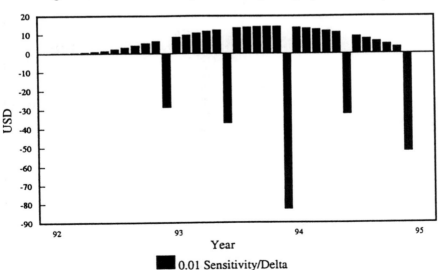

Figure 16.8.2: 3-Year Cap Amortizing Hedging 3 Bullet Caps

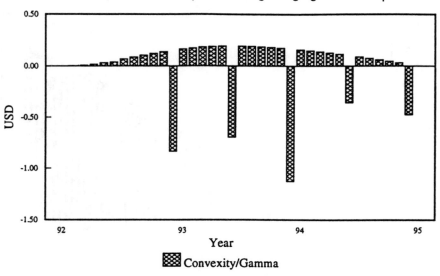

Description of Methodology

The hedge recommendations are expressed in terms of 0.01 sensitivity against a given maturity of any yield to maturity instrument, such as a fixed rate bond, used to construct the master zero curve. It is assumed for

Figure 16.8.3: 3-Year Cap Amortizing Hedging 3 Bullet Caps

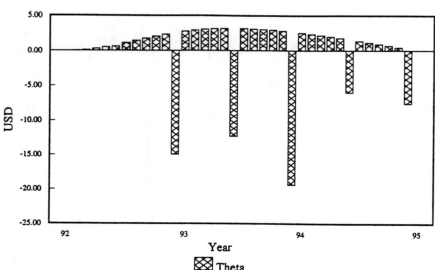

Figure 16.8.4: 3-Year Cap Amortizing Hedging 3 Bullet Caps

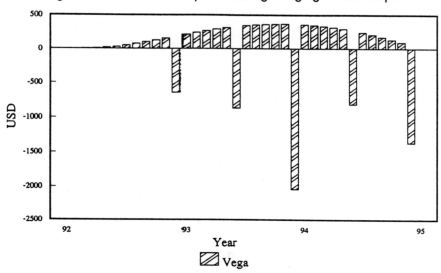

the purposes of these graphics that the yield to maturity instruments in the hedge set are also being used to construct the master zero curve.

To test the sensitivity of the portfolio against a change in yield at a single point along the yield to maturity (YTM) curve, the yield of the YTM instrument concerned is increased by one basis point while the yields of all other instruments used to construct the master zero curve are held constant. The master zero curve is then re-calculated and the portfolio revalued using the revised curve.

The difference in the value of the portfolio as a result of the revaluation with the adjusted curve is the partial differential hedge result for the maturity of the YTM instrument whose yield was increased by one basis point. This process is repeated for all of the instruments used to construct the master zero curve, and produces a partial differential hedge result for all points along the curve at which there are YTM instruments used to construct the master zero curve.

The hedge implemented as a result of the partial differential hedge (PDH) calculations described above provides a degree of protection against changes in the value of the portfolio as a result of non-parallel shifts in the yield curve. In reality, if the hedge instruments are different from the instruments in the portfolio (for example if bonds are used to hedge swaps) then there are other risks such as basis risk to contend with in addition to the risks associated with changes in the shape of the yield curve.

The PDH methodology described above provides no protection

against gamma, vega, and theta exposures which may also be contained in the portfolio to be hedged. Of course, there is a lot more involved in the hedging of options positions than just delta hedge considerations such as described here.

Examples Involving Swaps and Caps

Figure 16.9.1 shows the PDH results for a forward start 5-year bullet swap when viewed from the swap fixed payer's perspective. If the hedge instruments are fixed rate bonds of various maturities, then the hedge involves net purchase of bonds. The reason for the short position recommendation for '92 is that a forward start swap rather than a spot start swap is being hedged. The maturity of the swap is after the maturity of the '97 hedge instrument, accounting for the additional and smaller hedge recommendation in '99. There is no hedge recommendation for '98 because there is no '98 maturity bond in the hedge set.

Figure 16.9.2 shows the PDH results for a 5-year bullet monthly cap. The hedge recommendations primarily involve buying the '97 maturity fixed rate bond, but there is sensitivity to earlier points along the YTM curve which require short positions. Note that if the maturity of the cap was reduced to 3 years from 5 years, then a long bond hedge position would still be required—it is not as simple as cutting off the '96 and '97 hedge recommendations derived for the 5-year cap.

Figure 16.9.1: 5-Year Bullet Swap Par Semi-annual Coupons

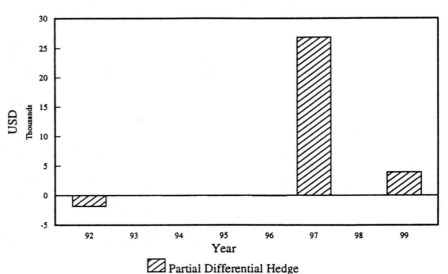

Partial Differential Hedge

Figure 16.9.2: 5-Year Bullet Monthly Cap (Buyer's Perspective)

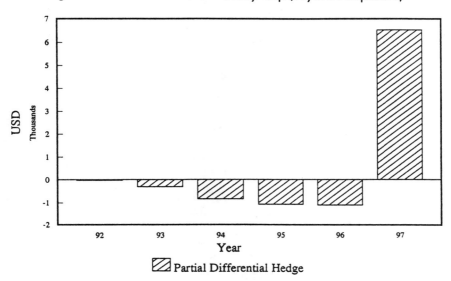

Delta Hedge Variances for Different Swaption Valuation Models

In this section graphical views are taken of different PDH recommendations which can arise when the same swaptions are valued using three different published swaption valuation models. The swaptions are all single exercise European style, and the inputs to the models are adjusted in each case until the NPVs produced by each of the three models are identical. Then the PDH analysis is performed on the same portfolio three different times using a different model each time, in order to expose differences in hedge recommendations which can emerge between the models.

In Figure 16.10.1 a PDH analysis is performed on a 1-month European-style single exercise swaption. The analysis is from the perspective of the option seller, where the option which gives the counterparty the right but not the obligation to receive fixed on a 2-year swap of fixed tenor (sometimes referred to as a short position in a payer swaption). The PDH recommendations from use of the three different swaption valuation models are shown in the one graphic for comparison. The reason for the short position recommendations in '92 is to eliminate those components of the long hedge which are not required at the short end of the curve (the period up until exercise date in '92).

The three different models produce PDH results which have differ-

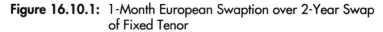

Figure 16.10.1: 1-Month European Swaption over 2-Year Swap of Fixed Tenor

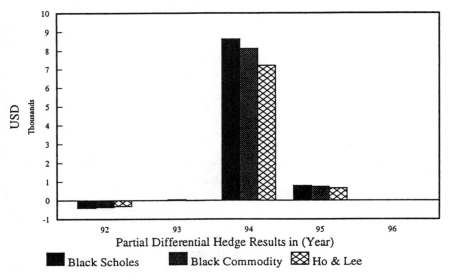

Figure 16.10.2: 2-Year European Swaption over 2-Year Swap of Fixed Tenor

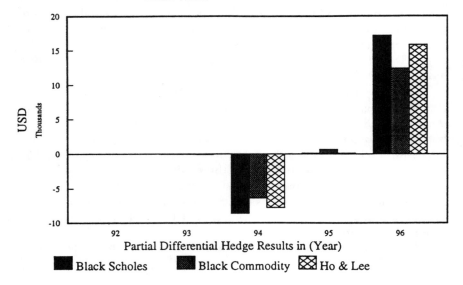

Figure 16.10.3: 5-Year European Swaption over 2-Year Swap of Fixed Tenor

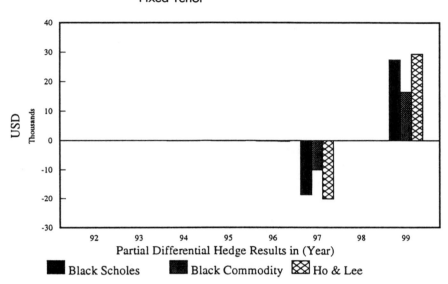

Partial Differential Hedge Results in (Year)

■ Black Scholes   ▦ Black Commodity   ⊠ Ho & Lee

ences of up to a maximum of 20%, with the Ho and Lee model[16] producing the smallest hedge recommendation and the Black and Scholes model[17] producing the largest recommendation. The reason for the smaller long positions in the '95 maturity bonds is that the term of the underlying swap extends beyond the maturity of the '94 maturity bonds.

In Figure 16.10.2 the analysis is the same as for Figure 16.10.1 but the term of the swaption is extended from 1 month to 2 years. The underlying swap remains the same fixed tenor of 2 years. In this case the short hedge position in '94 is larger because the '92 and '93 effects of the long position in the '96 maturity bonds need to be removed.

By extending the term of the swaption the three different models produce PDH results which have differences of up to a maximum of 40%, with the Black Commodity[18] model producing the smallest hedge recommendation and the Black and Scholes model producing the largest hedge recommendation.

In Figure 16.10.3 the analysis is the same as for Figure 16.10.2 but the

---

[16] See T. S. Y. Ho and S. B. Lee, "Term structure movements and pricing interest rate contingent claims," Journal of Finance, Vol 41 (1986), pp 1011–1029.

[17] See F. Black and M. Scholes, "The valuation of option contracts and a test of market efficiency," Journal of Finance, Vol 27 (1972), pp 399–418.

[18] See F. Black, "The pricing of commodity contracts," Journal of Financial Economics, Vol 3 (1976), pp 167–179.

term of the swaption is extended from 2 years to 5 years. In this case, as might be expected, the PDH recommendations produced using the different models show substantial differences in some areas. There are differences of up to a maximum of 70%, with the Black Commodity model producing the smallest hedge recommendation and the Ho and Lee model[19] producing the largest recommendation.

---

[19] The input to the Ho and Lee model used a single volatility figure from which estimates of pseudo-probability and pseudo-volatility were estimated. Thus, when balancing the NPVs under each of the three models the only setting that needed to be varied was volatility input. The volatility inputs were of course quite different due to the different forms in which volatility is expressed to the different models.

THE DEFAULT RISK OF SWAPS*

Ian A. Cooper and
Antonio S. Mello**

17

Swaps have been one of the most explosive and important innovations in international capital markets in the last 10 years. In its simplest form, a swap consists of an agreement between two entities (called counterparties) to exchange in the future two streams of cash flows. In a currency swap, these streams of cash flows consist of a stream of interest and principal payments in one currency exchanged for a stream of interest and principal payments of the same maturity in another currency. In an interest rate swap they consist of streams of interest payments of one type (fixed or floating) exchanged for streams of interest payments of the other type in the same currency. The two types of swap are shown in Appendix 1.[1]

The economic importance of swap transactions is the fact that they can be combined with debt issues to change the nature of the liability for the borrower. The sum of a bond issue and a currency swap gives a net liability stream which is equivalent to transforming the bond liability into a different currency. A floating rate note combined with an interest rate swap results in a liability equivalent to fixed rate debt.

Two issues have dominated the academic literature on swaps. The first concerns the reasons for their use. Arbitrage of imperfections in capital markets was the original cause of their appearance (Price and Hend-

* This article originally appeared in *The Journal of Finance*, vol. xlvi, no. 2, June 1991. Reprinted with permission.
** The authors are grateful to participate at workshops at Bristol University, Cambridge University, HEC, London Business School, LSE, MIT, and Warwick University for comments. We are especially grateful to Dick Brealey, Bernard Dumas, Michael Selby, René Stulz, and two anonymous referees for suggestions.
[1] For an excellent summary of swaps see Wall and Pringle (1988).

erson (1984)). Turnbull (1987) shows that lowering borrowing costs by a synthetic transaction involving a swap is not possible in a complete, integrated capital market. Subsequent authors (Wall and Pringle (1988); Arak, Estrella, Goodman, and Silver (1988); Smith, Smithson, and Wakeman (1987)) observe that market incompleteness or agency costs may provide an alternative explanation for the continued growth of the swap market.

The second part of the literature on swaps concerns pricing and hedging, including the pricing of default risk. Bicksler and Chen (1986) analyze the valuation of default-free interest-rate swaps and demonstrate that the swap is equivalent to holding one type of bond (fixed or floating) financed by selling short the other type. Several papers (Arak, Goodman, and Rones (1986); Federal Reserve Board and Bank of England (1987); Belton (1987) estimate the maximum probable loss on swaps but do not attempt to value the default risk using an equilibrium model. Whittaker (1987) values the credit exposure of interest rate swaps using option pricing but does not endogenize the event triggering the swap default. His results are, therefore, the value of swap default assuming that the probability of the event triggering default is independent of the size of the default. Sundaresan (1989) models the default risk premium as a function of an "instantaneous default premium" that follows an exogenous stochastic process. This gives an equilibrium structure of default premia across different swaps but does not determine the level of the premium.

The purpose of this paper is to develop a partial equilibrium model for the swap default that: a) is consistent with equilibrium rates for risky debt and enables the comparison of swap default risk with debt market default risk; b) makes clear the wealth transfers between corporate claim holders, if any, arising from swaps; and c) is applicable to both interest rate swaps and currency swaps. This analysis is important for at least three types of capital market participants. Banks holding portfolios of swaps need to be able to measure the value of these transactions net of default risk. Bank regulators require a consistent way of measuring the potential default risk so that they can set appropriate capital requirements. Corporations borrowing and using swaps to transform their liabilities should include an allowance for default risk in their comparison of the cost of direct and synthetic borrowing.

The paper is organized as follows: Section I discusses swap risk. Section II analyzes a simplified single-period swap to highlight the wealth transfers taking place. Section III discusses alternative treatments in default. Section IV analyzes a swap using a contingent claims analysis similar to the Merton (1974) model of risky debt to enable comparison of swap market spreads with debt market spreads. Section V applies the model to interest-rate swaps. Section VI contains the concluding comments.

I. Swap Risk

There are two types of risk in swap transactions: rate risk and default risk. Rate risk arises because, during the life of the swap, exchange rates and interest rates vary so that the default-free present value of the cash flows remaining to be paid and received through the swap also varies. This rate risk can be hedged by taking offsetting positions in some combination of currency futures, bond and interest rate futures, currency forward contracts, and spot currency and bond markets.

The second type of swap risk, default risk, is much more difficult to hedge. This risk, sometimes called replacement risk, is complex to evaluate because the cost of default by the counterparty to a swap depends upon four things: the value of the swap at the default date, the event that will trigger the swap default, the relationship between the value of the swap and the event triggering default, and the rule for sharing claims in default. In swap defaults there is the added complication that the counterparty that is in default on its original debt could be due either to make or to receive a swap payment. If it is due to make a payment, it will, presumably, default on the swap contract as well as on the debt if the swap payment is subordinated to the debt. Alternatively, it could be due to receive a swap payment, in which case the swap payment could be received (increasing the value of the bankrupt firm) or withheld.

Although the treatment of swaps in default is not yet certain, the consensus appears to be consistent with the following assumption (Henderson and Cates (1986)):

A1: Swaps are subordinate to debt in bankruptcy. In the event of a default on its debt by a counterparty that is owed value in a swap, the value of the swap will be paid to the bankrupt firm. The swap contract will be treated as a contract for the net cash flows due in the swap, not as an exchange of gross amounts.

This assumption is used throughout this paper except where it is explicitly stated otherwise. We assume that no collateral is held by the counterparty exposed to default risk. The assumption that the swaps are not collateralized is important in comparing the sizes of the swap spreads and the debt market spreads.[2] In the limit, collateralization could reduce the equilibrium swap spread to zero. Our analysis could be extended to include collateral, but such an extension is beyond the scope of this paper.

---

[2] In the recent default by a Local Authority in England, collateralization did not seem to be important. By some estimates, bank counterparties in the swap contracts stand to lose around £200M.

II. Analysis of Default Risk: Distribution-Free Results for Single-Period Swaps

In this section we analyze the impact of settlement rules on the default risk of the swap and on wealth arising from the swap. Since we are interested in the simplest possible swap that will highlight the economic substance of the analysis, we focus on single-period swaps. At this stage, we make no distinction between interest-rate swaps and currency swaps because the qualitative substance of the results is not different for the two types. The stylized single-period setting that we analyze is characterized by the following assumptions:

A2: Capital markets are perfect and competitive. There are no deadweight costs to bankruptcy.

A3: There is one risky counterparty, called firm 1. It has real assets with current value V_0. At the maturity date of the debt T, the random value of the firm will be $\tilde{V}_T$.

A4: It has raised funds of amount B in a 'variable' debt market by issuing a zero coupon variable bond with face value $\tilde{X}_T$ and maturity T. The remainder of the firm is financed with equity. Equity pays no dividends prior to the debt maturity.

A5: There is a swap counterparty Z which is riskless. Firm 1 can contract with Z a swap which pays at time T the amount $(F - \tilde{X}_T)$ from firm 1 to Z. If $(F - \tilde{X}_T)$ is negative, the amount $(\tilde{X}_T - F)$ is paid at T from Z to firm 1.[3]

Debt in this case is zero coupon, and 'variable' debt involves a promise to pay, at the debt maturity date T, an amount which is equal to the realization of a random variable $\tilde{X}_T$. If no default occurs on the debt or the swap, the net effect of the swap is to convert the variable liability X_T to the fixed liability F. In the case of a currency swap, X_T will be equal to a fixed amount of foreign currency translated into dollars at the random exchange rate at time T (the payoff to a zero coupon foreign bond). In the case of an interest-rate swap, X_T will be equal to the principal amount in dollars multiplied by the cumulative wealth relative on a random interest rate between time zero and time T (the payoff to a rolled-up deposit). Although this treatment of the swap omits the important feature that net coupon flows occur throughout the life of the swap, introduced later in Section V, it does retain two important characteristics of swaps. The first is the fact that the swap is a net contract. The second is the economic setting characteristic of swaps, that they are most frequently used in conjunc-

---

[3] In each equilibrium we analyze we assume that the proceeds from the bond issue are unaffected by the swap and the swap proceeds are zero on the initiation of the swap. This means that the operations fo the firms are not affected by the type of liability issued.

Table 17.1: Cash Flows to Swap Participants at the Swap Maturity, Time T

Firm 1 issues a debt liability of face value X. It enters a swap with firm Z whereby the net swap payment is $(F - X)$ from firm 1 to Z. In the swap, firm 1 owes $(F - X)$ in states 1–3 and Z owes $(X - F)$ in states 4–6. The table shows the cash flows to the bondholders of firm 1 (B), the equity holders of firm 1 (E), and the riskless counterparty to the swap (Z). V is the value of the operating assets of firm 1. The table also shows the payoffs to two other claims: $C(V, F)$ a European call option on V with exercise price F, and $PX(V, X, F)$ a European put option on the maximum of V and X, with exercise price F.

Cash Flow

State	1 B_S	2 E_S	3 Z_S	4 $C(V, F)$	5 $PX(V, X, F)$
1 $V > F > X$	X	$(V - F)$	$(F - X)$	$(V - F)$	0
2 $F > V > X$	X	0	$(V - X)$	0	$(F - V)$
3 $F > X > V$	V	0	0	0	$(F - X)$
4 $V > X > F$	X	$(V - F)$	$-(X - F)$	$(V - F)$	0
5 $X > V > F$	X	$(V - F)$	$-(X - F)$	$(V - F)$	0
6 $X > F > V$	$(V + X - F)$	0	$-(X - F)$	0	0

tion with debt market instruments to change the characteristics of the debt.[4]

The way we analyze the net wealth transfers from the swap is to segment the future into six different states. These cover the following possibilities at the maturity date of the swap:

a) $F \gtreqless X_T$ determines who is the net payer,

b) $X_T \gtreqless V_T \gtreqless F$ determines the solvency status of firm 1.

Table 17.1 columns 1–3 show the payoffs to the bondholders and shareholders of firm 1 and the shareholders of the riskless counterparty in the swap. In this case, firm 1 issues a variable bond and swaps it for fixed with

---

[4] To illustrate that net settlement is preserved in this context, consider an interest rate swap with principal amount P, a fixed amount of interest of C per \$1 of principal during the period $[0, T]$, and variable interest of $\tilde{R}$ per \$1 of principal. In the stylized swap investigated in this section, the fixed and variable payments would be defined by: $F_T = P(1 + C)$ and $X_T = P(1 + \tilde{R})$, respectively, Thus, the contact is equivalent to a net exchange of coupons (with no principal exchange) at maturity.

the riskless counterparty. The settlement rule for the swap requires that Z makes the swap payment even when firm 1 is insolvent. Swap default can in this case result only in Z receiving a swap payment lower than promised in the swap contract. In state 6, for instance, Z makes a swap payment $(X_T - F)$ even though firm 1 is already bankrupt. This payment is then transferred to the bondholders of firm 1 as an addition to the liquidation value of the firm, V_T. In case 2 firm 1 is solvent until it has to make the swap payment. The residual claim after the bondholders have been paid is $(V_T - X_T)$, but this is not large enough to make the full swap payment. This amount is then paid to the swap counterparty Z, and the firm is bankrupt after the swap payment has been taken into account, even though it could afford to pay its bondholders. We assume that V_T and X_T are sufficiently variable to give positive probability to each state in Table 17.1:

A6: There is a positive probability of each state in Table 17.1.

For most realistic distributions of V and X, this assumption is innocuous.

Table 17.1 also shows the payoffs to two other claims, a European call option on V_T with exercise price F denoted $C(V, F)$, and a European put option on the maximum of V_T and X_T with an exercise price of F denoted $PX(V, X, F)$. By inspection, the following valuation relationships hold from Table 17.1:

$$E_S = C(V, F) \tag{1}$$

$$B_S = V_O - C(V, F) + X_0 - F_0 + PX(V, X, F) \tag{2}$$

$$Z_S = F_0 - X_0 - PX(V, X, F) \tag{3}$$

where E_S is the value of the equity of firm 1; B_S is the value of the risky debt of firm 1; X_0 is the value of a default free claim on X_T; F_0 is the value of a default free claim on F; Z_S is the value of the claim held by the swap counterparty Z. These pricing results are distribution-free and can be used to price the stylized type of swap discussed in this section.

To facilitate the analysis, we define four more values: $E_F = C(V, F)$ and $B_F = F_0 - P(V, F)$ are the values of the equity and debt resulting if firm 1 issues zero coupon debt of face value F and does not swap it, and $E_X = C(V, X)$ and $B_X = X_0 - P(V, X)$ are the values of the equity and debt resulting if firm 1 issues zero coupon variable debt with a promised payment of X_T and does not swap it. $P(V, F)$ and $P(V, X)$ are the values of European puts on V_T with exercise prices F and X_T, respectively. In the cases of $C(V, X)$ and $P(V, X)$, the exercises prices are stochastic.

The situation where the firm does not swap its debt is important because it enables us to compare the swap claim with debt market claims.

The value B_X is particularly important, since the holders of firm 1's debt do not control the decision to swap unless the debt contains a covenant to force the swap. They will, therefore, pay only the minimum of B_X (its unswapped value) or B_S (its swapped value) when the debt is issued. We now define the equilibrium swap rates and characterize the wealth transfers resulting from the swap.

The equilibrium swap rate $\bar{F}$ is the solution to the following expression:

$$Z_S\left(\bar{F}\right) = \bar{F}_0 - X_0 - PX\left(V, X, \bar{F}\right) = 0. \tag{4}$$

In a competitive swap market, this is the rate that would be set by Z in the swap settlement formula $(F - X_T)$. We now show the wealth effects resulting from firm 1 entering the swap.

PROPOSITION P1: *Any swap results in a wealth transfer to the debtholders of firm 1.*

Proof: If the debt is not swapped, its payoffs are identical to those in Column 1 of Table I except in states 5 and 6. In these states the payoff is V_T, which is lower than the payoff to the swapped debt. Using A6 proves the proposition that $B_S > B_X$.

COROLLARY C1: *An equilibrium swap results in a wealth transfer from the shareholders to the debtholders of firm 1 of a claim with value* $C(V, X) - C(V, \bar{F})$, *where $\bar{F}$ is the rate that solves expression* (4).

Proof: The value of the equity claim before the swap is $E_X = C(V, X)$. After the swap it is $E_S = C(V, \bar{F})$. Prior to the swap $E_X + B_X = V_0$. After the swap, $E_S + B_S + Z_S = V_0$. Using equation (4) and P1, $E_S < E_X$ for $F = \bar{F}$.

This result is a consequence of three important assumptions. First, the swap is subordinated to the debt and so cannot expropriate any rights of the debtholders.[5] Second, the debtholders do not control the decision to swap and will, therefore, not pay for any value added as a result of the swap, unless a covenant requires the swap. Finally, the default rule for the swap requires payment by Z even when the debt is in default, which results in the wealth transfer. Note that none of these assumptions are peculiar to the particular style of swap we are currently analyzing. This same

---

[5] Bondholders could be hurt by the swap if the swap payments are due before the debt matures. If, for instance, a swap were designed so that the firm makes payments before the debt matures and receives payments after, bondholders would be hurt by the swap payments and receive limited benefits in exchange. The swap we analyze is, however, of the same maturity as the debt because it is explicitly tailored to match the debt and change it from floating to fixed.

result holds for the usual coupon-bearing swaps, but a proof for coupon-bearing swaps involves solving complex algebraic expressions without generating further insight into this particular issue.

Proposition P1 and its corollary are a stronger version of the Turnbull (1987) argument that swaps are a zero sum game in a complete market. Here, the zero sum is the total of the wealth effects on shareholders and debtholders and the swap counterparty. Without the swap, the debtholders have a claim that pays $\min[V, X]$. With the swap, the debt claim pays $\min[\max(V, V + X - F), X]$. The swap raises the value of the total assets over which the debtholders have a claim, because $\max(V, V + X - F)$ dominates V.

This analysis raises two important questions. One is why the shareholders want the debt to be swapped when it has a negative effect on their wealth. Although our model cannot directly answer this question, it suggests what circumstances are necessary for shareholders to be willing to swap. Note that the wealth effect of the swap arises when variable debt is transformed to fixed. For a firm with a preference for fixed debt liabilities, the comparison that is relevant is the choice between issuing fixed rate debt directly and issuing variable debt and swapping it. The latter could be the preferred alternative under some circumstances. If the swap is covenanted at the time the variable rate debt is issued, then there will be no wealth effect, and the shareholders will be indifferent. There may, however, be agency effects of the type suggested by Wall and Pringle (1988) and Arak, Estrella, Goodman, and Silver (1988) whereby swaps, for instance, enable the borrower to take advantage of private knowledge concerning future creditworthiness. This may give rise to a preference for swapped variable rate debt rather than fixed rate debt, and the equity holders may prefer the swap despite its negative wealth effect in the absence of such agency considerations. Finally, if there is a pricing inefficiency between the variable and fixed debt markets that is larger than the wealth transfer caused by the swap, the swapped debt could have a positive wealth effect for equity when compared with unswapped fixed debt.

The second issue is whether the second wealth effects occur if the swap is from fixed to variable rather than from variable to fixed. To see that this is, indeed, the case, note that all the results so far are true (with appropriate modifications) if X and F are interchanged in Table 17.1. Thus, the wealth effects we are considering arise from the general nature of the swap contract and not from the specific circumstances of its use.

To clarify the nature of the wealth transfers and the relationship between swap rates and debt market rates, we now consider a swap that is not an equilibrium swap, but an exchange of equal market values of debt. Suppose that the firm enters a swap to exchange floating payments for fixed that does not change the value of the equity. This swap corresponds to an exchange of T_T for a fixed amount $\hat{F}$ defined by:

$$C(V,\hat{F}) = C(V,X).\tag{5}$$

In the absence of a swap, the value of debt and equity must sum to the value of the firm, so:

$$B_{\hat{F}} = B_X.\tag{6}$$

Thus the exchange of X and $\hat{F}$ is the exchange of amounts which, if issued as unswapped promised debt payments by the firm, would have equal values. We define the rate $\hat{F}$ as the equal value swap rate, and the following proposition holds:

PROPOSITION P2: *A swap that exchanges debt payments of equal value results in a wealth transfer from the counterparty Z to the debtholders of firm 1 of a claim with value* $PX(V, \hat{F}, X)$, *where* $\hat{F}$ *is the rate that solves expression* (6), *and* $PX(V, F, X)$ *is the value of a European put on the maximum of* V *and* F *with exercise price* X.

Proof: From equation (6), the value of the equity claim is unchanged by the swap. The value of the swap claim given by (3) is shown, in Appendix 2, to be equal to:

$$F_0 - X_0 - PX(V,X,F) = C(V,X) - C(V,F) - \left[C(X,F) - M(V,X,F)\right]\tag{7}$$

where $M(V, X, F)$ is the value of a European call on the minimum of V and X with exercise price F. Using (6) gives:

$$F_0 - X_0 - PX(V,X,\hat{F}) = -\left[C(X,\hat{F}) - M(V,X,\hat{F})\right].\tag{8}$$

From Stulz (1982), the right hand side is equal to $- PX(V, \hat{F}, X)$, which, by A6, is negative.

An equal value swap thus has negative value to the swap counterparty because the swap rate does not provide compensation for the incremental default risk arising from the way the swap is settled. This wealth transfer results from the subordination of the swap to the debt and the inability of Z to withhold the swap payment when firm 1 is in default on its debt. Default occurs if $V_T < X_T$. Firm 1 is owed a swap payment if $F < X_T$. Thus, both V_T and F must be lower than X_T for the wealth transfer to occur, and the resulting wealth transfer takes the form of an option that pays only if both V and $\hat{F}$ are less than X. The value of this option is $PX(V, \hat{F}, X)$.

The swap that exchanges debt payments with equal values results in a wealth transfer from Z to the debtholders of firm 1. Clearly Z would not be willing to enter into this swap without promised compensation in the form of the additional amount $(\bar{F} - \hat{F})$. This is summarized by the following:

PROPOSITION P3: *The equilibrium swap rate $\bar{F}$ is greater than the swap rate $\hat{F}$ that exchanges debt payments with equal market value.*

Proof: From P1, $C(V, X) - C(V, \bar{F}) > 0$. From equation (5) $C(V, X) = C(V, \bar{F})$. Consequently, $C(V, \bar{F}) < C(V, \bar{F})$, which implies $\bar{F} > \hat{F}$.

By analogy with P3, the opposite swap where firm 1 pays floating and receives fixed will have an equilibrium rate below $\hat{F}$. Thus, there will be a bid-ask spread in the swap market arising from the requirement to compensate the bank for the fact that it subsidizes the debtholders of firm 1 if the swap takes place at $\hat{F}$, regardless of the direction of the swap.

We can now derive the relationship between swap market default spreads and debt market default spreads. For the fixed rate debt market we define the default spread in a way equivalent to Merton (1974):

$$S_F = ln\left[\hat{F}_0 / B_{\hat{F}}\right] / T \tag{9}$$

where r is the continuously compounded riskless interest rate for maturity T, and:

$$\hat{F}_0 = \hat{F}e^{-rT}. \tag{10}$$

The spread is thus the interest rate equivalent to the discount of the bond's market value from the value it would have if there were no default risk. We define the variable spread in the same way:

$$S_X = ln\left[X_0 / B_X\right] / T \tag{11}$$

where X_0 is the default-free value of the promised variable payment, and B_X is its value including default risk.

The conventional way to define a swap spread is as the rate that must be added to the riskless fixed interest rate to obtain the swap quote, with the variable payment being treated as riskless. In the swap we are considering, the riskless value of the variable side of the swap is X_0, and the swap spread S_S is defined by:

$$F = X_0 e^{(r+S_s)T}. \tag{12}$$

Rearranging:

$$S_S = \ln[F_0/X_0]/T. \tag{13}$$

Given these definitions, it is now possible to derive the relationship between the swap market spread and the debt market spreads. Combining equations (9), (11), and (13) gives:

$$S_S = S_F - S_X + \ln[F_0/\hat{F}_0]/T. \tag{14}$$

The swap spread is made up of two components. The first, $(S_F - S_X)$, is the difference between equilibrium spreads in the fixed and variable interest rate markets. If the swap was equivalent to an exact exchange of the cash flow streams arising from the two types of risky debt, the swap spread would be equal to $(S_F - S_X)$. A swap with this rate would, however, from P2, have negative value to the bank. The swap rate contains a second element, which we call the pure swap spread S'_S. This arises from the incremental default risk in the swap, given the settlement rule in bankruptcy:

$$S'_S = \ln[F_0/\hat{F}_0]/T. \tag{15}$$

This is the additional rate required to compensate the swap counterparty for the value loss resulting from the way the swap is settled in bankruptcy. If the swap rate is the equilibrium rate $\bar{F}$, then from P3, $S'_S > 0$. Using equation (14) then yields, in equilibrium:

$$S_S > S_F - S_X \tag{16}$$

In equilibrium the swap spread should exceed the difference between the fixed and variable debt market spreads. The conventional test for swap arbitrage involves finding violations of the inequality (16). Such violations should not be observed in a perfect market, so the conventional arbitrage test is valid in our model, in the sense that violations of (16) indicate arbitrage opportunities.

III. Alternative Settlement Rules

In this section we analyze three possible treatments of the swap in default. These are not the most likely cases, but, given the uncertainty about the precise treatment of swap defaults, they illustrate the size of the risk introduced by alternative settlement rules. The swap we analyze is the same swap as in Section II. We analyze the following three alternative rules: (1) swap payments are made only if both counterparties to the swap are solvent prior to the swap payment (cross default); (2) the net payment is made before any cash flows are paid to the bondholders (prior settlement); and (3) the swap is treated as an exchange of gross amounts; the counterparty Z pays X_T to firm 1 and is then a subordinated creditor for the amount F (gross settlement).

Table 17.2 shows the cash flows to the debtholders and shareholders of firm 1 and to the swap counterparty Z at the maturity of the swap for each settlement rule. To analyze the equilibrium swap rate and wealth transfers in each case, we first prove the following proposition:

PROPOSITION P4: *Under any rule, an equilibrium swap results in a net wealth change of* $C(V, \hat{F}) - C(V, F^i)$ *for shareholders, where* F^i *is the equilibrium swap rate under that rule. Debtholders wealth changes by an equal amount in the opposite direction.*

Proof: From inspection of Table 17.2, it is clear that the value of the equity claim after the swap is $C(V, F^i)$ under all rules. The value of the equity claim before the swap is $C(V, X)$. From the definition of the equal value swap rate, $C(V, X) = C(V, \hat{F})$. So the shareholders net wealth change is $C(V, F^i) - C(V, \hat{F})$. Before the swap, the value of the debt and equity sum to V_0. After the swap, the value of the debt and equity and the swap value $Z_S(F^i)$ sum to V_0. The definition of the equilibrium swap rate is $Z_S(F^i) = 0$. So the wealth gain or loss of the equity is a transfer from or to the debt.

We now characterize the equilibrium swap rates and wealth transfers under the three alternative default rules.

PROPOSITION P5: *With cross-default, the equilibrium swap rate* F^c *solves:*

$$C(V,X) - C(V,F^c) = W(V,X,F^c) \qquad (17)$$

where $W(V, X, F^c)$ *is a claim that pays* $(X_T - V_T)$ *if* $X_T > V_T > F^c$. *An equilibrium swap results in a wealth transfer from shareholders to debtholders of firm 1 of value* $W(V, X, F^c)$.

Proof: From Table 17.2A, $Z_S(F^c) = C(V, X) - C(V, F^c) - W(V, X, F^c)$. The equilibrium condition is $Z_S(F^c) = 0$. Combining these gives equation (17). The wealth transfer from equity is $C(V, F^c) - C(V, X)$, equal to $W(V, X. F^c) > 0$.

The impact of cross default is that the swap is canceled when the firm is in default on its debt. This enables the bank to withhold the swap payment due in state 6. In state 5, the value of the firm's assets is less than its

Table 17.2: Cash Flow to Swap Participants at the Swap Maturity Time T, Alternative Settlement Rules

Firm 1 issues a debt liability of face value $\tilde{X}$. It enters a swap with firm Z whereby the net swap payment is $(F + X)$ from firm 1 to Z. In the swap, firm 1 owes $(F - X)$ in states 1–3 and Z owes $(X - F)$ in states 4–6. The table also shows the payoffs to the following claims: $C(V, X)$ is a European call option on V with exercise price X; $C(V, F)$ is a European call option on V with exercise price F; $W(V, X, F)$ is a claim that pays $(X - V)$ if $X > V > F$; F_0, X_0, and V_0 are unconditional claims on F, X_T, and V_T, respectively; $P(V + X, F)$ is a European put option on $(V + X)$ with exercise price F. In Panel A State 2, the equity holders of firm 1 pay in $(X - V)$ to prevent bankruptcy.

Panel A: Cross-default: swap payment made only if both counterparties solvent prior to the swap payment

State	B	E	Z	$C(V, X) - C(V, F)$	$W(V, X, F)$
1 $V > F > X$	X	$(V - F)$	$(F - X)$	$(F - X)$	0
2 $F > V > X$	X	0	$(V - X)$	$(V - X)$	0
3 $F > X > V$	V	0	0	0	0
4 $V > X > F$	X	$(V - F)$	$-(X - F)$	$-(X - F)$	0
5 $X > V > F$	X	$(V - F)$	$-(X - F)$	$-(V - F)$	$(X - V)$
6 $X > F - V$	V	0	0	0	0

Panel B: Prior settlement: net swap payment made before any payments to bondholders

State	B	E	Z	$(F_0 - X_0)$	$P(V + X, F)$
1 $V > F > X$	X	$(V - F)$	$(F - X)$	$(F - X)$	0
2 $F > V; F > X;$ $V + X > F$	$(V + X - F)$	0	$(F - X)$	$(F - X)$	0
3 $F > V; F > X;$ $V + X < F$	0	0	V	$(F - X)$	$(F - V - X)$
4 $V > X > F$	X	$(V - F)$	$-(X - F)$	$-(X - F)$	0
5 $X > V > F$	X	$(V - F)$	$-(X - F)$	$-(X - F)$	0
6 $X > F > V$	$(V + X - F)$	0	$-(X - F)$	$-(X - F)$	0

Panel C: Gross settlement: swap is treated as an exchange of gross amounts

State	B	E	Z	$(V_0 - X_0)$	$C(V, F)$
1 $V < F$	X	0	$(V - X)$	$(V - X)$	0
2 $V > F$	X	$(V - F)$	$(F - X)$	$(V - X)$	$(V - F)$

debt market liability, but it benefits the shareholders to contribute enough to save the firm from bankruptcy and receive the swap payment.

PROPOSITION P6: *With prior settlement, the equilibrium swap rate* F^P *solves:*

$$V_0 - C\left(V + X, F^P\right) = 0 \tag{18}$$

where $C(V + X, F^P)$ *is the value of a European call on* $(V_T + X_T)$ *with exercise price* F^P. *An equilibrium swap results in a wealth transfer of* $C(V, F^P) - C(V, X)$ *between debtholders and shareholders of the firm.*

Proof: From Table 17.2B, $Z_S(F^P) = F_0^P - X_0 - P(V + X, F^P)$. The equilibrium condition is $Z_S(F^P)$. From put-call parity:

$$P\left(V + X, F^P\right) = C\left(V + X, F^P\right) - V_0 - X_0 + F_0^P.$$

Substitution for $P(V + X, F^P)$ in $Z_S(F^P) = 0$ yields equation (18). The wealth transfer between debt and equity cannot be signed in this case.

The equilibrium swap rate with prior settlement F^P is lower than the equilibrium swap rate $\bar{F}$. The equilibrium conditions are:

$$\bar{F}_0 - X_0 - PX\left(V, X, \bar{F}\right) = 0 \tag{19}$$

$$F_0^P - X_0 - P\left(V + X, F^P\right) = 0 \tag{20}$$

From inspection of Tables 17.1 and 17.2B, $P(V + X, F^P) < PX(V, X, \bar{F})$. Thus:

$$\bar{F}_0 = X_0 - P\left(V + X, \bar{F}\right) > 0 \tag{21}$$

From the proof of P6:

$$V_0 - C\left(V + X, \bar{F}\right) > 0 \tag{22}$$

The value of the call in equation (22) is decreasing in F. The condition for F^P is (18). Thus:

$$F^P < \bar{F}.$$

Prior settlement is advantageous to the swap counterparty and enables him to offer a lower swap rate than the equilibrium swap rate $\bar{F}$. Prior to settlement also potentially results in a wealth transfer from debt to equity, since it appropriates part of the debtholders prior claim on a firm's assets. If debtholders believe that prior settlement is possible, however, they will price their debt claim accordingly, and the resulting wealth transfer from swapping will again be from the equity to the debt.

With gross settlement of the swap, shown in Table 17.2C, the claims held are quite simple. The gross payment by Z of the variable cash flow due in the swap effectively fully guarantees the debt of firm 1. The swap counterparty Z then holds a fixed claim of face value F on the assets of the firm. This results in the following equilibrium:

PROPOSITION P7: *With gross settlement, the equilibrium swap rate* F^G *solves:*

$$V_0 - X_0 - C\left(V, F^G\right) = 0 \tag{23}$$

A swap at this rate results in wealth transfer of $P(V, X)$ *from the shareholders to the debtholders of firm* 1.

Proof: Equation (23) is obvious from inspection of Table 17.2C. The wealth change for the shareholders is $C(V, F^G) - C(V, \hat{F}) = C(V, F^G) - C(V, X)$. Substituting (23) gives a wealth change of $V_0 - X_0 - C(V, X)$. From put-call parity, this is equal to $- P(V, X)$.

This wealth transfer results from the fact that the swap effectively guarantees the debt. The debtholders will not, however, pay for this guarantee, since they may not receive it if the swap does not occur. Thus, when the swap occurs, the price of guaranteeing the debt, $P(V, X)$, is effectively paid by the equity holders.

IV. Determinants of the Equilibrium Swap Spread

The results in the previous sections were presented in terms of general contingent claims without making specific assumptions about the stochastic processes followed by the value of the firm V and the variable swap payment X. In this section, we specialize the analysis to the case of currency swaps. In Section V, interest-rate coupon swaps are analyzed in more detail.

The variable payment in a currency swap is a fixed amount of foreign currency, with a corresponding value in dollars solely dependent on the exchange rate. We assume that the value of the firm's assets V and the present value in dollars of the foreign currency payment X follow joint geometric Brownian processes:

$$dV/V = \mu_V\, dt + \sigma_V dz_V \tag{24}$$

$$dX/X = \mu_X\, dt + \sigma_X dz_X \tag{25}$$

where dz_V and dz_X are increments to standard Wiener processes with $dz_V dz_X = \sigma dt$. At earlier dates $t \in [O,T]$, X_t is defined as the value of a default-free claim on X_T. This is the value in dollars of a fixed amount of foreign currency to be received at time T. The final assumptions are:

A7: Trading in assets takes place continuously.

A8: The continuous interest rate in dollars, r, is constant.[6]

Given these assumptions, all of the contingent claims arising from the default-risk of the swap are continuously spanned by a combination of the riskless security, the asset V_t, and the asset X_t. The swap can be valued using the results in Black and Scholes (1973), Margrabe (1978), and Stulz (1982). The value of the swap is, from Appendix 2:

$$Z_S = C(V,X) - C(V,F) - C(X,F) + M(V,X,F) \tag{26}$$

The values of the components of this expression are (see Appendix 3):

$$C(V,X) = V_0 N(d_w + \overline{\sigma}_w) - X_0 N(d_w) \tag{27}$$

$$C(V,F) = X_0 N(d_v + \overline{\sigma}_v) - F_0 N(d_v) \tag{28}$$

$$C(X,F) = X_0 N(d_x + \overline{\sigma}_x) - F_0 N(d_x) \tag{29}$$

$$M(V,X,F) = V_0 N_2\left(d_v + \overline{\sigma}_v, -(d_w + \overline{\sigma}_w), \rho_k\right) \\ + X_0 N_2\left(d_x + \overline{\sigma}_x, d_w, \rho_w\right) - F_0 N_2\left(d_x, d_v, \rho\right) \tag{30}$$

with:

$$F_0 = Fe^{-rT}\,;\, \overline{\sigma}_v = \sigma_v \sqrt{T}\,;\, \overline{\sigma}_x = \sigma_x \sqrt{T}\,;\, \overline{\sigma}_v^2 = \overline{\sigma}_v^2 + \overline{\sigma}_x^2 - 2\rho\overline{\sigma}_v\overline{\sigma}_x\,;\\ \rho_w = \left(\rho\sigma_v - \sigma_w\right)\,\sigma_w\,;\, \rho_k = \left(\rho\sigma_x - \sigma_v\right)/\sigma_w$$

---

[6] This assumption is, of course, unsustainable for interest-rate swaps. Currency swaps are, however, those where the default risk problem is greater.

and:

$$d_x = \left[ln(X_0/F_0) - \bar{\sigma}_x^2/2 \right]/\bar{\sigma}_x \tag{31}$$

$$d_v = \left[ln(V_0/F_0) - \bar{\sigma}_v^2/2 \right]/\bar{\sigma}_v \tag{32}$$

$$d_w = \left[ln(V_0/X_0) - \bar{\sigma}_w^2/2 \right]/\bar{\sigma}_w \tag{33}$$

Where $N_2[d_1, d_2, \sigma]$ is the standard bivariate normal distribution function with correlation σ evaluated at d_1 and d_2. $N[d]$ is the standard univariate normal distribution function evaluated at d.

When the swap contract is to exchange debt payments with equal market value, the claim that is transferred from the swap counterparty to the debtholders of firm 1 is equal to:[7]

$$
\begin{aligned}
PX(V,\hat{F},X) = {} & X_0 \left[d_x - \bar{\sigma}_x \right] - \hat{F}_0 N[d_x] - X_0 N_2 \left[d_x + \bar{\sigma}_x, d_w, \rho_w \right] \\
& + \hat{F}_0 N_2 \left[d_x, d_v, \rho \right] - V_0 N_2 \left[d_x + \rho\bar{\sigma}_v, d_v + \bar{\sigma}_v, \rho \right] \\
& + V_0 N_2 \left[d_x + \rho\bar{\sigma}_v, d_w + \bar{\sigma}_w, \rho_w \right]
\end{aligned}
\tag{34}
$$

Table 17.3 shows representative values of the swap spread. Panel A shows the effect of changing the leverage of the risky counterparty for the cases where the assets of firm 1 are uncorrelated with the variable debt payment and the case where default spreads are equal in the fixed and floating markets. Increased leverage increases spreads in both debt markets and in the swap market. Similarly, in Panel B where the maturities of the debt and swap are varied, a longer maturity raises all spreads. Panel C shows the effect of changing the correlation of the assets of the firm with the payment due on the variable debt. As this correlation rises the pure swap spread falls. The total swap spread is compensation to the counterparty Z for the default by firm 1 when it owes a swap payment. This occurs if both V and X are low. As the correlation between V and X rises, this is more likely, and the swap spread rises. Note, however, that the total swap spread rises because the decline in the variable spread dominates the decline in the pure spread in the expression $S_S = S_F - S_X + S'_S$. In all cases, the swap spread is lower than the debt market spreads, often by a considerable margin. This results from the different amounts of exposure in the

---

[7] There is a corresponding set of expressions for a risky counterparty issuing fixed-rate debt and swapping it for floating with a riskless counterparty.

Table 17.3: Equilibrium Swap Spreads in Basic Points per Annum

Firm 1 issues a debt liability of face value $\tilde{X}$. It enters a swap to exchange this for a fixed liability F. S_X and S_F are default spreads in the variable and fixed rate debt markets. S_S is the equilibrium swap spread quoted as a rate per annum by which the default free value of F exceeds the default free value of X. $S'_X = S_S - (S_F - S_X)$ is the pure swap spread which compensates the swap counterparty for the incremental default risk arising from the difference between the way that the swap is settled and the way that risky debt is settled. σ_V is the volatility of the firm's assets, σ_X the volatility of $\tilde{X}$, and ρ the correlation between V and X. r is the riskless interest rate, T the maturity of the debt and the swap, and B / V the market value of debt divided by the market value of assets of the firm.

Panel A: $\sigma_V = 0.3$; $\sigma_X = 0.1$; $r = 0.1$; $T = 5$

	B/V	0.10	0.20	0.30	0.40	0.50
$\rho = 0$	S_X	1	12	49	117	222
	S_F	0	8	36	93	186
	S_S	0	2	10	25	50
	S'_S	1	4	23	49	66
$\rho = 0.167$	S_X	0	8	36	94	186
	S_F	0	8	36	94	186
	S_S	0	3	14	33	62
	S'_S	0	3	14	33	62

Panel B: $\sigma_V = 0.3$; $\sigma_X = 0.1$; $r = 0.1$; $B/V = 0.04$; $\rho = 0$

T	1	3	5	10	20
S_X	3	59	117	207	289
S_F	1	44	93	174	250
S_S	0	12	25	52	88
S'_S	2	27	49	85	127

Panel C: $\sigma_V = 0.3$; $\sigma_X = 0.07$; $r = 0.1$; $T = 5$

B/V	0.30	0.30	0.30	0.50	0.50	0.50
ρ	0.25	0.00	−0.25	0.25	0.00	−0.25
S_X	30	42	56	166	204	242
S_F	36	36	36	186	186	186
S_S	12	8	4	51	37	24
S'_S	6	14	24	31	55	80

two contracts. The debt contract exposes the entire repayment to default. The swap, however, only exposes the net difference between the cash flows due to two debt contracts.[8]

Clearly, the inclusion of coupons in the model would reduce default spreads. This will, however, affect both the bond and the swap contract. Thus, it will not necessarily reduce the swap spread relative to the debt spread. To do so it would be necessary for the reduction of default risk due to the coupon stream to be greater for a swap contract than for a debt contract. Since the swap is subordinated to the debt, this may well be the case, as part of the cash flow to the swap will occur prior to part of the cash flow to the debt when there is a coupon stream.

V. Swaps of Coupon-Bearing Debt

In this section we examine interest rate swaps of debt with coupons. We replace equation (24) with the following:

$$dV = (\alpha V - C)dt + \sigma_V V dz_V \qquad (35)$$

The coefficient α is the instantaneous expected rate of return on the firm, and C represents the total dollar payout by the firm per unit of time.

Instead of A8 we now assume that the term structure of interest rates is fully specified by the instantaneous riskless rate r. Its dynamics are given by:[9]

---

[8] With two risky counterparties engaged in the swap, there is a possibility of default by either. The claims exchanged in the swap now depend upon the values of the assets of both firms engaged in the swap. Against a risky counterparty firm 1 can now swap at an apparently more favourable rate (a lower value of F) than with a riskless counterparty. This is, however, simply compensation for the extra default risk. With two risky counterparties we can split the change in the value of the equity resulting from the swap contract into two components. The first component is the gain that would arise from swapping with a riskless counterparty. The second component, which is always negative, is the loss from the fact that the counterparty is risky. We have solved for these values by Monte Carlo simulation. The Monte Carlo results indicate that the gain to the equity holders of a firm swapping with a risky counterparty is increasing in the asset value of the counterparty firm, decreasing in ρ_{VX} of the counterparty firm if the counterparty issued variable rate debt and is paying fixed in the swap, and increasing in ρ_{VX} of the counterparty firm of the counterparty issued fixed rate debt and is paying variable in the swap. The effect of the correlation between the counterparty asset value and the variable payment occurs because X determines who is due to pay in the swap. If the counterparty is due to pay when X is high and has assets highly correlated with X, this makes the swap more valuable. If the counterparty is due to pay when X is low and has assets highly correlated with X, this makes the swap less valuable.

[9] These dynamics are similar to those used by Brennan and Schwartz (1982). An alternative interest rate process is used in Ramaswamy and Sundaresan (1986). These papers contain discussion of the relative merits of different processes.

$$dr = m(\mu - r)dt + \sigma_r r\, dz_r, \quad m > 0, \mu > 0, dz_r dz_V = \rho_{Vr} dt \tag{36}$$

The instantaneous drift term $m(\mu - r)$ represents a force that pulls the interest rate towards its long-term value μ with magnitude proportional to the current deviation.

For any security issued by the corporation, its market value at any point in time can be written as a function of V and r alone. For a fixed rate corporate bond, with value B, the dynamics are, using Ito's Lemma:

$$dB = [B_V(\alpha V - C) + B_r m(\mu - r) + B_t + 1/2(B_{VV}\sigma_V^2 V^2 + B_{rr}\sigma_r^2 r^2 \tag{37}$$
$$+ 2B_{Vr}Vr\sigma_V\sigma_r\rho_{Vr})]dt + B_V V\sigma_V dz_V + B_r r\sigma_r dz_r$$

Using the traditional argument that results in a no-arbitrage condition for the price gives:

$$B_V\left[(\alpha V - C) - K_1\sigma_V V\right] + B_r\left[m(\mu - r) - K_2\sigma_r r\right] + B_t \tag{38}$$
$$+ \frac{1}{2}\left(B_{VV}\sigma_V^2 V^2 + B_{rr}\sigma_r^2 r^2 + 2B_{Vr}Vr\sigma_V\sigma_r\rho_{Vr}\right) + C - rB = 0$$

where $K_1 = (\alpha - r)/\sigma_V$.

We assume that the market is risk-neutral with respect to nominal interest rate risk, so the Local Expectation Hypothesis of the term structure holds, and $K_2 = 0$. The corporate bond price must then satisfy the following equation at all times:[10]

$$B_V(rV - C) + B_r m(\mu - r) + \frac{1}{2}\left(B_{VV}\sigma_V^2 V^2 + B_{rr}\sigma_r^2 r^2 + 2B_{Vr}Vr\sigma_V\sigma_r\rho_{Vr}\right) \tag{39}$$
$$+ C - rB = -B_t$$

The terminal condition is:

$$B(V, r, T, C) = \min(F, V) \tag{40}$$

We assume that coupons are paid semiannually and that the firm will default on the coupon if the value of the firm at any coupon date falls below the coupon payment. In that case the value of the firm's assets V is

---

[10] As Dothan (1978) points out, the term structure of interest rates will, in general, depend upon the risk preference parameter K_2. Equilibrium swap spreads will also depend upon this parameter. We leave open the question of how large this dependence is.

paid to the debtholders, and the firm is liquidated. Thus $B(V, r, T, C) = V$ if $V \le C$, $t < T$, and t is a coupon date.

To define the interest rate spreads, we also need the coupons on default-free government bonds. For a coupon-paying government bond with value $G(r, t, C)$ the corresponding PDE is:

$$G_r\left[m(\mu - r)\right] + 1/2 G_{rr}\sigma_r^2 r^2 + C - rG = -G_t \qquad (41)$$

with terminal condition $G(r, T, C) = F$.

To determine the value of the default risk spread in the fixed and variable markets we use the following procedure. First, we determine the fixed coupon rate that makes a default-free bond sell at a price equal to its face value F. For variable coupon bonds this is simply r_t. For fixed rate bonds it is the coupon rate g, such that $G(r, 0, g, F) = F$. We then determine the coupon rate required for a bond subject to default risk to sell at par at the date of issuance. Bond prices depend on the short term interest rate, the value of the firm, time to maturity, and how the processes z_V and z_r are correlated. Accordingly, the default risk spreads will reflect these characteristics. The spread for risky variable bonds is defined by the fixed mark-up to the coupon rate that reflects the credit risk of a particular bond. This spread S_X is defined by $B(V, r, 0, (r + S_X)F) = F$. Similarly, the spread for the default risk of fixed coupon bonds is given by the coupon rate differential S_F such that $B(V, r, 0, (g + S_F)F) = F$. To determine these spreads we use the Hopscotch method. This method, developed by Gourley (1970) can be applied to solve parabolic and elliptic equations in two dimensions with a mixed derivative term (see Gourley and McKee (1977)).[11]

In Table 17.4 we present the equilibrium spreads for both fixed coupon and variable coupon bonds. The parameters for the interest rate process are $m = 0.72$, $\mu = 0.09$, and $\sigma_r^2 = 0.006$. The instantaneous variance of the return on the firm is $\sigma_V^2 = 0.09$.[12] Table 17.4 reports the spreads for a current value of $r = 10\%$ and different values of the debt to firm value ratio and the correlation parameter ρ_{Vr}. All bonds have five years to maturity. For both fixed and variable bonds, the spread increases with the debt to firm value ratio. A lower value of the correlation parameters also raises

---

[11] More specifically, we have used the "line" version of the Hopscotch method, appropriate in applications with mixed derivative terms and variable coefficient (see Gourlay and McKee (1977)). In the first time step we solved explicitly for bond values at alternating values of r for all firm values. Then we used these calculated values to set up the tridiagonal equation system of the remaining values of r and solved it by elimination. The second step is solved implicitly in the direction of V. For any particular grid point, explicit and implicit calculations are used at alternating time steps. At coupon dates implicit replacements were used.

Table 17.4: Fixed Coupon Spreads and Variable Coupon Spreads due to Default-Risk in Basis Points per Annum

A firm has assets of value V and a single debt issue of value B. B/V is the market-value leverage; ρ_{Vr} is the correlation between the firm value and the interest rate; S_F is the default spread in the fixed debt market; and S_X is the default spread in the floating rate market. The volatility of firm value is 30 percent per annum. Bonds pay coupons twice a year and have a 5-year maturity. The instantaneous interest rate is r. Its dynamics are given by: $dr = m(\mu - r)dt + \sigma_r dz_i$. The parameter values are: $m = 0.72$, $\mu = 0.09$, and $\sigma_r^2 = 0.006$.

	B/V = 0.30			B/V = 0.50		
ρ_{Vr}	0.25	0.00	−0.25	0.25	0.00	−0.25
S_F	16	18	20	66	69	72
S_X	12	19	27	57	71	87
$S_F - S_X$	+4	−1	−7	+9	−2	−15

the floating rate spread, indicating a higher credit risk. The spread in the variable rate market is more sensitive to changes in the value of the correlation parameter. Thus, for $\rho_{Vr} = -0.25$, the spread in the variable rate market is bigger than the spread in the fixed rate market, and the opposite occurs for $\rho_{Vr} = 0.25$.

To compute the swap spread in a way that is consistent with the debt market spreads, we use the following procedure. Suppose that the firm issues bonds that promise to pay a coupon rate of $(r_t + S_X)$, and at the same time it agrees to a coupon swap of $(r_t + S_X)$ for $(g + S_F)$ with a riskless counterparty. If, at coupon dates, $(r_t + S_X) < (g + S_F)$ and the firm is solvent, it pays the counterparty a net amount of $[g + S_F - r_t - S_X]F$. Conversely, if $(r_t + S_X) > (g + S_F)$, the bank will pay the firm an amount equal to $[r_t + S_X - g - S_F]F$. This swap corresponds to the swap of equal values of debt discussed in Section II. Once the firm enters the swap it promises to pay a total coupon rate of $(g + S_F)$, to be divided between the bondholders and the swap counterparty. Ex post, shareholders of the firm are worse off if the firm enters the swap and happens to be the net payer and are better off if the firm enters the swap and becomes the net receiver. Ex ante, since the present values of two bonds issued by the firm, one paying a fixed coupon rate of $(g + S_F)$ and other paying a variable

---

[12] Except for m, the speed of reversion, we have used parameter values similar to those in Ramaswamy and Sundaresan (1986). The low rate of mean reversion was used so that short rate behavior resembles a random walk.

coupon rate of $(r_t + S_x)$ would be equal, shareholders are indifferent when the firm agrees to this swap contract. Bondholders, however, gain because the cash flow to service the debt will be increased by the counterparty payment when the firm is due to receive on the swap. Consequently, whereas the straight floating rate notes sell at par F the swapped floating rate notes will be worth more than par. At any point in time the swapped price must satisfy the following equation:

$$B_V \left[rV - (g + S_F)F \right] + B_r m (\mu - r) +$$
$$\frac{1}{2} \left(B_{VV} \sigma_r^2 V^2 + B_{rr} \sigma_r^2 r^2 + 2 B_{Vr} V r \sigma_V \sigma_r \rho_{Vr} \right) + (r + S_x)F - rB = -B_t \quad (42)$$

Because there is no swap cash flow at the maturity date, the terminal condition (40) still holds.

At any time the firm will default on the bond if it cannot pay the promised amount of $[r_t + S_x]F$ to the debtholders. But now the cash flows to service the debt can come from two different sources: the firm's assets with value V and the claim on the assets of the swap counterparty. We assume, therefore, a default boundary on the debt $t < T$ which is given by:

$$B(V, r, r + S_x, t) = \begin{cases} \min \left[V + (r_t + S_x - g - S_F)F, (r_t + S_x)F \right] \\ \qquad \text{if } r_t + S_x > g + S_F \\ \min \left[V, (r_t + S_x)F \right] \\ \qquad \text{if } r_t + S_x \le g + S_F \end{cases} \quad (43)$$

The first inequality refers to the case where the firm is receiving a swap payment. It then defaults on its debt if its assets plus the swap payments at the current rate will not cover the coupon payments on the debt. The second applies when the firm is due to make a swap payment. It then defaults on its debt when its assets will not cover the coupon payments on the debt.

This equal value swap is not an equilibrium transaction, since it has a negative value for the riskless counterparty. As a result, the firm must increase the fixed coupon it offers in exchange for $r_t + S_x$. The equilibrium swap rate is the agreement to exchange $r_t + S_x$ for a fixed coupon rate c_s, such that the swap claim has zero value. By deviating from a total cash flow per unit time of $g + S_F$, the value of the equity will fall. Similarly, by paying a higher coupon rate on the swap c_s, the value of the debt will decrease relative to the equal value swap, both because the likelihood of the firm being the net receiver will go down and because the net amount received in that swap will drop.

To solve for the equilibrium swap rate we use the Hopscotch algorithm referred to above. First, we solve for the value of the bonds according to equation (42) for a given debt to value of the firm ratio B / V. We then increase the fixed spread by S'_S, such that $c_s = g + (S_F + S'_S)$ and solve for new values of the debt and equity. We repeat this procedure until, for the particular value of the pure swap spread S'_S, $V = \bar{B} + \bar{E}$. The corresponding coupon rate c_S is the equilibrium swap quote that makes the value of the swap claim zero, since the values of the swapped debt, the equity, and the swap itself must sum to the value of the firm.

We then compare the equilibrium spread in the swap market with the bond market spreads. The equilibrium swap is an offer to exchange c_S for $r_t + S_X$. This is equivalent, because of net settlement, to an offer to exchange $c_S - S_X$ for r_t. We, therefore, define the swap spread as:

$$S_S = c_S - S_X - g \qquad (44)$$

This is the coupon that must be added to the government bond rate in an equilibrium swap offered in exchange for r_t. The fixed swap coupon c_S is equal to $g + S_F + S'_S$, so that:

$$S_S = S_F - S_X + S'_S \qquad (45)$$

This expression is identical to equation (14) for the zero coupon swap analyzed in Section III.

Table 17.5 reports the values of swap market spreads in six different situations. As in the currency swap case, the pure swap spread S'_S is inversely proportional to the correlation parameter ρ_{Vr}. The total swap spread is an increasing function of ρ_{Vr} because a rise in the correlation of the firm's assets with the variable payment reduces the variable spread S_X. This effect dominates the rise in the pure swap spread in expression (45). The order of magnitude of the relationship between the pure swap spread S'_S, the swap spread S_S, and the debt market spreads S_F and S_X is similar in Table 17.5 to the relationship in Table 17.3 for zero coupon currency swaps. Although the two tables are not strictly comparable, both suggest that the equilibrium swap spread is significantly lower than debt market spreads.

VI. Summary and Conclusions

We have characterized the exchange of financial claims arising from risky swaps. These transfers are between three groups: shareholders, debt-

Table 17.5: Interest Rate Swap Market Spreads in Basis Points per Annum

A Firm has assets of value V and a single debt issue of value B. B/V is the market-value leverage; ρ_{Vr} is the correlation between the firm value and the interest rate; S_F is the default spread in the fixed debt market; and S_X is the default spread in the floating rate market. The volatility of firm value is 30 percent per annum. Bonds pay coupons twice a year and have a 5-year maturity. The instantaneous interest rate is r. Its dynamics are given by: $dr = m(\mu - r)dt + \sigma_r dz_r$. The parameter values are: $m = 0.72$, $\mu = 0.09$, and $\sigma_r^2 = 0.006$. The firm swaps from a floating rate debt issue to a fixed rate, paying C_S fixed in exchange for $(r + S_X)$. A default free fixed rate bond pays a coupon of g. The equilibrium swap spread is $S_S = C_S - S_X$ quoted as a rate annum by which the default free value of the fixed side of the swap exceeds the default free value of the floating side. The pure swap spread is S'_S which compensates the swap counterparty for the incremental default risk arising from the difference between the way that the swap is settled and the way that risky debt is settled.

	B/V = 0.30			B/V = 0.50		
ρ_{Vr}	0.25	0.00	−0.25	0.25	0.00	−0.25
S_X	12	19	27	57	71	87
$c_S - g$	18	23	30	77	89	104
S_S	6	4	3	20	18	17
S'_S	2	5	10	11	20	32

holders and the swap counterparty. Swaps generally result in wealth transfers from shareholders to debtholders.

We have derived equilibrium swap rates and related them to debt market spreads. In the case of geometric Brownian motion we obtained closed form solutions for the value of the default risk in the swap. These values are of a significantly lower order of magnitude than debt market spreads. We extended the analysis to include coupon payments and to analyze swaps between two risky counterparties. It remains to be tested whether this model can explain such empirical features of swap markets as the level of swap spreads and their relationship to the variables that determine them in equilibrium. Other extensions would be to include the effects of collateralizing the swap and then to embed this analysis in a model with agency effects or other imperfections that can provide a motivation for the swap transaction.

Appendix 17.1: Net cash flow for $1 of principal due to the receiver of fixed rate dollars in a swap

A: Interest-rate swap

Time	1	. . .	$N-1$	N
Cash Flow	$(C - \tilde{R}_1)$		$(C - \tilde{R}_{N-1})$	$(C - \tilde{R}_N)$

B: Currency swap

Time	1	. . .	$N-1$	N
Cash Flow	$C - C_F \tilde{E}_1$		$C - C_F \tilde{E}_{N-1}$	$(C + 1) - (C_F + P_F)\tilde{E}_N$

Time is in units equal to the coupon frequency.

C: Coupon in dollars per $1 principal value
R_i: Variable rate at time i (random)
E_i: Exchange rate in dollars per unit of foreign currency at time i (random)
C_F: Coupon in foreign currency per $1 principal value
P_F: Principal in foreign currency per $1 principal value
N: Maturity of swap.

Appendix 17.2: From Stulz (1982) equations (14), (12), and (11)

$$PX(V, X, F) = F_0 - MX(V, X, 0) + MX(V, X, F) \tag{A2.1}$$
$$MX(V, X, F) = C(V, F) + C(X, F) - M(V, X, F) \tag{A2.2}$$
$$M(V, X) = V_0 - C(V, X) \tag{A2.3}$$

Where $MX(V, X, F)$ is a European call option on the maximum of V and X with an exercise price of F.

Substituting (A2.2) in (A2.1) and using $C(V, 0) = V_0$, $C(X, 0) = X_0$, and (A2.3) gives:

$$PX(V, X, F) = F_0 - X_0 - C(V, X) + C(V, F) + C(X, F) - M(V, X, F) \tag{A2.4}$$

Rearranging gives equation (7). Using (4) gives:

$$Z_S = C(V, X) - C(V, F) - C(X, F) + M(V, X, F) \tag{A2.5}$$

Appendix 17.3: From Stulz (1982) equation (11), with the correction noted in Johnson (1987)

$$M(V, X, F) = X_0 N_2(\gamma_1 + \sigma_x\sqrt{T}, (\ln(V_0/X_0)$$
$$- 1/2\,\sigma_w^2 T) / \sigma_w\sqrt{T}, (\rho\sigma_V - \sigma_x) / \sigma_w)$$
$$+ V_0 N_2(\gamma_2 + \sigma_V\sqrt{T}, (\ln(X_0/V_0)$$
$$- 1/2\,\sigma_w^2 T) / \sigma_w\sqrt{T}, (\rho\sigma_x - \sigma/v) / \sigma_w)$$
$$- F_0 N_2(\gamma_1, \gamma_2, \rho)$$

where:

$$\gamma_1 = (\ln(X_0/F_0) - 1/2\,\sigma_x^2 T) / \sigma_x\sqrt{T},$$
$$\gamma_2 = (\ln(V_0/F_0) - 1/2\,\sigma_V^2 T) / \sigma_V\sqrt{T},$$
$$\sigma_w^2 = \sigma_V^2 + \sigma_x^2 - 2\rho\sigma_{Vo}x,$$

substituting for γ_1, γ_2, $\bar{\sigma}_V$, $\bar{\sigma}_x$, $\bar{\sigma}_w$, ρ_w, ρ_x, d_x, d_V, d_w gives equation (30).

REFERENCES

Arak, Marcelle, Laurie S. Goodman, and Arthur Rones. 1986. Credit lines for new instruments: Swaps, over-the-counter options, forwards and floor-ceiling agreements, Conference on Bank Structure and Competition, Federal Reserve Bank of Chicago, 437–456.

———, Arturo Estrella, Laurie S. Goodman, and Andrew Silver. 1988. Interest rate swaps: An alternative explanation, *Financial Management* 117, 12–18.

Belton, Terrence M. 1987. Credit risk in interest rate swaps, Unpublished working paper, Board of Governors of the Federal Reserve System.

Bicksler, James and Andrew H. Chen. 1986. An economic analysis of interest rate swaps, *Journal of Finance* 41, 645–655.

Black, Fischer and Myron S. Scholes. 1973. The pricing of options and corporate liabilities, *Journal of Political Economy* 81, 637–654.

——— and John C. Cox. 1976. Valuing corporate securities: Some effects of bond indenture provisions, *Journal of Finance* 31, 351–368.

Brennan, Michael J. and Eduardo S. Schwartz. 1982. An equilibrium model of bond pricing and a test of market efficiency, *Journal of Financial and Quantitative Analysis* 17, 301–329.

Cox, John C. and Stephen A. Ross. 1976. The valuation of operations for alternative stochastic processes, *Journal of Financial Economics* 3, 145–166.

————, Jonathon E. Ingersoll, Jr. and Stephen A. Ross. 1985. A theory of the term structure of interest rates, *Econometrica* 53, 385–407.

Dothan, L. Uri. 1978. On the term structure of interest rates, *Journal of Financial Economics* 6, 59–69.

Federal Reserve Board and Bank of England. 1987. Potential credit exposure on interest rate and foreign exchange rate related instruments, Unpublished staff paper.

Gourlay, A. R. 1970. Hopscotch: A fast second-order partial differential equation solver, *Institute of Mathematics Applications Journal* 6, 375–390.

————, and S. McKee. 1977. The construction of hopscotch methods for parabolic and elliptic equations in two space dimensions with a mixed derivative, *Journal of Computational and Applied Mathematics* 3, 201–206.

Henderson, Schuyler K. and Armed C. Cates. 1986. Termination provisions of swap agreements under U.S. and English insolvency laws, in Boris Antl, eds.: *Swap Finance*, vol. 2 (Euromoney Publications, Ltd., London).

Johnson, Herb. 1987. Options on the maximum or the minimum of several assets, *Journal of Financial Quantitative Analysis* 22, 277–283.

Margrabe, William. 1978. The value of an option to exchange one asset for another, *Journal of Finance* 33, 177–198.

Merton, Robert C. 1974. On the pricing of corporate debt: The risk structure of interest rates, *Journal of Finance* 29, 449–470.

Mitchell, Andrew R. 1969. *Computational Methods in Partial Differential Equations,* (John Wiley and Sons, New York).

Price, John A. M. and Schuyler K. Henderson. 1984. *Currency and Interest Rate Swaps* (Butterworths, London).

Ramaswamy, Krishna and Suresh M. Sundaresan. 1986. The valuation of floating-rate instruments, *Journal of Financial Economics* 17, 251–272.

Smith, Clifford W., Jr., Charles W. Smithson, and Lee M. Wakeman. 1986. The evolving market for swaps, *Midland Corporate Finance Journal* 3, 20–32.

————, Charles W. Smithson, and Lee M. Wakeman. 1987. Credit risk and the scope of regulation of swaps, Conference on Bank Structure and Competition, Federal Reserve Bank of Chicago, 166–185.

Stulz, Renæa M. 1982. Options on the minimum/maximum of two risky assets, *Journal of Financial Economics* 10, 166–185.

Sundaresan, Suresh. 1989. Valuation of swaps, First Boston Working paper, 89–15.

Turnbull, Stuart M. 1987. Swaps: A zero sum game?, *Financial Management* 16, 15–21.

Wall, Larry D. and John J. Pringle. 1988. Interest rate swaps: A review of the issues, Federal Reserve Bank of Atlanta Economic Review, 22–40.

Whittaker, J. Gregg. 1987. Pricing interest rate swaps in an options pricing framework, Unpublished working paper, Federal Reserve Board of Kansas City.

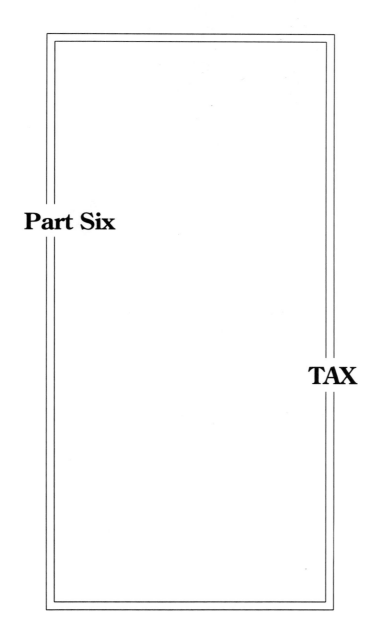

Part Six

TAX

EQUITY DERIVATIVE PRODUCTS: FINANCIAL INNOVATION'S NEWEST CHALLENGE TO THE TAX SYSTEM*

Edward D. Kleinbard**

18

I. Equity Derivative Products

A. Overview

Viewed from the perspective of a tax practitioner, the federal income tax system has not been particularly adept at coping with financial innovation in the capital markets. Our tax system works by describing a finite number of idealized transactions and attaching to each a set of operative rules—what might be termed a set of tax cubbyholes.[1] Tax professionals spend a modest amount of time learning to identify these tax cubbyholes and their consequences, and a great deal of time massaging reality to fit within the desired cubbyhole. As new financial products and strategies are developed in the domestic and international capital markets, the tax system attempts to respond by assigning each new product to

---

*Published originally in *69 Texas Law Review* 1319–68 (1991). Copyright 1991 by the Texas Law Review Association. Reprinted by permission.

**The author wishes to acknowledge the counsel of Suzanne F. Greenberg, Vice President, Salomon Brothers Inc., and Russell E. Makowsky, Vice President, Goldman, Sachs & Co., and the assistance of his colleague Nicholas L. Gunther, in the preparation of this Article. The opinions expressed herein remain solely those of the author.

[1] This process is more formally referred to in the literature as *mapping. See, e.g.,* Hu, *Swaps, the Modern Process of Financial Innovation and the Vulnerability of a Regulatory Paradigm,* 138 U. PA. L. REV. 333, 393 (1989) (describing the difficulty of classifying financial products within a regulatory scheme as a mapping problem); Powers, *Formalism and Nonformalism in Choice of Law Methodology,* 52 WASH. L. REV. 27, 30–31 (1976) (explaining that the mapping problem arises when a "formal rule" is used to determine results in particular cases, because relevant information is necessarily excluded and accordingly the result in a particular case may be contrary to the policies underlying the rule).

an appropriate cubbyhole, which in turn determines the tax consequences to users of that product.

Theoretically, the tax system should respond to financial innovation
by promptly formulating clear substantive tax rules that produce after-tax
results commensurate with each new product's pretax economics. Yet, as
this Article will demonstrate, the analytical tools available for this task are
not very powerful. The resulting tax uncertainty causes market inefficiency, which means that the tax system is failing the capital markets. This
result cannot be the intended consequence of sound tax policy.[2]

To take one example, the aggregate notional principal amount of all
outstanding notional principal contracts (interest rate swaps, currency
swaps, etc.) now totals roughly 2.5 trillion dollars.[3] Yet comprehensive tax
rules governing these contracts have not yet been promulgated, and
within the last few months sharp intra-agency controversy has apparently
broken out over whether pension funds and other tax-exempt investors
can use swaps as asset management tools without running afoul of the unrelated business taxable income (UBTI) provisions of the Internal
Revenue Code.[4]

---

[2] During 1990, some proponents of a federal tax on transfers of securities—termed a
Securities Transfer Excise Tax, or STET—argued that the tax could be justified not simply as a revenue-raiser, but also as a necessary corrective to capital markets that had become *too* efficient. Under this view, "excessive" liquidity in the stock markets had caused
an increase in price volatility; by throwing "sand into the gears" of the equity markets
through the introduction of a STET (which would increase the cost of transacting securities purchases and sales), short-term speculative trading could be reduced and price
volatility modulated. *See* Summers & Summers, *The Case for a Securities Transactions Excise
Tax*, 48 TAX NOTES 879, 883–84 (1990); Summers & Summers, *When Financial Markets
Work Too Well: A Cautious Case for a Securities Transactions Tax*, 3 J. FIN. SERVS. RES. 261,
275–85 (1989). Ironically, one of the points missed by these commentators is how easily
the STET can be avoided, particularly in the international context, by the use of the derivative equity products that are the subject of this Article. These arguments were elo-
quently rebutted in Schaefer, *Arguments Against a STET: A Response to the Summers Paper*, 48
TAX NOTES 1187 (1990), and empirically questioned in Kiefer, *The Security Transactions
Tax: An Overview of the Issues*, 48 TAX NOTES 885, 890–91 (1990). Moreover, even where
taxes deliberately levied for the purpose of creating market inefficiency in an effort to
modulate price fluctuations, it is impossible to imagine that creating a system of random
tax uncertainties would be an acceptable means of achieving that end.
[3] Hansell, *Is the World Ready for Synthetic Equity?*, INSTITUTIONAL INVESTOR (int'l ed.), Aug.
1990, at 54, 55.
[4] Although the Internal Revenue Service initially ruled that payments received under an interest rate swap agreement by an institution exempt from federal income tax under I.R.C.
§ 501(c)(3) (1988) did not constitute UBTI, *see* Priv. Ltr. Rul. 90–42–038 (July 23, 1990),
the Service later announced that the ruling is being reconsidered, *see* Priv. Ltr. Rul.
90–46–066 (Oct. 26, 1990); Announcement 90–134, 1990–50 I.R.B. 18. For professional
reaction to both the initial ruling and the IRS's subsequent pullback, see Liebowitz,
Ruling May Open Swap Mart to Tax-Exempt Organizations, INVESTMENT DEALERS' DIG., Oct. 29,
1990, at 17, and Liebowitz, *IRS Reconsiders Ruling on Charity's Swap Income*, INVESTMENT
DEALERS' DIG., Nov. 12, 1990, at 10. *See also infra* notes 65–68 and accompanying text (noting the uncertainty in this area and arguing that swap payments probably do not involve
sales or exchanges of property).

At the other end of the spectrum, tax uncertainty creates the opportunity for some taxpayers to use new financial products to obtain (or at least claim to obtain) after-tax results that are disproportionately better than the pretax economics of those strategies. If participants in such strategies are relatively few in number, their activities result only in a loss of tax revenues; if, however, they are numerous, their activities may actually distort the capital markets, by introducing a noneconomic incentive to enter into various transactions. The results obtained by such taxpayers typically are labelled "loopholes," and the users thereof "exploiters" of these loopholes; the notoriety surrounding these transactions usually sparks Congress's only interest in overhauling the Internal Revenue Code to respond to financial innovations.[5]

In the capital markets, loopholes and their exploiters thrive on an atmosphere of tax uncertainty.[6] Their presence is simply a symptom of a failing in the tax system, and they should no more be held responsible for the tax system's shortcomings than the insect kingdom should be blamed for spoiling improperly refrigerated meat.

This Article examines the application of the federal income tax system to an important new area of financial innovation: the development of a new generation of equity derivative products. Just as the development of

---

[5] In each of the last two tax acts, Congress has eliminated perceived "loopholes" that arguably were the result of uncertainty in fundamental tax policy. As part of the Revenue Reconciliation Act of 1989, Pub. L. No. 101–239, § 7211(a), (b), 103 Stat. 2301, 2342–45, Congress enacted I.R.C. § 172(b)(1)(E), (h) (Prentice Hall 1991), which generally prohibits net operating loss carrybacks from years after a corporate equity reduction transaction (CERT) to years before the CERT. Presumably, the motivation for these provisions was general concern over the dramatic increase in the amount of corporate indebtedness generated by highly leveraged buyouts and recapitalizations. Presumably also a product of the same concern, another part of the 1989 legislation enacted I.R.C. § 163(e)(5), (i) (Prentice Hall 1991), imposing a limitation on the deductibility of interest in respect of "high yield original issue discount obligations," based in part on the excess of the yield to maturity of such an obligation over the "applicable Federal rate" plus five percentage points. *See* Revenue Reconciliation Act of 1989, Pub. L. No. 101–239, § 7202(a), (b), 103 Stat. 2301, 2330–32; *see also infra* note 129 (noting the elimination of tax consolidation benefits for "subsidiary preferred stock" offerings). Similarly, as part of the Revenue Reconciliation Act of 1990, Pub. L. No. 101–508, § 11325(a)(2), 104 Stat. 1388–400, 1388–466, Congress repealed former I.R.C. § 1275(a)(4) (1988) in order to require issuers to recognize cancellation of indebtedness income on certain exchanges of debt securities, as discussed further *infra* at note 91. Interestingly, former § 1275(a)(4) was itself the end product of reactions against perceived abuses. *See* Haims & Schaumberger, *Restructuring the Overleveraged Company*, 48 TAX NOTES 91, 95–96 (1990); New York State Bar Ass'n Tax Section, *Report of Ad Hoc Committee on Provisions of the Revenue Reconciliation Act of 1990 Affecting Debt-for-Debt Exchanges*, 51 TAX NOTES 79, 83 (1991).

[6] As discussed above, "loopholes" result from the use of uncertainty in tax treatment to create unintended tax consequences. By contrast, taxpayers' ability to engage in "line-walking" to their own advantage will exist whenever there are formal rules which by their nature offer comparative certainty and thus are either "underinclusive as to purpose, overinclusive as to purpose, or both." M. KELMAN, A GUIDE TO CRITICAL LEGAL STUDIES 40 (1987); *see* Hu, *supra* note 1, at 398.

derivative interest rate products, such as interest rate swaps, caps, and floors,[7] revolutionized liability management in the 1980s,[8] so too the burgeoning equity derivative marketplace will (if the interest rate swap market is a guide) revolutionize investment in, and issuance of, corporate equity in the next few years.

This Article first describes briefly the market for equity derivative products and highlights some of the policy issues these products raise for the tax system. The Article then considers in detail how the paradigmatic new equity derivative product—the equity index swap—should be analyzed under current tax law. Finally, the Article turns to the broader theme of the methodology by which the tax system currently copes with financial innovation, and how that methodology might be improved.

B. The Marketplace for Equity Derivative Products

In the broadest sense, equity derivatives are not new. One recent source explains:

> An equity derivative is a security or private contract whose cash value rises or falls depending on what happens to the one or more stocks or market indexes to which it is tied. A derivative can take the form of an option, a warrant, a swap, a bond, a certificate of deposit or any manner of hybrid.[9]

By this definition, a convertible bond, for example, is an equity derivative product. This broad understanding of the term conforms with market practice: many market participants view the decision to invest in a convertible bond not as the acquisition of a debt obligation with a stapled opportunity to roll the dice on equity prices, but as the de facto purchase of the underlying equity at an above-market price in return for an above-market current yield. Securities firms, for example, underwrite convertible bonds through their equity syndicate desks rather than their debt syndicate desks, and the National Association of Security Dealers Automated Quotation System (NASDAQ), which operates as a computerized bid-ask pricing system for over-the-counter equity securities, lists convertible bonds (but not straight debt).[10]

---

[7] For practical definitions of options, forwards futures, and the standard "notional principal amount" products (interest rate swaps, caps, floors, and collars), see Kleinbard & Greenberg, *Business Hedges After* Arkansas Best, 43 Tax L. Rev. 393, 394–95 nn.3–4 (1988).

[8] For an overview of the use of derivative interest rate products and similar tools such as liability management tools, see generally Management of Interest Rate Risk (B. Antl ed. 1988).

[9] Hansell, *supra* note 3, at 55; *see also* Donnelly & Torres, *Sluggish Wall Street Is Rushing into 'Derivatives'*, Wall St. J., Nov. 30, 1990, at C1, col. 3 ("Derivatives are not exactly stocks, not exactly bonds. They are customized securities designed to act a certain way when an underlying security, index or commodity moves in price.").

[10] Interestingly, the tax law traditionally has characterized convertible bonds in precisely the opposite fashion, treating a convertible bond as debt until it actually is converted into eq-

Examples of more modern, but equally straightforward, equity derivative products are the cash-settlement put and call options on widely followed stock indices (such as the Nikkei 225 stock index[11]) recently issued by several United States securities firms in United States public offerings. In addition, new forms of equity derivatives (and new uses for them) have been developed recently, largely as a result of three factors: the incorporation into the equity arena of swap terminology and technology developed in the interest rate derivatives area, the increasing globalization of the equity markets, and the ability of securities firms to profit through advanced proprietary hedging techniques for equity-based products.[12]

As in the early years of the interest rate swap market,[13] many new equity derivatives are designed to arbitrage differences between various capital markets. An example of such intermarket arbitrage is the "covered warrant," a hugely profitable business for some securities firms during the 1984–1989 period.[14] In a typical covered warrant program, a securities firm would arbitrage the difference between wholesale and retail markets for an issuer's equity warrants. To accomplish this arbitrage, the securities firm would acquire, in the secondary market, a large block of outstanding warrants to purchase the underlying equity securities of an issuer. Typically, the warrant issuer was a Japanese corporation that had issued the warrants previously as part of a bond-warrant unit in the Euromarkets. The securities firm then would issue its own warrants to purchase the same underlying securities, using the purchased warrants as a hedge (or "cover"). The new warrants would be issued in smaller denominations than the cover warrants, and might be exercisable in a different currency—such as Swiss Francs—with a higher exercise price than the under-

---

uity. *See* B. BITTKER & J. EUSTICE, FEDERAL INCOME TAXATION OF CORPORATIONS AND SHAREHOLDERS ¶ 4.60, at 4–73 (5th ed. 1987) (explaining that before conversion, the debt "genes" of a convertible bond are treated as dominant and the equity "genes" are treated as recessive). For further discussion, see *infra* Part I(C). Arguably, Prop. Treas. Reg. § 1.1275–4(g), 56 Fed. Reg. 8308 (1991) represents a different view of the economics of a convertible bond. That proposed regulation, which would apply to some (but not all) convertible bonds, and to all "exchangeable" bonds (that is, bonds convertible into stock of a corporation other than the issuer of the bonds), would require that a debt instrument within its scope be bifurcated into its constituent components—in the case of a convertible bond, a discount bond and a warrant. This proposed regulation is discussed *infra* at note 105.

[11] The Nikkei 225 Index is the best known index of Japanese equity securities. A number of firms have offered cash-settlement put and call options on that index. *See* Parker, *Index Warrant Use Grows,* PENSIONS & INVESTMENT AGE, Apr. 2, 1990, at 10.

[12] The current state of the marketplace for equity derivatives is summarized in Hansell, *supra* note 3.

[13] *See* Taylor, *Understanding Interest Rate Swaps and Contracts,* in NEW FINANCIAL INSTRUMENTS AND TECHNIQUES 1989, CORPORATE LAW AND PRACTICE COURSE HANDBOOK SERIES No. 630, at 493, 496 (1989).

[14] *See* Ipsen, *The Biggest Pool in Town,* INSTITUTIONAL INVESTOR (int'l ed.), June 1990, at 100, 100–01.

lying cover warrants (thereby reducing the up-front premium required to purchase a warrant and leaving the issuing securities firm with the potential to capture as profit the difference in strike prices).[15] The repackaged warrants would be sold, in the usual case, to retail investors, at substantial mark-ups from the trading price of the original large denomination, less liquid cover warrants.[16] By employing its capital to acquire and finance the cover warrants and using its distribution network to locate retail market customers, the securities firms were able to earn a merchant's mark-up with minimal exposure to the underlying equity risk. It has been estimated that roughly $5 billion in covered warrant transactions were consummated in the public capital markets in 1989 and the first quarter of 1990.[17]

One obvious limitation on the growth of covered warrants was the finite supply of large blocks of illiquid warrants in the secondary marketplace to serve as "cover." Bankers Trust Company is widely credited with developing an innovative response to this dilemma when, in 1988, it issued the first "faux covered warrant"—a warrant whose "cover" was not a perfectly offsetting actual warrant, but rather a sophisticated melange of actively managed financial instruments, including futures contracts, over-the-counter options, and positions in the underlying physical securities.[18] Unlike a covered warrant, these complex hedges required careful monitoring and constant adjustment to respond to changes in the equity market. With the introduction of these sophisticated hedging techniques, however, securities firms could offer to investors virtually any saleable investment opportunity, and reserve for themselves the economic opportunity (and risk) of their "imperfect" hedging strategies.

Although the covered warrant and faux covered warrant programs are of little direct interest to United States tax regulators, they do illumine several key characteristics of the developing market for equity derivatives. First, cross-border equity markets currently are relatively inefficient and cumbersome for investors. Some of these inefficiencies are attributable to information shortages and high transaction costs: for retail investors, in particular, it can be very difficult to gather information on equity issuers domiciled in foreign markets, and foreign currency transaction costs must be added to retail brokerage commissions.[19] Other inefficiencies are attributable to nontax regulatory constraints: regulated entities,

---

[15] The issuing securities firm would also hedge its currency exposure through currency forward or swap contracts.

[16] *See* Ipser, *supra* note 14, at 101–02.

[17] *Id.* at 100.

[18] *Id.*

[19] *See* Donnelly & Torres, *supra* note 9, at C17, col. 3 ("[D]erivatives also offer investors a way to venture into unfamiliar foreign markets at a lower cost—and often lower risk—than in using the conventional route.").

such as pension funds or insurance companies, often are subject to limitations on investment in foreign equity securities.[20] Derivative instruments can be used to overcome these inefficiencies, by enabling parties to take an economic position in an equity security without actually owning it.[21] Canadian pension funds, for example, are not permitted to invest more than ten percent of their assets in non-Canadian equities, but that limitation does not apply to equity-indexed contingent debt arrangements.[22] For a securities firm—with its superior access to information and ability to manage risk—these inefficiencies give rise to arbitrage opportunities and corresponding arbitrage profits.

Second, the bulk of equity derivative counterparties, apart from the securities industry, are equity investors, rather than equity issuers. Equity derivatives are used for the most part to make efficient equity investments, to hedge existing investment portfolios, or to earn an incremental return on those portfolios. In this respect, the current state of the equity derivative marketplace is the opposite of the early years of the interest rate swap market, where the majority of participants were debt issuers looking to arbitrage differences in access to funds in different debt markets. Just as the interest rate swap market rapidly evolved into an asset management tool, however, so too will the equity derivative marketplace likely take on increasing importance for equity (or quasi-equity) issuers over time.

Third, the current equity derivative marketplace exhibits a remarkable symbiotic relationship between securities firms and the investor community. Although most equity derivatives are designed to appeal to one segment or another of the investor community, it nonetheless remains true that every derivative instrument requires two parties. The counterparties to many equity derivatives are securities firms, which view the equity derivatives that they market to investors as opportunities to create substantial profits through "dynamic" (read imperfect) hedges of the underlying risks. These hedges typically employ a wide range of equity and nonequity instruments, including interest rate sensitive instruments and foreign-currency contracts.[23] The hedges are designed with the assistance of computers and sophisticated mathematical analyses, and are constantly

---

[20] *Cf.* London, *Tailored Securities Cutting a Dash*, Fin. Times, Oct. 23, 1990, at 32, col. 5 (observing that United States institutional investors have turned to structured private placements because such investors are often denied access to overseas equity markets).

[21] Eric Seff, Managing Director of Chase Investors Management Corp., observes: "I can use [swap-based equity derivatives] for anything I would previously have used futures, options or the stocks themselves for. In most cases it is more economical than using the listed markets, easier than the listed markets and relatively free of cumbersome regulation." Hansell, *supra* note 3, at 56.

[22] *See id.*

[23] *See* Torres, *'Synthetic' Stock: Future Stand-In for the Real Thing*, Wall St. J., Oct. 19, 1990, at C1, col. 3.

adjusted over their lives to respond to changing market conditions. Dynamic hedging carries considerable risks, but has been a significant source of profits for several securities firms in recent years.[24] Such a firm satisfies its appetite for dynamic hedge proprietary trading opportunities by acting as the issuer of equity derivatives to customers, and then using that economic exposure as the vehicle around which its proprietary hedging revolves.

In addition to equity warrants (both covered and faux), two other equity derivative products deserve special attention because of the interesting issues that they raise for tax advisors and tax authorities alike. The equity index swap is perhaps the most complex and interesting equity derivative product. The market is sufficiently new that no standard form of equity index swap has emerged. In one common variant, however, one party (the "equity payor") agrees to make periodic payments over a fixed term of (1) amounts based on the *increase* in value, if any, during each period of a specified index of equity securities (e.g., the Standard & Poor's 500 Index), and (2) dividends on that index, in each case as applied to a notional principal investment in that index. The counterparty (the "floating-rate payor") agrees to make periodic payments determined by applying to the same notional principal amount (1) a specified floating rate of interest (e.g., a rate based on LIBOR), and (2) amounts based on the *decrease* in value during each period of the equity index. The notional principal amount itself typically adjusts each period to reflect changes in the value of the underlying equity index. A typical equity index swap is documented in a fashion similar to an interest rate swap, and as in the case of interest rate swaps, cash flows typically are netted.[25]

The "money-back warrant," or "principal-indexed note," as its name suggests, presents unique characterization issues.[26] This instrument may be denominated as a warrant or as a note, and has a fixed maturity. The instrument pays no interest prior to maturity; at maturity, it pays stated principal amount together with contingent interest (if any) measured by

---

[24] *See* Siconolfi & Power, *U.S. Securities Industry Expected to Post Worst Results Since 1974*, Wall St. J., Jan. 3, 1991, at C1, col. 3 ("One of the biggest money-makers for Wall Street firms in the fourth quarter and throughout 1990 was trading, particularly for their own accounts. So-called derivative products . . . also were lucrative for [certain] firms. . . ."); *see also* Ipsen, *supra* note 14, at 100 ("[The] equity derivatives group [is] Bankers Trust's largest single money-churner."); Torres & Donnelly, *Rivals Challenge Bankers Trust in Derivative-Securities Business*, Wall St. J., Dec. 6, 1990, at C1, col. 5 ("[T]hrough November [of 1990] Bankers Trust racked up about $500 million of revenue in the derivatives business," with estimated profits from derivatives "approach[ing] $250 million. . . .")

[25] The equity index swap is considered in detail in Part II below.

[26] *Cf.* Bensman, *Tax Questions May Blur Appeal of Money-Back Warrants*, INVESTMENT DEALERS' DIG., Feb. 22, 1988, at 48 (discussing whether a money-back warrant should be taxed like a traditional warrant or like a bond). It should be noted that the term "money-back warrant" is securities industry slang. Recent issues have used a variety of tradenames to describe these products. *E.g.*, $100,000,000 Stock Index Growth Notes ("SIGNs") due August 15, 1996 issued by the Republic of Austria (Prospectus Supp. Jan. 28, 1991) (copy on file with the *Texas Law Review*).

the price fluctuation of a specified equity index or equity security.[27] The tax uncertainties surrounding money-back warrants are considered in more detail below.

C. Tax Issues Raised by Equity Derivatives

The equity derivative marketplace today is not large—probably under $100 billion in off-exchange contractual products (measured by the value of the underlying equity).[28] As the equity derivative market matures, however, it is likely to expand dramatically in size, to the point where the United States tax system will not be able to ignore it.

It obviously is impossible to predict in advance all the pressure points on the tax system that will emerge as the equity derivative marketplace matures, but some issues are reasonably foreseeable. In the international context, and as described in detail in Part II, equity derivatives may be used by foreign investors to earn an economic return measured, in part, by dividends on an index of United States equities without incurring United States withholding tax liability.[29]

In the domestic context, the Internal Revenue Code often imposes certain constraints, or grants certain benefits, to taxpayers measured partly on the amount of their dividend income. It is unclear, at best, whether payments received in respect of a derivative contract (such as equity-based payments received by the floating-rate payor in the equity index swap described above) would be treated as dividend income for these purposes.[30] Similarly, it is not clear whether a corporate investor that was

---

[27] An early example is the Yen Foreign Exchange Warrants Expiring February 11, 1993 issued by the Student Loan Marketing Association (Prospectus dated Feb. 2, 1988) (copy on file with the *Texas Law Review*). The "warrants" were issued to the public at $9.25 per warrant, and paid at maturity the greater of $9.25 or an amount indexed to relative yen/dollar values. The prospectus disclosed that counsel to the issuer thought "the better view" was that the warrants constituted debt for federal income tax purposes. *Id.* at 36.

[28] Estimates vary. *Compare* Ipsen, *supra* note 14, at 100 (estimating that as much as $70 billion in outstanding privately negotiated long-dated covered options were issued in 1989) *with* Hansell, *supra* note 3, at 54–55 (estimating that the dominant houses had booked $30 billion to $40 billion in equity derivatives by August 1990). One difficulty in assessing the size of the marketplace is informational: many derivatives are privately negotiated contracts, and no clearing house for data on such arrangements exists. Another difficulty is definitional: neither of the above estimates, for example, appears to include convertible bonds or conventional exchange-traded products. A comprehensive definition would result in a much larger estimate.

[29] A similar issue would be raised if Congress were to seek to impose a capital gains tax on foreign portfolio investors in United States equities.

[30] For example, a corporation's status as a "personal holding company" under I.R.C. § 542 (1988) (and therefore the applicability of the personal holding company tax under I.R.C. § 541 (1988) to that corporation) depends in part on the proportion of the corporation's income that consists of dividends, as does a corporation's status as a "regulated investment company" under I.R.C. § 851 (Prentice Hall 1991) (and therefore the availability of the deduction for dividends paid). Dividends received by a corporate shareholder are eligible for the dividends-received deduction under I.R.C. § 243 (Prentice Hall 1991) and dividends are excluded from the "unrelated business taxable income" of a tax-exempt institution under I.R.C. § 512(b)(1) (Prentice Hall 1991).

the equity payor in an index swap would lose the benefits of the dividends-received deduction[31] if the investor also owned the underlying stocks making up the equity index.[32] In the case of pension funds and other tax-exempt investors, certain contractual equity derivatives raise, in a new context, a UBTI issue similar to the controversy that has deterred many tax-exempt investors from using interest rate swaps and similar notional principal contracts as asset management tools.[33]

From the perspective of corporate issuers, the tax system also appears at risk. As noted earlier, receipt by a corporate issuer of an interest deduction on convertible debt has traditionally been tolerated, even though many market participants view that instrument as a de facto equity investment. Increasing sophistication in hedging techniques and investor acceptance of new equity derivative products will lead to new structures that will place even more tension on current law's frayed distinctions between debt and equity instruments.

Consider, for example, the money-back warrant and its economic identical twin, the principal-indexed note. Most tax advisors believe, with varying degrees of fervor, that money-back warrants that are denominated as debt instruments and treated as such for debtor-creditor law purposes are debt instruments under current tax law classification principles, but even the most ardent believer pauses when told that these debt instruments will be offered for sale in $20 denominations and listed on a na-

---

[31] I.R.C. § 243 (Prentice Hall 1991).

[32] Under I.R.C. § 246(c)(1)(B) (1988), a taxpayer loses the benefit of the dividends-received deduction to the extent the taxpayer is obligated to make related payments with respect to positions in substantially similar or related property. While the payments made by the equity payor under an equity index swap are similar in amount to dividends on the underlying equities, it is uncertain whether the swap contract, which provides for bilateral payments between the parties, can be viewed as "substantially similar" to a short position on physical equities. In addition, to qualify for the dividends-received deduction, a taxpayer must have held the related stock for at least 46 days, and the taxpayer's holding period will be reduced in a manner to be prescribed under Treasury regulations for any period in which the "taxpayer has diminished his risk of loss of holding [one] or more other positions with respect to substantially similar or related property." I.R.C. § 246(c)(4)(C) (1988). Although the Service's regulatory authority under § 246(c)(4)(C) might be adequate to prohibit the dividends-received deduction in this context, the Conference Committee Report to the Tax Reform Act of 1984, Pub. L. No. 98–369, 98 Stat. 494, provides two specific examples of transactions within the scope of the rule for substantially similar or related property to which the regulations should be retroactive and states that, as to other transactions, the regulations should apply only on a prospective basis. *See* H.R. CONF. REP. NO. 861, 98th Cong., 2d Sess. 757, 818, *reprinted in* 1984 U.S. CODE CONG. & ADMIN. NEWS 1445, 1506. Because the terms of the equity index swap do not conform to either of the examples in the Conference Committee Report, any such swaps entered into before the promulgation of regulations under § 246(c)(4)(C) arguably are beyond the reach of such subsequent regulations.

[33] *See supra* note 4 and accompanying text; *infra* note 68 and accompanying text.

tional options exchange.[34] Most issues of money-back warrants to date have involved options on commodities or currencies, and most recent interest in issuing such instruments has come from nontaxable institutions (such as foreign entities). Very recently, however, the first public offering of an equity-based, principal-indexed note (on the Standard & Poor's 500 Index) by a United States domestic issuer was filed with Securities and Exchange Commission.[35]

Finally, the Treasury Department is expected to release a study on the integration of the corporate tax system early in 1991.[36] Regardless of the study's conclusions, it is likely to spur debate on whether the United States should move towards a system of corporate integration, as have many other major economic powers.[37] Equity derivative products will raise difficult issues for many corporate integration proposals, because those products will enable taxpayers in effect to invest either in actual equity (with its attendant integration consequences) or in synthetic equity. In the absence of thoughtful policing mechanisms, taxpayers may be able to

---

[34] The more familiar "exchangeable bonds" (i.e., bonds convertible into stock other than that of the obligor) are treated for tax purposes as debt until conversion, at which point they are treated as exchanged for the stock in a taxable transaction. At least prior to Prop. Treas. Reg. § 1.1275–4(g), 56 Fed. Reg. 8308 (1991), the Internal Revenue Service has treated a holder of such a bond as recognizing gain on the exercise of the exchange privilege equal to the difference between the fair market value of the stock received and the holder's tax basis in the bond. See Rev. Rul. 69–135, 1969–1 C.B. 198; Priv. Ltr. Rul. 85–50–022 (Sept. 13, 1985); Gen. Couns. Mem. 39452 (Dec. 4, 1985); see also Estate of Timken v. Commissioner, 47 B.T.A. 494 (1942) (holding that the excess of the fair market value of shares received over the cost of the convertible bond was taxable income), nonacq. on other grounds, 1942–2 C.B. 32, aff'd on other grounds, 141 F.2d 625 (6th Cir. 1944). Viewed from the perspective of the obligor, such a theory would result in gain (presumably capital gain) measured by the value of the stock at the time of the exchange over the obligor's basis in that stock, and an ordinary deduction for redemption premium measured by the excess of the value of the stock over the face amount of the bonds.

In my view, this analysis gives insufficient weight to the general rules for the taxation of options transactions. A more satisfactory result would follow if the exchangeable bonds were viewed for the purposes of measuring the amount and character of gain or loss as representing an option, the exercise of which on the exchange of the bonds for stock results in (1) no tax consequences to the holders, who take a basis in the stock equal to the face amount of the bonds exchanged therefor, and (2) gain recognized by the obligor in an amount equal to the excess of the face amount of the bonds over the obligor's basis in the stock. Prop. Treas. Reg. § 1.1275–4(g) radically alters the tax analysis of exchangeable bonds. See infra note 105.

[35] Standard & Poor's 500 Index-Linked Notes Due 1996, to be Issued by Salomon Inc. (Preliminary Prospectus Supp. Jan. 28, 1991). These proposed securities have not to date been issued, presumably at least in part because of the promulgation of Prop. Treas. Reg. § 1.1275–4(g), 56 Fed. Reg. 8308 (1991), discussed infra at note 105.

[36] See Rosen, Treasury's Corporate Integration Study Back on Track, 49 TAX NOTES 956 (1990); see also infra note 135.

[37] The United Kingdom, France, and Germany, to take but a few examples, all tax corporations and their shareholders through one variation or another of a partial integration scheme. See Gourevitch, Corporate Tax Integration: The Corporate Tax Experience, 31 TAX LAW. 65 (1977).

separate the tax consequences associated with the ownership of equities in an integration model (e.g., a deemed-paid tax credit) from the economic risks of such ownership.

II. Equity Index Swaps—A Case Study

A. Overview

Imagine the case of three hypothetical investors. The first, a foreign tax-exempt institution, wishes to invest in the United States equity market, but is constrained from doing so by its country's regulatory concerns. Moreover, as a tax-exempt institution in its home jurisdiction, the investor will suffer a pure out-of-pocket expense in respect of any United States withholding tax imposed on dividends received by it. Finally, the investor would prefer to leverage its equity investment, but is prohibited from borrowing under its articles of association. The second hypothetical investor is a United States pension plan with substantial money market investments. The pension plan wishes to move some of these assets into an investment in a broad base of United States equity securities in a cost-efficient manner, without running afoul of the UBTI provisions of the Internal Revenue Code.[38] Finally, the third hypothetical investor is a United States taxpaying corporation with capital loss carryovers and with similar investment goals to that of the United States pension plan; unlike the pension plan, however, this investor is primarily interested in deriving capital gains from its investment (rather than interest or dividend in-

---

[38] I.R.C. §§ 511–515 (Prentice Hall 1991). These provisions effectively impose net income tax on the income of otherwise tax-exempt institutions to the extent attributable to any "unrelated trade or business," as defined in I.R.C. § 513 (Prentice Hall 1991). Broadly speaking, the purpose of the UBTI provisions is to prevent tax-exempt organizations from using their tax-favored status to compete unfairly with taxpaying business organizations.

Section 513(a) defines an "unrelated trade or business" as "any trade or business the conduct of which is not substantially related (aside from the need of such [exempt] organization for income . . .) to the exercise or performance by such organization of its [exempt] . . . purpose. . . ." I.R.C. § 513(a) (Prentice Hall 1991). The Internal Revenue Service and the courts generally take the view that, in contrast to the law for individuals, any concerted profit-motivated activity by an exempt organization (*including* the active management of an investment portfolio) constitutes an unrelated trade or business for purposes of § 513(a). *See, e.g.,* Gen. Couns. Mem. 39615 (Mar. 12, 1987) (stating that stock index arbitrage activity constitutes a trade or business); Louisiana Credit Union League v. United States, 693 F.2d 525 (5th Cir. 1982) (finding that serving as a "middleman" between credit unions and commercial vendors of insurance, debt collection, and electronic data processing services, is motivated by profit and is thus a trade or business).

Accordingly, as a practical matter most UBTI analysis by practitioners consists of searching for an *exception* to the broad scope of the definition of an unrelated trade or business. The most useful constellation of exceptions is contained in I.R.C. § 512(b) (Prentice Hall 1991), which excludes from the scope of the UBTI rules (among other categories) interest, dividends, and gains from the sale of noninventory property.

come), because it can use its capital loss carryover to shelter the current year's capital gain net income from tax.[39]

Each of these investors can accomplish its economic purpose by entering into the floating-rate payor side of an equity index swap. The equity payor (typically a United States securities firm) will agree to make periodic payments for a specified term of (1) amounts based on the *increase* in value, if any, during each period of a specified equity index—for purposes of this case study, the Standard & Poor's 500 Index—and (2) amounts equal to dividends paid on that index. In exchange, the floating-rate payor (the hypothetical investor) will agree to make periodic payments of X, a floating rate of interest pegged (by way of example) to LIBOR, and Y, amounts based on the *decrease* in value during each period of the Standard & Poor's 500 Index. The notional principal amount against which all payments are calculated will be adjusted each period to reflect the change in value in the equity index from the prior period.[40]

While the economic goals of each of the three investors can be satisfied through an equity index swap, the tax analysis applicable to each investor varies somewhat. At the outset, however, all three investors face the same fundamental dilemma: does there exist a tax cubbyhole under current law into which the equity index swap can be assigned?

B. Swap or Leveraged Purchase of Equities?

The first order conceptual issue raised by an equity index swap is whether the economic analogy to a leveraged purchase of equity securities should drive the United States tax analysis, or whether, instead, the formal differences between the swap and an actual leveraged investment require that the swap be analyzed as a novel form of financial investment for tax purposes.

As an economic matter, by entering into the floating-rate payor side of an equity index swap on a domestic United States equity index, such as the Standard & Poor's 500 Index, each investor will create cash flows that closely approximate the cash flows that would be obtained if the investor actually borrowed the notional principal amount from its counterparty and then invested that amount in the equity securities that make up that

---

[39] *See* I.R.C. § 1212 (1988). As in the case of the foreign tax-exempt investor, the domestic pension plan and taxpaying corporation would each suffer adverse tax consequences from making a leveraged investment in equity, because of the rules treating "debt-financed income" as UBTI. *See infra* note 63 (discussing the potential classification of debt-financed income as UBTI under I.R.C. § 514 (Prentice Hall 1991)); I.R.C. § 246A (Prentice Hall 1991) (reducing or eliminating the dividends-received deduction in the case of debt-financed portfolio stock).

[40] This fluctuation in notional principal amount mimics an investment in a constant quantity of "units" of the index, in which the units hypothetically are sold at the end of each period and immediately repurchased at their market value, thereby affecting the amount of deemed cash invested in the hypothetical transaction.

equity index. Thus, each investor can be viewed in economic terms as paying amounts equal to a floating rate of interest to the equity payor counterparty in each period and receiving amounts equal to the dividends paid on the underlying equity securities. The equity-indexed payments received or made by the floating-rate payor would correspond to the economic gains or losses on a hypothetical basket of equities, if those equities were sold for cash at the end of each measurement period under the swap. Similarly, the equity payor can be viewed as having a dual role: (1) as a money lender that collects periodic floating-note interest, and (2) as an effective custodian of the equity securities acquired by the investor, passing through to the investor at specified intervals the economic return on those securities.

Despite the similarity of cash flows, there are several important structural differences that distinguish an equity index swap from a fully leveraged purchase of actual equity securities. First, the floating-rate payor, unlike an actual equity investor, will not acquire any of the voting or other management rights of a corporate shareholder. Second, the equity-indexed amounts under the swap will be determined by reference to the performance of the specified equity index as a whole. The composition of the equity index over time, of course, is wholly outside the control of the investor/floating-rate payor.[41] Third, unlike the owner of an actual basket of equity securities, the floating-rate payor will have no power to fine tune its investment portfolio by acquiring or disposing of individual equity securities in response to market charges. Fourth, dividend-equivalent amounts paid by the equity payor will not be limited to the funds legally available for the payment of dividends by the underlying equity issuers; moreover, in some equity swap contracts, such dividend-equivalent amounts are calculated by reference to historic dividend yields, not actual dividends during the term of the swap. Finally, and perhaps most important, the parties to an equity index swap face a different set of credit concerns than would arise from actually borrowing and directly investing in equity securities. The floating-rate payor, in contrast to the direct equity investor, is exposed not only indirectly to the credit quality of the corporations whose stock constitute the equity index, but also directly to the credit of the equity payor under the swap. For these reasons, the better analysis under current law is to view an equity index swap as a novel form of notional principal contract that provides for unique, equity-based bilateral payments, rather than as a disguised, fully leveraged purchase of equity securities.

The general point that follows from this conclusion is that, under current law, similarity of economic results is not sufficient to require identity of tax analysis: where there is no actual indebtedness and no actual in-

---

[41] *See infra* note 81 and accompanying text.

dicia of ownership of equities, current tax law does not determine the tax consequences of an equity index swap by recasting the contract into a different (albeit economically similar) form.[42]

The immediate consequence of the conclusion, by contrast, is to throw into doubt the tax analysis of an equity index swap, because the appearance of a novel form of notional principal contract does not automatically stimulate the production of a comprehensive tax cubbyhole into which to place that product. Accordingly, the tax analysis of an equity index swap will consist of attempting to force that financial product into existing tax cubbyholes, where the fit may be less than perfect. The resulting tax conclusions will also vary somewhat from investor to investor. It will prove fruitful to demonstrate this point by going through that analysis (under the theory that an equity index swap is properly characterized as a novel form of "notional principal contract") for each of our three hypothetical investors.

1. The Foreign Investor. A foreign investor entering into an equity index swap with a United States counterparty in the first instance is interested primarily in ascertaining the *source* (United States or foreign) of income earned in respect of that swap. If the investor's income is treated as foreign-source income for United States tax purposes, then, as a general matter, income earned by the foreign investor will not be subject to United States withholding tax.[43] Conversely, if that income is treated as United States source income, then payments to the foreign investor by

---

[42] *See infra* Part III.

[43] Most practitioners would conclude that a foreign investor that enters into a swap contract with a United States counterparty would not, simply by virtue of that contract, be treated as engaging in a trade or business in the United States, even without regard to the application of the "safe harbor" of I.R.C. § 864(b)(2) (Prentice Hall 1991), which treats certain securities and commodities trading as not constituting a United States trade or business. In the case of income that is not trade or business income, the Code imposes tax on non-United States persons only in respect of certain categories of United States source income. *See* I.R.C. § 871(a)(1) (1988) (imposing tax on nonresident alien individuals' income other than capital gains); I.R.C. § 881(a) (1988) (imposing substantive tax liability on income from sources outside the United States received by foreign corporations); I.R.C. § 1441(a) (1988) (withholding of tax on nonresident aliens); I.R.C. § 1442(a) (1988) (withholding of tax on foreign corporations). Moreover, even if a foreign investor were treated as engaged in a trade or business in the United States by virtue of entering into a swap contract, the United States imposes tax only on income "effectively connected" with the conduct of that trade or business. *See* I.R.C. §§ 871(b), 882(a) (1988). Foreign-source income is treated as effectively connected with the conduct of a trade or business only if, among other factors, the foreign investor has an "office or other fixed place of business within the United States to which such income . . . is attributable." I.R.C. § 864(c)(4)(B) (Prentice Hall 1991). *But cf. infra* note 51 (describing the more stringent regulations that specifically address sourcing of notional principal contracts). Accordingly, as a practical matter, if one can conclude that income earned by a foreign investor is not derived from sources within the United States, that income generally will not be subject to United States net income tax or withholding tax.

the United States counterparty to the swap conceivably could be subject to United States withholding tax.[44]

Prior to January 1991, foreign counterparties to equity index swaps and other exotic notional principal contracts had no source rules on which they could rely to conclude that income earned on such contracts with United States counterparties gave rise to foreign-source income. From 1989 to January 1991, the only regulatory authority that addressed the source of swap income or expense was former Temporary Treasury Regulation Section 1.863–7T,[45] which provided special sourcing rules for certain United States dollar-denominated notional principal contracts, such as interest rate swaps. Those rules generally sourced income from a notional principal contract by reference to the residence of the recipient.[46] Under this approach, notional principal contract payments received by a non-United States counterparty that had no other United States connections were treated as foreign-source income and therefore were exempt from United States withholding tax, without regard to whether the non-United States party was otherwise eligible for tax treaty benefits or other withholding tax exemptions.[47]

Simply denominating an equity index swap as a "swap," however, did not ensure that these favorable sourcing rules applied. In particular, the definition of "notional principal contract" in former Temporary Treasury Regulation Section 1.863–7T did *not* include equity-based notional principal contracts, such as equity index swaps, because that regulation required that payments under a "notional principal contract" be determined by reference to an *interest rate index.*[48]

---

[44] This risk is borne by the foreign investor as a matter of law, but typically is shifted to the United States counterparty as a matter of contract through a "gross-up" provision.

[45] Temp. Treas. Reg. § 1.863–7T (1989).

[46] *See id.* Section 1.863–7T was itself the successor to I.R.S. Notice 87–4, 1987–1 C.B. 416 (containing prior sourcing rules for dollar-denominated interest rate swap income and expenses). Temp. Treas. Reg. § 1.988–4T (1989) contains a similar source rule for "section 988 transactions," which, in general, include most foreign-currency transactions, including currency swaps. Those rules generally have no application to the type of swap discussed in subpart II(A), which normally would consist solely of United States dollar flows determined by reference to United States dollar-based equity and debt indices.

[47] Section 892, for example, exempts from United States taxation any income of foreign governments derived from "financial instruments held in the execution of governmental financial or monetary policy. . . ." I.R.C. § 892(a)(1)(A)(ii) (Prentice Hall 1991). Temp. Treas. Reg. § 1.892–3T(a)(4) (1988) clarifies that this reference covers swaps and similar financial products.

[48] More specifically, the temporary regulation defined a notional principal contract covered by its sourcing rules as

> an interest rate swap, cap, floor, collar, or similar financial instrument that provides for the payment of amounts by one party to another at specified intervals calculated by reference to an *interest rate* index upon a notional principal amount in exchange for specified consideration or a promise to pay similar amounts.

Temp. Treas. Reg. § 1.863–7T(a)(1) (1989) (emphasis added). The definition was further limited to notional principal contracts denominated in, and determined by, refer-

With the promulgation of final Treasury regulations in January 1991, the uncertain sourcing rules of prior law have now been resolved favorably to foreign investors. New Treasury Regulation Section 1.863–7 expands the source rule of the former temporary regulations to any "financial instrument that provides for the payment of amounts by one party to another at specified intervals calculated by reference to *a specified index* upon a notional principal amount in exchange for specified consideration or a promise to pay similar amounts."[49] The preamble to the final regulations explains that the expansion of the definition to include *all* index-related payments, whatever the index, was intended to bring "commodity swaps" within the scope of the regulation's source rules.[50] The preamble does not contain a similar reference to equity derivative products, and the term "index" is not defined by the regulation, but there does not appear to be any basis for excluding from its scope a well-known and heavily publicized equity index such as the Standard & Poor's 500.

Accordingly, it would appear that our hypothetical foreign investor should now be able to conclude that any income attributable to an equity index swap with a United States counterparty will be characterized for United States tax purposes as derived from sources outside the United States, and therefore will not be subject to United States withholding

---

ence to the "functional currency" of the United States party (normally United States dollars). *Id.*

An equity index swap did not come within this definition of a "notional principal contract," because the equity-indexed component of the parties' swap payments cannot properly be viewed as either calculated by reference to an *interest rate index* or as "specified consideration" for the floating-rate amounts. (I view the term "specified consideration" to mean a fixed amount of money, whether paid in one lump sum (as in the case of a typical interest rate cap or floor) or over time (as in the case of the fixed-rate leg of a standard interest rate swap).) Consequently, the residence-based sourcing principles of Temp. Treas. Reg. § 1.863–7T did not provide a safe harbor that would eliminate United States withholding tax risk for payments made by the United States securities firm as equity payor under the swap.

In the absence of a consensus view about the metaphysical nature of derivative products *not* covered by the pragmatic guidance of Temp. Treas. Reg. § 1.863–7T, practitioners had no choice but to analogize to more clearly understood categories of income. *Cf.* Bank of Am. v. United States, 680 F.2d 142, 150 (Ct. Cl. 1982) (determining source of income from "confirmation" and "acceptance" of letters of credit "by analogy to interest [sourcing rules]," even though the income was not actually interest). For example, service income generally is sourced where the services are performed, *see* I.R.C. §§ 861(a)(3), 862(a)(3) (Prentice Hall 1991), insurance premiums are sourced at the situs of the insured risk, *see* I.R.C. §§ 861(a)(7), 862(a)(7) (Prentice Hall 1991), and interest generally is sourced by the residence of the obligor, *see* I.R.C. § 861(a)(1) (Prentice Hall 1991).

[49] Treas. Reg. § 1.863–7(a)(1) (1991) (emphasis added). The new rules are effective for notional principal contract income includible in income on or after February 13, 1991, subject to a taxpayer election to apply the rules retroactively. *Id.* § 1.863–7(a)(2).

[50] Explanation of Provisions, T.D. 8330, 1991–7 I.R.B. 10. "Commodity swaps" are another example of a novel form of notional principal contract. A commodity swap might look much like an equity index swap, except that one party would pay an amount of cash measured by the then-current spot price price of, for example, crude oil applied to a notional quantity of that commodity, while the counterparty would pay a fixed number of dollars (or dollars measured by a floating-rate interest index).

tax.[51] Thus, a foreign investor can resolve its pragmatic United States tax concern (the possible imposition of United States withholding tax on swap payments) without ever struggling with—or needing to struggle with, for that matter—the more difficult question of the metaphysical tax cubbyhole into which equity index swaps should be placed for United States tax purposes.[52]

2. *The United States Investors.* One of the most interesting aspects of Treasury Regulation Section 1.863–7 (and its predecessor temporary regulation) is that it represents a purely pragmatic result, without all the metaphysical trappings that would be required in a comprehensive approach to the taxation of the financial products covered by the regulation. Commentators have applauded the Treasury and the Internal Revenue Service for that pragmatism, because it improves the economic efficiency of the international capital markets.[53] At the same time, it must be admitted that pragmatism has a price; in this case, by limiting guidance to the international capital markets in a purely pragmatic fashion, the Treasury and the Internal Revenue Service have offered no guidance at all to domestic parties entering into equity index swaps. As the discus-

---

[51]As noted earlier, foreign-source income of a foreign investor will not be treated as "effectively connected" with the conduct of a United States trade or business (and hence subject to net income tax) unless, among other factors, the foreign investor maintains an office or other fixed place of business in the United States. *See supra* note 43. Treas. Reg. § 1.863–7 (1991) (as well as the predecessor temporary regulation) effectively turns the statutory rule on its head by providing that if income derived by a foreign entity from a notional principal contract "arises from" the conduct of a United States trade or business, as determined under principles "similar to" those described in Treas. Reg. § 1.864–4(c) (as amended in 1984) (which does not deal specifically with income from notional principal products), then that income will be treated as derived from sources within the United States and will be treated as effectively connected with the conduct of a United States trade or business. A foreign investor must, therefore, still be on guard that its dealings with United States counterparties not rise to the level of a trade or business in the United States.

[52] One interesting question that remains is whether Treas. Reg. § 1.863–7 (1991) changes settled law in areas not within its apparent intended scope. Virtually any cash-settlement futures contract on a financial index, for example, could theoretically come within the scope of the regulation, which in turn might affect the source of income from such a contract (or its characterization as effectively connected with the conduct of a United States trade or business). One counterargument is that, when the regulation defines the term "notional principal contract" by reference to the "payment of *amounts*," that definition requires that at least one of the parties to a notional principal contract be obligated to make more than one payment to its counterparty. This hyper-literal reading in turn would transform Treas. Reg. § 1.863–7 into a quasi-elective system for forward contracts. By structuring a contract with two payments rather than one, a contract could be brought within the definition of a notional principal contract.

[53] The change on sourcing rules made in the permanent regulation was itself in response to input on the shortcomings of the temporary regulation. *See Allocation of Income Attributable to Notional Principal Contracts—Final Regulations Under Section 863,* 50 TAX NOTES 237, 237 (1991); *cf.* Kleinbard, Duncan & Greenberg, *U.S. Reduces Tax Risk for Swaps,* INT'L FIN. L. REV., Feb. 1987, at 26, 27.

sion that follows demonstrates, the resulting lacuna compels taxpayers to follow a tortuous path through Internal Revenue Code provisions that were not drafted to deal with equity derivative products.

I began by postulating two United States investors in equity index swaps: a tax-exempt pension plan that wished to avoid the UBTI provisions of the Internal Revenue Code, and a taxpaying corporation that could increase its after-tax returns by deriving capital gains, rather than ordinary income, from an equity index swap. By coincidence, the same convoluted tax analysis can provide favorable conclusions for both investors.

Section 512(b) sets out a series of statutory exceptions from the scope of the UBTI provisions of the Internal Revenue Code.[54] On the theory that an equity index swap represents a novel form of notional principal contract, sections 512(b)(1) through (3), which exclude interest, dividends, rents, and royalties from the scope of UBTI, cannot help the tax-exempt investor.[55] Section 512(b)(5), however, is potentially relevant. That provision excludes from UBTI gain from the "sale, exchange or other disposition" of property other than inventory (or other property held primarily for sale to customers in the ordinary course of business).[56] (For the sake of clarity, inventory and property held primarily for sale to customers in the ordinary course of business hereinafter are collectively referred to as "dealer property.")

The taxable corporation, of course, has no direct interest in section 512(b)(5).[57] Instead, to derive capital gain from an equity index swap, the corporation must recognize "gain from the sale or exchange of a capital asset."[58] A "capital asset" in turn means any property held by the taxpayer, other than dealer property (and certain other types of property not relevant to the present analysis).[59]

Thus, both the tax-exempt pension plan and the taxable corporation can achieve their tax objectives if income from an equity index swap constitutes gain from the "sale or exchange" of property (other than dealer property).[60] An equity index swap (or other equity derivative product)

---

[54] I.R.C. § 512(b) (Prentice Hall 1991). Whether these exceptions are exclusive or are a series of safe harbors lies at the heart of the current debate over the application of the UBTI provisions to interest rate swaps. *See infra* note 68.

[55] *See supra* note 38. Phrased differently, having rejected the analysis that an equity index swap in fact is an investment in equities, a tax-exempt institution cannot then seek shelter in a statutory exclusion for actual dividends.

[56] I.R.C. § 512(b)(5) (Prentice Hall 1991).

[57] *See supra* note 39 and accompanying text.

[58] I.R.C. § 1222(1), (3) (1988).

[59] I.R.C. § 1221 (1988); *see also* Arkansas Best Corp. v. Commissioner, 485 U.S. 212 (1988) (limiting extra-statutory exceptions to the definition of "capital asset").

[60] Because I ultimately favor the "sale or exchange" solution, I do not consider the alternative argument available to a tax-exempt institution that income from an equity index swap is gain from the "other disposition" of property, within the meaning of § 512(b)(5).

quite clearly constitutes property under tax common law.[61] Moreover, in the hands of an institutional investor (whether tax-exempt or taxable), an equity index swap ordinarily will not constitute dealer property, because the investor does not hold itself out to customers as a market-maker in such contracts.[62] As a result, the fundamental tax issue raised by an equity index swap for both hypothetical United States investors is simply whether income from an equity index swap can be characterized as gain from the "sale or exchange" of property.[63]

---

[61] Although contract rights do not invariably constitute property for tax purposes, financial instruments such as equity derivative products typically do. For example, a debenture is property in this sense. *See* Commissioner v. Ferrer, 304 F.2d 125, 129–30 (2d Cir. 1962); *see also* Commissioner v. Gillette Motor Transport Co., 364 U.S. 130, 134 (1959) (describing the typical characteristic of a "capital asset" as the potential for appreciation in value over a substantial time); International Flavors & Fragrances, Inc. v. Commissioner, 524 F.2d 357, 360 (2d Cir. 1975) (noting the Service's withdrawal of reliance on the theory that a forward contract was *not* a capital asset for tax purposes); Hoover Co. v. Commissioner, 72 T.C. 206, 243–48 (1979) (holding a forward contract to be property), *nonacq.*, 1980–1 C.B. 2; Turzillo v. Commissioner, 346 F.2d 884, 889 (6th Cir. 1965) (finding that rights under a buy-sell agreement for stock constitute property); Dorman v. United States, 296 F.2d 27, 29 (9th Cir. 1961) (finding that an executory contract to acquire capital in a partnership constitutes property); Anderson v. United States, 468 F. Supp. 1085, 1096–98 (D. Minn. 1979) (holding a right of first refusal to be a capital asset), *aff'd mem.*, 624 F.2d 1109 (8th Cir. 1980); Vickers v. Commissioner, 80 T.C. 394, 405 (1983) (noting the settled law that a futures contract is a capital asset); Estate of Shea v. Commissioner, 57 T.C. 15, 23–25 (1971) (holding that a ship charter constitutes property, based in part on the market for the existence of such charters), *acq.*, 1973–2 C.B. 3.

[62] As applied to the securities industry, both categories of dealer property (property properly includible in inventory and property held for sale to customers in the ordinary course of business) require that a taxpayer have *customers* from which it seeks to earn a "middleman's" bid-asked profit. *See* Treas. Reg. § 1.471–5 (as amended in 1987) ("[A] dealer in securities is a merchant of securities . . . regularly engaged in the purchase of securities and their resale to customers; that is, one who as a merchant buys securities and sells them to customers with a view to the gains and profits that may be derived therefrom"); Kemon v. Commissioner, 16 T.C. 1026, 1032–33 (1951) (distinguishing securities traders from securities dealers on the basis that, while both are engaged in a trade or business, securities traders do not have customers).

The traditional tax definition of a securities dealer cannot literally be applied to a dealer in notional principal contracts, because even the most active market participants cannot be said to actively hold out their "books" of open contractual positions for sale to customers in the ordinary course of business. Although swap dealers occasionally do sell (or consent to the assignment of) swaps in the secondary market (usually at the behest of their counterparties), the vast bulk of a swap dealer's activity consists of entering into new contracts with customers. In recognition of this fact, Temp. Treas. Reg. § 1.954–2T(a)(4)(iii) (1988) defines a "regular dealer," for purposes not directly relevant here, as a "merchant" that either functions as a merchant in the sense used by Treas. Reg. § 1.471–5 (as amended in 1987), *or* "makes a market in derivative financial products . . . by regularly and actively offering to enter into positions in such products to the public in the ordinary course of business."

Under any of these definitions, an institutional investor should not be viewed as a dealer in notional principal products. Accordingly, contracts held by such an investor should not constitute dealer property—or, phrased positively, such contracts should constitute capital assets in the hands of the investor.

[63] In the case of the tax-exempt pension plan, income that otherwise cannot be classified as UBTI might nonetheless be swept within those provisions if that income is "debt-financed

As might be suspected, the term "sale or exchange" is charged with tax meaning. In particular, under the so-called "extinguishment" doctrine, a long line of case law has held that, in the absence of a statute to the contrary, payments from one party to a contractual counterparty in consideration of the termination of the underlying contractual arrangement are not considered to arise from the "sale or exchange" of property, because the property (*viz.*, the bundle of contract rights) does not survive the transfer.[64]

---

income," within the scope of I.R.C. § 514 (Prentice Hall 1991). Essentially, § 514 treats income earned by a tax-exempt institution as UBTI to the extent that such income is attributable to the investment of the proceeds of borrowings by the tax-exempt entity.

If one proceeds on the basis that an equity index swap is a novel form of notional principal contract, rather than a leveraged investment in equities, it should follow that there can be no § 514 issue, because the contract does not create any "acquisition indebtedness." This is, of course, the correct answer. The Internal Revenue Service, however, apparently prefers to follow a more overgrown path to reach this straightforward conclusion.

In a General Counsel Memorandum, the Service considered at great length whether a simple "long" commodity futures contract (that is, an executory contract to purchase a fixed quantity of a commodity at a specified price at a fixed date in the future) contains a component of acquisition indebtedness. *See* Gen. Couns. Mem. 39620 (Apr. 3, 1987). The Memorandum correctly concludes that "variation margin" is not evidence of any indebtedness, but then proceeds down a path that is as novel as it is confused. To the extent that its argument can be restated, the Memorandum appears to argue that, since a futures contract is "property," entering into a long futures contract must be tantamount to purchasing property today (the futures contract itself, *not* the underlying commodity) in exchange for a promise of deferred payment (the purchase price of the *underlying commodity* at maturity of the contract).

Why a party that simply enters into an executory contract should be viewed as "buying" a bundle of contract rights at all is not explained by the Memorandum, nor is its basis for concluding that the promised future payment for the underlying commodity is itself the measure of the purchase price of these intangible rights. *Cf.* Lucas v. North Texas Lumber Co., 281 U.S. 11, 13 (1930) (finding that an executory sales contract is not a current sale); Commissioner v. Olmsted Inc. Life Agency, 304 F.2d 16, 23 (8th Cir. 1962) (finding no tax consequences from the modification of an executory contract). In fact, the purchase price of these intangible rights, if meaningful at all, can only be zero—the amount paid by the parties for the privilege of entering into the contract. This bizarre confusion of the purchase price of the contract rights with the purchase price of the underlying commodity covered by that contract leads the Memorandum to conclude that there is no difference between an executory contract to sell a house in the future and a current sale of that house, with the seller taking back a purchase money mortgage—a proposition that the drafters of the Memorandum, were they to implement their example, would find sorely tested on the first rainy day.

In the end, the Memorandum comes to the correct answer that executory contracts, including commodity futures contracts, do not give rise to "acquisition indebtedness," although it does so only on the grounds of the purported policy goals of the statute and an overdeveloped concern for the technical problems its analysis raises (which technical problems, of course, are simply evidence that the analysis itself is faulty).

[64] *See* Kleinbard & Greenberg, *supra* note 7, at 436–37 & n.136; *see also* Stoller v. Commissioner, 60 T.C.M. (CCH) 1554 (1990) (holding that a fee paid to a counterparty to terminate various forward contracts to purchase and sell United States Treasury securities gave rise to ordinary, rather than capital, loss, because the party's contract rights did not survive their cancellation). *Stoller* involved a taxable year prior to the effective date of I.R.C. § 1234A (1988), described at note 69, *infra*.

The application of the "sale or exchange" doctrine to notional principal contracts most charitably can be described as uncertain. The Internal Revenue Service has never explicitly addressed the issue; indeed, on those few occasions the Service has addressed cross-border swap transactions, it has specifically avoided any resolution of the question.[65] In the case of traditional interest rate swaps, most observers nonetheless have concluded that fixed-for-floating swap payments do not involve sales or exchanges.[66] The theory underlying this conclusion is that the United States dollar is not "property" for tax purposes, and therefore the "exchange" of floating-rate dollars for fixed dollars does not involve the sale or exchange of property.[67] One important result that follows is that interest rate swap income probably does *not* fall within section 512(b)(5)'s exception from UBTI for gains from the sale, exchange, or other disposition of nondealer property.[68]

The application of the "sale or exchange" doctrine to the equity index swap, however, is considerably more complex than its application to a traditional interest rate swap. Section 1234A provides in part that gain at-

---

[65] *See, e.g.*: Rev. Rul. 87–5, 1987–1 C.B. 180 (concluding that a traditional interest rate swap gives rise to "industrial and commercial profits" in the hands of a bank for purposes of the United States Netherlands Income Tax Convention); I.R.S. Notice 87–4, 1987–1 C.B. 416 (refusing to take a position on whether swap income is "fixed or determinable annual or periodic income").

[66] *See* Battle, Schultz & Mangieri, *Tax Considerations in the United States,* in THE HANDBOOK OF CURRENCY AND INTEREST RATE RISK MANAGEMENT 26–5, 26–6 (R. Schwartz & C. Smith eds. 1990); Note, *Tax Treatment of Notional Principal Contracts,* 103 HARV. L. REV. 1951, 1958 n. 33 (1990).

[67] For a more comprehensive discussion of the application of the "extinguishment" doctrine to payments to terminate interest rate swaps (as well as to interim swap payments), see Kleinbard & Greenberg, *supra* note 7, at 436–37.

[68] An early report by the New York State Bar Association argued that an interest rate swap had substantial economic similarity to a series of cash-settlement financial futures contracts, but even that report did not argue that an interest rate swap was in fact a series of cash-settlement futures (or forwards) contracts on existing financial instruments. *See* New York State Bar Ass'n Tax Section, Report on the Withholding Tax Consequences of Interest Rate Swap Agreements under the Internal Revenue Code (June 6, 1985) (unpublished) (copy on file with the *Texas Law Review*). Accordingly, the economic similarity of results (which, in any event, has never been explicitly conceded by the Internal Revenue Service) is of limited utility in constructing a "sale or exchange" argument for interest rate swap income.

I do not consider, of course, the more difficult policy question (adverted to briefly in note 54, *supra*) of whether I.R.C. § 512(b) should be read as a series of safe harbors or as a list of exclusive exceptions from the definition of UBTI. *Compare* Rev. Rul. 78–88, 1978–1 C.B. 163 (ruling that income from securities lending is not UBTI because it is similar in nature to other investment activities) *with* Gen. Couns. Mem. 36948 (Dec. 10, 1976) (stating that such income is UBTI—prior to the Internal Revenue Code's amendment to deal with this issue—because it does not fall within any statutory exception to UBTI, and "exemptions from taxation are to be strictly construed"). Gen. Couns. Mem. 37313 (Nov. 7, 1977) and the attached Conference Memorandum offer interesting insights into the deliberations that led to the effective reversal of Gen. Couns. Mem. 36948.

See *supra* note 4 for the recent history of the Service's indecision on this issue.

tributable to the "cancellation, lapse, expiration, or other termination of . . . a right or obligation with respect to personal property (as defined in section 1092(d)(1)) which is (or on acquisition would be) a capital asset in the hands of the taxpayer . . . shall be treated as gain or loss from the sale of a capital asset."[69] Section 1234A by its terms does not require a current or future possessory interest in underlying "personal property" for the section to apply; if bilateral cash payments are made by reference to fluctuations in the value of "personal property," and the section's other requirements are satisfied, section 1234A will create a deemed "sale or exchange" of personal property.[70]

---

[69] I.R.C. § 1234A (1988). Section 1234A was enacted in 1981 as one of the tax straddle provisions of the Economic Recovery Tax Act of 1981, Pub. L. No. 97–34, § 507(a), 95 Stat. 172, 333. It was intended to "prevent tax-avoidance transactions designed to create fully-deductible ordinary losses on certain dispositions of capital assets, which if sold at a gain, would produce capital gains." H.R. REP. NO. 201, 97th Cong., 1st Sess. 212 (1981); see JOINT COMM. ON TAXATION, 97TH CONG., 1ST SESS., GENERAL EXPLANATION OF THE ECONOMIC RECOVERY ACT OF 1981, at 313 (Comm. Print 1981) [hereinafter 1981 BLUEBOOK]. Prior to the enactment of § 1234A, taxpayers would, for example, enter into largely offsetting long and short forward contracts for foreign currency or securities; the taxpayers would then claim ordinary loss (under the extinguishment doctrine) on the cancellation of the loss leg and capital gain on the sale of the gain leg.

Then, as now, § 1234A applied to "a right or obligation with respect to personal property (as defined in section 1092(d)(1))." I.R.C. § 1234A(1) (1988). As originally enacted, however, the scope of the personal property reference was narrower, because § 1092(d)(1)'s definition of personal property contained a comprehensive carve-out for stock, including stock options. See Tax Reform Act of 1984, Pub. L. No. 98–369, § 101(b)(1), 98 Stat. 494, 618.

[70] It is theoretically possible to understand § 1234A as requiring a possessory interest in personal property. The argument might run as follows. First, § 1234A requires a "right" to control or "obligation" to deliver property, and a contractual right to cash based on fluctuations in the value of property arguably is not such a right or obligation. Rather, a right to cash in an amount equal to the value of specified property is a "position" or an "interest" in personal property, a formulation used in § 1092 but not in § 1234A. Second, if § 1234A did not require a possessory interest, it would govern cash-settlement equity index options. If that were the case, the "cash settlement" amendment made by the Tax Reform Act of 1984, Pub. L. No. 98–369, § 105(a), 98 Stat. 494, 629, to I.R.C. § 1234 (1988) (the general option provision) should have been limited to stock options not covered by § 1234A. Finally, § 1234A was enacted to deal with abuses involving contracts to deliver property. See 1981 BLUEBOOK, supra note 69, at 313.

Such a reading, however, would (1) be inconsistent with the breadth of § 1234A's language, (2) overlook evidence of an overlap between § 1234 and § 1234A, and (3) defeat the anti-abuse purpose for which § 1234A was enacted. As to § 1234A's language, Congress could have written a delivery requirement into § 1234A (as it originally did for § 1256) had it wished to. Instead, the provision applies to a right or obligation "with respect to" personal property, and "with respect to" is perhaps the broadest formulation that the tax law envisions.

The argument that § 1234 and § 1234A are mutually exclusive does not take account of the murky state of the law in 1984. Since "personal property" at that time included neither stock nor (in most cases) stock options, it understandably was not clear whether § 1234A applied to equity index options. Moreover, § 1234A does not apply to contracts held as a dealer (such as an options dealer); I.R.C. § 1234(c) (1988) in effect addresses the character (but not the timing) of income from that class of options contracts. Accordingly, there is no inconsistency in having some overlap between these two

As applied to an equity index swap, section 1234A could be viewed as treating *each* interim swap payment as a payment in termination of a right or obligation with respect to property (either the specified equity index itself or the stocks constituting that equity index).[71] If section 1234A applied to the equity index swap payments, the result would be that each payment to the investor would be treated as attributable to a "sale or exchange." In turn, gain from the "sale or exchange" of nondealer property would not be UBTI to a tax-exempt investor and would be capital gain to a taxable investor.

---

provisions, since both lead to capital gain or loss, and no principle of tax law mandates exclusive application of either one provision or the other.

This overlap between § 1234 and § 1234A is demonstrated by Rev. Rul. 88–31, 1988–1 C.B. 302. One part of the Ruling deals with the character, holding period, and timing of recognition of gain or loss from a contingent payment right that the Service has determined should be characterized as a cash-settlement put option. While the ruling relies primarily on § 1234 for the character issue, it also cites § 1234A specifically with respect to the character of loss to the holder on the lapse of the option. *See infra* notes 79–80 and accompanying text. This citation is incomprehensible unless § 1234A (as well as § 1234(c)) in fact applies to cash-settlement options.

Finally, perhaps the most telling argument against the importation of a delivery requirement into § 1234A is that such a reading would thwart the purpose for which § 1234A was enacted. If § 1234A does not apply to cash-settlement contracts, then taxpayers may use cash-settlement forwards to convert capital loss into ordinary loss (and thereby evade the capital loss limitation), just as they used forwards on currency and securities to convert losses before § 1234A was enacted. While it is of course not unknown for Congress to enact a provision that turns out to be too narrow to halt the abuse at which it is directed, the anti-abuse purpose of § 1234A should guide the understanding of its language. Since it does not by its terms require a possessory interest in personal property, and since reading in such a requirement would defeat its purpose, a possession requirement should not be read into § 1234A.

[71] The fact that § 1234A applies to a "termination" of a right or obligation with respect to personal property does not mean that § 1234A does not apply to each periodic payment under an equity index swap. The "termination" language of § 1234A should be understood as excluding interest, rents, and similar periodic payments for the use of property from the scope of § 1234A, not as applying to a case that, like the equity index swap, is closer to a series of discrete forward contracts.

In economic substance, the equity index swap is a series of independent periodic "bets" on an index. Each payment is made in respect of changes in the value of the equity index (and in respect of prevailing interest rates) for the period to which the payment relates. At the start of each period, the equity index benchmark effectively is reset to the current market levels, so that the performance of the index in prior or subsequent periods has no effect on the payments made with respect to the current period.

In this sense, then, each payment terminates the rights of the parties in respect of the "bet" they have made for the period to which that payment relates. One does not have to determine that an equity index swap is in fact a series of forward contracts for all tax purposes to conclude that each payment made under the swap is sufficiently independent of any other to be described by § 1234A's language as a *termination* of a right with respect to personal property (the underlying index). Any other reading would lead to the absurd result that the final payment under an equity index swap could be treated as a sale or exchange under § 1234A, but that none of the preceding payments could.

In the case of interest on a bond, by contrast, each interest payment does not "terminate" any party's rights with respect to the underlying property; it is only the return of principal that is a termination event. Thus, a final interest payment on a bond is still not a termination payment (even without regard to § 1234A's carve-out for debt obligations).

Section 1234A imposes two prerequisites to its application. First, the underlying property (either the equity index itself or the stocks constituting that equity index) must constitute a capital asset in the hands of a counterparty: to the extent that an equity index swap serves as an investment substitute, this criterion almost invariably will be satisfied. Second, section 1234A requires that either the equity index or the basket of stocks composing the equity index constitute "personal property (as defined in section 1092(d)(1))."[72] This latter requirement is the source of much of the ambiguity in the analysis as applied to an equity index swap.

Section 1092(d)(1) generally defines "personal property" as "any personal property of a type which is actively traded."[73] An equity index swap itself will not be personal property as defined in section 1092(d)(1), because the swap is not "actively traded." In the hands of either of the hypothetical domestic investors, however, the equity index swap is "a right or obligation with respect to" the specified equity index (or to the stocks constituting that index), as required under section 1234A.[74] In most cases, the stocks that make up the index that serves as the basis for an equity index swap will be both "personal property" (in the vernacular sense) and "actively traded." For swaps based on a recognized index such as the Standard & Poor's 500 Index, forwards, futures, and options in that index also will be actively traded. Accordingly, payments to an investor/floating-rate payor in respect of such publicly traded equity index swaps would appear to be covered by section 1234A.

Section 1092(d)(3), however, provides: "[F]or purposes of [section 1092(d)(1)] . . . the term 'personal property' does not include stock [unless that stock is part of a straddle described in section 1092(d)(3)(B)]. The preceding sentence shall not apply to any *interest in stock.*"[75]

---

[72] I.R.C. § 1234A (1988).

[73] I.R.C. § 1092(d)(1) (1988).

[74] I.R.C. § 1234A (1988).

[75] I.R.C. § 1092(d)(3) (1988) (emphasis added). The "interest in stock" language in § 1092(d)(3) stems from a technical amendment to the Tax Reform Act of 1984. Prior to 1984, stock and exchange-traded stock options were expressly excluded from the straddle rules. The 1984 Act dropped the language excluding exchange-traded stock options from the straddle rules, but did not affirmatively provide that stock options were subject to those rules (although that was clearly Congress's intent). The language excluding stock was narrowed but not dropped. *See* Tax Reform Act of 1984, Pub. L. No. 98–369, § 101(a), (b), 98 Stat. 494, 616–19; STAFF OF JOINT COMM. ON TAXATION, 98TH CONG., 2D SESS., GENERAL EXPLANATION OF THE REVENUE PROVISIONS OF THE DEFICIT REDUCTION ACT OF 1984, at 308–11 (Comm. Print 1984). In 1986, Congress clarified § 1092(d)(3) by providing that although the straddle rules do not, in general, apply to "stock," they do apply to an "interest in stock." *See* Tax Reform Act of 1986, Pub. L. No. 99–514, § 1808(c), 100 Stat. 2085, 2817–18; STAFF OF JOINT COMM. ON TAXATION, 100TH CONG., 1ST SESS., EXPLANATION OF TECHNICAL CORRECTIONS TO THE TAX REFORM ACT OF 1984 AND OTHER RECENT TAX LEGISLATION 43–44 (Comm. Print 1987). While the legislative history of this technical amendment refers only to stock options, Congress's use of the term "interest in stock" rather than "stock option" suggests that Congress intended to reach all "interests" in stock other than outright ownership.

The application of section 1234A to an equity index swap therefore turns on two questions: (1) whether section 1234A's reference to section 1092(d)(1) is meant to include section 1092(d)(3)'s carve-out for "stock"; and, (2) assuming that the section 1092(d)(3) carve-out is relevant, whether the equity index swap should be viewed as a right or obligation with respect to "stock" (in which case section 1234A would have no application to the equity index swap, and swap payments might be UBTI), or as a right or obligation with respect to an "interest in stock" (in which case, as further described below, section 1234A would apply to create a "sale or exchange" on every swap payment, thereby causing those payments to be characterized as non-UBTI to a tax-exempt investor, and as capital gain to a taxpaying investor).

Section 1234A's cross-reference to "personal property (as defined in section 1092(d)(1))" should be read as importing the limitations of section 1092(d)(3). The stock carve-out was part of section 1092(d)(1) when that provision was originally enacted in 1981 as part of the same legislation that enacted section 1234A.[76] Section 1092(d) was then revised in 1984 to render the straddle rules applicable to straddles composed of stock and stock options (or substantially similar property).[77] Nothing in the legislative history suggests that this rewriting of section 1092(d) was intended to affect the scope of section 1234A. Furthermore, in its current form, section 1092(d)(3) applies by its terms "for purposes of" section 1092(d)(1). It is therefore difficult to separate the two paragraphs in the absence of a specific statutory directive to do so. This analysis also appears to be consistent with the Internal Revenue Service's approach to section 1234A in Revenue Ruling 88–31.[78]

Revenue Ruling 88–31 analyzes, in a variety of different factual circumstances, the tax consequences of payments to a holder of a cash-settlement put option on publicly traded stock of a corporate issuer. Revenue Ruling 88–31 first quotes sections 1234 (the general option taxation rule), 1234A, 1092(d)(1), and 1092(d)(3) (among other provisions), and examines, in particular, the legislative history of section 1234's cash-settlement option rules.[79] Among its other fact patterns, the ruling then considers the tax consequences to the issuer and to a holder of a naked cash-settlement put option of a payment by the issuer at maturity of the option contract. The ruling explicitly concludes that the issuer's tax consequences are governed by the general option rules of section 1234 (not section 1234A); moreover, Revenue Ruling 88–31 appears to rely on those general option rules—not on section 1234A—for the proposition that the

---

[76] *See* Economic Recovery Tax Act of 1981, Pub. L. No. 97–34, § 501(a), 95 Stat. 172, 325.
[77] *See* Tax Reform Act of 1984, Pub. L. No. 98–369, § 101(a), (b), 98 Stat. 494, 616–19.
[78] *See* Rev. Rul. 88–31, 1988–1 C.B. 302; *supra* note 70.
[79] *See* Rev. Rul. 88–31, 1988–1 C.B. 302, 303–04.

holder has a deemed sale or exchange on the receipt of payment from the issuer.[80]

Thus, publicly traded stock (unless part of certain specified straddles) is not "personal property" for purposes of section 1234A, because section 1092(d)(3) excludes stock from the term "personal property" for purposes of section 1092(d)(1). As described above, however, section 1092(d)(3) carves out from section 1092(d)(1) only "stock," and not an "interest in stock." The question remains whether an equity index swap should be viewed as a right or obligation with respect to "stock," or to an "interest in stock"—and, if the latter is correct, whether a recognized index, such as the Standard & Poor's 500 Index, itself can be said to be "actively traded" for purposes of the definition of "personal property" under section 1092(d).

The differences between a right or obligation with respect to a bundle of stocks and an index comprising that bundle can only be described as metaphysical. On balance, however, an equity index swap should be viewed as a right or obligation with respect to "an interest in stock." The specified equity index is itself an artificial construction whose constituent securities—and the relative weighting given each of them—are determined by the rules of the compilers of that index. Those compilers can modify their own rules, or add or drop securities from the index, without directly affecting the underlying equity securities in any way.[81] Thus, the equity index can fairly be viewed as separate from the underlying equity securities that compose the index at any given point in time.

Moreover, a recognized index, such as the Standard & Poor's 500 Index, itself can reasonably be viewed as "actively traded" personal prop-

---

[80] See id. at 304–05. Any other reading would render superfluous Revenue Ruling 88–31's discussion of the legislative history of the general option rules of § 1234 as applied to holders of cash-settlement options. If the Service in fact believed that § 1234A looked solely to § 1092(d)(1) without regard to § 1092(d)(3), then a holder of the cash-settlement put option considered in Revenue Ruling 88–31 would have been treated as a party to a sale or exchange by virtue of § 1234A, without any need to consider the full scope of the general option rules of § 1234.

This reading of Revenue Ruling 88–31 creates in turn some uncertainty as to why the Service quoted § 1234A in setting out the statutory provisions relevant to its analysis, and in its analysis of the tax consequences to a holder of the lapse of an option. It seems to me incredible, however, that the Service would have relied on § 1234A to characterize termination payments to a holder of a naked cash-settlement put option as a "sale or exchange" without discussing the application of § 1092(d), while at the same time quoting excerpts from the legislative history to § 1234 that are relevant solely for purposes of determining that the termination payment should be characterized as a sale or exchange.

[81] Thus, in January 1991, when Pan Am Corporation filed for a bankruptcy reorganization under Chapter 11 of the Bankruptcy Code, the compilers of the Standard & Poor's 500 Index dropped that company from the index and substituted Blockbuster Entertainment Corporation in its place. See Wall St. J., Jan. 10, 1991, at C20, col. 3. The compilers of the Dow Jones Transportation Average also dropped Pan Am, and substituted for it Roadway Services, Inc. See Wall St. J., Jan. 11, 1991, at C1, col. 3.

erty. Certainly the Standard & Poor's 500 Index is actively traded in the futures and options markets. It is true that in the cash markets the Standard & Poor's 500 Index and the stocks constituting that index meld into complete identity, but the existence of actively traded, very short-dated forwards, futures, and options should be sufficient to conclude that the Standard & Poor's 500 Index (or a similar index) can itself be viewed as actively traded personal property separate and apart from the stocks composing that index at any given point in time.

Consequently, a persuasive (albeit convoluted) argument can be made that, in the case of an equity index swap, the second sentence of section 1092(d)(3) trumps the carve-out for "stock" in the first sentence of section 1092(d)(3). As a result, an equity index swap can be viewed as a "right or obligation with respect to personal property (as defined in section 1092(d)(1))"—that is, the underlying equity index itself. Accordingly, section 1234A should apply to treat each interim payment in respect of the swap as a "sale or exchange."

If the above analysis is correct, every payment under an equity index swap based on a publicly traded index is a sale or exchange. Such income therefore does *not* constitute UBTI to a domestic tax-exempt investor, and does constitute capital gain to a domestic taxable investor.[82] The conclusion that would follow from this analysis is that, assuming the swap's form is respected (and the transaction not recharacterized as a leveraged purchase of equities, as described above), the two hypothetical United States investors should be able to achieve their different tax objectives through entering into equity index swaps.[83]

C. Variations on a Theme

The above analysis considered only one type of equity index swap, and only with respect to one category of investor. Different federal income tax issues arise using equity index swaps in other contexts.

1. Foreign Currency Denominated Swaps. United States parties have entered into equity index swaps on non-United States equity indices (such as the Nikkei 225). Where one party's payment obligations are in one currency, and the counterparty's obligations in a different currency, the "sale or exchange" analysis set out earlier be-

---

[82] Another logical argument against treating equity-based payments under an equity index swap as ordinary income is that the equity payments to be made under the swap economically are indistinguishable from gains (or losses) on the underlying equities. This argument comes dangerously close, however, to conceding that the equity index swap should be viewed for tax purposes as a leveraged purchase of the underlying stocks composing the relevant equity index. Accordingly, I have not relied on this argument in the above analysis.

[83] Obviously, it is assumed that the taxable investor in this example recognizes gain from its equity index swap position; a recognized loss would be characterized as a capital loss.

comes more straightforward. Since foreign currency is viewed as property for United States tax purposes,[84] a contract to exchange a variable amount of United States dollars for a variable number of units of a foreign currency should always give rise to a sale or exchange. Conversely, in the case of domestic tax-exempt investors or taxable investors seeking capital gains, swaps in which all cash flows are in a single foreign currency (e.g., Yen LIBOR versus the Nikkei 225) require the same section 1234A analysis as that summarized above.[85]

2. *Non-Publicly Traded Equity Indices.* If an equity index swap is written on an index that is not publicly traded—for example, a securities firm's proprietary equity index—then the section 1234A analysis would lead to the opposite conclusion. In the absence of a publicly traded index, payments made under the swap would not be accorded sale or exchange treatment under section 1234A. The parties to the swap should therefore recognize ordinary income or loss (as probably also is the case in interest rate swaps[86]). This result might be troublesome to a United States tax-exempt investor (who might have more difficulty analyzing swap payments as non-UBTI), but might be desirable to a United States taxable institutional investor without capital losses (who would typically prefer ordinary loss to capital loss, and who would usually be indifferent to earning capital gain as opposed to ordinary income). Different tax objectives could be satisfied, then, by using (or creating for the occasion) different equity indices.

III. Financial Innovation and the Tax System

A. Limitations of Current Law

The above case study of equity index swaps points out some important lessons that recur in the tax analysis of many new financial products. First, and perhaps most important, identifying an economic similarity between different financial strategies does little to advance the tax analysis:

[84] *See* Hoover Co. v. Commissioner, 72 T.C. 206 (1979), *nonacq.,* 1980–1 C.B. 2; Rev. Rul. 78–281, 1978–2 C.B. 204; Rev. Rul. 74–7, 1974–1 C.B. 198.
[85] Some taxpayers have attempted to turn swaps in which all cash flows are in a single foreign currency into cross-currency transactions in order to come within the sale or exchange learning that applies to cross-currency exchanges. *See* Cole, *Strong Pound Offers Special Opportunities; Robert Cole Examines Why Managed Currency Funds Have Found Renewed Favour,* The Independent, July 14, 1990, at 25. For example, the gross cash flows under a swap might be calculated as an economic matter in a single foreign currency, and then one party's payment obligations converted into a different currency (at current spot rates) so that an actual exchange of one currency for another is made. In my view, however, this arrangement can be attacked as a single currency swap and a separate purchase or sale of currency at spot rates.
[86] *See supra* text accompanying notes 65–68.

where two strategies are different in fact (that is, produce similar results through different bundles of contractual rights and obligations), the tax analysis of one will not determine the tax analysis of the second.

Second, the tax system typically has no mechanism to ask, much less answer, the tax policy questions raised by new financial products. Reasonable tax policy makers might disagree whether dividend-equivalent payments made to a foreign counterparty to an equity index swap should be subject to United States withholding tax in the same manner as dividends,[87] whether such payments should be UBTI in the hands of a domestic tax-exempt institution, and whether they should give rise to ordinary income or capital gain. However, policymakers might not wish to create a tax system that encourages investors to purchase equity derivatives rather than the real thing; on the other hand, if an equity swap in tax reality is different from a leveraged investment in equities, why should any portion of the swap's flow be taxed, for example, as dividends? The actual tax analysis of equity index swaps, however, proceeds without regard to these policy questions. Instead, the analysis follows a highly technical route through Internal Revenue Code provisions whose purposes and premises may have little to do with the issues raised by the new instrument.[88] It should not be surprising, then, that this technical analysis reaches answers that appropriately reflect sound tax policy only occasionally, and then only by coincidence.

It also should not be surprising that the tax conclusions reached through this technical analysis are easily manipulated. Complex Internal Revenue Code provisions invariably offer opportunities to opt in or out of the resulting analysis, as these provisions—tailored for highly particularized transactions—lose coherency in new and unintended contexts.

Finally, while the current tax system may answer some important tax questions raised by a new financial product incorrectly, the system does not purport to answer other important questions at all. Thus, the Internal Revenue Code may offer some suggestions as to whether income from a particular equity index swap should be treated as gain from the sale or exchange of property, but, until the recent promulgation of Treasury Regulation Section 1.863–7, offered few clues as to the source (domestic or

---

[87] The same issue arises daily in the more straightforward context of income in lieu of dividends paid to a foreign lender of United States equities under a securities loan of the type generally studying the question for the last several years. *See* Priv. Ltr. Rul. 88–22–061 (Mar. 7, 1988); Sheppard, *Tax Officials Consider Debt Securities Questions*, 47 TAX NOTES 1044, 1044–45 (1990); *IRS Makes Progress on Rules on Interest Rate Swaps*, 54 BNA's BANKING REP. 866, 866 (1990).

[88] As discussed at notes 69–70, *supra*, the background and policy behind I.R.C. §§ 1092 and 1234A concern the taxation of straddles and the elimination of specific abuses perceived by Congress in that area. It is not surprising, therefore, that the application of these provisions to equity index swaps should be technical, convoluted, and devoid of any discernible policy. This theme is discussed further in subpart III(B), *infra*.

foreign) of that income, and does not even hint as to the rules that should govern the timing of inclusion of income or loss from complex swap instruments.

B. Legislation and "Legislative" Regulations

One approach to addressing financial innovation in the tax system would be for Congress simply to create new tax cubbyholes for new financial products. In theory, Congress could regularly enact legislation that defines each financial innovation and prescribes a set of operative rules for its users, but Congress in fact has done so infrequently, at best.

Congress's principal contributions to the area in the 1989 legislative process, for example, were two belated and piecemeal limitations on the deductibility of interest expense incurred in the context of leveraged buyouts—provisions that were variously described as limiting abuses or curbing loopholes,[89] but that in fact suggested to many outside observers that Congress was unable to formulate any consensus views as to the role that the corporate interest deduction played (or should play) in shaping the capital structure of American corporations.[90]

Similarly, the 1990 Congress's change to the Internal Revenue Code of principal concern to the capital markets was a technical provision that redefined the implicit yield to maturity of debt obligations issued (or deemed issued) through certain exchanges or modifications of outstanding debt obligations trading at a discount.[91] This provision already has been roundly criticized as encouraging troubled companies to enter

---

[89] *See Financial Products, ABA Tax Section Panel Comments on 1989 High-Yield Debt Restrictions,* Daily Rep. for Executives (BNA) No. 249, at 6–2 (Dec. 27, 1990).

[90] The Revenue Reconciliation Act of 1989, Pub. L. No. 101–239, 103 Stat. 2301 enacted (1) rules prohibiting net operating loss carrybacks from years following a "corporate equity reducing transaction," *see id.* § 7211(a), (b), 103 Stat. at 2342–45 (codified at I.R.C. § 172(b)(1)(E), (h) (Prentice Hall 1991)), and (2) a limitation on the deductibility of interest in respect of "high yield original issue discount obligations," *see id.* § 7202(a), (b), 103 Stat. at 2330–32 (codified at I.R.C. § 163(e)(5), (i) (Prentice Hall 1991)), each discussed in *supra* note 5. The 1989 Act also enacted I.R.C. § 1503(f) (Prentice Hall 1991), *see* Revenue Reconciliation Act of 1989, Pub. L. No. 101–239, § 7201(a), 103 Stat. 2301, 2328–29, an "anti-loophole" provision that eliminated the tax advantages of "subsidiary preferred" offerings. *See* Ginsburg, Levin, Welke & Wolfe, *CERTs: The New Limitations on NOL Carrybacks,* 46 Tax Notes 1315 (1990); Zonana, *Revenue Reconciliation Act of 1990,* N.Y.L.J., Jan. 18, 1990, at 5, col. 1.; *infra* note 129.

[91] *See* Revenue Reconciliation Act of 1990, Pub. L. No. 101–508, § 11325(a)(1), 104 Stat. 1388–400, 1388–466 (codified at I.R.C. § 108(e)(11) (Prentice Hall 1991). Although former I.R.C. § 1275(a)(4) (1988) (repealed 1990) applied specifically to original issue discount rather than cancellation of indebtedness (COD), prior to its removal by the Revenue Reconciliation Act of 1990, this provision was generally thought to imply that upon the exchange of an outstanding debt security for a new debt security having a value less than the "adjusted issue price" of the old debt security, no COD income would result to the issuer because under § 1275(a)(4) the "issue price" of the new debt security could not be less than the adjusted issue price of the old debt security. The 1990 Act amended § 1275 by deleting former § 1275(a)(4), *see* Revenue Reconciliation Act of 1990, Pub. L. No. 101–508, § 11325(a)(2), 104 Stat. 1388–400, 1388–466, and it provided explicitly in

bankruptcy reorganization (to avoid the new rule's sting) rather than to negotiate an out-of-bankruptcy workout, for no particularly clear tax policy reason.[92]

Congress on occasion has attempted to deal with financial innovation through the delegation of "legislative" regulation-making authority to the Treasury Department and Internal Revenue Service, but even those expert agencies have been slow to utilize whatever authority has been delegated to them. For example, the administrative agencies have left largely untouched a large set of proposed regulations dating back nearly five years addressing, in effect, all aspects of the timing of interest income or expense for debt instruments.[93] These proposed regulations represent virtually the only guidance on a range of issues that affect billions of dollars of debt offerings; yet, because the regulations exist only in proposed form (and because they have been extensively criticized in the academic literature), taxpayers routinely rely on, or alternatively ignore, the proposals, as suits their circumstances.[94]

Similarly, in 1983, proposed regulations were promulgated under Internal Revenue Code Section 1058, which deals with the federal income tax consequences of securities lending.[95] Since that time, both the volume of securities lent and the purposes for those loans have mushroomed, giving rise to a number of interesting tax questions.[96] Moreover, as the equity

---

I.R.C. § 108(e)(11) (Prentice Hall 1991) that, for purposes of determining COD income in the case of a debt-for-debt exchange, an issuer is deemed to have satisfied its outstanding debt with an amount of cash equal to the fair market value of its new debt.

[92] See, e.g., Cohen, The Repeal of Section 1275(a)(4), Tax Forum Paper No. 464 (Dec. 1990) (unpublished) (copy on file with the Texas Law Review); New York State Bar Ass'n Tax Section, supra note 5, at 79.

I suspect that a considerable amount of the impetus for this amendment came because, during 1989 and 1990, investment banking firms began actively to intermediate debt-for-debt exchanges by buying up the discount debt of an issuer in the secondary marketplace and then negotiating an exchange with the issuer. Viewed cynically, the 1990 deletion of § 1275(a)(4) can be viewed as investment banker bashing in the guise of legislative oversight of the capital markets.

[93] See Prop. Treas. Reg. §§ 1.1271–1.1275, 51 Fed. Reg. 12022–12096 (1986); I.R.C. § 1275(d) (Prentice Hall 1991).

[94] See Knoll, The Second Generation of Notes Indexed for Inflation, 39 EMORY L.J. 499, 503 (1990); Kwall, The Income Tax Consequences of Sales of Present Interests and Future Interests: Distinguishing Time from Space, 49 OHIO ST. L.J. 1, 31 n.172 (1988). The recent amendment of these proposed regulations through the addition of Prop. Treas. Reg. § 1.1275–4(g), 56 Fed. Reg. 8308 (1991), has done nothing but increase the controversy over the proposed regulations package. See infra note 105.

[95] Prop. Treas. Reg. §§ 1.1058–1, 1.1058–2, 48 Fed. Reg. 33912 (1983). As described by I.R.C. § 1058 (Prentice Hall 1991), "securities lending" is a temporary transfer of securities, during which the transferor is entitled to receive all payments of interest, dividends, and other distributions which the owner of the securities is entitled to receive.

[96] These questions include: (1) a metaphysical inquiry into whether there is any difference between a securities loan of a United States Treasury obligation and a "repo" (more formally, a "sale-repurchase agreement") thereof, and, if not, whether anyone should care; and (2) whether a non-United States lender of a United States equity security that receives a payment in lieu of a dividend from a United States borrower should be treated for United States withholding tax purposes as having earned United States-source dividend income. See supra note 87.

derivative market matures, stock lending activities can be expected to increase. Yet, despite the receipt of a significant number of learned proposals and comment letters from tax professionals, the administrative agencies have neither finalized nor updated the proposed regulations to reflect the experience of the last eight years.[97]

When pressed in private conversations, staffers at the various congressional taxwriting committees, the Treasury Department, and the Internal Revenue Service typically explain the glacial pace of legislative and regulatory responses to financial innovation as the result of a lack of adequate information about the capital markets, or a shortage of resources, or (in the case of the most cynical) the belief that the absence of regulation has a greater *in terrorem* effect than do clear guidelines.[98] To an outsider, however, these explanations readily distill into the observation that, as an institutional matter, tax policy makers have chosen not to invest very much energy in developing rules to ensure that after-tax results of financial innovations are consistent with their pretax economics.[99]

---

[97] It is my vivid recollection that the draftsman of the proposed § 1058 regulations later was pulled off the project to turn to the more pressing problems of drafting regulations implementing I.R.C. § 278 (repealed in 1986), dealing with the amortization of certain citrus and almond grove expenditures. These regulations were in turn promulgated in proposed form in 1983, three years before § 278 was repealed, and were never finalized. Prop. Treas. Reg. § 1.278–2, 48 Fed. Reg. 51936 (1983).

To mention but a few additional examples: in 1980, eleven years after enactment of I.R.C. § 385 (Prentice Hall 1991) (authorizing the Treasury to distinguish between debt and equity by regulation), regulations under § 385 were first promulgated, *see* Prop. Treas. Reg. §§ 1.385–1 to 1.385–12, 45 Fed. Reg. 18957 (1980), then finalized, *see* Treas. Reg. §§ 1.385–1 5o 1.385–10 (1980), then reissued in proposed form, *see* Prop. Treas. Reg. §§ 1.385–0 to 1.385–10, 47 Fed. Reg. 164 (1982), only to be withdrawn in 1983, *see* T.D. 7920, 1983–2 C.B. 69, and no regulations have been issued pursuant to the authorization contained in I.R.C. § 246(c) (1988), enacted in 1984.

[98] It is a corollary of this last, cynical, rationale that clear guidelines can always be "gamed" by taxpayers to produce results not anticipated by the drafters of these guidelines. *See infra* note 100 and accompanying text.

[99] Obviously, one must distinguish between *institutional* and *individual* commitments to advancing tax policy in this area. It is my assertion that the institutional commitment has not been sufficient to the task; conversely, every tax practitioner in the field would agree that there are many tax policy professionals in the government who have brought tremendous energy and initiative to the (frequently overwhelming) tasks assigned them.

For those regulators whose feelings nonetheless may be hurt by my assertion, I would suggest comparing the state of the rules for the taxation of international securities loans, on the one hand, with the rules under I.R.C. §§ 6038A, 6038C (Prentice Hall 1991), governing information reporting for transactions between foreign-owned United States companies and their affiliates, on the other. The first set of rules, as noted earlier, consists of eight-year-old proposed regulations of limited sophistication, *see supra* note 97; the latter rules have been addressed twice by Congress in the last two years in the Revenue Reconciliation Act of 1989, Pub. L. No. 101–239, § 7403(a)-(d), 103 Stat. 2106, 2358–61, and the Revenue Reconciliation Act of 1990, Pub. L. No. 101–508, § 11315(a), (b), 104 Stat. 1388, 1388–456 to 457, and have been the source of two complete sets of proposed regulations, Prop. Treas. Reg. § 1.603A, 55 Fed. Reg. 50706 (1990), Prop. Treas. Reg. §§ 1.6038–2, 1.6038A–1, 48 Fed. Reg. 56076 (1983), and one complete set of final regulations since the end of 1983, Treas. Reg. §§ 1.6038–2, 1.6038A–1 (1985).

C. The Limitations of Tax Reasoning

1. The Need for a Contextual Analysis. No single convincing theory exists to explain why tax policy makers assign such a modest priority to responding to financial innovations. In my own experience, however, three principal factors appear to be at work. First, many tax policy makers appear to suffer from the impression that the taxation of the financial strategies and products that emerge from the process of financial innovation is a matter of interest only to a highly specialized (and geographically concentrated) industry—the banks, securities firms, and other financial intermediaries that are actively involved in developing financial innovations. From this perspective, investing precious tax policy resources in the financial innovation area appears to be only marginally more important to the national interest than, for example, taking up whatever tax accounting issues confront the legalized gaming industry.

While it may be true that the financial services industry confronts tax issues unique to it, it is also true, for example, that many of the counterparties to the $2.5 trillion in outstanding notional principal contracts are nonindustry participants. Indeed, the view that the taxation of innovative financial strategies is a matter of concern only to the financial services industry phrases the issue precisely backwards. Many financial innovations are developed to meet the financial objectives of nonindustry participants (e.g., corporate issuers of debt or investors with special goals or restrictions); the financial services industry earns fees from selling such strategies, and exports the tax uncertainties to the capital markets generally.

Second, a significant number of tax policy makers in fact believe that all clear tax guidelines in general, and tax rules governing financial products in particular, are easily "gamed"—that is, used by taxpayers in contexts not anticipated by policy makers to produce results of which they would not approve.[100] I have always thought this argument suffers from a number of defects. In the first place, it assumes away the duty of tax policy in this area of the law, which is to ensure that the capital markets are as efficient after-tax as they are pretax. Moreover, the fear of "gaming" appears to value more heavily the negative impact on the tax system of the relatively few taxpayers who may stray away from an intended result than it does the positive impact of herding the majority of taxpayers into the corral of conformity with fair tax rules. Finally, the argument reflects a bewildering admission of impotence to revise rules to respond to unanticipated issues, despite the traditional self-compulsion of the financial and

---

[100] For instance, Internal Revenue Service Commissioner Fred Goldberg recently remarked: "I am absolutely convinced . . . that the way to deal with the gaming-the-system problem is not more rules. It is clear that the more rules we write, the more we're going to get gamed." *IRS: Rules Projects. Consolidation of Organizational Changes Top Agenda,* Daily Tax Rep. (BNA) No. 10 (Jan. 15, 1991).

legal community to tout publicly the exploitation of each newly discovered loophole in the Internal Revenue Code.

Third, and finally, there is a belief that the tax system will sort itself out. Through an incremental accretion of rulings and case law, the system, it is thought, will slowly but inexorably reduce each new financial innovation to a recognizable variant (or combination of variants) on one or more familiar tax cubbyhole themes. I would respond that this philosophy fails to address the ever-accelerating pace of financial innovation and its overall benefits to the United States economy.[101] Both the fisc and the taxpayers end up poorer if the utility of every financial innovation is clouded by tax uncertainties for an extended period of time.

More important, this philosophy misses two fundamental points about financial innovation. First, financial innovation can lead to entirely new categories of financial products that do not fit neatly into traditional tax cubbyholes. Thus, interest rate swaps, which were the paradigmatic financial innovation of the 1980s, have at various times and for various applications been analyzed for tax purposes as futures contracts, bonds, and dancing lesson contracts[102]—all of which acknowledges that no one analogy is particularly persuasive in all contexts. The incremental process of rulings and litigation is ill-equipped to develop a comprehensive set of tax rules governing this novel type of instrument.

The more fundamental problem in relying on an incremental approach to the taxation of financial innovation is that, at its core, this approach rests on a premise that is simply untrue in the contemporary capital markets: that financial products, once correctly placed in a given tax cubbyhole, fill the same financial role for all taxpayers in all circum-

---

[101] Professor Henry Hu convincingly makes this point. *See* Hu, *supra* note 1, at 335–39, 392–412. The volume of mortgage-backed securities issued each year has grown from a trickle in the early 1980s to approximately $136 billion in 1990. *Kidder Rises to Top of MBS Market*, MORTGAGE-BACKED SECURITIES LETTER, Jan. 7, 1991, at 1. *See generally* Shenker & Colletta, *Asset Securitization: Evolution, Current Issues, and New Frontiers*, 69 TEXAS L. REV. 1369, 1383–88 (1991). Securitization of residential mortgages is widely believed to have reduced significantly the cost of such mortgages to the homeowner.

[102] *See*, e.g., New York State Bar Ass'n Tax Section, *supra* note 68, at 14–20 (analogizing interest rate swaps analogized to futures contracts); I.R.S. Notice 89–21, 1989–1 C.B. 651 (rejecting the analogy of lump sum notional principal contracts to the dancing lesson contracts in Schlude v. Commissioner, 372 U.S. 128 (1963)); Cantrell, Hanna & Kurtz, *Notice 89–21 Crashes the Interest Rate Swap Party*, 45 TAX NOTES 337, 338–40 (1989) (arguing that prepaid interest rate swaps should be analyzed as loans rather than sales of future income); *id.* at 340–42 (stating that if such swaps are not analyzed as loans, subject to the potential application of I.R.C. § 446(b) (1988), *Schlude* should apply to permit acceleration of income by the recipient of the lump sum prepayment, and distinguishing Artnell Co. v. Commissioner, 400 F.2d 981 (7th Cir. 1968) (holding that a lump sum prepayment need not be accelerated if the extent and the time of future performances are certain, and related items are accounted for with clarity) and Boise Cascade v. United States, 530 F.2d 1367 (Ct. Cl. 1976) (holding that recognition of income from prepaid payments can be deferred in accordance with generally accepted accounting principles)).

stances. For example, institutional investors frequently purchase a portfolio of stocks whose performance tracks that of the Standard & Poor's 500 Index, because those investors in fact wish to invest in the index. Yet that same portfolio investment, when combined with a "short" futures position in the Standard & Poor's 500 Index, becomes what the financial industry terms a "conversion"—a synthetic money market instrument whose economic return is governed by short-term interest rates rather than equity prices.[103] Similarly, a taxpayer looking to borrow short-term funds can enter into a "reverse conversion," under which the taxpayer borrows a basket of stocks that closely tracks an index, sells those stocks short, and enters into an actual or synthetic futures contract to purchase the index at a future date.

As these simple examples demonstrate, the economic consequences of a financial product—and therefore any rational tax analysis of that product—depends entirely on context. Sometimes an equity index futures contract is a speculative investment, and sometimes it is a component of a fixed-rate, short-term borrowing. The available analytical tools simply cannot cope with the need for context-specific analysis.

2. The Pitfalls of Reasoning by Analogy. One of the favorite pastimes of tax professionals and policy makers is reasoning by analogy, in which new financial products or transactions are compared to simpler and better understood financial arrangements. Thus, for 600 years the common law has recognized that what purports to be a lease of real property sometimes in fact is a mortgage. When applied in the tax context, at least one court— fortunately overturned—has directed taxpayers to resolve this conundrum of lease or loan by an adult version of the children's game of pickup sticks, in which analogies are drawn between the transaction in question and more paradigmatic loan and lease arrangements. Each correspondence that can be identified is awarded a stick, and whichever cate-

---

[103] A taxpayer can establish a "short" futures position—that is, an obligation to sell the Standard & Poor's 500 Index—by entering into a futures contract on the Standard & Poor's 500 Index on the Chicago Mercantile Exchange. Alternatively, that taxpayer could establish a synthetic futures position by writing a call option on the Index and buying a put option on the Index with the same strike prices. If, at maturity of the option contracts, the Index's price is above the strike price, the put option will expire worthless, but the taxpayer will be obligated to satisfy the call option it concurrently wrote; conversely, if the Index's price is lower than the strike price, the counterparty to the taxpayer's call option will not exercise the call, but the taxpayer will profit by exercising its put. In either case, then, the taxpayer will sell the Index for an amount equal to the strike price, just as if the taxpayer had sold a futures contract. Moreover, under the doctrine of "put-call parity," the strike price at which the taxpayer's premium to purchase the put option offsets its income from writing the call option (so that the taxpayer has no out-of-pocket expense for the put-call pair) should be the same as the price for an at-the-money futures contract. *See* C. JOHNSON, AN INTRODUCTION TO OPTIONS 10–11 (1987) (published by Salomon Brothers Bond Portfolio Analysis Group, copy on file with the *Texas Law Review*).

gory has the larger bundle of sticks at the conclusion of the analysis is declared the cubbyhole into which the transaction is placed.[104]

Reasoning by analogy is a potent tool when applied to incremental variations on a familiar theme, but it fails miserably when applied to genuine innovations. First, as noted above with respect to the example of interest rate swaps, reasoning by analogy simply cannot expand the number of tax cubbyholes to deal with a genuine innovation. Instead, reasoning by analogy works best to make binary categorization decisions between two well-known and preexisting cubbyholes (e.g., Is this instrument debt or equity? Loan or lease?).

Second, as the discussion in Part II with respect to equity index swaps suggests, it proves too much to claim that reasoning by analogy means that bundles of transactions that are different in fact but that yield economically similar results should be taxed identically. This argument leads imperceptibly into an argument for a tax common law of economic integration, a theme that is taken up below.

3. Deconstruction. If reasoning by analogy cannot cope with genuine financial innovation, what analytical tools are left? Perhaps the most popular is "bifurcation"—or, more generally, "deconstruction,"—in which one complex financial instrument is split into many simpler and better understood instruments. Under a deconstructionist approach, by way of example, a convertible bond should be analyzed for tax purposes as a combination of the simpler building blocks of a bond and a separate warrant.[105]

---

[104] *See* Frank Lyon Co. v. United States, 536 F.2d 746, 751 (8th Cir. 1976), *rev'd,* 435 U.S. 561 (1978).

[105] The proponents of deconstructionism have scored a very recent triumph of ideology with the release of Prop. Treas. Reg. § 1.1275–4(g), 56 Fed. Reg. 8308 (1991). Very briefly, that proposed regulation would take a debt instrument with contingent payments and bifurcate the instrument into its constituent parts. Those constituent parts then would be taxed "in accordance with their economic substance" as if they were separately issued instruments.

More specifically, Prop. Treas. Reg. § 1.1275–4(g) generally would apply to any debt instrument that (1) is issued for cash or publicly traded property, (2) provides for noncontingent payments at least equal to the instrument's issue price, and (3) provides for one or more contingent payments determined, in whole or in part, by reference to the value of publicly traded stock, securities, commodities, or other publicly traded property. Under an important exception, the proposed regulations would not apply to a debt instrument "merely because" the instrument may be converted into stock or another debt instrument of the issuer. (The preamble to the proposed regulations warns, however, that this exception for "plain vanilla" convertibles may be revisited.)

Debt instruments within the scope of the proposed regulations would be bifurcated into noncontingent and contingent components. The noncontingent payments would be taxed as a separate hypothetical debt obligation, which generally would be treated as having been issued with significant original issue discount. As noted above, the contingent components would be taxed according to their economic substance. For example, the contingent components could be taxed as options or swaps, among other possibilities.

The early reviews of the proposed regulations have been mixed. *See,* e.g., Hariton,

A description of the many problems caused by an over-reliance on deconstruction theory is beyond the scope of this Article.[106] It is worthwhile noting, however, that deconstructionism suffers one fundamental flaw, in that it is totally insensitive to context. Thus, to return to the earlier example of a "conversion"—a simple combination of the ownership of stocks and a forward contract to produce a synthetic money market instrument—no amount of deconstruction will produce a tax analysis consistent with the transaction's economics. What is wanted in this case is tax fusion, not fission.

4. The Missing Doctrine of Tax Integration. The above discussion has sought to suggest that both reasoning by analogy and deconstructionism ultimately fail as analytical tools for financial innovation, because they do not treat a bundle of transactions as a synthetic whole. The importance of contextual analysis obviously suggests the need for a doctrine of integration, in which courts and the Internal Revenue Service analyze the federal income tax consequences of financial strategies by considering the overall economic result achieved, rather than by engaging in an instrument-by-instrument analysis. Yet a doctrine of financial product integration certainly does not exist in current tax law, at least not by that name.[107] Phrased generally, I am not aware of any case or ruling in which a court or the

---

New Rules Bifurcating Contingent Debt—A Mistake? 51 TAX NOTES 235 (1991); Lawrence, *New Rules Bifurcating Contingent Debt—A Good Start,* 51 TAX NOTES 495 (1991). Some of the objections are technical; others can be said to go to the heart of whether bifurcation is feasible or desirable.

　　Prop. Treas. Reg. § 1.1275–4(g) is the first attempt to apply a deconstructionist approach to a wide range of financial instruments, and many observers believe that the proposed regulation is at least as much a trial balloon for the whole proposition of deconstructionism as it is an attempt to resolve the five-year-old impasse of the former proposed regulations' unsatisfactory treatment of contingent payment obligations. *See,* e.g., Lawrence, *supra.* As a result, practitioners and academics alike can be expected to follow closely the evolving debate as to the success or failure of Prop. Treas. Reg. § 1.1275–4(g) to produce feasible and appropriate results. If the proposed regulations are judged workable (or fixable), subsequent regulations (and legislation) can be expected to expand the scope of deconstructionist analysis. If, conversely, the proposed regulations are judged too broken to fix (or are judged fixable only by adopting so many simplifying assumptions that the original purpose is lost), then the current ideological triumph of deconstructionist thinking will fade into a historical curiosity.

[106] See Kau, *Carving Up Assets and Liabilities—Integration or Bifurcation of Financial Products,* 68 TAXES 1003 (1990), and Kleinbard, *Beyond Good and Evil Debt (and Debt Hedges): A Cost of Capital Allowance System,* 67 TAXES 943, 947–52 (1989), for discussions of some of the principal shortcomings of aggressive reliance on deconstructionism as a means of coping with financial innovation.

[107] This assertion presents the classic problem of trying to prove the negative. *Cf.* Kau, *supra* note 106, at 1007–09; McCawley, *Tax Aspects of Interest and Currency Exchange Rate Hedging Transactions,* 31 TAX MGMT. MEMORANDUM 119, 128 (1990) (describing the problem of tax integration and concluding that "[t]he validity of these arguments has been recognized to a limited extent by the IRS where it has been specifically authorized by Congress to provide rules implementing them").

Internal Revenue Service has determined the federal income tax analysis of several real transactions entered into by one taxpayer with *different* counterparties by considering the synthetic result achieved by that taxpayer.[108] This point is made forcefully in a recent article by Randall Kau, where he sets out twelve alternative ways of replicating the cash flows of an investment in a United States dollar fixed-rate debt instrument, none of which is uniformly treated as an investment in synthetic fixed-rate debt for tax purposes.[109]

One simple example of this premise is the established tax treatment of a "short against the box" transaction. If a taxpayer holds appreciated securities and wishes to defer recognition of gain on the disposition of those securities, the taxpayer can enter into a short sale of identical securities. The taxpayer thereby has sold its securities in an economic sense, by locking in the current value and insulating itself from future price fluctuations. The taxpayer nonetheless will recognize gain for tax purposes only when the taxpayer closes out its short position, because tax law requires a separate analysis of the taxpayer's offsetting long and short positions.[110]

Similarly, sophisticated corporate issuers routinely issue complex debt instruments which they then hedge (through swaps, options, and other instruments) into "plain vanilla" debt obligations. Yet, outside the narrow scope of certain recent regulations concerning specified foreign currency hedges, the issuer's tax results are determined without regard to the issuer's synthetic objectives.[111] "Conversions" and "reverse conversions" are another straightforward example; while taxpayers have argued that the economic similarity of these instruments to short-term loans and borrowings should determine the *character* of any gain or loss recognized by the taxpayer, no one has suggested that such strategies constitute loans and

---

[108] One arguable exception to this assertion is Monfort of Colorado, Inc. v. United States, 406 F. Supp. 701 (D. Colo. 1976), *aff'd*, 561 F.2d 190 (10th Cir. 1977), in which gains and losses from futures contracts used to hedge inventory prices were integrated into the cost of that inventory. *Monfort* is contrary to a long line of other authority, which treats hedges as separate from the property being hedged. *See, e.g.*, Edward R. Bacon Grain Co. v. Reinecke, 26 F.2d 705 (N.D. Ill. 1928) (holding that sales of futures and the hedging contracts for such sales should be treated separately for tax purposes if they are closed out in separate years), *aff'd mem.*, 54 F.2d 1078 (7th Cir. 1929); Rev. Rul. 74–227, 1974–1 C.B. 120, 121 (stating that potential losses or gains from futures contracts have no effect on the cost of the physical inventory created when the commodity which is the subject of the futures contracts is on hand at the end of the year); Rev. Rul. 74–223, 1974–1 C.B. 23, 24 (stating that "speculative" futures transactions not offset by actual spot or cash transactions may not be included or taken into income in any manner until such futures transactions are actually closed).

[109] Kau, *supra* note 106, at 1004–05.

[110] *See* Treas. Reg. § 1.1233–1(a)(1) (as amended in 1980).

[111] *See* Kleinbard, *supra* note 106, at 952–54; Kleinbard & Greenberg, *supra* note 7, at 432–36.

borrowings for all tax purposes.[112] Indeed, to the extent that the Supreme Court's decision in *Arkansas Best Corp. v. Commissioner*[113] can be said to divorce the determination of the character of gain or loss recognized in respect of a financial instrument from the use to which that instrument is put, the cause of a doctrine of integration of financial instruments has suffered a considerable setback.[114]

A general doctrine of the tax integration of financial products also cannot be read into current law by recourse to either "substance-over-form" or "step-transaction" learning. As the term "substance-over-form" is generally used, it is a shorthand for the issue of whether a transaction is real or fictitious, and whether it has pretax economic consequences.[115] The substance-over-form doctrine can be applied to financial innovation to determine whether each component of a complex financial strategy is real, but once the reality of those components has been confirmed, the substance-over-form doctrine has not been invoked to merge these separate and real components into a different synthetic financial instrument.[116]

Similarly, the step-transaction doctrine cannot be used to supply the missing doctrine of tax integration. The step-transaction doctrine typically is invoked when a taxpayer, dealing in effect with himself (or one other party), engages in a circuitous series of transactions in the hopes of accomplishing a tax objective that would not have been available had the taxpayer structured his affairs more straightforwardly. Two common versions of the step-transaction test have been formulated: whether the steps taken were "interdependent" steps towards an agreed-upon conclusion, and whether the "end result" was preplanned.[117] The effect of the doc-

---

[112] Taxpayers that enter into a "reverse conversion," for example, are at risk that the locked-in loss on their "long" stock futures position (which is economically analogous to interest) will be characterized as capital loss under the principles of Arkansas Best Corp. v. Commissioner, 485 U.S. 212 (1988). Indeed, an individual Internal Revenue agent's memorandum reaching just that conclusion has been widely circulated among Wall Street tax professionals.

[113] 485 U.S. 212 (1988).

[114] *See* Kleinbard & Greenberg, *supra* note 7, at 432–40 (discussing the different tax treatment of liability hedges before and after *Arkansas Best*).

[115] For example, in applying the doctrine of substance-over-form in *Frank Lyon Co. v. United States*, the Supreme Court rejected the claim of the Internal Revenue Service that a sale/leaseback was a sham disguising a loan and mortgage agreement, because the parties' risk, rights, and obligations were different from those of a loan and mortgage, and the transaction therefore had economic substance. 435 U.S. 561, 581–84 (1978).

[116] It is precisely the absence of this result that has bedeviled corporate issuers engaged in liability hedging strategies.

[117] *See generally* Chirelstein & Lopata, *Recent Developments in the Step-Transaction Doctrine*, 60 TAXES 970, 970 (1982) ("The step-transaction doctrine is a judicially developed concept which . . . permits a series of separate steps to be recharacterized and treated as a single integrated transaction if the steps are closely related and focused toward a particular end result."); Mintz & Plumb, *Step Transactions in Corporate Reorganizations*, 12 N.Y.U. ANN. INST. ON FED. TAX'N 247, 250 (1954) ("Under [the 'end result'] test, a given intended re-

trine is that where the intended and actual result of a sequence of steps is clear, the courts view the transaction as a whole for tax purposes, rather than fragmenting the sequence into its individual steps and applying the tax laws to each step individually.[118]

The step-transaction doctrine is not, however, applied to collapse the tax consequences of what in fact are separate transactions into a single, integrated transaction. In the leading tax straddle case of *Smith v. Commissioner*,[119] for example, the Tax Court found that a taxpayer that entered into a typical commercial straddle on a bona fide exchange created legally binding rights and obligations that would have ripened into the obligation to make and take delivery of the underlying commodity in different months had the taxpayer not independently later entered into offsetting trades.[120] The government argued for disallowing the loss recognized by the taxpayer in closing out one leg of its straddle and replacing it with a new leg obligating (presumably) a different ultimate counterparty.[121] The government's argument relied in part on a step-transaction argument.

The Tax Court summarized the step-transaction doctrine as follows:

> The step transaction doctrine generally applies in cases where a taxpayer seeks to get from point A to point D and does so stopping in between at points B and C. The whole purpose of the unnecessary stops is to achieve tax consequences differing from those which a direct path from A to D would have produced. In such a situation, courts are not bound by the twisted path taken by the taxpayer, and the intervening stops may be disregarded or rearranged.[122]

---

sult would have the same tax effect whether achieved directly or by circuitous steps."). A third test, the "binding commitment" test used in *Commissioner v. Gordon*, requires the transaction to be characterized as a single integrated whole if the organization makes a binding contractual promise, at the time the initial step in the transaction is taken, to complete the remaining steps to accomplish the end goal of the transaction. 391 U.S. 83, 96 (1968). The same analysis would apply for this test as for those discussed above.

[118] *See*, e.g., Kuper v. Commissioner, 533 F.2d 152 (5th Cir. 1976) (holding that a transaction in which a corporation became a wholly owned subsidiary for one day, followed by exchange of its shares for shares in the parent, was in substance an exchange by the shareholders of shares in both corporations); Commissioner v. Transport Trading & Terminal Corp., 176 F.2d 570 (2d Cir. 1949) (finding that the distribution of stock by a corporate taxpayer to the parent company, and subsequent sale of that stock by the parent company, was in substance a sale of the stock by the corporate taxpayer, rather than a dividend to, and a sale by, the parent company).

[119] 78 T.C. 350 (1982).

[120] *Id.* at 385. The economic theories and tax objectives of straddle transactions are summarized in the case; those tax objectives, in turn, have been substantially eliminated by the introduction of I.R.C. § 1092 (1988). *See supra* notes 75–81 and accompanying text.

[121] *Smith*, 78 T.C. at 370.

[122] *Id.* at 389 (citing Gregory v. Helvering, 293 U.S. 465 (1935)).

The Tax Court held, however, that the doctrine does not apply to a tax straddle that produces losses in one year and a corresponding amount of income in a subsequent year, noting that the doctrine had never been applied to tax shelters simply because they were tax shelters and that "such an argument would go far toward undermining the very system of annual tax accounting."[123]

A very recent tax straddle case also helps to make this point. In *Stoller v. Commissioner*,[124] the Tax Court considered a complex series of tax straddles involving long and short forward and futures positions in United States Treasury bonds and GNMA certificates. Although the case is interesting for a number of reasons,[125] what is particularly relevant in this context is that the Tax Court correctly concluded that the economic substance of the taxpayer's trading strategy in forward contracts was to create the economic equivalent of short-term loans and borrowings:

> For example, by entering into a contract to purchase 15-year T-Bonds for delivery on a specified date and simultaneously entering into a contract to sell 15-year T-Bonds for delivery six months later, Holly created the economic equivalent of a contract to purchase a six-month T-Bond. Holly then arbitraged that [effectively, locked in the financing to carry that synthetic six-month "T-Bond"] against simultaneous contracts to sell GNMAs on that specified date and purchase them six months later.[126]

Although the Tax Court found the "integrated" economic substance of the taxpayer's trades highly relevant in determining whether the taxpayer had the requisite pretax profit motive (so that its losses would be recognized as bona fide for tax purposes), it never occurred to the Tax Court to treat these transactions in forward contracts as *actual* short-term loans and borrowings for purposes of determining the character of payments made to terminate those contracts.

---

[123] *Id.*

[124] 60 T.C.M. (CCH) 1554 (1990).

[125] The case is relevant, for example, to the continuing scope of the extinguishment doctrine, discussed *supra* at text accompanying note 64. The case clearly holds that one $10,000 payment made by the taxpayer to cancel four related long and short forward contracts gave rise to ordinary loss, by virtue of the extinguishment doctrine, but then concludes that the other terminations by the taxpayer gave rise to capital loss, apparently because those positions, once terminated, were replaced with new positions (called "switch transactions" by the court). *See id.* at 1566–67. The Tax Court concluded that these contracts were not "closed by cancellation," but rather were "closed by offset." *Id.* at 1566. A more straightforward way of expressing this conclusion would be to state that where, as here, the taxpayer purported to cancel existing contracts for a fee and then immediately replaced those contracts with the same counterparty, and where the contracts were not separately valued, but rather were priced to preserve the preexisting spread between the two legs of the straddle, the substance-over-form doctrine requires the conclusion that the taxpayer exchanged a new contract (and cash) for the old contract.

[126] *Id.* at 1558.

Even if a generalized doctrine of the tax integration of financial instruments did exist, it is by no means clear that the doctrine could be sufficiently responsive to the pace of financial innovation. The dynamism of contemporary financial strategies means that a financial position might appropriately be viewed as part of a larger synthetic unity today, and a stand-alone position tomorrow. Similarly, contemporary "dynamic hedge" technologies deliberately seek enhanced profitability through imperfect syntheses; a securities firm intentionally might create, for example, an agglomeration of positions that performs roughly like an investment in an equity index, but outperforms or underperforms that index, depending on Treasury interest rates. A sophisticated tax analysis, then, should address in a dynamic fashion the context in which a financial instrument is employed, to respond to rapid changes in context and to synthetic results that are similar, but not identical, to more straightforward instruments.

IV. Moving Forward

The tax system to date has been slow to respond to financial innovation. A simple acceleration of existing extra-statutory methodologies will not resolve the problem, because those methodologies do not offer a basis for dynamic and contextual analysis.[127] The result is economic inefficiency. In many cases, economically rational transactions are not entered into for fear of tax costs disproportionate to economic returns.[128] In other cases—in my own experience much less common than tax policy makers typically believe—taxpayers can use the current approach to the tax analysis of complex financial instruments to produce, through synthetic arrangements, after-tax results superior to more straightforward transactions. In either case, the current tax system distorts the capital markets.

These issues raise a frightening and depressing prospect for the future: the specter of a wave of sophisticated new equity derivative products further blurring the already frayed distinction between debt and equity, and underscoring the impotence of current analytical tools to handle that onslaught. Fear and depression among tax policymakers, however, appear to be the prerequisites to the radical revisions required to make the tax system responsible to financial innovation.

The first step toward revising the tax system to address the looming problems of financial innovation is to recognize that symmetry of tax re-

---

[127] I include as a "statutory" approach the promulgation of "legislative" regulations, such as Temp. Treas. Reg. § 1.988–5T (1989), dealing with the integration of nonfunctional currency debt instruments and hedging transactions. See supra note 46 and accompanying text.

[128] Many well-advised taxpayers, for example, no longer enter into "reverse conversions" for fear that the transaction will generate capital, rather than ordinary, loss. See supra note 112.

sult between issuers and investors is a false goal. The capital markets in general increasingly are dominated by tax-exempt or tax-insensitive institutions, and the markets have proved themselves extremely efficient at matching up the tax profiles of issuers and investors to reduce the overall tax burden imposed on investment capital.[129] These problems are compounded, of course, by some of the strategies described earlier, in which a series of separate transactions are combined to achieve a completely different synthetic economic result; in such cases, there is no relationship between the overall results achieved by the taxpayer and the economic position of its various counterparties.[130]

In light of market realities, then, symmetry of tax result imposes little meaningful tax discipline. Conversely, by abandoning the false comfort of symmetry of result between issuers and investors, it is possible to develop more useful tax policy strategies to deal with the problems unique to each.

A. The Taxation of Corporate Issuers

Corporate issuers have been substantial users of derivative interest rate financial products (such as interest rate swaps), primarily as devices to hedge or otherwise manage their liabilities.[131] Issuers increasingly find, however, that many sophisticated liability strategies currently being developed, while appearing very elegant on a pretax basis, simply cannot be implemented once tax costs are taken into account, because the instrument-by-instrument approach required by current law leads to a wide variety of anomalous (and expensive) results. As applied to corporate issuers, current tax law also places enormous stress on whether a particular capital market instrument is deductible debt or nondeductible equity, again without regard to the overall economic result achieved by that instrument in the context of the issuer's other positions. As the equity derivative product marketplace matures, corporate issuers can be expected to use those products more frequently, not only to manage their cost of equity

---

[129] The most common cases are straightforward corporate bonds issued by taxpaying corporations and held largely by tax-exempt investors. More elegant examples were the "subsidiary preferred" offerings of the 1980s. Subsidiary preferred stock transactions took advantage of the dividends-received deduction under I.R.C. § 243 (Prentice Hall 1991) to maximize tax efficiency where the investor was a tax-paying corporation and the issuer did not currently pay tax, typically because of net operating loss carryforwards. *See generally* Warren, *Recent Corporate Restructuring and the Corporate Tax System,* 42 TAX NOTES 715, 715–17 (1989); Jassy, *Issuances of Floating Rate Preferred Stock by Special Purpose Subsidiaries of Loss Corporations,* 39 TAX LAW. 519 (1986). The subsidiary preferred structure effectively was eliminated by I.R.C. § 1503(f) (Prentice Hall 1991), enacted in 1989.

[130] For a long-winded example of a complex series of transactions through which a corporate issuer might achieve low-cost funds and investors an equity-based return, see Kleinbard, *supra* note 106, at 954–55.

[131] *See generally id.* at 952–55.

capital but also to seek to convert nondeductible equity expenses into deductible derivative payments.

These anomalies and tensions could be resolved, and a source of substantial inefficiency in the capital markets eliminated, if the current tax system for corporate issuers were entirely scrapped, and replaced by a statutory Cost of Capital Allowance (COCA) system.[132] Under the COCA system, a corporation would be allowed to deduct each year an amount equal to the product of (1) its "Invested Capital," and (2) a statutory COCA. A corporate issuer would not recognize deductions, loss, income, or gain in respect of its actual interest expense *or* in respect of cash flows payable or receivable on any liability management tool. Thus, for example, gain or loss recognized by an issuer on an interest rate swap that related to the issuer's outstanding liabilities, or gain or loss on an equity index swap used as a cost of equity management tool, would be excluded from net income. The COCA system thus would provide a corporate taxpayer with a uniform annual deduction for all the capital employed by that corporation in its income-producing activities, regardless of whether that capital is denominated debt or equity.

"Invested capital" in effect would include an issuer's outstanding equity as well as debt. Since balance sheets, by definition, balance, a corporation's outstanding capital (i.e., the right side of its balance sheet) must equal its assets (i.e., the left side). Accordingly, under the COCA system, a corporation's invested capital in each year would equal the aggregate adjusted tax bases of all its assets.[133]

The COCA would be an annual percentage determined pursuant to a statutory formula based on that year's current Treasury obligation yields.[134] An issuer's annual deduction in respect of its cost of capital would equal its Invested Capital multiplied by this cost of capital allowance. The deduction, like interest, would fully offset ordinary income, and would be subject to the current rules that allocate interest for foreign tax credit purposes.

The statutory formula would remain constant from year to year, but a corporation's annual cost of capital allowance would fluctuate with changes in prevailing Treasury interest rates and changes in the corpora-

---

[132] I first made this proposal in an earlier article. *See id.* My summary here is a condensation of the arguments presented therein.

[133] See *id.* at 958 for a discussion of some ancillary issues relating to the definition of Invested Capital, such as the application of the rule to affiliated groups.

[134] For example, the formula could be a specified weighted average of each year's average short-term, medium-term, and long-term federal rates, multiplied by a specified percentage (presumably less than 100 percent). The federal rate is a monthly computation of the average yields on selected short-, medium-, and long-term Treasury securities. *See* I.R.C. § 1274(d) (Prentice Hall 1991); Prop. Treas. Reg. § 1.1274–6, 51 Fed. Reg. 12077 (1986). The purpose of multiplying the Treasury rate by a factor of less than 100% would be to ensure revenue neutrality at the time the COCA system is introduced.

tion's investment in assets. Because United States corporations generally borrow at a spread over Treasury rates for comparable maturities, the annual cost of capital allowance would generally move in tandem with changes in a taxpayer's actual borrowing costs (or the implicit interest costs of its actual equity capital).

No separate or additional deduction would be allowed for a taxpayer that incurred actual interest or equity expense in excess of the cost of capital allowance. Similarly, a taxpayer whose actual cost of capital was lower than the statutory allowance nonetheless would be entitled to its full annual COCA deduction.

Since the whole purpose of the COCA system would be to substitute an arbitrary annual deduction for all the various components of a corporate taxpayer's actual annual cost of capital, under the COCA system corporations would not recognize gain or loss on any liability management transaction, just as corporations currently recognize no gain or loss on trading in their own stock. Similarly, gain or loss attributable to any designated liability management tool employed by a corporate issuer to manage capital costs (e.g., an equity swap, or an interest rate swap, cap, or forward contract), once identified as part of a taxpayer's cost of capital "account," would simply generate tax-free cash flows.

It is interesting to note that the COCA system produces results that are more consistent with various corporate integration goals than are achieved under the current tax system.[135] Specifically, the COCA system tends to assure that at least some tax burden is shouldered by corporate debt (by functioning like a partial interest expense disallowance system), and that at least some relief from double taxation is afforded corporate equity (through the cost of capital allowance on equity). At the same time, because the COCA system by itself would change very little in the current taxation of investors, the COCA system should prove to be more politically feasible than would a more explicit integration agenda. Moreover, regardless of one's feelings about corporate integration, the COCA system resolves the absence of substantive tax rules and the lack of

---

[135] "Corporate integration" refers, of course, to proposals that have as their goal the elimination (or reduction) of the double tax burden that the current "classical" system imposes on corporate profits. Corporate integration should be distinguished from the doctrine (or, more accurately, nondoctrine) of the integration of financial instruments, discussed in section III(C)(4), which addresses the issue of the combination of different financial instruments to produce a synthetic unity.

For an extensive and thoughtful review of the competing arguments for various forms of corporate integration, see Rudnick, *Who Should Pay the Corporate Tax in a Flat Tax World?*, 39 CASE W. RES. L. REV. 965 (1989). That article neatly summarizes the financial theory underpinning the COCA system, *id.* at 1037–38, and points out the similarities between that proposal and the work of other authors, *id.* at 1243 n.995. Professor Rudnick ultimatley concludes that corporate issuers should be permitted a deduction for the "interest component of the return to equity capital"—a result that moves in the same direction as the COCA system proposal. *Id.* at 1268.

contextual analysis for new financial products—issues that traditional integration models leave untouched.

In the year since I first made this specific proposal, no objection has been raised to it that has deterred me from repeating it. Proponents of corporate integration have observed, in private conversations, that the proposal is no more than a mediocre success when measured solely against the objectives of comprehensive corporate integration schemes. In response, it can be observed that the COCA system would perform a great deal better as a corporate integration model than any such corporate integration scheme would perform as a vehicle to resolve the current tax system's inability to deal with financial innovation. Moreover, because the COCA system by itself does not require a revision of the tax rules governing investors, it has at least a glimmer of political feasibility to it—a point to which some proponents of corporate integration seem curiously insensitive.

In a recent and thoughtful article, two economists distinguish between an issuer's cost of *capital* and its cost of *funds;* under their definition, the proposal should be renamed a Cost of Funds Allowance System.[136] I am delighted to accept this emendation if doing so would advance the cause, although a more terminologically precise "COFA" system offers fewer opportunities for amusing acronyms than does the original proposal.

B. The Taxation of Investors

By definition, a COCA system does not purport to address the taxation of investors, except that it would contemplate the elimination of the intercorporate dividends-received deduction.[137] Most radical and systematic solutions on the investor side would require investors to be taxed on some imputed or theoretical return on investment—a result that I have assumed to be politically infeasible. If this assumption is correct, a different, less systematic approach is required to deal with the taxation of financial innovation at the investor level.

Most investor-level tax policy concerns can be addressed by a three-pronged strategy: (1) the amendment of the Internal Revenue Code to eliminate some existing statutory anomalies and to delegate comprehensive rule-making authority to the Treasury Department and the Internal Revenue Service, (2) the regular use by those agencies of that delegated authority, and (3) the increased reliance on taxpayer identification to resolve tax integration problems.

Some suggested amendments to the Internal Revenue Code follow

---

[136] McCauley & Zimmer, *Explaining International Differences in the Cost of Capital,* FED. RES. BANK N.Y. Q. REV., Summer 1989, at 7, 8.

[137] *See* Kleinbard, *supra* note 106, at 960.

directly from the particular problems identified in this Article: for example, Section 1234A should be amended to eliminate the extinguishment doctrine in all contexts,[138] and Section 512 should be amended to broaden the base of investment vehicles that tax-exempt institutions may hold[139]—ideally, by granting authority to the Internal Revenue Service to designate the new financial products whose economic purposes are consistent with the current exceptions to the definition of UBTI.

More generally, Congress should confront the realities of the torrid pace of financial innovation and the institutional sophistication required to address many new financial products by delegating to the Treasury Department and the Internal Revenue Service comprehensive authority to address all the relevant aspects of financial innovation—the *character* (capital or ordinary, interest or noninterest, etc.) of income or loss, the *source* (foreign or domestic) of that income or loss, and the *timing* of income or expense recognition. Congress has already delegated the authority to determine the source of financial product income or expense,[140] but in the absence of comprehensive authority to address all the tax aspects of financial products, the Treasury and the Internal Revenue Service have been slow to use this limited authority.[141]

It goes without saying that the delegation of authority will accomplish little good if that authority is not regularly and thoughtfully exercised. It is my hope, however, that if the administrative agencies were empowered with comprehensive authority, their current institutional frustration at being able to address only fragments of the questions raised by financial innovation would disappear, and the agencies would expand their institutional ability to understand and give appropriate guidance to the capital markets.

These solutions still do not deal terribly satisfactorily with the problem of contextual analysis. I would suggest that the person best equipped to supply that context is the taxpayer himself. Accordingly, the Internal Revenue Service should develop procedures (relying on the delegation of authority described above) to enable taxpayers to identify tax components of synthetic investments and to have the transaction taxed in accordance with that synthetic result. (Such a rule would not be required for synthetic *liabilities*, because corporate liabilities would be governed by the

---

[138] *See supra* text accompanying note 64; *supra* note 125.

[139] *See supra* notes 54–55 and accompanying text.

[140] *See* I.R.C. § 865(j)(2) (1988) (enabling the Secretary of the Treasury to prescribe regulations applying the rules of § 865 to income derived from trading in futures contracts, forward contracts, and other instruments).

[141] *See supra* notes 93–97 and accompanying text. It goes almost without saying that, even if the COCA proposal were dismissed, Congress nonetheless could—and should—grant broad regulatory authority along the lines suggested in the text.

COCA system.[142]) The Internal Revenue Service already has gained significant experience with just such an approach in the foreign-currency arena,[143] where the principal taxpayer comment has been a chorus of requests to expand the identification-election program still further.[144] Such an election should be available on a synthetic investment-by-investment basis, but required to be made at the outset of each such investment to preclude "gaming" opportunities.

By electing into such a system—perhaps termed an "Investment Account"—a taxpayer could be assured that its tax results would be commensurate with its pretax economic strategy. Conversely, if a taxpayer sought to avoid being taxed by reference to the synthetic instrument it had created, the Internal Revenue Service would retain the authority in the audit process to place the taxpayer's positions in an investment account—just as is true today in the foreign-currency arena.[145] In response to the objection that this would impose strains on the audit process, one can only observe that the result cannot help but be better than the current system, under which the Internal Revenue Service generally is powerless to treat most integrated series of transactions in accordance with their overall economic results, even if taxpayers gain a significant advantage by treating the different components of such strategies separately for tax purposes.

---

[142] One exception would be the debt-financed income rules of I.R.C. § 514 (Prentice Hall 1991); if, for example, a pension fund enters into a "reverse conversion," that synthetic borrowing should be subject to the special constraints of § 514.

[143] See Temp. Treas. Reg. § 1.988–5T (1989); Temp. Treas. Reg. § 1.861–9T(b)(6) (as amended in 1989).

[144] NYSBA Tax Section Reports on Foreign Currency Temporary Regulations, Highlights & Documents, May 21, 1990, at 1753.

[145] See Temp. Treas. Reg. § 1.988–5T(a)(8)(ii) (1989).

UNCERTAIN FUTURES: THE TAX
TREATMENT OF HEDGING*

**Robert J. Mackay and
Phoebe A. Mix**

19

Volatile interest rates and prices, if left unmanaged, expose even the best-run businesses to the risk of financial loss and possible bankruptcy. Take the following examples. A spike in interest rates can destroy the spread between a finance company's cost of financing and the yield earned on its assets. An oil supply shock that drives up the cost of fuel or a shift in exchange rates can quickly erode the profit margin and competitive position of an airline or a manufacturer. Businesses have dealt with these risks by hedging, that is, by structuring financial arrangements that produce gains (or losses) that offset or counterbalance, at least in part, the losses (or gains) arising from interest-rate or price volatility. Hedging protects the owners, managers, and employees of U.S. businesses—small enterprises as well as corporate giants—from price risk and the threat of financial distress or bankruptcy.

The continued viability of hedging as a means of controlling the risks of ordinary business operations has been thrown into doubt by a 1988 Supreme Court decision. In *Arkansas Best Corporation v. Commissioner of Internal Revenue,* a case having nothing to do with hedging, the Court overturned the prevailing doctrine governing the tax treatment of hedging. For reasons it has chosen not to reveal, the Treasury Department, for the past four years, has steadfastly refused to clarify the reach of *Arkansas Best,* leaving companies in the dark about the tax treatment of hedges—hardly an environment in which hedging can flourish. In this uncertain atmosphere, IRS auditors have been reviewing corporate income tax re-

* This article originally appeared in *The American Enterprise,* May/June 1992. Reprinted with permission.

turns (in some cases, back as far as the early 1980s) and disallowing deductions that were allowable for over 50 years. Notices of past-due taxes—in amounts reaching hundreds of millions of dollars for some large corporations—are arriving in corporate headquarters across the nation. The prospect of hostile audits and lawsuits is causing nightmares for corporations that use hedging strategies to protect themselves against price fluctuations.

Tax Policy Before 1988

At issue is the tax treatment of losses and gains on hedges of ordinary business expenses (not of capital assets, such as pension funds, which are treated appropriately as capital gains and losses). Until 1988, gains and losses on these hedge transactions were treated symmetrically as ordinary gains or losses. From an economic perspective, this was sound tax policy consistent with efficient business decision-making.

To see this, consider the case of a hypothetical airline, Mid-America Airline (MAA), that uses large amounts of refined jet fuel. MAA's fuel requirements subject it to substantial price risk, particularly in times of unexpected turmoil in the oil markets like the Persian Gulf War. To ensure a more stable cost of fuel, MAA can hedge its price risk by using a wide array of instruments, including forward contracts with refineries, futures or options contracts traded on an organized exchange, or customized commodity swaps or caps traded over the counter. Suppose MAA entered into a series of futures contracts to purchase for a fixed sum of money a specified amount of heating oil during each month of 1990 and 1991. (Heating oil futures are commonly used to hedge jet fuel prices since jet fuel futures are not traded and heating oil and jet fuel prices are highly correlated.) The futures contracts generated gains and losses that offset, in part, the increases and decreases in the cost of jet fuel during these years. MAA was thus protected from volatile fuel prices during the Gulf War.

In assessing its tax liability, the airline could deduct the cost of acquiring jet fuel as an ordinary and necessary business expense (as it can today), and under the tax doctrine prevailing until 1988, it could treat any gains or losses on the futures contracts as ordinary income or loss in the tax year it incurred the fuel expense. From a tax perspective, the ordinary losses (or gains) on the futures contracts offset the ordinary gains (or losses) on the jet fuel purchases. The tax code was neutral in its effect on businesses' hedging decisions. What made good economic sense on a before-tax basis made good economic sense on an after-tax basis.

This tax policy stemmed from a 1955 Supreme Court case, *Corn Products Refining Company v. Commissioner of Internal Revenue*, which was broadly interpreted to mean that property that was integrally related to the taxpayer's trade or business generated ordinary income or loss. The taxpayer, Corn Products Refining Company, lacked adequate storage space for all the corn it anticipated using, so it purchased corn futures contracts, giving it the right to receive corn in the future rather than having to build new storage facilities. The futures contracts increased in value, and the company reported the gains as capital gains. (At the time, capital gains were taxed more favorably than ordinary gains.) The IRS disagreed, arguing that the futures were hedges that should be characterized as ordinary income or loss. (Since 1936, the IRS had asserted—quite appropriately—that hedges were a form of business insurance that generated ordinary income or loss.)

The Supreme Court found in favor of the IRS, holding that the corn futures were not separate and apart from the taxpayer's manufacturing activities. The Court concluded that "Congress intended that profits and losses arising from the everyday operation of a business be considered ordinary income or loss rather than capital gain or loss." This statement became the basis of the Corn Products Doctrine, under which a taxpayer's subjective intentions or business motivations for acquiring and holding property determined the character of gains and losses.

The Case in Question

Corn Products gave a green light to legitimate hedging transactions—meaning those that reduce or offset a business's price risks—not because they were hedges but because they met the business motive test. It no longer mattered whether a transaction was, in fact, a hedge.

Arkansas Best was a case testing the limits of the business motive doctrine from *Corn Products*. At issue were the losses sustained by a diversified holding company, Arkansas Best Corporation, on its shares of the National Bank of Commerce in Dallas. After the holding company acquired 65 percent of NBC stock in 1968, NBC's financial condition deteriorated. Hoping to prevent NBC's failure and to protect its own business reputation, Arkansas Best bought additional NBC stock. Eventually, NBC stock became unmarketable. In 1975, Arkansas Best disposed of a substantial portion of its NBC stock at a loss, which it reported as an ordinary loss.

The Supreme Court found that the losses were capital losses and, in a sweeping reversal of tax practice, removed the business motive test. The Court stated that taxpayers must look to the literal language of the Internal Revenue Code to determine the tax character of an asset. Section 1221 of the tax code defines a capital asset as "property held by the taxpayer (whether or not connected with its trade or business)" and lists five exceptions to capital asset treatment, one of which is "property of a kind which would properly be included in the inventory of a taxpayer."

As an aside, the Court squared its opinion in *Arkansas Best* with its prior opinion in *Corn Products* by stating that the corn futures in *Corn Products* were an integral part of the taxpayer's inventory purchase system and as such were surrogates for inventory, one of the five exceptions to capital asset treatment.

So while *Corn Products,* a case dealing directly with hedging, gave a green light to all hedging transactions, including surrogates for inventory as well as traditional offsets to inventory. *Arkansas Best,* a case having nothing to do with hedging, is read by some as giving a green light to only one type of hedge—surrogates for inventory. Under this interpretation, the airline in our first example could find its futures contracts reclassified by IRS auditors as capital assets that generate capital gains and losses. The airline cannot rely on the inventory-surrogate argument since, for tax purposes, the jet fuel is ordinary property used in the normal course of the airline's business, not inventory of raw materials, such as the corn in *Corn Products,* or inventory of finished goods. Such an interpretation would have major repercussions for the airline's tax liability—and thus for its willingness to enter into new hedge transactions—since, under the tax code, there is a limitation on the deductibility of capital losses: capital losses are deductible only to the extent of any capital gains. This limitation does not apply to ordinary losses, which are fully deductible. With ordinary and capital income taxed at the same rate, the only real tax advantage of capital gains over ordinary gains is to mop up otherwise unusable capital losses.

Herein lies the potential for the tax system to impede hedging. If losses on the futures contracts are deemed capital losses, there is nothing in the hedge transaction generating a capital gain that would render that loss deductible. The (capital) losses on the futures contracts could not be used to offset the (ordinary) gains on fuel purchases; in effect, the unprofitable half of the hedge is ignored while the profitable half is exposed to taxation. The failure to tax symmetrically the gains and losses on the two halves of the hedge—the hedged item (fuel purchases) and the hedging instrument (futures contracts)—creates a tax bias against otherwise efficient hedging activities. Business will hedge less, shift into other more costly or less effective hedging strategies (such as holding inventories), or stop hedging altogether. On net, businesses will be exposed to greater financial risk as they are forced to take on risk that could be efficiently reduced or shifted to other parties.

The bias against hedging could be even worse than indicated above. If IRS auditors really run amok, they could use a technical provision in the tax code to classify the gains on futures contracts as ordinary while leaving the losses on those contracts as capital. Asymmetrical treatment of the two halves of the hedge would be compounded by asymmetrical treatment of the gains and losses on one half. Were this to happen, hedging losses on one futures transaction could not even be offset by hedging gains on other futures transactions.

Liability Hedges and Short-Inventory Hedges

One of the most important and widespread uses of hedging is reducing the interest rate risk associated with debt issuance. To see how *Arkansas Best* may affect liability hedges, consider a hypothetical example.

The XO Corporation regularly issues five-year debentures to fund its manufacturing operations. Currently, XO is paying 8.5 percent interest on this debt. To hedge against the risk that interest rates will rise before its next debenture offering in 30 days, XO enters into a short futures position, agreeing to sell at par $100 million of five-year Treasury notes earning 8 percent. If interest rates fall to, say, 7.5 percent within 30 days, XO will realize a loss (equal to the difference between the market value and the face value of the Treasury notes) when it closes out the futures contracts. That loss will offset XO's reduced interest cost associated with the $100 million debt offering. The hedging loss effectively reduces the proceeds from the hedged debt offering, increasing the effective cost of borrowing above the realized cost.

Prior to *Arkansas Best,* the hedging loss would have been treated as generating an ordinary business expense and could offset, for tax purposes, the gains resulting from the reduced interest cost. The tax system would have been neutral in its effect on the corporation's decision to hedge.

After *Arkansas Best,* IRS auditors seem inclined to treat the futures contracts as capital assets. Capital losses on the futures position could not be used to offset the ordinary gains from lower borrowing costs. The use and effectiveness of futures as hedges of interest rate risk would be impaired significantly as businesses would seek other hedging instruments, such as interest rate swaps, that appear to be treated more favorably by the IRS.

As a final example of the possible effect of *Arkansas Best,* consider this case of a classic short hedge of inventory. Double Bar Ranch has livestock on hand that it plans to sell in October in the cash market. Concerned with the possibility of a decrease in the price of livestock before the sale, Double Bar sells a short live-cattle futures contract for delivery in October. If cash prices for cattle fall before October, Double Bar will be largely protected from the price decline because the gain on its short futures position will offset the decreased value of the cattle. If, instead, cattle prices increase, losses on the futures position will effectively reduce Double Bar's gain when it takes the cattle to market.

Prior to *Arkansas Best,* Double Bar's losses on its futures contracts would have been ordinary expenses and thus fully deductible against ordinary income. Since *Arkansas Best,* it is unclear how the futures contracts will be treated. Tax lawyers generally assume that hedges such as this, classic short hedges of inventory, will continue to generate ordinary income or loss. However, there are reports that some IRS auditors have even disallowed losses generated in these hedges because they are not surrogates for inventory positions.

While *Arkansas Best* can be read narrowly to foreclose ordinary treatment of most hedges—and the actions of IRS auditors are certainly consistent with such a reading—a good case can be made for a broader reading. Importantly, the Supreme Court did not overturn, nor did it even address, a long line of lower court decisions and Treasury statements stretching from 1936 to 1987 that accord ordinary treatment to hedges under a business insurance rationale. Further, the Court explicitly acknowledged extra-statutory exceptions to capital treatment in articulating the inventory surrogate rationale for the *Corn Products* decision. It is also worth noting that Congress, in 1981 and 1984, noted and approved of the ordinary treatment of hedging transactions. (These instances involved the exemption of hedging transactions from statutory provisions affecting straddles and regulated futures contracts.)

Massive Uncertainty

To date, the IRS and the Treasury Department that oversees it have refused to step into the breach and eliminate the uncertainty that now plagues decisions about whether or not to hedge ordinary business expenses. They have taken no steps—other than permitting IRS auditors to challenge past hedging transactions—to clarify the reach of *Arkansas Best* or the tax treatment of hedges.

While lawsuits are pending that should help clarify the issue, no case has yet been decided. (Litigation is a slow and expensive way to make policy.) The present situation is one of massive uncertainty that, if left unaddressed, could be as detrimental to hedging as a final unfavorable ruling on the tax treatment of hedges. Businesses have been left to guess what the tax implications of their recent or possible future hedging transactions will be. Businesses unwilling to proceed before they know the outcome of audits and litigation will stop hedging or search for other instruments subject to less legal and financial risk.

The problem seems to be more than one of benign neglect by the IRS. One possibility is that the IRS believes that the Supreme Court intended to overturn 50 years of accepted IRS practice regarding the treatment of hedges as business insurance. This makes no sense, however, since the issue of hedging was not raised by any party to the suit in *Arkansas Best;* moreover, the Court specifically cited the business insurance doctrine without suggesting in any way that it was no longer valid.

Another possibility is that the Treasury Department has a myopic concern with preventing the loss of taxes that would be due under a narrow reading of *Arkansas Best*.

Whatever the reason for its inaction to date, the administration should move quickly to clarify the tax treatment of hedges and to restore the symmetrical treatment of hedging losses and gains. It can do this quite simply by announcing that the IRS will continue to follow its 1936 policy statement that characterizes bona fide hedging transactions as generating ordinary business income or loss, not capital gain or loss, or it could adopt the view that any hedge that is a surrogate for, or an adjustment to, an item that generates ordinary income, loss, or expense is treated as generating ordinary business income or loss, not capital gain or loss. Either way, the pre-1988 status quo would be restored for bona fide hedges without disturbing the decision rendered in *Arkansas Best*.

The uncertainty that now surrounds the tax treatment of hedging impacts thousands of U.S. businesses, including some of the nation's largest manufacturing and financial firms, who either wait anxiously to see if their prior hedges will survive a tax audit or must now decide whether to protect shareholders, managers, and workers through hedging against the next shock to oil prices or jump in interest rates. If these businesses decide not to hedge because the legal and financial risks are too great, the economy as a whole will suffer: the cost of capital will increase, too many firms will experience financial distress, and some may go bankrupt. The costs to the economy of this policy failure are, and will continue to be, substantial.

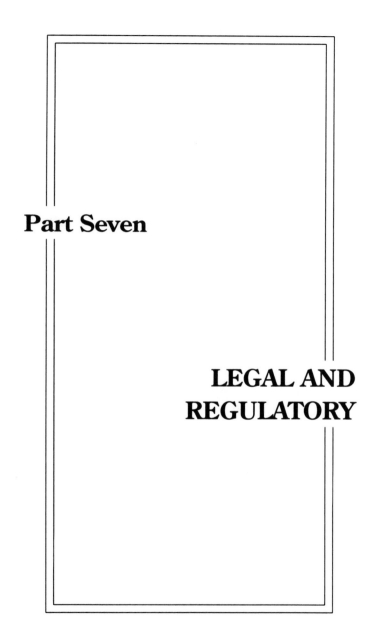

Part Seven

LEGAL AND REGULATORY

A REVIEW OF INTERNATIONAL AND U.S. CASE LAW AFFECTING SWAPS AND RELATED DERIVATIVE PRODUCTS

Anthony C. Gooch
Linda B. Klein*

20

Introduction

Only a few disputes involving swaps and related derivative products have come before the courts,[1] and many of those suits have been settled out of court. In addition, the legislature changed the applicable law after the court's decision in some of the cases, so the issue examined in the case must now be analyzed under different rules. Market practitioners are actively lobbying for still further legislative changes to the law applied in some of the cases. Nevertheless, there are ample lessons to be learned from studying the sorts of disputes that have found their way before judges and juries, and the court decisions in some of the cases will be the applicable law for the future in the jurisdictions where they were decided. This chapter is intended as an overview of some of those lessons and a summary of those rules.[2]

---

* The authors of this material are partners in law firms that advise various market participants mentioned herein on legal issues arising in connection with their derivatives activities. One of those firms, Cleary, Gottlieb, Steen & Hamilton, represented parties in certain of the proceedings discussed herein. The authors wish to express their thanks to Seth Grosshandler for his thoughtful comments on the section of this chapter that relates to termination of swap agreements upon a counterparty's bankruptcy or insolvency.

[1] By far the largest group of cases relates to transactions with English local authorities, which are discussed in the text accompanying notes 45–91 below.

[2] The selection of cases discussed in this chapter does not purport to be exhaustive, although the authors believe that they have covered most of the cases that have directly involved swaps or related derivatives transactions. The authors would be grateful for citations to or reports of other such cases. This material is current as of August 1, 1992.

The Cases in Their Contexts

It is not unusual to find lawyers wondering or disagreeing about what a court decision means or whether the same judge, or panel of judges, would have reached another result if the facts had been different. When the forum is a jurisdiction other than one's own, the difficulties in understanding the potential impact of a court decision are compounded by the intricacies of the foreign legal system. As a result, there may be many qualifiers to the answer a market participant will hear if it asks counsel whether the institution's swap "book" will be affected by the decision in a particular lawsuit, or whether the institution should change its form of agreement or some current practice in light of that decision.

The cases described in this chapter and the lessons we have gleaned from them therefore may or may not have relevance for any given institution, and in forming a view on the subject a market participant will want to consult counsel about the contexts in which each of the cases must be understood. At a minimum, these contexts will include the role of the court or the jury in the particular case and the particular facts presented as the basis for the decision.

When a case is decided by a jury in the United States, the result will have little predictive value for other cases if the judge does not render a written opinion, because the function of the jury is to apply the law as stated to it by the court to the particular facts of the case as the jury finds them; juries do not explain either their verdicts or how they reached them.

Even when the decision is rendered by the court without a jury, exactly what function the court is fulfilling may be important in a different way. For example, in some instances a court may be acting as the interpreter of a codified rule of law, and in others it may be acting as law maker in an area left to the courts by the legislature. In either circumstance, although the opinion may speak in more sweeping terms in stating the law being applied by the court in the case, unless the court is rendering an advisory opinion, the court will be performing its function of resolving a concrete dispute between the parties to a lawsuit, perhaps by deciding a motion that does not require passing on all the issues raised by the parties. To evaluate whether the case has any relevance for its own derivatives business, a market participant may have to know how much of the court's opinion may be binding as a statement or interpretation of the law: all or only the parts that the court had to decide in order to dispose of a particular motion or resolve the particular dispute brought before it by the parties to the case? The answer can easily differ in different legal systems.

Another limiting context is the sphere within which the court's decision is law in interpreting or enforcing a contract. Whether a court is acting as an interpreter of the law or laying down a rule of judge-made law, another court may always interpret the same codified rule, or an identically worded rule or contractual provision, differently. The decision of a trial court may be subject to appeal to one or more higher courts, and two courts of equal ranking in different jurisdictions may differ in their reading of the same or an identical provision of law or contract. For example, the federal circuit courts (which are courts of appeal) in two U.S. circuits may have different views of the meaning of a single provision of U.S. federal law (such as the U.S. Bankruptcy Code), and the highest courts of two different states within the United States may adopt different interpretations of identically worded versions of a provision of a uniform code (such as the Uniform Commercial Code) adopted in their respective states, even though there may be a practice, or a rule, leading the courts to give some deference to each other's view in these circumstances.

Although our discussion of the cases below may not always repeat these considerations of context, they should always be thought of as the backdrop for the discussion.

The Cases in the Context of the Swap Agreement

The format in which we have presented the various cases discussed below follows generally the order in which the relevant issues may arise for the swaps practitioner. The first set of cases involves disputes over the formation and existence of the contract. Our discussion of those cases is presented against the backdrop of a common practice in the market, which has been for the parties to reach agreement over the telephone with respect to a particular transaction and to confirm the terms of that transaction by telex or telecopy before negotiating a full-blown agreement. In the second set of cases, the parties admittedly reached an agreement, but one of them challenged the binding nature or validity of their contract. The remaining cases relate to disputes that arise over defaults and early termination, and the calculation of damages and handling of collateral in these circumstances.

Formation of the Swap Contract; Statutes of Frauds and Parol Evidence Rules

During the early years of the swap market, the parties to a swap generally documented their understanding with respect to each transaction in a separate agreement. To avoid the waste that was produced by this practice, the master swap agreement came to be the general vehicle for documenting swaps (and, later, other swap-related derivatives) between parties that expected to enter into more than one transaction with each other.[3] Once the master framework is in place to govern the overall relationship between the parties with respect to the kinds of transactions that are included, the parties need only bring the specific terms of any particular transaction under the master agreement through the appropriate mechanism. Since the parties usually enter into each transaction over the telephone, this mechanism generally consists of a written "Confirmation," which is to be sent (by telex, facsimile transmission[4] or hand or mail delivery) promptly after the deal is struck on the telephone and will form an integral part of and supplement to the master agreement. The master agreement is, however, often not in place by the time the parties wish to enter into their first transaction. In these circumstances, until execution of the agreement, the parties will generally rely on a brief confirmation of the financial terms of their swap, perhaps adding reference to a few additional terms thought to be particularly important and referring to their intent to execute a fuller agreement promptly.

The market has always been aware of the potential for danger posed by oral agreements to be memorialized temporarily through a short confirmation; the most obvious concerns included the possibility of default or repudiation of the swap by a counterparty before it has delivered a satisfactory confirmation and the lack of sufficient detail in the confirmation

---

[3] Although the initial impetus for the master agreement was the desire to reduce paperwork, professional swap market participants also sought, for U.S. bankruptcy purposes, to have all their swaps with a given counterparty constitute a single agreement and thus to avoid "cherry-picking" among the swaps by a trustee in bankruptcy or debtor in possession—that is, rejection of swaps unfavorable to the debtor and preservation of those favorable to it. This single-agreement approach was later adopted in the swap agreement forms published in 1987 by the International Swap Dealers Association, Inc. ("ISDA"). Through amendments adopted in 1990 to the U.S. Bankruptcy Code (11 U.S.C. § 101 *et seq.*, hereinafter referred to as the "Bankruptcy Code"), the single-agreement approach has been recognized as beyond attack for debtors in a Bankruptcy Code proceeding. This is achieved through the last part of the definition of "swap agreement," Bankruptcy Code § 101(55(C)), which provides that "swap agreement" means "a master agreement" for any of the transactions elsewhere defined in that provision as a "swap agreement" "together with all supplements" (*i.e.*, the confirmations supplementing the master agreement with the terms of each swap). The single-agreement concept has received the same kind of recognition in the law most likely applicable since August of 1989 to the insolvency of federally-insured depository institutions in the United States, the Financial Institutions Reform, Recovery, and Enforcement Act of 1989 ("FIRREA")which amended the Federal Deposit Insurance Act to deal, among other things, with swaps and other "qualified financial contracts." 12 U.S.C. § 1821(e)(8). As amended, the act expressly provides that "[a]ny master agreement for any agreements [described as a swap agreement] . . . shall be treated as a swap agreement." 12 U.S.C. § 1821(e)(8)(D)(vii). In both statutes, "swap agreement" is broadly defined to include rate and currency swaps, caps, floors, collars, FRAs, futures and similar agreements. Bankruptcy Code § 101(55); 12 U.S.C. § 1821(e)(8)(D)(vi). The 1992 ISDA master agreement form for multicurrency and cross-border transactions is designed to accommodate many of these derivative products so as to extend the benefits of the single-agreement approach to them.

[4] Some market participants are beginning to use electronic messaging to exchange confirmations, and this practice is reflected in ISDA's 1992 master agreement forms.

to clarify what would constitute default and the parties' rights and remedies in case of default.[5] Most participants correctly expected that, if detected early, misunderstandings over the terms of the oral agreement could generally be resolved through amicable negotiations; however, most also realized that litigation could be required to resolve an occasional dispute over the terms agreed to, or whether agreement had been reached, particularly if the misunderstanding was discovered only after a significant movement of rates in favor of one of the parties.

Where the London swap market is concerned, "The London Code of Conduct—Part 2: The Swap Market," released by the Bank of England in 1988,[6] provides that principals subject to that Code[7] must send written confirmations of each swap transaction concluded orally as soon as possible and, in any case, within one business day, but that they should treat themselves as bound to a swap contract "at the point where the terms of the transactions are agreed."[8] The London Code of Conduct also contains guidelines relating to the confirmation of transactions negotiated by such principals through brokers and states that when the parties to a swap disagree over the terms of their transaction, the Bank of England will stand ready to arbitrate.[9]

Whether or not terms like those included in the London Code of Conduct apply to any particular segment of the market or transaction, it is everywhere understood by swaps professionals that the market could not operate unless the parties to a swap intended to be bound from the moment they reached agreement orally. This is so because the market depends on the participation of the swap professional or "dealer," and the

---

[5] In various jurisdictions the local association of bankers has adopted recommended terms for swaps, or at least short-term swaps, between banks in that jurisdiction, and under those terms member institutions are deemed to adopt them (subject to express reservations or changes) to govern their swaps with each other unless they specify otherwise in effecting the swap trade. An example is the "BBAIRS terms" produced by the Interest Rate Swaps Working Party of the British Bankers' Association, which include minimal provisions relating to defaults and damages, as well as recommended terms and conditions on other subjects. Therefore, an oral agreement on a short-term swap between two BBA banks in the London market followed by a brief confirmation of the financial terms of the transaction, unless otherwise agreed during the trade, would also be subject to the fuller BBAIRS terms on defaults and other subjects.

[6] Parts of The London Code of Conduct deal with other subjects involving the wholesale markets in Sterling, foreign exchange and bullion. Only Part 2, relating to the swap market, is referred to herein as the "London Code of Conduct."

[7] Paragraph 2 of the London Code of Conduct states that it applies to all listed institutions subject to the supervisory jurisdiction of the Bank of England. On the procedures for becoming a listed institution and the advantages to a professional swap market participant of being one, see Canby & Pilley, "Regulatory Issues: United Kingdom," in The Handbook of Currency and Interest Rate Risk Management, Chapter 38, pp. 38–5 to 38–8 (New York Institute of Finance, Schwartz & Smith eds. 1990).

[8] London Code of Conduct ¶¶ 31 and 35. This same understanding has been made part of ISDA's 1992 master agreement forms.

[9] London Code of Conduct ¶ 33.

swap business of such an institution, simply stated, consists of making a profit as an intermediary through the spread between the payments it agrees to make and receive in one transaction and the payments it agrees to make and receive in one or more swap, futures or other transactions entered into as hedges; a swap professional could not take on its obligations to the parties to any of these transactions with any reasonable expectation about whether the business would prove sufficiently profitable unless it could rely on the existence of the transactions on the other side starting at the same, or approximately the same, time.[10] Swaps and related derivatives exist, at least in part, because of volatility in the rate and price indices (such as interest and foreign exchange rates and commodity prices) used in these transactions; that same volatility would make it impracticable for the market to exist with any depth if the parties to the transactions did not view themselves as bound by the terms of their oral trades until they had executed a full-fledged contract for each transaction.

The cases discussed in this section illustrate some of the circumstances that may give rise to disputes over the formation of enforceable derivatives contracts in the absence of formal, executed agreements or in the event of an alleged misunderstanding as to the parties' agreement.

Homestead: The Existence of an Enforceable Agreement

Homestead Savings v. Life Savings and Loan Association[11] involved two swaps between American thrift institutions for which final documentation was never completed. Homestead sought damages for anticipatory breach of contract and breach of implied covenants of good faith and fair dealing from Life Savings, which denied the existence of an enforceable contract for either swap. Both were transactions with $20 million notional amounts and five-year terms under which the parties' semiannual payment obligations were to be calculated on the basis of floating rates, in the case of Homestead, and fixed rates, in the case of Life Savings; the former was using the swaps to hedge against the risk of loss or lower re-

---

[10] The situation of the "end-user" of swaps can in substance be the same insofar as the binding nature of the oral agreement is concerned. For example, if an end-user has committed itself to issue fixed-rate bonds in, say, Swiss francs, with the understanding that a swap will enable it to exchange the bond proceeds for U.S. dollars on the issue date and to effect a reverse exchange at an agreed rate when the bonds mature, and further to synthetically convert its Swiss franc debt service obligations to an obligation to make fixed-rate payments in dollars, the end-user will want to know that the swap provider will consider itself bound with respect to the swap from the date the end-user commits itself with respect to the issuance of the bonds and agrees on their coupon rate, even if only an oral agreement on the swap exists at the time.

[11] Commenced in the U.S. federal District Court for the Northern District of California, as Case No. C 85 1690 SAW, the case was transferred to the District Court for the Northern District of Illinois, Western Division, where the action is identified as Case No. 86 C 20268. The case is unreported.

turns on a pool of variable-rate mortgage assets in a declining rate environment, and the latter to hedge against the risk of loss on a pool of fixed-rate mortgage assets in a rising rate environment.

The trade for the first swap occurred in mid-May of 1984, and the dispute between the parties crystallized in November of the same year. Over the six intervening months, there was correspondence between the parties relating to the transactions and some negotiation of draft documentation for the swaps and related security agreements, including a proposal by Life Savings of some changes and completions for the drafts, as well as indications that it would provide letter-of-credit support instead of collateral in connection with its obligations. However, during the same period rates declined considerably, placing Life Savings in the position of net payer under the swaps for the imminent first payment date. In the face of these circumstances, it gave notice that it was not prepared to go forward since the final documentation had not been agreed. Although the parties entered into negotiations to structure another transaction that would enable Life Savings to mitigate its losses, the transaction was not consummated and Homestead commenced the lawsuit. Subsequent settlement discussions foundered and the court action moved forward to a jury award for the plaintiff for some $6.2 million of damages. The defendant institution became insolvent soon thereafter and its receiver, the Federal Savings and Loan Insurance Corporation ("FSLIC"), moved to vacate the judgment, but the motions were rejected by the trial court and the verdict in favor of the plaintiff was left standing.[12]

Because the outcome was reached through a jury verdict, rather than a decision of the court, and because juries do not explain the reasons for their verdicts, the action offers less guidance for other market participants than might otherwise have been the case. Nevertheless, the lawsuit serves as a reminder of the importance of ensuring that a swap trade is quickly memorialized in writing in a form that will preclude or overcome a challenge on the ground that the trade is unenforceable as a mere oral contract. In *Homestead* the challenge was made through the affirmative defense of the statute of frauds asserted by Life Savings, a defense which Life Savings had the burden of proving.

The Nature of a Signed Writing under a Statute of Frauds. Most jurisdictions have statutes of frauds applicable to at least some kinds of agree-

---

[12] Order of August 12, 1987, declining to reconsider the court's order of July 1, 1987, denying FSLIC's motion to vacate judgment and relinquish jurisdiction. This description of the facts is based on information in the complaint filed by Homestead Savings and documents attached thereto, as well as a Memorandum of Points and Authorities in Support of Issuance of Writ of Attachment filed by Homestead when it sought to attach property of the defendant after the settlement negotiations failed. The defendant's positions in the case differed primarily in the light in which it cast the same facts or the legal conclusions it argued should be drawn from them.

ments (such as the sale of land), but the requirements of the statutes and the kinds of contracts to which they apply can differ widely from jurisdiction to jurisdiction. As suggested by the name,[13] the statutes are intended to protect against fraudulent claims based on alleged oral contracts and, although in the extreme case the statute may only be satisfied by a contract or deed executed under seal, in many cases far less than a full-blown agreement is required.[14] For example, as stated by the judge in *Homestead* in his instructions to the jury, the statute of frauds applicable in that case provided that,

> if an agreement cannot be fully performed within one year from its effective date, there must be some memorandum or note thereof in writing, signed by the person to be obligated.
>
> The memorandum or note must contain the essential terms of the agreement but it is not necessary to provide for every collateral matter or every future contingency. The memorandum may be composed of more than one document.

To establish its statute-of-frauds defense, Life Savings had the burden of proving that this kind of written note or memorandum signed by it could

---

[13] Rules with the effects of a statute of frauds are not necessarily expressly identified as such. For example, the Federal Deposit Insurance Act, 12 U.S.C. §§ 1821(d)(9), 1821(n)(4) & 1823(e), includes certain writing requirements that must be satisfied to permit enforcement of a claim against the Federal Deposit Insurance Corporation (the "FDIC") when it is acting as conservator or receiver for a failed federally-insured depository institution. On these requirements and a "safe harbor" clarifying how they may be deemed satisfied in connection with swaps and other "qualified financial contracts," *see* Gooch & Pergam, "Legal Aspects of Swap Agreements: United States and New York Law," in *The Handbook of Currency and Interest Rate Risk Management,* Chapter 34, p. 34–17 (New York Institute of Finance, Schwartz & Smith eds. 1990). The safe harbor is set forth in a Policy Statement Regarding Qualified Financial Contracts adopted on December 12, 1989. Notice of adoption of the Policy Statement, and of an identical statement adopted by the Resolution Trust Corporation, appears at 55 Fed. Reg. 7,027 (Feb. 28, 1990) (identifying the sources at those agencies from which copies may be obtained). A reference at 57 Fed. Reg. 17,756 (Apr. 27, 1992) indicates that a proposed "rule stage" for the safe harbor was on the unified agenda for those agencies on April 27, 1992 and that, when published, the text of the safe harbor will appear at 12 C.F.R. 1622. In the meantime, it may be consulted as reproduced in *Advanced Swaps and Derivative Financial Products* 195–203 (Practising Law Institute 1991) and in the FDIC loose-leaf reporting service at 5901.

[14] Under the statute of frauds set forth in Section 2–201(1) of the Uniform Commercial Code as in effect in New York (which, as explained below, has been found applicable to foreign currency forwards and may apply to currency swaps governed by New York law), "[a]ll that is required is that the writing afford a basis for believing that the offered evidence rests on a real transaction." N.Y. U.C.C. § 2–201(1) Official Comment 1 (McKinney 1964) (describing the philosophy behind the requirement of the provision). *See Iandoli v. Asiatic Petroleum Corp.,* 57 A.D.2d 815, 816, 315 N.Y.S.2d 15, 16 (1st Dept.) (citing that Official Comment as support for its holding), *appeal denied,* 42 N.Y.2d 1011, 398 N.Y.S.2d 535, 368 N.E.2d 285 (1977).

not be shown to exist, either through a single document or by looking at the documents together.[15]

From the record of the case it does not seem that there were very many documents signed by the defendant or that they included a detailed confirmation of the sort generally used in the swap market today, although the term and fixed and floating rate indices for the first of the swaps were set forth in a signed letter sent by Life Savings to Homestead and confirmed by it in a brief reply.[16] It seems, however, that the jury must have concluded that the statute of frauds requirement was met in part by looking at some documents that were not executed by the defendant in the light shed on them by others it did execute. Specifically, it would appear, at least with respect to the second of the swaps, that the jury found the statute's requirements to be satisfied by a signed letter from an officer of the defendant stating the changes the defendant would require to the draft agreement sent by the plaintiff.

Insofar as this part of the analysis required by the case is concerned, *Homestead* merely illustrates how a contract enforceable against a counterparty may be found to exist, through an examination of all the correspondence and other documents exchanged by the parties, even if the counterparty has failed to sign a confirmation of the transaction. Since it is obviously undesirable, however, to run the risk that a judge or jury may find that a statute of frauds has not been satisfied, *Homestead* should serve as a vivid reminder of the importance of obtaining at least a signed confirmation of each swap promptly after the oral agreement is reached.[17]

Under some statutes of frauds the recipient of a confirmation sufficient to be enforceable against its sender may not mount a successful statutes-of-fraud defense by proving it never signed the confirmation or

---

[15] A similar statute of frauds is generally applicable under New York law (N.Y. Gen. Oblig. § 5-701(a)(1) (McKinney 1989)) to contracts that cannot, by their terms, be performed within one year from their making (which would include derivatives with terms longer than one year and, possibly, "delayed start" transactions with terms shorter than one year but ending more than one year from their trade date). *See* Gooch & Klein, *Swap Agreement Documentation* 81–82 (2d ed., Euromoney Publications, 1988) (hereinafter cited as Gooch & Klein, *Swap Documentation*). If enacted, a proposed amendment to that provision of the General Obligations Law would create an exception for "qualifying financial contracts," including swaps, entered into orally or through electronic communication if sufficient evidence of the existence of an agreement could be established in any of several ways, including the transcript or written output of the oral or electronic communication (if otherwise admissible under applicable rules of evidence). The April 23, 1992 draft of the proposed amendment is reproduced in *Swaps and Other Derivatives in 1992*, 365–68 (Practising Law Institute 1992).

[16] The letter from Life Savings did not, however, specify which of the parties was the fixed and which the floating rate payer.

[17] Some statutes of frauds, including the New York statute in Section 5–701(a)(1) of the General Obligations Law, provide that the required documentation be "subscribed" rather than simply signed. *See* Gooch & Klein, *Swap Documentation* 84 on the interpretation that has been given to the term "subscribed."

any other record of the terms orally agreed. This is the case under Section 2–201(2) of the Uniform Commercial Code as adopted in the State of New York[18] (the "UCC") where the contract concerned is a transaction "between merchants," as the term is defined in Section 2–104 of the UCC,[19] the confirmation is sent within a reasonable time after the trade occurs and the recipient has reason to know of the contents of the confirmation and fails to object within 10 days.[20] A transaction will be "between merchants" for these purposes if both parties are chargeable with the knowledge or skill of merchants in the transaction,[21] and "merchants," in this context, means "a person who deals in goods of the kind or otherwise by his occupation holds himself out as having knowledge or skill peculiar to the practices or goods involved in the transaction or to whom such knowledge or skill may be attributed by his employment of an agent or broker or other intermediary who by his occupation holds himself out as having such knowledge or skill."[22]

When foreign currency is treated in a transaction as a commodity rather than as medium of payment, it can constitute "goods" under the UCC for purposes of the provisions described above.[23] Therefore, if currency swaps are viewed as involving foreign currency as a commodity and within Article 2 of the UCC, in currency swaps "between merchants"— which should include sophisticated market participants, whether or not swap professionals—it may not always be strictly necessary to obtain a signed return confirmation from a counterparty,[24] unless the parties' agreement suggests otherwise. Indeed, some market participants include

---

[18] N.Y. U.C.C. § 2–201(2) (McKinney 1964).

[19] N.Y. U.C.C. § 2–104 (McKinney 1964).

[20] N.Y. U.C.C. § 2–201(2) (McKinney 1964).

[21] N.Y. U.C.C. § 2–104(3) (McKinney 1964).

[22] N.Y. U.C.C. § 2–104(1) (McKinney 1964).

[23] This is the underpinning of the *Intershoe* case discussed below, which treats another provision of Article 2 of the UCC as applicable to a forward contract for the purchase and sale of a foreign currency for U.S. dollars. *See Intershoe, Inc. v. Bankers Trust Co.,* 77 N.Y.2d 517, 521, 571 N.E.2d 641, 644, 569 N.Y.S.2d 333, 336 (1991) ("There seems to be no question that the UCC applies to foreign currency transactions. . . ."). *See also* N.Y. U.C.C. § 2–105 Official Comment 1 (McKinney 1964).

[24] In a recent case involving foreign currency forward and option contracts, the court analyzed Section 2–201(2) of the Uniform Commercial Code, as adopted in both New York and Virginia, in rejecting the defendant's statute-of-frauds defense and expressly found the defendant, a wealthy surgeon who engaged regularly in swaps and foreign currency transactions with the plaintiff and other major financial institutions, to be a merchant for purposes of Section 2–201(2). *Salomon Forex Inc v. Tauber,* Civ. No. 91–1415–A (E.D. Va.) (order of March 24, 1992 granting, *inter alia,* the plaintiff's motion for partial summary judgment on its claim for breach of contract and denying the defendant's motion for partial summary judgment on certain counts of his counterclaim). In so doing, the Court cited *Armco, Inc. v. New Horizon Dev. Co. of Virginia,* 331 S.E.2d 456 to the effect that "a merchant is 'a business professional as opposed to a casual or inexperienced seller or buyer.' " Other aspects of the *Tauber* case are discussed in the text accompanying notes 97–133 below.

in their master swap agreements contractual provisions that establish a rule like that set forth in UCC 2–201(2), where necessary expressly overcoming any suggestion elsewhere in the agreement that an exchange of confirmations is required for a binding swap.[25] To avoid problems like that described in the foregoing discussion of *Homestead,* however, the market can be expected to continue to operate, as it now does, on the basis of the general, prudent, conclusion, that a signed, return confirmation of each transaction should always be sought.[26]

The Parties' Intent to Be Bound Absent a Formal Agreement. There is a second worthwhile lesson to be learned from *Homestead:* Life Savings based its defense in part on the argument that the parties did not intend to be bound with respect to the swaps until they executed a formal agreement for each swap. With respect to this defense, the judge described the applicable law to the jury in two sets of instructions. According to the first:

> An oral agreement which contemplates the signing of a written agreement may or may not be binding, depending on the intent of the parties. The intent of the parties is evidenced by their conduct.
>
> On the one hand, there is no enforceable agreement if the parties intend not to be bound until a formal writing has been executed.
>
> On the other hand, there is an enforceable agreement if the writing is intended to memorialize a bargain already made.

The second, related set of instructions offered the following further principles about how the parties' intent might be established:

---

[25] This kind of provision might be viewed as a waiver of any applicable statute of frauds or as an attempt by one party—the recipient of the confirmation—to appoint the other as its agent for purposes of satisfying the statute of frauds. It appears that the defense of the statute may be waived in various ways (including failure to raise it at an appropriate stage of litigation), at least after the fact, so, viewed as a contractual waiver, this kind of provision might prove enforceable; if it were viewed as an appointment of the other party as agent, the provision might prove more problematical. *See* Gooch & Klein, *Swap Documentation* 115–16, and cases there cited. In the *Tauber* case cited in the preceding note, the confirmations of some of the relevant foreign exchange forward transactions sent by the plaintiff, Salomon Forex Inc, to the defendant expressly recited as a contractual provision the substance of U.C.C. § 2–201(1): "You shall be deemed to have signified your acceptance of the terms and conditions of the transactions as described on the face hereof unless we receive written notice of your objections within ten days after your receipt of this confirmation." Memorandum in Support of Plaintiff's Motion for Summary Judgment at 13.

[26] The proposed amendment to New York's General Obligations Law referred to in note 15 above would extend a rule like that set forth in N.Y. U.C.C. § 2–201(2) to all swaps and related derivatives, as well as other kinds of transactions. It would also shorten the period for objection and effect other liberalizing changes that would facilitate the use of electronic recordings and electronic messaging records to satisfy the statute of frauds.

In determining whether either party intended that an agreement be reduced to writing and signed by the parties before it becomes effective, you may consider, along with all the other evidence in the case, the following factors:

1. Whether the agreement is one usually put into writing;

2. Whether the purpose of the agreement would be defeated if the oral agreement were not binding;

3. Whether there are few or many details in the contract;

4. Whether custom and practice in interest rate swap transactions is that oral agreements are binding;

5. Whether the amount involved is large or small;

6. Whether the contract requires a formal writing for a full expression of the covenants and promises in the contract; and

7. Whether negotiations themselves indicate that a written draft is contemplated as the final conclusion of negotiations.

Again, bearing in mind that the applicable law in any given jurisdiction may be different and that the enforceability of one's swaps ought not to be left to the weighing of these kinds of factors by the trier of fact (judge or jury), a valuable lesson to be learned from *Homestead* is that, where the parties do not already have a master agreement for their swaps in place, they should be scrupulously careful to establish in the confirmation of each trade that it memorializes the terms of their binding agreement on the relevant swap. If reference is made to the parties' intention to enter into a more formal agreement, it should be clear that the confirmation will constitute a binding agreement until it is either superseded by that formal document or deemed to become a confirmation under, and part of, it, in the case of a master agreement.

Intershoe: Contradicting a Written Agreement

It is not unheard of for a market participant to discover after the fact that the signed confirmation of a swap does not correctly reflect its understanding of what the parties agreed. In many instances the relevant part of the confirmation is acknowledged by both parties to be a mistake and a substitute confirmation is executed. A recent court action involving an FX transaction illustrates the application of New York law in a case where the parties did not agree a mistake had been made.

As described by the court in *Intershoe, Inc. v. Bankers Trust Co.,*[27] the plaintiff, a shoe importer that used foreign currencies, including lire, in its business, "placed a telephone order with the defendant concerning a foreign currency futures transaction involving the exchange of Italian lira

---

[27] N.Y.2d 517, 571 N.E.2d 641, 569 N.Y.S.2d 333 (1991).

[*sic*] for United States dollars."[28] The defendant, Bankers Trust Company, sent a confirmation slip to the plaintiff indicating that the requested transaction was a sale of lire by the plaintiff to the defendant, and the plaintiff signed and returned the confirmation. As the settlement date for the transaction approached, some seven months later, Bankers Trust asked Intershoe for the details relating to delivery by Intershoe of the lire, and Intershoe responded "that the transaction was a mistake and that it would not go through with it."[29] To cover commitments in other currency transactions, Bankers Trust purchased lire on the open market at a price higher than that in effect when the trade with Intershoe was done and the confirmation was sent, "resulting in a loss of $55,019.85."[30] Shortly afterwards, Intershoe commenced the lawsuit "claiming that it had purchased, not sold, lira and that it had sustained damages of $59,336.40."[31] Bankers Trust counterclaimed for its damages resulting from Intershoe's refusal to sell the lire as agreed. The only evidence offered by Intershoe in support of its position was an affidavit of its treasurer to the effect that, although he could not recall every conversation he had had with Bankers Trust regarding lira transactions, he unequivocally knew that Intershoe did not agree to sell lire in the transaction in question or any other transaction that year.[32]

There was, therefore, no dispute over satisfaction of the applicable statute of frauds; rather, the question was whether the relevant signed confirmation was subject to challenge through extrinsic evidence as an incorrect statement of the terms agreed. The question was answered in the negative by New York State's highest court when Bankers Trust appealed a denial of its motion to dismiss Intershoe's complaint and for summary judgment on its own counterclaim for damages against Intershoe.[33] In giving its answer the court was interpreting UCC 2–202, which provides as follows with respect to the use of parol or extrinsic evidence:

> Terms with respect to which the confirmatory memoranda
> of the parties agree or which are otherwise set forth in a writing

---

[28] 77 N.Y.2d at 519, 571 N.E.2d at 642, 569 N.Y.S.2d at 335. Throughout the court's opinion, reference is made to "lira," regardless of whether the singular or plural is intended. The form used by the court will be transcribed without further comment in quotations from the reported opinion.

[29] 77 N.Y.2d at 520, 571 N.E.2d at 643, 569 N.Y.S.2d at 335.

[30] *Ibid.*

[31] *Ibid.*

[32] *Ibid.* The affidavit also indicated that Intershoe had sold foreign currency to Bankers Trust Company in only one of nearly 1,000 currency transactions between them and that the confirmations for two other transactions between them on the same day had been for purchases of foreign currency by Intershoe.

[33] As a procedural matter, the question certified to the court, by permission of the intermediate appellate court, was whether the trial court's order, as affirmed below, was properly made.

intended by the parties as a final expression of their agreement with respect to such terms as are included therein may not be contradicted by evidence of any prior agreement or of a contemporaneous oral agreement but may be explained or supplemented

(a) by course of dealing or usage of trade . . . or by course of performance. . . ; and

(b) by evidence of consistent additional terms unless the court finds the writing to have been intended also as a complete and exclusive statement of the terms of the agreement.[34]

Intershoe's claim and its defense to the Bankers Trust counterclaim were not based on an attempt to explain or supplement the signed confirmation as contemplated in the cited provision; rather, the plaintiff clearly sought to contradict the terms of the confirmation. Under the rule applied by the court, Intershoe could not do so through extrinsic evidence of the parties' contemporaneous oral agreement on terms covered in the confirmation except in very limited circumstances. Because the function of the Court of appeals was to determine whether the lower court's order was properly made, and the lower court had focused only on whether the confirmation was a final expression of the parties' agreement, it was on that basis alone that the appellate court analyzed whether the lower court had properly denied the Bankers Trust motions.

In deciding that it had not and reversing the lower court's order, the Court of Appeals analyzed Intershoe's position that was apparently adopted below: in the plaintiff's view the confirmation should not be viewed as a final expression of the parties' agreement, unless the confirmation itself contained an express statement to that effect (which it did not) or there was uncontroverted evidence that the confirmation was so intended. In the absence of either, the plaintiff argued that there were factual issues about the parties' intent sufficient to warrant denial by the lower court of the summary judgment requested by Bankers Trust.[35] The Court of Appeals found the contents of the confirmation to be complete as to all essential terms of the transaction and no indication that the confirmation was of a bargain to be made in the future; rather, in the court's view, it expressed "the parties' meeting of the minds as to a completed bargain's essential terms."[36] The court also rejected the plaintiff's argument that a writing must include express language that it represents the parties' final agreement, because to accept the argument would be to "introduce a technical, formal requirement not contemplated by the [UCC]

---

[34] N.Y. U.C.C. § 2–202 (McKinney 1964).
[35] *Intershoe Inc. v. Bankers Trust Co.*, 77 N.Y.2d 517, 521–22, 571 N.E.2d 641, 644, 569 N.Y.S.2d 333, 336.
[36] *Id.*, 77 N.Y.2d at 522, 571 N.E.2d at 644, 569 N.Y.S.2d at 333.

. . . and one that would frustrate the Code's purpose of facilitating sales transactions by easing the process of contract formation," as well as creating " 'a particularly troublesome precedent for commercial practice in currency futures transactions by providing a convenient "hedge" for one party or the other against currency fluctuations.' "[37]

It should be remembered that *Intershoe* was decided under Section 2–202 of the UCC, which applies to sales of goods.[38] As noted above, transactions in foreign currency, like the FX transaction involved in the case, can fall within the purview of Article 2 of the UCC if the foreign currency is treated as a commodity, as opposed to a medium of payment, in the transaction.[39] The rule of the case may, therefore, also be applicable to currency swaps and some other currency derivative transactions.[40] If the same kind of dispute arose under New York law in connection with a swap or related derivative of another kind, the source of the applicable parol evidence rule would be different, although the applicable principles appear to be generally the same.[41]

Since no degree of additional care can perfectly guard against a mistake of the kind involved in *Intershoe*, in the light of the case the market has focused on whether practice should somehow change insofar as the drafting of confirmations is concerned. One possibility is that confirma-

---

[37] 77 N.Y.2d at 523–24, 571 N.E.2d at 644–45, 569 N.Y.S.2d at 337 (quoting from the dissent in the lower court, in the second part of the quoted text).

[38] The same UCC provision was applied in the *Tauber* case referred to in note 24 above and further described below in the text accompanying notes 97–133, in the court's order granting the plaintiff's motion for partial summary judgment and denying the defendant's motion for partial summary judgment on certain counts of his counterclaim. The defendant contended, among other things, that the plaintiff had breached an express representation of "best pricing" made by one of the plaintiff's sales persons, by overcharging the defendant for the options and foreign currency forwards purchased by the defendant. Citing *Intershoe*, the court found that this UCC parol evidence rule barred the defendant from introducing extrinsic evidence to support this contention, which was an attempt to add new or contradictory terms to contradict the final expression of the parties' agreements as embodied in the written confirmations of the transactions.

[39] *See* note 23 *supra* and accompanying text.

[40] This is not, however, necessarily the case. It should be noted that at least one commentator has questioned whether the provisions of Article 2 of the Uniform Commercial Code have been correctly applied to foreign exchange forward transactions in *Intershoe* and other cases. *See* Scarborough, "Statute of Frauds' Issues and Foreign Exchange Transactions/Contracts," *Swaps and Other Derivatives in 1992*, 331, 345–46 (Practising Law Institute 1992).

[41] As stated by the courts in New York, the applicable parol evidence rule provides that, when the parties have reduced their agreement to writing, extrinsic evidence of prior or contemporaneous agreements may not be offered to contradict, vary or subtract from the terms of the writing, *Aratari v. Chrysler Corp.*, 35 A.D.2d 1077, 316 N.Y.S.2d 680 (4th Dept. 1970); however, where the writing does not appear to express the entire agreement of the parties, evidence that the writing which purports to be a contract is in fact not a contract at all, or to explain any ambiguities or omissions in the writing, is admissible. *Jamestown Bus. College Ass'n v. Allen*, 172 N.Y. 291, 294 (1902); *Mitchill v. Lath*, 247 N.Y. 377, 383, 160 N.E. 646 (1928); *Frasca v. Metropolitan L.I. Co.*, 272 N.Y. 588, 4 N.E.2d 816 (1936).

tions could begin to include the kind of "merger" or "integration" clause that is contained in most formal swap agreements: an express statement something to the effect that the confirmation, together with the terms of the master agreement it supplements, where applicable, constitutes the entire agreement of the parties with respect to the terms of the transaction covered by the confirmation and, as to those terms, supersedes all prior agreements and contemporaneous oral agreements with respect to that transaction. *Intershoe* stands for the proposition that such a provision is not necessary under Section 2–202 of the UCC, but the applicable law in some cases and jurisdictions may be different.[42] The parties must weigh the potential benefit of the provision, and the element of finality it may lend to the debate,[43] against the desire in the market to keep the confirmation as brief as possible. However, inclusion of such a provision may be attractive to entities that believe they themselves will make few mistakes and, in any event, would prefer to live with mistakes so as to avoid litigation if necessary. The other possibility, for institutions particularly concerned about the high cost of mistakes, is to consider a contractual provision that would expressly permit the contradiction of a signed confirmation through at least certain kinds of contemporaneous extrinsic evidence. Market participants that electronically record their swap trades may consider this kind of provision desirable, subject to appropriate safeguards relating to the legality and integrity of the recording.[44]

Market participants that consider altering the text of their confirmations to deal with mistakes and attempts to contradict the terms of a signed confirmation should bear in mind the distinction between contradicting and clarifying the terms of a confirmation through extrinsic evidence. Because confirmations—even those prepared on standardized forms—are often completed with less than complete precision in the use of technical terminology (such as the terms defined in the 1991 ISDA Definitions and its predecessors, the SWAPS Code and the 1987 Interest Rate and Currency Exchange Definitions), extrinsic evidence on the course of dealing or usage of trade, or evidence of consistent additional terms, may prove extremely useful to explain or clarify an ambiguity in a confirmation. If a market participant so believes, it would want to avoid precluding itself from using extrinsic evidence for those purposes, even if

---

[42] *See* Wigmore, *Evidence in Trials at Common Law* (rev. ed., J. H. Chadbourn 1982) § 2425, for a discussion of and citations to similar parol evidence rules in the United States.

[43] There are well-established exceptions to the courts' willingness to allow general "merger" clauses to preclude extrinsic evidence, where the evidence is proposed, not to contradict the written agreement, but to attack its character as an agreement at all, on grounds such as fraud in the inducement of the contract. *Sabo v. Delman*, 3 N.Y.2d 155, 164 N.Y.S.2d 714 (1957).

[44] The electronic recording of telephone conversations raises several complex legal issues that are beyond the scope of this chapter.

it chose to provide in the confirmation that extrinsic evidence could not be used to contradict a term in the confirmation.

Power and Authority to Enter into Swaps; Legality—Broad Challenges to Derivatives Transactions

Since the inception of the swap market, and particularly as it has grown to involve new varieties of swaps and related derivatives and new and different kinds of end-users, counsel have spent a good deal of time analyzing whether agreements that their clients are considering are legal, valid and binding agreements that they can expect to be able to enforce against their counterparties.

The cases discussed in this section deal with some typical concerns of counsel in this regard. The first subsection describes cases in which the defense was based on a challenge to the power and authority of an entity to enter into swaps; the second describes a case in which the defense was based in part on challenges to the legality of transactions alleged to have been entered into in violation of statutory prohibitions of off-exchange commodity futures and options transactions, "bucketing" and wagering contracts. In all these cases, the challenges were broadly based, in that they went to the enforceability of the agreement as a whole, whereas the cases reviewed in the following section will deal with narrower challenges to the enforceability of specific provisions relating to early termination and damages, particularly in the context of a swap with a counterparty that has become insolvent.

Hammersmith and Fulham:[45] Power and Authority to Enter into Swaps

Because swaps are relative newcomers to the world of commercial agreements, legal counsel for market participants have generally recommended to their clients a high degree of care in analyzing whether potential counterparties have the power and authority to enter into swaps. This diligence is called for because swaps do not always fall neatly into any of the categories of actions or contracts with respect to which the entity's power is clear and for which the procedures to obtain authorization are well established.

The power of an entity to enter into a transaction generally flows from its charter and by-laws or, in some cases, the special or organic law under which it was created. Where sovereigns and public-sector entities are concerned, a local or national constitution may also be relevant, or a

---

[45] *Hazell v. Hammersmith & Fulham London Borough Council*, [1990] 2 W.L.R. 17, [1992] Q.B. 697 (Div'l Ct. 1989), *aff'd in part and rev'd in part*, [1990] 2 W.L.R. 1039, [1992] Q.B. 697 (C.A. 1990), *reinstated*, 2 A.C. 1, [1991], All E.R. 545, [1991] 2 W.L.R. 372 (H.L. 1991), hereinafter cited as *"Hazell."*

charter or statute, in the case of a public corporation, and, where trusts are involved, the deed of trust will be the source of power. In many cases the powers of entities are expressly limited by their organizational instruments or by applicable law and regulation; in others, the entity may also have the additional power to take such actions and enter into such contracts as may be necessary or incidental to the exercise of a power expressly granted to it, so long as the action or contract does not involve a power expressly prohibited to the entity.[46]

The same and additional sources, as well as applicable law and regulation, can govern whether an entity has taken all action necessary to authorize its entering into a transaction. Just as a resolution of the board of directors may be required for a company to enter into a swap, an action of a particular official or decision-making body or administrative agency may be required to authorize a swap for a public-sector entity or for a company in a regulated industry, even if the relevant entity or company has the general power to engage in swap transactions. In addition, in some jurisdictions that have exchange controls, prior authorization may be required from the central bank or a special governmental agency charged with the administration of the exchange controls.

It is not always necessarily the case that a party to a swap or related transaction will suffer adverse consequences if its counterparty lacked the power to enter into the transaction or failed to obtain the proper authorization to do so. When one deals with an ordinary business corporation, the contract may nonetheless be enforceable, especially if one has reasonably relied on written assurances that all was in order and the persons who acted on behalf of the corporation had apparent authority to do so.[47] Whether or not this will be case, however, should always be explored, and particularly before a market participant engages in a swap with an entity from the public sector. As the lawsuit discussed in this section illustrates, the consequences for a market participant can be exceedingly grave if its public-sector counterparty enters into a swap that is beyond its powers—*ultra vires*—or fails to obtain all the necessary authorizations.

The London Borough of Hammersmith and Fulham (the "Borough") began entering into interest rate swap agreements in December 1983.[48]

---

[46] For a discussion of these issues as they relate to municipalities in the United States, *see* McGavin, "Interest Rate Swaps in the Municipal Markets," *Swaps and Other Derivatives in 1992*, 267, 274–81 (Practising Law Institute 1992). For a discussion of the situation in France, *see* Boulat & Chabert, *Les Swaps* 194 (Masson 1992).

[47] This approach is also taken in the "safe harbor" for qualified financial contracts (including swaps and related derivatives) on which a market participant may seek to base a claim in connection with the receivership or conservatorship of a federally-insured depository institution in the United States. *See* note 13 *supra*.

[48] Two swap transactions were entered into on behalf of the Borough in its 1983–84 financial year; two were entered into in the following financial year; three were entered into in

Virtually all of the Borough's funding consisted of borrowings bearing interest at a fixed rate, and the Borough's early swaps appear to have consisted of transactions in which the Borough agreed to make swap payments at a floating rate and to receive payments at a fixed rate, so the transactions had the effect of converting the interest rate on a portion of the Borough's debt to a floating rate.[49]

Beginning in April 1987, the volume of the Borough's derivatives transactions increased, as did the variety of types of transactions entered into.[50] At some point during this period, the Borough began to enter into matched pairs of swaps as an intermediary; it also appears that the Borough began to lock in its profits on certain earlier swap transactions by entering into "reverse" swaps under which it agreed to make payments at a fixed rate and to receive floating-rate payments.[51]

The Borough was not the only English local authority to use swaps and related derivatives during this period, though it seems to have been the largest user. The House of Lords decision in the case stated (using the term "swap transactions" to refer generically to derivatives transactions and referring to the Borough's Council as "the council") that: "[f]rom investigations made by the auditor it appears that 77 local authorities entered into about 400 swap transactions, nearly all between 1987 and 1989. Only 10 local authorities (other than the council) entered into more than 10 swaps and only 18 (other than the council) entered into more than five. By 31 March 1989 the council had entered into 592 swap transactions and 297 of those were still outstanding."[52] There is ample evidence that the use of derivative products by local authorities was widely known; it was referred to in publications of the Audit Commission of Local Authorities in England and Wales (the "Audit Commission") and the Bank of England.[53]

In the course of an audit of the accounts of the Borough for its

---

1985–86; and seventeen were entered into in 1986–87. *Hazell*, [1990] 2 W.L.R. 17, 25, [1992] Q.B. 697, 710 (Div'l Ct. 1989). Most of the agreements were expressed to be made with the "London Borough of Hammersmith and Fulham"; others were stated to be with the Borough's Council. *Hazell*, [1990] 2 W.L.R. 1038, 1062, [1992] Q.B. 697, 778–79 (C.A. 1990).

[49] *Hazell*, [1990] 2 W.L.R. 17, 24, [1992] Q.B. 697, 710 (Div'l Ct. 1989). Although the opinion is not entirely clear on this point, there is a suggestion that at least some of the swaps were "parallel contracts" that were matched with particular borrowings of the Borough. *See* [1990] 2 W.L.R. at 34, [1992] Q.B. at 721.

[50] [1990] 2 W.L.R. 17, 25, [1992] Q.B. 697, 710 (Div'l Ct. 1989). The Borough also entered into interest rate caps, floors and collars, options on swaps, forward rate agreements and gilt and cash options. *Hazell*, [1990] 2 W.L.R. 17, 22, 52–53, [1992] Q.B. 697, 708, 742–43 (Div'l Ct. 1989).

[51] *Hazell*, [1990] 2 W.L.R. 17, 54, [1992] Q.B. 697, 742 (Div'l Ct. 1989).

[52] *Hazell*, [1992] 2 A.C. 1, _, H.L. (E.), [1991] All E.R. 545, 552, [1991] 2 W.L.R. 372, 380–81 (H.L. 1991).

[53] *Hazell*, [1990] 2 W.L.R. 1038, 1051–52, [1992] Q.B. 697, 767 (C.A. 1990).

1987–88 financial year, the auditor became aware of the derivatives transactions that the Borough had entered into. In July 1988 the auditor received copies of somewhat conflicting legal opinions that had been received by the Audit Commission on the legality of transactions of the kind that had been entered into on behalf of the Borough. Leading counsel was of the view that these transactions were unlawful except when they consisted of "parallel" swaps that were closely tied to borrowings; junior counsel was of the view that all of these derivatives transactions were unlawful.[54] The auditor advised the Borough of the legal advice that had been received and sought confirmation that the Borough would not enter into any further derivatives transactions other than that would be lawful in the opinion of leading counsel. The Borough's Director of Finance agreed in July 1987 to cease entering into derivatives transactions on behalf of the Borough except as necessary to manage the existing portfolio and to avoid losses to the Borough—the so-called "Interim Strategy."[55]

In October 1988, the Borough's Council consulted legal counsel for the first time[56] regarding the legality of these derivatives transactions and, in December, was advised that the transactions were lawful if they were undertaken "as part of the proper management of the council's fund . . . so long as all relevant market factors are taken into account" but not if the Council was "carrying on a business of interest rate swaps."[57] The auditor took the position at a meeting with the Director of Finance in February 1989 that the Borough should not engage in further derivatives transactions except when they were supported by favorable legal opinions. On the same day, the Council's legal adviser rendered a further opinion to the effect that "looking at the totality of the transactions it is not possible to say that these transactions were part and parcel of debt management so as to be lawful."[58] The Council then decided to suspend all payments on its derivatives transactions, absent approval of the transactions by the Secretary of State for the Environment or a favorable court decision on the legality of the transactions.[59]

Until February 1988, no report was made by the Borough's officers to the members of its Council regarding these derivatives transactions, which were not authorized by the Council or its committees or sub-committees.[60] At that time, a report to the Borough's Finance Administration Sub-Committee stated that "[t]he director of finance has also continued to arrange where applicable, transactions in the London Money/Capital

---

[54] *Hazell,* [1990] 2 W.L.R. 17, 25, [1992] Q.B. 697, 711 (Div'l Ct. 1989).
[55] *Hazell,* [1990] 2 W.L.R. 17, 25, 26, [1992] Q.B. 697, 711, 712 (Div'l Ct. 1989).
[56] *Hazell,* [1990] 2 W.L.R. 17, 27, [1992] Q.B. 697, 712 (Queen's Bench Division 1989).
[57] Opinion of council quoted at *Hazell,* [1990] 2 W.L.R. 17, 27, [1992] Q.B. 697, 713, (Div'l Ct. 1989).
[58] *Ibid.*
[59] *Hazell,* [1990] 2 W.L.R. 17, 28 [1992] Q.B. 697, 713 (Div'l Ct. 1989).
[60] *Hazell,* [1990] 2 W.L.R. 17, 24, [1992] Q.B. 697, 709 (Div'l Ct. 1989).

Markets in order to maximise gains on favourable interest rate movements."[61] The Council authorized the Director of Finance to arrange such transactions.[62] A similar report was made in February 1989, and the Council took similar action.[63] The auditor took the position (according to the Divisional Court, "with obvious justification") that "the information as supplied to the Council, its committees and sub-committees in the reports in 1988 and 1989 was . . . inadequate to enable members of them to consider properly the legality, reasonableness and prudence of the activities in the London Money/Capital Market."[64]

The auditor applied to the Divisional Court in May 1989 for a declaration that the Borough's derivatives transactions in its 1987–88 and 1988–89 financial years were "contrary to law." Several banks that had been parties to derivatives transactions with the Borough applied to be joined as respondents in the proceedings, and their applications were granted.[65] The court decided, after an extensive examination of the relevant statutes and precedents, that none of the derivatives transactions entered into on behalf of the Borough and in effect during those financial years "are capable of being lawfully entered into by the council." The court held (i) that the Borough should be regarded as a statutory corporation with limited powers rather than a chartered corporation with the same power to enter into contracts as a natural person,[66] and (ii) that the transactions under review were not within the Borough's statutory powers.[67]

The Divisional Court went on to express its views on certain other issues presented by the case, noting that this was not "strictly speaking" necessary, but stating that it wished to do so for the purpose of "assisting the parties and superior courts if this case goes to appeal."[68] The more important of those views may be summarized as follows: (1) Even if the derivatives transactions were lawful, they were not properly authorized by the Borough's Council.[69] (2) With respect to the Borough's early swaps (December 1983 to March 1987) the Borough's derivatives activities were not such as to enable the court to hold that the Borough was not engaged in interest risk management.[70] (3) At some point around April 1987, "[t]he

---

[61] *Hazell*, [1990] 2 W.L.R. 17, 26, [1992] Q.B. 697, 712 (Div'l Ct. 1989).
[62] *Ibid.*
[63] *Hazell*, [1990] 2 W.L.R. 17, 28, [1992] Q.B. 697, 714 (Div'l Ct. 1989).
[64] *Ibid.*
[65] *Hazell*, [1990] 2 W.L.R. 17, 22, 46, [1992] Q.B. 697, 707, 733–34 (Div'l Ct. 1989).
[66] *Hazell*, 2 W.L.R. 17, 30–34, [1992] Q.B. 697, 716–721 (Div'l Ct. 1989).
[67] *Hazell*, [1990] 2 W.L.R. at 34–39, [1992] Q.B. at 721–26 (Div'l Ct. 1989).
[68] *Hazell*, [1990] 2 W.L.R. 17, 39, [1992] Q.B. 697, 726 (Div'l Ct. 1989).
[69] *Hazell*, [1990] 2 W.L.R. 17, 38–41, [1992] Q.B. 697, 726–28 (Div'l Ct. 1989). The Divisional Court also considered the possible impact on its conclusions of the purported establishment of a "capital market fund" for the Borough and concluded that "no capital market fund was ever validly established." [1990] 2 W.L.R. at 42, [1992] Q.B. at 729.
[70] *Hazell*, [1990] 2 W.L.R. 17, 44, [1992] Q.B. 697, 731 (Div'l Ct. 1989).

scale and range of transactions makes it clear that the council was not engaged in interest risk management but engaged in a trade designed to exploit the market in these transactions with a view to profit."[71] (4) Regarding the period of the "Interim Strategy":

> the evidence . . . indicates that the council was seeking to re-
> duce its exposure as a result of its earlier activities which it by
> that time appreciated were arguably beyond its powers. If trans-
> actions which were undertaken as part of interest risk manage-
> ment were capable of being within the powers of the Act, then in
> our view so must activities which the council undertook with a
> view to minimising the risks to which the council was exposed by
> earlier transactions.[72]

(5) "Where the council was acting as an intermediary and merely entering into swaps with a view to obtaining a 'turn,' for example to assist another council which was rate capped or whose credit standing was not as
high as that of the council, then in our view the transactions are self-evi-
dently nothing to do with interest rate management."[73] (6) When the Borough *sold* swap options, gilt options, cash options and interest rate caps,
floors and collars, it was not engaged in interest rate management.[74] (7)
Swaps, forward rate agreements, and purchases of swap options and interest rate caps and floors are capable of being used for interest rate management.[75] The Divisional Court's decision does not deal, as such, with
the question of the enforceability against the Borough of individual derivatives transactions or the rights of the Borough or its counterparties to
restitution of amounts paid in connection with the transactions that were
held to be outside the powers of the Borough. Hearing on those issues

---

[71] *Hazell*, [1990] 2 W.L.R. 17, 44, [1992] Q.B. 697, 731 (Div'l Ct. 1989). The Divisional Court
stated that it could not identify precisely when the Borough began to engage in trade
rather than interest risk management beyond finding that it was "towards the beginning
of this period," and that further evidence would be required to establish the exact date.

[72] *Hazell*, [1990] 2 W.L.R. 17, 44, [1992] Q.B. 697, 731–32 (Div'l Ct. 1989).

[73] *Hazell*, [1990] 2 W.L.R. 17, 45, [1992] Q.B. 697, 732 (Div'l Ct. 1989).

[74] *Hazell*, [1990] 2 W.L.R. 17, 45, [1992] Q.B. 697, 732–33 (Div'l Ct. 1989). The Divisional
Court noted that these transactions could be linked to interest risk management, but
stated that "we do not regard the link as being sufficiently close." The argument for link-
age could go along the following lines: An entity with extensive ability to borrow at fixed
rates might prudently decide to include a portion of floating rate debt in the mix to protect itself against a fall in rate levels. In some circumstances it would be cheaper to accomplish this by entering into a swap rather than an actual floating rate borrowing. If rates
then fell, the swap would become an asset of the entity. At some point it might be prudent to cash in some or all of that value, for example, by accepting a cash payment from
the counterparty to cancel the swap or by entering into a reverse swap. It might be, however, that the entity could maximize its gain from cashing in on the swap with some less
direct approach, such as selling an option on the reverse swap or entering into some combination of cap, floor and collar transactions or cash and gilt option transactions.

[75] *Hazell*, [1990] 2 W.L.R. 17, 45–46, [1992] Q.B. 697, 733 (Div'l Ct. 1989).

was ordered to be deferred, though the Court of Appeal stated that "[a]ll parties before us accepted that . . . [the Divisional Court's decision], if correct, renders unenforceable any outstanding claim by the banks . . . against the council and must . . . preclude successful claims on similar facts by any other bank against the council or by any bank against any other local authority."[76]

The banks that had been granted leave to join the proceedings as respondents appealed the decision to the Court of Appeal; the Borough's auditor and its Council contended that the decision of the Divisional Court should be affirmed.[77] The Court of Appeal reversed the Divisional Court on the fundamental lawfulness of derivatives transactions entered into by local authorities, holding that they may lawfully "enter into swap transactions as part of interest rate risk management" in certain circumstances,[78] and stated that its conclusion applied to "all the categories of swap transactions which have featured in these proceedings."[79] The court then turned to the "question of where precisely the boundary line is drawn between interest rate risk management, which is permissible, and trading, which is not,"[80] and found that all the Borough's derivatives transactions during the 1983–87 period (that is, the first period during which the Borough engaged only in swap transactions, and the second, in which the range of its transactions broadened considerably) consisted of trading and not interest rate risk management, basing itself on a finding that "there was, in short, no attempt to match the council's actual debts and investments, either singly or in the aggregate, with any of these transactions."[81] With respect to the period of the "Interim Strategy," during which the Borough's transactions were limited to those necessary to man-

---

[76] *Hazell*, [1990] 2 W.L.R. 1038, 1048, [1992] Q.B. 697, 763–64 (C.A. 1990) (*dictum*).

[77] *Hazell*, [1990] 2 W.L.R. 1038, 1044–47, [1992] Q.B. 697, 743–46 (C.A. 1990). The Council also contended that "so much of the decision of the Divisional Court as adjudged that the transactions entered into during the interim strategy period (August 1988 to 23 February 1989) were lawful be reversed on the grounds that all of the transactions entered into by the council were ultra vires as they were not undertaken for the purpose of legitimate debt management and that the transactions undertaken during the interim management period were themselves ultra vires and did not become intra vires because they were undertaken in an attempt to mitigate previous ultra vires transactions." *Hazell*, [1990] 2 W.L.R. 1038, 1047, [1992] Q.B. 697, 746 (C.A. 1990).

[78] *Hazell*, [1990] 2 W.L.R. 1038, 1067, [1992] Q.B. 697, 784 (C.A. 1990).

[79] *Hazell*, [1990] 2 W.L.R. 1038, 1071, [1992] Q.B. 697, 788 (C.A. 1990). The court expressly reversed on sales of swap options, gilt options, cash options and interest rate caps, floors and collars, saying: "There may be circumstances in which a local authority is entitled, by way of interest rate risk management, to *buy* a swap option, or a gilt option, or a cash option or interest rate caps and floors and collars. If that is so, it must follow there may be circumstances in which a local authority is entitled to *sell* such options, if only by way of a 'mirror' transaction should an option which has been bought be found later to be unwanted." [1990] 2 W.L.R. at 1071, [1992] Q.B. at 788.

[80] *Ibid.*

[81] *Hazell*, [1990] 2 W.L.R. 1038, 1073, [1992] Q.B. 697, 790–91 (C.A. 1990).

age its existing portfolio, the Court of Appeal held that the auditor was not entitled to a declaration that the Borough's derivatives transactions were unlawful.[82] On the issue of authorization of the Council's officers, the court stated that a council meeting should have been called to authorize the steps that were taken during the period, but that it would not invalidate the transactions on the basis of the failure to call such a meeting since the court found it probable that the steps would have been authorized had the meeting been called.[83] The Court of Appeal affirmed the decision of the Divisional Court to the effect that, where the Borough was acting as an intermediary between two other parties, the transactions constituted impermissible trading and not lawful interest rate risk management.[84] Finally, the court noted that "[t]he question whether any outstanding contract is enforceable as between the council and any other party is not before us and we express no opinion upon it."[85]

The Borough's auditor, and its Council, entered an appeal to the House of Lords. The bank parties appear to have conceded on appeal that the Borough's swaps entered into before July 25, 1988 were outside its powers,[86] so the decision of the House of Lords focused on the period of the "Interim Strategy." The Law Lords held "that a local authority has no power to enter into a swap transaction,"[87] thus reinstating the decision of the Divisional Court. The Law Lords found (i) that there was no express authority for local authorities to enter into swap transactions and (ii) that entering into such transactions was not "calculated to facilitate," "conducive to" or "incidental to" the borrowing function of local authorities; accordingly, there was no reason to treat transactions entered into pursuant to the Borough's Interim Strategy any differently from those entered into during the preceding years: "Since I have concluded that a local authority has no power to enter into swap transactions, it must follow that a swap transaction entered into pursuant to the interim strategy was also unlawful. . . . No authority was cited which suggested that in certain circumstances an ultra vires transaction could be remedied by another ultra vires transaction, possibly with different parties."[88] Like the courts below, the House of Lords left unanswered the question of the effect of its

---

[82] *Hazell*, [1990] 2 W.L.R. 1038, 1077, [1992] Q.B. 697, 794 (C.A. 1990).

[83] *Hazell*, [1990] 2 W.L.R. 1038, 1082, [1992] Q.B. 697, 800 (C.A. 1990).

[84] *Hazell*, [1990] 2 W.L.R. 1038, 1070–71, [1992] Q.B. 697, 787–88 (C.A. 1990).

[85] *Hazell*, [1990] 2 W.L.R. 1038, 1083, [1992] Q.B. 697, 801 (C.A. 1990).

[86] Reporter's notes, *Hazell*, [1991] All E.R. 545 (H.L. 1991); *see Hazell*, [1992] 2 A.C. 1, _, H.L. (E.), [1991] All E.R. 545, 549, [1991] 2 W.L.R. 372, 377 (H.L. 1991).

[87] *Hazell*, [1992] 2 A.C. 1, _, H.L. (E.), [1991] All E.R. 545, 561, [1991] 2 W.L.R. 372, 390 (H.L. 1991).

[88] *Hazell*, [1992] 2 A.C. 1, _, H.L. (E.), [1991] All E.R. 545, 561, [1991] 2 W.L.R. 372, 391 (H.L. 1991) (Lord Templeman, J.).

decision on individual derivatives transactions that had been entered into with the Borough.[89]

Press reports indicate that numerous proceedings have been begun against British local authorities by their swap counterparties seeking to obtain repayment of amounts paid to the authorities on derivatives transactions.[90] Those reports also suggest that the cases are being settled at a rapid clip.[91]

The morals to be drawn from the Hammersmith and Fulham situation are not hard to find. Standard practice in documentation for swaps and related derivatives (sometimes relaxed for transactions between established dealers) has always required that each party to an agreement deliver to the other evidence of the steps taken by the party to authorize its execution and delivery of the agreement and any confirmations thereunder, together with incumbency and specimen signature certificates for the persons signing the documentation on its behalf. Legal opinions, though often dispensed with in transactions between dealers, should be required in most cases of transactions with end-users, especially if the counterparty (i) is organized in a jurisdiction other than one of the leading financial jurisdictions, (ii) operates in a regulated industry or (iii) is a public-sector or supranational entity. Legal opinions of inside counsel are normally accepted, particularly if they are negotiated with experienced counsel who can probe the contents of the opinion to be sure that the special concerns that arise in the area have been given informed attention.[92]

In contemplating swaps and related derivatives transactions with end-users of the kinds referred to above, a discussion of these concerns and of the contents of the legal opinion being requested may be the best place to start, because it may not be prudent to enter into the transaction if the end-user or its counsel cannot furnish adequate assurance of the power and authority of the end-user to enter into transactions of the kind. If the

---

[89] *Hazell,* [1992] 2 A.C. 1, _, H.L. (E.), [1991] All E.R. 545, 561, [1991] 2 W.L.R. 372, 390 (H.L. 1991). The decision is said to have caused "consternation" in the City of London. A Legal Risk Review Committee established to "find a permanent way to tackle the legal uncertainties of the wholesale market, including better communications between City institutions and the government," is reportedly seeking market reactions to various proposals, including the establishment of a special Financial Law Panel to work on standard documentation and the like and a Financial Law Liaison Group to conduct studies and propose remedial legislation from time to time. The Committee's proposals include abolition of the *ultra vires* doctrine. "Less Risk, More Cover," *The Times,* July 21, 1992.

[90] *See, e.g.,* "UK swap deals to be settled in court," *The Financial Times,* May 8, 1991.

[91] The High Court judge charged with about 200 outstanding actions between swap dealers and local authorities initially selected six representative "lead cases" to be tried first, but all six were settled out of court; six other lead cases have been selected. "Council rate swap cases resume," *The Financial Times,* June 11, 1992. The same article reported that the hearing date for the first of these cases is set for January 11, 1993.

[92] On closing documents and legal opinions, *see generally* Gooch & Klein, *Swap Documentation* 20–21, 26–27, 168–69; Gooch & Pergam, *supra* note 13, at 34–8 to 34–9.

power and authorization issues cannot be clearly disposed of in a favorable manner, the potential counterparty to a derivatives transaction with such an end-user should explore what the consequences could be if the transaction proved to be *ultra vires* for the end-user or is not properly authorized. Would the law entitle the end-user to deny its liability with respect to the transaction at any time? If so, what relief, if any, might the counterparty obtain—only recovery of payments made by it? Not even that, with any certainty? Under the applicable law, could the end-user be estopped from denying its liability in respect of an *ultra vires* or improperly authorized transaction in some circumstances? If so, what are they, and do they exist in connection with the proposed transaction? In each of these areas, is there a difference between transactions that are *ultra vires* and those that suffer from some irregularity in the authorization process?[93] If satisfactory answers to all these and related questions cannot be obtained, the end-user should be asked to seek a change in the law relating to its powers or to correct any lapse in the authorization process before the transaction is consummated.[94] If this is not possible, or if the end-user is unwilling to attempt it, then the market participant should carefully weigh the wisdom of entering into the transaction in the light of the answers it has obtained about the consequences of entering into an *ultra vires* or improperly authorized transaction with that end-user.[95]

Tauber: Legality of Off-Exchange Transactions in Foreign Currency

In determining whether to engage in business with a particular kind of counterparty, or with counterparties generally in a particular jurisdiction, the swap market participant must also consider whether the proposed transactions may violate prohibitions against certain kinds of transactions. In many legal systems the analysis may begin with a general principle that private parties should have broad freedom to contract; according to a secondary principle, however, that freedom can be limited to

---

[93] For some general discussion about these and related issues and references to cases in which they have arisen in the United States, *see* 56 Am.Jur.2d (on Municipal Corporations) §§ 523, 526 & 527 (1971).

[94] Discussion of these issues at the earliest possible stage is particularly important if authorization may require further action. For example, if it appears that the transaction would be permissible only if entered into to further a specific goal, it can be critical to establish that the appropriate body—a council, board or committee of authorized decision makers—has, on the basis of characteristics of the transaction described to it, made the necessary finding that the transaction will further that goal. If those decision makers meet before counsel reviews the description of the transaction and the proposed findings, it may be politically or logistically difficult to convene a new meeting to correct any lapse that counsel may perceive.

[95] In some cases purely technical flaws in the authorization process can be corrected after the fact through ratification of the transaction. It is obviously not desirable, however, for either party to have a cloud hanging over the legality of a transaction that has already been consummated.

protect the public against perceived evils or to further public goals, and the limitations may be embodied in criminal or civil statutes that prohibit offending contracts, impose sanctions against the parties to them or render such contracts void or voidable.

Probably every major institution that participates as a professional in the swap and related derivatives market has, over the years, engaged counsel more than once to advise it on the applicable limitations on its freedom to engage in the business and how it can conduct the business with minimal risk that it will run afoul of the limitations. In addition, in entering into an agreement with a counterparty of a new kind, or from a new jurisdiction, professional market participants often require the counterparty to furnish an opinion of counsel addressing the legality of the agreement under the law of the relevant jurisdiction. Unfortunately, however, the limiting rules of the kinds we have described are often drafted in very broad and general terms, so counsel may be unable to reach an unqualified conclusion and, where the law is not clear, there is always some risk that a counterparty may seek to avoid liability under a contract by invoking the limitation.[96]

This is precisely what occurred in *Salomon Forex Inc v. Tauber*,[97] an action commenced in September 1991 to recover close to $26 million in damages, plus interest, for wrongful refusal to pay amounts due in respect of 68 Swiss franc and Australian dollar foreign currency forward and option agreements between the parties. The defendant filed a counterclaim in the action challenging the validity of over 2700 over-the-counter such transactions with the plaintiff, including the 68 on which the plaintiff's claim was based; he did not challenge the validity of his swaps with the plaintiff. To the extent his defenses raised issues that have concerned the swap and derivatives market generally, however, the case and authorities cited by the court in deciding it should be of interest to market participants.[98]

The defendant, described by the court as a surgeon and a major real

---

[96] In some cases another problem is that the applicability of the statute in question may turn on the intent with which a party enters into a transaction. *See* text accompanying notes 122–133 *infra* relating to the gambling and bucket-shop law defenses raised in the *Tauber* case referred to below. The issue of intent may also arise in connection with the power of an entity to enter into transactions. *See, e.g.,* Canby & Pilley, *supra* note 7, at 38–11 to 38–13, on the role of intent in determining whether building societies in the U.K. have the power to enter into derivatives transactions. *See also* note 94 *supra*.

[97] Civ. No. 91–1415–A (E.D. Va. 1992), appeal filed April 3, 1992. Only part of the ruling in the case was set forth in a Memorandum Opinion of the Court. *See* [Current] Comm. Fut. L. Rep. ("CCH") ¶ 25,310 at 39,012, 1992 U.S. Dist. LEXIS 8787 (June 1, 1992).

[98] The following description of the facts is based generally on the court's description of them in its Memorandum Opinion (hereinafter referred to as "Mem. Op."), rejecting defenses and counterclaims based on alleged violations of the Commodity Exchange Act. *See* note 97 *supra*.

estate investor,[99] at the time of the court's decision had also engaged in currency trading involving billions of dollars of foreign currencies since 1981 with at least 14 well known market participants in addition to the plaintiff and used the Telerate service from computer terminals in his home and elsewhere in connection with these trading activities. The defendant also owned a foreign currency trading company, Westwood Options, Inc., "holder of a seat on the Philadelphia Stock Exchange, the nation's largest foreign currency exchange," according to the court. From 1987 to 1991 he was plaintiff's only non-institutional client. The transactions in question in the suit were foreign exchange forwards that matured and foreign currency options that were exercised in July and August of 1991. To secure his obligations under his transactions with the plaintiff, Tauber was required to post collateral or provide letter-of-credit support. His failure to do so at the plaintiff's request during the fall of 1990 led to interim arrangements that were to have continued until August 31, 1991. Despite these arrangements and subsequent written and oral agreements to post additional collateral, the defendant failed to do so. Against this background, and finding itself inadequately secured, Salomon Forex commenced the action when almost $26 million fell due in July and August of that year.

As summarized by the court, Tauber's defenses consisted of "allegations of common law and statutory fraud, violations of state 'bucketing' and gambling laws, negligence, breach of fiduciary duty, duress, failure to mitigate damages, estoppel, waiver, statute of frauds violations, breach of an implied covenant of good faith and fair dealing, breach of an express warranty of 'best pricing,' and breach of a duty to disclose material information relating to purported market manipulation,"[100] as well as an argument that the transactions were void or voidable as off-exchange foreign currency futures and options entered into in violation of Section 4(a) and Section 4c(b) of the Commodity Exchange Act (the "CEA").[101] All of the defenses, as well as the multiple counts of a counterclaim based on the same theories and the issue of damages, were disposed of on summary judgment in favor of the plaintiff ordered on May 24, 1992. The following discussion is limited to the broad-based challenges to the legality and enforceability of the transactions through defenses based on the CEA and state bucket-shop and gambling laws.[102] Since the court's reasoning on

---

[99] At the time the court wrote the Memorandum Opinion referred to above, Tauber's real estate interests included a 75% share in Laszlo N. Tauber & Associates, described by the court as one of the federal government's largest private landlords. Mem. Op. n. 3, [Current] Comm. Fut. L. Rep. ("CCH") ¶ 25,310 at n. 3.

[100] Mem. Op. n. 2, [Current] Comm. Fut. L. Rep. ("CCH") ¶ 25,310 at 39,013 n. 2.

[101] 7 U.S.C. §§ 1 *et seq.* (1980 & Supp. 1992).

[102] As noted above, the court's treatment of the statute-of-frauds defense was based on a finding that the requirements of the applicable statute, Section 2-201(1) of the UCC, had

the state-law defenses and related counterclaims was stated from the bench and not described in an opinion, the discussion here of those defenses and counterclaims is based on the transcript of the proceedings available in the record; the discussion of the court's reasoning with respect to the CEA defenses and counterclaims is, however, based on its Memorandum Opinion of June 1, 1992.

The Commodity Exchange Act Defenses. The first of the defenses that broadly challenged the legality of the foreign currency forward and option transactions was based on the Commodity Exchange Act; Tauber asked the court to find that the transactions were void or voidable and subject to rescission by Tauber, as futures and options entered into in violation of Sections 4(a) and 4c(b) of the CEA.[103] Section 4(a), among other things, makes it unlawful for any person to enter into "a contract for the purchase or sale of a commodity for future delivery" unless the transaction is conducted on or subject to the rules of a foreign board of trade, exchange or market or on or subject to the rules of a board of trade that has been designated by the Commodity Futures Trading Commission (the "CFTC") as a "contract market" for that commodity.[104] Section 4c(b), as implemented through CFTC regulations, has the same substantive effect as applied to "any transaction involving any commodity regulated under [the CEA] . . . which is of the character of, or is commonly known to the trade as, an option. . . ."[105] The court disposed of both defenses by finding that the transactions in question were expressly

been satisfied: Tauber himself had signed the confirmations sent by the plaintiff for most of the transactions, and he failed to object in writing to the remainder within the prescribed period of 10 days allowed to "merchants" under that provision. *See* note 24 *supra.* Other claims of Tauber failed because they could only be established by extrinsic evidence that would contradict or vary the terms of the confirmations, which were found to express the parties' final agreement, and the parol evidence rule of UCC § 2–202 was held by the court to preclude the introduction of such evidence. *See* note 38 *supra* and the accompanying discussion of UCC § 2–202. Briefly stated, the claims of duress, common-law fraud, negligence, breach of fiduciary duty, and implied covenant of good faith were all rejected as without basis in the facts, since there was no evidence that Salomon Forex owed any special duty to Tauber that could be characterized as fiduciary or that its conduct involved duress, fraud, negligence or bad faith of any sort. The defenses of estoppel and waiver could not stand once the court rejected any theory of wrongful conduct by the plaintiff, since the theory of the defenses was that Salomon Forex should be estopped from making, and deemed to have waived, any claim by virtue of its own wrongful conduct in its dealings with Tauber.

[103] Tauber's counterclaim also included counts in which he sought damages in an amount to be determined at trial, but estimated to exceed $20 million, as a result of Salomon Forex's having entered into the allegedly illegal transactions. Answer to amended complaint, filed December 9, 1991, ¶¶ 56 & 62. Tauber's defenses based on statutory fraud and related counterclaims also depended on a finding that the relevant transactions violated anti-fraud provisions of the CEA and regulations thereunder. *Id.,* ¶¶ 63–77.

[104] 7 U.S.C. § 6(a) (1980). The provision also imposes certain other requirements for futures transactions conducted on a regulated exchange in the United States.

[105] 7 U.S.C. §§ 6c(b) & 6c(d) (1980).

removed from the reach of the CEA through the so-called "Treasury Amendment," embodied in Section 2 of the CEA.[106]So named because it was adopted after lobbying by the U.S. Treasury Department, the relevant part of Section 2 provides in relevant part: "Nothing in this Act shall be deemed to govern or in any way be applicable to transactions in foreign currency . . . , unless such transactions involve the sale thereof for future delivery conducted on a board of trade."[107] The court therefore did not analyze whether the transactions were, as argued by plaintiff, also exempt under other provisions of the CEA and regulations thereunder.[108]

In reaching its conclusion, the court rejected the defendant's argument that, whatever the apparent breadth of the words of the Treasury Amendment, the Congressional intent was that the exemption should apply only to transactions in foreign currency between financial institutions. In support of his position, Tauber cited both portions of the legislative history and a statutory interpretation of the CFTC, which similarly suggests that the Treasury Amendment is limited in its application to interbank trading of currencies regulated by the banking agencies.[109] The court reached its conclusion first by applying a well-established principle of statutory interpretation to the effect that "legislative history may not be invoked to create an ambiguity where none otherwise exists,"[110] and, second, by finding that, even if resort to legislative history had been appropriate in the circumstances, nothing in it indicated to the court a congressional intent to exempt only the interbank market in currency transactions and, indeed, portions suggested that a broader exemption was intended.[111] The court also found "[e]specially instructive" *Bank Brussels Lambert, S.A. v. Intermetals Corp.,*[112] a recent case in which the federal District Court for the Southern District of New York reached the same result in holding that the Treasury Amendment is not limited to the inter-

---

[106] 7 U.S.C. § 2 (1980 & Supp. 1992).

[107] *Ibid.*

[108] These other exclusions are discussed below in the text accompanying notes 115–120. The court noted in *dictum* that the disposition of the defenses and claims based on those exclusions would have required the resolution of disputed material issues of fact and, therefore, would have precluded summary judgment. Mem. Op., n. 8, [Current] Comm. Fut. L. Rep. ("CCH") ¶ 25,310 at 39,015 n. 8.

[109] Mem. Op. notes 14 & 15 and accompanying text, [Current] Comm. Fut. L. Rep. ("CCH") ¶ 25,310 at 39,016–17. For an expression of the CFTC's view of the limited application of the Treasury Amendment, *see* CFTC, Statutory Interpretation on Trading in Foreign Currencies for Future Delivery, 50 Fed. Reg. 42,983, 42,985 (Oct. 23, 1985). The Statutory Interpretation was issued in response to off-exchange foreign currency futures contracts offered to the general public and intended to make clear that they fell outside the Treasury Amendment. *Id.* at 42,985.

[110] [Current] Comm. Fut. L. Rep. ("CCH") ¶ 25,310 at 39,016, citing *Railroad Comm'n of Wisconsin v. Chicago, Burlington and Quincy R.R.,* 257 U.S. 563, 589 (1922) and other authority.

[111] *Ibid.*

[112] 779 F.Supp. 741 (S.D.N.Y. 1991).

bank market in spot trades of foreign currency, "In so doing, the court concluded that 'even if it is correct that Congress' *motivation* . . . was to exempt interbank trading . . . statutory history of this nature cannot be a substitute for express terms of the statute' (emphasis in the original)."[113]

The finding of the District Court, which has been appealed by Tauber to the Fourth Circuit Court of Appeals,[114] is of interest to the swap market because, although the *Tauber* case related only to foreign exchange forward transactions and exercised currency options, the analytical underpinnings of the decision would seem equally applicable in an action involving an attempt to avoid liability on a currency swap on the theory that the swap constituted an illegal off-exchange futures contract. Because the court disposed of Tauber's defenses by finding the relevant transactions to be transactions in foreign currency exempt from the CEA's bans on off-exchange commodity futures and options, the court did not address the parties' arguments on the applicability of two other exclusions from those prohibitions—the forward contract exclusion[115] and the so-called "trade option exemption"[116]—that were cited by Salomon Forex in support of its position that the forward currency exchange transactions and the currency options, respectively, were outside the reach of the CEA. A discussion by the court of the merits of the par-

---

[113] Mem. Op. [Current] Comm. Fut. L. Rep. ("CCH") ¶ 25,310 at 39,016–17, quoting from *Bank Brussels Lambert, S.A. v. Intermetals Corp.*, 779 F.Supp. 741, 751 (S.D.N.Y. 1991). The court also rejected Tauber's argument that the Treasury Amendment is inapplicable to the foreign currency options involved in the case because options are not "transactions *in* foreign currency," within the requirements of the Treasury Amendment, but, rather, transactions *in* rights to exercise options that merely "involve" foreign currency. Noting in *dictum* that it thought the distinction lacked real substance, the court disposed of this argument on the basis of the fact that all the relevant options had already been exercised and, "[u]nder the exercised options, the parties had the obligation and capacity to deliver or accept delivery of the specified foreign currency at the set prices on the fixed dates," so the exercised options became transactions *in* foreign currency. Mem. Op. [Current] Comm. Fut. L. Rep. ("CCH") ¶ 25,310 at 39,017, citing, *inter alia, Board of Trade of City of Chicago v. S.E.C.*, 677 F.2d 1137, 1154 (7th Cir.), *vacated as moot*, 459 U.S. 1026 (1982).

[114] The appeal was filed on April 3, 1992.

[115] Under the forward contract exclusion, "any sale of any cash commodity for deferred shipment or delivery" is expressly stated to be outside the CEA's ban on off-exchange futures contracts. 7 U.S.C. § 2 (1980 & Supp. 1992).

[116] Under the "trade option exemption" certain over-the-counter commodity options are permitted if the party offering the option "has a reasonable basis to believe that the option is offered to a producer, processor, or a commercial user of, or a merchant handling, the commodity which is the subject of the commodity option transaction, or the products or by-products thereof, and that such producer, processor, commercial user or merchant is offered or enters into the . . . transaction solely for purposes related to its business as such." CFTC Regulation 32.4, 17 C.R.F. § 32.4(a) (1992). Certain restrictions on the applicability of the trade option exemption (*e.g.,* its inapplicability to agricultural commodities) would be eliminated by proposed amendments to Part 32 of the CFTC's Regulations. *See* 56 Fed. Reg. 43,560 (Sept. 3, 1991) (noting, at 43,563 n. 39, that this limitation does not apply to swaps).

ties' arguments on those exclusions[117] would have been of interest to the
derivatives market because both are viewed by the market and the CFTC
to be applicable to at least some swaps, in the case of the forward contract
exclusion, and some caps and floors, in the case of the trade option exemption.[118]

Although the CFTC has given market participants assurance that it
will not treat certain kinds of swaps and related derivatives as illegal, off-

---

[117] Tauber argued that the transactions with the plaintiff did not fall within either exclusion
because both apply only to commercial transactions, whereas his transactions with the
plaintiff were purely speculative, as the plaintiff knew, and, in the case of the foreign exchange forwards, because Tauber took delivery of foreign currency under only four, set-
tling the others through offsetting transactions pursuant to a general understanding with
the plaintiff that offset would be the normal procedure. Laszlo N. Tauber, M.D.'s Reply to
Salomon Forex Inc.'s Opposition; and in Support of his Own Motion for Partial Summary
Judgment, at 4–8; Laszlo N. Tauber, M.D.'s Memorandum in Support of Motion for Partial Summary Judgment, at 36–37. To support its position that both exclusions applied,
the plaintiff pointed the court to evidence supporting the commercial motivation behind
the transactions with Tauber (including Tauber's own admissions that his currency trading activities were not speculative) and to the modern and still evolving view that the forward contract exclusion does not require actual, physical delivery of the relevant commodity in all cases, as well as case law supporting the position that offset constitutes
delivery. Plaintiff's Mem. at 12–15. Among the sources cited was the CFTC's Statutory Interpretation Concerning Forward Transactions, 55 Fed. Reg. 39,188 (Sept. 25, 1990), in
which the CFTC stated that the forward contract exclusion is applicable to certain private,
individually negotiated commercial transactions in Brent crude oil entered into by the
parties in connection with their business, where the parties are capable of accepting delivery of the relevant commodity, even if they forego delivery through individually negotiated "book-outs" involving cash payments. In the contracts examined by the CFTC in issuing the interpretation, the parties were not required by their contracts to enter into such
offsetting and cash settlement terminations. Id. at 39,190–92. The Statutory Interpretation was adopted by the CFTC in response to the market's concern over Transnor
(Bermuda) Ltd. v. BP North America Petroleum, 738 F. Supp. 1472 (S.D.N.Y. 1990), a case in
which certain Brent crude oil contracts, always thought of as within the forward contract
exclusion, were treated by the court as futures contracts. For a summary of the evolution
of the CFTC's position on the issue of delivery under the forward contract exclusion and
its relation to the Transnor case, see Raisler & Morgen, "Legal Aspects of Commodity
Derivatives," in Swaps and Other Derivatives in 1992, 235–37 (Practising Law Institute
1992).

[118] In 1989 the CFTC adopted a "Policy Statement Concerning Swap Transactions" establishing a "safe harbor" for certain swaps that it would not seek to treat as illegal, off-exchange
futures. 54 Fed. Reg. 30,694 (July 21, 1989). In so doing the CFTC expressly noted that
the forward contract exclusion "may encompass certain swap transactions" but expressed
its belief that the safe harbor was required because the forward contract and other exclusions established by the CEA and regulations thereunder "are not sufficiently broad to
provide clear exemptive boundaries for many swaps." Id. at 30,696. For example, some of
the exemptive criteria seem inapposite to certain kinds of swaps, such as the delivery requirement for the forward contract exclusion (see note 117 supra), in the case of rate
swaps. Many of the swap safe-harbor requirements are based on the established criteria
for excluded forward contracts. For a summary of the safe harbor, see Cunningham,
Rogers & Bilicic, "Interest Rate and Currency Swaps and Related Transactions," in Swaps
and Other Derivatives in 1992, 9, 39 (Practising Law Institute 1992) (transcribing the text of
the Policy Statement as an appendix).

exchange futures,[119] the CFTC's pronouncements on the subject are not binding on the courts and cannot be counted on to preclude attempts by private litigants to seek to avoid liability under their derivatives transactions through defenses like those raised by Tauber.[120] Ultimately, the market may obtain protection from this risk through proposed amendments to the CEA that, as currently contemplated and adopted by the U.S. Senate, would direct the CFTC to exempt over-the-counter swap agreements between most institutional parties from the CEA if the CFTC determines that the exemption is consistent with the public interest and creditworthiness of a party to the swap is a material consideration taken into account by the other party in entering into the transaction or determining its terms, including pricing, cost or credit enhancement terms.[121]

   The Gambling Law Defense. In many jurisdictions there are laws that prohibit unregulated gambling and impose sanctions on its promoters as a means of protecting the general public. Lawyers therefore shudder at the reaction, "Why that's gambling!" or "That's speculation!" when they first explain swaps to an innocent friend. That precisely was Tauber's characterization of his foreign currency forward and option transactions with the plaintiff and, on the theory that they violated the gaming laws of New York and Virginia, Tauber sought to have the court rule that the transactions were void.[122] The New York statute invoked, Section 225.00(2) of the New York Penal Law, provides in relevant part: "A person engages in gambling when he stakes or risks something of value upon the outcome of a contest of chance or a future contingent event not under his control or influence, upon an agreement or understanding that he

---

[119] *See, e.g.,* the CFTC's Policy Statement Concerning Swap Transactions cited in note 118 *supra* and CFTC-OETF Interpretative Letter No. 90–1, Eligibility of "Collar Agreements" for Safe Harbor Treatment Under the CFTC's Policy Statement Concerning Swap Transactions, [1987–1990 Transfer Binder] Comm. Fut. L. Rep. ("CCH") ¶ 24,583 at 36,512 ("CFTC-OETF" Jan. 18, 1990).

[120] *See* Raisler & Morgen, *supra* note 117, at 235–37, for a discussion of two recent cases interpreting the forward contract exclusion and the deference paid to the CFTC's Statutory Interpretation Concerning Forward Contracts in one of them (*In re Bybee*, 945 F.2d 309, 314–15 (9th Cir. 1991)). Whether a court would give a CFTC Policy Statement the same weight it would an official Statutory Interpretation is unclear.

[121] For further details and the text of the proposed legislation, *see* Cunningham, Rogers & Bilicic, *supra* note 118, at 40 & 93. The CFTC does not currently have the power to grant an exemption for swaps from the CEA's ban on off-exchange commodity futures, although it has the power to grant exemptive relief from the ban on off-exchange commodity options.

[122] In *Marsh & McLennan Cos. v. Evans Railcar Leasing Co.,* 87 Civ. 204 (S.D.N.Y. 1987), the defendant initially sought to defend against an action seeking a judgment for overdue payments under an interest rate exchange agreement on the ground that the agreement was "unenforceable and void as illegal" under the Illinois gambling statute, Answer at 4, but that allegation was withdrawn after a pre-motion conference, Affidavit of Mitchell J. Auslander at 3, and the Court granted plaintiff's motion for summary judgment. Judgment dated June 29, 1987.

will receive something of value in the event of a certain outcome."[123] The Virginia statute is less ambiguous in its prohibition of "all contracts and securities whereof the whole or any part of the consideration be money or other valuable thing won, laid, or bet, at any game, horse race, sport or pastime. . . ."[124] Tauber's characterization of the transactions as within the reach of these statutes rested on evidence going to his speculative intention in entering into the transactions. The plaintiff referred to Tauber's use of foreign currency trading in connection with his real estate and other investments and as a business itself, and to Tauber's own admissions that he was not a speculator or gambler while engaged in his currency trading, in order to bring the currency transactions within judge-made exceptions to the gambling statutes: case law in New York has created an exception to that state's gambling statute for contracts between parties who have some genuine interest in the outcome of future events, such as an insurable interest or an investment,[125] and case law in Virginia has treated as presumptively valid, notwithstanding the statute, commodities contracts in connection with which performance is secured with collateral and credit.[126] The court found that the transactions between the plaintiff and the defendant fell within these exceptions.[127]

The Bucket-Shop Law Defense. The Commodity Exchange Act did not preempt the laws in effect in almost half the states in the United States to prohibit certain unregulated over-the-counter transactions in commodi-

---

[123] N.Y. Penal Law § 225.00(2) (McKinney 1989). This provision of the Penal Code sets forth definitions for terms such as "gambling" that are used in related, operative provisions that actually define offenses, such as promoting gambling and knowingly holding gambling records. Tauber did not cite any of those statutes. The unstated basis for his defense must have been one of the provisions of New York's General Obligations Laws that provide that gambling contracts are unlawful and void. *See* N.Y. Gen. Oblig. §§ 5–401 & 5–411 (McKinney 1989). For an analysis of the application of gambling laws to swaps in France, *see* Boulat & Chabert, *Les Swaps* 46–56 (Masson 1991). On the situation in Japan and Canada, *see* Yoshida, "Legal Aspects of Currency and Interest Rate Swaps: Japan," and McKee & Graham, "Regulation of Currency and Interest Rate Transactions in Canada," in *The Handbook of Currency and Interest Rate Risk Management,* Chapters 36 and 39, respectively, at 36–9 and 39–5 (New York Institute of Finance, Schwartz & Smith eds. 1990). On the situation in various other jurisdictions, *see* Brown, "Non-Tax Issues in Cross-Border Transactions," *Interest Rate and Currency Swaps 1987* (Practising Law Institute 1987).

[124] Va. Code § 11–14, cited in Memorandum in Support of Plaintiff's Motion for Summary Judgment (hereinafter referred to as "Plaintiff's Mem.") at 48, n. 49.

[125] *Liss v. Manuel,* 296 N.Y.S.2d 627, 631 (N.Y. Sup. Ct. 1968); *see also O'Farrell v. Martin,* 292 N.Y.S. 581, 584 (N.Y. City Ct. 1936) ("[A] gambling contract generally exists only between parties who have no interest in the subject-matter except as to the possible gain or loss resulting")—both sources cited to the court by the plaintiff.

[126] *See Allen's Ex'x v. Virginia Trust Co.,* 116 Va. 319, 82 S.E. 104, 105–6 (1914). The plaintiff also cited to the court several cases supporting plaintiff's position that forwards and options contracts between commercial parties have never been regarded as wagers, whether they are satisfied through actual delivery of the commodity or offset. Plaintiff's Mem. at 48–49 n. 50.

[127] Transcript of proceedings on March 24, 1992, at 60–61.

ties and securities and the shops set up to engage in them.[128] These laws were adopted to protect the public against unscrupulous practices that involved taking orders for the purchase or sale of commodities or securities without actually effecting the transactions on an exchange or arranging for delivery; the orders were actually, or for all practical purposes, thrown in the "bucket," so the laws are referred to as "bucket-shop" laws.[129] One of Tauber's defenses was based on New York's version, which prohibits making or offering to make contracts for the purchase or sale of commodities or securities upon credit or margin, if the person offers or makes the contract "not intending the actual bona fide receipt or delivery of any such securities or commodities, but intending a settlement of such contract based upon the difference in [the] . . . public market quotation of [prices made on any board of trade or exchange or market upon which such commodities or securities are dealt in] or such prices at which said securities or commodities are, or are asserted to be, bought or sold."[130] As described above, Tauber characterized his intent to be purely speculative in his transactions with Salomon Forex and argued that, although he took delivery of foreign currency to settle four of the contracts, all the others were settled, and the parties always intended they be settled, without actual delivery.[131] The plaintiff argued that the statute did not give rise to a private cause of action and that the transactions were bona fide commercial transactions of the kind excluded from the statute, since the statute's requirement as to intent with respect to delivery was satisfied even when actual delivery of currency was not made, because the offsetting of transactions, like that used to settle most of the transactions with Tauber, is recognized as a valid means of making delivery.[132] The court rejected the defense merely by stating that it believed there was no violation of the New York statute.[133] If the subject is explored on appeal, its treatment will be of interest to the swap market, which has been concerned that a swap counterparty might some day seek to avoid its obligations by invoking a bucket-shop law.

Whatever the outcome on appeal, the mere fact that the *Tauber* case could have been brought is a valuable lesson for market participants.

---

[128] *See* 7 U.S.C. § 16(e) (Supp. 1991). For discussion of these laws and the interplay between them and the Commodity Exchange Act, *see* Taylor, "Swaps: Commodities Laws in Transition" and Russo, Mitchell & Shainberg, "Federal and State Regulation of Swap Transactions," in *Advanced Swaps and Derivative Financial Products* at 43 & 133, respectively (Practising Law Institute 1991).

[129] *See* Taylor, *supra* note 128, at 55.

[130] N.Y. Gen. Bus. § 351(3) (McKinney 1988). The statute sets forth other, similar offenses, all of which constitute felonies.

[131] *See* note 117 *supra.*

[132] Plaintiff's Mem. at 46–47 and cases cited in note 48 on page 47.

[133] Transcript of Proceedings on March 24, 1992, at 59.

Some may argue that a case like *Tauber* is unlikely to arise in connection with a swap because the swap market, as a general rule, does not deal with individuals, and companies and other legal entities that use swaps for asset and liability management are unlikely to risk their ability to continue to do business by seeking to avoid liability on a swap. That may be so,[134] and it is certainly the case that all market participants select each counterparty with the expectation that it will never seek to avoid its obligations without good cause. Because the courts are filled, however, with disappointed expectations, *Tauber* is a reminder that swap market participants should continue to be diligent in weighing the legal risks of engaging in transactions with new kinds of counterparties and in new jurisdictions. In particular, in each case the market participant will want to ascertain whether any law embodying the public policy of a relevant jurisdiction might be interpreted to render swaps void or voidable or might otherwise provide a basis for avoidance of liability by a counterparty.[135]

---

[134] Even if the market in general could count on this assumption, it does not necessarily follow that individual market professionals will avoid litigation of other sorts relating to their derivatives transactions with institutional counterparties. A case in point is *Bankatlantic v. Blythe Eastman Paine Webber*, 955 F.2d 1467 (11th Cir. 1992), which involved an action brought by a savings and loan institution which, at the time it commenced the suit, was one of the largest in Florida and the United States, seeking damages for losses in excess of $30 million that the plaintiff claimed it incurred as a result of the defendant's alleged breach of fiduciary duty, fraud, fraudulent concealment, negligence and negligent misrepresentation, in connection with failure to disclose, among other things, the risks involved in interest rate swaps. The claims were decided in favor of the defendant at the trial and appellate levels but the mere fact that they were brought suggests that market participants should take a somewhat closer look at the potential litigation risks involved in their derivatives business with institutional counterparties and the additional steps they may be able to take to reduce those risks. *See* the discussion in the following footnote.

[135] Although the public policy areas discussed in the *Tauber* case are among those most frequently thought of as raising a risk of attempts by counterparties to avoid liability, at least in the United States, there may be other bodies of law that should be examined closely, at least in the context of certain kinds of derivatives. For example, if a market participant proposes to engage in equity-index based transactions of certain kinds, it would undoubtedly want to consider whether the securities laws applicable in its own or its counterparties' jurisdictions might be invoked by the counterparty as a basis for seeking to avoid liability or rescind a transaction. It should also be remembered that both the common law applicable to contracts in general and the statutory frameworks applicable to transactions of certain regulated kinds (such as securities) may afford a party a right to seek rescission if it can prove that it was fradulently induced to enter into the transaction. In light of considerations like these, some participants in the market have recently begun to incorporate into their swap and related agreements provisions specifically crafted to establish that they have made no representations to their counterparties other than those expressly set forth in the agreement and to obtain the acknowledgment of each counterparty that it understands the risks involved in the transactions contemplated in the agreement and has entered into the agreement and transactions under it solely on the basis of its own independent analysis of those risks and such other factors as the counterparty has deemed appropriate. *See* Gooch & Klein, *Loan Documentation* 228–29 (2d ed. Euromoney Publications 1991) on such provisions and the circumstances in which they have been enforced.

Termination of Swap Agreements and Damages—Challenges to the Enforceability of Specific Provisions

The cases described in this section deal with challenges to the enforceability of two of the most important parts of the swap agreement: the provisions on early termination and the provisions on the calculation of damages upon early termination. Because swap and similar agreements, and master agreements covering multiple derivatives transactions, can at any point involve contingent obligations of both parties to make future payments depending on movements in the rates and prices used in the transactions, at any point during the life of the master agreement one or the other of the parties will almost certainly be exposed to the risk that its counterparty may cease to be able to make those payments. The provisions of those agreements on early termination are included to permit management of that risk to some extent; if a party is able to terminate all future scheduled payment obligations under all transactions when it appears that its counterparty may no longer be able to perform, it can effectively "cut its losses"—or avoid any losses at all—that may subsequently arise if rates or prices move so as to increase the magnitude of the future payment obligations the counterparty may miss. Apart from any payments that may already have been missed by the counterparty and interest on those payments, the size of the loss will be quantifiable at the point of early termination on the basis (simply stated) of the cost of replacing the counterparty in the terminated transactions. If the right to terminate contemplated in the agreement, or the selected measure of damages upon early termination, is not enforceable, the whole structure of risk management for the swaps and other transactions is weakened or may fall apart.[136] Thus, the subject matter of the cases described below is of great interest to the derivatives market. The first set of cases relates to early termination rights; the second, to provisions on damages upon early termination. In each of the cases the challenge arose in connection with the insolvency of one of the parties.

Termination Upon Bankruptcy or Insolvency of the Counterparty

In swap documentation, the occurrence of bankruptcy, insolvency or a similar event with respect to a party has usually been treated as an event of default with respect to that party and, moreover, at least until recently,

---

[136] This is not to say that early termination is always the only appropriate route for a non-defaulting party. A non-defaulting party might choose to leave a swap agreement in place and sue for amounts not paid thereunder when due. *See, e.g., Marsh & McLennan Cos. v. Evans Railcar Leasing Co.,* 87 Civ. 204 (S.D.N.Y. 1987).

as an event that led to immediate and automatic termination of that party's swap transactions.[137] There have, however, been serious doubts as to the enforceability of this provision in some jurisdictions, and concerns about the potentially adverse effects that automatic termination could have on a non-defaulting party.[138] In the United States, many of the doubts have now been resolved by legislation.[139]

By way of background, bankruptcy and insolvency laws override certain kinds of contractual agreements of the debtors that become subject to their protection, to insulate the debtors' property from the claims of creditors pending an orderly and equitable disposition of all claims. Under the U.S. Bankruptcy Code, once bankruptcy relief has been applied for, certain kinds of action to enforce claims against the debtor's property are prohibited, under Section 362 of the Bankruptcy Code, through an "automatic stay" unless they have first been approved by a court or other competent authority or an applicable exception to the automatic stay exists.[140] In addition, under Section 365(a) of the Bankruptcy Code, which relates to "executory contracts" with a Bankruptcy Code debtor[141] (generally speaking, agreements that involve unperformed obligations of both parties), the bankruptcy trustee or the "debtor in possession" of its own bankruptcy estate may elect, in certain circumstances, to assume an executory contract and realize upon its value by assigning the debtor's position under the agreement to a third party, notwithstanding a provision in the agreement entitling the other party to terminate the executory contract in connection with the insolvency of the debtor, the commencement

---

[137] The master swap agreements published by ISDA in 1987 provided for automatic early termination upon the occurrence of most insolvency-related events. A somewhat revised list of those events can result in automatic early termination under the 1992 ISDA forms too, but the forms recognize that the parties may wish to opt out of that result, so it only applies if the parties actively elect "Automatic Early Termination."

[138] Automatic early termination may expose the nondefaulting party to significant risks if its claim for damages will be determined as of the time of the automatic termination but it learns of the triggering insolvency event—and therefore is able to enter into a replacement transaction—only later and after an unfavorable movement in rates. *See* Gooch & Klein, *Swap Documentation* 31–32, 92.

[139] The legislation that has removed the doubts relating to the right of early termination in certain circumstances has not relieved the doubts about the potentially adverse effects of automatic termination described in the preceding footnote. However, because the legislation has protected the right to terminate as described in this section, provisions relating to automatic termination with most U.S. counterparties seem to offer no further advantage. Many participants in the market have, therefore, elected to opt out of automatic early termination in their agreements with U.S. counterparties acting domestically so as to avoid the potentially adverse effects automatic termination can have.

[140] Bankruptcy Code § 362(a).

[141] In this discussion the terms "Code debtor" and "Bankruptcy Code debtor" will be used to refer to entities that are eligible to be, or are, the subject of proceedings under the U.S. Bankruptcy Code.

of proceedings under the Bankruptcy Code or similar circumstances.[142] In the alternative, the trustee or debtor in possession may reject the contract and, if it does, the contract will be treated as if it had been breached by the debtor just before the filing of the bankruptcy petition, so the solvent counterparty should be entitled to claim damages.[143] However, those damages may be measured as of the date just before the proceedings are commenced and not the date of the decision to reject, and the Code debtor's counterparty may not know for some time which of the two elections has been made, leaving the solvent party in doubt as to whether and when to treat the executory contract as terminated and cover the resulting open position.[144] Until the adoption in 1990 of amendments to the Bankruptcy Code relating to swaps, the automatic stay and these provisions relating to executory contracts appeared to be an obstacle to the exercise by a swap party of a contractual right to terminate a swap if its counterparty became the subject of proceedings under the Bankruptcy Code.[145] As a result of those 1990 amendments, the automatic stay and the executory contract provisions of Section 365(a) no longer bar the exercise of a contractual right to terminate swaps and other derivatives[146] with most, if not all, Code debtors on the ground of the insolvency or financial condition of the debtor, the commencement of proceedings under the Bankruptcy Code or the appointment of a trustee or custodian in connection with or before the commencement of the proceedings.[147] In addition, under the

---

[142] Bankruptcy Code § 365(a). If the contract is assumed, or assumed and assigned, the counterparty must in certain circumstances be given some assurance that future performance owed to it will be forthcoming. Bankruptcy Code § 365(b)(1).

[143] Bankruptcy Code § 365(a).

[144] See Gooch & Pergam, supra note 13, at 34–14.

[145] In addition, until the 1990 amendments it was not clear that the trustee or debtor in possession would not be allowed to "cherry pick" among the swaps under a master agreement with a debtor, rejecting those of value to its counterparty and assuming, or assuming and assigning, those favorable to the debtor. See note 3 supra. The amendments provide that a master swap agreement with any kind of a Bankruptcy Code debtor as counterparty, including all supplements thereunder relating to swaps, will be treated as a single agreement with the debtor, so the danger of cherry picking has ceased to exist under the Bankruptcy Code. The 1990 amendments also introduced other provisions that are favorable to the swap counterparties of Code debtors. See generally Cunningham, Rogers & Bilicic, supra note 118 at 25–27.

[146] See Section 560 of the Bankruptcy Code, which expressly preserves a swap participant's contractual right to terminate a swap agreement and to offset or net out any termination values or payment amounts arising under or in connection with any swap agreement, and see note 3 supra with respect to the broad definition of "swap agreement" in the Bankruptcy Code as amended in 1990.

[147] Section 560 of the Bankruptcy Code, which was added by the 1990 amendments, provides that a "contractual right" to terminate a swap agreement upon the insolvency of the debtor may be exercised notwithstanding the automatic stay and the powers of the trustee or debtor in possession referred to in the next paragraph of the text. For purposes of that provision, "contractual right" is defined to include "a right, whether or not evidenced in writing, arising under common law, under law merchant, or by reason of normal business

1990 amendments the automatic stay will not prevent a Code debtor's swap counterparty from exercising a contractual right "to offset or net out any termination values or payment amounts arising under or in connection with any swap agreement," or from setting off "any mutual debt and claim under or in connection with any swap agreement that constitutes the setoff of a claim against the debtor for any payment due the debtor" from the swap participant under or in connection with any swap agreement, or against collateral held to secure the debtor's obligations under any swap agreement.[148]

Federally-insured banks and savings and loan institutions organized in the U.S. are not eligible to be Code debtors. Until the adoption of FIRREA in 1989, it was unclear whether the regulators that would act as receivers for those institutions in insolvency would be deemed to have powers and rights like those described above of Bankruptcy Code trustees and debtors in possession. Under FIRREA, the rights—including the right to terminate a swap or similar derivative transaction—and obligations of the counterparty will depend on whether the relevant regulator (almost always the FDIC or the Resolution Trust Corporation)[149] chooses to operate the failed institution as a going concern, to carry out a merger or purchase and assumption transaction through which assets of the insolvent entity are transferred, or to liquidate the failed institution.[150] Swaps and other derivatives are, as noted, included in a category referred to as "qualified financial contracts"[151] to which FIRREA extends certain special protections that, in some cases, are like those afforded to the same kinds of transactions under the 1990 Bankruptcy Code amendments. If the insolvent depository institution is placed in conservatorship, its counterparty in a qualified financial contract will be entitled to exercise a contractual right to terminate the contract if the sole ground for termination is not the appointment of the conservator.[152] If the only contractual ground for

---

practice." Bankruptcy Code § 560. By its own terms, Section 560 should apply notwithstanding any other provision in the Bankruptcy Code, including the provisions of Chapter 9, which relate to bankruptcies of municipal entities; however, in listing other provisions applicable to proceedings under Chapter 9, Section 901(a) of the Bankruptcy Code does not refer to Section 560. Some are, therefore, concerned about whether the relief afforded by Section 560 applies in proceedings under Chapter 9.

[148] Bankruptcy Code §§ 560 and 362(b)(14).

[149] The provisions of FIRREA do not appear to apply to banks and thrift institutions that are not FDIC insured. They also may not apply if neither the FDIC nor the Resolution Trust Corporation (the "*RTC*") acts as conservator or receiver for an FDIC-insured institution. For some circumstances in which neither the FDIC nor the RTC might act as conservator, *see* Eccard & Grosshandler, "Qualified Financial Contracts with FDIC-Insured Banks and Thrifts," 7 *Rev. Banking & Financial Services* 49 n. 2 (Apr. 10, 1991).

[150] For a discussion of the FIRREA provisions, *see* Gooch & Pergam, *supra* note 13, at 34–13 to 34–17.

[151] 12 U.S.C. § 1821(e)(8)(D)(i). *See* note 3 *supra*.

[152] 12 U.S.C. §§ 1821(e)(8)(E) & 1821(e)(12)(A).

termination is the appointment of the conservator, the counterparty will be unable to exercise the right;[153] however, if qualified financial contract with an insolvent institution affords the counterparty another ground for termination that is enforceable under applicable noninsolvency law, under FIRREA the counterparty's exercise of that right will be protected.[154] If the insolvent institution is placed in receivership, the counterparty will be entitled to exercise a contractual right to terminate its qualified financial contracts with the institution, but only if the receiver fails (1) to transfer all qualified financial contracts between the institution and that counterparty and its affiliates, and all subordinated claims of the counterparty and its affiliates thereunder, by the close of business on the business day after the receiver's appointment, through a purchase and assumption or similar transaction, or (2) fails to notify the counterparty of the transfer by that time.[155] The depository institution's counterparties in qualified financial contracts will be entitled under FIRREA to exercise contractual rights to set off or net all amounts payable in respect of qualified financial contracts with the insolvent institution, including the termination values of multiple swaps under a master agreement.[156]

---

[153] 12 U.S.C. § 1821(e)(12)(A). The counterparty will, however, be protected against cherry picking by the conservator through selective transfers of qualified financial contracts with a counterparty, because the conservator is not permitted to transfer any such contract with a counterparty unless it transfers all such contracts with the same counterparty to the same transferee. 12 U.S.C. § 1821(e)(9).

[154] 12 U.S.C. § 1821(e)(8)(E). *See* the discussion in Eccard & Grosshandler, *supra* note 149 at 53.

[155] The relevant provision, 12 U.S.C. § 1821(e)(10), requires a depository institution's receiver to use best efforts to give notice of such a transfer to the institution's counterparty to any qualified financial contract involved in the transfer by noon of the business day following the transfer. However, FDIC and RTC policy statements on the subject clarify that they interpret the statutory provision to have the effect described above in the text, and that they would not view a counterparty's exercise of a contractual right to terminate a swap involved in a transfer, or its action against collateral securing the depository institution's obligations under such a swap, as protected if the right were exercised on the ground of the appointment of a receiver, or the action were taken, before the close of business on the business day following the appointment of the receiver. *See* Gooch & Pergam, *supra* note 12, at 34–16 and note 12 *supra,* and Eccard & Grosshandler, *supra* note 149 at 53 and note 27, on these issues and the relevant policy statements. The counterparty will have the benefit of the protection against cherry picking described in note 153 *supra.* The statute does not deal expressly with whether the one business-day waiting period applies when a receiver is appointed for the depository and the counterparty has a contractual right to terminate the transaction on a ground other than the appointment of the receiver. Commentators have expressed the belief that the waiting period would not apply in these circumstances. *See,* e.g., Cunningham, Rogers & Bilicic, *supra* note 118, at 23.

[156] 12 U.S.C. § 1821(e)(8)(A)(iii). In addition, the counterparty will be entitled to exercise its rights under security arrangements relating to qualified financial contracts, 12 U.S.C. § 1821(e)(8)(A)(ii), subject to the right of a receiver or conservator to obtain a stay of all judicial actions involving the insolvent depository, for a period of 90 days, in the case of a receivership, and 45 days in the case of a conservatorship. 12 U.S.C.§ 1821(d)(12)(A) & 1821(e)(8)(B). Therefore, collateral that is available without judicial action can be applied without that delay against the depository's swap obligations, including obligations in respect of early termination settlement, where early termination is permitted as described above.

The cases described in this section shed some light on the problems that may arise in connection with swap contract provisions allowing for early termination when one is confronted with an insolvent or bankrupt swap counterparty. The first deals with, and upholds, a contractual right to terminate exercised before the commencement of bankruptcy proceedings relating to the counterparty although on the basis of a decline in its financial condition that soon thereafter led to the initiation of such proceedings. The second deals with, and enjoins, the exercise of a contractual right to terminate after the appointment of a receiver for the counterparty.

Drexel Burnham Lambert Products Corp. v. MCorp[157] was an action brought to recover approximately $1.8 million calculated by the plaintiff ("Drexel Products") as damages in connection with early termination of a seven-year rate swap with the defendant, plus interest at a rate specified in the swap agreement. The agreement contemplated automatic early termination in connection with events of default related to a party's insolvency. One of those events was, "The Defaulting Party . . . fails or is unable to pay its debts generally as they become due." The agreement also provided that the termination date in such an event would be deemed to be the day on which the event occurred and that the nondefaulting party was required to give the defaulting party oral notice of automatic early termination, followed by confirmation in writing. Drexel Products gave MCorp the required oral notice on October 24, 1988 (following it with written notice on October 25), citing as the event that triggered the automatic early termination the declaration by MCorp's Board of Directors of a "moratorium on payment of preferred stock dividends and of principal and interest on all parent company public and privately placed indebtedness for borrowed money." The moratorium was announced in a press release on October 24 but was stated to be effective October 21, 1988. The release was followed by a press report that MCorp's president had said that there was "a high probability" that proceedings under Chapter 11 of the Bankruptcy Code would be filed with respect to MCorp within 30 days. Pursuant to the moratorium, MCorp failed to make a swap payment due to the plaintiff on October 21, and Drexel Products' notice advising MCorp of the early termination also cited that payment failure as an event of default under the agreement. By letter of October 26, 1988 MCorp admitted the existence of the moratorium and its failure to make the October 21 payment but refused to pay the amount calculated by Drexel Products as the damages payable to it under the agreement as a result of the early termination. Drexel Products filed the complaint in the action a few weeks later.[158]

---

[157] No. 88C-NO-80 (Super. Del. Feb. 23, 1989), *motion for reargument denied,* 1991 Del. Super. LEXIS 298 (Aug. 13, 1991).
[158] This description of the facts is based on the court's unreported opinion granting the plaintiff's motion for summary judgment.

In its attempt to defeat the plaintiff's motion for summary judgment, MCorp contended that it was not in default under the cited provision of the agreement because it was only unwilling, not unable, to pay its debts, as required by the contract, and that, even if it was in default, it should be given the opportunity to test Drexel's calculation of damages, so summary judgment was inappropriate. In granting the motion,[159] the court found, as Drexel products argued, that the event of default had been triggered by adoption of the moratorium, since the moratorium legally disabled MCorp from generally paying its outstanding obligations, and that MCorp had in fact failed to pay its debts affected by the moratorium since its October 21 effective date. MCorp contended that the language in the agreement should be read in accordance with cases interpreting a similarly-worded provision in the Bankruptcy Code involving situations where the debtor fails to pay its debts generally as they become due; the court rejected the argument noting that the contractual provision had a broader reach and was clearly intended to afford a party the opportunity to terminate before the other party actually became bankrupt. In denying MCorp's motion for reargument of the same issues, the court again ruled that the moratorium coupled with MCorp's actual failure to pay debts was a sufficient basis on which to find an event of default for purposes of triggering the automatic early termination provision of the agreement.[160]

The *MCorp* case illustrates the willingness of a court to enforce the parties' agreement on early termination of a swap agreement when not constrained by overriding rules applicable in bankruptcy proceedings. Indeed, language in the court's opinion granting Drexel Products' motion for summary judgment illustrates an understanding of the need for early termination provisions in similar agreements:

> The efficacy of an agreement of this type as a planning device depends on the financial ability of the parties to perform the agreement. If one party . . . should be unable to perform, the other party could discover itself with an increasing uncovered exposure to adverse changes in interest rates. Under such circumstances, the party at risk must be free to terminate the interest rate swap agreement and to take steps to cover against any exposure to market risk.

On May 29, 1990, Drexel Products itself became a debtor in Bankruptcy Code proceedings, a little over three months after a voluntary petition was filed by The Drexel Burnham Lambert Group Inc., which had provided guaranties for swap obligations of Drexel Products. The filing by the guarantor was cited by some of Drexel Products' swap counterparties as an event of default leading to automatic early termination of the swaps

---

[159] The court's handling of MCorp's arguments relating to the amount of damages claimed by Drexel is discussed in the next section. *See* note 167 and accompanying text.

[160] *Drexel Burnham Lambert Products Corp. v. MCorp*, 1991 Del. Super. LEXIS 298, at *2.

with those counterparties, and the available papers do not indicate that Drexel Products challenged the assertion, although it seems to have resisted attempts to obtain release of collateral that had been delivered by the counterparties when release was sought on the ground that the early termination ended all obligations of the counterparties requiring security.[161] Similarly, the appointment of administrators for one English company and the appointment of a statutory administrator for a New Zealand development bank have led swap counterparties to those entities to assert that their respective swap agreements terminated automatically, but in those cases too[162] the dispute seems to relate wholly to the provisions of the agreements on payments in connection with early termination, and not to the provisions on automatic early termination. The circumstances were different, however, in the *Beverly Hills* case described below, where the applicable insolvency law was invoked to prevent the exercise of a contractual termination right.

Beverly Hills Savings v. Renault Acceptance B.V.[163] was a case that arose before the adoption of FIRREA and involved an insolvent California savings and loan association. The thrift, which had a swap agreement with Renault Acceptance B.V., was placed in receivership by the Federal Home Loan Bank Board, and FSLIC immediately effected a transfer of assets and liabilities of the insolvent thrift to a new, federally chartered institution. The swap agreement provided (i) that insolvency of a party would entitle the other party to terminate the agreement and (ii) that neither party could assign its rights under the agreement without the other party's consent. The thrift's rights and obligations under the swap agreement were nonetheless included in the transfer arranged by FSLIC. The obligations of Beverly Hills under the agreement were secured by collateral held by Bank of America, as agent for the purpose.

After learning of the insolvency, Renault sought to terminate the swap and realize on the collateral to satisfy its claim for damages resulting from the early termination. The new Beverly Hills sought a preliminary injunction barring the early termination and liquidation of the collateral.

---

[161] *See, e.g.*, the complaint filed by the Resolution Trust Corporation, as conservator for Western Empire Federal Savings and Loan Association, in *RTC v. Drexel Burnham Lambert Products Corp.*, No. 6332, at ¶¶ 13–16 (seeking return of collateral delivered to Drexel Products on the ground that further security was no longer required since the early termination ended all obligations under the swaps of the thrift for which the RTC was acting). It appears that Drexel Products settled all but three claims relating to its swap agreements prior to its own Chapter 11 filing. *See* Asquith & Cunningham, "Swaps and Termination Events: Legal and Business Considerations," unpublished paper delivered at ISDA's Annual General Meeting in Paris on March 13, 1992, pp. 19–24 (summarizing information in the Debtors' First Amended and Restated Disclosure Statement Pursuant to Section 1125 of the United States Bankruptcy Code, as filed with the court).

[162] *See* notes 176–184 *infra*.

[163] No. C–549–684 (Super. Ct. Los Angeles County 1985).

The court's opinion granting that relief concluded that the contractual clause prohibiting the assignment should not be given effect in these circumstances, and that Renault should, as requested by the plaintiff, be enjoined from terminating the swap and realizing on the collateral because to deny the relief sought by the new Beverly Hills and enforce the provisions of the contract would interfere with FSLIC's successful reorganization of the insolvent entity. The court also concluded that the assumption by the new entity of the insolvent thrift's obligations under the swap agreement cured any default caused by the insolvency and in no way impaired Renault's position. The lawsuit was settled in September 1987.

Until FIRREA there was some uncertainty about the powers of FSLIC as receiver for an institution like the thrift in *Beverly Hills,* and there were no precedents other than that case relating to swaps. The law has since changed, as noted above, with the adoption of FIRREA and its statement of the powers of receivers and conservators with respect to FDIC-insured U.S. depository institutions, including their powers relating to swap agreements and other qualified financial contracts. In fact, under FIRREA a case like *Beverly Hills* should never arise, because under FIRREA the receiver for a federally-insured U.S. depository is required to give the depository's swap counterparties notice of a transfer like that contemplated by FSLIC in *Beverly Hills* before the close of business on the business day following the appointment of the receiver, but subject to that notice requirement, the right of the receiver to effect such a transfer appears to be clear, and pending the expiry of the one business-day period provided to the receiver, a swap counterparty would be unprotected if it sought to terminate its swap and collect an early termination settlement from collateral delivered by the depository.[164]

Damages upon Termination

When the right to terminate swap and related agreements with insolvent counterparties was partially recognized, as described above, through recent amendments to the U.S. Bankruptcy Code and through the adoption of FIRREA, the recognition of that right was not conditioned on any particular provisions for payments upon termination of the transactions. FIRREA does provide that, if an insolvent depository's contracts are repudiated by a receiver or conservator, the damages payable to the other party to the transactions will be limited to "actual and direct compensatory damages," and FIRREA further provides that, where qualified financial contracts such as swaps are concerned, damages will be measured as of the date of the repudiation, and "normal and reasonable costs of cover or other reasonable measures of damages utilized in the industries

---

[164] *See* note 155 *supra* and accompanying text.

for the contracts" will be deemed to be compensatory.[165] As a general matter, however, at least in the United States, the enforceability against an insolvent counterparty of a contractual provision relating to payments in connection with early termination will, subject to applicable limitations imposed by bankruptcy law, be governed by the same non-bankruptcy law in the field of contracts that would apply in an action brought outside insolvency proceedings, including principles of contract law that render penalty provisions unenforceable.[166]

In one of the cases described earlier, *Drexel Burnham Lambert Products Corp. v. MCorp*, the court was asked, in the defendant's motion for reargument, to deny the plaintiff's motion for summary judgment and plea for damages based on the contract's "Agreement Value" measure on the theory that the damages provision was unenforceable as a penalty. This theory was based on MCorp's belief (for which it offered no supporting evidence) that Drexel Products had not actually entered into a replacement swap as "cover" for the terminated transaction with MCorp.[167] Earlier in the proceedings, MCorp had requested that the court order discovery on whether actual cover was obtained, and the request was denied, because MCorp offered no evidence to suggest that actual cover was required by the parties' agreement; like most agreements used in the market in recent years, the MCorp agreement provided that a nondefaulting party would be entitled to determine its damages on the basis of quotations obtained from leading participants in the swap market of their fees for entering into a substitute agreement with the nondefaulting party. Finding that the agreement did not require a nondefaulting party to enter into a substitute agreement, the court denied the discovery request. The later argument that the agreement's approach to damages constituted an unenforceable penalty because Drexel Products did not (MCorp asserted) actually enter into a replacement swap was merely a new attempt, in another guise, to obtain discovery on the point. The court rejected the argument, describing the agreement value approach embodied in the agreement as a market-based measure of the actual loss of the nondefaulting party based on quotes developed at the time of the default with tight time constraints imposed on the nondefaulting party. The court therefore found no basis for the argument that the provision was invalid as a penalty.[168]

The *MCorp* decision was welcomed in the swap market as upholding the agreement value approach to damages that many participants in the market have adopted for many of their agreements over recent years, although the particular agreement involved in the case adopted a variant of

---

[165] 12 U.S.C. §§ 1821(e)(3)(A)(i) & 1821(e)(3)(C)(i).
[166] *See* Gooch & Klein, *Swap Documentation* 39–40.
[167] 1991 Del. Super. LEXIS 298 at *5.
[168] 1991 Del. Super. LEXIS 298 at *7.

the approach under which the party determining its damages would do so by taking the lowest of the quotations for replacement transactions obtained by it from leading participants in the market, so the decision does not actually stand for approval of the generally used approach that involves averaging market quotations. The decision is also important for its rejection of an attempt to characterize the approach as a penalty provision merely because it does not require the nondefaulting party to obtain actual cover.[169]

Other cases outside the United States appear now to be testing whether another aspect of the damages provisions contained in many swap agreements may act as an unenforceable penalty: the so-called "Limited Two-Way Payments" approach to payments upon early termination.

In swap documentation, a distinction is drawn between early termination arising from a default by one of the parties (an "Event of Default") and early termination that comes about as a result of a no-fault "Termination Event," such as the imposition of withholding tax or supervening illegality.[170] Bankruptcy, insolvency and similar events with respect to a party have generally been treated in swap documentation as Events of Default rather than Termination Events. Most market practitioners have (until recently, as discussed below) adopted the "Limited Two-Way Payments" approach to the payment of damages, under which a party that became insolvent or bankrupt would, in some circumstances, not be entitled to receive the value of swaps that were "in-the-money" to it at the time of its insolvency or bankruptcy.

The main features of the Limited Two-Way Payments approach, simply stated, are as follows: (i) If a swap is terminated as a result of an Event of Default at a time when the swap is of value[171] to the nondefaulting party, the defaulting party is required to pay damages to the nondefaulting party to compensate it for its loss resulting from the termination of the swap. (ii) If there is an Event of Default and the swap is in the money

---

[169] The court pointed to other aspects of the approach that seemed to support its view that the approach did not involve a penalty. These included, as noted, the time and other constraints imposed on the nondefaulting party in obtaining its quotations, as well as the fact that the provision applied equally to both parties.

[170] See Gooch & Klein, *Swap Documentation* 34–35; Gooch & Klein, "Damages provisions in swap agreements," *International Financial Law Review* (Oct. 1984).

[171] This simplified explanation does not take into account that this value element (which represents the net value at the time of all the regular swap payments scheduled to be made after the early termination date) is not the only element to be considered in determining what payment, if any, is to be made upon early termination of a swap agreement. Another element consists of any swap payments relating to earlier calculation periods that remain unpaid on the early termination date. Such unpaid amounts, if owed to the defaulting party, are generally taken into account to reduce any settlement amount that must be paid to the nondefaulting party; however, the question whether there should be a cash payment by the nondefaulting party to the defaulting party in respect of such unpaid amounts if the balance is in the latter's favor has been controversial. See Gooch & Klein, *Swap Documentation* 32–37, 149.

to the defaulting party, the nondefaulting party will not be obligated to pay the corresponding value over to the defaulting party.[172] (iii) If the cause of early termination is a no-fault Termination Event, whichever party stands to benefit from early termination is required to pay that benefit over to the other party, regardless of the identity of the party that is affected by the Termination Event.[173] Certain commentators have long questioned the fairness of the Limited Two-Way Payments approach, particularly as applied to bankruptcy and insolvency situations,[174] and have championed the alternative "Two-Way Payments" approach which treats Events of Default in the same general manner as Termination Events affecting the defaulting party, so that neither party is allowed to retain benefits that it obtains from early termination.

There have been few court challenges to the Limited Two-Way Payments provision as applied in the insolvency context, even though there have been numerous insolvencies of counterparties to swaps that were

---

[172] If several swaps are being terminated, the value of the swaps that are in the money to the defaulting party is credited against the value of the swaps that are in the money to the nondefaulting party, but no payment is made if the net amount is in favor of the defaulting party.

[173] If only one party is affected by the Termination Event, the amount to be paid, under the calculation mechanics of the 1987 ISDA forms, is calculated from the perspective of the other party; if both parties are so affected, the mechanics are designed to find the middle-of-the-market value of the swap. For example, if the value of the swap to one party were 100, and if it represented a liability of 110 to the other party, the amount to be paid would be 105. See Gooch & Klein, *Swap Documentation* 63–65, 150–51, 170–71.

[174] See Price & Henderson, *Currency and Interest Rate Swaps* 115–19 (Butterworths 1st ed. 1984). There has been some movement in the market toward using the Two-Way Payments approach across the board and not just in the insolvency context. Significant movement in this direction first took place when market participants sought to document essentially unilateral agreements, such as caps, floors and "swaptions," with the same master agreements that they were using for swaps. Since well-advised purchasers of those instruments would not agree to have the Limited Two-Way Payments approach apply to them, some market participants began to shift to a full Two-Way Payments approach in their master swap documentation; others adopted an approach that treats "fully paid for" transactions such as caps, floors and swaptions in one way and swaps and other executory transactions in another. Banking regulators have begun to discourage the use of the Limited Two-Way Payments approach, in part by expressing concern over the extent to which the "walk away" aspect of that approach "might materially adversely affect the financial condition of an already weakened bank," see Patrikis, "Bank Regulatory Issues Relating to Swaps," *Swaps and Other Derivatives in 1992,* 295, 315 (Practising Law Institute 1992), and, in part by contemplating regulatory responses that would disfavor Limited Two-Way Payments, *e.g.,* through the imposition of increased capital requirements for swaps documented under that approach (*see ibid.* at 315). This would be the effective result of a measure that bank regulatory authorities have recently suggested they might take with respect to a bank's measurement of credit exposure on swaps for purposes of compliance with capital adequacy rules. See issues paper on "Netting" dated April 21, 1992 prepared by technical experts from bank supervisory authorities in the Group of Ten Countries, suggesting that a bank might be permitted to measure its exposure vis-à-vis a counterparty to a master swap agreement on a net basis for capital adequacy purposes if the agreement provided for early termination settlement on a full Two-Way Payments basis but that the exposure would have to be calculated on a gross basis if the bank's agreements adopted the Limited Two-Way Payments approach.

documented in the standard way and were in the money to the insolvent counterparties at the time of the insolvency. In the authors' experience, this is so because the solvent counterparties have preferred to reach negotiated settlements with the representatives of the insolvent counterparties in cases where the swap or swaps are in the money to the insolvent counterparties; the accepted market wisdom is to the effect that the solvent counterparty can negotiate a favorable settlement in these cases, at least in part because of the *in terrorem* effect of the Limited Two-Way Payments clause. Although, of course, any negotiated settlement is not as favorable as keeping the entire windfall resulting from termination, the risks and costs of potentially prolonged litigation provide an incentive for the solvent party to settle. From the point of view of the insolvent party, the *raison d'être* for the swap transactions has often disappeared at this point, since the characteristics of the liabilities being hedged with the swaps have been radically changed as a result of the insolvency. The insolvent party can be further motivated to settle with its swap counterparty because cashing in (at least partially) on the valuable swaps offers a ready source of funds, whereas a court challenge to the Limited Two-Way Payments provision of the swap agreement can be expected to involve significant cost and delay, and the outcome will be uncertain.[175]

Although these factors have generally resulted in few challenges, as noted, to the Limited Two-Way Payments approach, there are currently two pending cases that we know of in which the approach is being tested: *DFC New Zealand vs. Security Pacific Australia* and *Atlantic Computer Systems v. Hill Samuel Bank Limited.*

The challange in *DFC New Zealand vs. Security Pacific Australia Ltd.,*[176] came about after DFC New Zealand ("DFC") "collapsed" and was placed under statutory management in October 1989, at a time when it had more than 100 swap agreements in effect with 70 counterparties.[177] With the approval of its regulator, the Reserve Bank of New Zealand, DFC re-

---

[175] It appears that similar motivations led the FDIC, as receiver for the Bank of New England ("BNE"), to transfer all of BNE's qualified financial agreements (swaps, caps, floors, repurchase agreements and foreign exchange contracts) to a bridge bank established to assume BNE's assets and liabilities, even though, under FIRREA, the receiver could have repudiated all such contracts with a particular counterparty if they had been burdensome. The FDIC seems to have concluded that assuming all such contracts was the most cost-effective way to preserve for the bridge bank assets with a net market value of some $185 million. *See* the discussions and quotations from hearings on the case in Asquith & Cunningham, *supra* note 161, at 6–11.

[176] The statement of claim and the other documents filed in the case are not publicly available, so this description of the action is based on newspaper accounts of the case. We are assuming for purposes of this discussion that the provisions for Limited Two-Way Payments in the relevant agreement are like those contained in ISDA's 1987 forms of master agreement, but it may be that there are differences that will affect the outcome of the proceedings.

[177] *National Business Review,* July 12, 1991.

solved to continue to perform its FX, swap and option agreements, and, on the same day that DFC was placed under statutory management, the regulator notified the counterparties that it expected DFC's payments under those agreements would be made when due.[178] In the following month, Security Pacific Australia Ltd. ("SecPac") sent a telex to DFC to the effect that SecPac's obligations under their swap agreement had terminated because of DFC's insolvency.[179] DFC reached negotiated settlements with its swap counterparties other than SecPac; in some cases DFC's rights and obligations were assigned to Barclays Bank; in others, the agreements were terminated and cash payments were made.[180] When negotiations with SecPac regarding an assignment or a cash settlement failed, DFC began legal proceedings seeking damages from SecPac. SecPac is reported to be defending the suit on jurisdictional grounds,[181] and press accounts state that DFC has amended its statement of claim to increase the amount claimed as damages.[182]

Atlantic Computer Systems PLC v. Hill Samuel Bank Limited[183] is a similar case. The complaint, which was filed in April 1991, recites that the plaintiff, Atlantic Computer Systems ("Atlantic") entered into two interest rate swap transactions in May 1988 with the defendant, then known as Hill Samuel & Co. Limited ("Hill Samuel"), that were subject to ISDA's 1987 Definitions and documented by confirmations sent by Hill Samuel to Atlantic by facsimile and then by confirmation letter. Both swap transactions had final payment dates on May 4, 1990. In April 1990, administrators were appointed for the property of Atlantic. The complaint further recites that on May 2, 1990, Hill Samuel gave notice that the appointment of the administrators constituted an event of default under the swap agreements and designated an early termination date for them. Hill Samuel also enclosed a calculation of the settlement amount for each of the two swaps, showing a gross amount payable by Atlantic of £581,643.84 and a gross amount payable by Hill Samuel of £911,643.84, leaving a net payable by Hill Samuel of £330,000 on each swap. Hill Samuel apparently took the position that no payment was due in respect of the swaps because of the operation of the Limited Two-Way Payments provision de-

---

[178] *The Examiner,* September 5, 1991.

[179] *Ibid.*

[180] *Ibid.*

[181] *The Examiner,* September 5, 1991.

[182] *National Business Review,* July 12, 1991. This press report suggests that the amended claim is for the full amount that would have been due from SecPac under the agreement, which related to a currency swap, without netting out the amounts due to SecPac from DFC, on the theory that such netting involves a setoff or counterclaim that would be available to SecPac only with the consent of DFC's statutory manager, thus raising a highly interesting new issue in the case.

[183] In the High Court of Justice, Chancery Division, CH 1991 A No. 4645 (April 26, 1991).

scribed above. Atlantic contends that the Limited Two-Way Payments provision is void as a penalty and is seeking payment of the settlement amounts on the two swaps, plus interest and costs.[184]

For a variety of reasons, some of which have been described above, the trend in swap documentation has been moving towards adoption of the full Two-Way Payments approach to damages in connection with early termination,[185] and with this movement perhaps lawsuits like the *DFC* and *Hill Samuel* cases will remain rare. From its experience with insolvencies of entities that were parties to swaps with many participants in the market, the market seems to have come to a consensus that, whether or not the Limited Two-Way Payments approach is enforceable, in practice the market as a whole stands to benefit more if the insolvent entity can realize on the net value of its swaps, since with those payments it may be able to pay the claims of market participants against it and its swap book as a whole will be disposed of with the least possible disruption to the market.[186]

Conclusion

It is perhaps only predictable that sophisticated financial transactions will sometimes lead to disputes, and that some of those disputes will not be resolved without the intervention of an impartial third party. Perhaps this is even more predictable where derivatives like swaps are concerned, since adverse movements in the rates, prices and indices used in these transactions may provide a strong motivation for one or the other of the parties to seek a way out of a deal that, in hindsight, it wishes it had never struck. The fact that there has been so little litigation (leaving aside *Hammersmith and Fulham* and its fall-out) is a tribute to the efforts of the pioneers in the market, who devoted much time and effort to the careful examination of the specific legal and documentation issues that might be

---

[184] An interesting sidelight to the *Hill Samuel* case is the way in which the derivatives portfolio of Atlantic Computer's parent, British & Commonwealth Merchant Bank ("BCMB") was handled by the receivers appointed for BCMB. Among other things, because some of the swaps were documented under agreements prepared on ISDA's 1987 master forms calling for automatic early termination, it appears that the receivers concluded that they had to cease making payments under those agreements, because the appointment of the receivers acted to trigger the automatic early termination and the receivers were only empowered to make payments to preserve the value of continuing assets. For a discussion of the matter and the apparent attempts of some counterparties to walk away with the value of their swaps with BCMB under the Limited Two-Way Payments provisions in their agreements, *see* Asquith & Cunningham, *supra* note 161, at 12–18.

[185] The most recent evidence of this movement is that the approach will be applicable under the 1992 ISDA master agreement forms unless the parties expressly agree otherwise.

[186] *See* Asquith & Cunningham, *supra* note 161, at 19–24, on the ability of Drexel Products to dispose of its swap portfolio effectively as the result of the willingness of most counterparties to pay over settlement amounts that the Limited Two-Way Payments approach provided they would be permitted to keep.

raised in a dispute. As the market's understanding of those issues evolves, in connection with changes in the law and experience with lawsuits like those described above, it should be expected that the documentation used and trading practices followed for swaps and related derivatives will also evolve in response. The authors hope that this chapter will be of use to market participants in their ongoing consideration of their own documents and practices.[187]

---

[187] As noted above, the material and analysis included in this chapter was current at August 1, 1992. Subsequent amendment of the U.S. Commodity Exchange Act will substantially alleviate the commodity law, gaming law and bucket-shop law concerns discussed in the text accompanying notes 96–135 in many, although not all, circumstances involving swaps as they are generally used in the U.S. market today. In addition, subsequent developments have occurred in some of the cases and other areas dealt with above, including a trial court grant of a motion of summary judgment, effectively upholding the Limited Two-Way Payments approach discussed in the text accompanying notes 170–86, in the case of *Drexel Burnham Lambert Products Corp. v. Midland Bank, PLC*, 92 Civ. 3098 (S.D.N.Y. 1992). These and other developments will be discussed in the authors' forthcoming book on Derivatives Documentation.

FINANCIAL INNOVATION AND UNCERTAIN REGULATION: SELECTED ISSUES REGARDING NEW PRODUCT DEVELOPMENT*

Thomas A. Russo
and Marlisa Vinciguerra

21

I. Introduction

Today, the fundamental question confronted in the development of an innovative financial product is not how the product could be developed to be efficient, to meet investors' needs, and to enhance U.S. competitiveness in the world financial market. Rather, the central issue has become whether or not a new product will ever be permitted to be offered or sold in the United States. This uncertainty stems from an ongoing controversy between the Commodity Futures Trading Commission (CFTC) and the Securities and Exchange Commission (SEC) over the scope of each agency's jurisdiction over new financial products.[1]

Currently, the SEC and CFTC exercise jurisdiction over instruments generally characterized, respectively, as "securities" and "futures." The distinctions between futures and securities, however, have become ambiguous in light of the development of products, such as exchange-traded op-

---

* Published originally in *69 Texas Law Review* 1431–1538 (1991). Copyright 1991 by the Texas Law Review Association. Reprinted by permission.
[1] A discussion of the application of state laws to new financial instruments is beyond the scope of this Article.

tions,[2] index participations (IPs),[3] and stock index futures,[4] that combine
characteristics of both. Until this statutorily required and increasingly

---

[2] For a thorough discussion of the historical evolution of exchange-traded options, see
Markham & Gilberg, *Stock and Commodity Options: Two Regulatory Approaches and Their Conflicts*, 47 ALB. L. REV. 741 (1983) [hereinafter *Two Regulatory Approaches*]. Options, generally, are transactions in which one party (the "holder") is granted the right—but does not
incur the obligation—to buy or sell a specified quantity of the underlying product
(e.g., individual stocks, commodities, foreign currency, stock indices, or stock index futures contracts) at an agreed-upon price (the "exercise" or "strike" price) from or to a
second party (the "writer"). The option right exists for a particular period of time, measured by its expiration date. For the option right, the holder will pay the writer consideration known as the option "premium." "Call" options entitle the holder to receive the specified quantity of the underlying product upon payment of the exercise price. "Put"
options entitle the holder to sell the specified quantity to the writer at the agreed-upon
price during the term of the option. *See id.* at 743. Exchange-traded options are made
"fungible" by, *inter alia*, limiting their variables (expiration date, strike price, and premium). *See* Study of Option Trading, Exchange Act Release No. 10490, 38 Fed. Reg.
32020, 32020 (1973). Exchange-traded index options do not require transfer of the products composing the index, but rather are settled in cash and may be offset by entering
into an opposite transaction. Fungibility enables a secondary market in exchange-traded
options, i.e., allows such options to be traded on the relevant exchange prior to expiration. For further discussion of stock index options and futures, see *infra* notes 4, 6, 95 and
accompanying text.

[3] See *infra* note 18 for a description of specific IPs. IPs generally are cash-settled contracts
of indefinite duration based on the value of an index of securities. During the life of an
IPs contract, the seller of an IP (who need not own the securities underlying the index) is
required to make payments to the buyer of the IP equivalent to the value of dividends
paid for stocks in the index during that quarter. The buyer pays for the IP in cash on the
date of sale, and may buy on margin. The seller receives the purchase price on the day
the contract is entered into, in return for undertaking the obligation to pay dividend
equivalents during the life of the contract. Consequently, during the life of the contract,
the buyer is in the same position as the purchaser of stock in a portfolio of stocks, and the
seller is in the same position as a "short seller" of stocks (i.e., one who does not own the
stock at the time the contract to sell is entered into). IPs, because they are fungible, may
be traded on the relevant exchange, and both buyers and sellers can liquidate their contracts by entering into offsetting positions. IPs are cleared and settled through the Options Clearing Corporation (OCC), which coordinates the payment of dividends from
sellers to buyers as well as the clearing and settlement of purchases and sales of IPs. *See*
Chicago Mercantile Exch. v. SEC, 883 F.2d 537, 539–40 (7th Cir. 1989), *cert. denied*, 110 S.
Ct. 3214 (1990); *see also infra* note 12 (describing the operation of the OCC).

[4] Traditionally, futures contracts have been described as contractual obligations between
two parties to exchange a stated quantity of a commodity at a fixed price in a future delivery month. *See* Gilberg, *Regulation of New Financial Instruments Under the Federal Securities
and Commodities Laws*, 39 VAND. L. REV. 1599, 1603 (1986). Futures contracts are traded in
the United States on exchanges and are made "fungible" by their stated quantity, quality,
and future delivery month, and by the fact that they are selected and cleared through
clearinghouses that become the buyer to every seller and the seller to every buyer. Stock
index futures, however, "differ from traditional futures contracts in that settlement at maturity can be made only in cash"; thus, no stock index futures contract involves physical
delivery of any of the securities that compose the underlying indices. B. BYRNE, THE STOCK
INDEX FUTURES MARKET 34 (1987). Mr. Byrne explains that "[c]ash settlement is employed
because the alternative would be physical delivery of a large stack of stock certificates for
full or fractional shares in all stocks composing the index." *Id.* Like agricultural futures,
however, stock index futures impose contractual obligations on both parties to perform
on the contract on its settlement date. For a discussion of the early development of stock
index futures trading, see T. RUSSO, REGULATION OF THE COMMODITIES, FUTURES AND

meaningless dichotomy between futures and securities is rejected as the touchstone for determining regulatory jurisdiction over new products, the jurisdictional conflict and innovation-inhibiting trends that this conflict has engendered undoubtedly will persist.

In the past, the development of financial instruments that have characteristics of both futures contracts and securities, such as options on GNMA certificates[5] and IPs (i.e., "derivative products"),[6] has led to costly and protracted litigation, followed by legislative and regulatory compromises that temporarily calm the jurisdictional storm with respect to limited categories of new products. Although these short-term resolutions have allowed the development of certain new products, the fact is that such compromises have been largely reactive measures aimed at resolving a current dispute, as opposed to proactive initiatives that anticipate and encourage new product innovation. More importantly, these measures have failed to revise the underlying premise of federal financial market regulation—that regulatory responsibility over new financial instruments should be allocated based upon whether an instrument falls within the definition of "security" or "futures contract."[7]

The long-standing and currently inflamed debate among the SEC, CFTC, legislators, and policy makers over the regulation of new derivative

---

OPTIONS MARKETS § 1.45 (1983 & Supp. 1990). Although stock index futures were among the first futures contracts that did not provide for physical delivery of the underlying commodity, cash settlement of futures contracts had always been the pervasive means of fulfilling the obligations of futures contracts. The "high incidence of settlement by liquidation occurs because futures contracts are traded primarily for the purpose of hedging price risks or speculating against price fluctuations, rather than for purchasing or selling physical commodities." Gilberg, *supra,* at 1603–04. It also is important to note that the Commodity Exchange Act (CEAct) *requires* that stock index futures be cash-settled in order to trade on U.S. futures exchanges. CEAct § 2(a)(1)(B)(ii)(I), 7 U.S.C. § 2a(ii)(I) (1988).

[5] GNMA certificates or "Ginnie Maes" are issued by private mortgage bankers under a program of the Government National Mortgage Association. The certificates represent interests in pools of government-underwritten mortgages, and the certificates' owners receive a portion of the income generated as mortgagors in the pool repay their mortgage loans. The monthly payment of principal and interest is guaranteed by the Government National Mortgage Association. *See* 24 C.F.R. § 390.1 (1991).

[6] The term "derivative products" generically means products whose prices are dependent upon the price of "cash" market items (e.g., stock, foreign currency, pork bellies). Thus, all futures and options contracts are "derivatives." Stock derivatives are a specific category of derivatives that includes only products whose value is dependent upon the price of stock, such as options on single stock, *or,* whose value is dependent upon changes in the value of indices of stocks, such as IPs. Stock index futures, stock index options, and IPs fall within this category. *See generally* OFFICE OF TECHNOLOGY ASSESSMENT, ELECTRONIC BULLS AND BEARS: U.S. SECURITIES MARKETS AND INFORMATION TECHNOLOGY (Sept. 1990) [hereinafter ELECTRONIC BULLS AND BEARS]. Exchange-traded stock index derivatives share certain features arising from exchange trading, such as the ability of parties to these transactions to "offset" by entering into an opposite transaction and the ability to trade such instruments in the secondary market, i.e., on the exchange on which they are traded. *See id.* at 69–70 (futures); *id.* at 94 (options); *id.* at 171–72 (IPs).

[7] For a discussion of the source of this underlying premise, see *infra* notes 92–104 and accompanying text.

products illustrates a consensus concerning the need for changing the current system.[8] The present debate, however, like the existing compromises, has failed to set forth a permanent workable solution to the SEC-CFTC turf battle. This is so because the usefulness of regulatory categorizations based upon imprecise legislative definitions has not been rethought.

This Article, therefore, seeks to focus attention upon the causes and effects of regulatory fragmentation and its relationship to financial innovation by examining the flaws inherent in the present "definitional" approach to market regulation. In this regard, the Article addresses how theories to justify and proposals to resolve jurisdictional turf battles would not meaningfully alter the definitional impediments to financial innovation. The Article then proposes a solution that rejects the present approach and, to this end, contains a comparison of the regulatory regimes of the SEC and CFTC in six key areas.

This regulatory comparison was prepared from work provided by volunteers from Cadwalader's Summer Associate Class of 1990 with a view toward objectively identifying the relevant distinctions between the regimes rather than toward uncovering which regime in each area facilitates innovation. The Article, consequently, departs from prior comparisons[9] by consciously refusing to analyze how the differences in each key area affect, for example, participants' entry into one market or the other. By contrast, the analysis applies the comparison, as an independent whole, to reach conclusions for resolving the SEC-CFTC jurisdictional dispute.

---

[8] For example, the 1987 market break generated numerous stock reports and studies regarding the appropriate regulation of derivative products, including: REPORT OF THE PRESIDENTIAL TASK FORCE ON MARKET MECHANISMS (the "Brady Report") (Jan. 1988) [hereinafter BRADY REPORT]; COMMODITIES AND FUTURES TRADING COMM'N, FOLLOW-UP REPORT ON FINANCIAL OVERSIGHT OF STOCK INDEX FUTURES MARKETS DURING OCTOBER 1987 (1988); General Accounting Office, Financial Markets: Preliminary Observations on the October 1987 Crash (JAN. 1988); AND SEC Division of Market Regulation, The October 1987 Market Break (FEB. 1988). THE OCTOBER 1989 MARKET BREAK LED TO FURTHER REPORTS AND STUDIES IN THIS CONNECTION. *See*, e.g., GAO ASSESSMENT OF SEC AND CFTC STUDIES OF 1989 MARKET VOLATILITIES. BRIEFING REPORT TO THE CHAIRMAN, SENATE SUBCOMMITTEE ON SECURITIES, COMMITTEE ON BANKING, HOUSING AND URBAN AFFAIRS (July 1990), *reprinted in* 2 Comm. Fut. L. Rep. (CCH) ¶ 24890 (Aug. 1990) [hereinafter GAO ASSESSMENT]; CFTC DIVISION OF ECONOMIC ANALYSIS, REPORT ON STOCK INDEX FUTURES AND CASH MARKET ACTIVITY DURING OCTOBER 1989 (May 1990); SEC DIVISION OF MARKET REGULATION, TRADING ANALYSIS OF OCTOBER 13 AND 16, 1989 (May 1990). See *infra* notes 179–92 and accompanying text for a discussion of legislative efforts in this area.

[9] *See*, e.g., Johnson, *Federal Regulation in Securities and Futures Markets*, in FUTURES MARKETS: THEIR ECONOMIC ROLE 291, 306–18 (A. Peck ed. 1985) [hereinafter ECONOMIC ROLE] (analyzing how regulatory differences create a "competitive advantage or a competitive disadvantage" regarding market participation); Seeger, *The Development of Congressional Concern About Financial Futures Markets*, in FUTURES MARKETS: REGULATORY ISSUES 1, 24 (A. Peck ed. 1985) [hereinafter REGULATORY ISSUES] (raising questions concerning how the different rules on margin, suitability, etc., affect investors' choices and "favor one market over another").

Through this analysis, we discovered that, even in areas that have inspired great debate regarding the differences in the SEC and CFTC's regimes, such as customer suitability and margin, the two regimes often contain substantively compatible regulatory approaches.

This discovery challenges the continued usefulness of analyses aimed at comparing the systems to uncover areas of regulatory superiority, and also reveals that the distinctions in these areas do not justify maintaining a dual system of financial regulation.

This Article begins in subpart I(A) by briefly describing the current state of financial markets, in which the statutory division between futures and securities has become obsolete. Subpart I(B) demonstrates that, viewed against this background, popular justifications for the current regulatory bifurcation prove meaningless or unworkable. In Part II, the Article examines the jurisdictional issues arising from the potential application of both the SEC and CFTC regulatory structures to new financial products. Focusing primarily upon the futures exchanges' suit that halted the trading of IPs on securities exchanges, Part III explores the manner in which the bifurcated statutory structure thwarts innovation. Part IV contains a proposed solution drawn from a comparison of the SEC and CFTC regulatory regimes in the areas of customer suitability, supervision, broker and dealer regulation, segregation, frontrunning, and margin, contained in the Appendix to this Article.* The results of this comparative analysis are applied to develop a workable solution to the current conflict.

A. Today's Financial Markets: Legal Bifurcation and Practical Conflation

Prior to examining the legal aspects of new product development, it is necessary to briefly describe the practical reality of today's financial marketplace. At the heart of the debate concerning regulatory bifurcation remains one undeniable fact: the proliferation of new derivative financial products over the past two decades has obviated the once separate boundaries between the securities industry and the futures industry. Industry interrelatedness is evidenced, in part, by the phenomenon that "futures exchanges now trade products closely related to traditional securities industry products, and stock exchanges have created futures exchange subsidiaries."[10]

---

* Because of space limitations, the Appendix, which was prepared from work by Cadwalader's Summer Associate Class of 1990, is not reprinted herewith. The reader interested in this SEC-CFTC comparison should refer to *69 Texas Law Review* (1991), pp. 1501–1538.

[10] Smidt, *Trading Floor Practices on Futures and Securities Exchanges: Economics, Regulation, and Policy Issues*, in REGULATORY ISSUES, *supra* note 9, at 111. For example, the New York Stock Exchange and the Philadelphia Stock Exchange have created the New York Futures Exchange and the Philadelphia Board of Trade, respectively, which are regulated by the CFTC. In addition, the Brady Report, which provided a comprehensive analysis of financial markets, concluded that there exists "one market" for stock derivative products. BRADY REPORT, *supra* note 8, at vi.

There exists no greater example of the practical conflation of the two industries than that presented by the development and implementation of exchange-listed options on the Chicago Board Options Exchange (CBOE), which is regulated by the SEC.[11] CBOE options trading involves futures-style characteristics, such as the competitive bidding for contracts, the ability to offset such contracts, and the standardization of contracts, the last being accomplished through the creation of the Options Clearing Corporation (OCC).[12] This practical convergence of the industries, although it entailed a fundamental transformation of the SEC's regulatory function,[13] did not inspire a basic alteration in the allocation of jurisdiction over new products.[14] Instead, the regulation of exchange-traded options as well as other derivatives was uncomfortably divided between the SEC and CFTC based upon pigeonholing these instruments into the categories of "securities" and "futures."[15]

This unfortunate trend persisted and remains in place today, exemplified by the Seventh Circuit's decision in *Chicago Mercantile Exchange v. SEC* (the "IPs case"),[16] in which IPs, designed to trade as securities on securities exchanges, were deemed "futures contracts" and, as such, were required to be offered and sold solely upon CFTC-designated[17] futures exchanges. Because the SEC-regulated exchanges trading IPs[18] could not

---

[11] For a discussion of the development of the CBOE, see *infra* notes 69–74 and accompanying text.

[12] The OCC performs a function for options trading analogous to that of clearinghouses, which "clear" futures trades "by comparing the reports submitted to them by buyers with those submitted by sellers and accepting for clearance only those trades for which both reports match." T. Russo, *supra* note 4, § 2.01. Futures clearinghouses, upon accepting trades for clearance, become "the seller to every buyer and the buyer to every seller" and, consequently, a "party to every trade." *Id.* For a thorough discussion of the operation and functions of futures clearinghouses, see *id.* §§ 2.01–.02. The OCC, in a related manner, is the issuer and guarantor of all SEC-regulated exchange-traded options and therefore a party to every such option trade. *See* Electronic Bulls and Bears, *supra* note 6, at 94, 190–93.

[13] *See infra* note 73 and accompanying text (discussing the SEC's role transformation in its regulation of exchange-traded options).

[14] *See infra* section II(C)(4) (discussing the current legislative structure that divides jurisdiction based upon whether a product is a "security" or a "futures contract"); *see also* Johnson, *supra* note 9, at 304–05 (noting that the SEC, in regulating exchange-traded options, first employed a regulatory structure similar to that applicable to stocks and bonds).

[15] *See infra* notes 92–94 and accompanying text.

[16] 883 F.2d 537 (7th Cir. 1989), *cert. denied,* 110 S. Ct. 3214 (1990). For an analysis of this case, see *infra* notes 124–77 and accompanying text.

[17] For a discussion of CFTC designation, see *infra* notes 50–51, 117–23 and accompanying text.

[18] The Philadelphia Stock Exchange's IP was called a Cash-Index Participation (CIP). It allowed the buyer to cash out on any business day at a discount of 0.5% from the value of the index, or, alternatively, on the quarterly payment date with no penalty. For purposes of the cash-out, the OCC would randomly match a seller with the cashing-out buyer and require the seller to pay the buyer the cash-out value, thereby liquidating both positions. The purpose of the cash-out was to tie the trading price of the CIP to the underlying index value. A buyer, knowing that the CIP carried with it a cash-out right on index value,

continue to do so, and CFTC-regulated exchanges have not offered IPs, these products "are not trading today in any U.S. financial market *in any form*."[19] The failure of CFTC-regulated exchanges to trade IPs in conjunction with their bringing suit to thwart SEC-regulated exchanges from trading this product has led SEC Chairman Breeden to note that "[a]pparently, the futures exchanges have no desire to trade IPs themselves—they just want to make sure that securities exchanges cannot trade them."[20]

Although it is true that futures exchanges are not trading IPs, it is more useful to examine the forces that lead to innovation-inhibiting results such as the IPs case than it is to question the desire of the futures exchanges to offer new products. Ironically, the energy and creativity that have thrust U.S. futures exchanges into the forefront of financial innovation over the past two decades also "have blurred the [definitional] distinctions assumed in statutes, and thus the allocation of responsibility of the CFTC and SEC."[21] Similarly, the methods used by the futures exchanges in successfully developing and implementing new products, including the clever use of statutory provisions in conjunction with the articulation of persuasive rationales for allowing innovative products to trade, have ended up being anticompetitive when results such as the IPs case have the effect of impeding innovation. Innovation-inhibiting results, then, should be viewed as an outgrowth of innovation in the context of competing agencies as opposed to being caused by competition between agencies and exchanges performing their assigned roles in the statutory environment imposed upon them. It is, therefore, as inappropriate to

---

would be willing to pay index value for the CIP in the open market. Likewise, the seller, aware that it might be compelled to pay a buyer index value in connection with a cash-out, would not be willing to sell an IP for less than index value. It was not intended that the cash-out would become the primary means of realizing value from a CIP. Rather, by this device the market for CIPs was made to match cash-out value, with the intent to promote exchange trading and liquidation by offset.

Moreover, it must be kept in mind that cash-out was a *right* held by the buyer, not an obligation. A buyer was entitled to hold a CIP in perpetuity and was never required to cash out. Thus, a CIP involved no expiration or settlement date as these terms are understood with respect to futures and options.

The IP traded on the American Stock Exchange was called an Equity Index Participation (EIP) and allowed the buyer to cash out quarterly for money or for a portfolio of stock shares matching the index. Holders of certain EIPs could exercise the right to receive delivery of securities. The CBOE's IP was called a Value of Index Participation (VIP); it allowed both buyer and seller to cash out and provided for a semiannual rather than a quarterly payment date. *See* Order Approving Proposed Rule Changes Relating to the Listing and Trading of Index Participations, Exchange Act Release No. 26709, 54 Fed. Reg. 15280, 15280–81 (1989) [hereinafter IPs Order].

[19] Testimony of Richard C. Breeden, Chairman, U.S. Securities and Exchange Commission, Concerning the Futures Trading Practices Act of 1991 Before the Committee on Agriculture, Nutrition, and Forestry, United States Senate, at 17 (Feb. 7, 1991) (transcript on file with the *Texas Law Review*) [hereinafter Breeden Testimony].

[20] *Id.*

[21] ELECTRONIC BULLS AND BEARS, *supra* note 6, at 170.

blame the CFTC or futures exchanges for vigorously representing their interests as it is to criticize the SEC or exchanges it regulates for having asserted jurisdiction over IPs in the first place. Viewing regulatory bifurcation from a blameless perspective sets the stage for identifying the cause of burdens on innovation as a means to creating workable solutions.

The primary mechanism that inhibits innovation today is the Commodity Exchange Act (CEAct), not because it vests exclusive authority over "futures contracts" in the CFTC and demands that all futures be traded on CFTC-designated exchanges,[22] but rather because these principles no longer prove justified when balanced against the costs associated with their burdens on innovation. These key aspects of the CEAct—exclusive CFTC jurisdiction over futures contracts and exchange trading—have been transformed from a sword that enabled innovation throughout much of the CFTC's existence[23] to a shield with which futures exchanges preserve a statutory monopoly. As a result of the CEAct's unique structure, a determination that an instrument is a futures contract carries extraordinary burdens and subjects the viability of new instruments to the discretion of the futures exchanges.[24]

The fact that futures exchanges have succeeded in protecting their interests by litigating the meaning of the CEAct should not be construed as a shortcoming to be remedied by making *them* stop doing so. Alternatively, results such as the IPs case that have exposed an innovation-inhibiting structure should be used as a learning device in an era in which the United States is rethinking its role in the world economy. Because the problem exists in the legislative framework that, among other things, allocates jurisdiction based on definitions, the best approach toward reaching solutions is to emphasize that *we*—that is, all U.S. exchanges, trading firms, and market participants—must work together with Congress and federal bodies to fashion a structure governing our financial markets that enhances U.S. competitiveness while preserving the safety and soundness of our markets.

Significantly, U.S. competitiveness in the world financial market has been threatened under the present structure because, in order to avoid the CEAct's burdens and the delays and expense of potential litigation by futures exchanges, trading firms that can afford to do so take their innovative products to overseas markets. Firms that cannot afford to export in-

---

[22] *See infra* notes 39–53 and accompanying text.
[23] *See* ELECTRONIC BULLS AND BEARS, *supra* note 6, at 20 ("Futures exchanges have been highly innovative in developing new products and the CFTC has been flexible and responsive in approving them."); Seeger, *supra* note 9, at 5, 8 (noting that the futures exchanges used the CEAct structure to offer innovative products following the creation of the CFTC in 1974. See *infra* notes 39, 42 and accompanying text, concerning the 1974 amendments to the CEAct that created the CFTC.
[24] *See infra* notes 110, 122 and accompanying text.

novation simply refuse to offer new products.[25] Additionally, when innovation travels to overseas markets, U.S. participants lose control of the innovative process and sacrifice their economic self-determination. In this environment, the potential for losses of creativity as well as jobs and business has become a reality.

B. Justifications of Bifurcation

These constraints on innovation in the financial markets make it imperative to scrutinize the rationales for a statutory structure that allocates exclusive jurisdiction based on whether or not an instrument is a futures contract. Theories that seek to justify or allocate regulatory jurisdiction typically rely upon functional grounds. These theories fall into two categories: (1) those that vest regulatory authority based upon whether instruments perform the same economic function ("functional-instrument")[26]; and (2) those that determine whether an agency's traditional function justifies regulation of a product because the product falls within the province defined by that function or affects the performance of such function ("functional-agency").[27] None of these functional rationales adequately accounts for the current structure, and initiatives founded on these rationales do not provide sensible solutions in light of industry interrelatedness and the complex universe of stock derivative products.

That the functional-instrument framework fails to explain regulatory bifurcation is evident from the existence of products that perform substantially similar economic functions, but are regulated by different agencies. For example, stock index futures contracts, which are traded on fu-

---

[25] See Breeden Testimony, *supra* note 19, at 17–18.

[26] See, e.g., IPs Order, *supra* note 18, at 15285–86 (presenting the SEC's determination that IPs are "securities" because their economic function is equivalent to that of stock). The SEC concluded that IPs are "stock" because they are negotiable, pay dividend-equivalent amounts, may appreciate in value, and may be hypothecated. The fact that IPs have no voting rights, as stock often does, was not viewed as determinative by the SEC.

[27] See, e.g., Statement of Dr. Wendy L. Gramm, Chairman, Commodity Futures Trading Commission, Before the Senate Committee on Agriculture, Nutrition, and Forestry, at 24 (Feb. 7, 1991) (transcript on file with the *Texas Law Review*) [hereinafter Gramm Testimony] (proposing an approach where the CFTC would be the regulatory body if the investor's primary purpose is to profit from future commodity price fluctuations and the SEC would be the regulator if the investor's primary purpose is to profit from the success of a single issuer's business). This approach would combine functional-agency and functional-instrument rationales because the CFTC could claim jurisdiction over instruments that are used to profit from future price fluctuations (functional-instrument) as well as claim jurisdiction as the agency whose traditional function as the regulator of agriculture futures is to regulate such instruments. Indeed, these theories converge, as suggested by this example. A second twist to the functional-agency rationale, moreover, is allocating jurisdiction based upon the agency's responsibilities concerning the product underlying the derivative, i.e., granting the SEC authority over all stock derivatives based upon the notion that such derivatives affect its traditional role as the regulator of stocks. The SEC has used this rationale to support transferring jurisdiction over margins on stock index futures from the CFTC to the SEC. See Breeden Testimony, *supra* note 19, at 26.

tures exchanges such as the Board of Trade of the City of Chicago (CBOT) and the Chicago Mercantile Exchange (CME) and regulated by the CFTC, and options directly on stock indices, which are traded on the CBOE and regulated by the SEC, perform substantially similar economic functions.[28]

Similarly, basing regulatory jurisdiction upon agency function has been rendered practically unworkable in the context of industry interrelatedness and the proliferation of new stock derivative products. Under this approach, either the SEC or CFTC could justify its jurisdictional authority over numerous new stock derivative products. In this regard, the CFTC could argue that its jurisdiction extends to all instruments that manage risk[29] because traditional futures contracts, the paradigm of

---

[28] *See,* e.g., Board of Trade of Chicago v. SEC, 677 F.2d 1137, 1152 n.28 (7th Cir.) (*GNMA Options*), *vacated as moot,* 459 U.S. 1026 (1982), in which the Seventh Circuit quoted the 1978 statement of SEC Chairman Harold M. Williams before a congressional subcommittee as to the general economic equivalence of options and futures:

> [D]espite the technical differences between futures on securities and options on securities, in a pragmatic vein the two investment vehicles are distinctly similar. At the most basic level, the prices of both futures on securities and options on securities are primarily dependent on the same factor—the price of the underlying security.

(quoting *Extend Commodity Exchange Act: Hearings on H.R. 10285 Before the Subcomm. on Conservation and Credit of the House Comm. on Agriculture,* 95th Cong., 2d Sess. 194–95 (1978)); *see also infra* note 29 (describing how futures and options are used to manage risk). There is no doubt, however, that stock index futures and stock index options do not perform the exact same economic functions. For a discussion of the technical differences between these instruments, see B. BYRNE, *supra* note 4, at 311–13. Stock index options and options on stock index futures, additionally, perform similar economic functions. *See id.* at 314 n.1 (noting that "options on stock index futures are valued in essentially the same manner as stock index options"). Both instruments are options whose value is based upon movements on the prices of stock underlying the index upon which the instruments are derived. Options on stock index futures, however, are derived from stock index futures contracts, while stock index options are derived directly from the stocks underlying the index. As is the case with stock index options and stock index futures, stock index options and options on stock index futures do not perform precisely the same economic functions. For a discussion of the technical differences between these two instruments, see *id.*

[29] Risk management shall be used hereinafter to describe the process through which participants in one market seek to minimize their risk of loss in that market by making transactions in a second market. For example, participants in the grain industry (a cash market) such as farmers who produce grain and bread manufacturers who buy grain may engage in transactions in futures or options markets to protect against price increases or decreases in grain. To manage price risk, a farmer who wishes to protect against a price decrease in grain could enter into a "short" futures contract under which he agrees to sell a specified amount of grain at a later date. The short grain futures will insure that the farmer could sell his wheat at the specified contract settlement date at the agreed-upon price which, if the price of grain drops, will be greater than he could receive in the cash market for grain. Similarly, the farmer could purchase a "put" option on grain and, as holder of the put, he could exercise the option and sell the specified quantity of grain to the option writer at the exercise price if the price of grain in the cash market drops below the exercise price plus the option premium and the farmer's transaction costs. In a related manner, the bread producer, who seeks to protect against a price increase in the grain he needs to manufacture his product could enter in a "long" futures contract or

CFTC jurisdiction, do so. The SEC, on the other hand, could contend that its traditional authority to regulate stock extends to any instrument derived from stock, or could argue that SEC regulation of stock derivatives is necessary because of the effect such stock derivatives have upon equity markets.[30] Given that both agencies' traditional functions could be valid bases for exercising jurisdiction over new stock derivative products, it is clear that the functional-agency approach does not explain the current structure in which the SEC regulates stock index options (which are risk management instruments) and the CFTC regulates stock index futures (which are instruments whose value derives from stock prices). As a result, functional justifications of bifurcated regulation prove incompatible with the practical conflation of financial markets and new products.

The failure of these functional approaches to explain or justify the current system does not, standing alone, render these approaches ineffective as *resolutions* to existing jurisdictional problems. Rather, the functional approaches are destined to provide an incomplete resolution to the SEC-CFTC turf battle because they, by definition, presuppose the existence of multiple agencies and take for granted that any new instrument will have an identifiable function, or easily fall within the ambit of a single agency's function, allowing neat categorization.

By rejecting outright the possibility that one agency could be a workable solution, both functional approaches circumscribe their own utility and ensure some degree of regulatory fragmentation. In addition, by allocating jurisdiction based upon specific functional categories, a resolution based upon the functions of instruments would confront the same hurdles presented by the present definitional approach, namely, that specific categories, once adopted, would become too narrow to accommodate innovation or too broad to provide meaningful guidelines.[31] A functional-

---

purchase a call option. *See* CFTC No-Action Letter No. 91-1 (May 29, 1991), *reprinted in* 2 Comm. Fut. L. Rep. (CCH) ¶ 25065 (discussing agricultural options). The type of risk management activity in which the farmer and bread producer would engage is referred to as "hedging." It should be emphasized, however, that hedging is not limited to transactions in which delivery occurs. Indeed, stock index futures and exchange-traded stock index options for which delivery of the stocks underlying the indices never occurs are used by pension funds and other institutional investors that own large stock portfolios to "hedge" against stock price decreases. Pension funds, thus, could "short" an S&P 500 futures contract to realize a gain at settlement represented by the amount by which the value of the index decreases. By doing so, the pension fund may offset the losses in the value of its stock portfolio. For a discussion of futures' risk management functions, see Silber, *The Economic Role of Financial Futures*, in ECONOMIC ROLE, *supra* note 9, at 83, 91. For a discussion of the economics of options, see Stoll & Whaley, *The New Option Markets*, in *id.* at 205, 226-34.

[30] *See* ELECTRONIC BULLS AND BEARS, *supra* note 6, at 174-76.

[31] *See id.* at 175 (noting that "[i]nstruments that provide both capital formation and risk shifting functions (to different investors) would still pose problems" under a functional-instrument scenario).

agency resolution would prove similarly inadequate because it would require, again, drawing a line between agency functions that would either be too rigid to accommodate instruments whose characteristics are unknown or too ambiguous to prevent a turf war between agencies.[32]

Industry interrelatedness under a system of regulatory bifurcation has not only undermined the premises of the present definitional framework and functional justifications thereof, but also has led to significant regulatory problems. For example, numerous trading firms must now register both as broker-dealers and as the futures analogue—futures commission merchants (FCMs)—and must comply with two sets of regulations in order to serve their customers' financial needs.[33] The outcry for coordinated clearing and settlement procedures between securities and futures exchanges[34] and the controversy surrounding the effect stock derivative products have upon stock market volatility[35] are additional problems engendered by bifurcation in the context of industry interrelatedness.

Numerous legislative initiatives and regulatory proposals regarding the types of regulatory standards that should be applied to new financial products have been forwarded to remedy the U.S. bifurcated regulatory structure that has become obsolete. These initiatives and proposals fall generally into two categories: (1) the establishment of one "super-regula-

---

[32] See Chicago Mercantile Exch. v. SEC, 883 F.2d 537, 544 (7th Cir. 1989) ("Functional separation is hard to achieve (new instruments will appear at any border)."), cert. denied, 110 S. Ct. 3214 (1990).

[33] See Breeden Testimony, supra note 19, at 3.

[34] See, e.g., Order Approving OCC Proposed Rule Change on Cross-Margining, Exchange Act Release No. 26153, 53 Fed. Reg. 39567, 39567 (1988) (approving the OCC's application to provide cross-margining of OCC-cleared securities options with futures positions executed and cleared by the Intermarket Clearing Corporation (ICC)); Order Granting the ICC Temporary Registration As a Clearing Agency, Exchange Act Release No. 26154, 53 Fed. Reg. 39556, 39557 (1988) (approving the ICC's application as a clearing agency). The ICC, which is a division of the OCC, clears for the New York Futures Exchange, the Philadelphia Board of Trade, and the American Stock Exchange Commodities Corporation. ELECTRONIC BULLS AND BEARS, supra note 6, at 10. "Clearing" is explained supra at note 12. "Settlement" is the procedure through which payment in exchange for a financial product occurs. See ELECTRONIC BULLS AND BEARS, supra note 6, at 181-93, for a thorough discussion of clearing and settlement. Coordinated clearing and settlement remains a hotly debated topic that has spawned legislative initiatives, although to date none of these initiatives has been adopted. See S. 648, 101st Cong., 2d Sess., § 5, 136 CONG. REC. S12548, S12550 (daily ed. Aug. 4, 1990) (Market Reform Act of 1990) (directing the SEC and CFTC to facilitate linked or coordinated exchanges for the clearance and settlement of securities, futures, and options transactions); H.R. 3656, 101st Cong., 2d Sess., 136 CONG. REC. H2062 (daily ed. May 8, 1990) (Coordinated Clearance and Settlement Act of 1990) (same). Studies have also called for coordinated clearing and settlement systems. See, e.g., BRADY REPORT, supra note 8, at 64. Because of the complexity of the subject, this Article will not further expand upon coordinated clearing and settlement. For a thorough discussion of issues arising in this area, see the reports accompanying S. 648 and H.R. 3656, supra, as well as ELECTRONIC BULLS AND BEARS, supra note 6, at 107-25.

[35] There have been numerous studies in connection with this issue. See, e.g., BRADY REPORT, supra note 8, at 64; GAO ASSESSMENT, supra note 8.

tor" that would perform the functions currently assigned to both the SEC and CFTC,[36] and (2) dividing regulatory responsibilities among the SEC, CFTC, and other governmental bodies and unifying regulation over certain areas or products such as margin on stock index products.[37] It will be demonstrated that these initiatives, in their present forms, derive from the functional and definitional approaches. Consequently, they limit the debate regarding regulatory reform by foreclosing an approach to market regulation that industry interrelatedness demands.

II. The Evolution of the SEC-CFTC Jurisdictional Debate

As noted above, jurisdiction over new financial instruments is based upon the categorization of the instruments as "securities" or "futures contracts." Past experience demonstrates that the introduction of derivative products such as stock index futures required that the traditional definitions regarding whether a product qualified as a "futures contract" or a "security" be reanalyzed and refined because such products did not fall neatly into the traditional definitional categories.[38] To understand the issues that arise in debates over the regulation of new products, it is necessary to have a general understanding of the evolution of the definitional structure underlying the current SEC-CFTC jurisdictional conflict. In this

---

[36] *See, e.g.,* H.R. 965, 102d Cong., 1st Sess., 137 CONG. REC. H1004 (daily ed. Feb. 19, 1991) (Markets and Trading Reorganization and Reform Act of 1991). This bill, which was recently referred to the Energy and Commerce Committee and Agriculture Committee of the U.S. House of Representatives, seeks to establish a Markets and Trading Commission to combine in one agency the functions of the SEC and CFTC. *See infra* notes 190–92 and accompanying text for a description of the bill. *See also* BRADY REPORT, *supra* note 8, at 59–63 (calling for the establishment of a single regulatory agency that rationalizes intermarket issues, but rejecting the view that the Federal Reserve, the Treasury Department, the SEC, a joint Federal Reserve-SEC-CFTC committee, or an SEC-CFTC merger would necessarily produce effective intermarket regulation).

[37] Other initiatives currently pending in Congress fall into this category. On March 5, 1991, the House passed H.R. 707, the Commodity Futures Improvements Act of 1991. *See* 137 CONG. REC. H1350 (daily ed. Mar. 5, 1991). In acting on H.R. 707, the Senate substituted the provisions of related legislation that had been under consideration by that body, S. 207, the Futures Trading Practices Act of 1991, and passed the bill as amended on April 18th. *See* 137 CONG. REC. S4708 (daily ed. Apr. 18, 1991). Among other differences, the House version of H.R. 707 does not contain intermarket provisions like those in the Senate bill. *See* S. 207, 102d Cong., 1st Sess. §§ 301–304, 137 CONG. REC. S4423, S4432–33 (daily ed. Apr. 16, 1991) (Futures Trading Practices Act of 1991). For a discussion intermarket provisions of the Futures Trading Practices Act of 1991, see *infra* notes 184–89 and accompanying text. The two versions of H.R. 707 have currently been referred to a joint committee for resolution. At the time of printing of this Article, no date had been set for conference.

Recent initiatives that have not been enacted include H.R. 4997, 100th Cong., 2d Sess. (1988) (Securities Market Reform Act of 1988), and H.R. 5265, 100th Cong., 2d Sess. (1988) (Commodity Exchange Option Amendments of 1988).

[38] For a discussion of the definition of "security" under the federal securities laws, see *infra* notes 56–59 and accompanying text.

connection, subparts II(A) and II(B) below describe, respectively, the CFTC's and SEC's traditional jurisdictional authority. Subparts II(C) and II(D) examine how the current structure evolved to inhibit new product development.

A. The CFTC's Traditional Jurisdiction

Under section 2(a)(1)(A) of the CEAct, the CFTC possesses *exclusive* jurisdiction to regulate "transactions involving contracts of sale of a commodity for future delivery" (i.e., futures contracts) and options thereon.[39] This "exclusive jurisdiction clause" lurks at the core of the jurisdictional controversy and remains, undoubtedly, the single most important statutory provision in the context of new product development. It should be noted that the exclusive jurisdiction clause was intended to play an innovation-enhancing role by preempting conflicting state laws governing futures trading and by facilitating a competent scheme of federal regulation and self-regulation for the futures industry.[40]

The exclusive jurisdiction clause's importance results, first, from the fact that the CEAct casts a broad and undefined net over the instruments

---

[39] With respect to futures contracts and options thereon, § 2(a)(1)(A) of the CEAct specifically provides:

> [T]he [CFTC] shall have exclusive jurisdiction with respect to accounts, agreements (including any transaction which is of the character of, or is commonly known to the trade as an "option," "privilege," "indemnity," "bid," "offer," "put," "call," "advance guaranty," or "decline guaranty"), *and transactions involving contracts of sale of a commodity for future delivery*, traded or executed on a contract market designated pursuant to [§ 5] of [the CEAct] or any other board of trade, exchange, or market. . . .

CEAct § 2(a)(1)(A), 7 U.S.C. § 2 (1988) (emphasis added). This provision was adopted to give a single agency responsibility for regulating the commodities industry and to prevent potentially conflicting regulation by the states. *See* 120 CONG. REC. 30458–59 (1974) (statement of Sen. Talmadge); H.R. REP. NO. 975, 93d Cong., 2d Sess. 48 (1974). Section 4c(b) of the CEAct, relating to commodity options, provides:

> No person shall offer to enter into, enter into or confirm the execution of, any transaction involving any commodity regulated under [the CEAct] which is of the character of, or is commonly known to the trade as, an "option," "privilege," "indemnity," "bid," "offer," "put," "call," "advance guaranty," or "decline guaranty," contrary to any rule, regulation, or order of the [CFTC] prohibiting any such transaction or allowing any such transaction under such terms and conditions as the [CFTC] shall prescribe.

7. U.S.C. § 6(c)(b) (1988).

It must be noted, however, that § 12(e) of the CEAct provides that it does not preempt, *inter alia*, state or federal laws governing off-exchange futures, options on futures, or commodity options transactions. *CEAct § 12(e), 7 U.S.C. § 16(e) (1988). Section 2(a)(1)(B)(i) of the CEAct, moreover, prevents the CFTC from regulating stock options and thereby limits CFTC regulatory authority over futures contracts to those that are not also stock options. 7 U.S.C. § 2a(i) (1988). Although these provisions should be kept in mind, this Article refers to CFTC jurisdiction over futures and options thereon as "exclusive."*
[40] *See* T. RUSSO, *supra* note 4, §§ 10.02–.03.

within the CFTC's exclusive ambit. Thus, the scope of the term "commodity" is statutorily defined to include all "goods and articles, except onions. . . , and all services, rights, and interests in which contracts for future delivery are presently or in the future dealt in."[41] This broad range of commodities was set forth in the 1974 amendments to the CEAct when the CFTC was created as an independent agency, and was intended to be a sword that led the way to product innovation within a regulated environment. The extensive range of commodities encompassed by the CEAct, moreover, was specifically intended to counter fraudulent schemes through which "boiler-room" operators exploited the previous framework of limited federal authority over futures contracts on agricultural commodities by offering and selling to the public unregulated futures on metals, lumber, coffee, and other goods not enumerated under the former law.[42]

In contrast to the CEAct's explicit yet broad definition of commodity, the CEAct and CFTC regulations conspicuously omit *any* definition of the term "futures contracts." Once again, the breadth of the term "futures contracts" should also be understood as a means to strengthen the basis of federal regulation over fraudulent activities involving futures and to enhance the safety and soundness of the U.S. futures markets. As a result of this statutory ambiguity, however, the responsibility for determining which new products qualify as futures contracts under the CEAct remains initially the province of the CFTC. Ultimately, this task has been thrust upon the courts.

From 1974, when the CFTC was created, until 1989, there evolved a construct for defining a futures contract that was based upon the existence of specific elements.[43] Although courts and the CFTC consistently claimed that these elements were merely guideposts rather than determinative elements, this approach generally provided a consistent and understandable definition of the term "futures contract."

Under this approach, the CFTC and the courts generally defined fu-

---

[41] CEAct § 2(a)(1)(A), 7 U.S.C. § 2 (1988); *see* Board of Trade of Chicago v. SEC, 677 F.2d 1137, 1142 (7th Cir.) (*GNMA Options*), *vacated as moot*, 459 U.S. 1026 (1982) ("By this amendment, literally anything other than onions could become a 'commodity' and thereby subject to CFTC regulation simply by its futures being traded on some exchange.") (footnote omitted).

[42] Prior to 1974, the Commodity Exchange Authority, the CFTC's predecessor, had authority to regulate futures trading only on certain agricultural products defined as "commodities." As a result, a number of futures contracts were traded in the United States without the benefit of federal regulation. Congress's concern regarding potential expansion of unregulated futures trading led to the adoption, in 1974, of an expanded definition of "commodity" to increase the scope of the CFTC's jurisdiction. *See* S. REP. No. 1131, 93d Cong., 2d Sess. 19, 46 (1974).

[43] See *infra* subpart III(B) for a discussion of how the IPs case altered this traditional framework in 1989.

tures contracts as bilateral contracts[44] for the purchase or sale of commodities for future delivery that are: (1) standardized, (2) directly or indirectly offered to the general public, (3) generally secured by "earnest money" or margin,[45] (4) entered into for managing price risk rather than for transferring ownership of actual commodities, and (5) generally extinguished by entry into offsetting contracts prior to the date on which delivery is called for and by payment of a cash amount representing the difference in price between the initial and offsetting transactions.[46]

The CEAct also contains certain exclusions and exemptions from regulation under its provisions, which are again the responsibility of the CFTC and courts to interpret. For example, contracts relating to the sale of any cash commodity for deferred shipment or delivery (i.e., "forward contracts") are excluded from the CEAct's definition of futures con-tracts.[47] Additionally, certain transactions covered by the

---

[44] "Bilateralism" means that a contract imposes a performance obligation in the future on both parties, such as when parties to an agricultural futures contract agree to deliver and pay or settle in cash on a future settlement date. *But see infra* notes 156–58 and accompanying text (discussing instances in which bilateralism was not deemed essential to a futures contract).

[45] See Appendix Part VI for a discussion of futures margins.

[46] *See,* e.g., *In re* First Nat'l Monetary Corp., [1984–1986 Transfer Binder] Comm. Fut. L. Rep. (CCH) ¶ 22698, at 30974–75 (CFTC Aug. 7, 1985); *In re* Stovall, [1977–1980 Transfer Binder] Comm. Fut. L. Rep. (CCH) ¶ 20941, at 23777 (CFTC Dec. 6, 1979); *see also* CFTC v. Co Petro Mktg. Group, Inc., 680 F.2d 573, 579–81 (9th Cir. 1982) (finding that although an investment company's contracts were not completely standardized in terms of quantity and delivery date, a provision in the contract obligating the company to engage in an offsetting transaction for the customer sufficed to make then "contracts of sale of a commodity for future delivery" within the meaning of § 2(a)(1) of the CEAct); CFTC v. National Coal Exch., Inc., [1980–1982 Transfer Binder] Comm. Fut. L. Rep. (CCH) ¶ 21424, at 26053 (W.D. Tenn. May 7, 1982) (comparing deferred delivery contracts with commodity futures). Similarly, the CEAct does not define the term "commodity option." Commodity options, nevertheless, have been characterized by courts as contracts in which: (1) the initial charge is a nonrefundable premium payable by the purchaser; (2) the purchaser has the right, but not the obligation, to purchase or sell the underlying commodity or futures contract; and (3) the purchaser's profit is determined by the extent to which any change in price of the underlying commodity or futures contract exceeds the cost of the premium and any related charges, while its loss is limited to the amount of the premium and such charges. *See,* e.g., United States v. Bein, 728 F.2d 107, 111–12 (2d Cir.), *cert. denied sub nom.* De Angelis v. United States, 469 U.S. 837 (1984); CFTC v. United States Metals Depository Corp., 468 F. Supp. 1149, 1155 (S.D.N.Y. 1979). Hence, it has been noted that a commodity option, unlike a futures contract, imposes an obligation on only one party. The regulation of commodity options has been the subject of great controversy because those instruments have a long history of serious abuses. *See,* e.g., Gilberg, *supra* note 4, at 1612. The controversy regarding such abuses led, in the era following the Great Depression, to a 30-year blanket prohibition on the sale of any options on agricultural commodities. For a discussion of the history of commodity option regulation under the CEAct, see *id.* at 1612–15.

[47] *See* CEAct § 2(a)(1)(A), 7 U.S.C. § 2 (1988). This exemption is known as the "cash forward" exclusion. The CFTC has stated that this exemption covers only contracts entered into with the expectation that delivery of the actual commodity will occur. *See,* e.g., *Stovall,* [1977–1980 Transfer Binder] Comm. Fut. L. Rep. (CCH) ¶ 20941, at 23777–78; Characteristics Distinguishing Cash and Forward Contracts and "Trade" Options, 50 Fed. Reg. 39656, 39657 (CFTC 1985) (Office of the General Counsel Interpretative Statement).

so-called Treasury Amendment are exempt from CEAct regulation.[48]

Another essential component of the CFTC's regulatory structure is section 4(a) of the CEAct, which by and large restricts futures trading in the United States to transactions effected on futures exchanges "designated" by the CFTC.[49] The exchange trading requirement is incorporated in the CFTC's regulatory regime through the requirement that each futures contract meet certain criteria before a CFTC-regulated exchange will be "designated" as a contract market upon which that futures contract may be traded.[50] The designation requirements relate to the intrinsic merit of new futures or options on futures and require that each new transaction have an "economic purpose" and be "not contrary to the public interest."[51]

---

[48] "[T]ransactions in foreign currency, security warrants, security rights, resales of installment loan contracts, repurchase options, government securities, or mortgages and mortgage purchase commitments, unless such transactions involve the sale thereof for future delivery conducted on a board of trade," are exempt from the coverage of the CEAct. CEAct §2(a)(1)(A), 7 U.S.C. § 2 (1988). This exemption, known as the Treasury Amendment, was proposed by the Department of the Treasury during the amendment of the CEAct in 1974. *See* Letter from Donald Ritger, Acting General Counsel of the Treasury Department to Sen. Herman Talmadge, Chairman of the Senate Committee on Agriculture and Forestry (July 30, 1974), *reprinted in* 1974 U.S. CODE CONG. & ADMIN. NEWS 5887, 5887–89. The CFTC has interpreted this provision to apply only to transactions between banks and other sophisticated and regulated institutions. *See* Trading in Foreign Currencies for Future Delivery, 50 Fed. Reg. 42983, 42984 (CFTC 1985). For an interesting discussion of the Treasury Amendment as it applies to banks trading foreign-currency options, see COMMITTEE ON FUTURES REGULATION OF THE ASS'N OF THE BAR OF THE CITY OF NEW YORK, REGULATORY FRAMEWORK FOR FOREIGN CURRENCY TRADING 54–59 (Dec. 1986). This provision also has been interpreted by courts to be inapplicable to options transactions based upon the view that options are transactions *involving* rather than *in* the underlying instruments. *See, e.g.,* CFTC v. American Board of Trade, 803 F.2d 1242, 1248–49 (2d Cir. 1986).

[49] *See* CEAct § 4(a), 7 U.S.C. § 6(a) (1988). *Futures contracts, furthermore, must be traded openly and competitively on the floors of CFTC-regulated exchanges. See* 17 C.F.R. § 1.38 (1991). In a related manner, the CFTC's option regulations prohibit over-the-counter commodity option transactions, except with respect to options that qualify for an exemption as "dealer" or "trade" options. *See id.* § 32.12 (dealer options); *id.* § 32.4 (trade options). The CFTC also has jurisdiction to regulate foreign futures under §§ 2(a)(1)(A) and 4(b) of the CEAct and has promulgated regulations governing the offer and sale of foreign futures and foreign exchange-traded options to persons in the United States. *See* Foreign Futures and Foreign Options Transactions, 17 C.F.R. §§ 30.1–.11 (1991). It must be emphasized that the Futures Trading Practices Act of 1991, discussed *supra* at note 37, does not address designation and exchange trading, but only seeks to exempt certain transactions from CFTC regulation, including designation and exchange trading. Thus, it would not solve this essential barrier to innovation and U.S. competitiveness in the world financial market. *See infra* notes 184–88 and accompanying text.

[50] CEAct § 5, 7 U.S.C. § 7 (1988).

[51] *Id.* § 5(g), 7 U.S.C. § 7(g) (1988); *see* Guideline on Economic and Public Interest Requirements for Contract Market Designation, 40 Fed. Reg. 25850 (CFTC 1975) [hereinafter Guideline 1]. Guideline 1 is not a CFTC Rule, but rather is an interpretive statement. *See* Economic and Public Interest Requirements for Contract Market Designation, 47 Fed. Reg. 49832, 49833 (CFTC 1982) (revising Guideline 1 and expressing the CFTC's view that it should be readopted as an interpretive statement rather than codified as a Rule). For a discussion of the designation requirements and Guideline 1, see T. RUSSO, *supra* note 4, § 1.39.

This exchange trading requirement, like the exclusive jurisdiction clause, the broad definition of "commodity," and the absence of a definition of "futures contract," was designed to maintain and preserve the safety and soundness of the futures markets and limit fraud by requiring that futures contracts traded in the United States be subject to CFTC oversight and the control of CFTC-regulated futures exchanges.[52] The structure of the CEAct originated at a time when there was general agreement over the meaning of "futures contract," and this general agreement continued to exist in 1974 when the CEAct was amended to include virtually all commodities. This structure encouraged new traditional futures contracts on numerous nontraditional commodities, such as futures on GNMA certificates and Treasury Bills,[53] to be developed pursuant to federal regulation.

B. The SEC's Traditional Jurisdiction

SEC jurisdiction, on the other hand, extends to all instruments that fall within the definition of a "security" *and* that are not exempt under sections 3(a)(2)–3(a)(8) of the Securities Act of 1933 ("1933 Act")[54] or section 3(a)(12) of the Securities Exchange Act of 1934 ("1934 Act").[55] To laypersons, the term "security" is associated with either equity instruments, such as IBM stock, that represent shares in the ownership of corporations, or debt instruments, such as corporate, municipal, and U.S. Treasury notes and bonds.[56] The federal securities laws, however, also traditionally defined "security" to include any right or contract to purchase a security—namely, stock options.[57]

It has been observed that the definition of a security under the federal securities laws "has been the subject of extensive judicial and legal debate and has spawned probably the most extensive literature in the areas of securities and commodities regulation."[58] This uncertainty has resulted in large part from questions regarding the scope of the definitions of tra-

---

[52] *See* 1 P. JOHNSON & T. HAZEN, COMMODITIES REGULATION § 1.06 (2d ed. 1989) (discussing how the exchange trading requirement originated from a desire to prevent the "bucketing" of customer orders, in which a futures trader promises to execute a customer order but pockets the customer's cash without making a transaction).

[53] *See* Seeger, *supra* note 9, at 10.

[54] Securities Act of 1933 § 3(a), 15 U.S.C. § 77c(a) (1988). For a thorough discussion of exemptions regarding securities under § 3 of the 1933 Act, see T. HAZEN, THE LAW OF SECURITIES REGULATION 127–69 (1990). Section 4 of the 1933 Act contains exemptions regarding certain transactions. *See* 15 U.S.C. § 77d (1988); T. HAZEN, *supra*, at 185–202.

[55] *See* Securities Exchange Act of 1934 § 3(a)(12), 15 U.S.C. § 78c(a)(12) (1988).

[56] *See* ELECTRONIC BULLS AND BEARS, *supra* note 6, at 3 n.3.

[57] *See* Securities Act of 1933 § 2(1), 15 U.S.C. § 77b(1) (1988).

[58] Gilberg, *supra* note 4, at 1622 & n.122 (collecting citations). For a thorough discussion of the numerous definitions of a "security" under the federal securities laws, see T. HAZEN, *supra* note 54, at 22–41.

ditional securities such as "investment contracts," "stock," and "notes."[59] Although the definition of a traditional security remains elusive, the effect of an instrument's characterization as a security is not whether the instrument may be offered but rather the manner in which it will be offered.[60] This is so because, unlike the CEAct's regulatory regime, which requires that new futures contracts must be designated prior to trading on a CFTC-regulated exchange, the federal securities laws are primarily concerned with regulating the "types and distribution of information provided to prospective investors" through registration requirements for nonexempt securities.[61]

Provided a financial product is a security under the 1933 Act and the 1934 Act, its offer or sale is subject to the comprehensive framework of SEC regulation, which, as indicated above, is designed "[t]o provide full and fair disclosure of the character of securities sold" to public investors.[62] Under this regime, in contrast to the CEAct, trading off-exchange, i.e., over-the-counter (OTC), has been institutionalized.[63] Further, although the rules of various SEC-regulated exchanges had restricted the off-exchange trading of certain listed securities, SEC regulations and industry practice have allowed OTC trading of many stocks that are also traded on an exchange.[64]

It should also be noted that OTC stock options existed when the CFTC was created in 1974, but were traded in a dealer market that remained unregulated by the SEC as a market.[65] Accordingly, the SEC's traditional jurisdiction over stock options included the premise that stock options qualified as "securities," but the SEC had not exercised its traditional authority to regulate the market for OTC options.[66]

In addition, it has been noted that, historically, the "SEC has been more cautious [than the CFTC] in approving new products for exchange trading."[67] Such historical reluctance on the part of the SEC to regulate

---

[59] *See* T. HAZEN, *supra* note 54, at 24–39 (discussing the development of judicial tests for identifying these instruments).

[60] *See* Gilberg, *supra* note 4, at 1621.

[61] *Id. But see infra* note 232 and accompanying text.

[62] Securities Act of 1933, Pub. L. No. 73–22, preamble, 48 Stat. 74, 74.

[63] *See infra* note 199 (discussing the self-regulatory regime of the OTC market in securities). For a discussion of the operation of the OTC market in stocks, see ELECTRONIC BULLS AND BEARS, *supra* note 6, at 45–47.

[64] *See* T. HAZEN, *supra* note 54, at 492 (noting that the pre-1976 practice of SEC-regulated exchanges prohibiting the off-exchange trading of listed securities "has now been abolished"). *But see* Rule 390, New York Stock Exchange, Inc., Constitution and Rules (CCH) ¶ 2390 (Feb. 1, 1989) [hereinafter NYSE Rules] (prohibiting, *inter alia*, exchange members from making off-exchange markets for listed stocks); ELECTRONIC BULLS AND BEARS, *supra* note 6, at 48–49 (discussing initiatives to abolish Rule 390).

[65] *See* ELECTRONIC BULLS AND BEARS, *supra* note 6, at 93–94.

[66] *See id.*

[67] *Id.* at 20.

markets in innovative instruments is illustrated through its declining to develop a market in futures contracts on mortgage certificates when approached by the Federal Home Loan Mortgage Corporation in 1972 regarding this prospect.[68]

C. *Regulation of Exchange-Traded Options: A Clash of Traditions*

Two jurisdictional regimes, emanating from the definitions of futures contracts and securities, might have coexisted without much controversy if these definitions had remained understandable as a means to distinguish between instruments. Bifurcation would make sense in a world in which futures contracts were the only instruments for managing price risk and there was a consensus that risk management instruments should be traded on an exchange and in which regulated securities markets solely involved corporate ownership, debt, or "investment contracts."

The possibility for a lasting peaceful coexistence, however, first became doubtful with the development of exchange-traded options and the establishment of the CBOE in 1973, one year prior to the CFTC's creation. A review of the CBOE experience illustrates the origins of the SEC-CFTC jurisdictional conflict concerning stock derivatives and highlights the process of financial innovation.

The process of financial innovation that resulted in the CBOE followed an elementary path presently applicable to all controversial (i.e., important) new product developments: (1) an idea, (2) falling outside of the current framework, (3) spawning conflict, and (4) resulting in a regulatory or legislative compromise that led to future jurisdictional disputes.

1. The Idea. The concept of exchange-traded options originated with a special committee of the CBOT, a prominent futures exchange, and came to fruition in 1973. The committee's objective, as it was later described by the CBOT, was to "develop *futures contracts* in securities."[69] Hence, it should be noted that the futures exchanges took the lead in developing this first revolutionary innovation in new products.

The general idea was to create an analogue to futures contracts on another type of financial instrument, securities, based upon the notion that investors needed a hedging tool (like futures) to manage the price risk of securities, just as grain producers had needed futures contracts on

---

[68] *See* Russo & Lyon, *The Exclusive Jurisdiction of the Commodity Futures Trading Commission,* 6 HOFSTRA L. REV. 57, 61–62 (1977). In 1975, the CFTC designated the CBOT as a contract market for futures contracts on GNMA certificates, described *supra* at note 5. For a discussion of the SEC-CFTC conflicts concerning jurisdiction over GNMA futures, see Russo & Lyon, *supra,* at 65–66.

[69] Board of Trade of Chicago v. SEC, 677 F.2d 1137, 1140 n.2 (7th Cir.) (*GNMA Options*), *vacated as moot,* 459 U.S. 1026 (1982) (quoting the CBOT's comments to the SEC objecting to the CBOE's proposed rule change to accommodate the trading of exchange-formed offset options on GNMAs).

grain to hedge against price fluctuations in that market.[70] The novelty of the exchange-traded option arises from its premise: to create a hedging instrument that functions like a futures contract but is not a futures contract and whose price derives from a financial instrument rather than an agricultural commodity. The idea, therefore, arose in an effort to design something truly groundbreaking, a product whose usefulness depended upon its unique attributes.

2. *A Regulatory Misfit.* It is this novelty that led to the next phase of innovation and regulatory complication: fitting this new idea into the existing structure. This step may be viewed as relatively simple in hindsight, because in 1973 the CBOT and other futures exchanges were regulated by the Department of Agriculture, whose statutory jurisdiction over futures contracts extended only to futures on agricultural commodities.[71] The SEC as regulator of the underlying commodity, in this case securities, became the chosen regulator by necessity. Indeed, the 1933 and 1934 Acts authorized this result by defining rights or contracts to buy securities as "securities."[72]

By becoming the regulator of exchange-traded options, however, the SEC's traditional role of regulating capital formation was transformed into overseeing the regulation of standardized risk management instruments.[73] As noted above, in 1973 OTC stock options constituted a small and rather unimportant market and were not regulated by the SEC as a market. Thus, when regulation of exchange-traded options was thrust upon it in 1973, the SEC did not even have meaningful experience regulating a market for "primitive" risk management instruments such as OTC dealer options. The SEC's role transformation, however, may have been justified at that time upon the grounds that exchange-traded options involved only options on corporate and debt securities and that regulation of these underlying instruments appeared to be the rightful province of the SEC.

Accordingly, the SEC's jurisdiction over exchange-traded options obviated any hope that regulatory jurisdiction over new products would be based upon the functional-instrument approach; exchange-traded stock options were specifically designed to "approximate" futures on stock.[74]

---

[70] See *supra* note 29 for a discussion of hedging.

[71] *See supra* note 42.

[72] *See supra* note 57 and accompanying text.

[73] *See generally* Chicago Mercantile Exch. v. SEC, 883 F.2d 537, 543 (7th Cir. 1989) ("[T]he distinction between capital formation and hedging falls apart when it comes time to allocate the regulation of options"), *cert. denied*, 110 S. Ct. 3214 (1990).

[74] Former CFTC Chairman Philip Johnson has stated that CBOE "options could approximate the desired instrument" (i.e., futures on securities). Johnson, *supra* note 9, at 305. He has suggested also that the CBOT abandoned its original idea to offer futures contracts on individual equity securities because of the limited scope of the CEAct at that

Similarly, by creating a securities exchange to trade such options, the futures exchanges effectively divorced the regulation of risk management instruments from the futures regulatory regime, thereby eliminating the possibility of regulation by traditional agency function. The regulation of the CBOE, however, did not vitiate a functional-agency framework based upon an agency's expertise regulating the product *underlying* a derivative instrument, because the SEC regulated all derivatives based upon stock, while the Agriculture Department regulated derivatives of specific agricultural commodities.

3. Conflict. Then the structure changed and the third stage of innovation under bifurcated regulation—conflict—arose. The structural change that provoked conflict was the amendment of the CEAct in 1974. The amendments established the CFTC in 1974 as an independent agency with exclusive jurisdiction over "futures contracts" on virtually all things that could fall under the rubric of the term "commodity." The 1974 CEAct amendments, however, also included a "savings clause" that stated "except as hereinabove provided, nothing contained in this section shall . . . limit the jurisdiction at any time conferred on the" SEC.[75] The savings clause was inserted below the CFTC's exclusive jurisdiction clause in the statute, bringing the exclusive jurisdiction clause within the terms "hereinabove provided" of the savings clause. Consequently, the savings clause, on its face, appeared to preserve the SEC's jurisdiction over contracts to purchase securities (options) that are not also futures contracts. The challenge then (and now) became drawing a definitional line between contracts to purchase securities (stock options) and futures contracts.[76]

Conflict inevitably resulted in 1975 when the CFTC permitted the trading of futures contracts on GNMA certificates (a government security) based upon the determination that these securities constituted "commodities" within the meaning of the CEAct.[77] The SEC, in response, chal-

---

time. *See id.* at 304–05. This rationale, however, does not support a decision to transform futures on equities into options on equities. The decision to offer options instead of futures, according to Johnson, resulted from the absence of a futures regulator in combination with the fact that "the securities industry was better acquainted with securities options," because of the OTC market. *Id.* at 305. The fact that the SEC did not regulate the OTC market as a market casts doubt upon the implication that the SEC was better equipped to regulate the market for securities options than securities futures at that time. Accordingly, it may have been partially because of a misperception that the SEC was prevented from becoming the regulator of futures contracts on individual corporate and debt securities in 1973.

[75] Commodity Futures Trading Commission Act of 1974, Pub. L. No. 93–463, § 201(b), 88 Stat. 1389, 1395 (codified as amended at CEAct § 2(a)(1)(A), 7 U.S.C. § 2 (1988)).

[76] *See infra* notes 135–53 and accompanying text (analyzing how the differences between futures and stock options are crucial to maintaining bifurcated regulation).

[77] For a discussion of the SEC-CFTC conflicts between 1975 and 1981, see T. RUSSO, *supra* note 4, §§ 10.22–.23. GNMA certificates are described *supra* at note 5.

lenged the CFTC's authority to trade futures on GNMA certificates. This challenge was based on the view that the SEC's authority to regulate securities, including contracts to buy securities, was preserved in the CEAct (even though the savings clause appeared to exclude SEC jurisdiction over securities futures). This agency conflict, however, did not discourage the futures exchanges from offering futures based on securities. To the contrary, CFTC-regulated exchanges created futures on governmental securities such as U.S. Treasury bonds and bills from 1975 to 1981.

Litigation, nevertheless, arose in 1981 when the SEC approved the trading of options on GNMA certificates on the CBOE.[78] The SEC's approval of CBOE options on GNMA certificates provided the first instance in which an option traded on an SEC-regulated exchange was based upon something deemed a "commodity" by the CFTC. Prior to 1981, CBOE options had been based upon nongovernmental single securities, and the futures exchanges had not traded futures contracts on these nongovernmental securities.

The CBOT challenged the SEC's jurisdiction over GNMA options based on the principle that because the CFTC interpreted the CEAct to include GNMA certificates as "commodities," the CFTC had exclusive jurisdiction over options on such commodities. Although the Chairmen of the SEC and CFTC reached an accord (the "SEC-CFTC Accord" or "Accord") regarding jurisdiction over new products such as GNMA futures and options, the Accord had not been legislatively enated[79] when the Seventh Circuit reached a decision concerning jurisdiction over GNMA options.

In its *GNMA Options* decision, the court determined that the CFTC had exclusive jurisdiction over GNMA options as commodity options, and concluded that because of the CFTC's commodity option ban then in existence, the CBOE could not trade the options.[80] The legal rationale for the court's decision opened the door to the trap of definitional and, to a certain extent, functional reasoning. The court's reasoning exemplifies both the superficial attractiveness of allocating jurisdiction upon definitional and functional grounds, and the pitfalls of this attraction.

With respect to definitions, the court determined that GNMA options were commodity options and were subject to the CFTC's jurisdiction through that agency's option ban.[81] This conclusion was based upon the

---

[78] Board of Trade of Chicago v. SEC, 677 F.2d 1137 (7th Cir.) (*GNMA Options*), *vacated as moot*, 459 U.S. 1026 (1982).

[79] See *infra* section II(C)(4) for a discussion of the SEC-CFTC Accord as codified.

[80] *GNMA Options*, 677 F.2d at 1144.

[81] *Id.* at 1143–44. The court also noted that trading in GNMA options would violate the newly adopted CFTC regulations which prohibited options directly on "commodities" and only permitted options on futures contracts that met certain criteria to be traded. *See id.* at 1144 & n.15; Regulation of Exchange-Traded Commodity Options: Final Rules, 46 Fed. Reg. 54500, 54530 (CFTC 1981) (codified as amended at 17 C.F.R. § 33.4 (1991)).

notion that because GNMA certificates had been deemed "commodities" by the CFTC, options on such "commodities" fell within the definition of "commodity option."[82] This line of reasoning, however, if taken to its logical conclusion, could have resulted in CFTC jurisdiction over the options on debt and equity securities that were already trading on the CBOE under SEC oversight.[83] This analysis could have been adequate to resolving the issue before the court (i.e., to prevent the CBOE from trading GNMA options) but would have eviscerated the savings clause, noted above.[84]

Thus, the court needed to add a functional gloss to this aspect of its decision by noting that the savings clause was intended to preserve SEC jurisdiction over options on corporate and debt securities.[85] Accordingly, the court attempted to draw the jurisdictional boundaries between exchange-traded options by first concluding that GNMA options fit the definition of "commodity option," yet because this rationale could divest the SEC of any authority over options, it concluded that the SEC's traditional authority over corporate and debt securities required limiting the CEAct's jurisdiction over options on such securities.[86]

Having established CFTC jurisdiction over GNMA options pursuant to the option ban and the added agency-function gloss, the court also examined whether the exclusive jurisdiction clause granted the CFTC *exclusive* jurisdiction over commodity options. The court fashioned an "analysis" of the scope of the CFTC's jurisdiction over transactions "involving" futures contracts. Building upon its options analysis, the court stated: "Since GNMA's are not traditional stocks and GNMA options have the character of a legitimate commodity derivative, we hold that the proposed GNMA options 'involve' the pre-existing GNMA futures and therefore are within the exclusive jurisdiction of the CFTC."[87]

Through this determination, the court transformed GNMA options from instruments that may have been within the CFTC's jurisdiction due to the commodity option ban into commodity options within the CFTC's *exclusive* jurisdiction based almost entirely on its view that GNMA options

---

[82] *GNMA Options,* 677 F.2d at 1143–44 & n.13. The court determined that GNMA certificates became "commodities" under the CEAct when the CFTC designated the CBOT as a contract market for trading futures contracts on GNMA certificates. *See id.*

[83] All the CFTC would have needed to do to produce this result was designate futures contracts on these traditional securities, which was not proscribed then as it is today. *See infra* note 94 and accompanying text (discussing the prohibition on futures on individual debt and equity securities).

[84] *See GNMA Options,* 677 F.2d at 1145 ("[T]he savings clause may indeed limit the option ban.").

[85] *Id.* at 1148 n.22.

[86] *See id.* at 1150 (citing the 1974 legislative history to the CEAct to suggest that "only 'traditional' SEC authority over corporate securities was to be preserved").

[87] *Id.* at 1152–53. It should be noted that the CEAct amendments of 1974 established CFTC exclusive jurisdiction over all transactions "involving" contracts of sale for future delivery. *See supra* note 39 and accompanying text.

"involved" GNMA futures.[88] It is interesting to examine briefly the Seventh Circuit's strained reasoning in enlarging CFTC exclusivity in this connection and also to note that the court's proclivity for widening CFTC exclusivity by expansively interpreting the exclusive jurisdiction clause that later appeared in the IPs case[89] originated from *GNMA Options*.

Under the court's opaque exclusivity formulation, any "legitimate"[90] commodity derivative product that is not derived from "traditional stocks" and is derived from a "commodity" upon which a CFTC-approved futures contract is based would be a commodity option subject to CFTC exclusivity. Accordingly, the critical feature that distinguished commodity options subject to CFTC exclusivity from those that are not was the underlying commodity. The term "involving" contained in the exclusive jurisdiction clause, under the court's view, would bootstrap options on commodities upon which futures have been designated into CFTC exclusivity merely because such futures are within CFTC exclusivity. Effectively, the court held that CFTC exclusivity regarding designated futures would attach to commodities underlying such futures and give rise to CFTC exclusivity over options when derived from such commodities.

Clearly, the court's approach with respect to CFTC exclusivity, as well as with regard to SEC and CFTC jurisdiction over options, failed to distinguish instruments by function. Rather, the court in discussing CFTC exclusivity vested jurisdiction over options based solely upon whether the type of product underlying an option also had been the product underlying a CFTC-designated futures contract. Under the court's threshold options approach, SEC jurisdiction would depend only upon whether the underlying product is a traditional stock. The CFTC's exclusive jurisdiction over commodity options and the SEC's jurisdiction over stock options, thus, would hinge upon whether a designated futures contract on a product underlying an option predated an option on such product and on that product not being a traditional stock. In any event, it is apparent that the court's logic in reaching these confusing results did not derive from a functional-instrument approach.

It is also apparent that the court's conclusions regarding the scope of the SEC's jurisdiction as opposed to that of the CFTC were purely definitional and not the result of a functional-agency approach, given that drawing a line between each agency's jurisdiction depended not upon the function of each but upon whether GNMA options were stock options or

---

[88] Judge Cudahy, in dissent, aptly note that "[t]he majority's almost total reliance on the word 'involving' in the exclusive jurisdiction clause to bear the crushing burden of options on actuals is to rest the Rock of Gibraltar on a toothpick." *GNMA Options*, 677 F.2d at 1170 (Cudahy, J., dissenting).

[89] *See infra* notes 129–34 and accompanying text.

[90] The court expressly refused to articulate what "legitimate" meant in this regard. *See GNMA Options*, 677 F.2d at 1151 n.26.

commodity options. It should be noted that the court's deference to the
SEC's regulatory function concerning traditional stocks suggests a functional-agency (as opposed to a functional-instrument) justification of its
definitional conclusion regarding SEC-CFTC jurisdiction,[91] yet this functional-agency rationale was not explored by the court in its critical exclusivity analysis. The definitional approach of *GNMA Options* would have
created uncertainty regarding the status of stock index options, because
questions would have arisen regarding whether or not the SEC's traditional jurisdiction over stocks extended to such options, given that they
are based on *indices* of traditional securities rather than upon single traditional securities.

   4. Compromise. The *GNMA Options* decision, however, was rendered
moot by the legislative codification of the SEC-CFTC Accord, which compromise represents the fourth phase of innovation.[92] Although the SEC-
CFTC Accord avoided the specific conundrums created in the *GNMA Options* decision, it followed the definitional path forged by that decision
and added its own functional gloss. With the objective of preserving the
traditional functions of the two agencies,[93] the legislation amended the
CEAct and the federal securities laws to split jurisdiction by definition
over options and futures contracts on financial instruments between the
CFTC and the SEC.

   The SEC-CFTC Accord preserves the CFTC's exclusive jurisdiction
over *all* futures contracts and grants the CFTC exclusive jurisdiction over
all options on futures contracts. The Accord, however, limits the universe
of permissible futures contracts. In this connection, the Accord prohibits
the offer or execution of futures contracts on individual securities, except
individual securities that are "exempted" and are not municipal securities.[94] It also circumscribes the permissible types of stock index futures

---

[91] *See supra* note 86 (discussing the court's references to a congressional intent to preserve
the SEC's traditional authority over stocks).

[92] The SEC-CFTC Accord amended § 2 of the 1933 Act, § 3 of the 1934 Act, and § 2(a) of
the CEAct, and hereinafter will be used as reference to these statutory amendments. For a
discussion of the events giving rise to the SEC-CFTC Accord, see Markham & Gilberg,
supra note 2, at 776–79.

[93] *See* S. REP. No. 384, 97th Cong., 2d Sess. 22 (1982) (noting that one "objective is to maintain, to the extent practicable, the traditional roles of the two agencies"). In this regard,
the Senate Report indicated that "the CFTC would continue to regulate markets and instruments that serve a hedging and price discovery function and the SEC would regulate
markets and instruments with an underlying investment purpose." *Id.; see also* H.R. REP.
No. 565, Part II, 97th Cong., 2d Sess. 40–41 (1982) (reprinting Letter from CFTC Chairman Philip Johnson to Congressman Edward Madigan (June 15, 1982) (discussing the
SEC-CFTC Accord and opposing an amendment to give the SEC veto power over CFTC
decisions to designate a contract market in stock index futures)).

[94] *See* CEAct §§ 2(a)(1)(A), 2(a)(1)(B), 7 U.S.C. §§ 2, 2a (1988). Exempted securities are
defined in § 3 of the 1933 Act, 15 U.S.C. § 77c (1988), and § 3(a)(12) of the 1934 Act, 15
U.S.C. § 78c(a)(12) (1988). Notably, the agreement between the Chairmen did not contain this prohibition, but, upon codification, the legislation settled their inability to decide this issue. *See* ELECTRONIC BULLS AND BEARS, *supra* note 6, at 49.

contracts to contracts based on "broad-based" indices, settled in cash, that are not readily subject to manipulation.[95] Consequently, the CFTC retains exclusive jurisdiction over, *inter alia,* futures contracts on Treasury Bonds (an exempted security), futures contracts on the Standard and Poor's 500 (a broad-based index), and options on such futures, yet it cannot exercise its expansive jurisdiction to regulate futures on, for example, IBM and AT&T stock or narrow-based indices.

Because the SEC-CFTC Accord preserves the CFTC's exclusive jurisdiction over futures contracts, the SEC may not regulate *any* futures contract. The SEC, however, has *exclusive* jurisdiction vis-åa-vis the CFTC over options directly on securities (including all exempted securities[96]) or based on the value thereof, on certificates of deposit, and on all stock indices. Indeed, the Accord defines all such stock options as "securities" in and of themselves.[97] Hence, in contrast to the limitations on the characteristics of indices upon which futures and options on futures may be based, the Accord permits the trading of options directly on any stock index.[98]

The definitional classifications of the SEC-CFTC Accord—namely, that options directly on stock indices are "securities" and futures on stock indices are "futures contracts"—cannot be justified by an argument that jurisdiction is based upon the function of instruments. S&P 500 stock index futures, options on S&P 500 stock index futures, and options on the S&P 500 all serve similar risk management functions, although the Accord allocates jurisdictional authority over the first two to the CFTC and over the third to the SEC.[99]

Supporting this point is the most obvious example of how functional similarity of instruments was rendered irrelevant by the SEC-CFTC Accord: the regulation of foreign-currency options.[100] For foreign-currency

---

[95] *See* CEAct § (2)(a)(1)(B)(ii), 7 U.S.C. § 2a(ii) (1988). The CFTC is required to consult with the SEC prior to designating any contract market for stock index futures. *Id.* § (2)(a)(1)(B)(iv), 7 U.S.C. § 2a(iv) (1988). The SEC may object and the CFTC is given the right of judicial review over any SEC objection. *Id.*

[96] Under CEAct § 2(a)(1)(B)(i), 7 U.S.C. § 2a(i) (1988), the CFTC is prevented from exercising jurisdiction over options on "securities" or options based on the value of "securities." The term "security" is defined in § 3(a)(10) of the 1934 Act, which confers SEC jurisdiction over stock options but does not itself confer SEC exclusivity over stock options. *See* 15 U.S.C. § 78c(a)(10) (1988). The CEAct, because it divests the CFTC of jurisdiction over stock options, renders the SEC's jurisdiction over stock options in cases involving disputes with the CFTC "exclusive." For purposes of this Article, which deals solely with SEC-CFTC jurisdictional issues, the SEC's jurisdiction over stock options will be referred to as "exclusive." For a discussion of the application of state law to securities, including stock options, see T. HAZEN, *supra* note 54, at 367–84.

[97] *See* Securities Exchange Act of 1934 § 3(a)(10), 15 U.S.C. § 78c(a)(10) (1988).

[98] *See* Stoll & Whaley, *supra* note 29, at 226.

[99] *See supra* note 28 and accompanying text; *see also* Johnson, *supra* note 9, at 292 (noting that these three instruments "closely approximate each other").

[100] An option on foreign currency grants the holder the right, with no obligation, to purchase or sell (for a predetermined price) a stated amount of foreign currency at any point up until the agreed-upon expiration date of the option. *See* Gilberg, *supra* note 4, at 1648.

options, the exact product is regulated by a different agency depending solely upon where it is traded. The Accord does this by providing that the SEC's jurisdiction extends to foreign-currency options when traded on a national securities exchange,[101] while options on foreign currency that are not traded on a national securities exchange are subject to CFTC jurisdiction.[102] Foreign-currency options present the "only instance to date when jurisdiction is determined by the forum in which the instrument is traded."[103]

Significantly, the Accord also fails to withstand scrutiny as a framework for maintaining each agency's traditional functions. For example, the SEC's jurisdiction over risk management instruments such as S&P 500 options highlights the failure of the Accord to fulfill its objective of preserving the SEC's traditional role as the regulator of instruments with an underlying "investment purpose."[104] In fact, if the S&P 500 option (which, like all exchange-traded index options and futures, is cash-settled) were deemed an instrument with an underlying investment purpose, it would be difficult to explain why the S&P 500 future, which is based upon the same five hundred securities and is also cash-settled, would not likewise be an instrument with an investment purpose. Furthermore, although the S&P 500 index is composed of stocks, the Accord did not vest authority over the regulation of every instrument derived from stocks to their traditional regulator, the SEC.

In sum, because both the S&P 500 future and S&P 500 option are risk management vehicles that are derived from the value of traditional stocks, the definitional classification of the former as a "futures contract" and the latter as a "security" cannot be justified through distinctions in agency or instrument functions.

Admittedly, the Accord permitted numerous exchange-traded options and new futures to trade and also resolved agency disputes over the jurisdiction of other instruments already in existence, such as foreign-currency options. This compromise, nevertheless, proved reactionary and effectively froze financial innovation into a 1982 model by failing to revise the definitional premise of jurisdictional allocation, neglecting to define the term "futures contract," and preserving the CFTC's exclusive jurisdiction over instruments embraced by this term. The following Part of this

---

[101] *See* CEAct § 4c(f), 7 U.S.C. § 6c(f) (1988) ("Nothing in this chapter shall be deemed to govern or in any way be applicable to any transaction in an option on foreign currency traded on a national securities exchange.").

[102] Thus, the SEC regulates an option on the British pound traded on the Philadelphia Stock Exchange, and the CFTC regulates an option on the British pound future traded at the CME. In addition, the CFTC has approved an option on the British pound for listing on the CME. The CME has not yet listed that contract for trading.

[103] Gilberg, *supra* note 4, at 1640.

[104] *See supra* note 93.

Article describes how the Accord spawned future conflict over jurisdiction of innovative products.

III. The Resulting Innovation-Inhibiting Structure

The failure of the Accord to revise the definitional premise of bifurcated regulation has led to the current controversy, which largely involves the scope of the definition of "futures contract." The imprecision of the definitional framework[105] and the CEAct's exchange trading requirement,[106] in the context of industry interrelatedness,[107] has resulted in a regulatory structure that provides futures exchanges with a shield from competition in new product development without any justification other than exploiting what has become a legislatively conferred monopoly.[108] This result is virtually mandated by statute and remains problematic despite the numerous efforts by the CFTC, including restricting through interpretations its own jurisdiction over certain swaps and hybrids,[109] to ameliorate the negative effects of the current statutory framework.

In fact, the four-stage pattern of innovation under bifurcated regulation has repeated itself several times in the aftermath of the Accord. The period of conflict and uncertainty regarding innovative products such as swaps and "hybrid" products that do not fit within the traditional definitions of futures contracts or securities has not heretofore led to litigation. Grave uncertainty persists, however, over the CFTC's "compromise" of issuing interpretations[110] to allow off-exchange trading of swaps and hy-

---

[105] See supra notes 38–46, 54–61 and accompanying text.
[106] See supra notes 49–53 and accompanying text.
[107] See supra notes 10–13 and accompanying text.
[108] See 1 P. JOHNSON & T. HAZEN, supra note 52, § 1.06 (referring to the exchange trading requirement as a "contract market monopoly").
[109] See infra notes 110, 111.
[110] See Regulation of Hybrid Instruments, 17 C.F.R. §§ 34.1–.3 (1990) (indicating which hybrid instruments could be deemed exempt from regulation under the CEAct); Policy Statement Concerning Swap Transactions, 54 Fed. Reg. 30694 (CFTC 1989) (indicating which swap transactions could be deemed to fall outside the CFTC's jurisdiction). "Hybrid instrument" is defined as "a debt, preferred equity or depository instrument with a commodity-dependent payment that is not severable therefrom." 17 C.F.R. § 34.1(b) (1991). Presently, there is an extensive market in OTC trading of so-called hybrid products. Such hybrids often involve securities and bank deposits having debt and commodity features. Examples have included the introduction of oil-indexed swaps by The Chase Manhattan Bank, N.A., the offering of gold-indexed certificates of deposit by Wells Fargo Bank, N.A., Ford Motor Credit Company's issuance of debt instruments that returned principal to the investor based on fluctuations in the value of a notional amount of Japanese yen, and Standard Oil's debt instruments that granted the holder an option to purchase a quantity of oil at a fixed price which would only be settled for cash, with no actual delivery being contemplated. Hybrid instruments often have an element of futurity or an optional feature. For example, repayment of principal or interest, redemption prices, or other aspects may be subject to a floating rate, i.e., coupled with inflation, based on changes in the value of a designated physical commodity (such as oil), or geared to an economic or other index (such as the Consumer Price Index). Although section 303 of

brids. It is far from clear whether this system will remain in effect or will withstand judicial scrutiny if challenged by futures exchanges or other parties. Litigation, however, has created hurdles regarding the off-exchange sale of fifteen-day Brent oil contracts, because one federal court has deemed these instruments to be futures contracts. Fifteen-day Brent oil transactions, like swaps, nevertheless are presently being used in the OTC market under CFTC interpretations.[111] On the other hand, it has come to our attention that certain major U.S. oil companies no longer participate in the fifteen-day Brent market in the direct and efficient manner that they had prior to the court's decision even though the CFTC has used its best efforts to revise that decision and ameliorate its anticompetitive effects. The court's decision, because it renders the fifteen-day Brent oil transactions risky, makes clear that expansive readings of the CEAct not only stifle innovation, but also hamper U.S. corporations' ability to compete internationally.

With respect to swaps, hybrids, or Brent oil, the premise remains that the decision of whether to deem these instruments futures contracts remains with the CFTC and the courts. This enormous definitional power of the CFTC and courts, in conjunction with the CEAct's exchange trading requirement, enables the dismantling of the trading of all these instruments in the United States or by U.S. participants. The swaps and hybrid markets together represent a multitrillion dollar international market that could be shut to domestic participants by a mere definitional determination.

---

the Futures Trading Practices Act of 1991, discussed *supra* at note 37, would exempt certain hybrids from CFTC regulation, this provision would not remedy the innovation-inhibiting effects arising from the CEAct as presently construed. Rather, this initiative would only permit off-exchange trading of certain hybrids and does not account for innovative hybrids that do not fall within the enumerated criteria. *See* S. 207, 102d Cong., 1st Sess. § 303, 137 CONG. REC. S4423, S4433 (daily ed. Apr. 16, 1991).

A swap is defined in the CFTC's policy statement as "an agreement between two parties to exchange a series of cash flows measured by different interest rates, exchange rates, or prices with payments calculated by reference to a principal base." Policy Statement Concerning Swap Transactions, *supra*, at 30695. This description is sufficiently broad to include caps, floors, collars, and other swap-like instruments, even though there is no explicit reference to them. A thorough discussion of swaps is beyond the scope of this Article. For an interesting discussion of the economics, regulation, and innovation of swaps, see Hu, *Swaps, The Modern Process of Financial Innovation and the Vulnerability of a Regulatory Paradigm*, 138 U. PA. L. REV. 333 (1989).

[111] A federal district court in New York recently held on a motion for summary judgment that the Brent oil forward market constitutes an off-exchange futures market and that 15-day Brent oil contracts are futures contracts within the meaning of the CEAct. Transnor (Bermuda) Ltd. v. BP N. Am. Petroleum, 738 F. Supp. 1472, 1489 (S.D.N.Y. 1990). In response, the CFTC issued a draft statutory interpretation concerning forward transactions on June 29, 1990, and a final statutory interpretation concerning forward transactions on September 19, 1990. *See* Statutory Interpretation Concerning Forward Transaction, 55 Fed. Reg. 39188 (CFTC 1990). This interpretation contradicts the *Transnor* decision and seeks to allow 15-day Brent oil contracts to trade off-exchange, but is confined to these and a limited category of other instruments.

Undoubtedly, this omnipresent threat limits financial innovation by its mere presence, along with the historical proclivity of the futures exchanges to litigate the meaning of the term "futures contract."[112] In the areas of swaps and hybrids, further, the interpretations the CFTC has admirably developed to counter the negative effects arising from ambiguities in the CEAct, by definition explicitly circumscribe the innovation of such instruments to specific parameters simply by virtue of having to codify such parameters to make such interpretations meaningful.[113]

Unlike the trading of certain swaps and hybrids that is currently allowed (albeit under innovation-inhibiting conditions), the trading of IPs has been fully thwarted. The IPs case[114] has generated several legislative proposals that would clarify the regulation of IPs as well as swaps, hybrids, and Brent oil contracts,[115] but none have been adopted. One of them, the Futures Trading Practices Act of 1991, would exempt certain of the aforementioned transactions from CFTC regulation.[116] Even if a reactive "solution" such as this were adopted, the core problems of the CEAct would persist. Just like the Accord, the Futures Trading Practices Act of 1991 would straitjacket innovation to the standards existing upon adoption and would not foster the development of products in response to evolving needs. There remains no possibility of a final compromise in this session of Congress that escapes jurisdiction by definition, because in their present forms the pending proposals do not revise the definitional framework.

To demonstrate how the CEAct has been distorted to impede innovation of the aforementioned products, it is necessary to reanalyze the exclusive jurisdiction clause, the breadth of the term "futures contract," and the exchange trading requirement in light of current developments.

A. The Burdens of Designation

The exchange trading requirement, in combination with the exclusive jurisdiction clause and the broad ambiguity of the CFTC's jurisdiction over futures contracts, renders a CFTC determination that a new

---

[112] *See supra* notes 78–89 and accompanying text; *infra* notes 124–77 and accompanying text.

[113] *See supra* notes 110, 111. In addition to straitjacketing innovation, the CFTC's interpretations have unintended negative effects. For example, the CFTC's Policy Statement regarding swaps sets forth certain criteria that must be met for transactions to be free from regulation under the CEAct, one of which is the absence of a margining system. Therefore, in order to remain subject to the policy statement, counterparties who desire to set up margining systems to limit their credit risk (thereby decreasing the risk of default) cannot do so, even if such margining increases the safety and soundness of the swaps market. Interestingly, effects such as this thwart the safety and soundness aims associated with a successful regulatory structure.

[114] Chicago Mercantile Exch. v. SEC, 883 F.2d 537 (7th Cir. 1989), *cert. denied*, 110 S. Ct. 3214 (1990); *see infra* notes 124–78 and accompanying text.

[115] *See infra* notes 184–92 and accompanying text.

[116] *See infra* notes 185–87 and accompanying text.

product is a futures contract today, in many instances, tantamount to a death sentence for trading that product in the United States. Exchange trading itself is incompatible with many OTC risk management instruments. Privately negotiated swaps, for instance, have flourished because, in contrast to traditional futures, they are neither standardized nor fungible, and they are used efficiently to manage risk on a transaction-by-transaction basis.[117]

This death sentence also results with respect to instruments designed to be traded on an exchange, because, as noted above, new instruments deemed to be futures contracts cannot automatically be traded on a CFTC-regulated exchange. Instead, such instruments must satisfy the "designation" requirements contained in section 5 of the CEAct.[118] Examination of the designation requirements illustrates how the CEAct's regime thwarts innovation.

The CFTC has required that each new futures contract, as a *precondition* to designation (as well as a continuing obligation), satisfy an "economic purpose" test. This test, as developed by the CFTC years ago, has created significant barriers to financial innovation today largely without flexibility as to safety and soundness purposes in that each and every new futures contract or option thereon must be individually justified through a protracted, costly, and cumbersome procedure. It has been noted that this "complicated justification process . . . often takes years on innovative contracts."[119]

The CFTC's procedure, which is mandated not by the CEAct itself but by agency interpretations, requires that each futures contract be proved to perform the economic function of either hedging or price discovery.[120] This test creates an insurmountable barrier to the trading of instruments for which an expensive and lengthy economic justification is not economically feasible (as well as instruments that fail to provide either hedging or price discovery functions). It is, therefore, overbroad because it excludes even new products that have a requisite economic purpose if demonstrating such functions is impractical. In fact, former CFTC Chairman Johnson has explained the role of the CFTC's economic justification requirement in impeding new product development by noting that, "[u]nlike the SEC, . . . the CFTC can prevent new products from entering the futures market, even though investor interest is keen and full disclosure is made, if the product's economic benefit . . . has not been persuasively documented."[121]

---

[117] *See*, e.g., *supra* note 110. *See generally* Hu, *supra* note 110, at 364 & n.81.
[118] For a thorough explanation and application of these requirements, contained in § 5(a)–(f), see T. RUSSO, *supra* note 4, §§ 1.37–.49.
[119] Seeger, *supra* note 9, at 9.
[120] *See* Guideline 1, *supra* note 51, at 25850.
[121] Johnson, *supra* note 9, at 302.

Significantly, the "designation" procedure also imposes substantial burdens upon financial innovation by requiring that any new instrument deemed to be a futures contract be brought under the CFTC's regulation by an exchange.[122] Thus, by equating the ability to trade an instrument with contract market designation, the CEAct effectively permits only CFTC-regulated exchanges to offer new products to the public. Designation, therefore, restricts the process of innovation by mandating that futures exchanges affirmatively undertake to offer new products to U.S. market participants. As a result of designation, the CEAct not only creates a regulatory monopoly over futures contracts, but also a de facto futures exchange monopoly over financial innovation for products subject to being labeled "futures contracts."

Given that numerous new products that could be deemed futures contracts by the CFTC or courts are not the types of products that the futures exchanges wish to trade (such as IPs) or are not amenable to exchange trading (such as most swaps), it is critical to understand that the CFTC or courts may prohibit their offer and sale in the United States by simply naming them "futures contracts."[123]

B. The IPs Case: Redefining Futures Contracts

Under this regime the crucial uncertainty faced in the development of new financial products has become whether such products will be deemed futures contracts, because this characterization triggers CFTC exclusivity and exchange trading. The scope of the term "futures contract," however, has been rendered boundless and incomprehensible by the recent judicial decision in the IPs case, *Chicago Mercantile Exchange v. SEC*.[124] In that case, the Seventh Circuit, in determining that IPs were futures contracts subject to the CFTC's exclusive jurisdiction and could not be traded by three SEC-regulated exchanges, departed from the traditional formulation of "futures contract."[125] The IPs case warrants elaboration[126] not only because it redefined the term "futures contract," but also because it reinforces the observations above concerning the innovation-inhibiting nature of the CEAct regime. The case also paradigmatically represents the pitfalls of jurisdiction by definition, because it preserves the

---

[122] *See generally* Seeger, *supra* note 9, at 9.

[123] It should be noted that in June 1991 the CBOT began trading "swaps futures," which differ from typical individually negotiated swap transactions.

[124] 883 F.2d 537 (7th Cir. 1989), *cert. denied*, 110 S. Ct. 3214 (1990).

[125] See *supra* notes 44–46 and accompanying text for the traditional elements of futures contracts.

[126] The authors have consciously avoiding setting forth a technical description of IPs in order to explore the IPs case from a jurisprudential and regulatory standpoint. Thus, the economic attributes of IPs are set forth in the context of discussing the court's judicial reasoning. For a brief description of IPs, see *supra* notes 3, 18.

fiction that there exist separate definable categories of derivatives and does so without a modicum of interpretive consistency.

1. To Define or Not to Define. One of the most interesting aspects of the IPs case is the Seventh Circuit's suggestion that construing the CEAct to define IPs as futures contracts was virtually preordained and that the court was not responsible for impeding innovation by its interpretation. The court's intimation was that, even though its decision "[d]oubtless . . . gives the futures markets the opportunity to block competition from an innovative financial product,"[127] the CEAct somehow required this result. In this regard, it noted: "We do not conceive it our function . . . to invent counterweights to statutes; judges should be interpreters rather than sappers and miners."[128] By reading the CEAct to require that IPs are futures requiring CFTC exclusivity, however, the court wasted an opportunity to add a new interpretive gloss to a persistent definitional problem. Instead, by adhering to definitional dichotomies without valid justifications, it exacerbated the innovation-inhibiting effects of jurisdiction by definition.

The court was not constrained to reach the conclusion that IPs were futures contracts by the CEAct (which fails to define the term) or by previous case law. Rather, it was through a convoluted interpretive methodology that the court determined IPs were futures.

The court reached this conclusion by, first, citing *GNMA Options* and the Accord and contending that these authorities preserved the fundamental premise that "if an instrument is *both* a security and a futures contract, then the CFTC's jurisdiction is exclusive."[129] Even this overbroad formulation,[130] however, does not compel a particular result on the threshold issue of defining an instrument as a futures contract, or any other instrument. The court could have refused to define IPs as either futures contracts or securities and, indeed, described its definitional task as "whether tetrahedrons belong in square or round holes."[131] Alternatively, the court decided to define IPs as *both* "securities"[132] and futures, which, of course, led to the court's preordained result: IPs as futures contracts must be subject to exclusive CFTC regulation.

2. Dual Categorization. This judicial approach of placing one instrument into two statutory categories (the "dual category approach" or "dual

---

[127] *Chicago Mercantile Exch.*, 883 F.2d at 548–49.

[128] *Id.* at 549.

[129] *Id.* at 544.

[130] *See infra* notes 133–34 and accompanying text (illustrating the overbreadth of this statement).

[131] *Chicago Mercantile Exch.*, 883 F.2d at 539.

[132] See *infra* notes 133–34 and accompanying text for a discussion of the court's limited and semantically incorrect formulation of "securities" in its discussion of jurisdiction over products that are both "securities" and futures.

categorization") provides the key to assessing the validity of the court's conclusion that IPs are futures contracts and require CFTC exclusivity.

Because the court broke new judicial ground in characterizing IPs as both futures contracts and securities, it is necessary to scrutinize this approach. To this end, the court overlooked a curious semantic aspect of the Accord when it made sweeping observations concerning the CFTC's monopoly over the regulation of futures contracts: the Accord defines stock options as securities and ousts the CFTC from exercising jurisdiction over stock options.[133] Thus, the court's references to "securities" in its generalizations concerning the CFTC's regulatory hegemony over instruments that are both futures and securities are either blatantly and strategically erroneous, or the result of sloppy draftsmanship. It should be emphasized, therefore, that the court's dual category approach *only* demands CFTC exclusivity when one category is futures and the other is non-stock option securities. When the categories are futures and stock options, dual categorization leads to the result of SEC exclusivity.[134] The case, consequently, must be read with the understanding that, in the court's dialectic regarding IPs as "securities" and futures contracts, the court meant non-stock option securities.

Aside from the court playing fast and loose with semantics, the court's dual category approach, as an intellectual framework, becomes self-consuming under the rationale of the case. To demonstrate how dual categorization renders the court's conclusions anomalous, the category of stock options warrants analysis.

3. The Omitted Category: Stock Options The court's conclusions, as a fundamental matter, depended upon how to categorize IPs. Because there exist three relevant categories—futures, stock options, and non-stock option securities—the court's definitional task involved not placing tetrahedrons in round or square holes, but in triangular holes as well. The court, however, created a narrow dialectic concerning the categorization of IPs as futures and non-stock option securities and concluded that an IP is "no less a future than it is a [non-stock option] security, and no more."[135] In fact, because of the CEAct's exclusive jurisdiction clause, the court found the fact that IPs were also non-stock option securities to be "neither here nor there."[136]

---

[133] *See supra* note 96.

[134] Indeed, the court expressly recognized this result and identified SEC exclusivity over stock options in one portion of its opinion, but failed to adequately analyze stock options thereafter. *Chicago Mercantile Exch.*, 883 F.2d at 545; *see infra* note 147 and accompanying text. For ease of reference, this Article will refer to options on securities as "stock options" and securities that are not stock options as "nonstock option securities."

[135] *Chicago Mercantile Exch.*, 883 F.2d at 546.

[136] *Id.* at 545.

Reference to the court's analysis of the characteristics IPs share with non-stock option securities such as stock,[137] thus, is unnecessary in light of the reality that a dual categorization concerning nonstock option securities and futures leads to CFTC exclusivity. Whether IPs are nonstock option securities or not becomes superfluous *provided* that the court's analysis of IPs also appropriately categorizes IPs as futures and not stock options.

By establishing a limited dual categorization, the court divorced its analysis of stock options from its primary discussion of the "securities" versus "futures" dilemma. Perhaps the most obvious indication of the court's exclusion of stock options from its primary dual categorization was its observation that "[t]he only thing of which we are sure is that an IP is not an option on a security."[138]

The court supported this observation by comparing IPs with "traditional" stock options. Concluding that because IPs differed in certain respects from what it deemed to be tradition, the court held that IPs were not stock options. Once again, however, the court either deliberately avoided making the proper comparison or simply erred in formulating the issue by comparing IPs to "options on a security" as opposed to options on the value of an index of securities. The Accord does not confine SEC exclusivity to options on a security, but rather extends expressly such exclusivity to "option[s] on one or more securities, including any group or index of such securities . . . or any interest therein or *based on the value thereof.*"[139]

Omitting to mention options based on the value of securities enabled the court to transform the analysis into whether IPs fell into the "option on a security category" or not. Not even a casual observer, however, would deem IPs to be anything derived from a single security, as IPs only involve indices of securities. As a predicate matter, then, the court's stock option analysis originates from an erroneous comparison of IPs and options on single securities.[140] The general, sweeping nature of the court's elimination of stock options from its dual categorization is underlined by the blunt statement that "IPs are not options."[141]

---

[137] *See id.* at 545–46.

[138] *Id.* at 546.

[139] CEAct § 2(a)(1)(B)(i), 7 U.S.C. § 2a(i) (1988) (emphasis added).

[140] In an earlier portion of the opinion, in which the court addressed whether IPs belonged in "any of the other pigeonholes of § 3(a)(10)" of the 1934 Act (which defines "security") the court noted that the "closest match" was language in the Accord that defines a security as a "privilege on any security . . . or group or index of securities (including any interest therein or *based on the value thereof*). *Chicago Mercantile Exch.,* 883 F.2d at 545. Because this category of "securities" consists of non-stock option securities, if IPs were to fall into this category as well as the category of futures contracts, CFTC jurisdiction would be exclusive. Reference to this aspect of the decision, however, illustrates that the court was well aware of the "based on the value thereof" language of the Accord but failed to incorporate such a concept in its stock options discussion.

[141] *Id.* at 547.

In noting that IPs do not have any of the distinguishing characteristics of options, the court focused upon the fact that IPs are not written "out of the money,"[142] are not limited in time, and do not establish a careful balance among premium, strike price, and duration.[143] There is no dispute that the "careful balance" noted by the court generally remains a traditional distinguishing characteristic of any option, including both commodity and stock options. With regard to the court's "out of the money" criterion, it is safe simply to say that this characteristic does not apply to all options and that such a statement by the court highlights its lack of familiarity with an instrument essential to its decision.[144] Similarly, the limited duration criterion cannot be an appropriate bar to IPs being characterized as stock options under the court's rhetoric because the court found IPs to be futures contracts even though futures contracts, to this day, are limited in time.[145]

Assume for the moment that all of the court's stock option criteria were accurate. Under this assumption it is clear that the court created a test for stock options based solely on whether an instrument had certain traditional features of stock options; the court concluded that because IPs lacked certain traditional features, IPs were not options. In particular, the court determined that if IPs were to be deemed stock options without these features, the term "stock option" would be meaningless. Specifically, the court held that "[w]ords are only useful to the extent they distinguish some things from others; symbols that comprise everything mean nothing."[146]

Underlying this terse and facially neutral interpretation that IPs do not qualify as options was the court's reluctance to engage in a robust stock options analysis and address the jurisdictional implications arising therefrom. Instead, the court held, in effect, that for SEC exclusivity to arise an instrument must strictly comport with certain court-appointed attributes of instruments within the SEC's traditional jurisdiction. The implications of a more robust analysis, however, are that a dual categorization of IPs as stock options that require SEC exclusive regulation and futures contracts that mandate CFTC exclusive regulation requires that SEC exclusivity must prevail. Although the court recognized in an early part of its opinion that a dual categorization of IPs as stock options and

---

[142] "Out of the money" in the case of a call option means the option's strike or exercise price exceeds the market price at the creation of the contract.

[143] *Chicago Mercantile Exch.,* 883 F.2d at 546.

[144] It is clear from this statement that the court failed to understand options or how they function. Neither put nor call options *must* be written "out of the money." Options also may be written "at the money" (equal to the exercise price) or "in the money" (above the exercise price).

[145] The court noted the "limited duration" criterion of futures in its futurity analysis when it noted that futures contracts have defined settlement obligations. *See Chicago Mercantile Exch.,* 883 F.2d at 542. For a discussion of options, see *supra* note 2.

[146] *Chicago Mercantile Exch.,* 883 F.2d at 547.

futures contracts demands SEC exclusivity,[147] it neglected to accurately define the features of stock options. Thus, the court restricted its analysis of IPs as stock options to three features, two of which were not appropriate. The court, moreover, failed to identify certain important features IPs *share* with stock options, such as unilateralism, i.e., the imposition of contractual obligations on only one party to the contract.[148] It is also not unfair to note that in the court's initial description of options it completely missed the boat in stating, "[u]nlike financial and index futures, options call for delivery of the underlying instrument—be it a share of stock or a futures contract."[149] Like the court's reluctance to compare IPs to options based on the value of indices of securities, its refusal to recognize that exchange-traded index options are cash-settled like stock index and financial futures and most IPs,[150] highlights the superficial nature of the case's approach toward the stock option category.

By disposing of the stock option issue through strict adherence to limited, and in two cases dubious, traditional criteria, and otherwise neglecting to accurately describe stock options, the court completely severed stock options from its dual categorization dichotomy. In so doing, it is apparent that the court embraced a limited framework that fails to accommodate jurisdictional realities. The case's shortcomings are well illustrated by declarations such as the following, "An instrument either is or is not a futures contract. If it is, the CFTC has jurisdiction; if it is not, the CFTC lacks jurisdiction; if the CFTC has jurisdiction, its power is exclusive."[151] This is unambiguously wrong in a circumstance in which an instrument is both a stock option and a futures contract, and the court's brief early acknowledgment of SEC exclusivity over stock options does not justify such flagrantly inaccurate subsequent observations.

To the extent an instrument is deemed to be a stock option, the fact that it is also a future is, borrowing the court's words, "neither here nor there."[152] It must be emphasized, therefore, that the court's disposal of the stock option issue provided the critical foundation for the conclusion that IPs are futures. Banishing the option question not only facilitated the court's conclusion but also proved necessary to it.

For the reasons explained above, the case rests upon both the court's disposal of the category of stock options that require SEC exclusivity and the court's characterization of IPs as futures contracts. Eliminating SEC

---

[147] *Id.* at 545; *see supra* note 134.

[148] *See supra* notes 2, 3 (describing stock options and IPs).

[149] *Chicago Mercantile Exch.*, 883 F.2d at 543.

[150] *See id.* at 546 n.3 (discussing the delivery feature of the American Stock Exchange's IP).

[151] *Id.* at 548. The court added: "If the CFTC may approve [IPs] trading because they are futures contracts, the CFTC's jurisdiction is exclusive." *Id.*

[152] *See supra* note 136 and accompanying text.

exclusivity, in turn, resulted from the court's inability to identify more than one accurate traditional characteristic of stock options as well as its heightened scrutiny of IPs with respect to their status as stock options. For futures, by contrast, the court adopted a liberal, flexible, and expansive analysis that departed substantially from traditional futures analyses.[153] Essentially, the court not only avoided a meaningful dual categorization concerning IPs as futures and stock options, but it also discriminated against stock options in its brief analysis thereof. In disposing of stock options too hastily, however, the court laid the foundation for the fallacy of its conclusion. Namely, the court interpreted the term "futures contract" to become a symbol that could define stock options, thereby rendering it meaningless.

The reason a definition of "futures contract" that fails to distinguish stock options is meaningless derives from the clash of exclusivity in which the SEC wins under the Accord. The validity of the court's conclusion that IPs are futures requiring CFTC exclusivity, thus, rests upon distinctions between stock options on one hand and futures and IPs on the other, as opposed to whether IPs are both futures and nonstock option securities. Accordingly, the next question to be resolved is the extent to which the court's definition of the term "futures contract" excludes stock options. Even though the court refused to adequately examine IPs as stock options and futures contracts, this exercise demands consideration. In fact, if the court had travelled the road set forth below, the IPs case would have been, at minimum, differently drafted, and perhaps differently decided.

4. How an IP Became a Future and a Stock Option

(a) *Discarding the futures tradition.* The court based its definitional task concerning IPs as futures on the premise that IPs "have all attributes of neither" nonstock option securities nor futures.[154] In so doing, it implied that there exists something readily definable as a futures contract (instruments that have all the traditional elements of futures developed in prior case law?) and that IPs are not such a something. It could have stopped at this point and held, in a manner similar to its stock options approach, that IPs, because they lacked certain distinguishing features of both non-stock option securities and futures, were neither.

If the court had reached this conclusion that was consistent with its stock options reasoning, it would have simply deprived IPs of a regulator. From an interpretive standpoint, the court's strict stock options analysis

---

[153] See *supra* notes 44–46 and accompanying text for a description of the traditional elements of futures contracts.

[154] *Chicago Mercantile Exch.*, 883 F.2d at 548.

implied that where an instrument is subject to exclusive jurisdiction, the court would hold that instrument to traditional court-appointed elements of the exclusive category. In calling IPs futures, however, the court departed from this approach. The effect of its decision was to restrict IPs to a regulatory regime that did not wish to trade them and to jeopardize the status of existing derivative instruments and the development of new products, without an interpretive or policy justification for doing so. With regard to policy, the court's lamentation concerning the innovation-inhibiting effects of its decision demonstrates that it deemed policy considerations irrelevant.[155] The decision, thus, must rest upon its interpretive coherence.

The court's sleight of hand in interpreting IPs that lacked all the attributes of futures to be futures contracts was largely drawn by analogy from one prior case involving nontraditional futures. The fundamental premise of the analogy was that because another court examining a different transaction found the transaction to be a futures contract without that transaction meeting all the traditional elements of a futures contract, then IPs could also be futures contracts without all traditional elements.

In this regard, the court held that although IPs lacked bilateralism, a traditional element of a futures contract, IPs were futures contracts because the Ninth Circuit had determined in *CFTC v. Co Petro Marketing Group, Inc.*[156] that certain gasoline contracts that lacked bilateralism were futures contracts.[157] It is beyond comprehension that the mere fact that a sister court had abandoned bilateralism in a different context in 1982 mandated that the Seventh Circuit do the same in categorizing IPs. The court cited *Co Petro* for the proposition that the court would not confine the definition of futures solely to instruments having every attribute of a "conventional" future.[158]

There were, however, a number of bases on which the court could have applied the traditional framework for defining futures contracts to the case before it without having to reject *Co Petro*'s flexible approach. In this connection, former CFTC Chairman Johnson has noted that in determining whether an instrument is a futures contract "[t]he critical inquiry is to look at all the surrounding circumstances in light of the [CEAct's]

---

[155] *See supra* note 127 and accompanying text; *see also Chicago Mercantile Exch.*, 883 F.2d at 549 ("[O]ur task should not reflect a value judgment as to which of the competing agencies is best equipped to regulate these [products].") (citing Board of Trade of Chicago v. SEC, 677 F.2d 1137, 1161 (7th Cir.) (*GNMA Options*), *vacated as moot*, 459 U.S. 1026 (1982)).

[156] 680 F.2d 573 (9th Cir. 1982).

[157] *Id.* at 580–81.

[158] *Chicago Mercantile Exch.*, 883 F.2d at 548–49. The court also supported its approach by noting that the Supreme Court has been flexible in interpreting the term "security." *See id.* at 549–50 (citing Landreth Timber Co. v. Landreth, 471 U.S. 681 (1985); SEC v. W. J. Howey Co., 328 U.S. 293 (1946); SEC v. C. M. Joiner Leasing Corp., 320 U.S. 344 (1943)).

purpose."[159] So, for example, the court could have taken the position that when, as in *Co Petro*,[160] a product is not being traded pursuant to another agency's regulation or does not share attributes of stock options or stock, the surrounding circumstances support an expansive approach toward defining a "futures contract." By contrast, where the product has many characteristics of stock and stock options and is already being traded under another agency's regulations—as was the case with IPs—the surrounding circumstances could support retaining the traditional elements of a futures contract. This example, at minimum, demonstrates that the court had a choice in deciding whether to depart from the traditional elements of futures in analyzing IPs.

Having identified the court's ability to deem IPs futures contracts without requiring them to satisfy all traditional elements of a futures contract, we must now examine the substantive rationale supporting the court's choice to deem IPs futures. As noted previously, it is necessary to expose how the court's substantive justifications for calling IPs futures contracts fail to distinguish futures from stock options.

(b) Conjuring up a new element: "futurity." It must be reiterated that the CEAct and case law did not *require* the conclusion that IPs be characterized as futures contracts. Because the decision does not specify the precise basis of its conclusion, it is necessary to speculate. The court's focus upon "futurity" as the defining element of a futures contract suggests that the "futurity" of IPs provided the key to the court's conclusion. Futurity is rooted in the CEAct's reference to contracts of sale for "future" delivery.[161]

In defining IPs' futurity, the court described two aspects of this criterion: (1) the absence of an obligation by either party to the contract to pay current value, and (2) valuation at a future date.[162] Because the purpose of the court's futurity analysis was to rebut the SEC's argument that IPs lacked futurity and were stock because they represented a "present obligation to pay current value,"[163] the two aspects of futurity the court chose serve to distinguish futures and IPs from stock. They do not, how-

---

[159] 1 P. JOHNSON & T. HAZEN, *supra* note 52, § 1.05. Without doubt, *Co Petro* supported the court's decision to not require that all futures have traditional futures attributes. Yet it would be unwarranted to imply that the Ninth Circuit case or a lofty judicial principle that refuses to circumscribe the CEAct to its traditional elements rendered the IPs result inevitable. Frankly, the court's reliance upon a seven-year-old case by another court becomes increasingly suspect in light of its paltry, strict, and inaccurate analysis of stock options.

[160] *See Chicago Mercantile Exch.*, 883 F.2d at 548 (discussing the facts of *Co Petro*).

[161] *See supra* note 39 and accompanying text.

[162] *Chicago Mercantile Exch.*, 883 F.2d at 546.

[163] *Id.*

ever, provide a definition of futures or IPs that meaningfully distinguishes them from other transactions, such as stock options.

As an initial step, the failure of either party to pay current value demands discussion. In examining this first prong of futurity, the court determined that "IPs are no more a 'present obligation to pay current value' than are futures contracts."[164] By virtue of SEC exclusivity over stock options, it is necessary to examine whether stock options, too, are no more a present obligation to pay current value than futures contracts or IPs.

With respect to futures and IPs, the court concluded that although the "holder" of either "an IP or a stock-index futures contract may go to market and trade it" and thereby "the price necessarily tracks current value," neither the "long on an IP nor the long on a futures contract can compel the short to *pay* current value."[165] Because IPs and futures, as well as exchange-traded options, are cleared through central clearing agencies that become a party to all such transactions, parties to none of these contracts could *compel* the opposite parties to pay anything, let alone current value.[166] Accordingly, the court's assertion that IPs and futures have futurity to the extent "longs" cannot compel "shorts" to pay current value applies with equal force to holders and writers of exchange-traded options. Although the court's use of the word "compel" may have been yet another semantic misstep, its current value analysis rested on this one sentence, which again illustrates the court's lack of understanding of how the products it analyzed are traded, cleared, and settled.

Similarly, the court's second and crucial prong of futurity—that valuation comes at a defined future date—applies to futures and IPs as well as, for instance, certain stock index options. The court did not explain what it meant by this indicator, but used analogies relating to the obligations of parties to IPs and futures contracts to demonstrate why IPs have this second type of futurity.

---

[164] *Id.*

[165] *Id.* It should be noted that the court could not decide how to label parties to various contracts in, for example, calling a futures long and IPs buyer a "holder" (which is a term of art that relates accurately to one party to an option contract, i.e., the one who has purchased the option). Also, the court generally referred to IPs buyers and sellers as, respectively, "longs" and "shorts," which are terms characteristically used to define parties to futures—perhaps to reflect its conclusion that IPs were futures contracts.

[166] See *supra* notes 12, 34 and accompanying text for a discussion of the OCC, which clears both IPs and exchange-traded options, as well as futures clearinghouses, which clear futures contracts. It should be noted, however, that under the Philadelphia Stock Exchange's "cash-out" IP, described *supra* at note 18, there existed a clearing mechanism through which a buyer who wished to cash out at a penalty had the opposite side of his contract randomly assigned to a seller, who would then need to pay dividend equivalents, as of the next day, minus a penalty. *Chicago Mercantile Exch.*, 883 F.2d at 540. Cash-out contracts with no penalty, further, could be construed to enable the OCC to have some seller pay *current value.* Notwithstanding this OCC obligation to select a seller to pay current value, it remains true that even under a cash-out contract that pays current value, a buyer cannot *compel* a seller to do anything.

In analogizing the obligations of IPs sellers to those of futures shorts, the court focused upon the notion that "[b]oth the futures contract and the IP are settled quarterly."[167] The concept of settlement, however, does not apply to IPs, because they are contracts of indefinite duration, under which the *buyer* has the right to cash out with no penalty on certain dates. Only if the buyer exercises this right does any obligation to pay arise for the seller.

The court further stated that the seller of an IP has an "obligation to pay the value of the index" on the IP's settlement date—"which [obligation] lies in the future to the same extent as the settlement date of any futures contract."[168] On rehearing, however, the court described the IP's futurity in this regard as follows: "IPs are valued as of a future date."[169] This generic phraseology clarifies that valuation on a future date, rather than predetermined contractual settlement obligations, was what futurity in this sense meant to the court.[170] Indeed, because IPs do not have settlement dates, this generic construction could be the only factually accurate analysis in this regard.

Such futurity, stated differently, means that IPs have futurity to the seller of the contract because he has an obligation, if a buyer chooses to cash out, to pay an amount whose value depends upon changes in the value of the underlying product subsequent to the time at which the contract is entered into. Stock index call options writers, nevertheless, have an obligation determined by future value like IPs sellers as well as futures shorts. This is so because the writer of a stock index call option has an obligation, upon the holder's exercise, to pay the difference between the option's exercise price and the current price of the stocks composing the index at any time up to the option's expiration date.[171] The stock index call option writer's obligation, therefore, lies in the future and is based on future value—even if the future is one minute after the contract is created.

The court also analyzed the "value at a future date" prong of futurity with respect to IPs buyers and futures longs. In this respect, the court noted that an IPs buyer "pays up front . . . but the long on a futures contract *promises* up front to make a defined payment on the settlement date;

---

[167] *Chicago Mercantile Exch.*, 883 F.2d at 546.
[168] *Id.*
[169] *Id.* at 550 (per curiam, on reh'g).
[170] *See infra* text accompanying note 175 (noting that the court needed to abandon predetermined future settlement obligations as an element of futurity with regard to buyers of the Philadelphia Stock Exchange's cash-out IPs contracts).
[171] The IPs seller's obligation is to pay a dividend-equivalent amount based upon changes in dividends of the stocks comprised in the index. The futures short's obligation is to deliver the product or settle the contract at the contract price on a future date, the value of the contract being determined by whether the price of the product underlying the contract is greater than or less than the contract price on the date of settlement.

the difference in the timing of the payment does not affect the fact that valuation comes at the defined future date."[172] Valuation from this perspective could again only mean that the value of the IPs transaction or futures contract to the buyer depends upon the value of the underlying product changing after the time at which the transaction is entered into. Futurity to IPs buyers, then, could not be contingent upon whether *payment* comes in the future because the IPs buyer pays up front. The court's rehearing decision also makes this interpretation clearly correct.

The amorphous concept of future value that became the key factor in the court's analysis of IPs buyers is in need of expansion. For the IPs buyer, the "value" of the up-front payment would depend upon the amount of future dividend-equivalent payments of the stocks composing the index. For the stock index futures long, the value of the obligation would depend upon whether the index of stocks increases or decreases in value from the time the contract is entered into.[173] Valuation of stock index call options, for example, would also come at a future date because the determination of the call index option holder to exercise the option will depend upon the future price movement of the stocks underlying the option. Indeed, the court, in describing call options, noted this feature: "[T]he buyer of the [call] option hopes that the market price will rise above the strike price by enough to cover the premium, the time value of money, and the transactions costs of executing the option."[174]

The only feature that distinguishes the call stock index option holder from the futures long in this regard, consequently, is that such option holder pays a premium up front and is not *obligated* by his contract to do anything at the option's maturity date. An option holder may merely allow the option to lapse, losing only his premium, interest that could have been earned on the premium, and the option's transactions costs. Yet is not the stock index option holder's decision to refuse to exercise the option a valuation determination that depends upon the future price movements of the stocks composing the index? Certainly, the option holder must continuously track the value of the option, from the date the contract is created until the option's expiration. The mere fact that an ultimate valuation determination may be *not* to exercise the option does not obviate the fact that the value of the call option to its holder depends upon the future value of the underlying stock.

Significantly, this continuing valuation process coupled with the contractual ability of the stock index call option holder to extinguish his obligations at any time up to the option's expiration resembles that of the IPs buyer under a "cash-out" contract. In this connection, the IP traded

[172] *Chicago Mercantile Exch.*, 883 F.2d at 546.
[173] *See supra* note 171 (describing future value regarding futures shorts).
[174] *Chicago Mercantile Exch.*, 883 F.2d at 543.

on the Philadelphia Stock Exchange (PHLX) enabled buyers to "cash out" contracts on any business day prior to the contractually assigned cash-out dates and receive 0.5 percent less than the value of the index as of the next day.[175] Upon "cash-out" at a penalty, such IPs buyers extinguish their contractual obligations before the specified cash-out day. Thus, such IPs buyers and call index option holders may extinguish their contractual obligations, under the terms of their contracts, prior to the IPs' "cash out at no penalty" dates or the options' expiration date, respectively. Cash-out IPs, moreover, indicate that the court's concept of futurity, in order to encompass all IPs, could not depend upon predetermined "settlement" obligations, notwithstanding dicta to the contrary. As a consequence, stock index call options, whose "value" is determined in the future for both writers and holders, but not on a defined date, would fall within the court's second formulation of futurity.

In stark contrast, the value of a futures contract to a futures long may be tracked continuously over time, but is determined only on *one* particular future date and is not extinguishable under the terms of the contract. Although it is true that a futures long (or short) may offset his contract by entering into another opposite contract or trade his contract in the secondary market, these alternatives apply to both parties to exchange-traded stock index options and IPs. Therefore, IPs and such stock index options contracts, by their own terms, enable buyers to extinguish their obligations prior to a contractually assigned date, while futures longs do not retain this contractually conferred ability to extinguish their obligations prior to the settlement date set forth in their contracts.

Clearly, then, *both* formulations of the court's definition of futurity—a failure of either party to pay current value and valuation at a future date—would apply to, for example, exchange-traded stock index call options as well as to futures and to IPs. Taken to its logical conclusion, the court's futurity reasoning would transform such stock options into futures contracts. Because of the SEC-CFTC Accord, this broad and nebulous formulation of futurity would not affect the jurisdiction of stock options. There remain, nevertheless, important repercussions of the court's failure to define IPs as futures to the exclusion of stock options through its futurity analysis.

5. *Repercussions.* The error of the court in failing to identify futurity characteristics that IPs share with futures to the exclusion of, for example, exchange-traded stock index call options turns the decision on its head. If

---

[175] *Id.* at 546–47. The court did not consider whether an IP with a daily cash-out at no penalty would have futurity. *Id.* at 550. Such no-penalty cash-out IPs are currently pending SEC approval. The CFTC, however, has stated that an IP's status as a futures contract does not depend upon whether the cash-out is quarterly or daily. *See* Breeden Testimony, *supra* note 19, at 16 n.9; *infra* note 178 and accompanying text.

futurity cannot separate one agency's exclusive jurisdiction from that of another, then the court had no basis for calling IPs futures as opposed to stock options.

Of course, the court could have avoided the judicial morass it created in extending the definition of futurity to encompass IPs, futures, and certain stock options by simply embracing bilateralism as a necessary criterion of futures contracts. But accepting bilateralism would have rendered IPs something other than futures, a contingency the court avoided at every turn.

In the process of attaching the label "futures contract" to IPs, however, the court reinforced the meaninglessness of definitional categorizations by discarding the one nearly universal defining element of a futures contract—bilateralism. The court, thus, created a paradox: in seeking to maintain definitional separations between futures and nonstock option securities, it levelled the separations between futures and stock options. Because of SEC exclusivity over stock options, it is apparent that the court should be scrupulously avoided erasing the definitional distinctions between futures and stock options. Yet by *both* elevating futurity to be the defining criterion of futures contracts and rejecting bilateralism as a necessary element of futures, the court fabricated a definition of futures contract that unravels when it is time to distinguish futures from stock options.

Futurity not only exposes the case's inability to distinguish between futures and stock options, but also increases the characteristics IPs share with stock options.[176] This inability of futurity to distinguish stock options from futures and IPs, in turn, undermines the critical assumption that permitted the court to construct the limited dual categorization between futures and nonstock option securities in the first place, i.e., that IPs were not stock options.

The danger of using the court's definition of futurity as the touchstone for analyzing new financial products is apparent: just as futurity cannot distinguish futures from stock index call options, futurity will demand

---

[176] It should be emphasized that the foregoing analyses do not seek affirmatively to categorize IPs as stock options but simply aim to demonstrate that the court's futurity analysis failed to establish a definition of futures contract that excluded stock options. It is not inconceivable, however, that another court examining new types of IPs in a subsequent case could deem IPs to be stock options and not futures. In fact, a court in a circuit that has recognized bilateralism as a distinguishing element of a futures contract could easily reject IPs as futures because they are not bilateral. Having disposed of the futures issue, a court could construe unilateralism as the primary indicator of an option and conclude that IPs are stock options because they are unilateral contracts based on the value of indices of securities. In view of the court's cavalier rejection of the traditional elements of futures in the IPs case, it is eminently feasible that another court could similarly abandon certain traditional elements of stock options (such as the "careful balance" the IPs case noted) in order to define IPs as stock options.

that any new risk management or derivative instrument is a futures contract. This result is inevitable, because nearly all innovative instruments, dating from exchange options in 1973 to IPs, contain aspects of valuation coming at a future date.[177] It is this specific problem that lies at the heart of the uncertainties arising in the swaps market, the 15-day Brent oil market, and the market for numerous bank products. Exacerbating the problem for new innovations is the fact that the court itself could not specifically identify exactly what futurity meant or how it makes futures contracts different from virtually all risk management instruments. In view of this ambiguity, the CFTC has stated that valuation after one day would be sufficient futurity to make an IP a futures contract.[178]

As a result, the court's nebulous interpretation of futurity and its elevation of futurity to be the defining feature of a futures contract not only prevented SEC-regulated exchanges from trading IPs, but also laid the foundation for CFTC-regulated exchanges to challenge practically all innovative products as futures contracts. Due to the CEAct's designation requirements, moreover, the court's futurity element will confine the development of virtually any new innovative instrument to the control of futures exchanges. It is the new uncertainty created by the IPs case that has inspired Congress's recent proposals to resolve the SEC-CFTC jurisdictional dispute.

C. Legislative Efforts

Numerous legislative proposals regarding the continuing SEC-CFTC jurisdictional conflict have been introduced in the years following the SEC-CFTC Accord and, more recently, in the aftermath of the IPs case.[179] None, however, have yet become law. Throughout this legislative debate, the SEC typically has indicated that the CEAct and the securities laws should be amended to transfer jurisdiction over stock index futures and options on stock index futures from the CFTC to the SEC, based upon the functional similarity between these products and stock index op-

---

[177] See ELECTRONIC BULLS AND BEARS, supra note 6, at 170 ("Most new contracts, if they are not standard corporate stock or bonds, have some aspects of 'future delivery,' and the likelihood that they will be found by the courts to fall under the CFTC's jurisdiction may effectively discourage stock markets from product innovation.").

[178] See Letter from Jean A. Webb, Secretary, Commodities Futures Trading Commission, to Jonathan G. Katz, Secretary, Securities and Exchange Commission (Nov. 28, 1990), cited in Breeden Testimony, supra note 19, at 16 n.9.

[179] See, e.g., S. 207, 102d Cong., 1st Sess., 137 CONG. REC. S4423 (daily ed. Apr. 16, 1991) (Futures Trading Practices Act of 1991); S. 2256, 100th Cong., 2d Sess., 134 CONG. REC. S3641 (daily ed. Mar. 31, 1988) (Intermarket Coordination Act); S. 1891, 100th Cong., 1st Sess., 133 CONG. REC. S16675 (daily ed. Nov. 20, 1987) (Financial Services Oversight Act); see also supra notes 36–37.

tions.[180] The functional-instrument initiatives supported by the SEC have been opposed by the CFTC, which has generally favored a functional-agency approach based upon each agency's traditional functions.[181] It is clear, however, that the definitional dichotomies engraved in statutes in connection with the CEAct's curious structure warrant Congress's intervention. This necessity was recognized in the IPs case, where the Seventh Circuit's conclusion that IPs were futures spurred the court's suggestion that:

> Congress might think it wise to relax the exclusivity clause that lies at the heart of this dispute; so long as that clause remains, however, jurisdictional clashes of the sort represented here are inevitable. . . .[182]

As a result of the IPs case and in an effort to resolve the ongoing jurisdictional dispute between the SEC and CFTC, compromise legislation was introduced on October 18, 1990 by Senators Leahy, Lugar, Dodd, Bond, and the late Senator Heinz.[183] This legislation was not enacted, but legislation relating to SEC-CFTC jurisdictional issues has been passed recently by the Senate as the Futures Trading Practices Act of 1991.[184] This bill provides, *inter alia,* that: (1) hybrid commodity instruments that derive less than fifty percent of their value from the date of issuance from the value of a commodity option component, or instruments for which it is expected that less than 50 percent of the change in value of the instrument will be due to movement in the price of a commodity or commodities underlying the instrument, would not be subject to CFTC regulation;[185] (2) IPs that are traded on a national securities exchange that were approved for trading by the SEC in its order dated April 11, 1989 or were pending approval on or prior to December 31, 1990 would be excluded from regulation under the CEAct;[186] (3) the CFTC would be granted limited exemptive authority applicable to certain institutions as well as the

---

[180] In May 1988, in the wake of the October 1987 crash, the SEC Commissioners voted to propose the transfer to the SEC of CFTC jurisdiction over stock index futures contracts and associated options. *See SEC Submits Legislation to Impose Post-October Market Crash Reforms,* 20 Sec. Reg. & L. Rep. (BNA) No. 26, at 1020 (July 1, 1988). This change in jurisdiction was proposed again in 1990. *See CFTC to Propose Language to Address Hybrid Financial Products, Gramm Says,* 23 Sec. Reg. & L. Rep. (BNA) No. 6, at 166 (Feb. 8, 1991); Breeden Testimony, *supra* note 19, at 21–27.

[181] *See* Gramm Testimony, *supra* note 27, at 23–25. *But cf. supra* note 27 (describing convergence of the functional-instrument and functional-agency theories).

[182] Chicago Mercantile Exch. v. SEC, 883 F.2d 537, 550 (7th Cir. 1989), *cert. denied,* 110 S. Ct. 3214 (1990).

[183] *See* Compromise Amendment No. 3031 to S. 1729, 101st Cong., 2d Sess., 136 CONG. REC. S16035 (daily ed. Oct. 18, 1990).

[184] *See* 137 CONG. REC. S4708 (daily ed. Apr. 18, 1991); *supra* note 37.

[185] S. 207, 102d Cong., 1st Sess. § 303, 137 CONG. REC. S4423, S4433 (daily ed. Apr. 16, 1991).

[186] *Id.* § 304, 137 CONG. REC. at S4433.

specific authority to exempt currency and interest rate swaps and hybrid instruments and must exclude certain bank deposits and loans from CFTC regulation if certain criteria are met;[187] and (4) the Federal Reserve Board (FRB) would set margin guidelines on stock index futures.[188] There is no general authority contained in this bill to exempt publicly offered products.

The Futures Trading Practices Act of 1991, as illustrated above,[189] fails to amend the CEAct's exclusive jurisdiction clause. Rather, it merely carves out exemptions and exclusions from such exclusive jurisdiction with respect to certain IPs and a limited number of other products. For example, this legislation, because it is directed at ameliorating the results of the IPs case, would allow IPs with the precise characteristics contained in SEC approvals or proposals prior to 1991 to trade pursuant to SEC regulation. The bill therefore permits IPs to trade under SEC oversight *only* if such IPs already had been approved by the SEC or had been pending SEC approval at a particular time, without permitting any flexibility for SEC-regulated exchanges to make such IPs more efficient or desirable to investors. By its terms, then, the legislation freezes the innovation of IPs to those previously developed and straitjackets securities exchanges into offering solely IPs that have been developed in the past or that are in proposal form, without any room for future innovation. For any new IPs, the IPs case would apply, thereby mandating that all new IPs (even those with minor distinctions from pre-1991 IPs) be traded pursuant to CFTC regulation.

The bill, in other words, would preserve the concept of futurity as articulated in the IPs case and would allow the CFTC to assert exclusive jurisdiction over any new product that falls outside the law's specific IPs criteria. In this connection, the 50 percent commodity option or futures component test for hybrids could become a new litigation minefield, given the obvious differences of opinion that could arise in dissecting a product for jurisdictional purposes with mathematical formulas. Indeed, one could clearly imagine a scenario in which the judicial forum becomes the locus of evaluating whether a hybrid derives 50 percent of its value from the value of a commodity option component so as to be subject to CFTC regulation, or merely 49 percent of such value from such component so as to be free to trade OTC. Compelling courts to apply this test will transform the judiciary—which, when it comes to futures exchanges' challenges to enlarge CFTC jurisdiction, means the Seventh Circuit—into a technical evaluation panel that determines jurisdiction over new products by percentage points.

---

[187] *Id.* § 302, 137 CONG. REC. at S4433.
[188] *Id.* § 301, 137 CONG. REC. at S4432.
[189] *See supra* note 110; *supra* text accompanying note 116.

It must be noted, moreover, that the 50 percent hybrid test would apply solely to the present concept of "hybrid" products, which products involve component parts. It would not, consequently, cover any innovative hybrid that is not easily divisible into components. The bill, therefore, ensures that the innovation of hybrids cannot include noncomponent instruments and mandates that new hybrids adhere to the 50 percent test. Furthermore, it is necessary to emphasize that the 50 percent hybrid test would not cover "true" derivatives such as new IPs, because such derivatives are not made up of components. For the same reason, innovative derivatives could be subject to the IPs case holding. As a result, the initiative clearly preserves the underlying definitional dichotomy between "securities" and "futures"that impedes innovation and therefore will not end the ongoing SEC-CFTC turf battle.

In addition, the Markets and Trading Reorganization and Reform Act, which would establish a Markets and Trading Commission to perform the task of the SEC and CFTC, was recently introduced by Congressman Glickman and referred jointly to the House Committees on Energy and Commerce and Agriculture.[190] This bill, by creating one agency, would prevent disputes between the two agencies, because both would no longer exist. Although the bill assigns the functions of the SEC and CFTC to a new agency, it does not articulate how such a transfer of functions would occur. It does not specify any substantive characteristics of the new agency, such as whether the agency will be required to write a new set of regulations applicable to both SEC- and CFTC-regulated exchanges and entities or whether the regulations of either existing agency will be adopted. Nevertheless, this bill represents a positive step in the evolution of thought regarding regulatory bifurcation by setting forth a challenge to the status quo at the congressional level. Indeed, this initiative directly addresses the core issue, which, in Congressman Glickman's words, is that "[t]he United States has a regulatory structure rooted in the 19th Century and financial markets already well into the 21st Century."[191]

The bill, however, does retain regulatory distinctions with regard to "futures" and, consequently, preserves the fiction that there exists a definable instrument called a futures contract. In the area of margin, the bill grants the Markets and Trading Commission the authority to set margins on products presently regulated by the SEC, but empowers the Commission only to "adjust" or "limit" margins set by "contract markets" (futures exchanges) with respect to futures.[192] Accordingly, the bill would require

[190] See 137 Cong. Rec. H1023 (daily ed. Feb. 19, 1991) (introduction and referral of H.R. 965).
[191] Hearings Before the Subcomm. on Telecommunications and Finance of the House Comm. on Energy and Commerce, on H.R. 4477, 101st Cong., 2d Sess. 34 (1990) (statement of Rep. Glickman). (H.R. 4477 was the predecessor to H.R. 965.)
[192] See H.R. 965, 102d Cong., 1st Sess. § 203, 137 Cong. Rec. H1004, H1005 (daily ed. Feb. 19, 1991).

the new Commission to determine which new financial instruments are "futures" as a precondition to the Commission's margin duties. It is easy to envision a Commission determination that a new product is one for which the Commission is authorized to set margin sparking a challenge by a futures exchange that the new product is a future and that margins on such product may be set only by the exchange. Therefore, this proposal would not prevent suits based upon an instrument being a futures contract, which, of course, has been the result all along.

IV. Solutions

A. Background

At this point it is useful to reflect upon the foregoing analyses. It has been demonstrated that regulatory bifurcation based upon legislative definitions cannot be justified through functional-instrument or functional-agency rationales. Case law such as *GNMA Options* and legislation such as the Accord that sought to maintain definitional separations using functional grounds have been exposed to be unworkable solutions to the SEC-CFTC jurisdictional conflict. The paradigmatic failure of the Accord to accommodate innovation is reflected in the analysis of the IPs case.

Examination of the IPs case, furthermore, aptly illustrates the innovation-inhibiting uncertainty arising from regulation by definition. Indeed, in that case, because of the anomalies presented by functional rationales, the court supported its definitional conclusion by grasping at what could be perceived to be the last remaining justification for legislative categorization: futurity. The fallacy of using futurity both as the primary factor that defines a futures contract and as the rationale for bifurcation has been highlighted. Finally, the failure of legislative proposals responding to the IPs case to adquately eliminate the barriers to innovation in the current fragmented system has been examined.

The key issue, therefore, becomes how to create a workable solution to the jurisdictional battles that encourages innovation and maintains the safety and soundness of the United States financial marketplace. Accordingly, we decided to adopt, as a theoretical framework, the goal of creating a system based upon how well it accommodates innovation (as opposed to whether a structure maintains regulatory distinctions based upon definitions, agency functions, or instrument functions). At the same time, this structure must reflect and maintain the safety and soundness provisions integral to any effective system of market regulation. To do so, however, we needed to identify any practical impediments to fundamentally revising the two-agency definitional system or, alternatively, any practical reasons for preserving this system. Clearly, theories may be abandoned and legislation could be rewritten, but if there exist extrinsic limitations on solutions, the.solutions must incorporate these limitations.

The first practical limitation on revising the current structure is politics. In view of each agency's political clout as well as that of their constituents, this limitation is real. Neither agency, nor the industries they regulate, should be expected to encourage any loss of jurisdictional authority. In particular, futures exchanges such as the CBOT and CME have demonstrated their substantial political acumen on numerous occasions and their ability to mount an effective battle to preserve their short-term interests should never be underestimated. This limitation, however, is not insurmountable and should not inhibit the development of new solutions. If proposals remain captive to politics, the debate on regulation will be closed, because generally both agencies publicly refuse to accept dilutions of their current jurisdictional authority.[193] To ameliorate certain adverse political repercussions, the appropriate proposal should, at minimum, attempt to maintain the self-regulatory organizations (SROs)[194] of both industries to the extent feasible. Such SROs are the securities and futures exchanges themselves, as well as the National Association of Securities Dealers (NASD) and the National Futures Association (NFA). Fundamentally, political considerations demand the least disruption to the current system necessary to effect innovation-enhancing regulation, which means that preserving SROs must be a goal of any new structure.

The second and most relevant practical limitation in formulating a new structure is the degree to which the regulatory and self-regulatory frameworks of the SEC and CFTC regimes are compatible. The extent to which these regimes are compatible, without doubt, determines the proper solution to the ongoing turf battle. For example, if the regimes are compatible, merger of the two agencies along with an adoption of harmonized regulatory standards becomes a true alternative. Such a merger would prevent interagency litigation, would bring all instruments currently traded pursuant to SEC and CFTC oversight under one roof, and would be based upon compatible federal regimes.

Provided the regimes cannot be combined for compatibility reasons, the focus of a restructuring to end jurisdictional squabbles must be shifted. Thus, if the two agencies could not be appropriately merged, the solution may be to establish a decision-making panel through which interagency disputes could be resolved in an expedited manner. Alternatively, the appropriate solution in the context of incompatibility may be to preserve each agency's current jurisdiction but permit new products to trade pursuant to either agency's oversight. Unless the degree of regulatory

---

[193] *See generally* Breeden Testimony, *supra* note 19; Gramm Testimony, *supra* note 27. It must be emphasized that the CFTC has voluntarily restricted its jurisdiction over certain swaps, hybrids, and 15-day Brent oil contracts. *See supra* notes 110–11 and accompanying text.

[194] See *infra* note 199 for a discussion of SROs. For a discussion of futures SROs, see T. Russo, *supra* note 4, §§ 1.02–.04. For a discussion of securities SROs, see T. Hazen, *supra* note 54, at 494–505.

compatibility were addressed, therefore, a proper solution could not be discovered.

In examining the available materials concerning comparisons between the SEC and CFTC regimes, it soon became clear that there existed no current in-depth comparison to assist in this endeavor.[195] Accordingly, prior to commencing this Article, we elicited the able assistance of volunteers from Cadwalader's 1990 Summer Associate class.[196] These volunteers objectively analyzed the two regimes with a view toward identifying regulatory distinctions in the areas of customer suitability, supervision, broker versus dealer functions, segregation of customer funds, frontrunning, and margin. The results were startling.

In commissioning this comparative analysis, it was believed that the Summer Associates would arrive at the same conclusions that pervade popular notions of SEC and CFTC distinctions. Instead, it was discovered that even in areas that are regularly cited as "different," such as margin and customer suitability,[197] the goals of the two regimes were surprisingly similar. It became abundantly apparent that the distinctions relating to each agency's traditional regulatory ambit (stock and debt securities for the SEC and futures on agricultural commodities for the CFTC) often obscured the similarities in the two agencies' regulatory aims.[198]

Of course, even with respect to nonagricultural derivatives, in none of the areas were the regimes exactly the same. We discovered not that each regime attached the same labels or instituted the same procedures towards regulating the various areas, but that both regimes shared common goals for regulating the six areas analyzed in the appendix to this article. In this connection, examining the shared goals concerning regulation of these areas led to the conclusion that there are enough regulatory similarities in the federal regimes to provide a foundation upon which a merged agency with one basic set of standards could exist. Because regulatory innovation seeks to improve the present structure, it is necessary to note that the merged agency model set forth below represents an effort to find solutions rather than aims to be the *only* solution to the SEC-CFTC turf war. In essence, the model is intended as a means to generate debate and creative solutions concerning the critical problem of innovation-inhibiting regulation.

B. *The Importance of SROs*

As an initial matter, in creating one agency with harmonized standards, the "basic" nature of one set of federal standards should be empha-

---

[195] *See supra* note 9 (discussing previous comparisons).

[196] Summer Associates were chosen for this analysis in order to gain insights into the two regimes from sources unsullied by prejudices.

[197] *See*, e.g., Gramm Testimony, *supra* note 27, at 17.

[198] *See*, e.g., *infra* notes 272–75, 287 and accompanying text (concerning heightened suitability determinations for options under both regimes).

sized. As the comparative analysis contained in the appendix makes clear, there remain certain differences within each agency's regime concerning, for example, the regulatory standards applicable to different products. This result occurs both because of different laws and agency regulations as well as because both agencies rely, to a large degree, upon SROs to assume regulatory responsibilities in numerous areas.[199]

That both agencies rely upon a broad system of self-regulation reflects the essential role the SROs play in the current bifurcated system. In view of the political importance of SROs and their self-regulatory functions, such SROs must be incorporated into a unified system. In fact, the result that each agency has been able to fulfill its regulatory function more efficiently and effectively because of SROs is beyond doubt, even though SROs under each agency's oversight have adopted disparate self-regulatory standards in many areas.[200]

The present system of self-regulation under two agencies, therefore, also indicates that there does not exist one unified set of standards under either regime today. The challenge then becomes how to merge the two agencies and maintain the viability of an increasingly disparate regime of self-regulation under one agency. The comparison in this regard indicates that, in connection with self-regulation as well as federal regulation, the two regimes retain similar goals. As a result, a new system under which one federal agency has oversight over both securities and futures SROs becomes a workable alternative.

Having generally outlined the conclusion that the SEC and CFTC regulatory and self-regulatory systems prove compatible, it is necessary to first demonstrate how these similarities arise in both regimes and how regulation of the six areas could be practically effectuated under the oversight of one federal agency. Following this predicate analysis of the six specific areas, the discussion will focus upon the broad issues relating to the benefits to financial innovation and challenges of unified regulation under one agency.

---

[199] Under §§ 6 and 19 of the 1934 Act, SEC-regulated exchanges are charged with a primary responsibility for disciplining member conduct inconsistent with "just and equitable principles of trade." 15 U.S.C. §§ 78f(b)(5), 78s (1988). In 1938 similar legislation was adopted for the regulation of the OTC markets. This so-called Maloney Act was enacted as § 15A of the 1934 Act and led to the creation of the NASD. 15 U.S.C. § 78o-3 (1988). In addition to NASD, there are presently ten SROs registered under § 6. Under § 17 of the CEAct, the CFTC has authority to oversee any registered futures association that satisfies the criteria contained therein. Currently, the NFA is the only futures association registered under the CEAct and is required to promulgate rules to, *inter alia*, "promote just and equitable principles of trade." 7 U.S.C. § 21(b)(7) (1988). Futures exchanges, moreover, are required to perform numerous self-regulatory functions. *See*, e.g., *id.* § 7(c)-(e); CFTC Regulation 1.52.

[200] *See*, e.g., Appendix subpart III(B) (discussing different rules of SEC-regulated exchanges concerning the regulation of broker versus dealer functions).

C. Unified Regulation of the Six Areas

With respect to the analysis of the six areas, it is essential to keep in mind that the success of disparate systems of self-regulation within each current regime provides a framework for establishing one agency with authority over a wider range of SROs with greater self-regulatory differences. Additionally, in proposing regulatory alternatives under a merged agency, the analysis below distinguishes between federal regulations and SRO rules that differ because of the inherent characteristics of either industry or the instruments each currently regulates (i.e., intrinsic differences) and differences that relate to "policy" reasons unrelated to such inherent characteristics. With respect to the former, it will be necessary to either retain different regulatory standards to accommodate such differences or articulate why maintaining different standards is inappropriate. For the latter so-called "policy" differences, the fact that such differences do not derive from intrinsic factors will be explained, yet the disposition of such differences will be left to the discretion of the new, merged agency. The innovation-enhancing merged agency model regarding the six areas set forth below aims to be a thought-provoking beginning to establishing a unified structure. Thus, it will not provide "all the answers" but will leave certain policy decisions to the agency, discuss the disposition of intrinsic differences, and offer proposals concerning both.

1. Suitability.[201] Suitability, loosely defined, encompasses the obligations of broker-dealers and FCMs when making recommendations to, or opening the accounts of, customers.[202] Under the SEC and CFTC regimes, neither agency directly regulates suitability. Rather, in both cases, SROs have defined these obligations as involving making disclosures and inquiries regarding the trading of instruments and the customer's trading objectives. The two self-regulatory regimes differ, however, in that broker-dealers are required either to have a reasonable basis for recommendations or determine that recommendations are not "unsuitable"[203] for a customer, while FCMs need not reach such determinations if proper disclosures and inquiries are made.[204] As a result, in dealing with SEC-regulated instruments, broker-dealers must have some justification for recommendations, whereas FCMs do not.

Given that both broker-dealers and FCMs make inquiries and disclosures, the key regulatory difference becomes the absence of justifications for recommendations by FCMs. This difference may be more superficial than real. Implicit in FCMs' disclosure and inquiry duties upon opening

---

[201] *See* Appendix, Part I.
[202] *See infra* note 240 and accompanying text. (All notes from 240 onward are part of the Appendix and, therefore, are not included in this reprint.)
[203] *See infra* notes 249–75 and accompanying text.
[204] *See infra* notes 286–89 and accompanying text.

customer accounts exists the root of the concept that there are limits to the types of transactions an FCM should execute for customers. In addition, because suitability requires mental determinations rather than specific actions, the self-regulatory distinctions ultimately relate to what the broker-dealer or FCM *thinks* rather than how each *acts* toward customers.

The question arises whether FCMs, like broker-dealers, should be compelled to make justifications for recommendations under a merged agency either at the federal or SRO level. Because of the fact that futures trading is inherently risky and involves the possibility of losses greater than a customer's investment of funds, any FCM justification for recommendations should probably *not* contain an express suitability determination.[205] Such a difference between futures trading and options or stock trading is "intrinsic," thereby requiring accommodation under a unified structure in a manner that does not inhibit innovation.

To effect this accommodation, FCMs may, under a single merged agency, be required by their SROs to have a "reasonable basis" for recommendations of all transactions in a manner similar to the New York Stock Exchange (NYSE) rule applicable to stock trading.[206] However, because certain SEC-regulated exchanges such as the American Stock Exchange (AMEX) do not require suitability or even "reasonable basis" determinations for stock recommendations,[207] it is eminently feasible that CFTC-regulated exchanges could retain their *current* duties of inquiry and disclosure or apply such duties to recommendations as well as to account openings with respect to existing products. The essential goal would be to reject imposing distinct requirements upon FCMs with regard to new instruments based upon such an instrument being characterized as a futures contract or a commodity option. In this regard, the merged agency, in its oversight role, could determine whether the current standards relating to futures or commodity options are appropriate for a new instrument on a case-by-case basis.

Under a merged agency, further, it would be appropriate to retain an SRO approach to suitability, because this approach has worked under the bifurcated framework. Given that the SEC does not *require* the SROs it regulates to adopt suitability rules and the CFTC and the NFA have rejected suitability rules,[208] it is apparent, for these reasons as well, that suitability regulation should remain at the SRO level. The single agency, however, would retain an important oversight role in ensuring that SRO suitability rules do not hinge upon defining new instruments and should encourage

---

[205] *See infra* notes 284–86 and accompanying text.
[206] *See infra* notes 262–65 and accompanying text.
[207] *See infra* text accompanying note 263.
[208] *See infra* text accompanying note 248; *infra* notes 276, 284 and accompanying text.

the adoption of nondefinitional provisions applicable to new products as they arise.

In sum, because both regimes require inquiries and disclosures, there exists a firm basis for uniting the present SRO rules in this area. SRO regulation, in its present form, could be the first step in a merged agency framework and not necessarily the final outcome. The merged agency could, in the future, experiment with requiring FCMs to make inquiries and disclosures when making recommendations or with requiring a reasonable basis for FCM recommendations. To the extent different suitability rules among what are currently securities SROs and futures SROs become problematic, the one agency would be able, as the SEC and CFTC are today, to promulgate federal suitability rules or to direct SROs to adopt certain types of suitability standards that are not based on the definition of instruments.

2. *Supervision.*[209] In contrast to suitability, the regulation of which mainly occurs at the self-regulatory level, the two agencies directly regulate the supervision of employees of broker-dealers and FCMs. SROs, however, have been actively involved in implementing and enforcing such supervisory requirements.

Under both regimes, strict liability is not imposed upon either broker-dealers or FCMs.[210] Each regime contains flexible standards of supervisory responsibilities that involve written procedures, a chain of command, and approval of certain trading practices.[211] Nevertheless, pursuant to the present CFTC regime, in contrast to the SEC regime, FCMs may be held directly liable for failing to adequately supervise employees, while broker-dealers' supervisory liability remains purely derivative of a violation by employees.[212]

Despite this direct liability distinction, the comparative analysis indicates that supervisory standards and procedures under both regimes prove so similar as to enable one federal standard under a merged agency.

In determining whether to incorporate the CFTC's direct liability standard into the new framework, in light of these similarities, it should be recognized that direct liability under the CFTC regime is not due to inherent differences in the types of employees working at FCMs or the transactions involved in an FCM's business. This distinction is instead a pure policy determination that a failure to supervise should be deemed a regulatory violation, standing alone, without an employee having commit-

---

[209] *See* Appendix, Part II.
[210] *See infra* note 303 and accompanying text.
[211] *See infra* notes 311, 341, 342 and accompanying text.
[212] *See infra* note 302 and accompanying text.

ted an underlying violation. As a result, the new agency would be in the best position to make this determination. Minor differences relating to whether written procedures are necessary in connection with specific transactions, or the degree to which senior personnel must be involved in supervising employees,[213] are largely technical determinations that also could be resolved by the agency.

Consequently, supervisory procedures, under a merged agency, could be unified at the federal level without regard to the nature of a trading firm's business. SRO rules, of course, should reflect such unified rules and should not be derived from the types of instruments with which employees are involved. At both the federal and self-regulatory levels, minimal alterations in the current approaches could give way to one set of streamlined supervisory federal regulations that could replace the two sets of standards presently applicable to firms that trade both SEC- and CFTC-regulated products.

3. Broker and Dealer Functions.[214] At the federal level, both regimes regulate the extent to which a broker-dealer or FCM may trade as a broker on behalf of customers and trade for its own account as a dealer. Both regimes attempt to minimize the conflicts of interest that arise from both brokering and dealing.

The SEC and CFTC regimes currently limit broker-dealers' and FCMs' dealing activities on exchange floors by generally requiring that customer orders be executed prior to the dealer's own "proprietary" orders. Although these limitations are statutorily imposed under the SEC regime[215] and adopted through regulation under the CFTC regime,[216] the limitations emanate from the federal level and not from SROs. As is the case with most federal provisions, however, SROs have adopted distinct standards relating to how these provisions are enforced.

Because the common goal of minimizing broker versus dealer conflicts generally requires that customer orders be executed before proprietary orders, it is possible that a merged agency could regulate this area through one statutory provision or one regulation relating to exchange trading activities. The distinctions between SRO rules as well as OTC and exchange trading, nevertheless, may require differences in how this regulatory goal is implemented.

The differences in the two regimes relate mainly to the fact that OTC trading is permissible under the SEC structure and prohibited under that of the CFTC. For example, the requirement that futures trading occur

---

[213] *See infra* note 364 and accompanying text.
[214] *See* Appendix, Part III.
[215] *See infra* notes 370–71 and accompanying text.
[216] *See infra* notes 416–19 and accompanying text.

through "open and competitive outcry" and the pandemonium in futures pits arising from this requirement has led the CFTC to link dual trading (i.e., brokering and dealing) with exchanges maintaining verifiable audit trails.[217]

Accordingly, unified regulation of broker and dealer activities must accommodate and reflect OTC trading of instruments. The new agency will confront challenges similar to the SEC today in establishing general rules in this area while overseeing SRO regulation of exchange and OTC trading practices. Also, a unified federal system must initially be, as the present systems are, flexible enough to allow SRO regulations to reflect different exchange floor trading practices. Such current practices include the presence of a specialist system at securities exchanges and the need for contract liquidity on futures exchange floors.[218]

4. Segregation.[219] At the federal level, both regimes protect customers' funds from misuse by broker-dealers and FCMs through segregation requirements. This common goal of segregation, however, is implemented in distinct manners through equally complex formulas. Such distinctions do not present a hurdle to unified federal regulation of segregation because the distinctions are by and large technical and aim to fulfill the same goal of protecting customers' funds and property.[220]

One difference between the SEC and CFTC segregation requirements, however, demands attention. Under the SEC rules, broker-dealers may not invest segregated funds even in certain "safe" investments, as FCMs may,[221] but are authorized to use customer securities as collateral for loans to customers.[222] Broker-dealers' ability to use customer securities as collateral for loans and FCMs' ability to invest customer funds, nevertheless, lead to a similar outcome in that trading firms under both regimes are permitted to earn interest in segregated funds.

The difference in the means by which such interest may be earned relates in part to intrinsic differences in the industries. That is, there are inherent characteristics of futures trading that facilitate investing of funds rather than lending on collateral, and there are qualities of stock trading that demand broker-dealers to engage in lending activities as opposed to safe investments. In creating a unified rule, the agency could incorporate both the SEC lending provision and the CFTC investment provision. Conversely, it could permit one method or the other, or even fashion a new approach to allowing interest on segregated funds.

---

[217] *See infra* notes 421–22 and accompanying text.
[218] *See infra* note 382 and accompanying text (specialists); *infra* note 414 and accompanying text (contract liquidity).
[219] *See* Appendix, Part IV.
[220] *See* Appendix, subparts IV(A), IV(B).
[221] *See infra* note 496 and accompanying text.
[222] *See infra* note 475 and accompanying text.

Therefore, segregation, because of its complexity and the similarity between the current regimes, becomes an area in which one set of federal regulations could be appropriate. Under one regime, trading firms would need only confront one set of complicated formulas. Despite certain distinctions, the core goals and procedures of the two regimes, because of their focus on protecting customer funds and property and their allowance of interest, provide a strong foundation upon which to accomplish unification. By eliminating duplication in this area, the merged agency could create regulatory efficiencies without sacrificing the safety and soundness aims of protecting customers' segregated funds.

5. *Frontrunning.*[223] Because frontrunning is an area that neither federal regime has directly regulated, frontrunning regulation presents a unique opportunity for a merged agency to step forward and assume a leadership role. The absence of entrenched or specific SRO policies concerning frontrunning, as well as the need for an understandable definition of frontrunning, makes this opportunity particularly attractive.

Given that frontrunning (which currently is defined as trading in securities, options, or futures while in possession of material nonpublic information concerning these instruments) often involves intermarket transactions, the benefits of assigning frontrunning regulation to a merged agency are obvious.[224] The possibility of frontrunning regulation at the federal level is underscored by the fact that the pending House bill, the Commodity Futures Improvements Act of 1991, contains criminal "insider trading" provisions that would amend the CEAct and render certain forms of frontrunning felonies.[225]

In tackling frontrunning regulation at the federal level, several important issues arise. The first issue is whether Congress should pass legislation defining frontrunning or whether this task should be left to the unified agency. Either alternative or a combination of both would resolve the absence of federal standards in this area. For example, the Commodity Futures Improvements Act of 1991 defines frontrunning, but provides that violations of the statute are dependent upon whether the statutory elements are satisfied in addition to the presence of a CFTC rule violation.[226] The Commodity Futures Improvements Act of 1991, thus, defines

---

[223] *See* Appendix, Part V.

[224] *See infra* notes 504–10 and accompanying text.

[225] H.R. 707, 102d Cong., 1st Sess. § 213, 137 CONG. REC. H1350, H1354 (daily ed. Mar. 5, 1991). The Futures Trading Practices Act of 1991, passed by the Senate, also contains an "insider trading" provision that is less directly applicable to frontrunning than that of the House bill. *See* S. 207, 102d Cong., 1st Sess. § 268, 137 CONG. REC. S4423, S4432 (daily ed. Apr. 16, 1991).

[226] H.R. 707, 102d Cong., 1st Sess. § 213, 137 CONG. REC. H1350, H1354 (daily ed. Mar. 5, 1991).

potential frontrunning violations but delegates the ultimate responsibility for defining such violations to the CFTC.

Second, the question arises whether frontrunning violations should give rise to criminal or civil sanctions or both. This determination relates to whether the penalties should be purely punitive, as the Commodity Futures Improvements Act of 1991 provides, or aim to preserve market integrity, as civil sanctions would.

Finally, frontrunning regulation could provide an opportunity for Congress and the merged agency to review the issue of whether insider trading, as the offense has developed in case law under section 10(b) of the 1934 Act and SEC Rule 10b-5, should be incorporated into a federal frontrunning standard.[227] The Commodity Futures Improvements Act of 1991, in this regard, fails to incorporate a Rule 10b-5 concept because it is limited to felonies and depends upon rule promulgation by the CFTC. To the extent any frontrunning or insider trading provisions derived from Rule 10b-5 are adopted, further, such prohibitions should not apply to bona fide hedging transactions, because of the important role hedging plays in the futures and options markets.[228]

6. *Margin.*[229] In light of the continuing controversy over margin regulation and the SEC and CFTC's diametrically opposed views regarding the proper regime of margin regulation in connection with stock derivatives, it is clear that integrating margin regulation would present a great challenge to a one-agency system. Nevertheless, because margins in both the securities and futures industries perform the common functions of protecting the integrity of markets and their participants, providing market liquidity and supplying leverage, there exists a foundation upon which to work toward a coordinated solution that is politically feasible.

Although the focus of the margin public policy debate has been the effect of so-called "low" futures margin upon stock market volatility, we have declined to address this issue in an effort to analyze narrowly the functions and regulation of margins within both the SEC and CFTC regimes. This somewhat artificial approach, however, has revealed that notwithstanding intermarket volatility issues, margin regulation under the current regimes warrants reanalysis. Notwithstanding the external effects margins in one market may have on another, a coordinated system of margins could benefit both the SEC and CFTC regimes, even if viewed independently, and could thereby improve the overall efficiency of our unified marketplace.

In fact, because both regimes share common participants, it is logical

---

[227] *See infra* notes 514–24 and accompanying text.
[228] See *supra* note 29 for a discussion of hedging.
[229] *See* Appendix, Part VI.

to strive to improve the efficiency of such participants' activities in the marketplace through cross-margining efforts. Through cross-margining and the related initiatives concerning coordinated clearing and settlement, both the securities and futures regimes could be strengthened without sacrificing their ability generally to regulate margin levels in the manner each has seen fit over time.

Under a cross-margining system, the politically explosive question of whether to impose governmental regulation of futures margins need not be addressed. Alternatively, a one-agency system could preserve the traditional role of futures exchanges in setting margin levels, yet require broker-dealers and FCMs to assess the risk of customers' positions across markets when requiring additional margin payments. In this manner, both broker-dealers and FCMs would acquire greater information regarding current market forces, the liquidity of markets, and a customer's ability to perform his obligations. Armed with such increased knowledge, it is probable that markets could better accommodate market stress while improving the overall safety and soundness of our unified financial marketplace.

D. Conclusion

The foregoing analysis illustrates the practical alternatives available in merging the SEC and CFTC into one agency and adopting certain basic federal rules in several key areas. That these alternatives—ranging from permitting SROs to continue to individually regulate suitability to empowering a merged agency to develop a set of frontrunning regulations—prove amenable to unification highlights the potential for a variety of regulatory approaches under the oversight of one agency. Certainly, addressing the alternatives in the six areas merely provides a framework for integrating numerous other regulatory areas that are not addressed in the Appendix, such as registration of broker-dealers and FCMs, antifraud and manipulation rules, and exchange arbitration rules. The fact that the regulatory approaches in these six "controversial" areas are compatible indicates that it may be possible for full unification of regulation in all relevant areas.

Now that the potential for unified regulation has been revealed, it is necessary to articulate the benefits and challenges relating to a unified structure.

As a principal matter, a single merged agency will prevent interagency squabbles and related lawsuits, because jurisdiction over all instruments currently traded pursuant to the SEC and CFTC regimes will be under the oversight of a single regulator. This fundamental transformation will eliminate regulation by definition at the jurisdictional level and the innovation-inhibiting effects arising therefrom that have been described at length above.

Second, by virtue of the compatibility between the two regimes illustrated in the comparative analysis, there exists a basic foundation upon which to unify regulation in a manner that does not retain regulatory distinctions concerning new financial products based upon the definition of instruments at the regulatory and self-regulatory levels. As the compatibility analysis above makes clear, there are numerous methods through which the agency and SROs of the two industries could retain significant roles without basing regulatory and self-regulatory approaches to new products upon definitional distinctions.

A unified structure based upon compatibility that retains the various SROs, however, will confront numerous challenges as well as opportunities. For example, the agency should seek to develop a long-range plan for merging the NFA and NASD as well as consolidating futures and securities exchanges to create truly "one market." The agency could begin by directing securities exchanges that have futures subsidiaries, such as the NYSE and the PHLX, to merge with such subsidiaries and use these instances as models for subsequent mergers of nonaffiliated entities.[230] Most importantly, the agency and Congress would have to address how the agency would use its expanded jurisdictional power to regulate where all instruments trade. In this regard, the unified agency must face the challenge of adopting regulations or exempting from regulation OTC instruments such as swaps and hybrids.[231] The CFTC's commendable efforts in issuing interpretations that circumscribe its jurisdiction and in supporting legislation doing the same reflect a cooperative spirit that recognizes that issues such as the competitiveness of our market prove far more important than a turf war.

The possibility that new products could be permitted to trade on any exchange or OTC will create difficult questions for Congress and the agency with regard to regulating existing products. Such issues would include highly sensitive matters, such as whether to permit stocks to trade on futures exchanges as well as OTC and securities exchanges, and similarly whether to permit agricultural futures contracts to trade OTC or on a securities exchange in addition to on futures exchanges. In resolving such questions, the lessons of bifurcated regulation must not be forgotten. Hence, the new agency should not determine the forum in which products trade simply by virtue of past jurisdictional boundaries. As a starting point, it may be wise to restrict most existing instruments to the forum in which they presently trade and permit new or controversial instruments, such as IPs, to trade either OTC, on securities exchanges, on futures exchanges, or on all three. The goal, however, ultimately should be to eliminate distinctions based upon the past definitions of instruments and encourage a fully integrated operating structure under a unified federal statutory and regulatory framework.

---

[230] *See supra* note 10 and accompanying text (discussing securities exchanges' futures subsidiaries).
[231] *See supra* note 110 and accompanying text.

At the center of this structure must be a system to determine the manner in which new products are offered. As explained above, the CFTC designation process has become more burdensome with regard to financial innovation in the past few years than it had in the CFTC's early heyday of approving innovative contracts. The SEC's alternative structure of requiring disclosure for new products also does not appear to be the most useful approach in designing a new regulatory framework. In fact, even though the SEC is not compelled to analyze the economic value of new securities, it has evaluated the economic purpose of proposed options, such as those involving stock indices and Treasury securities.[232] Furthermore, there appear to be efforts by the CFTC to "streamline" its designation procedure for new products in an effort to make U.S. futures exchanges more competitive with their overseas counterparts.

As a result, there exists a movement in both regulatory regimes toward revising the traditional methods of offering products. These efforts indicate that there is the potential for achieving a unified framework applicable to offering new products. Such a framework may incorporate aspects of both the registration requirements of the SEC regime and the designation requirements of the CFTC regime to assess whether, how, and when new products may be offered and traded.

Resolving these difficult issues could lead to a unified federal agency that would create parity among U.S. markets and those of other jurisdictions, in which futures and securities markets operate under the auspices of a single regulatory body. This parity, in turn, will diminish the attractiveness of exporting innovation that the bifurcated structure creates. At the most basic level, a unified agency with harmonized regulations will nurture and encourage the development of new financial products in the United States and provide a flexible structure under which any innovation will be accommodated by eliminating the rigid "round and square holes" that the definitions of futures contracts and securities have become.

The time is now and the place is Congress to begin the process of regulatory reevaluation. From a 1991 vantage point, the convergence of U.S. markets through the innovation of financial derivatives cannot remain captive to an early 1900s concept of market regulation. With the onset of creative instruments that consistently challenge the ability of the terms "futures" and "securities" to define their characteristics and functions, such as IPs, swaps, warrants, and variations thereof, it is necessary that Congress, the originator of definitional regulation in a bygone era, reconsider its premise today.

---

[232] Compare the SEC's traditional orientation toward information disclosure, discussed *supra* at notes 61–62 and accompanying text.

Responsibility for reform remains with Congress not simply because the definitional statutes it passed no longer reflect practical realities, but also because efforts from other quarters cannot provide forward-looking alternatives while the specter of legislative definitions looms overhead. More importantly, Congress and only Congress can reclaim its rightful control over financial market policy in this era in which courts, through judicial fiat as highlighted in the IPs and *Transnor* cases,[233] pronounce public policy in this essential area. It is holdings such as these, as opposed to the acts or intent of Congress, that have established a structure of uncertainty in which instruments having any element of future valuation may be cast as futures contracts (which could include most derivative instruments), thereby confining their development, offer, and sale to U.S. futures exchanges.[234]

This judicially created uncertainty has arisen against a background in which there exists a demand for complex derivative products, whose usefulness depends upon elements of future valuation but whose characteristics and functions make exchange trading and designation inefficient or impossible. This anomaly becomes a severe impediment to the hallmark of U.S. financial markets: product innovation.

Yet it is Congress, as the common voice of sometimes competing interests in a private market-based democracy, that must resume its proper role of articulating our common goals of preserving and encouraging the competitiveness of the U.S. financial marketplace through legislation in a rapidly changing global environment. Ultimately, Congress, not the courts or federal agencies, will be called upon to redress the repercussions of regulation by definition, including the obvious effect of a loss of U.S. regulatory control over innovative products and markets that find a comfortable home elsewhere, as well as attendant costs, such as a loss of jobs in the U.S. financial services industry.[235]

We have set forth in this Article one approach for Congress to consider: namely, to incrementally strive for one agency to oversee our unified financial market. However, we have emphasized that the primary focus of reform should be upon revising the status quo to encourage innovation without sacrificing public protection and the safety and soundness of our market. Mindful of real political impediments, we have also suggested that alternative positive steps toward achieving this primary

---

[233] *See supra* note 111; *supra* notes 127–32 and accompanying text.

[234] As noted above, the Futures Trading Practices Act of 1991, by granting the CFTC exemptive authority over certain instruments, would allow such instruments to trade, but would not address the legislative problems regarding innovation in the future. *See supra* notes 184–88 and accompanying text.

[235] *See supra* note 25 and accompanying text (discussing loss of U.S. competitiveness under the current structure). In fact, markets in various transactions are travelling abroad on a daily basis.

goal should be encouraged. Under any approach, however, regulatory flexibility should occur such that effective regulation need not be the same for all participants or instruments. To be sure, different participants and different instruments may require distinct approaches, with safety and soundness achieved through stringent direct federal oversight in some cases, while industry practices and a lack of any meaningful problems in others may make federal control unnecessary.

Interestingly, the seeds of reform have been germinating for quite a while, but such alternatives have not yet been implemented. For example, serious studies such as the Brady Report contributed enormously to the creation of a common body of knowledge regarding the evolution of our once disparate markets toward one, integrated market. The Brady Report's main goal of intermarket coordination, however, has not been implemented, despite the efforts of Secretary of Treasury Brady in forwarding the debate in this area. Impetus for reform is also evident at the Federal Reserve Board, with David Mullins, formerly the Associate Director of the Brady Commission, currently advocating positive change in his capacity as a Federal Reserve Board Governor.[236] Individual members of Congress such as Congressman Glickman, Congressman Schumer, and Senator Wirth, have made efforts at placing market reform on the front burner of public debate. Indeed, Congressman Schumer has called for a unified clearing system for derivatives as well as interagency coordination.[237] Alternatives also have included Congressman Glickman's pending bill, discussed above, and Senator Wirth's bill that would have established an independent oversight commission to define the types of activities in which a particularly important sector, financial institutions, may engage.[238] Similarly, Under Secretary of the Treasury for Finance, Robert Glauber, has been a vocal advocate of market reform who has emphasized the necessity for coordinating market mechanisms and removing statutory barriers to innovation.[239]

Other alternatives may also warrant reexamination, such as the implementation of a congressionally created independent decision-making panel that would be free to determine jurisdictional disputes in a way that permits new products to trade as long as sufficient regulatory protections exist. Additionally, Congress may consider it appropriate to mandate that the SEC and CFTC, in conjunction with a working group, coordinate an

---

[236] See Nasar, *For Fed, a New Set of Tea Leaves*, N.Y. Times, July 5, 1991, at C1 (nat'l ed.).

[237] See Schumer & Russo, *It's Time to Put the Brady Plan into Effect*, N.Y. Times, Nov. 26, 1989, § 3, at 3, col. 1.

[238] See S. 1891, 100th Cong., 1st Sess., 133 CONG. REC. S16675 (daily ed. Nov. 20, 1987) (Financial Services Oversight Act).

[239] See Statement of the Honorable Robert R. Glauber, Under Secretary of the Treasury for Finance Before the Senate Committee on Agriculture, Nutrition, and Forestry (Feb. 7, 1991) (transcript on file with the *Texas Law Review*).

effort to unify regulation in certain areas, such as customer protection, off-exchange and computerized trading, account opening procedures, testing and registration requirements, and clearing and settlement. This approach would integrate the efforts of the SEC and CFTC, both of which, through their Chairmen, Breeden and Gramm, respectively, have made great strides in addressing the core problem of regulation by definition in recent times.

Despite these alternatives, the Futures Trading Practices Act of 1991 promises to repeat 1982 efforts by grandfathering innovation as it exists today and effectively straitjacketing innovation, possibly into the twenty-first century. Such endeavors, in allowing certain instruments to trade, are more helpful than not except to the extent their codification inspires us to lose sight of the inherent statutory problems of our bifurcated system.

Addendum

The "Futures Trading Practices Act of 1992" (FTPA), which was enacted on October 28, 1992, marks a significant development in financial market regulation since the original publication of the article reprinted herein. Title V of the FTPA establishes a new procedure under the Commodity Exchange Act, as amended (CEAct) that authorizes the Commodity Futures Trading Commission (CFTC) to exempt futures and products with futures-like characteristics from most requirements of the CEAct. Essentially, Title V empowers the CFTC, for the first time, to exempt covered products from the CEAct's exchange-trading requirement if certain criteria are met and the CFTC determines the exemption would be in the public interest and would not impair the ability of the CFTC or any self-regulatory organization to fulfill its responsibilities under the CEAct. On November 12, 1992, the CFTC published proposed swaps and hybrids rules under Title V in the Federal Register. For a discussion of Title V and the CFTC's proposed rules see T. Russo and M. Vinciguerra, "Financial Regulation and Title V of the Futures Trading Practices Act of 1992," Futures International Law Letter, November-December 1992.

HYBRID INSTRUMENTS AND THE COMMODITY EXCHANGE ACT— A PRACTICAL GUIDE

Joanne T. Medero*

22

In the past few years several commentators have described the reach of the Commodity Exchange Act (CEA) as overbroad or proposed alternatives in restructuring regulation over derivative products.[1] Jurisdictional disputes are perhaps an inevitable consequence of banking, securities and commodity futures regulatory schemes which have their modern origin in the early decades of this century. However, until the United States Congress enacts true financial services reform, and, in particular overhauls the CEA and the securities laws, new product developers and their lawyers must cope with the practical reality of existing law.[2]

Background

Congress has given the Commodity Futures Trading Commission (CFTC or Commission) exclusive jurisdiction over futures contracts, op-

---

* The views herein are those of the author and do not necessarily reflect the views of the Commodity Futures Trading Commission, its Commissioners or staff. This article is current as of June 1992.
[1] Russo & Vinciquerra, "Financial Innovation and Uncertain Regulation: Selected Issues Regarding New Product Development," 69 Tex. L. Rev. 1431 (1991); Markham, "Regulation of Hybrid Instruments Under the Commodity Exchange Act: A Call for Alternatives," 1 Col. Bus. L. Rev. 1 (1990); Young & Stein, "Swap Transactions Under the Commodity Exchange Act: Is Congressional Action Needed?," 76 Geo. L. J. 1917 (1988); Gilberg, "Regulation of New Financial Instruments Under the Federal Securities and Commodity Laws," 39 Vand. L. Rev. 1599 (1986).
[2] H.R. 707/S.207, the Commodity Futures Improvement Act of 1991 is pending as of June 1, 1992 before a Conference Committee. Title III, if enacted in the form passed by the Senate, would substantially change CFTC regulation of hybrids and swaps.

tions on futures and commodity options. All contracts for sale for future delivery must be traded on a contract market designated by the CFTC and all commodity option transactions are prohibited unless specifically permitted by CFTC rule, regulation or order.[3]

Section 2(a)(1) of the Act defines the term *commodity* to include, in addition to specifically enumerated agricultural commodities, "all other goods and articles . . . and all services, rights, and interests, in which contracts for future delivery are presently or in the future dealt in." However, the CEA does not provide a definition of a futures contract and thus the definition has been left to CFTC and judicial interpretation. Most of the interpretative opportunities have arisen in the context of enforcement cases where a broad definition has been espoused in order to protect the public from fraud.[4] Characterization of an off exchange transaction as a futures contract has serious consequences: the contract is illegal and thus void *ab initio*. More recently the Commission has recognized that a broad definition may unnecessarily impinge upon legitimate business transactions not intended to be encompassed by the CEA.[5]

There are two exclusions from the prohibition against off-exchange futures transactions. Sales of "any cash commodity for deferred shipment or delivery" are not required to be traded on a designated contract market.[6] This is known as the "forward contract exclusion." The other exclusion is provided by the so-called Treasury Amendment.

The most recent case to discuss the forward contract exclusion is *In re Bybee*.[7] This case arose out of the bankruptcy of a retail precious metals dealer where the bankruptcy trustee sought to have certain contracts between the retail dealer and a wholesale dealer voided as illegal off-exchange futures contracts. The court, relying in part on the Commission's recent Forward Contract Interpretation, declined to void the contracts by finding that the contracts were forwards because the agreement provided a "forced burden of delivery." The court also stated that the contracts were also futures because of an implicit guarantee of offset. In the Commission's view these inconsistent findings of fact result in an error of law, as a transaction cannot be *both* a futures and a forward.

The Treasury Amendment was proposed by the Department of Trea-

---

[3] *See* 7 U.S.C. § 2, 6c.

[4] *See CFTC v. CoPetro Marketing Group, Inc.*, 680 F.2d 573 (9th Cir. 1982); *In re Stovall* [1977–1980 Transfer Binder] Comm. Fut. L. Rep. (CCH) ¶ 20,941 (1979).

[5] *See,* Policy Statement Concerning Certain Swap Transactions, 54 Fed. Reg. 30,694 (1989) ["Swap Policy Statement"]; Interpretation Concerning Certain Forward Transactions, 55 Fed. Reg. 39,188 (1990) ["Forward Contract Interpretation"].

[6] 7 U.S.C. § 2. *See also*, Forward Contract Interpretation, 55 Fed. Reg. 39,188 and cases cited therein; Committee on Commodities Regulation of the Association of the Bar of the City of New York, "The Forward Contract Exclusion: An Analysis of Off-exchange Commodity based Instruments," 41 Bus. Law 853 (May 1986).

[7] 945 F.2d 309 (9th Cir. 1991).

sury in 1974 out of an expressed concern that the newly expanded definition of "commodity" could grant jurisdiction to the CFTC over the trading of a wide range of instruments. The provision provides that nothing in the CEA shall be deemed to govern or in any way be applicable to "transactions in foreign currency, security warrants, security rights, resales of installment loan contracts, repurchase options, government securities, or mortgage and mortgage purchase commitments" unless such transactions involve the sale thereof for future delivery conducted on a board of trade.[8]

In one of the few cases to consider the Treasury Amendment, it was held that the exclusion does not apply to options on foreign currency as options *involve* foreign currency but are not transactions *in* foreign currency.[9] For its part, the CFTC has interpreted the Treasury amendment to apply to markets not involving participation by the general public and otherwise limited to transactions between "sophisticated and informed institutions."[10]

In addition to the two statutory exclusions, the Commission has exercised its authority under the CEA to permit off exchange trading of certain "trade options." Trade options are those that are offered to a person who is "a producer, processor, or commercial user of, or a merchant handling, the commodity which is the subject of the option and who enters into the option solely for purposes related to the person's business as such."[11] Only the "offeree" of the option need meet these requirements and Commission staff has allowed some flexibility in the concept of "offeree" when "master agreements" are involved.[12]

The Hybrid Rules and Interpretation

The CFTC uses the term "hybrid instrument" to encompass those debt, preferred equity or depository instruments which contain elements

---

[8] 7 U.S.C. § 2. Certain transactions in these instruments may also be covered by the forward contract exclusion.

[9] *CFTC v. American Board of Trade*, 473 F. Supp. 1177 (S.D.N.Y. 1979). The CFTC did not base its enforcement action on this reading of the Treasury Amendment and has not brought any enforcement cases on reliance thereon.

[10] *See* CFTC Interpretative letter, No. 77–12 [1977–1980 Transfer Binder] Comm. Fut. L. Rep. (CCH) ¶ 20,467 (Aug. 17, 1977); CFTC Release, Trading in Foreign Currencies for Future Delivery, 50 Fed. Reg. 42,983 (1985); CFTC Off-Exchange Task Force ("OETF") Letter No. 90–1, [Current Binder] Comm. Fut. L. Rep. (CCH) ¶ 25,064 (May 30, 1991). *But see Salomon Forex, Inc. v. Tauber*, Civ. 90–1415 A (E.D. Va. June 1, 1992) (applies "plain meaning" of Treasury Amendment); *Bank Brussels Lambert, S.A. v. Intermetals Corp.*, 779 F. Supp. 741 (S.D.N.Y. 1991) (in *dicta* the District Court supports "plain meaning" for the Treasury Amendment).

[11] 17 C.F.R. § 32.4(a) (1991).

[12] Swap Policy Statement, 54 Fed. Reg. at 30695, n.14; CFTC OETF Letter No. 90–3, Comm. Fut. L. Rep. (CCH) ¶ 24,807 (Mar. 27, 1990).

or characteristics of futures or commodity option instruments. Swaps are not hybrids but raise some of the same issues under the CEA.[13] Index participations, the stock index based instruments listed briefly on several securities exchanges, are futures.[14] Options on individual securities, options on stock indices and currency options traded on a national securities exchange are securities.[15] However, options on all other commodities, even if issued as "warrants" by a single issuer, remain within the exclusive jurisdiction of the CFTC.[16]

The CFTC initial response to the emergence of hybrid instruments was a series of staff no-action letters and an advance notice of proposed rulemaking.[17] The Advance Notice and the no-action letters are instructional as to the staff and Commission views at that time, but have been largely superseded by a statutory interpretation concerning hybrid instruments ("Hybrid Interpretation")[18] and rules for the regulation of hybrid instruments ("Hybrid Rules").[19] As with most regulatory agency pronouncements, the explanation and footnotes accompanying the Hybrid Interpretation and Hybrid Rules are nearly as important as the Rules or Interpretation itself.

The CFTC has premised both the Hybrid Rules and the Hybrid Interpretation on two grounds: that the commodity play is incidental to the instrument and that an adequate alternative regulatory scheme exists. Thus the CFTC has limited its relief to hybrid instruments which are bona fide debt securities, depository instruments and preferred equity securities. Depository instruments must be issued by an institution insured by a U.S. government agency or by certain U.S. branches or agencies of foreign banks.[20]

The Hybrid Rules govern hybrids with "commodity dependent" option components. The commodity price play is measured by reference to the implied option premium. In order to be within the Hybrid Rules the value of the implied option premium must be no greater than 40% of the

---

[13] *See*, e.g., Swap Policy Statement, 54 Fed. Reg. 30694; Young & Stein, *supra*, note 1.

[14] *Chicago Mercantile Exchange v. Securities Exchange Commission*, 883 F.2d 537 (7th Cir. 1989).

[15] 7 U.S.C. § 2; 15 U.S.C. 77b. These provisions codify the 1982 Shad Johnson Accord.

[16] *See*, e.g., *Board of Trade of the City of Chicago v. SEC*, 677 F.2d 1137 (7th Cir. 1982); *CME v. SEC*, 883 F.2d at 544. *See also*, Meer, "Hybrid Instruments: Their Treatment Under Recent Commodity Futures Trading Commission Releases" 46 Bus. L. 405, 421 (1991).

[17] Advance Notice of Proposed Rulemaking, 52 Fed. Reg. 47,022 (1987). The Advance Notice and various no-action letters are discussed in Markham, *supra* note 1, at 20–40. *See also*, Meer, *supra* note 16, at 410–414.

[18] 54 Fed. Reg. 1139 (1989); 55 Fed. Reg. 13582 (1990) (Reissued).

[19] 54 Fed. Reg. 1128 (1989) (proposed); 54 Fed. Reg. 30684 (1989) (final). Codified at 17 C.F.R. Part 34.

[20] 17 C.F.R. § 34.2(a)(1) (1991); Statutory Interpretation, 55 Fed. Reg. at 13586. *See also*, CFTC OETF Letter No. 90–2, [1987–1990 Transfer Binder] Comm. Fut. L. Rep. (CCH) ¶ 24,425 (March 2, 1990) (NY state chartered branches or agencies of foreign banks may issue hybrid depository instruments).

issue price of the instrument.[21] In addition, any *one* of four performance criteria must be met. These criteria are: 1) a credit rating for the instrument (or comparable securities of the issuer) in one of the four highest categories; 2) an issuer with $100 million in net worth; 3) the issuer maintains cover equal to the amount of its commodity-related commitments; or 4) the instrument is eligible for insurance by the U.S. government or agency thereof.[22] The performance criteria is intended to provide some assurance that the issuer will be able to meet the obligations of the option component. This criteria can be criticized as imposing the regulator's view as to a "quality investment" or what is often referred to as "merit regulation." Three of the alternative performance criteria and the value of the implied option premium are determined as of the time of issuance, but "cover" must be maintained throughout the life of the instrument.

In addition, the Hybrid Rules also require that the commodity dependent component not be severable from the instrument; that the terms of the hybrid do not call for delivery by means of an instrument specified in the rules of a futures exchange; and that the hybrid is not marketed as being or having the characteristics of a futures contract or commodity option.

The Commission has by order permitted severability in the context of several "Brady bonds" based upon its determination that such commodity options are "in the public interest."[23] Trading restrictions imposed on these options are narrower than those imposed under federal securities laws for private placements. Although the CFTC has not formally stated a position, it is not unreasonable to conclude that the subsequent transfer of a commodity option pursuant to the terms of *another* exemption (i.e., the trade option exemption) is not inconsistent with the purpose of the non-severability requirement and therefore legally permissible.

The Hybrid Interpretation contains the same restrictions as the Hybrid Rules as to marketing, delivery and nonseverability of the commodity dependent component.[24] However, as the Hybrid Interpretation sets forth the Commission's views as to its jurisdiction over hybrid instruments

---

[21] Issuers may rely on the underwriter's good faith opinion as to the offering's compliance with the quantitative conditions. For the economics and mathematic calculations for "implied option premium" *see,* Jordan, Mackay and Moriarty, "The New Regulation of Hybrid Debt Instruments," Journal of Applied Corporate Finance; Furbush and Sackheim, "US Hybrid Instruments: Evolving Legal and Economic Issues" 6 Journal of Int'l Banking and Financial Law 450 (1991).

[22] 17 C.F.R. 34.2(a)(3) (1991).

[23] *See* Order (Mexico) [1987–1990 Transfer Binder] Comm. Fut. L. Rep. (CCH) ¶ 24,801 (Mar. 6, 1990); Order (Uruguay) Comm. Fut. L. Rep. (CCH) ¶ 25,008 (Feb. 6, 1991). Orders have also been issued for Venezuela (Dec. 3, 1990) and Nigeria (Jan. 10, 1992).

[24] Hybrid Interpretation, 55 Fed. Reg. at 13587.

which contain commodity futures and option characteristics, the economic calculations of the Hybrid Interpretation are more complex. The Commission, in effect, has concluded that instruments meeting the criteria of the Hybrid Interpretation are not futures contracts or commodity options.

The economics are as follows: 1) the percentage change in the payment due to movements in the indexed commodity may not exceed the percentage change in the commodity price to which the payment is indexed ("one-to-one" indexing); 2) maximum loss is limited to the greater of either the commodity-independent payment or the purchase price of the instrument; and 3) the commodity-dependent payment must be at least 50 percent but no more than 150 percent of the estimated annual yield at the time of issuance for a comparable non-hybrid instrument ("50–150 test").[25]

These three tests work together to preserve the character of the hybrid instrument as a debt security or deposit. Limiting maximum loss to the purchase price is the most obvious distinguishing feature between futures and bonds or deposits. The one-to-one indexing limits the extent to which the instrument's commodity play is "leveraged" for example, where a 1% increase in commodity price would result in a 20 percent increase in the commodity dependent component. Thus, the one-to-one indexing limits the potential impact of price changes for the life of the instrument. The 50–150 test applies at issuance and acts to restrict the value of the commodity interest which can be imbedded in an instrument.[26]

Application

As can be seen from the discussion, determining whether and how the Commodity Exchange Act applies is largely determined by the economic reality of the instrument—*albeit* the economic reality as seen by the CFTC.

It is important to identify the nature of the indexing, i.e., whether it is futures-like or option-like. The Hybrid Rules apply to options; the Hybrid Interpretation analysis is used for embedded futures and for options which do not meet the 40 percent premium test of the Hybrid Rules. A commodity "option based payment" is one in which the "commodity price indexing or referencing results in the indexing of payments for commodity prices *either* above or below the indexing reference price but not *both*.[27]

---

[25] Hybrid Interpretation, 55 Fed. Reg. at 13586–87.

[26] Calculation examples for one-to-one indexing and the 50–150 test are given in the Hybrid Interpretation, 55 Fed. Reg. at 13588–89. For further examples, *see* Jordan, Mackay & Moriarty, *supra*, note 21.

If the indexing results in the possibility of payments both above and below the indexing reference price, Commission staff will consider it to be futures-like and apply the criteria of the Hybrid Interpretation.

Indexing which appears to be option-like may be treated as futures-like if there is not limited risk of loss to the investor. For example, option components which are capped and/or floored cannot at issuance have strike prices that are too far out of the money.[28]

The nature of the indexing can be jurisdictional in result if the commodity dependent payment is calculated in reference to an equity index such as the S&P 500 Index. If the component is an option on an equity index, jurisdiction lies with the Securities and Exchange Commission (SEC) but if the component is futures-like, the analysis of the Hybrid Interpretation must be applied. This is a result of the Shad Johnson Accord which gives the SEC jurisdiction over options on equity indices and the CFTC jurisdiction over futures on equity indices.[29]

The CFTC has also stated that its jurisdiction does not extend to lending or deposit instruments in which the interest payments are measured by reference to published interest rates or indices of interest rates such as the prime rate, LIBOR and Treasury bill rates.[30] The basis for the exclusion of these instruments and others enumerated in the Hybrid Interpretation is that such instruments have *de minimus* commodity option and futures features.[31] Another perspective for this exclusion is that when a coupon is periodically reset by reference to a then prevailing interest rate or indices of interest rates, the instrument does not embed a commodity play. Thus, it may also follow that an instrument whose coupon is calculated by reference to a multiple of LIBOR on a particular date, or by reference to a multiple of LIBOR minus the T-bond rate, is not within the purview of the CEA. This analysis may not hold true for principal indexation.

If a particular hybrid instrument does not fall within the economic parameters of the Hybrid Rule or Interpretation, the first recourse would be to redesign the economic terms, subject of course, to market accep-

---

[27] 17 C.F.R. § 34.1(e) (1991) (emphasis added). A hybrid instrument which has only the coupon indexed to a commodity price may appear to always be option-like indexing as the principal will be repaid in full. One should analyze, however, the indexing in reference to the commodity independent component (coupon or principal) rather than the instrument as a whole.

[28] Hybrid Rules, 54 Fed. Reg. at 30685; *see also,* CFTC OETF Letter 90–1 [1987–1990 Transfer Binder] Comm. Fut. L. Rep. (CCH) ¶ 24,583 (Jan. 18, 1990) (eligibility of collar agreements for safe harbor treatment under Swap Policy Statement).

[29] 7 U.S.C. § 2, 15 U.S.C. 77b.

[30] Hybrid Interpretation, 55 Fed. Reg. 13587, n.32. Staff Has informally advised that the use of the word "published" was intended to be descriptive, not definitional.

[31] Advance Notice, 52 Fed. Reg. at 47024.

tance. For example, instruments with shorter maturities are more likely to meet the 40 percent implied option premium test of the Hybrid Rule.

Another course of action is to request no-action or other relief from the CFTC or its staff. The Hybrid Interpretation indicates that the Commission will consider relief on a case by case basis. Staff preference is to grant no-action relief, but on one occasion since the Hybrid Interpretation was finalized CFTC staff has given interpretative advice.[32] The Commission may also issue orders permitting the offer and sale of options when it believes it to be in the public interest.[33] Counsel should be advised that formal no-action or interpretative relief can take several months from the time a request is initiated to the issuance of a letter.

A third alternative is to see whether the hybrid instrument can be analyzed consistent with the forward contract exclusion, the trade option exemption or the Treasury amendment. The Hybrid Rules and the Hybrid Interpretation are not intended to be the exclusive manner in which hybrid instruments may be exempted or excluded from CFTC regulation.[34]

Any hybrid offered and sold in response on any of these provisions must be privately placed and secondary trading restrictions imposed. As previously discussed, a trade option offeree must be a commercial user, the forward contract must be between commercial participants in connection with their business, and, at least in the CFTC's view, trading in the enumerated Treasury Amendment instruments is limited to "sophisticated and informed institutions." It should be further noted that CFTC enforcement interest is less if transactions occur between institutions who are capable of understanding the risks of the transaction.[35]

The trade option analysis is often the most promising as its parameters are more certain than the exclusions provided by the Treasury Amendment or by forward contracts. Purchasers of the hybrid would most likely be the "offerees" of the trade option and thus must meet the two prong test of being a commercial user of the commodity referenced in the option and entering into the option solely for purposes related to

---

[32] CFTC OETF Letter 91–3, Comm. Fut. L. Rep. (CCH) ¶ 25,182 (Oct. 8, 1991). These commodity indexed hybrid notes raised an issue concerning the application of the one-to-one indexing and commodity independent yield criteria where interest is imputed daily based on the T-bill rate but remains at risk during the life of the instrument. Staff concluded that, when viewed as a whole, that the notes are more appropriately treated as securities.

[33] 17 CFR 32.4(b) (1991), 7 U.S.C. § 6c.

[34] The Swap Policy Statement, a non-exclusive safe harbor for certain swap transactions, provides good source material to use in analyzing instruments under these exemptions and exclusion.

[35] In any particular transaction, issuers should evaluate the likelihood of claims of illegality by purchasers. *Cf. Bank Brussels Lambert, S.A. v. Intermetals Corp.*, 779 F. Supp. 741 (S.D.N.Y. 1991).

its business as such. The second prong has been interpreted (too narrowly) as limiting trade options to nonspeculative transactions.[36]

Whether an offeree is a producer, processor or merchant handling a commodity is usually obvious when nonfinancial tangible commodities are involved. The question is more difficult when one must rely on a purchaser being a "commercial user" and financials or intangibles (e.g., interest rates) are the subject of the option. Although it is consistent with the policies underlying the exemption and the plain meaning of the regulation, the CFTC has not formally stated that banks, broker-dealers and other financial intermediaries are appropriate offerees for this type of trade option.[37]

The use of the forward contract exclusion is limited by the fact that the CFTC does not recognize the concept of a "cash settled" forward, except, perhaps, for currencies.[38] An ingenious use of forward contracts to provide a oil-linked return was the issuance by Phibro-Solomon in 1990 of certain trust units. The units themselves are not hybrids but their trading value reflects the market perception of the value of the underlying forward contract for oil. CFTC staff issued a no-action letter based upon its understanding that delivery of the oil occurs to the trust consistent with customary cash market practices.[39]

A Treasury Amendment analysis is probably best utilized for hybrids whose commodity dependent payments are linked to foreign currencies and government securities.[40] Reliance on the Treasury Amendment for option-like indexing is not advisable unless the issue of "in or involving" is more favorably decided.[41]

The Future

The Hybrid Interpretation and Hybrid Rule did much to alleviate uncertainty and permit increased development of hybrid instruments. However, the financial engineers already have designed, not more than two years after promulgation, products which were not contemplated by the CFTC. As previously noted, legislation pending as of June 1992 would

---

[36] Swap Policy Statement, 54 Fed. Reg. at 10396. It may also include transactions entered into for the purpose of minimizing a price risk. See 51 Fed. Reg. 12698 (1986).

[37] Pending amendments will broaden the trade option exemption to lift the ban on options on agricultural commodities and to eliminate a prohibition against pricing using exchange traded futures price information. 56 Fed. Reg. 43560 (1991). Further expansion is necessary to meet the realities for today's market.

[38] Swap Policy Statement, 54 Fed. Reg. at 10396.

[39] CFTC OETF Letter 90–4 Comm. Fut. L. Rep. (CCH) ¶ 24,866 (April 25, 1990).

[40] The CFTC has stated that swaps may be subject to the Treasury Amendment. Swap Policy Statement, 54 Fed. Reg. at 30696, n.16. It is equally logical that certain hybrids may also be included in this analysis.

[41] See note 10 and accompanying text.

substantially affect the regulatory analysis of these instruments. Its primary effect would be to simplify the analysis, based upon the "predominant purpose" of the instrument. Hybrids would be divided into those which predominantly reflect an investment, for example, in an enterprise and those which predominantly represent an interest in commodity movements.

An objective test is contemplated, with the CFTC having jurisdiction only if, at issuance, the expected commodity price play associated with the option and/or futures component is greater than the non commodity component.[42] Any instrument in which the non-commodity component predominates would be excluded from CFTC jurisdiction, and most likely would be regulated by the SEC or bank regulatory authorities.

Failing enactment of this legislation, the Commission must move quickly to resolve the regulatory uncertainty surrounding hybrid instruments that are a generation (or two) beyond prior regulatory pronouncements. Without resolution, hybrids will be developed and marketed offshore, to the great disadvantage of the U.S. financial industry.

---

[42] *See* Furbush and Sackheim, *supra,* note 21, for further explanation on how the calculations might be done.

US HYBRID INSTRUMENTS: EVOLVING LEGAL AND ECONOMIC ISSUES*

Dean Furbush and Michael Sackheim

23

Introduction

If you are a businessman, banker, or broker developing a new financial product for the United States, you must grapple with the issues of which laws and which regulators will have jurisdiction over the product. If you are an investor considering the range of your investment choices, you should be aware of hybrid instruments which have some of the features of fixed income investments while providing limited exposure to movements in commodity prices. And if you are an observer of financial markets you should be aware of the derivative markets which have come to account for $3 trillion of business worldwide. The regulation of derivative products has been the topic of heated debate in the U.S. media, among government agencies, and in Congress. Even if strong special interests were absent, the regulatory issues would be thorny.

Essentially, the Securities and Exchange Commission (SEC) regulates securities and options on securities, while the Commodity Futures Trading Commission (CFTC) regulates contracts derivative to commodities, including commodity futures, commodity options, and options on commodity futures. This jurisdictional division is premised on the idea of functional regulation: the SEC regulates markets and instruments that are designed to raise capital and that serve a public investment function; and the CFTC regulates markets and instruments that primarily serve a hedging and price-discovery function. But the current jurisdictional division does not adequately account for the hybrid instruments that institutions and investors are finding to be so economically appealing.

---

* An earlier version of this article was published in *Butterworths Journal of International Banking and Financial Law*, September 1991. Reprinted with permission.

Over the last decade, banks and brokerage houses have developed numerous hybrid financial products that fall in the regulatory twilight zone between the SEC and the CFTC, either because they contain both security-derivative and commodity-derivative components or because the overall product characteristics are not easily identified as belonging to one category or the other. The lack of product conformity along established regulatory lines has engendered regulatory confusion, jurisdictional conflict, and now, something of a solution—compromise legislation that became law during the 1992 Congressional session.

This article discusses the background and regulatory context of the compromise legislation. We explain how the legislation applies to hybrid instruments, outlining the factors that determine whether or not a hybrid instrument will receive regulatory relief and showing the adjustments that are possible. Those factors have always been of critical *economic* interest in the design of a hybrid product. Under the 1992 legislation, the factors also take on critical *regulatory* importance as well, determining whether or not the instrument must be traded on a CFTC-regulated exchange.

Hybrid Instruments

Imagine an oil company that is planning to raise capital through a debt offering—call it Shamacon. If Shamacon's cost of capital is 10 percent and it issues a five-year, $1,000 principal, zero-coupon bond, it will be able to raise $621. But Shamacon can raise more capital by offering a hybrid instrument with some elements of a bond and some elements of a derivative product. A hybrid instrument including a call option on oil, for example, allows Shamacon to raise more capital at the offering (by the value of the option) without increasing the bond component of their principal repayment. An increase in the price of oil necessitates a higher payout by Shamacon because investors exercise their options, but higher oil prices also increase Shamacon's revenue and thus their ability to pay the higher amount.

With this bond-option hybrid, Shamacon can raise additional capital without increasing the hardship associated with paying their debt, and investors have the opportunity to augment the yield that would be available to them from a fixed income investment alone. The rationale for futures-like hybrid instruments is similar, but commodity price movements in both directions affect the value of the instrument. Although hybrid products are conceptually simple, the specific terms of each product tend to be complex, making it difficult to define a clear and objective regulatory system to determine the product's regulation.

The CFTC's Regulation of the Commodity Exchange Act

The U.S. Commodity Exchange Act (CEA) generally defines all goods, articles, services, and interests as "commodities." To the extent that (i) an instrument derives its value from the price of a commodity rather than from an individual stock or small group of stocks, (ii) is sold to the general public for non-hedging purposes, and (iii) does not primarily envision the delivery of the underlying commodity, it may be subject to the requirements and prohibitions of the CEA as administered by the CFTC. Before the CFTC designates a new commodity futures or option product, the CFTC-regulated commodities exchange must submit a petition detailing, among other things, the economic benefits of the product and the enforcement mechanism used by the exchange to protect the public from fraudulent trading practices.

The most prohibitive feature of the CEA is that a commodities instrument containing any or all of the classic indicia of a futures contract may be required to be traded only on or subject to the rules of a CFTC-regulated exchange. The usual features of a futures market include:

   (i)   standardized terms;

   (ii)   marketing to the public;

   (iii) margining;

   (iv) centralized clearing and settlement; and

   (v)   use for purposes other than for transfering ownership of the underlying commodity.

While courts have concluded that there is no brightline test for whether a product should be regulated by the CFTC, the courts have advised that an examination must be made concerning the underlying purpose of the product to determine whether or not the product is a commodity futures contract, which may only lawfully be traded on or subject to the rules of a CFTC-designated exchange. The primary exclusion from the CEA's off-exchange prohibition for futures contracts applies to cash forward contracts which contemplate actual delivery of the underlying commodity, although delivery may not ultimately occur.

Similarly, an option on a commodity futures contract or directly on a commodity (except for an option on a stock, on a stock index, or on a foreign currency traded on a national securities exchange) may only be offered on a CFTC-designated exchange, subject to such exemptions and conditions as the CFTC permits. The primary exception to the exchange requirement for options is the "trade option" exemption which applies to options on commodities entered into by commercial entities for nonspeculative purposes.

In the same way that certain product characteristics allow some commodities transactions to be excluded from CFTC regulation, developers of hybrid financial products, which combine elements of commodity futures or options contracts within traditional securities, debt, and depository instruments, have requested regulatory relief.

Recall Shamacon's hybrid instrument. If the instrument is mostly a bond with only a trivial option kicker, it would be reasonable to exempt it from CFTC regulation; but if the hybrid is mostly an option on the price of oil, and has only incidental bond characteristics, it would fall under CFTC jurisdiction. The question facing the CFTC is a tough one. How do you provide a test to determine where, in the vast area between those two extremes, the CFTC should begin to regulate? When, in the words of former CFTC Chairman Wendy Gramm, does the instrument become "mostly not a future [or an option]?" Any answer is necessarily arbitrary but does not need to be ambiguous. The CFTC's approach to the question evolved over the last decade.

In 1980, the CFTC did not prohibit a silver mining company from raising capital by publicly offering a bond which was partially indexed to the price of silver. Purchasers could redeem the bond at either $1,000 or the market value of 50 ounces of silver, whichever amount was greater at the time of redemption. In effect, this product was part bond and part option. The mining company's interests were served because they were able to raise capital more cheaply by sweetening their bond offering with an option that diminished some of their upside potential. The very circumstances that would increase the mining company's debt service costs— higher silver prices—would increase their ability to service their debt. The CFTC did not prohibit purchasers of these instruments, members of the general public, from speculating in the price of silver through an investment in a bond which was not traded on a CFTC-designated exchange and which contained some, but not all, of the features of a commodity options contract.

Through the mid-1980s, similar debt instruments and securities were offered which were indexed to fluctuations in the price of oil, various stock indices, and one or more foreign currencies. The CFTC permitted the off-exchange public offerings of such instruments through the issuance of case-by-case "no-action" letters by a special CFTC "Task Force on Off-Exchange Instruments." In 1987, however, the CFTC commenced a federal court action against a major U.S. bank for offering and selling to the general public a certificate of deposit indexed to the price of gold. Before adjudication and without admitting any CEA violation, the bank settled with the CFTC and consented to an injunction prohibiting it from selling gold-indexed certificates of deposit or other off-exchange commodity options.

These incidents and the resulting uncertainty in the marketplace prompted the CFTC to promulgate (i) a statutory interpretation concerning instruments containing *de minimis* commodity futures and option components, and (ii) alternative hybrid options rules. Both regulatory promulgations asserted CEA and CFTC jurisdiction over specified hybrid instruments while permitting a broad array of hybrid instruments to be offered free of the CEA's exchange-trading requirement.

The CFTC's Statutory Interpretation

The 1989 "*Statutory Interpretation Concerning Hybrid Instruments,*" revised in 1990, set forth the CFTC's understanding of its jurisdiction over instruments that combine incidental characteristics of commodity futures or option contracts with certain debt, depository, and equity instruments. The CFTC stated that its jurisdiction excluded certain stock, debt, and depository hybrid instruments with *de minimis* commodity futures and option features.

Such characterization is indicated by the following features:

(i) the percentage change in the interest payment due to movements in the indexed commodity may not exceed the percentage change in the commodity price to which the payment is indexed;

(ii) the maximum loss on the interest payment may not exceed the commodity-independent indexed interest payment or the purchase price of the instrument, whichever is greater;

(iii) the commodity-independent payment must be at least 50 percent but no more than 150 percent of the estimated annual yield at the time of issuance for a comparable non-hybrid instrument, i.e., the commodity-dependent factor may not account for more than half of the yield;

(iv) the commodity-dependent component may not be detachable;

(v) settlement may not be made by means of a CFTC-designated contract market's delivery instrument; and

(vi) the instrument may not be marketed as having the characteristics of a commodity futures or option contract.

For an instrument which qualifies for such an exclusion, none of the CEA's other provisions, including registration requirements, sales standards, recordkeeping rules, or capital maintenance requirements, apply. For those hybrid instruments which do not fit squarely within these conditions, the Statutory Interpretation states that the CFTC will continue to entertain case-by-case exclusionary relief.

The CFTC's 1989 Hybrid Rules

An alternative exemptive route is contained in Part 34 of the CFTC's rules and regulations, promulgated in 1989 and entitled *"Regulation of Hybrid Instruments."* Part 34, as adopted in 1989, exempts from the CEA's exchange-trading requirement and from regulation under the CEA, certain hybrid debt, equity, and depository instruments which have limited commodity option characteristics. Although the Statutory Interpretation actually applies to both futures-like and option-like hybrids, in practice it is applied to hybrids with futures characteristics while Part 34 is applied to hybrids with embedded option characteristics.

Such instruments are exempt if they meet criteria including:

  (i)   the "implied option premium," the issue price of the instrument less the present discounted value of the commodity-independent payments, must be no greater than 40 percent of the issue price of the entire instrument;

 (ii)   the issuer must either meet certain financial soundness conditions or the instrument's commodity-independent obligations must be "covered" by the issuer in the underlying physical futures or options markets; and

(iii)   if the commodity-dependent payment is indexed to the price of a commodity reported on a CFTC-designated contract market, an exemption notice must be filed with the CFTC.

A hybrid instrument which does not meet the criteria of Part 34 may nevertheless qualify for a discretionary exemption from the CEA's exchange-trading requirement if the CFTC determines that such an exemption is not contrary to the public interest.

1991 Legislative Proposal

The CFTC's promulgation of Part 34, along with their series of no-action letters, interpretative letters, and hybrid instrument statutory releases expanded the permissible use of commodity-indexed, off-exchange products through exclusions and exemptions, but did not resolve the jurisdictional uncertainties surrounding hybrid instruments. As a result, in 1991 the Senate proposed Title III of the Futures Trading Practices Act of 1991, entitled *"Intermarket Coordination."* Section 303, entitled *"Hybrid Commodity Instruments,"* was a provision of Title III. It mandated an objective test based on the predominant characteristics of a hybrid instrument to determine whether the instrument should be regulated under the CEA.

Under section 303, the CEA would not apply to a hybrid instrument based on certain values measured at the time the instrument was issued.

Section 303 stated that an option-like hybrid instrument was exempt "to the extent that . . . the instrument derives less than 50 percent of its value . . . from the value of the commodity option;" a futures-like hybrid is exempt "to the extent that . . . it is expected that less than 50 percent of the value gained from and payable on the instrument will be due to movement in the price of the commodity or commodities specified in the instrument or in the terms and conditions of the transaction pursuant to which the instrument was issued." This unfortunate language masked the simple intent and effect of Section 303.

The intent of Section 303 of Title III was to relieve from CFTC regulation a new hybrid product that is "mostly not a commodity futures or option product." The effect of Section 303 would have been to transfer the jurisdiction of more hybrid products from the CFTC to the SEC. Section 303 used the option pricing theory employed by financial practitioners to determine the "commodity price play" in the commodity derivative component of the hybrid. Put simply, under Section 303, if the dollar value of the measured commodity price play is less than the dollar value of the straight bond at time of issue, the instrument is not regulated by the CFTC; that is, its predominant purpose is not as an option or future. The 1991 legislation, though never enacted, served as the genesis of the *"Futures Trading Practices Act of 1992."*

CFTC Exemptive Authority Under the Futures Trading Practices Act of 1992

After three years of debating the form of a CFTC exemptive test for hybrid instruments, the *"Futures Trading Practices Act of 1992 "* ("FTPA") was finally passed by Congress and enacted into law on October 28, 1992, amending and supplementing the CEA.

Modeled after Title III of the 1991 legislation, FTPA section 502, which amends CEA section 4, grants broad exemptive authority to the CFTC with respect to hybrid instruments that are predominantly securities or depository instruments, to the extent that such instruments contain certain commodity futures-like or commodity option-like components and thus may be considered subject to the CEA's exchange-trading requirement and other CEA regulatory prohibitions. Under its new exemptive authority, in January 1993 the CFTC adopted a complete revision to its Part 34 exemptive rules.* Under the new rules, which replace the CFTC's 1989 hybrid rules and are entitled *"Regulation of Hybrid Instruments,"* a single predominance test is applied to hybrid depository, debt

---

* The CFTC's 1993 Part 34–*"Regulation of Hybrid Instruments"* rules are reproduced in the back of the book on page 653.

and preferred equity instruments containing either commodity futures-like or option-like components. Such a predominance test compares a measure of the commodity-dependent portion of the instrument to the value of the commodity-independent payments to determine the predominant nature of the instrument. The commodity price exposure is measured by first decomposing the commodity-dependent payout of the instrument into component option positions. The option prices will then be appropriately summed or netted to arrive at a measure of the commodity price exposure. Instruments having a commodity price exposure less than the present value of the commodity-independent payments, and meeting other criteria specified in the rules, will be exempted from the exchange-trading requirement contained in the CEA and from other CFTC regulatory requirements.

In addition to limiting the overall commodity-dependent component of the instrument, the new Part 34 rules require a limit on losses on the hybrid instrument. The rules exempt only debt, depository or security interest instruments regulated by another Federal or State regulatory body. The purchase or sale of such instruments is restricted to "appropriate persons" as set forth in CEA section 4(c), i.e., specified financial institutions and pension plans; specified large business entities; specified CFTC and SEC registrants; and other persons, including individuals, found to be "appropriate" by the CFTC in light of their financial or other qualifications or the applicability of appropriate financial safeguards. The CFTC's final Rule 34.3 limits the exemption to instruments initially issued or sold subject to applicable federal or state securities or bonding laws "to persons permitted thereunder to purchase or enter into the hybrid instrument."

The CFTC's new hybrid instruments rules, which replace the agency's 1989 Part 34 rules, became effective in February 1993. Section 502 of the FTPA also authorizes the CFTC to separately exempt any other agreement, contract or transaction (or class thereof) having a commodity component, either unconditionally or on stated terms and conditions, from any provision of the CEA, if the agency determines that the exemption is consistent with the public interest, will be entered into between "appropriate persons," and will not have a material adverse effect on the ability of the CFTC or any commodity exchange to discharge its regulatory duties. The CFTC's 1989 Statutory Interpretation will continue to be applicable as an alternative exclusionary test for any hybrid debt, depository on preferred equity instrument with a commodity-dependent component. Continuing to remain outside of the purview of the CEA will be non-transferrable life insurance contracts, adjustable rate mortgages, employment agreements, leases, floating interest rate lending instruments, securities, and certain traditional deposit instruments whose payments are indexed to an interest rate.

Applying the Predominance Test

We can see how the predominance test works by examining the oil option attached to the Shamacon debt instrument discussed earlier. Imagine a call option that raises the hybrid issuance price from $621 to $1,000. By construction, the option component of the hybrid has a commodity price play worth $379 ($1,000 – $621). Because $379 is less than $621, the product is mostly not an option and would not be regulated by the CFTC.

A bond-futures hybrid is somewhat less intuitive because, unlike the case of an option, arbitrage keeps the value of a futures contract equal to zero at its market price. Therefore a bond with an embedded futures contract at the market price would be the same price as the equivalent straight bond; the $621 bond would also be a $621 hybrid instrument. But the question facing the CFTC remains: when is the hybrid mostly not a future? The answer to the question lies in focusing on the commodity price play in the futures contract rather than on its economic value. An option contract's commodity price play is equal to its economic value. Such is not the case for a futures contract at the market price. To determine the commodity price play associated with a futures contract, it must be parsed into its option components. A long futures contract is equivalent to (and is often arbitraged with) the combination of a long call option and a short put option both with the same exercise price and expiration date. The measured commodity price play is relevant for price movements in both directions, so the commodity price play in a futures contract is the sum of the positive values of the call and the put, rather than their difference. The sum is applied in the same way as it is for option-like hybrids: if the dollar value of the commodity price play is less than the dollar value of the straight bond at time of issue, the instrument is not regulated by the CFTC.

The advantage of using option pricing theory to determine whether or not an instrument falls within CFTC jurisdiction is that the option pricing methodology parsimoniously accounts for the factors that determine the relationship between a commodity's price and a financial product derivative to that commodity. The same factors that are examined to determine the economic viability of a hybrid instrument are examined to determine its regulatory viability. The key factors are shown in Figure 23.1.

The fundamental point is that a hybrid may be exempted from CFTC regulation if, at issuance, (A) the value of the straight bond component exceeds (B) the value of the commodity price play. The bond and commodity components depend on other factors, most of which can be chosen in the design of the product. That is, the financial engineers will have several degrees of freedom to work with should they wish to design a product that is more bond than derivative product. Such design will not

Figure 23.1: Key Determinants of Hybrid Regulation

(Arrows indicate direction of change to avoid the exchange-trading requirement)

A. Value of the Straight Bond Component [↑]	**B. Value of the Commodity Price Play [↓]**

Depends on:

1. Firm's cost of capital [↓]

2. Time to maturity [↓]

3. Futurity of coupon structure [↓]

Depends on:

1. Commodity units in hybrid [↓] and

2. Derivative value [↓]

Depends on:
(long option position)
   i. Strike price less current commodity price [↑/↓, call/put]
  ii. Risk free rate [↑/↓, call/put]
 iii. Time to maturity [↓/↑, call/put]*
  iv. Commodity return volatility [↓]
   v. Other option features [↓/↑, call /put]

*The put relationship does not hold uniformly but does hold for typical values of the risk free rate, time to maturity, and commodity price volatility.

be just a bureaucratic exercise to dodge the regulators, it really will result in the design of more "bond-like" products if the products are to fall outside of the CEA's exchange-trading requirements.

The higher the value, at the time of issue, of (A) the straight bond component relative to (B) the commodity price play, the greater is the likelihood of the hybrid being exempted from CFTC regulation. The principal factors affecting the issuance value of the bond are (1) the firm's cost of capital, (2) the bond's time to maturity; and (3) the futurity of the bond's coupon structure. The lower is each of these values, the higher will be the issuance value of the bond. Clearly, shortening the time to maturity and lowering the futurity of the coupon structure (paying higher coupons sooner) are both choice variables available to the financial engineer. The firm's cost of capital is based on the market's perception of its solvency and reliability, operational verities generally beyond the realm of the financial engineer; but even the cost of capital can be lowered by raising the seniority of the instrument or entering other financial arrangements that diminish the debt burden of the firm.

For the commodity price play, the lower is its relative value, the greater is the likelihood of the hybrid instrument being exempted from CFTC regulation. The value of the commodity price play is lower, (1) the fewer commodity units are in the hybrid instrument, and (2) the lower is the derivative value of those units. The number of commodity units in the instrument is readily adjusted, and the value of the derivative component, which depends on several other factors, can also be adjusted.

The derivative value (2) depends on:

(i)   the difference between the strike price and the current commodity price;

(ii) the risk free rate;

(iii) the option's time to maturity;

(iv) the underlying commodity's return volatility; and

(v)   other option features.

A thorough examination of these factors is beyond the scope of this article, but a few implications are explicated here, based on a hybrid instrument whose commodity price play is due to a long option position.

The difference between the strike price and the price of the cash commodity at the time of issue (i) measures how far "in (or out) of the money" the option is. The farther from the money is the current commodity price, the lower is its value, other things equal, and the more likely the hybrid instrument is to receive regulatory relief. In the comment period prior to the 1989 promulgation of the CFTC's Part 34 hybrid rules, the Federal Reserve Board correctly commented that the rules favored out of the money options. The same is true for the 1992 legislation. That feature of the law is not a random and dysfunctional derivative of the CFTC's intention but is a fundamental characteristic of the option pricing methodology, capturing just what it is intended to capture: an out of the money option is less dependent on the price movements of the commodity than one that is closer to the money or one that is in the money. The strike price can be set by the financial engineer in order to lower the commodity price play of the hybrid and receive regulatory relief.

The risk free rate (ii) and the instrument's time to maturity (iii) are both factors that determine the value of the derivative component because they determine the value of the risk-free bond against which options can be arbitraged in order to determine their value. A lower risk-free rate and a shorter time to maturity are both associated with lower valued call-option hybrid instruments and higher valued put-option hybrids. The call-put asymmetry exists because the arbitrage for a long call includes selling a risk-free bond whereas the arbitrage for a long put includes buying a risk-free bond, so the factors that increase the value of the bond (a lower risk-free rate and a shorter time to maturity) decrease the value of a call and (for typical values of the input factors) increase the value of a put. The risk-free rate is outside the control of the financial engineer while the time to maturity is not.

Higher volatility commodities (iv) are unambiguously associated with higher valued options. Basically, a bouncy price is more likely to bounce into the money where it can be profitably exercised. The financial engineer cannot choose the volatility of the commodity, but depending on the purpose of the hybrid, may be able to choose a lower volatility commodity to lower the value of the option.

Finally, other option features (v) may determine the value of the derivative component. The choices are several, but one example deserves attention. The large upside potential that is available from holding a long option position can be attenuated by capping a call option, putting a floor on a put option, or a collar around both. Attenuating the upside potential diminishes the value of the derivative component and is readily accomplished by the financial engineer.

Most of the factors described here, and included in Figure 23.1, can be adjusted in order to balance the economic incentives of the hybrid issuer and of investors with the regulatory imperatives. The CFTC will be required to provide guidance for the methods to be used to calculate the commodity futures and options price play for hybrid instruments. For example, complex derivative positions can be associated with more than one option structure.

The issue of whether a new product falls under the jurisdiction of the CFTC or SEC is crucial, as such a determination will decide many issues, including:

(i)   federal and state regulatory requirements and prohibitions;

(ii)   registration and exchange-trading requirements;

(iii)   disclosure and prospectus requirements;

(iv)   sales activity restrictions;

(v)   investment and commodity trading advisor management capabilities;

(vi)   advisory fee restrictions;

(vii)   investor suitability requirements; and

(viii)   co-mingled investment fund uses for such instruments.

Conclusion

U.S. regulators have been reacting to evolving hybrid instrument proposals during the past 10 years by:

(i) issuing case-by-case exemptive relief;

(ii) excluding instruments from the definition of a futures contract through the issuance of "statutory interpretations;"

(iii) promulgating alternative rules for the exemption of hybrid instruments with *de minimis* embedded options; and finally

(iv) seeking the aid of Congress in amending the CEA to provide an objective test for exempting an instrument from the CEA's exchange-trading requirement.

The predominant purpose test will be subject to continuing regulatory and industry scrutiny as the CFTC develops guidelines and methodologies for assessing the various criteria needed to apply the test to new hybrid products. Including the predominant purpose test into the CEA enhances regulatory certainty and uniformity concerning the market for commodity-derivative instruments which has burgeoned in response to the needs of both issuers and investors.

Former CFTC Chairman Wendy Gramm enthusiastically endorsed and lobbied for the enactment of Section 502 of the FTPA. Former SEC Chairman Richard Breeden did not share her views on this matter. In a March 18, 1991 letter to Senator Donald Riegle, Chairman Breeden wrote that most new innovative hybrid securities products "would, in effect, become illegal if traded or sold anywhere other than on a futures exchange unless licensed or approved [by the CFTC] . . . New products would be barred from heretofore open and competitive markets unless market participants engaged in lengthy and expensive regulatory proceedings to prove to the CFTC that these products should be allowed to exist." Under the 1992 legislation and new CFTC rules however, new hybrid instruments could be developed based on an objective test and could be issued without the encumbrance of any pre-issue approval process.

In designing innovative debt, securities, or banking products, the international financial community must therefore be sensitive to the CFTC's new statutory exemptive authority and existing CFTC requirements, both of which affect hybrid instruments that are sold in the US or to US investors, regardless of whether the instrument is issued by a US or foreign entity.

THE NEW REGULATION OF HYBRID
DEBT INSTRUMENTS*

**James V. Jordan, Robert J. Mackay,
and Eugene J. Moriarty**

24

Commodities regulation, which is typically associated with the activities of futures markets, may affect your firm's next bond issue. This is certainly true if the debt is a hybrid offering with the principal or coupon linked to the price of raw materials, precious metals, foreign currencies, or the rate of inflation—because all are considered "commodities" under the Commodity Exchange Act (CEA). Bank deposits linked to such commodities would also be affected.

The development of commodity-linked debt and depository instruments during the 1980s has proceeded in the face of considerable regulatory uncertainty. The instruments cross boundaries that separate the regulatory jurisdictions of the Commodity Futures Trading Commission (or CFTC, which is the regulator of commodities markets), the Securities and Exchange Commission (SEC, the primary regulator of securities markets), and federal and state banking regulators. Under one interpretation of the CEA, the CFTC would have to prohibit the issuance of hybrids with futures-like components unless they are to be traded only on futures exchanges. Hybrids with option-like components would have to be approved for issuance by the CFTC, and their trading would also be regulated by the agency. The prospect of jurisdictional conflict under this restrictive interpretation, as well as the desire to avoid needless constraints on constructive financial innovation, has prompted a series of recent releases by the CFTC.[1]

---

* This article originally appeared in the *Journal of Applied Corporate Finance*, vol. 2, no. 4, Winter 1990. Reprinted with permission.
[1] See the following statements by the CFTC: "Regulation of Hybrid Instruments," *Federal Register*, 54, January 11, 1989(a), 1128–1138; "Statutory Interpretation Concerning Certain Hy-

In this article, we explain the implications of the recent CFTC statements for the design of hybrid debt securities. We also provide a short review of commodities regulation and a brief examination of the economic rationale for these new instruments.

Some Examples of Hybrid Instruments

The regulatory modifications issued by the CFTC were made necessary by the creation of new financial instruments that combine debt securities (and bank deposits) with commodity components similar to commodity futures and option positions. Three examples which illustrate hybrid design, as well as the regulatory questions, are Standard Oil of Ohio (SOHIO) oil-indexed notes, Wells Fargo gold-indexed certificates of deposit (CDs) and the Principal Exchange Rate Linked Securities (PERLS) and Reverse PERLS issued by several firms.

The bond issue offered by SOHIO in the summer of 1986 featured a special option-like payoff. In addition to a coupon instrument, the package included two zero-coupon notes, each of which was designed to trade separately. At maturity, the notes promise payment of the stated principal plus the excess of the price of oil over $25 per barrel (but capped at $40 per barrel) multiplied by 170 (barrels of oil). The notes appear to be both securities, which are regulated by the SEC, and commodity (oil) options, which are regulated by the CFTC. Particularly important was the lack of the periodic interest payment usually associated with debt instruments. Although zero-coupon debt had been issued prior to this time, the coupling of such debt issued at or near par with an option-like payoff seemed to invite interpretation as a contrivance for an off-exchange commodity option. Although the CFTC took no action against SOHIO, this instrument first brought into focus the difficult regulatory issues.

The "Gold Market Certificate" offered by Wells Fargo Bank called for a deposit of as little as $2500 to as much as $1 million plus a fee (or premium). At the end of the deposit period, the depositor received the deposit times either 50 percent or 100 percent (depending on the fee paid) of the increase in the price of gold. This CD combined with a commodity (gold) option crossed commodity and banking regulatory boundaries.

In 1987, the CFTC took its first hybrid-related enforcement action against this instrument. The case was settled under a consent decree enjoining Wells Fargo from issuing the certificates.

---

brid Instruments," *Federal Register*, 54, January 11, 1989(b), 1139–1142; and "Regulation of Hybrid Instruments," *Federal Register*, 54, July 21, 1989(c), 30684–30693. The CFTC has also recently addressed swap transactions, another difficult jurisdictional issue, in "Policy Statement Concerning Swap Transactions," Federal Register, 54, July 21, 1989(d), 30694–30697. Swaps are not discussed in this paper.

An important new type of instrument issued in 1988 had principal and/or coupon payments indexed to the price of foreign currencies. For example, the PERLS mentioned above defined the payment at maturity as principal plus the change in the spot value of a stated amount of foreign currency between the time of issue and maturity. This design introduced an embedded futures-like component referenced not to a futures price (observed or estimated), but to the current spot price. As we will show later, this feature built a current value into the futures-like component and thereby allowed the issuer to set a higher or lower coupon than the coupon on comparable non-hybrid debt. The design focused attention on the relative value of a futures-like component, much as the SOHIO design had raised questions about its option-like component.

In two separate instances, the CFTC took a no-action stance on PERLS-type instruments indexed to the dollar/yen exchange rate, but this stance left the issue of regulation and jurisdiction unresolved.

Before examining the new regulatory approach to hybrid debt instruments in detail, we will briefly consider the corporate motives for issuing these securities.

The Role of Hybrids in Financial Innovation

The financial environment of the 1980s has been marked by the emergence of a host of new financial instruments and financing techniques.[2] These include adjustable-rate preferred stock and intermediate-term debt, foreign-denominated bonds, interest rate and currency swaps, and the increased use of futures, forwards, and options.[3] In general, the same uncertainties about interest rates, foreign currencies, and commodity prices that have driven much of this innovation also underlie the emergence of hybrid financial instruments. To put it as succinctly as possible, companies issue hybrid instruments to hedge existing risks, to satisfy investor clienteles, and to capture the gains (in the form of lower capital costs) from product innovation.

For example, a company producing precious metals or raw materials obtains some hedging benefit by "going short" the same commodity through a hybrid debt issue. Similarly, if firms have determined that they are effectively in a long position with respect to changes in inflation, cur-

---

[2] Complex securities are not unique to the 1980s. For a description of securities issued by the Confederacy as dual currency (French francs and British pounds), cotton-indexed bonds, see Waite Rawls and Charles Smithson, "The Evolution of Risk Management Products," published in the Vol. 1 No. 4 (1989) of this journal.

[3] For a discussion of many of the new securities created in the 1980s, see John D. Finnerty, "Financial Engineering in Corporate Finance: An Overview," *Financial Management* 17, Winter 1988, 14–33.

rency, or interest rates, they may build an offsetting position into their debt.

In some cases, companies may have a short rather than a long exposure to such risks. For example, U.S. firms with foreign currency liabilities are effectively short the foreign currency. If the value of the foreign currency relative to the dollar increases, it takes more dollars to obtain the foreign currency to pay bills. One way to hedge this risk is to put a long foreign currency position into a hybrid.

The more puzzling question may be why companies hedge with hybrids rather than by using the existing futures, option, and forward markets. For most of the hybrids that have been issued (with the possible exception of oil-indexed bonds), there are active forward markets in the underlying commodity (at least for certain maturities). Because companies could participate in these markets either on their own or through intermediaries, there must be an important advantage to linking the financing instrument with the hedging instrument.

The advantage may involve the appeal of a linked instrument to certain investors. Diversification may be a primary factor. Many investors, both institutional and individual, may be unable to participate directly in commodity markets. The restrictions on widespread investor participation include institutional regulatory restrictions, transaction-size limitations for private investors, and general lack of familiarity with futures and forward markets. Even where these factors are not restrictive, contracts with desired maturities and other terms may not be available in existing markets. For example, designated futures and option markets have few contracts extending beyond one year. For all these reasons, the diversification from holding, for example, both a straight 5-year bond and a 5-year gold contract is not available to certain investors. A company that issues a hybrid has the opportunity to create a scarce risk-return combination and, to the extent the combination is indeed unique, the firm obtains the premium investors pay in the form of lower cost financing and hedging.

Taxation also plays a role in the uniqueness of hybrids. The preference of different investors for different combinations of income and capital gains is well-recognized. For example, U.S. corporations' investment preference for high dividends, due to the exclusion of 80 percent of dividend income from taxation, has led to "dividend-capture" strategies.[4] Similarly, U.S. tax-exempt pension funds have been advised to purchase "yield-tilted" portfolios of securities, or portfolios that have relatively high coupons and dividends but are otherwise matched to the funds' usual investment preferences (such as risk).[5] Conversely, high-tax-bracket individ-

---

[4] See Alan G. Seidner, *Corporate Investments Manual,* Boston: Warren, Gorham and Lamont, 1989, 5–25.

[5] See William F. Sharpe, *Investments.* Englewood Cliffs, N.J.: Prentice-Hall. 3rd Edition, 1985, 230–238.

uals in the U.S. would prefer lower income-producing securities, all things equal. Hybrid debt, with the potential for creating high or low coupons as illustrated below, is an ideal vehicle for appealing to tax-differentiated classes of investors. Again, issuing firms will gain the innovation premium.

Finally, hybrids provide a new means of changing the risk-sharing arrangement among managers, stockholders, and bondholders. An interesting explanation for the existence of convertible debt is that it provides debtholders with an equity stake in the firm. In so doing, it reduces managers' incentive (as representatives of shareholders) to transfer value from bondholders to shareholders by increasing the riskiness of the firm. (Witness the effect of the KKR buyout on RJR's existing bondholders.) For this reason, it may be the preferred form of debt financing for firms perceived to be facing "event risk," or other kinds of uncertainty.[6]

Hybrid debt may be considered an altered form of convertible debt, wherein the "equity" stake is not in the equity *per se*, but in a commodity whose price is expected to be a major determinant of the value of the equity. Certain bondholders may prefer debt that implies corporate hedging (negative correlation with equity). Others may prefer a futures- or option-like interest in an underlying factor positively correlated with the value of the firm.

Having considered the corporate reasons for issuing hybrid securities, we now provide a brief review of commodities regulation and then turn to the specific regulatory issues raised by commodity-linked securities.

The Regulatory Environment

Regulation of futures trading began with the Grain Futures Act in 1922, which was revised and renamed the Commodity Exchange Act in 1936.[7] The CEA prohibits the trading of futures contracts other than on a designated "contract market," or futures exchange. The requirement for exchange trading of futures contracts reflects both recognition of the economic benefits of trading in contracts for future delivery, including risk reduction (through hedging) and price discovery, and long-standing con-

---

[6] Michael Brennan and Eduardo Schwartz have shown that bond purchasers and managers can more easily agree on the price of convertible bonds than straight bonds under such conditions. See Brennan and Schwartz, "The Case for Convertibles," in Vol. 1 No. 2 of this journal, Summer 1988.

[7] An earlier attempt at regulation, the Futures Trading Act of 1921, had been declared unconstitutional by the Supreme Court. For a review of futures regulation, see Jerry W. Markham, *The History of Commodity Futures Trading and its Regulation*, New York: Praeger, 1987. For a comparison of the regulation of financial instruments under securities and commodities law, see David J. Gilberg, "Regulation of New Financial Instruments Under the Federal Securities and Commodities Laws," *Vanderbilt Law Review* 39, 1986, 1599–1689.

cerns about speculation, price manipulation and customer abuse in un-regulated futures markets.[8] The specific benefits of trading the contracts on exchanges include reduction of default risk, open price determination, rapid and wide price dissemination, enhancement of liquidity, customer protection, and market protection.

In 1974 the CFTC was created and given exclusive jurisdiction to enforce the CEA. In the same legislation that created the CFTC, the definition of "commodity" was broadened to include virtually everything on which a futures contract can be traded. With the emergence of new products, this broader definition can be seen in retrospect as an important development leading up to the recent jurisdictional conflicts. Prior to the 1974 amendments, hybrids indexed to such commodities as currencies and interest rates clearly would not have been subject to commodities law.

Commodity options, including both options on futures contracts and options on the underlying commodities, are regulated under the CEA, but under a different set of regulations. Options on commodities specifically cited in the 1936 CEA, all of which are agricultural commodities, were absolutely banned by that act.[9] Options on other commodities were not addressed by the Act. In the early 1970s, non-exchange-traded options on non-agricultural commodities such as silver, platinum, and coffee were the source of millions of dollars in customer losses because of option sellers' failures to satisfy exercises. With the broadening of the commodity definition in 1974, Congress gave the CFTC the authority to regulate option trading in commodities not cited in the original CEA.

At that time, the CFTC allowed off-exchange trading to continue. But in 1978, following further instances of customer abuse,[10] Congress imposed a moratorium on all options trading pending the development of a pilot program for exchange trading by the CFTC.[11] Following the pilot programs, the CFTC could proceed to permit either or both exchange trading and off-exchange trading of commodity options. Also, the ban on agricultural options no longer applied. By 1986, following successful pilot programs, CFTC regulations permitted the exchange trading of all commodity options.

---

[8] For reviews of the economic benefits, see the articles by Anne Peck, William Silber and Jerome Stein in *Futures Markets: Their Economic Role*, edited by Anne E. Peck. Washington, D.C.: American Enterprise Institute, 1985. For a review of the early history of alleged and documented problems, see Markham, particularly in Chapter 1, as cited in note 2.

[9] The 1921 act that was declared unconstitutional had sought to stop option trading with a prohibitive tax. Some exchanges and some states prohibited options trading throughout the period prior to the CEA. The 1934 National Industrial Recovery Act included a Code of Fair Competition for grain exchanges, which required an options ban. See Markham, cited earlier, p. 20 and p. 24.

[10] See Markham, pp. 79–80 and 194–195.

[11] The moratorium did not apply to "trade" options, which are options sold to commercial users of non-agricultural commodities, nor to "dealer" options, which are options written by metals dealers that were utilizing such options as of May 1, 1978.

The important distinction between futures and options regulation, which affects the CFTC's approach to hybrid instruments, is that off-exchange futures contracts are still prohibited by act of Congress whereas the CFTC has broad latitude to allow both on- and off-exchange trading of options. Currently, only trade and dealer options are permitted off-exchange. The emergence of hybrids forced the CFTC to fit these securities-like and commodities-like instruments into the prohibition on off-exchange futures contracts and the regulations specifying exchange trading of most options.[12]

The recent actions by the CFTC attempt to avoid unnecessary restriction of securities innovation while still attempting to bring commodities regulation to bear on hybrids with significant commodities elements.

The New Regulation of Hybrids

In January 1989, the CFTC issued a statutory interpretation of the Commodity Exchange Act that excludes certain categories of hybrid instruments from regulation under the CEA.[13] This "jurisdictional exclusion" applies to all hybrids meeting certain criteria, including both futures-like and option-like hybrids. On the same date, the CFTC proposed an exemption from options regulation for option-like hybrids that would not meet the criteria for jurisdictional exclusion.[14] The criteria for this "regulatory exemption" specifically address the option-like character of these instruments. The exemption was adopted with the issuance of final rules in July 1989.[15]

The details of the exclusion and the exemption are given below.

Jurisdictional Exclusion

This statutory interpretation recognizes a jurisdictional exclusion for two broad categories of hybrid instruments: (1) debt securities[16] and (2) time deposits offered by a bank whose deposits are insured by the Federal Deposit Insurance Corporation (FDIC) and marketed and sold directly to

---

[12] In contrast to the exchange-trading orientation of commodities regulation, securities regulation has little to say about where stocks and bonds are traded. The greatest dollar volume of bond trading takes place not on the organized exchanges but "over the counter," through a network of brokers and dealers electronically linked. The legal and regulatory philosophy is concerned primarily with disclosure of information about the issuer of a security. Such disclosure is accomplished through registration of the issue in accordance with the Securities Act of 1933. Even registration is not required for certain securities defined as exempt (generally government-issued securities, bank-guaranteed securities, and short-term commercial paper) and for private placements.

[13] CFTC (1989b), as cited in note 1.

[14] CFTC (1989a), as cited in note 1.

[15] CFTC (1989c), as cited in note 1.

[16] Securities within the meaning of Section 2(1) of the Securities Act of 1933.

a customer.[17] Hybrid instruments in these two categories are excluded from regulation under the CEA if the instruments:

1. are indexed to a commodity on no greater than a one-to-one basis;

2. limit the maximum loss on the instrument to a commodity-independent face value or coupon or both;

3. have a commodity-independent yield of at least 50 percent, but no more than 150 percent, of the yield on a comparable non-hybrid instrument;

4. do not have a commodity component that is severable from the instrument;

5. do not call for delivery of a commodity by means of an instrument specified in the rules of a futures exchange; and

6. are not marketed as being or having the characteristics of a futures contract or commodity option.

The last three items in this list need little explanation. Essentially, these are intended to maintain a clear separation between the excluded hybrids and exchange-traded commodity contracts and to avoid some possible effects of hybrids on those exchange markets. The nonseverability requirement prevents the separate off-exchange trading of a pure commodity contract. The restriction on deliverable instruments provides some protection against interference with deliverable supplies for settlement of exchange-traded contracts.[18] The restriction on marketing prevents misleading representations of the essential nature of the instruments, their legal status, and the regulatory supervision to which they are subject.

The first three items concern the economic features of the hybrids. Restricting any indexing to no greater than a one-to-one basis prevents design of an instrument that offers the equivalent of a levered position in the underlying commodity such that, for example, a 1 percent increase in the commodity price would produce a 10 percent increase in the commodity-dependent payment of the hybrid. This reduces the extent to which a hybrid instrument can be a "commodity play." Restricting the maximum loss due to a commodity price movement maintains the similarity between a hybrid instrument and traditional debt and depository instruments. It would indeed be unprecedented if a bond or bank deposit subjected the investor to a potential call for additional funds.

---

[17] Time deposits within the meaning of 12 C.F.R. 204.2(c)(1).
[18] It should be noted that this restriction is not intended to interfere with the ability of issuers to develop physical delivery alternatives to cash settlement.

The need for the commodity-independent yield (CIY) restriction, particularly the upper bound, may not be immediately obvious. The CIY is a yield-based indicator of the proportion of the value of the instrument that is not commodity-related. A CIY lower than the yield on comparable nonhybrid debt indicates that the commodity component has a positive current value and that noncommodity-related interest payments have been reduced. A CIY greater than the comparable non-hybrid yield indicates that the commodity interest has a negative current value and that the noncommodity-related interest payments have been increased. Thus, the CIY criterion acts to preserve the straight-debt character of a hybrid by restricting the absolute value of the commodity interest that can be built into it.

The one-to-one and CIY criteria also work in tandem to constrain commodity-related value in an instrument excluded from commodity regulation. As just noted, the CIY criterion constrains the value at the time of issue. The one-to-one criterion restricts the potential impact of commodity price changes on the value of the hybrid after issue.

The application of the one-to-one, maximum loss, and commodity-independent yield criteria are illustrated by a series of examples in the next section. But before proceeding to those examples, we turn to the exemption.

Regulatory Exemption

The exemption applies to debt securities, preferred equity securities, and bank deposits. Both securities registered in accordance with the Securities Act of 1933 and those qualifying for specified exemptions from such registration are included. Most demand deposits and transaction accounts offered by financial institutions whose deposits are insured by a U.S. government agency, or government-chartered corporation, or offered by a foreign bank in the United States (if supervised by Federal banking authorities) are also exempt. The intent of this section is to exempt registered securities, securities that are exempt from registration because of other indicators of soundness, and transactions for which such protections should be unnecessary, such as commercial paper and time deposits offered by banks with deposits insured by the FDIC.

Such securities would be exempt if the value of the *implied option premium* is no greater than 40 percent of the issue price of the instrument and if *any one* of the following requirements are satisfied:

1. the instrument has been rated in one of the four highest categories by a nationally-recognized rating organization, or if not rated, other comparable instruments of the issuer have been so rated;
2. the issuer maintains at least $100 million in net worth;

3. the issuer maintains cover equal to the amount of its commodity-related commitments; or

4. the instrument is eligible for insurance by a U.S. government agency or government-chartered agency. The exemption criteria also include the same restrictions on severability, deliverable instruments, and marketing as do the exclusion criteria.

These rules are self-explanatory except for the implied option premium. This requirement is similar to the CIY criterion applied in the exclusion. However, since the exemption test is specific to option-like instruments, measurement of the relative option component in terms of an option premium is a natural choice. The implied option premium is defined as the difference between the present value of the straight-debt portion of the hybrid instrument and the issue price of the hybrid instrument. The choice of 40 percent reflects a desire to place some reasonable limit on the proportion of the hybrid's value that is due to a commodity option-like payoff.

Effects of Criteria on Hybrid Instrument Design

The application of the criteria is best explained by examples. First, we present a relatively simple example of a foreign-currency, principal-indexed hybrid with a long futures-like commodity component—one which meets the exclusion test. We discuss in detail the influence of the one-to-one, maximum loss, and commodity-independent yield criteria on this design. We also develop simple rules for design parameters that keep the instrument within the exclusion criteria. We then consider the use of option-like components in the context of this example.

Second, we introduce variations in the way a futures-like commodity component might be defined and how these variations affect exclusion. Third, we discuss coupon indexing. Fourth, we discuss short futures-like commodity components. Fifth and last, we show a typical form of an option-like component and the application of exclusionary and exemptive criteria to this type of hybrid. Here, the implied option premium criterion is illustrated.

Let's start, then, with the case of a British pound, principal-indexed bond with a long futures-like commodity component and a coupon rate equal to a comparable nonhybrid coupon rate. This instrument has a $1,000 principal, a 10 percent coupon rate, and a 5-year maturity. This coupon is assumed to be the same that the issuer would pay on nonhybrid debt of comparable maturity and indentures. To keep the example simple, it is assumed that the coupon is stated as a percentage of the fixed principal, not the indexed principal. Indexation of the principal is defined as an adjustment to principal equal to the change in the dollar value of 500 British pounds from the reference price of the pounds at issue to the spot price at maturity.

A key feature of this example is that the reference price has been chosen so as to be equal to the price for future delivery of the commodity that could be obtained on a futures or forward contract of the same maturity as the bond. We adopt the generic term, *market forward price*, for this price.[19] (This choice of reference price, as you will see later, affects the maximum loss and the CIY criteria.)

The "commodity-independent" payments of this hybrid are the coupons of $100 and principal of $1000. The "commodity-dependent" payments will be equal to 500 times the difference between the spot price of pounds at maturity and the market forward price at issue.[20]

One-to-One Criterion

Under certain conditions, this bond meets the requirement for one-to-one commodity indexing as defined in the exclusion. One-to-one means that the absolute value of the change in any commodity-dependent payment as a percentage of its associated commodity-independent payment (in this example, the principal) may not exceed the absolute value of the percentage change in the commodity price to which the payment is indexed (in this example, the current spot price).

To illustrate this criterion, suppose the spot price of a pound at the time of issue is $2 and the market forward price is $1.90. If the spot price at maturity were $2.02, then this would represent a 1 percent increase in the commodity price to which the instrument is indexed. Considering the spot price at the time of issue of the hybrid, the commodity-dependent payment at that time is 500 ($2.00 – $1.90) = $50. At maturity, the commodity-dependent payment would be 500 ($2.02 – $1.90) = $60. Because this $10 increase amounts to only 1 percent of the principal of $1000, the one-to-one criterion is not exceeded.[21]

---

[19] This terminology is generic in the context of the economics literature that distinguishes futures and forward prices principally on the basis of daily resettlement (see, for example, J. C. Cox, J. E. Ingersoll, and S. A. Ross, "The Relation Between Forward Prices and Futures Prices," *Journal of Financial Economics*, 9, 1981, 321–346). It is not intended to evoke the regulatory distinction between futures and forward contracts. In some cases, futures and/or forward prices for contracts with the same maturity as the hybrid would be directly observable. In other cases such prices would have to be estimated.

[20] Mathematically, the indexed principal, H, may be written as: $H^* = \$1000 + 500(S_m - F)$ where S_m and F represent the price of pounds at maturity of the bond and the market forward price, respectively. A more general expression, with H as the non-indexed principal, N as the quantity of the commodity embedded in the hybrid, and R as the reference price, is as follows: $H^* = H + N(S_m - R)$ The commodity-independent payment is H (together with the coupons). The commodity-dependent payment is $N(S_m - R)$.

[21] A general form of the one-to-one criterion for this principal-indexed instrument is $N(S_m - R) - N(S - R)/H \leq (S_m - S)/S$ where S is the spot commodity price at the time of issue. This expression is satisfied only if $NS \leq H$, that is, if the value at the issue spot price of the number of units of the commodity does not exceed the principal of the instrument.

The number of forward contracts is clearly important in meeting this one-to-one criterion. In this example, if the number of contracts exceeded 500, then the criterion would not be met. As a general rule, the maximum number of commodity units cannot exceed the number of units that could purchased with the principal at the time of issue. In the example, given an issue spot price of $2, the $1,000 principal would buy at most 500 pounds.

Maximum Loss Criterion

Under certain conditions, this instrument has a maximum potential loss no greater than the principal. The maximum potential loss occurs when the spot price at maturity is zero. In the example, the commodity-dependent payment at a maturity spot price of zero is −500 times the market forward price. If this market forward price exceeds $2, this loss will exceed the principal.

Equivalently, as a general rule, the number of units of the commodity times the reference price cannot exceed the principal.[22] (Note that the reference price is defined at the time of issue and does not change as time passes.) If this condition were violated, however, the maximum loss criterion could still be satisfied simply by specifying in the bond contract that any reduction in principal due to indexation could not exceed the principal. This amounts, in effect, to introducing an option-like component into the instrument.

Commodity-Independent Yield Criterion

To understand this criterion, it is necessary to distinguish between the coupon rate, the yield-to-maturity, and the commodity-independent yield as defined in the exclusion. The coupon rate is defined as the coupon (or interest payment on a bank deposit) as a percentage of principal.[23] In our example, the coupon rate is 10 percent. The yield-to-maturity (YTM) is the single discount rate that discounts a bond's promised payments to its price. It is also known as the internal rate of return and as the dollar-weighted return. The YTM represents in effect the market's required rate of return on a bond. If the coupon rate on a bond is less than the YTM, then the bond will sell for less than par. If the coupon rate is more than the YTM, the bond will sell for more than par. Par bonds thus have a coupon rate equal to the YTM.

For the purpose of the exclusion, the concept of yield-to-maturity is applied only to comparable nonhybrid debt. It serves as the "bogie"

---

[22] That is, NR ≤ H

[23] The common terminology the "coupon rate" is not the same as the coupon yield, which is the coupon as a percentage of the bond price. The coupon yield is analogous to the dividend yield on preferred or common stock.

against which the commodity-independent yield is compared. In the precise language of the exclusion, it is "the estimated annual yield at the time of issuance for a comparable non-hybrid debt or depository instrument issued by the same or similar issuer."[24] Thus, it is the required rate of return of similar debt.

The commodity-independent yield (CIY) is the single discount rate that discounts a hybrid's commodity-independent payments to its price. Thus, the CIY is calculated in the same way as a yield-to-maturity. The CIY answers the question, what would be the yield on the hybrid if it had no commodity component. The criterion for exclusion is that this yield "without commodity component" must be no less than 50 percent and no more than 150 percent of the YTM, or required rate of return, on comparable nonhybrid debt.

The comparison criterion of CIY relative to YTM serves to indicate the value of the commodity component of a hybrid. When the embedded commodity component of a hybrid instrument is a futures-like component with a reference price equal to the market forward price, the value of the embedded commodity component is zero.[25] In this case, only the coupons and principal of the hybrid, discounted at the comparable non-hybrid YTM, determine the price. Then the CIY, which discounts those same payments to the hybrid price, must equal the YTM. In our example, if 10 percent is the YTM on nonhybrid debt, then CIY = YTM = 10 percent, and the CIY criterion is satisfied.

CIY as a Limit On Embedded Commodity Value

When the reference price of the hybrid is less than the market forward price, the hybrid will have a commodity component that has a positive value. In the vernacular of options traders, the commodity component is already "in the money."[26] The issuer can reduce the coupon rate and still sell the issue for the same price as comparable non-hybrid debt. The CIY on this lower-coupon debt will be less than the YTM on comparable nonhybrid debt.

---

[24] CFTC (1989b).

[25] As an example of this principle, consider a futures contract, which is a contract with a "reference price" equal to the market forward price. The contract has no current value. Only a good-faith margin deposit is required to enter into the contract.

[26] If an "in-the-money" commodity component did not have positive value, then an arbitrage opportunity would be available. Suppose an in-the-money futures or forward contract with reference price $R \leq F$ could be obtained for zero purchase price. This forward contract could be purchased and a conventional ("at-the-money") forward contract at price F could be sold (for zero). At delivery, the profit on the in-the-money contract would be $Sm - R$, and the profit on the conventional contract would be $(F - Sm)$ for a certain net profit of $F - R$. The market could not be in equilibrium if this certain cash flow could be obtained for zero investment. The value of the in-the-money contract must be the discounted value of $F - R$.

When the reference price is greater than the market forward price, the hybrid will contain a commodity component with negative value. The issuer can increase the coupon rate and still sell the issue for the same price as comparable non-hybrid debt. The CIY will then be greater than the YTM on comparable nonhybrid yield.

As illustrated in Figure 24.1, the CIY criterion thus limits the value of the embedded commodity component. The point labeled Å represents the combination of a CIY of 10 percent with a reference price (R) equal to the market forward price. The point labeled B is the combination of CIY and R in which the reference price (R′) is less than the market forward price. The CIY is assumed to be 2 percent, an unacceptable CIY under the interpretation because it is less than 50 percent of the comparable nonhybrid YTM of 10 percent. The vertical distance between points A and B (representing 8 percentage points) is a yield-based indicator of the positive value embedded in the futures-like commodity component.

The point labeled C is the combination of CIY and R in which the reference price (R″) is greater than the market forward price. The CIY for this case is assumed to be 18 percent, also an unacceptable CIY. Again, the difference of 8 percentage points from the comparable nonhybrid yield indicates the negative value of the commodity component.

Figure 24.1 illustrates several considerations in designing hybrids to meet the CIY criterion. One is the inclusion of option-like components in addition to futures-like components. Take point A. If a long option-like component were included in the hybrid, its value would increase the

Figure 24.1 Commodity Independent Yield (CIY) and Reference Price (R)

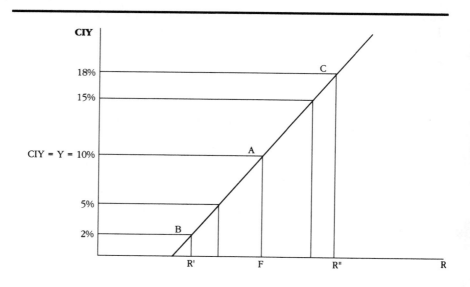

value of the hybrid unless the coupon were decreased. The coupon could be decreased until the CIY were 5 percent, and this permissible 5 percent decrease in the CIY limits the value of the embedded option-like component. A point to be emphasized here is that the CIY criterion accommodates both futures-like and option-like designs.

Also, a short option-like component could be embedded that would reduce the value of the hybrid and require an increase in the coupon if the nonhybrid issue price were to be maintained. The coupon could be increased until the CIY equals 15 percent. Thus, the upper bound on CIY limits the value of a short option-like component embedded in a hybrid.

The ability to adjust the CIY of a hybrid by adding long and short futures-like and option-like positions gives issuers considerable flexibility. For example, if the "first-pass" design of a hybrid with a futures-like component resulted in CIYs such as points B and C in Figure 24.1, then either long or short option components could be added to attain a CIY within the limits.

Contango and Backwardation

A typical choice of reference price when the market forward price is not chosen is the current spot price. In certain markets (known as "contango" markets), the market forward price typically exceeds the spot price. In such markets, this choice for the reference price might correspond to point B in Figure 24.1. Some typically contango commodities are gold and stock indexes. For markets in which the spot price typically exceeds the market forward price ("backwardation" markets), use of the spot price as the reference price might correspond to point C in Figure 24.1. Some typically backwardation markets are wheat (during the harvest season) and Treasury bills. In other commodities, the relationship between the spot price and the market forward price varies with market conditions. Examples include currencies and oil.

The CIY criterion will constrain designers of hybrids with embedded futures-like commodity contracts referenced to the spot price according to the degree of contango or backwardation in the commodity. If the hybrid is to be sold at the same price as comparable nonhybrid debt, then the decrease or increase in the coupon rate must equal the percentage contango or backwardation. If the issue price is par, the coupon rate is also the CIY. Then the difference between the CIY and the comparable nonhybrid YTM is the percentage contango or backwardation.

For example, in Figure 24.1 the 8 percent difference between points A and B is driven by an 8 percent contango market.[27] In such a market, the CIY criterion cannot be met on a hybrid issued at par if the spot price is chosen as the reference price for a futures-like embedded commodity component. Of course, the criterion could be met in this case by adding an option component that would subtract value, i.e., a short option-like

---

[27] This assumes par issue prices for both non-hybrid and hybrid.

Table 24.1: Coupon Rates for Hybrids Denominated in Selected Commodities and Foreign Currencies* February 8, 1989

Days	30	90	360
US Government YTM	9.25%	9.50%	9.94%
Yen	4.15%	4.54%	4.88%
Ausdollar	15.78%	16.37%	16.93%
Oil	44.82%	36.43%	23.33%
Gold	1.33%	1.46%	1.69%
Copper	41.68%	32.07%	32.72%
Silver	3.57%	.71%	.02%
Soybeans	−.07%	.37%	10.71%

*Hybrids contain only long futures-like component with reference prices equal to the current spot price. Hybrids sell at par. Comparable non-hybrid debt yield to maturity is yield to maturity on U.S. governments.

component. The vertical distance between point B and 5 percent CIY is the (negative) value the short option would have to contribute. Similar calculations for backwardation markets and long option-like components can be made.

Table 24.1 shows estimates, based on *Wall Street Journal* data, of what the hybrid-debt coupon rate would have to be in order to issue the debt at par if only a futures-like component with the reference price equal to the spot price were embedded, and if the comparable nonhybrid debt yield is the U.S. government security rate shown in the table. To illustrate how to interpret the estimates in Table 24.1, consider the following example. Assume the YTM on one-year comparable nonhybrid debt is 9.94 percent. If a futures-like component in yen were embedded with the current spot price as the reference price, the hybrid would sell at par at a coupon of 4.88 percent (because of the degree of contango of yen on this date), and this is also its CIY.

This yen-denominated hybrid would fail to meet the CIY criterion. The minimum permissible CIY (to be excluded from regulation under the CEA) is 50 percent of 9.94 percent, or 4.97 percent. (The maximum permissible is 14.91 percent.) However, the would-be issuer of a yen-denominated hybrid has alternatives. A short option-like component could be added to reduce the total value of the commodity component. Or the coupon could be set at 4.97 percent, in which case the hybrid would sell at a premium. In either case, the effect of the CIY criterion is to constrain the relative value of the commodity component.

The CIY criterion is perhaps the most controversial part of the exclusion criteria.[28] Some commentators argued, in effect, that all commodities are not treated equally by the criterion, as Table 24.1 illustrates. For example, one-year hybrids could not be issued in yen, the Australian dollar, oil, gold, or copper, but could be issued in silver and soybeans. The view underlying this differentiation among commodities is that large deviations of the CIY from the comparable nonhybrid YTM in certain commodities reflects an important distinction between commodity markets and traditional debt markets.

However, one exception was made. For hybrid instruments designed to afford a real rate of return relative to the Consumer Price Index or other broadly based inflation measures, the comparable debt yield is defined as a real yield relative to the inflation measures.[29] That makes the comparable debt YTM rather low so that low coupons ("real" rate coupons) can be used.

Par Bonds and CIY

For bonds issued at part, the CIY criterion creates an upper bound on the absolute value of the commodity component as a percentage of par. This is illustrated for hybrids with long futures-like components in Table 24.2. For example, at a CIY of 50 percent on a 10 percent YTM, 5-year bond, the commodity component as a percentage of par is only 19 percent. The commodity component as a percentage of par approaches (but does not exceed) 50 percent only at very long maturities and very high YTM.[30]

Variations in Indexing

The foregoing discussion has covered the essential characteristics of a principal-indexed hybrid with an embedded long futures-like position and the effects of the one-to-one, maximum loss and commodity-indepen-

---

[28] See the Goldman-Sachs comment letter, May 10, 1989. Also, the Federal Reserve Board is moving toward allowing foreign currency-denominated deposits, which behave essentially like PERLS. These would sometimes violate the CIY criterion unless the forward price is used as the reference price.

[29] More recently, senior staff of the Commission have indicated a willingness to go beyond even this exception for inflation-indexed instruments. They have indicated that the CIY criterion would not have to be met for CPI indexed instruments that meet the other criteria of the exclusion.

[30] A mathematical proof of this property will be provided by the authors on request. It should be emphasized that, although this characteristic of the criterion provides a useful insight for a large class of potential (par) hybrids, the CIY does not create an upper bound on the commodity percentage for non-par bonds. For example, consider a comparable non-hybrid zero-coupon bond. In order to attach a short futures-like commodity component, which would reduce the issue price, a greater-than-zero coupon could be paid in order to support the issue price at the non-hybrid level. Because the issue price is already relatively low, the absolute value of the commodity component can be shown to exceed 50% of the issue price even though the CIY does not exceed 150% of the non-hybrid yield.

Table 24.2: Maximum Commodity Component as Percentage of
Par Issue Price 50% – 150% CIY Criterion

Comparable Non-Hybrid Yield (Coupon)[*]	Years to Maturity						
	1	5	10	15	20	25	30
5%	.02	.11	.19	.26	.31	.35	.38
10%	.05	.19	.31	.38	.43	.45	.47
15%	.07	.25	.38	.44	.47	.48	.49
20%	.08	.30	.42	.47	.49	.49	.50
25%	.10	.34	.45	.48	.49	.50	.50
30%	.12	.37	.46	.49	.50	.50	.50

[*] Yield and coupon are equal for non-hybrid debt instruments selling at par.

dent yield criteria on this type of instrument. Some alternatives to indexing principal include different methods of defining the indexing feature, coupon indexing, and embedded short futures-like positions.

Defining the Indexation. Some possible variations include the following:

1. An adjustment to principal defined as the rate of change in the price of the British pound from the reference price, in turn defined as a percentage of the current price. Using our earlier example of a current price of $2 and a maturity price of $2.02, the adjustment would be $1,000 × ($.02/$2) = $10. This definition of the adjustment is really identical to the original definition because the $1,000 divided by the $2 (per pound) is 500 pounds. That is, in this variation the number of pounds involved in the forward contract is defined implicitly as the principal divided by the current price of the commodity. This particular definition ensures one-to-one indexing; but if the denominator of the adjustment calculation is less than the current spot price, then one-to-one indexing cannot be achieved.

2. A principal payment defined as a fixed dollar amount of principal times the ratio of the value of British pounds at maturity to the current value. Using the example, the principal becomes $1,000 × ($2.02/$2) = $1,010. This is another equivalent definition.

3. An adjustment to principal defined in terms of the change in a price other than the spot price. Although this variation has not been seen up to now, it is conceivable and the language in the release was deliberately chosen so as not to exclude such a design.

For example, the adjustment to principal might be based on the rate of change in the market forward price from the time of issue to maturity of the hybrid.

Coupon Indexing

Coupon indexation can be achieved either separately or in concert with principal indexation in any of the above forms. In one form, the coupon may vary as a fixed percentage of the indexed principal, where the indexation is computed based on the spot price of the commodity at each coupon payment. The example of the British pound-indexed principal instrument could be modified so that the 10 percent coupon becomes 10 percent of adjusted principal. This payment is the same as 10 percent of the fixed principal plus 10 percent of the price change on 500 pounds. The commodity-independent coupon payment is 10 percent of the fixed principal, and the commodity-dependent payment is 10 percent of the price change on 500 pounds. (Identical coupon indexation could be achieved by defining an indexed coupon rate to be multiplied times the fixed principal.) It is important to remember that when both coupons and principal are indexed, the one-to-one and maximum loss criteria apply separately to both the coupons and principal. This example satisfies these criteria. Indeed, the same analysis developed above in terms of how this type of indexation can be designed to satisfy these criteria for principal indexation applies also to coupon indexation.

Variations in which the coupon only, but not the principal, is indexed include all of the forms illustrated above. The adjustment in each case is simply applied to the coupon payment rather than the principal payment. An example of this type of instrument is a bank deposit with indexed interest.

Short Futures-Like Components

Short futures-like positions can be embedded in hybrids simply by reversing the definition of the adjustment to principal. Based on the analysis of the embedded long futures-like component, it is clear that this design will meet the one-to-one criterion as long as the value at the current spot price of the number of units of the commodity does not exceed the principal. However, the maximum loss criterion cannot be met without other contractual specifications, since the loss is unlimited as the spot price increases.

The application and effect of the CIY criterion are identical to the case of the long commodity position except that the effect of contango and backwardation is reversed. For example, in a contango market, choice of the spot price for the reference price builds a negative value into the embedded commodity position necessitating a higher coupon rate and higher CIY.

Option-Like Hybrids

All of the variations considered thus far were presented as primarily futures-like hybrids; option-like characteristics were added only to meet the maximum loss or CIY criterion. Now let's consider an option-like hybrid in more detail. We present an example that meets the exclusion criterion and then consider the application of the exemption criteria for a variation that fails the exclusion tests.

Consider a gold principal-indexed bond with a coupon rate below the nonhybrid rate of 10 percent (for par issues). This example is similar to the indexed certificates of deposit that have been the subject of interpretative letters. The instrument has a maturity of 5 years, a fixed coupon of 6 percent, principal of $1000, and an adjustment to principal equal to 2.5 ounces of gold times the change in the gold price above $400 per ounce.

If the spot price of gold at issue is $400 per ounce, then this hybrid will satisfy the exclusion criteria. The one-to-one criterion is satisfied because, at an issue spot price of $400 per ounce, the principal payment of $1000 is equivalent to 2.5 ounces of gold, the same amount as specified in the adjustment to principal.[31] This will ensure that the percentage change in the commodity-dependent payment as a percentage of the principal does not exceed the percentage change in the price of gold. The maximum loss criterion will be met by explicit design in this example because of the option-like payoff function. Finally, if issued at par, the commodity-independent yield will be 6 percent, or 60 percent of the comparable nonhybrid yield.

This example may be changed to fail the exclusion by increasing the number of ounces. Suppose, for example, 3 ounces were specified and that a 5 percent coupon would allow sale at par. Now the hybrid would fail only the one-to-one exclusion criterion because a 1 percent change in the price of gold would produce a 1.2 percent adjustment to principal.

But since the hybrid has the explicit option-like character, it could be subjected to the tests for exemption from the exchange-traded option regulations. We will assume that all of the criteria necessary for exemption have been successfully met except the implied option premium test. The application of that test proceeds as follows:

1. Determine the present value at 10 percent (the comparable nonhybrid yield) of the commodity-independent payments, which are the coupon stream (for five years) and the $1000 principal. This present value turns out to be $810.46. (This calculation is based on annual coupons for simplicity.)

---

[31] Note that if the price of gold increased by 1% to $404, the principal adjustment would be $10, or 1% of principal. The one-to-one criterion is also satisfied at lower exercise prices. At higher exercise prices more ounces could be specified.

2. The implied option premium is the difference between the issue price and that present value, or $1000 − 810.46 = $189.54.

3. Determine the proportion of the issue price represented by the implied option premium, which is 189.54/1000, or about 19 percent.

Since this proportion is not greater than 40 percent, the implied option preminum test is passed. Thus, this hybrid would be exempted from commodity option regulation.

In Closing

The regulation of off-exchange futures- and option-like instruments is one of the most complex and potentially controversial issues facing regulators in the commodities, securities, and banking agencies. The CFTC has addressed a significant component of the off-exchange market by providing certain hybrid debt and depository instruments with an exclusion from regulation under the CEA. It has also provided certain option-like hybrids that are not so excluded with an exemption from the exchange-trading requirement. This regulatory approach is intended to allow constructive financial innovation to proceed within the context of the CEA. The new framework will materially affect the design of future hybrids as well as the evolution of further regulation from this point.

||

MANAGING A DERIVATIVE PRODUCTS BUSINESS FROM A RISK-ADJUSTED RETURN PERSPECTIVE*

| **Ronald D. Reading and**
| **James C. Lam**

25

From many perspectives, the derivative products business is one of the most attractive lines of business in the financial services industry today. While many businesses are struggling to earn an adequate rate of return on capital, the best performing derivative products businesses are achieving returns significantly higher than their required return. Moreover, the business has been growing at over 40 percent per annum over the past several years (see Figure 25.1). Profit and growth potential should continue to be attractive as new product innovations are introduced, new customers are cultivated, and new applications are developed to match products to customer needs. The globalization of financial markets, and the need for both financial and nonfinancial institutions to manage their financial risks on an integrated, worldwide basis, should result in many more years of profit and growth opportunities in the derivative products business.

However, the derivative products business is not without risks and challenges. Several firms have recently reported unexpectedly high credit losses. Rating agencies, regulators, and other policy makers are closely scrutinizing the potentially large credit exposures in the derivative products market. Margins on "plain vanilla" products continue to decline as these products reach the mature stage of their product life cycles (e.g.,

*The authors would like to thank Alden Toevs, Managing Vice President and Co-Head of First Manhattan Consulting Group's Risk Management Practice for his significant contributions to the analytical framework and methodologies discussed in this chapter.

553

Figure 25.1: Notional Principal Amount of New Swap
Transactions (1987–1991) Compound Annual
Growth Rate [CAGR]

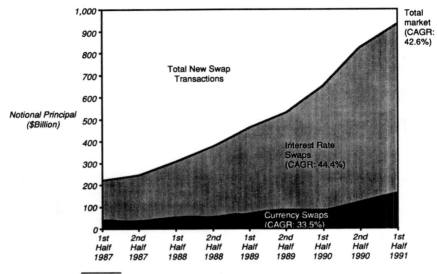

Source: International Swap Dealers Association, Inc. (ISDA).

see Figure 25.2 on the spread deterioration on U.S. dollar interest rate swaps). Lastly, the entry of new competitors in the derivative products business has further eroded margins on existing products, as well as shortened the product life cycles of new products.

In this environment, it has become increasingly important for managers of derivative products businesses to distinguish profitable versus unprofitable transactions and customers on a risk-adjusted ROE basis. However, it is our belief that current accounting conventions and practices do not provide this perspective. Revenues are calculated based on present valuing all future income, with no standard practices for reserving against future capital requirements, credit provision, and administrative expenses. Moreover, the amount of capital allocated to a derivative products business is usually based on regulatory guidelines or an average capital ratio, neither of which reflects underlying financial risks. Current accounting practices simply do not accurately measure the economic profitability of derivative products. This chapter focuses on establishing an economic framework for performance measurement and management decision making.

Methodologies for measuring the economic profitability of derivative products not only provide better management accounting information,

Figure 25.2: Spreads on Plain Vanilla Products Such as U.S. Dollar Interest Rate Swaps Continue to Narrow

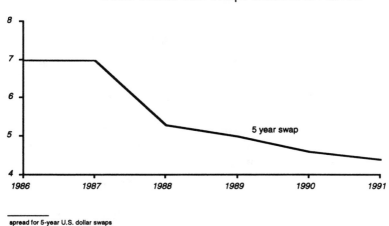

spread for 5-year U.S. dollar swaps

but also establish the fundamental basis for several key management processes critical to the success of the overall business:

- *Business segment profitability analyses.* On an economic basis, management of a derivative products business should be able to measure the risk-adjusted profitability of the business as a whole, as well as the key segments of the business, including organization units, customers, and products.

- *Risk-adjusted pricing models.* Prior to a transaction taking place, the trader should be able to use pricing models to quantify the expected profitability of a deal in two ways:

  –For a given price, measure the risk-adjusted ROE.

  –For a given target return, calculate the required pricing.

- *Meritorious incentive compensation programs.* To stimulate appropriate actions at the operating level, the incentive compensation system should also be based on a consistent set of methodologies for measuring performance as those used for management accounting and pricing models. This is the most effective way to develop congruence between the objectives of the owners and the objectives of the managers and employees of a derivative products business.

Two fundamental principles underlie sound methodologies for determining the economic profitability of a derivative products business:

A. The appropriate methodologies should be based on fundamental accounting and financial principles:

- *Matching Principle.* Revenues and costs should be matched to the extent they are related to the same transaction or activity.

- *Present Value Principle.* For evaluating ROE of derivative product transactions on a multiyear basis, the free cash flows available to equity shareholders should be discounted at the hurdle rate.

B. The appropriate methodologies should be risk-adjusted and fully allocated.

The economic profitability measure should incorporate all of the economic revenue and costs associated with a derivative product transaction. A schematic of the economic framework is shown in Figure 25.3, which shows the key drivers of risk-adjusted ROE, and thus economic value, of a derivative products business.

To measure accurately the economic profitability of derivative products, management needs to improve upon current management accounting practices and develop an integrated set of methodologies for its profitability MIS and pricing models. In the first three sections, we discuss the key methodologies that address the major shortcomings of current management accounting practices:

- Measuring the credit exposure created by derivative products.

- Accounting for the financial risks associated with running a derivative products business.

- Deferring sufficient income for future financial requirements.

In the final section, we discuss how to incorporate risk-adjusted profitability measurement into the day-to-day management of the derivative products business in order to maximize the risk-adjusted return to the shareholder.

Measuring the Credit Exposure Created by Derivative Products

A. Concept

Incremental credit risk exposure is created whenever a swap[*] is transacted. Unlike a loan, however, a swap's credit exposure cannot be precisely determined at inception because it is a function of future changes in market rates. The basic concept of the credit risk exposure calculation is that statistical models can be used to develop an estimate of the *expected* credit exposure for each swap over the life of the contract.

---

[*] The methodologies discussed in this chapter apply to all derivative products so the terms swap and derivative product are used interchangably.

Figure 25.3: Schematic of an ROE Calculation for a Derivative Products Business

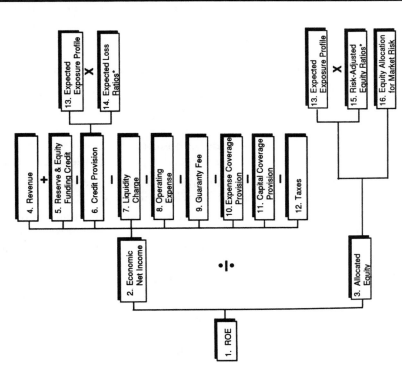

Definition of Terms

1. *ROE.* The economic return on equity

2. *Economic Net Income.* Risk-adjusted income available to common shareholders

3. *Allocated Equity.* Economic equity sufficient to cover a predetermined cumulative probability loss event (i.e. unexpected loss)

4. *Revenue.* Total product revenue, including hedging cost

5. *Reserve and Equity Funding Credit.* Funding credit for allocated reserve and equity (i.e., sources of interest-free funding on the balance sheet)

6. *Credit Provision.* Risk-adjusted reserve set aside for expected credit losses

7. *Liquidity Charge.* Cost of holding liquid assets and other types of liquidity

8. *Operating Expense.* The cost of originating the transaction(s) including attributed overhead plus the first year servicing cost

9. *Guaranty Fee.* Cost of excess capital allocated to the derivatives unit or a guaranty from the parent company (to ensure a triple-A or double-A rating)

10. *Expense Coverage Provision.* Deferred income to cover future operating expense.

11. *Capital Coverage Provision.* Deferred income to provide an acceptable return on capital in future periods. This will reduce income in year 1 and increase it in subsequent years

12. *Taxes.* Effective tax rate times pretax net income

13. *Expected Exposure Profile.* The expected replacement cost of the derivative over the life of the contract

14. *Expected Loss Ratios.* Expected credit loss for the relevant credit risk grade over the life of the contract

15. *Risk-Adjusted Equity Ratios.* The maximum present value of unexpected credit loss for each risk grade over the life of the contract

16. *Equity Allocation for Market Risk.* The market loss that would occur assuming risk exposures are at their limit and that there is a 3-sigma adverse rate move

* – Need to be differentiated by risk grade so the appropriate reserve and equity ratios can be applied.

P/O 174-20\104-3

The credit loss on a swap is the replacement cost of the swap contract at the time the counterparty defaults. This is equal to the mark-to-market gain on the contract at the time of default. Because the mark-to-market value of a swap is driven by future movements in interest rates and/or exchange rates, a swap's credit exposure can only be estimated through statistical analyses.

One of the key objectives of calculating the expected exposure of a swap is to establish a basis for allocating capital and credit reserve. Therefore, the methodology used to calculate the expected exposure should:

1. Be based on statistical analysis.

2. Be a dynamic process to capture the continual changes in market rates.

B. Methodology

The expected credit exposure of a swap can be defined as:

The Expected Replacement Cost Over the Life of the Swap

In the rest of this section, we will show that the expected replacement cost over the life of a swap is the best estimate, on a probability-weighted basis, of the credit exposure of a swap transaction over the life of the contract. The expected replacement cost is often referred to as the loan-equivalent amount.

The expected replacement cost has two components:

1. *The current replacement cost.* If a derivative product counterparty defaults today, the loss is equal to the current replacement cost of the derivative:

   • If replacement can be done in the market at no loss or at a gain, there is no *current* loss exposure to the counterparty.

   • If replacement can only be done in the market at a loss, this loss defines the *current* loss exposure.

2. *The potential for future exposure.* In addition, there is the potential for future exposure due to future movements in interest rates and/or foreign exchange rates. While future replacement costs are not known, they can be estimated using simulation-based or option-based models. The general process used to calculate the expected replacement cost curve for a swap is shown in Figure 25.4.

Example: Simulation Process

A simulation model can be used to calculate an expected replacement cost curve for a swap. The three basic steps are:

1. Calculate the mark-to-market value of a swap for each of, say, 1,000 randomly generated interest rate paths (see Figure 25.5).

Figure 25.4: Expected Exposure Calculation

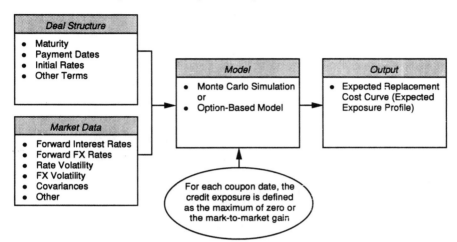

2. Set to zero all negative mark-to-market values (see Figure 25.6).

3. Calculate the expected replacement cost curve as the mean of all mark-to-market values, including those set to zero in Step 2 (see Figure 25.7).

As described above, the simulation model will generate an expected replacement cost curve for any given swap transaction. This expected replacement cost curve is the probability-weighted estimate for the replace-

Figure 25.5: Simulation for an Interest Rate Swap

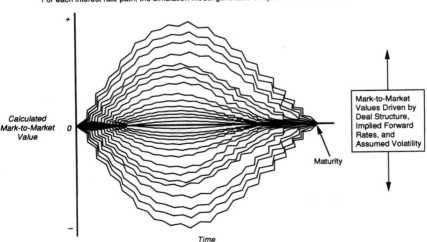

Figure 25.6:

Next, the simulation model sets all negative mark-to-market values to zero:

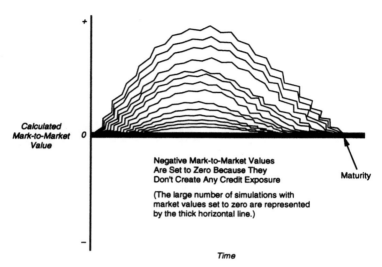

ment cost of the swap contract over time, and is driven by two opposing factors (see Figure 25.8):

- *Factor 1: Amortization Effect.* As time passes, the replacement cost of a swap declines until it reaches zero at maturity. This is because the

Figure 25.7

Lastly, the *expected* replacement cost curve is calculated as the mean of all mark-to-market values:

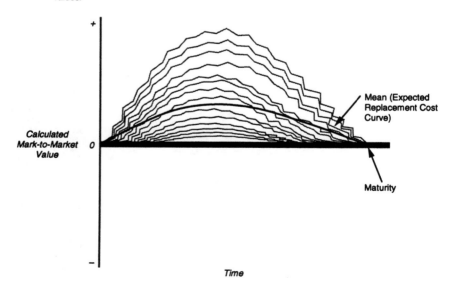

Figure 25.8: Factors Impacting the Expected Replacement Cost Curve. Example: Interest Rate Swaps

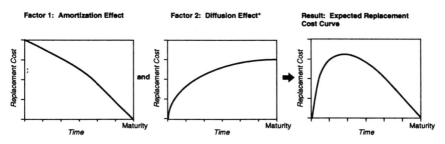

Factor 1: Amortization Effect   Factor 2: Diffusion Effect*   Result: Expected Replacement Cost Curve

* — Mathematically, volatility increases at the speed of the square root of time.

number of payments also declines with time until the last payment is made at maturity.

- *Factor 2: Diffusion Effect.* For a given volatility assumption, the expected replacement cost increases with time.

- *Result: Expected Replacement Cost Curve.* The interaction of the amortization effect and the diffusion effect results in the expected replacement cost curve.

Based on the simulation process described, the expected replacement cost curve of a new derivative transaction can be developed (see Figure 25.9 for examples of single- and cross-currency swaps).

A number of factors will influence this calculation. For example, key variables affecting the potential for future exposure of single and cross currency swaps are:

- *Interest rate volatility.* The higher the assumed volatility, the larger the future exposure of an interest rate and a cross currency swap.

- *FX volatility.* The higher the assumed volatility, the larger the future exposure of a cross currency swap.

- *Maturity date.* The more distant the maturity of the swap, the larger the future exposure of any swap.

- *Forward interest rates.* The higher the forward rates (i.e., the steeper the yield curve), the larger the future exposure of the fixed rate payer.

Figure 25.9: Expected Replacement Cost Curve over Time*

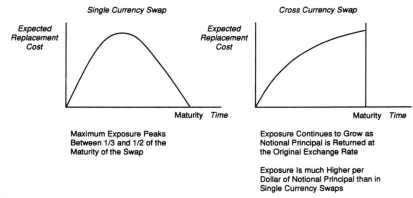

Single Currency Swap

Cross Currency Swap

Maximum Exposure Peaks
Between 1/3 and 1/2 of the
Maturity of the Swap

Exposure Continues to Grow as
Notional Principal is Returned at
the Original Exchange Rate

Exposure Is much Higher per
Dollar of Notional Principal than in
Single Currency Swaps

*Illustrations are for swaps with mark-to-market value of zero.

- *Forward FX rates.* The higher the forward exchange rates, the larger the exposure of the domestic currency payer.
- *Covariance.* The higher the covariance between interest rates and FX rates, the higher the future exposure of a cross-currency swap.

Accounting for Financial Risks

In the previous section, we discussed the loan equivalent concept for swap transactions, which is an estimation of the expected credit risk exposure. While credit risk is generally the greatest risk exposure for a derivative products business that is oriented towards customer business (as opposed to trading), there are other risk factors that should also be incorporated in performance measurement. To account for all of the financial risks of a derivative products business, the performance measurement system needs to include:

A. Capital allocation and charge for capital

B. Provision for credit losses

C. Charge for guaranty fee

D. Charge for liquidity/hedging costs

E. Allocation of expenses

A. Capital Allocation and Charge for Capital

Each business unit should be charged for the amount of economic capital needed to support the underlying risks associated with that business unit's activities. A significant number of leading banks have developed, or are in the process of developing, methodologies to allocate economic capital to business units and products based on underlying economic risks. In order to measure performance from a shareholder value perspective, this practice should also be extended to the derivative products business.

The charge for capital is determined by:

1. The amount of economic capital used by the business unit

2. The firm's cost of capital

Each of these factors is discussed below.

1. Economic Capital The amount of economic capital used by a business unit is driven by the need to cover the potential for unexpected losses due to financial risks. While capital is also needed to fund portions of fixed assets (e.g., buildings, equipment, etc.) that are not funded with debt, this amount is insignificant compared to the capital needed to cover financial risks.

To cover the underlying financial risks of a derivative products business, management needs to:

- Establish a cumulative probability of loss that management has determined is necessary to hold capital against. This would be a function of the risk aversion of management as well as key financial targets of management such as financial leverage risk and credit rating objectives.

- Calculate how much capital the selected probability level implies for each product by credit grade, as well as for noncredit types of risk (e.g., market risk) faced by the firm. This process can be thought of as equilibrating all risks to the same consistent cumulative loss probability level to determine the amount of capital the firm needs to hold against each risk (i.e., the unit cost of risk is measured by capital). Developing appropriate capital ratios is usually the most important and complex process in building a risk-adjusted profitability measurement system. This is because performance measurement is highly sensitive to capital assumptions. Many firms use external capital allocation "benchmarks" until they have fully developed internal data bases that can be used to determine appropriate capital ratios.

See Figure 25.10 for an illustration of the above process. For a derivative products business, the primary risk factors are credit risk and market risk.

The allocation of economic capital for credit risk involves five steps as illustrated in Figure 25.11:

Step 1: Calculate the expected replacement cost curve based on statistical processes discussed earlier.

Figure 25.10: Capital Allocation Based on Unexpected Loss

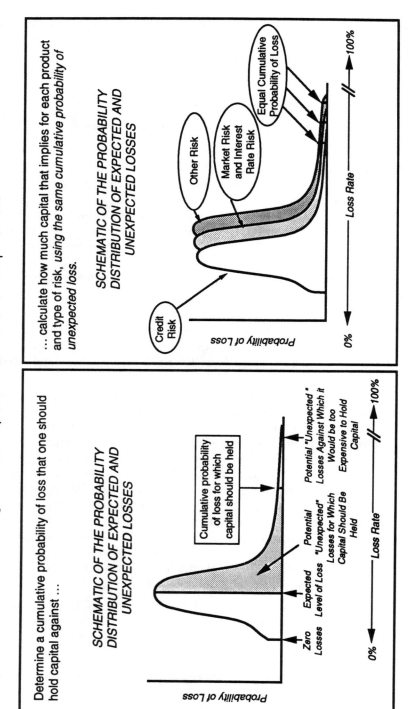

Figure 25.11: Capital Allocation for Credit Risk

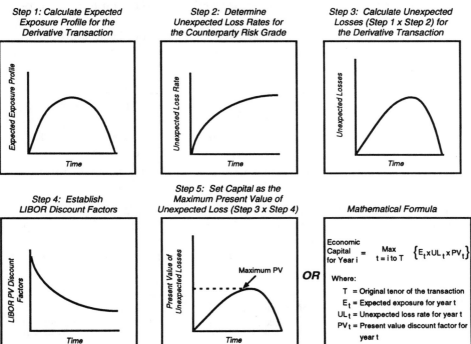

Step 2: Develop unexpected loss rates for each counterparty risk grade based on an internal credit loss database or an external data source. This is the loss rate at the point where the cumulative probability of loss is that for which capital should be held (see Figure 25.10).

Step 3: Calculate unexpected losses over the life of the transaction (step 1 times step 2).

Step 4: Establish the discount factors using, say, the LIBOR yield curve.

Step 5: Set the economic capital needed to cover the credit risk of this transaction as the maximum of the present value of unexpected losses (i.e., the maximum of step 3 times step 4).

The end result of this five-step calculation is an economic capital requirement that will cover an unexpected loss over the entire life of the transaction. To incorporate the diversification effect of multiple transactions and netting, the expected exposure profile should be calculated for all derivative transactions in a single currency with each counterparty. This is repeated for each currency and the results are added to obtain the economic capital for all transactions with a single customer. The economic capital for each customer is then added to obtain the total economic capital for credit risk.

Some firms multiply an average expected exposure by an average unexpected loss to derive economic capital. However, this approach has two important shortcomings:

- The credit exposure of a swap transaction varies over time, but this profile cannot be captured by an average expected exposure measure. As seen in Figure 25.9, the expected exposure of a single currency swap is greatest between one third and one half of its life, while for a cross currency swap it is greatest near maturity.

- The unexpected loss rate varies over time. This factor is not captured when using an average unexpected loss ratio.

To capture the time dimension of swap exposure and unexpected loss rates, as well as the interrelationship between the two factors, the five-step calculation described above is required.

The allocation of economic capital to cover market risk can be determined as follows:

The above process requires the following:

- Risk limits for the derivative products business
- The assumed market rate move at a confidence level equal to the cumulative probability of loss determined as needed to hold capital against
- Correlation assumptions for these risk factors

The economic capital allocated to a business unit is equal to the sum of the economic capital for credit risk and the economic capital for market risk (plus a small amount for fixed assets).

2. Capital Charge. For each business unit, the charge for capital is determined by multiplying the economic capital allocated to it by the firm's cost of capital.

In order to evaluate investment opportunities most firms establish a cost of capital, which can be defined in the following way. The overall corporate objective is to maximize the value for shareholders. This will be

---

*Instead of risk limits, some firms prefer to use actual positions.
**This factor will always be less than or equal to 1.

achieved if the corporation invests only in business opportunities that earn a long term return on equity that is at or above the minimum level needed for the investment's value to equal the amount of equity capital that has been invested in it. This "minimum" level of ROE is known as the firm's cost of capital and is the rate that should be used to calculate the capital charge.

B. Provision for Credit Losses

In addition to holding economic capital for unexpected credit losses, the firm should deduct from income and hold as a credit reserve an amount to cover *expected* credit losses for all credit grades.

The level of expected loss for each product by credit grade can be actuarially derived by using a database of actual historical losses. For each reporting period, the risk-adjusted credit reserve is calculated as follows:

a. Assign a credit grade to each counterparty.

b. Establish a required reserve level for each product using the firm's actual historical losses or an external database. This reserve level should reflect the expected loss of each product given its maturity and credit grade.

c. Calculate and allocate the required provision based on the following formula:

$$\boxed{\text{Required Provision}} = \boxed{\text{Required Reserve}} - \boxed{\text{Actual Reserve}} + \boxed{\text{Net Chargeoffs}}$$

The methodology for establishing credit reserve is as follows:

$$\text{Credit Provision for Year}_i = E_i \times EL_i$$

$$\text{Credit Reserve for Year}_i = \sum PV_i \times \text{Credit Provision}_i$$

Where:

$$E_i = \text{Expected exposure for year } i$$
$$EL_i = \text{Expected loss rate for year } i$$
$$PV_i = \text{Present value discount factor year } i$$

As with the capital calculation, the expected exposure profile should be calculated for all derivative transactions in a single currency with a single customer. The formula above is then used to determine the credit reserve.

C. Charge for Guaranty Fee

A critical factor for success in the derivative products business is a triple-A or double-A credit rating. This factor has a real economic cost that is not captured in the performance measurement systems of most derivative products businesses. Without adjusting for this cost, a firm's profitability is inflated because of the free capital subsidy from the parent company.

The cost of a triple-A or double-A credit rating can be measured in four ways:

1. If the parent chooses to allocate substantial capital (e.g., multiples of, say, a 3-sigma loss level) to the derivative products subsidiary, the associated cost is simply the cost of excess capital.

2. If the parent chooses to issue an unconditional guaranty for the performance of the derivative products subsidiary, the associated cost would be the cost of capital (residing on the parent's balance sheet) that supports the financial guaranty.

3. If the method used to achieve the desired rating is a credit enhancement contract from a third party, the associated cost is simply the cost of the credit enhancement contract.

4. If the swaps business is a division of the parent company, the associated cost is the cost of capital supporting the unconditional guaranty for performance.

Regardless of how the guaranty fee is measured, this cost should be incorporated in the performance measurement system of a derivative products business.

D. Charge for Liquidity/Hedging Costs

One of the key drivers of the profitability of a derivative products business is product development using advanced proprietary trading and simulation models. These highly structured and complex products add significant value to the customers by providing a customized solution to their financial needs. While these custom products represent high-margin business, they are usually illiquid and difficult to hedge. Therefore, for performance measurement purposes, the cost of maintaining liquidity (i.e., the negative carry on the investment portfolio) and the cost of hedging (e.g., option premiums, basis risk cost, etc.) should be charged to the products that create such requirements.

E. Allocation of Expenses

Noninterest expenses should be fully allocated to business units to ensure cost effectiveness by linking all expenses to revenue generation units. Without full allocation of expenses, business unit profitability would be overstated.

The expenses that should be fully allocated to business units include:

- Direct expenses
- Indirect expenses
- Corporate overhead

Factors that might be used to allocate indirect and overhead expenses include number of transactions, total volume traded, headcount, amount of capital allocated, and so on. The objectives of any cost allocation methodology should include:

- Full allocation of all expenses
- Consistent cost and revenue allocation methodologies

Deferring Sufficient Income for Future Financial Requirements

When a swap is transacted and hedged, it creates an income stream for each year over the life of the swap that is equal to the spread times the notional amount. The common accounting practice is to present value the expected income stream over the life of the swap using the yield to maturity or the zero coupon curve as the discount rate(s). This value, which is often referred to as the "day 1 NPV," is then recognized as income in the initial period.

While the present valuing of spread income is appropriate for the swaps business because it is a trading business that is marked to market regularly, the current accounting practice will inevitably lead to problems interpreting product profitability:

- ROE will appear to be higher than normal in periods when swap volume increases.
- ROE will appear to be lower than normal in periods when swap volume decreases.

The underlying reason for this is because derivative products originated in any period will continue to reside on the books until they mature or are terminated, and while they are on the books these transactions will continue to absorb financial resources. In other words, until they mature or are terminated, transactions executed in any period will have multi-year financial requirements such as:

- Credit provision in future periods
- Expenses that will be incurred to service and manage these transactions in future periods

- Liquidity and hedging costs in future periods
- Capital costs on future capital requirements
- Guaranty fee in future periods

In order to match revenue and cost recognition, the above costs should also be present valued, deducted from initial period income, and held as reserves for future financial requirements. Therefore, the types of reserves that should be held include:

1. Credit reserve
2. Administrative expense reserve
3. Liquidity/hedging reserve
4. Capital coverage reserve
5. Guaranty fee reserve

While most derivative products businesses establish credit reserves, and some even hold reserves for future administrative expenses, few hold reserves for the last three items above. In order to measure economic profitability on a fully-allocated and risk-adjusted basis, management of derivative products businesses need to ensure that all of these reserves are properly established and reflected in the performance measure system.

Incorporating Risk-Adjusted Profitability Measurement into the Management of the Derivative Products Business

In the previous sections, we have discussed the economic framework and methodologies for measuring the risk-adjusted profitability of a derivative products business. In this final section, we discuss how risk-adjusted profitability measurement can be applied to day-to-day management to maximize the risk-adjusted profitability of a derivative products business. These applications include:

- *Measuring usage of counterparty credit exposure limits.* The statistical process used for calculating expected exposure of a swap can be used to measure, on a dynamic basis, the credit exposure usage for each counterparty. To allow for the potential for an unexpected movement in market rates, many derivative products businesses use a 1, 1.65, or 2 standard deviation replacement cost curve to measure the usage of counterparty credit exposure limits (see Figure 25.12).
- *Developing pricing models.* The methodologies discussed in this chapter can be "reverse engineered" to produce pricing models for derivative product transactions (see Figure 25.13). A risk-adjusted pricing model can calculate the risk-adjusted ROE of a specific

Figure 25.12: Credit Exposure Calculations for Line Usage Purposes

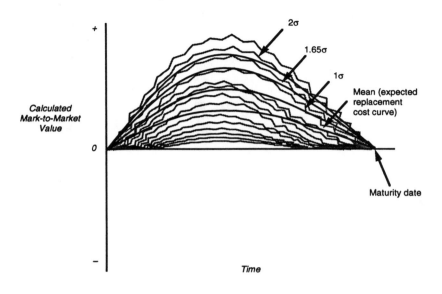

Figure 25.13: Pricing Model Applications

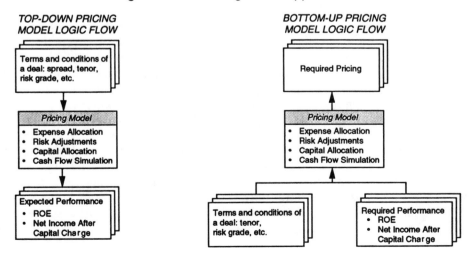

Figure 25.14: Illustrative Pricing Model for a 5-Year Single Currency Swap

		Calculate ROE Given a 5 bp Spread	Calculate Spread Given a 15% Required Return
	Notional Amount	$10 mm	$10 mm
	Swap Spread	5.0 bp	4.5 bp
	Revenue	$21,700	$19,500
Plus:	Capital Credit	600	600
Less:	Credit Reserve	500	500
Less:	Administrative Expense Reserve	13,700	13,700
Less:	Liquidity/Hedging Reserve	200	200
Less:	Guaranty Fee Reserve	1,700	1,700
Less:	Capital Coverage Reserve	1,500	1,500
	Pretax Income	4,700	2,500
Less:	Tax	1,880	1,000
	Net Income	$2,820	$1,500
	ROE	28 %	15 %

transaction for a given price, or calculate the required pricing to achieve a specific target return (see Figure 25.14 for examples of both applications).

- *Developing a swaps profitability MIS.* A swaps profitability MIS produces performance measurement reports for any segment of a derivative products business and the business overall. The swaps profitability MIS can be a powerful management tool for understanding the economic performance of a derivative products business by segmenting the overall business into its component parts, such as by product (see Figure 25.15), by customer (see Figure 25.16), and by risk grade (see Figure 25.17). These analyses can help management refocus their product, market, and pricing strategies. For example, our experience working with a number of derivative products businesses has shown that pricing on actual swap transactions is not fully differentiated to account for underlying credit risk (as indicated by the ROE by risk grade illustrated in Figure 25.17). As more competitors develop risk-adjusted return

Figure 25.15: Swaps Profitability by Product

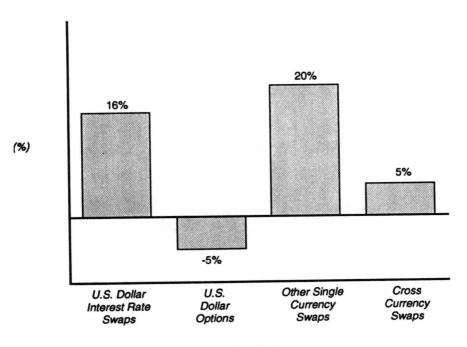

Product

Figure 25.16: Swaps MIS Report by Customer Profitability

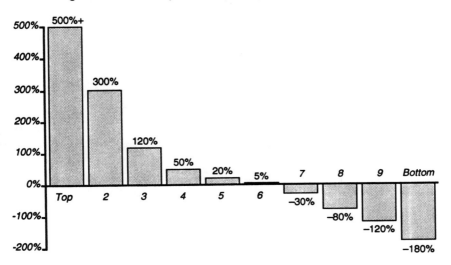

Customer Profitability by Decile

Figure 25.17: Swaps Profitability by Risk Grade

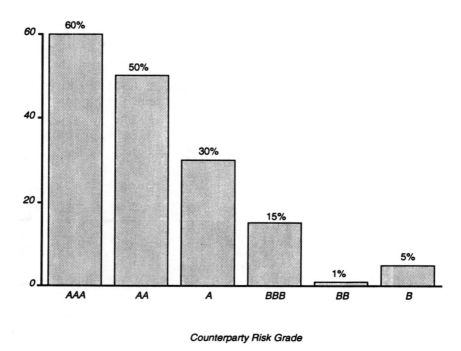

Counterparty Risk Grade

Figure 25.18: Adverse Selection Without Risk-Adjusted Pricing

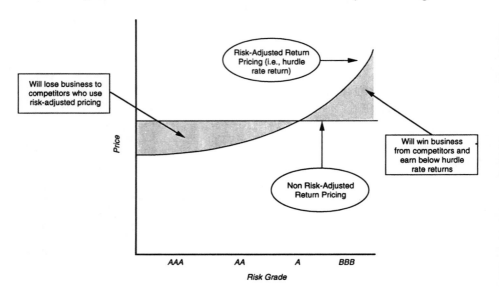

methodologies and pricing models, those without such tools will suffer adverse selection as shown on Figure 25.18. The result will be a lower credit quality portfolio of swaps that is systematically underpriced for the inherent risk.

- *Establishing incentive compensation formulas.* Key to motivating meritorious behavior at the operating level is establishing incentive compensation programs that are based on a consistent set of methodologies as those used for the MIS and pricing models (see Figure 25.19). This is the most effective way to develop congruence between the objectives of the owners (i.e., maximize shareholder value) and the objectives of the employees.

Summary

The derivative products business is fast growing and can be highly profitable for well managed operations, but it also involves complex financial risks. In this chapter, we have presented an economic framework and a set of methodologies that fully account for the risks and costs of running a derivative products business. These methodologies can help managers to answer three key questions:

1. What is the risk-adjusted profitability of my business units, customer relationships, and products?

2. How should I price this transaction given its inherent financial risks?

Figure 25.19: Consistent Application of Methodologies

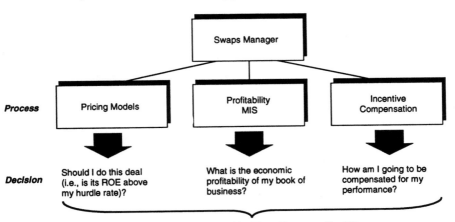

3. How should I reward my people based on merit and contribution to the overall objective of maximizing shareholder value?

We have shown that derivative products firms that adopt a risk-adjusted profitability measurement system will be able to develop significant competitive advantages. Firms that fail to manage their businesses from a risk-adjusted return perspective do so at their peril.

Part Eight

ACCOUNTING

HEDGE ACCOUNTING: A STATE-OF-THE-ART REVIEW*

J. Matthew Singleton

26

For many companies, hedge accounting is more than a mere consequence of a risk-management decision. It is a stated objective that, if not met, may result in the change or cancellation of an otherwise prudent strategy. Management declares, "We've made our funding decision. This combination of debt, swaps, and options results in the lowest all-in interest cost. How can we get hedge accounting?"

Today's accounting standards are inadequate to address the challenges of hedge accounting. While accountants have developed diverse tools with which to attack hedge accounting problems, many continue to struggle for lack of an overall accounting framework. This article will present an overview of practice today.

I will discuss the principal hedge accounting techniques used currently:

- traditional hedge accounting;
- targeted risk reduction, in which custom-designed products are used to hedge company- or product-specific risks;
- compound instrument accounting;
- synthetic instrument accounting, with a discussion of guidelines used to determine whether the effects of hedge accounting can be achieved through this technique.

What Is Hedge Accounting?

One way to define hedge accounting is that it allows the business entity to avoid mark-to-market results for a derivative position that is meant

---

*This article originally appeared in *Bank Accounting & Finance*, Fall 1991.

to hedge an asset, liability, or commitment carried at historical cost. In fact, hedge accounting generally would not be relevant were it not for our historical cost accounting framework.[1] Although the mechanics of hedge accounting for various derivatives differ, the key attribute is that *the income statement is not affected by changes in the market value of the hedging instrument alone.* In the income statement, the effects of the hedge generally are presented on a net basis—that is, as an adjustment to the income or expense item being hedged. In the balance sheet, however, hedges typically are presented on a gross basis in relation to the item being hedged when the hedge is with a different counterparty and no legal right of offset exists.[1]

For most people, it is not important to get hedge accounting for a derivative that is established as an economic hedge of a position that is marked to market; that is, to the extent that the correlation is good, the income-statement effect of the hedge and the income-statement effect of the position being hedged (both of which are marked to market) will offset each other. Mark-to-market, or nonhedge, accounting for derivatives is always available by default.

Traditional Hedge Accounting

This is the most familiar portion of hedge accounting practice. The authoritative literature covering hedge accounting is limited to Statement of Financial Accounting Standards (SFAS) No. 52, "Foreign Currency Translation," and SFAS No. 80, "Accounting for Futures Contracts." The Emerging Issues Task Force (EITF) has dealt with other questions on an ad hoc basis; these affect particular products. In addition, AICPA Issues Paper No. 86–2 covers options, but it is not binding (like FASB statements).

The authoritative hedge accounting literature applies only to a very limited set of instruments. The FASB has stated explicitly, for example, that SFAS No. 80 applies to futures but not to forwards or similar products. Likewise, SFAS No. 52 applies to most foreign currency transactions but not to foreign currency options.[2] In the last decade, the capital markets have produced an astounding array of financial products; the vast majority do not fit neatly into the parameters established by the authoritative accounting literature. Some of these instruments, such as basic interest-rate swaps, are now fundamental to the marketplace yet continue to exist, for the most part, in an accounting vacuum.

---

[1] There are exceptions to this generalization, for example, hedges of anticipated transactions. In these cases, hedge or deferral techniques may be applicable despite mark-to-market treatment of the risk transaction.

[2] The practice of not accounting for currency options under SFAS No. 52 has been reinforced by the EITF in its recent consensus on Issue 90–17, "Hedging Foreign Currency Risks with Purchased Options" (*Bank Accounting & Finance*, Summer 1991, p. 49).

Under the authoritative literature, the specific requirements for hedge accounting vary. In general, three elements must be present:

- *There is accounting risk.* If all else is held constant, changes in the interest rate, price, or foreign currency exchange rate being hedged would expose the company's earnings to fluctuations.

- *The hedge instrument is designated as a hedge of the risk.* This often occurs on a one-to-one basis, but portfolio, or macro, hedging occurs sometimes (discussed below).

- *The hedge is effective at reducing the identified risk.* Depending on the hedge instrument, this requirement may be applied on an enterprise basis (for example, futures) or on a transaction basis (for example, currency forwards). Cross-hedging may or may not be permissible, and correlation tests may or may not be specifically required.

With these explicit rules, it is relatively easy to determine whether or not a given transaction qualifies for hedge accounting.[3] The problem, as mentioned above, is that many hedge transactions today involve hedge instruments other than those covered by the authoritative literature. For these instruments, we must look elsewhere for answers.

Targeted Risk Reduction: Analogies to Traditional Hedge Accounting

Increasingly, bankers are developing customized hedging products to address very specific types of risk. Examples include commodity swaps that operate like interest-rate swaps but are designed to hedge a specific commodity price, such as fuel oil, and instruments to mitigate the risk of prepayments for mortgage bankers. For these innovations, authoritative pronouncements cannot be applied directly because the hedging instruments involved in a particular transaction are not within the scope of FASB or EITF documents.

Like most derivatives, these products involve an agreement between two counterparties, a notional principal amount, and some type of formula for periodic cash settlements based on reference to some measurable market benchmark. They can be designed on an asset- or a liability-specific basis or on a company-specific basis. As such, they offer a form of *targeted risk reduction.*

These products pose an accounting problem because traditional hedge accounting criteria cannot be applied to them directly, and synthetic instrument accounting (see below) may not fit either. Yet for many

---

[3] One not uncommon issue is determining whether there is adequate correlation between the risk position and the hedge.

of these instruments, it is apparent that an economic hedge has taken place. In practice, accountants make analogies to the traditional framework to determine whether some form of hedge accounting should be used for these instruments. In particular, accountants look for the familiar attributes of traditional hedges—risk identification, designation, and effectiveness in risk reduction—as conditions for achieving hedge accounting.

One of the more troublesome aspects of dealing with these special-purpose transactions is demonstrating the effectiveness of the hedge. For example, is complete risk elimination necessary or would partial risk reduction in limited scenarios be adequate to show effectiveness? And what happens when there are multiple risks, for example, interest-rate risk and prepayment risk?

In some instances, accountants have attempted to model the economic and accounting effects of the transaction to determine whether risk reduction has taken place. Typically, they take market data from recent periods and project the pro forma performance of the hedge against the risk position to see if a significant pattern of risk reduction can be established. In particular, they look at changes in cash flows and market values with and without the hedge and ascertain whether the addition of the hedge produces a demonstrably more stable pattern of income.

Compound Instrument Accounting

Compound instruments are single financial instruments that combine the elements of one or more basic cash instruments and derivatives. Instruments that involve a bond and an embedded option, for example, callable and convertible debt, are familiar compound instruments.

For decades, it has been acceptable for issuer and investor to account for compound instruments as if they were conventional debt securities—that is, these bond/option combinations are treated as bonds and accounted for at historical cost. Although some special accounting questions arise as a result of the possible option exerise,[4] the option still is accounted for as an integral part of the bond. Using this integrated approach, the option is not accounted for on a stand-alone basis; thus, it is in effect accounted for at historical cost, not market value.

Today, more and more financial instruments involve multiple, identifiable economic components (that is, cash instruments and embedded derivatives). Examples include puttable bonds, participating or shared appreciation mortgages, debt convertible into an asset of the issuer, and notes indexed to various market indices such as gold prices.

---

[4] These include amortization of premium or discount, debt extinguishment, and common stock issuance accounting.

Lately, accounting practice for these compound instruments has been mixed. Sometimes accountants split the instruments into their underlying components and account for them separately. For example, debt indexed to the Standard & Poors index (under which the investor is guaranteed par value but would receive more if the index increased) could be split into two components—straight debt and an option—for accounting purposes. Conversely, accountants may make analogies to traditional compound instruments (like convertible debt) and account for the new instruments on an integrated basis using historical cost. In this way, they can achieve a form of hedge accounting for the embedded derivative.

In deciding which type of accounting to use for a particular compound instrument, practitioners probably will rely primarily on the similarity of the instrument in question to those for which historical cost accounting is used. For example, say a gold producer plans to repay at so-called gold loan through future production. This loan probably would qualify for historical cost/hedge accounting because, in essence, the producer has locked in its price on sales of future production. In contrast, an S&P-indexed note with an embedded option written by an issuer with no related asset probably would not qualify for historical cost treatment.

Synthetic Instrument Accounting

In an increasing number of circumstances, two or more instruments are linked together to create the same economic result as that of one recognizable financial instrument. For example, say a company wants to obtain a particular asset or a liability. It can go about this in two ways—directly or indirectly (that is, synthetically)—depending on the most effective execution in the marketplace. The classic example is an entity that issues fixed-rate debt and enters into an interest-rate swap at the same time. In the swap, it receives fixed-rate interest and pays floating-rate interest on a notional principal amount equal to the principal on the debt. The combination of the debt and the swap converts fixed-rate debt to "synthetic" floating-rate debt.

Synthetic instrument accounting is the flip side of compound instrument accounting. Synthetic instrument accounting is treating the combination of instruments in the way that the instrument they replace would be treated—in this case, accounting for the fixed-rate debt and swap together as floating-rate debt. Other common examples of synthetic instruments follow:

- Callable debt synthetically changed to noncallable debt through writing (selling) an option on an interest-rate swap that permits the holder to pay floating and receive fixed on the call date.

- Callable debt with the mandatory maturity synthetically shortened by writing (selling) an option on an interest-rate swap permitting the holder to pay fixed and receive floating on the call date.

- Synthetic puttable debt created from callable debt by writing (selling) *both* of the options described above.

- Synthetic yen debt created from dollar-denominated debt and a currency swap.

All of these synthetic debt instruments behave like basic identifiable financial instruments in the marketplace. Because it believes that the total cost is lower, the borrower chooses a combination of instruments instead of one identifiable instrument.

In practice, synthetic instrument accounting is common. Sometimes the same results could be achieved by applying hedge accounting in other cases, the combination of instruments does not satisfy the criteria for hedge accounting. For example, the synthetic instrument may well *increase* transaction and enterprise risk.

Traditional hedge accounting analysis can be applied only to hedge vehicles covered by the accounting literature (among them futures contracts, foreign currency transactions, and certain options). Even in these instances, it is likely that some transactions designed to create a synthetic instrument would fail to achieve hedge accounting (for example, because accounting risk is increased, not decreased). Thus market-value accounting might be required for the hedge components of the synthetic instrument. This is a problem because the resulting hybrid accounting clearly does not reflect the essence of the transaction, that is, the creation of a single financial instrument.

Synthetic instrument accounting attempts to deal with this problem. Mechanically, synthetic instrument accounting involves accounting in the income statement for a combination of cash and derivative instruments in the same manner as one would account for the cash instrument that they replicate. To ascertain whether synthetic instrument accounting is appropriate, practitioners have applied some or all of the following informal guidelines.

It is better to create a familiar synthetic instrument than an unusual one. With familiar instruments, the accounting is better understood and analysis more easily accepted.

For example, synthetic instrument accounting is more understandable for a synthetic fixed-rate, noncallable bond than for a synthetic puttable, commodity-indexed bond. To assess familiarity, it is important not only to make a general assessment of the market for the synthetically developed instrument but also to assess the company's own experience with the instrument. For example, a synthetic put bond might be unconventional in general but not for a company that has a history of issuing put bonds directly and wants to improve the efficiency of future put bond issues by doing them synthetically.

It is best to have a synthetic instrument comprised of a mix of cash instruments and derivatives rather than of only one of these categories. Practice has been reluctant to accept the idea of a derivative as a hedge of another derivative or off-balance-sheet risk. Likewise, as alluded to in EITF Issue 87–1, "Deferral Accounting for Cash Securities that Are Used to Hedge Rate or Price Risk," hedge accounting is generally prohibited for cash instruments used as hedges.

It is better to reduce risk than to increase it. If you *do* increase risk, the smaller the increase the better.

The closer the matching of the terms (and cash flows) of the synthetic to the instrument it represents, the better.

The more explicit the existing accounting guidance, the less likely it is that synthetic instrument accounting concepts will apply. While practitioners can be somewhat pragmatic in developing accounting solutions for novel or unique transactions, existing rules cannot be ignored. For example, instruments clearly covered by SFAS No. 52, SFAS No. 80, and EITF issues must comply with those standards.

It is best to avoid situations involving a dangling, or unmatched derivative. Partial hedges, when the size of the position hedged exceeds the notional balance of the hedging instrument, generally are accepted. In contrast, many accountants would feel less comfortable using a derivative tall—that is, a derivative with a longer maturity than that of the hedged instrument—to extend the maturity of an identified cash instrument.

When selling an option, it is better to sell one that you already own. Selling, or writing an option involves risk taking; generally, this precludes hedge accounting. Some accountants will make an exception when the clear intent is to dispose of an option already owned. For example, many accountants will argue in favor of synthetic instrument accounting for a synthetic noncallable bond created by combining a callable bond and a written option on an interest-rate swap. Some of those accountants would not permit synthetic instrument accounting for a synthetic put bond created by combining a similar option with a noncallable bond issuance.

It is better to create the synthetic instrument earlier than later. The analogy to a familiar instrument is best made at inception and for the entire life of the security. Down-the-road synthetic creations are troublesome because the intent of the action—and therefore the appropriate accounting analogy—is less clear. For example, a decision to sell a call provision embedded in a callable bond issuance after the passage of time may take on characteristics of a bond issuance and refinancing, or a speculation, rather than characteristics of a synthetic noncallable bond created at inception.

The motive for the synthetic issue is important: economic motives are more compelling than accounting motives. For example, a company is more likely to achieve synthetic instrument accounting based on the argument that it can lower the overall cost of funds of a borrowing by doing it synthetically than based on the argument that it could produce a desired pattern of income.

The likelihood of achieving synthetic instrument accounting is greater if the underlying cash instrument is of a type similar to the synthetic instrument being created. Converting a bond into a different type of bond is more likely to achieve synthetic instrument accounting than converting an equity or a physical commodity into a synthetic bond.

Flowchart for Choosing the Accounting Method

Figure 26.1 shows the questions to ask in deciding whether any of these hedge accounting techniques applies to a particular transaction.

Hedging Indirect, or Strategic, Exposures

Corporate managers have become more sophisticated in their analysis of risk and increasingly have acted to hedge risk. For example, it is no surprise that most analyses of currency risk focus on a company's foreign-currency-denominated positions or operations. These typically include purchases, sales, investments, and anticipated transactions in currencies other than the company's own native, or functional, currency. But some have argued that even companies that purchase, sell, or invest only in their functional currency may be exposed to foreign-currency risk. This is because market prices may be driven primarily by foreign competitors whose local market pricing decisions (along with the relationship of currency rates) dictate the prices in *all* markets.

Consider the case of a U.S. car manufacturer that produces cars domestically using locally procured materials and sells them exclusively to U.S. consumers. Nevertheless, due to the intensity of competition with Japanese manufacturers, the company's sales margins vary directly in proportion to the dollar yen exchange rate.

From an accounting standpoint, this issue is troublesome because the U.S. manufacturer has no direct exposure to foreign markets. Accordingly, accountants have been reluctant to permit hedge accounting for transactions to protect against this type of risk. In fact, in Issue 90–17, the EITF recently concluded that hedge accounting would not be appropriate in this situation, thus adding to the frustration of those who seek to hedge broadly.

Figure 26.1: Flowchart for Choosing a Hedge Accounting Technique

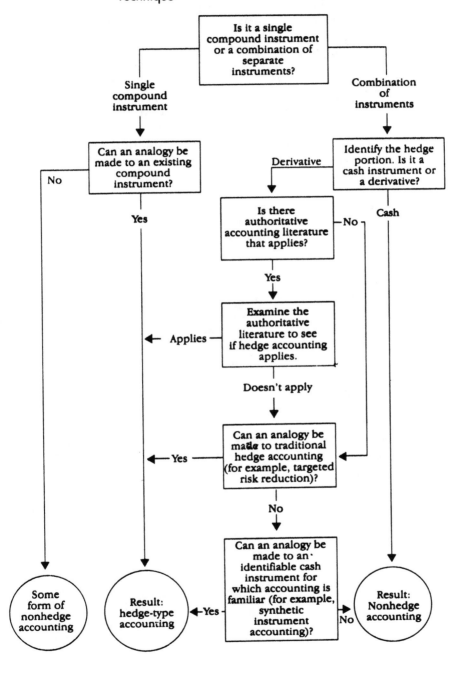

Macro Hedging, or Hedging on a Portfolio Basis

In some respects, portfolio hedging is widely accepted. For example, SFAS No. 80 specifically acknowledges that it is acceptable to hedge on a portfolio basis.[5]

The issue becomes more complicated for a bank that may enter into derivative positions for two reasons: either to make a market as a dealer in those instruments or to hedge the bank's own asset/liability interest-rate position. The potential accounting ramifications are enormous, because banks account for those two activities differently. Market-making or dealing activities are reported on a mark-to-market basis. Asset/liability management activities generally are reported on a historical cost, or accrual, basis of accounting. Radically different income-statement effects can result over the life of an interest-rate swap depending on which accounting basis is employed.

In the case of the market-making activities, there is no controversy about the use of market-value accounting for derivatives.[6] However, when banks undertake asset/liability management using derivatives, attitudes differ about the criteria that must be met to achieve historical cost accounting. At one end of the spectrum, some argue that management need do no more than merely *designate* the derivative as an investment or as part of the asset/liability management activities or treasury activities of the bank. (It is noteworthy that the designation would not necessarily link the derivative to any specific group of assets or liabilities.) These proponents argue that, de facto, the derivative exists solely to alter the bank's interest-rate profile to achieve management's objective; thus, no further justification is needed. Further, they argue that the direction of the change in the institution's interest-rate gap is not important (for example, risk can be increased, according to these proponents).

At the other extreme, some accountants argue that all the traditional identification and risk-reduction criteria must be met before hedge accounting can be used on a portfolio basis. In other words, an individual

---

[5] "One or more futures contracts may be designated as a hedge of either an individual item or an identifiable group of essentially similar items (for example, government securities that have similar maturities and coupon rates)," SFAS No, 80, Footnote 6.

"Some enterprises (for example, commodity dealers) may use futures contracts to hedge a net exposure comprising inventory held for sale and firm commitment to purchase and sell essentially similar assets. If associating individual futures contracts with the assets on hand or specific commitments is impractical because of the volume and frequency of transactions, reasonable allocations of the results of futures contracts between assets or commitments on hand at the end of a reporting period and assets sold during the period may be used. The method of allocation shall be consistent from period to period." SFAS NO. 80, Paragraph 8.

[6] There are questions about appropriate methods to calculate market value. These are beyond the scope of this article.

derivative would have to be linked to specific transactions and risk reduction would have to be demonstrated, at least on a transaction basis if not on a portfolio or enterprise basis.

Other accountants take positions between these two extremes. This issue has been simmering in recent years, since different banks (with the concurrence of their auditors) have followed different approaches. The question has also been an issue for regulators. This is a troublesome problem; discussion should continue.

Conclusion

Eventually, the FASB financial instruments project will settle these issues. Most of us are optimistic that clarity, consistency among products, and a closer alignment of accounting to the economics will result. Before that happens, the EITF or the regulators may take a more active role in shaping hedge accounting. In the meantime, companies and their auditors must do their best with the existing guidelines. While far from perfect (and they will evolve), the guidelines do a reasonable job of providing consistent, appropriate accounting for derivatives.

ACCOUNTING FOR FUTURES CONTRACTS AND THE EFFECT ON EARNINGS VARIABILITY*

Jennifer Francis

27

Most studies evaluating the effect of a regulatory accounting change on firm behavior focus on the information content of the security market's response to the announcement of the change.[1] If the regulatory change has no direct economic effect on the firm, market efficiency stipulates that no price reaction should occur. A price reaction may result, however, if accounting earnings are used by regulators or included in compensation or debt contracts. One problem with these studies is that because there is no well-articulated theory linking accounting measurement rules to capital asset prices, it is difficult to interpret any ensuing market reaction (Foster 1980).

This study describes an alternative approach to examining the information content of regulatory change that does not require specification of a link between accounting measurement rules and security prices. Using simulation and empirical tests, I compare the effects of alternative accounting rules on firms' reported earnings streams. Specifically, I examine how the reported earnings of two types of financial institutions (commercial banks and brokerage firms) are affected by the accounting procedures for futures contracts stipulated in the Board of Governors of

*This article originally appeared in *The Accounting Review*, vol. 65, no. 4, October 1990. Reprinted with permission. Financial support was provided by the Fuqua Center for Accounting Studies. Permission to use the data was granted by Sheshunoff, Inc. The assistance of both organizations is gratefully acknowledged. Helpful comments were provided by Dan Collins, Doug Foster, Donna Philbrick, and two anonymous referees.
[1] For example, see prior work on line of business reporting disclosures (Collins 1975); replacement cost disclosures (Beaver et al. 1980); FASB Statement No. 2 (Dukes et al. 1980); and FASB Statement No. 19 (Dyckman and Smith 1979).

the Federal Reserve System's "Policy Statement Concerning Forward Placement or Delayed Delivery Contracts and Interest Rate Futures Contracts" (Docket No. R-0261, March 1980) and in the Financial Accounting Standard Board's Statement No. 80, "Accounting for Futures Contracts" (SFAS No. 80). The Board of Governors statement, effective January 1, 1980, permitted commercial banks the option of carrying futures contracts used as hedges on a mark-to-market or lower-of-cost-or-market basis. Effective January 1985, SFAS No. 80 requires that commercial banks use "hedge accounting" for futures contracts used as "micro hedges," but that they recognize immediately in income any changes in the market value of futures contracts used as "macro hedges." Macro hedges reduce the sensitivity of a firm's income (or market value) to changes in interest rates but are not linked to identifiable assets or obligations; micro hedges focus on risk reduction in terms of a single, identifiable transaction. Hedge accounting requires firms to recognize changes in the market value of futures contracts that qualify as a micro hedge[2] as adjustments to the carrying amount of the hedged item. For example, if a bank uses futures contracts to micro hedge a variable rate loan from changes in interest rates, then changes in the value of the futures contracts are recorded as adjustments to the value of the loan. Alternatively, changes in the market value of futures contracts used as macro hedges are recognized currently in income regardless of whether the futures contracts are closed. This treatment is similar to the mark-to-market basis advocated in the Board of Governors statement.

Prior to SFAS No. 80, firms using futures contracts for investment or speculation (such as investment and brokerage companies) were required to account for changes in the market value of futures contracts using the lower-of-cost-or-market method. SFAS No. 80 replaces the lower-of-cost-or-market basis with the requirement that all gains and losses on futures contracts used for investment or speculation be recognized immediately in income.

In summary, SFAS No. 80 (1) retained the mark-to-market basis advocated by the Board of Governors for futures contracts used as macro hedges; (2) abolished the lower-of-cost-or-market basis for carrying futures contracts used as micro hedges, as macro hedges, or for investment or speculation; (3) required firms to use hedge accounting for futures contracts that qualify as hedges; and (4) required firms that use futures contracts for investment or speculation to switch from the lower-of-cost-or-market basis to the immediate recognition of changes in the value of futures contracts.

---

[2] A qualifying hedge must meet two criteria. First, the hedged item must expose the firm to price or interest rate risk. Second, the futures contracts must reduce that exposure and be designated as a hedge.

The problem with SFAS No. 80 and the Board of Governors statement, as perceived by some practitioners and researchers, is that recognizing changes in the value of futures contracts used to macro hedge immediately in income may require firms to recognize gains and losses on futures contracts and hedged items in different periods. Opponents argue that this asymmetry increases the variability of earnings and discourages effective use of futures contracts to hedge interest rate risk.[3] This argument implies that shareholders, managers, or investors perceive an increase in earnings variability as an undesirable event. This may be the case, for example, if political and contracting costs are positively associated with earnings volatility. Prior studies support these concerns: Benston and Krasney (1978) conclude that smooth earnings streams shield firms from regulatory intervention and its associated costs; Moses (1987) finds that lower earnings variability benefits managers via its relation with compensation and bonus schemes; and Diamond (1984) and Smith and Stulz (1985) argue that lower earnings variability reduces the probability and expected costs of bankruptcy. Private or closely held firms may also try to reduce the variability of income to reduce the unsystematic risk of the firm.

With respect to earnings variability, current accounting rules raise several questions. First, for a given macro hedge, does immediate recognition lead to a more variable earnings stream than hedge accounting? Since futures contracts are used to reduce interest rate risk, many critics have argued that immediate recognition is diametrically opposed to the perceived benefits of hedging. This phenomenon is particularly troubling to large users of macro hedges such as commercial banks.[4] A second question addresses a second group affected by SFAS No. 80: firms that invest or speculate with futures contracts. Specifically, I examine whether the reported earnings streams of a sample of brokerage firms increased following the implementation of SFAS No. 80. If SFAS No. 80 increases earnings variability, a third question is to what extent an increase in the variability of reported earnings influences hedging, investment, and speculation with futures contracts?

The purpose of this paper is to address the first and second questions to determine whether there is any reason for examining the third issue. I examine the association between the current accounting rules for futures contracts and the variability of reported earnings in two ways. First, I simulate the effect on earnings of using futures contracts to macro hedge the

---

[3] For example, see Booth et al. (1984).
[4] Commercial bankers are likely to use macro, rather than micro, hedges for two reasons. First, it is often difficult to identify the interest rate exposure of isolated transactions, and required disclosures provide a readily available measure of net exposure. Second, it is possible to *increase* the bank's exposure to interest rate risk by using micro hedges for some assets and liabilities without hedging others (Breeden and Giarla in Fabozzi 1988, 889–986).

interest rate exposure positions of a sample of commercial banks. The simulation results show that for a given level of hedging, immediate recognition significantly increases earnings variability vis-àg-vis hedge accounting. This finding, which is robust to the size of the hedge and the measure of earnings, suggests at least one motivation for a change in commercial bank hedging behavior following SFAS No. 80. Second, I examine the variability of reported earnings of a sample of broker-dealers before and after the effective date of SFAS No. 80 to determine whether immediate recognition of gains and losses on futures contracts used for investment or speculation increases earnings dispersion. The empirical tests show no significant difference between the variability of post-1984 and pre-1985 reported earnings streams.

The remainder of the paper is organized as follows. Section I describes prior research on futures contracts and the variability of earnings. Although these studies focus on the effect that hedging activity *per se* has on earnings volatility (rather than the influence that a change in the accounting treatment for hedges has on earnings variability), they provide a useful starting point for this research. Section II provides background information about how banks measure interest rate exposure and their hedge position. Section III discusses factors influencing the accounting for futures contracts used to macro hedge these positions. Section IV describes the simulation. Section V empirically examines the earnings variability of broker-dealers before and after the implementation of SFAS No. 80. Section VI summarizes the findings.

I. Prior Research

Prior research on the effectiveness of futures contracts in reducing volatility compares the variability of hedged and unhedged profits (Hill and Schneeweis 1984; Koppenhaver 1983). These studies define unhedged profits as the change in the value of the hedged item(s), and hedged profits as the change in the value of the hedged items plus the change in the value of the futures contracts. For example, suppose that a firm macro hedges $100 million in net interest sensitive assets with futures contracts. During the year, the value of the net asset position and the value of the futures contracts change as interest rates change. In fact, if the futures contracts are effectively hedging interest rate risk, gains and losses on the futures contracts offset losses and gains on the hedged items. If the value of the net asset position rises to $125 million and the value of the futures contracts declines to $140 million dollars, then unhedged profits are $25 million ($125 million less $100 million) and hedged profits equal –$15 million ($25 million less $40 million change on futures contracts). Using these definitions, prior studies simulate a series of macro hedges and compare the variability of hedged profits with the variability of unhedged profits. The studies find large reductions in variability in the presence of hedging: Hill and Schneeweis (1984) document declines in excess of 40 percent and Koppenhaver (1983) reports 80 percent reductions in the variability of hedged versus unhedged profits.

Two points regarding the definition of profits used in these studies are important. First, neither of the studies focuses on accounting earnings. Accounting earnings typically include a host of expense and revenue accounts that prior research ignores, e.g., interest income, depreciation, extraordinary items, etc. Accounting earnings may also exclude gains and losses that have not been realized, such as changes in the value of some hedged items. Second, prior research ignores the timing problems associated with income recognition.

This study addresses both of these issues in the context of commercial banks. This industry provides a sample of potential macro hedge users that is concerned about the income effects of SFAS No. 80.[5] In order to examine the income effects of mark-to-market accounting, more information about how commercial banks measure and report interest rate exposure positions and about the implementation of hedging strategies is required. These are detailed in the next section.

II. Hedging Interest Rate Exposure

Commercial banks earn profits by anticipating interest rate changes and constructing portfolios of assets and liabilities that benefit from these movements. Under "gap management,"[6] bankers set the desired interest rate exposure position by mismatching the maturities of rate-sensitive assets and liabilities. Assets and liabilities are sensitive to movements in interest rates over a particular period if they reprice (as a result of a change in interest rates) within that time frame. For example, a three-month certificate of deposit reprices within a three-month horizon and, therefore, is

---

[5] The Federal Reserve Bank of Kansas conducted a survey and found that 40 percent of the sample commercial banks using futures contracts believed accounting guidelines "significantly discourage" futures use, while another 36 percent were "somewhat discouraged" (Goodman and Langer 1983).

[6] Exposure to interest rate risk may be defined with respect to reported earnings or the market value of the firm. The focus on earnings versus value is an important one since each requires different management techniques: "gap management" insulates earnings from interest rate risk, while "duration analysis" protects the market value of the bank from unanticipated changes in interest rates. Although superior to gap management, duration analysis requires detailed information about the timing, amounts, and interest rate sensitivity of cash flows. For many banks, these data requirements and implementation difficulties render the application of duration analysis impractical. Gap management is a much simpler method of managing interest rate risk that has the implicit support of regulatory agencies that require certain gap-related disclosures. For these reasons, this study uses gap analysis to measure interest rate exposure.

sensitive to 90-day movements in interest rates. Gap management defines the bank's interest rate exposure position as the mismatch for each repricing horizon:

$$GAP(i)_t = RSA(i)_t - RSL(i)_t, \tag{1}$$

where:

$RSA(i)_t$ = book value of assets at time t repricing during horizon j;
$RSL(i)_t$ = book value of liabilities at time t repricing within horizon j; and
j = repricing horizon

The purpose of a hedging strategy is to mitigate the firm's exposure to anticipated or unanticipated changes in interest rates. Because of the risk-profit tradeoff, banks may hedge selectively in that they bear risk when they think they can forecast rate changes. For example, suppose management expects rates to decline but is unable (or it is too costly) to construct a negative gap position. By hedging, the bank mitigates the expected losses on the positive gap position. If careful gap management fails to insulate earnings, earnings may be protected with interest rate futures, swap and option contracts, and forward rate agreements.

This study focuses on hedging strategies that use interest rate futures contracts to protect earnings. An interest rate futures contract is an agreement made with a clearing corporation to buy or sell financial securities (e.g., Treasury securities, certificates of deposit, etc.) in the future. There are currently seven types of interest rate futures contracts traded on the two most active exchanges (Chicago Board of Options and International Monetary Fund): 91-day Treasury bill futures, ten-year Treasury note futures, 20-year Treasury bond futures, domestic certificates of deposit futures, 91-day Eurodollar time deposit futures, GNMA eight percent collateralized deposit receipts, and GNMA II futures. By far the most actively traded futures contracts are 91-day Treasury bills, 91-day Eurodollar time deposits, and 20-year Treasury bonds. Table 27.1 provides a summary of selected institutional features of these futures contracts. The feature of an interest rate futures contract most relevant to this study is its price: as rates fall (rise) the price of the futures contract rises (falls). Therefore, when using interest rate futures to hedge movements in interest rates, a bank will (1) buy futures contracts (i.e., take a long position) when hedging rate decreases, and (2) sell futures contracts (i.e., take a short position) when hedging rate increases.

The amount of exposure to hedge depends on the acceptable level of interest rate risk. Because regulatory constraints prohibit banks from

Table 27.1: Characteristics of Selected Futures Contracts

Futures Contract	Exchange Traded[a]	Contract Size	Last Trading Day	Margin Requirement[b]
91-Day Treasury Bill	IMM	$1,000,000	Wednesday following third Monday of delivery month	$3,500
91-Day Eurodollar Time Deposit	IMM	$1,000,000	Second London business day before third Wednesday of delivery month	$3,500
20-Year Treasury Bond	CBT	$ 100,000	Seven business days prior to last business day of delivery	$3,500

[a] Futures contracts are traded on the International Monetary Market (IMM), the Chicago Board of Trade (CBT), and the American Commodities Exchange, the Midamerica Commodity Exchange, the London International Financial Futures Exchange, and the Financial Instrument Exchange.
[b] Both the IMM and CBT require initial margins of $2,000 and maintenance margins of $1,500 per standard contract.

increasing their exposure to interest rate risk,[7] gap management defines an upper bound on the acceptable hedge. In the simulation, I assume initially that banks hedge their entire exposure position, $|GAP(j)_t|$; this assumption is later relaxed to consider partial hedges. The hedging strategy for an exposed position of length j at time t is as follows:

$$H(j)_t = \begin{cases} \text{long position of amount} \left|GAP(j)_t\right| & \text{if } GAP(j)_t > 0 \\ \text{short position of amount} \left|GAP(j)_j\right| & \text{if } GAP(j)_t < 0. \end{cases} \quad (2)$$

The hedging strategy of a hypothetical bank is illustrated in the Appendix.

III. Accounting for Futures Contracts by Commercial Banks

Commercial banks must recognize changes in the market value of futures contracts used as macro hedges immediately in income (SFAS No.

---

[7] Commercial banks are not permitted to invest or speculate with futures contracts (Office of the Comptroller of the Currency, Banking Circular No. 79, March 1980).

80). As previously noted, practitioners and researchers argue that this accounting treatment increases the variability of earnings. Whether immediate recognition affects the volatility of reported earnings, however, depends on several factors: (1) the correlation between the futures contract and exposure position; (2) the timing of the recognition of changes in the value of futures contracts and the profit from the exposure position; (3) unhedged earnings; and (4) the variability of unhedged earnings.

The correlation between the futures contracts and the exposed position determines the direction and magnitude of the profit from the hedging strategy. When the futures position is negatively correlated with the exposure position, gains offset losses. If the futures position is positively correlated with the exposure position, gains and losses are magnified, accentuating the exposure of bank earnings to interest rate movements. Besides direction and magnitude, the timing of the recognition of the profit from futures contracts and exposure positions affects earnings variability. Gains are *not* offset when profits from futures contracts are recognized in a different period than are profits on the exposure position. Finally, observed unhedged earnings and their variability also influence earnings. Consequently, while immediate recognition *may* increase the volatility of earnings, reported earnings are also affected by the magnitude and direction of profits from futures contracts, exposure positions, and the variability of unhedged earnings.

IV. Simulation

Data

In this section, I simulate the effect that immediate recognition versus hedge accounting has on reported earnings. To avoid creating unrealistic scenarios, I use empirical data collected from a sample of 76 non-hedging commercial banks located in Pennsylvania to calibrate the simulation.[8] Table 27.2 presents descriptive statistics characterizing the sample banks during 1983–1988. A comparison (not reported) of the sample banks with the population of U.S. banks showed that the sample

---

[8] Available information disclosed whether the bank did (did not) use a hedging strategy in 1986, 1987, and 1988. No information on the extent of their use was reported. While the use (nonuse) of a hedging strategy in these years does not imply their use (nonuse) in previous years, data about the sample banks use of interest rate hedging strategies in prior years are unavailable. Also, although a "no-hedging" strategy may be optimal for commercial banks, it is unlikely to be the case for the sample period. Francis (forthcoming) finds little association between either the direction or magnitude of commercial bank gap positions and either the perfect foresight or rational expectations forecast of interest rate changes during 1983–1986. These findings suggest that a "no-hedging" strategy is probably not optimal for most commercial banks. Consequently, critics' concern that the accounting treatment for futures contracts discourages firms from hedging takes on more significance.

Table 27.2: Descriptive Information About Sample Commercial Banks (in $000,000s Except as Indicated)

	1983		1984		1985		1986		1987		1988	
	Mean	Median	Mean	Median	Mean	Median	Mean	Median	Mean	Median	Mean	Median
Assets	914	269	1,101	291	1,220	338	1,352	357	1,331	353	1,430	358
Book Value of Equity	57	18	61	20	69	25	78	26	73	26	77	29
Net Interest Margins	27.7	8.8	31.8	9.8	35.5	12.3	39.4	13.3	40.1	12.6	43.7	13.8
Net Income Before Loan Loss Provision and Security Gains/Losses	7.1	2.2	11.3	3.5	13.7	4.4	15.7	5.0	17.4	5.8	20.1	6.2
Net Income Before Extraordinary Items and Taxes	6.9	2.2	7.8	2.9	10.9	3.9	11.4	4.5	1.6	4.1	10.1	4.4
Net Aftertax Income	6.5	2.3	7.3	2.8	10.4	10.6	4.0	1.6	4.0	9.9	4.3	
Return on Assets	.92%	.93%	.96%	.97%	1.06%	1.03%	1.06%	1.05%	1.09%	1.01%	1.10%	1.17%

banks are similar to the population based on size (total assets) and profitability (median return on asset) dimensions.

Design

In the simulation, the absolute value of the horizon j gap position at December 31 defines the hedge position.[9] $GAP(j)_t$ measures are examined for three repricing horizons: one-year, five-year, and over five-years. The one-year gap does not pose a timing problem because unhedged annual earnings contain gains and losses on rate sensitive assets and liabilities with maturities of one year or less; gains and losses on futures contracts used to macro hedge these items are also included in annual earnings because they are *realized* during the year. Five-year and over five-year repricing horizons pose a timing problem because gains and losses on rate-sensitive assets and liabilities maturing after one year are not recognized currently (except if they are sold prematurely); immediate recognition requires, however, that changes in the value of futures contracts be included in current reported earnings.

The macro hedge generated by the one-year, five-year, and over five-year gaps is termed the "full hedge," while the macro hedge generated by just the one-year gap horizon is termed the "restricted hedge." If immediate recognition increases earnings variability vis-à-vis hedge accounting, then the volatility of "full hedge earnings" (unhedged earnings plus the profit on the full hedge) will exceed "restricted hedge earnings" (unhedged earnings plus the profit on the restricted hedge) because the latter excludes gains and losses on futures contracts used to hedge items maturing after one year. Hence, restricted and full hedge earnings may be viewed as earnings reported under hedge accounting and immediate recognition accounting, respectively.

Table 27.3 describes the macro hedges simulated for the 1983–1987 period. Average hedge positions for each repricing horizon, as well as the number of banks taking long and short positions, are reported. Given the macro hedging strategy specified in equation (2), most sample banks had short positions to hedge one-year gaps and long positions to hedge five- and over five-year repricing horizons. These positions are consistent with the average negative one-year gap positions and positive five- and over five-year gap positions of the sample banks.

The gain or loss on futures contracts depends on the type and the number of futures contracts purchased or sold, the correlation of the futures contract with the exposure position interest rates, and the account-

---

[9] Although gap positions change between balance sheet dates to reflect changes in interest rate forecasts and gap management policies, year-end gap positions should reflect management beliefs conditional on information available at year-end. Year-end regulatory filings and examinations also motivate commercial bankers to construct exposure positions that are consistent with gap policies and interest rate expectations.

Table 27.3 Simulation Results: Size and Type of Hedge Position 1983–1988

	Average in $000s		Hedge Position $H(j)_t^b$			
	$\lvert GAP(j)\rvert_t$	$GAP(j)_t^a$	# Firms Short	# Firms Long	# Firms None	Average $N(j)_t^c$
Year: 1983						
1-year	$ 33,064	$-19,139	51	24	1[d]	(38)
5-year	66,004	65,839	2	74	0	16
+5-year	78,719	678,719	0	76	0	19
Year: 1984						
1-year	32,610	−22,086	54	22	0	(44)
5-year	78,511	78,364	2	64	0	19
+5-year	71,625	71,625	0	76	0	17
Year: 1985						
1-year	39,338	−23,064	49	27	0	(46)
5-year	78,997	78,750	2	74	0	19
+5-year	84,164	84,164	0	76	0	20
Year: 1986						
1-year	60,988	−53,367	64	12	0	(106)
5-year	101,700	101,016	2	74	0	25
+5-year	88,436	88,436	0	76	0	22
Year: 1987						
1-year	51,851	−44,830	59	16	1[d]	(89)
5-year	102,283	101,920	2	74	0	25
+5-year	88,549	88,549	0	76	0	22

[a] $GAP(j)_t = [RSA(j)_t - RSL(j)_t]$ where $RSA(j)_t$ = assets repricing within a horizon of length j; and $RSL(j)_t$ = liabilities repricing within a horizon of length j.
[b] $H(j)_t$ = hedge strategy for an exposed position of length j at time t; a long position of amount $\lvert GAP(j)_t\rvert$ if $GAP(j)_t < 0$.
[c] $N(j)_t$ = number of futures contracts purchased (sold).
[d] One sample bank perfectly matched its one-year rate sensitive assets and liabilities thus eliminating the need for a one-year hedge.

ing treatment for futures contracts. The type of futures contract to choose is the one whose implied yield shows the strongest correlation with the yield on the components of the exposure position. The majority of the assets and liabilities comprising the gap positions of the sample commercial banks are as follows:

1-year: short-term certificates of deposit, commercial paper, federal funds and short-term corporate borrowings.

5-year: Treasury securities maturing after one year, commercial and real estate loans, and mortgages.

over 5-year: Treasury securities maturing after one year, commercial and real estate loans, and mortgages.

Table 27.4 shows the correlations between the yields on these items and the yields on the most actively traded interest rate futures contracts computed from quarterly data from 1983–1988. The correlations are high, ranging from 0.8896 to 0.9913; all are significant at the 0.0001 level.

Table 27.4: Correlation Between Yield on Instruments Comprising Gap Positions and Yield on Most Actively Traded Futures Contracts During 1983–1988[a]

Most Actively Traded Futures Contracts

Commercial Bank Asset/Liability	91-Day Treasury Bill Futures	91-Day Eurodollar Futures	20-Year Treasury Bond Futures
Federal Funds	0.9551	0.9419	0.9093
Short-term corporate borrowings (at prime rate of interest)	0.9503	0.9448	0.9521
1-month commercial paper	0.9353	0.9220	0.9295
3-month commercial paper	0.9341	0.9298	0.9347
6-month commercial paper	0.9378	0.9362	0.9425
1-month CD[b]	0.9369	0.9270	0.9295
3-month CD[b]	0.9685	0.9715	0.9367
6-month CD[b]	0.9422	0.9412	0.9427
90-day Treasury bill	0.9720	0.9463	0.9437
1-year Treasury note	0.9477	0.9339	0.9629
2-year Treasury note	0.9536	0.9437	0.9790
3-year Treasury note	0.9064	0.8896	0.9839
5-year Treasury note	0.9461	0.9336	0.9903
10-year Treasury note	0.9436	0.9349	0.9083
30-year Treasury bond	0.9279	0.9140	0.9913
GNMA mortgages	0.9190	0.8973	0.9831
FHA mortgages	0.9583	0.9460	0.9789
Municipal bonds	0.9245	0.9108	0.9687

[a] Correlations are based on quarterly yields during 1983–1988. Monthly yield rates on each asset and liability instrument collected from Federal Reserve Bulletins are averaged to yield a quarterly time series. Prices and yields on futures contracts are from Fabozzi (1988, 898–99) and Breeden (forthcoming, figure 9).
[b] Certificate of Deposit (CD).

The items comprising the one-year gap exhibit a stronger association with the short-term futures contracts (0.9480 and 0.9395 on average for 91-day Treasury bill and Eurodollar futures contracts, respectively) than with the 20-year Treasury bond futures contract (0.9384 on average). The reverse is true for the five-year and over five-year gap positions; the average correlation between the yields on items comprising these positions and 20-year Trasury bond futures is 0.9814 (vs. 0.9395 for 91-day Treasury bill futures and 0.9272 for Eurodollar futures). Consequently, the simulation uses Treasury bill futures contracts to hedge the one-year gap[10] and 20-year Treasury bond futures contracts to hedge the five-year and over five-year gap positions.

The number of futures contracts to purchase, N(j), equals the average gap position divided by the size of the futures contract (CS), multiplied by the ratio of the length of time the gap position is to be hedged (k = 1-year for all j) to m, the maturity of the futures contract (Sinkey 1986, 112):

$$N(i)_t = \frac{GAP(i)_t}{2CS} \times \frac{k}{m}. \tag{3}$$

Table 27.3 reports the mean number of futures contracts purchased for each gap horizon. On average, the simulated hedge positions required an initial sale of \$38 million in Treasury bill futures contracts and an initial purchase of \$4.5 million (\$3.2 million plus \$1.3 million) in Treasury bond futures at the end of 1983.

SFAS No. 80 requires firms to include changes in the value of macro hedges constructed with interest rate futures contracts in current earnings, regardless of the maturity of the underlying asset or liability. The profit from the hedging strategy is computed as:

$$\pi = \sum_i N(i)_t \left[P(i)_{t+1} - P(i)_t \right]. \tag{4}$$

where:

π_t = profit (loss) at time t from futures contracts;
$P(j)_t$ = quoted price at time t of futures contract used to hedge repricing horizon of length j;
$j \in J$ = {one-year, five-year, over 5-year} for the full hedge, or {one-year} for the restricted hedge.

---

[10] Eurodollar futures contracts produced similar results and, therefore, are not reported.

Year-end prices of 91-day Treasury bill and 20-year Treasury bond futures contracts with delivery in March were collected from *The Wall Street Journal.* In the simulation, March $t + 1$ futures contracts are purchased on the last trading day of year t. The futures contracts are rolled over every three months until year end when March $t + 2$ contracts are closed.[11] The profit from this hedging strategy is computed by (1) multiplying the difference between the price of the appropriate March $t + 2$ futures contract on the last trading day of year $t + 1$ and the price of the March $t + 1$ contract on the last trading day of year t, $P(j)_{t+1} - P(j)t$, by $N(j)_t$, and (2) summing (1) over j, the repricing horizons hedged. This profit is added to unhedged earnings to yield either full or restricted hedge earnings.

Annual unhedged earnings of each bank are measured as: (1) net interest income less interest expense, NIM_t; (2) income before loan loss provision and security gains or losses, $NIBLS_t$; (3) net income after loan loss provision and security gains or losses but before taxes and extraordinary items, $NIBTE_t$; and (4) net income after taxes and extra-ordinary items, NI_t, $NIBLS_t$ (NIM_t plus any net noninterest income) and $NIBTE_t$ (the sum of $NIBLS_t$, the loan loss provision and any security gains or losses) provide information on the significance of two alternative sources of earnings variability: loan loss provisions and security gains and losses other than those realized on futures contracts. For the fourth earnings measures, the profit from the hedging strategy is adjusted for taxes prior to arriving at hedged earnings.[12]

Tests

The variability of reported earnings is measured by (1) the amount of dispersion in the reported earnings variable, and (2) the coefficient of variation. The coefficient of variation, a dimensionless statistic describing the variation in a population, is particularly useful in assessing consistency across different populations, such as hedged earnings computed using two accounting procedures. Dispersion ($VAR[^*]$) and coefficient of variation ($CV[*]$) measures are computed for each sample bank and each earnings variable for the full hedge (i.e., $VAR[F]$ and $CV[F]$) and the restricted hedge (i.e., $VAR[R]$ and $CV[R]$).

If immediate recognition increases earnings variability vis-àg-vis hedge accounting, then $VAR[F]$) will exceed $VAR[R]$ ($CV[R]$):

---

[11] December $t + 1$ *contracts are not closed because the last day of trading in December* $t + 1$ contracts precedes 31 December by as much as 12 days. In order to hedge the bank's exposure to a full year December $t + 1$ contracts are rolled over into March $t + 2$ futures contracts that may be traded through 31 December.

[12] For tax purposes, the gain on futures contracts used as hedges constitutes ordinary income (Internal Revenue Code, Section 582(c)).

H_o: For a given level of hedging, immediate recognition does not lead to a more variable earnings stream than hedge accounting, i.e., $VAR[F]/VAR[R] \leq 1$ ($CV[F]/CV[R] \leq 1$).

H_A: For a given level of hedging, immediate recognition leads to a more variable earnings stream than hedge accounting, i.e., $VAR[F]/VAR[R] > 1$ ($CV[F]/CV[R] > 1$).

Results

Table 27.5 reports the dispersion ratios for each of the four earnings variables. For every earnings measure the first, second, and third quartile dispersion ratios exceed one; in fact, more than 90 percent of the observations on each earnings measure exceed one. In comparing the dispersion of full hedge earnings to restricted hedge earnings, the average coefficient of variation is 12 percent higher for NIM_t, 18 percent for $NIBLS_t$, and 29 percent for $NIBTE_t$ and NI_t. The nonparametric Wilcoxon signed-ranks statistic is used to examine (1) the difference $CV[F]/CV[R] - 1$, and (2) the difference $VAR[F]/VAR[R] - 1$. 1. Positive differences indicate greater variability of full hedge earnings relative to restricted hedge earnings. the Wilcoxon signed-ranks statistic, which examines the sum of the ranks of sample banks with positive hypothesis (at the 0.001 level), favoring the alternative hypothesis that immediate recognition increases the dispersion of reported earnings vis-à-vis hedge accounting.

One problem with the Wilcoxon signed-ranks test is that the statistic is relatively insensitive to the magnitude of the change in variability. That is, many "small" positive deviations may lead to rejection of hypothesis H_o. One test that incorporates the size of the deviation is constructed by examining the ratio $VAR[F]/VAR[R]$ for each observation; this ratio has an F-distribution with (5, 5) degrees of freedom. Figure 27.1 illustrates the percentage of the observations rejecting the null hypothesis that $VAR[F]/VAR[R] \leq 1$ for various confidence levels and for each earnings measure. The graph indicates that more than 90 percent of the observations could *not* reject the null hypothesis at conventional levels for *any* earnings measure.

The fact that the individual observations fail to reject the hypothesis that $VAR[F]/VAR[R] \leq 1$ is not surprising: the small sample size (five degrees of freedom in numerator and denominator) lowers the power of the statistic in detecting deviations from the null hypothesis and contributes to the probability of Type II error.[13] An alternative test that uses the $VAR[F]/VAR[R]$ ratio examines the probability that the cumulative distribution of the sample $VAR[F]/VAR[R]$ ratios, $F(x)$, is less than (i.e.,

---

[13] Type I error is rejecting the null hypothesis when the null hypothesis is false. Type II error is accepting the null hypothesis when the null hypothesis is false.

Table 27.5: Effect of Hedging Strategy on the Variability of
Annual Earnings Hedging Strategy:
$H(i)_t = |GAP(i)_t|$

	NIM$_t$	NIBLS$_t$	NIBTE$_t$	NI$_t$
VAR [F]/VAR[R][a]				
First Quartile	1.158	1.261	1.305	1.303
Second Quartile	1.241	1.386	1.508	1.517
Third Quartile	1.388	1.675	1.721	1.721
Mean	1.321	1.673	3.075	2.930
Minimum	0.982	0.275	0.488	0.488
Maximum	2.559	8.181	98.139	98.139
Percent of obs.>1.0	99%	93%	96%	95%
Wilcoxon signed ranks				
statistic (α-level)	0.001	0.001	0.001	0.001
Kolmogorov goodness-of-fit				
statistic (α-level)	0.001	0.001	0.001	0.001
CV[F]/CV[R][a]				
First Quartile	1.054	1.056	1.064	1.064
Second Quartile	1.089	1.122	1.144	1.146
Third Quartile	1.149	1.213	1.232	1.228
Mean	1.120	1.178	1.294	1.286
Minimum	0.970	0.493	0.654	0.654
Maximum	1.574	2.644	8.975	8.975
Percent of obs.>1.0	99%	91%	92%	92%
Wilcoxon signed ranks				
statistic (α-level)	0.001	0.001	0.001	0.001

[a] *VAR[F]/VAR[R]* is the ratio of the variability of full hedge earnings to the variability of restricted hedge earnings. *CV[F]/CV[R]* is the ratio of the coefficient of variation of full hedge earnings to the coefficient of variation of restricted hedge earnings. Full hedge earnings are annual unhedged earnings plus changes in the value of futures contracts used to macro hedge one-year, five-year, and over five-year gap positions. Restricted hedge earnings are annual unhedged earnings plus changes in the value of futures contracts used to macro hedge just the one-year gap position.

has greater mass to the right of) the F-distribution with (5, 5) degrees of freedom, $F^*(x)$:

H_o: $F(x) \geq F^*(x)$ for all $x \varepsilon [-\infty, +\infty]$.

H_A: $F(x) < F^*(x)$ for at least one value of x.

The Kolmogorov goodness-of-fit test examines the statistic K, defined as the greatest vertical distance between the $F^*(x) = F_{(5,5)}$ distribution and the empirical distribution based on the sample observations, $S(x)$:

$$K = \sup \text{renum} \left[F*(x) - S(x) \right].$$

If $K > 0.174$, then hypothesis H_o is rejected in favor of the alternative hypothesis that the empirical distribution is "right-shifted" relative to the $F_{(5,5)}$ distribution.[14] That is, collectively the individual F-ratios indicate a significant increase in earnings variability under immediate recognition vis-åg-vis hedge accounting. Values of the Kolmogorov statistic reject the null hypothesis at the 0.001 level for each earnings measure.

In summary, although the individual F-ratios fail to reject hypothesis H_o: $VAR[F] / VAR[R] \leq 1$, the Wilcoxon and Kilmogorov tests support the

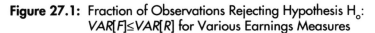

Figure 27.1: Fraction of Observations Rejecting Hypothesis H_o: $VAR[F] \leq VAR[R]$ for Various Earnings Measures

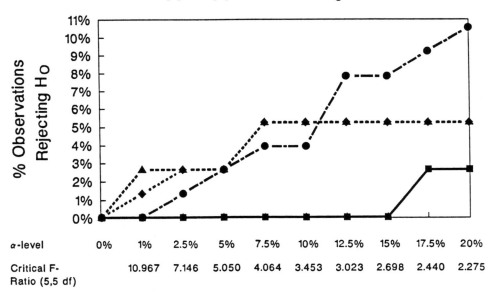

——■—— Net income margins (NIM)

--●-- Net income before loan provision and security gains/losses (NIBLS)

···▲··· Net income before taxes and extraordinary items (NIBTE)

···◆··· Net income after taxes and extraordinary items (NI)

[14] Conover's (1980) critical value computed using large sample approximation (n=76) and α=0.001.

alternative hypothesis that immediate recognition leads to a significantly more variable earnings stream than does hedge accounting. Given the low power and high probability of Type II error associated with the individual F-statistics, I conclude that the simulation results indicate a significant increase in earnings variability under immediate recognition vis-à-vis hedge accounting. I also reran the simulation and tests assuming that the sample banks hedged 50 percent and 75 percent of their gap positions. These results (unreported) support the findings obtained from the 100 percent hedge positions that immediate recognition leads to a more volatile earnings stream than hedge accounting.

V. Accounting for Futures Contracts by Broker-Dealers

A second group affected by SFAS No. 80 are broker-dealers, pension plans, and investment companies; these firms often invest or speculate using futures contracts. SFAS No. 80 specifies that immediate recognition of changes in the market value of futures contracts used for investment or speculation is preferred to the lower-of-cost-or-market method for marketable securities described in SFAS No. 12 "Accounting for Certain Marketable Securities." Briefly, the FASB concluded that futures positions are sufficiently dissimilar to equity securities (e.g., because of the reliability of futures contract markets and trading features) to warrant a departure from the lower-of-cost-or-market method. While the FASB also noted that reported earnings may fluctuate more between periods as a result of recognizing gains and losses currently, they argued that these results represent the true economics of the transactions and, therefore, provide more relevant information to users.

I examine the variability of reported earnings of a sample of brokerage firms before and after the effective date of SFAS No. 80 to determine whether immediate recognition of gains and losses on futures contracts used for investment or speculation increases earnings dispersion. Earnings information for a sample of 27 loan brokers (SIC code 6163), security and commodity brokers (SIC code 6200), and security brokers and dealers (SIC code 6211) is obtained from COMPUSTAT for the period 1982–1987.[15] Descriptive statistics about the sample firms are reported in panel A, Table 27.6.

Variability in reported earnings is measured as (1) the ratio of the dispersion in post-1984 earnings to pre-1985 earnings. $VAR[\text{post-}1984]/VAR[\text{pre-}1985]$, and (2) the ratio of the coefficient of variation in post-1984 earnings to pre-1985 earnings, $CV[\text{post-}1984]/CV[\text{pre-}1985]$). Percentile statistics, reported in panel B, Table 27.6, show that only 41

---

[15] COMPUSTAT includes 76 firms in these industries. Forty-nine firms were excluded, however, because of missing or incomplete data.

Table 27.6: Descriptive Data and Variability of Reported Earnings of Sample Brokerage Firms in Pre-1985 and Post-1984 Periods

Panel A. Average Values of Selected Financial Information (in $000,000s):

	1981	1982	1983	1984	1985	1986	1987
Total Assets	3,603	4,234	5,427	7,172	10,425	11,487	11,512
Total Debt	3,264	3,961	5,042	6,760	9,920	10,876	10,923
Market Value of Equity	512	853	569	708	1,014	1,012	685
Net Sales	2,197	1,627	1,857	1,976	2,035	2,151	2,347
Earnings Before Extraordinary Items	64	54	57	43	72	96	54
Earnings After Extraordinary Items	63	54	56	44	71	99	54

Panel B. Effect of Immediate Recognition Accounting on Variability of Reported Earnings:

	Earnings Before Extraprdomary Items	Earnings After Extraordinary Items
VAR[post-1984]/VAR[pre-1985][a]		
Sample Size	27	27
First Quartile	0.333	0.371
Second Quartile	1.300	1.640
Third Quartile	3.918	4.458
Mean	1.753	8.028
Minimum	0.051	0.051
Maximum	37.478	78.507
Percent of obs.>1.0	59%	59%
Wilcoxon signed ranks statistic (α-level)	0.786	0.746
Kolmogorov goodness-of-fit statistic (α-level)	>0.100	>0.100
CV[post-1984]/CV[pre-1985][a]		
Sample Size	27	27
First Quartile	0.128	0.104
Second Quartile	0.526	0.598
Third Quartile	1.812	1.969
Mean	2.237	1.380
Minimum	−6.044	−34.372
Maximum	25.484	37.848

Table 27.6 (continued): Descriptive Data and Variability of Reported Earnings of Sample Brokerage Firms in Pre-1985 and Post-1984 Periods

Percent of obs.>1.0	41%	41%
Wilcoxon signed ranks statistic (α-level)	0.806	0.806

[a] VAR[post-1984]/VAR[pre-1985] is the ratio of the variability of 1985–1987 (post-1984) earnings to the variability of 1982–1984 (pre-1985) earnings. CV[post-1984]/CV[pre-1985] is the ratio of the coefficient of variation of 1985–1987 earnings to the coefficient of variation of 1982–1984 earnings.

Figure 27.2: Fraction of Observations Rejecting Hypothesis H_o: VAR[post-1984]≤VAR[pre-1985] for Various Earnings Measures

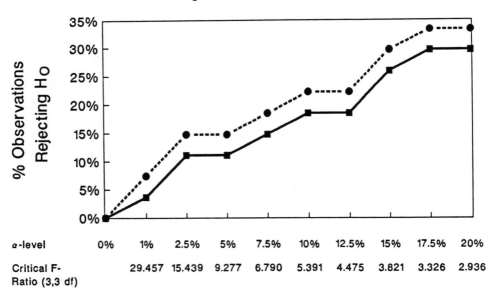

percent of the CV[post-1984]$/CV$[pre-1985] ratios exceed one. Overall, the Wilcoxon signed-ranks statistics show no difference between the variability of the sample firms' earnings before and after the effective date of SFAS No. 80. Also, while 59 percent of the VAR[post-1984]$/VAR$[pre-1985] ratios exceed one, the individual F-statistics (Figure 27.2) are not statistically significant for the majority of sample firms for earnings either before or after extraordinary items. Finally, the Kolmogorov goodness-of-fit test, comparing the empirical distribution of VAR[post-1984]$/VAR$ [pre-1985] to the $F^*(x)=F_{(3,3)}$ distribution, also indicates no difference in the variability of pre-1985 and post-1984 earnings streams of broker-dealers.

VI. Conclusion

This paper analyzes the information content of the change in accounting methods required by SFAS No. 80. Unlike prior studies of regulatory change that measure the stock market's response to the event, this study uses simulation and empirical tests to examine whether changes in the accounting treatment for futures contracts alter firms' reported earnings patterns. One advantage of this approach is that it requires no specification of the link between accounting measurement rules and capital asset prices. Simulation results support critics' concern over the accounting treatment for hedges; immediate recognition accounting led to a more variable earnings stream than did hedge accounting for more than 90 percent of the sample observations. Statistical tests also reject the hypothesis that the earnings stream simulated by immediate recognition accounting is less variable than the earnings stream generated by hedge accounting. However, empirical tests do not support critics' concern over the accounting treatment for futures contracts used for investment or speculation. These tests show that immediate recognition does not significantly increase the volatility of reported earnings for a sample of brokerage firms that invest or speculate with futures contracts.

The empirical results should be interpreted carefully for several reasons. First, the tests are based on a small number of time-series observations.[16] Second, because the sample firms are drawn from the same industry and time period, the earnings data may be cross-sectionally dependent or influenced by the same macroeconomic variables. Third, because

---

[16] Paucity of time-series data is also a problem with the simulation tests: (1) there are five observations of commercial bank gap positions, 1983–1987, and (2) there are three observations in each of the pre-1985 and post-1984 periods (1982–1984 and 1985–1987, respectively). It is not possible to extend the commercial bank time-series prior to 1983 since commercial banks began disclosing gap positions in that year. Therefore, although few in number, the 1983–1987 time-series is complete. Further, while the pre-1985 time-series of broker-dealers could be extended to years before 1982, the number of years in the post-1985 period is restricted to those years with available earnings information.

there is no time period diversification in the sample (all firms switched to immediate recognition accounting in 1985), it would be difficult to attribute differences in firms' reported earnings patterns only to the accounting change. The cross-dependence and omitted variables problems are common to tests of mandatory accounting changes. For example, one factor that is omitted from the analysis is the hedging behavior of broker-dealers. Unfortunately, firms are not required to disclose either the existence or extent of their hedging strategies. Hence, attempting to control for hedging behavior leads to making tradeoffs between the omitted variables problem and the biased sample of firms reporting hedging strategies. (Of the 27 broker-dealers, seven disclosed their use of futures contracts to hedge. The analysis, repeated on the 20 nonhedging firms, generated results very similar to the full sample of broker-dealers.)

Appendix

Example of Hedging Strategy Using Interest Rate Futures

Management expects interest rates to decline over the next month and constructs a negative $18 million gap position. If rates increase, however, bank profits are exposed to severe losses because interest expense on the rate-sensitive liabilities will exceed the income generated by rate-sensitive assets. Therefore, management wishes to hedge an unanticipated rate increase over this period. The 91-day Treasury bill futures contracts are currently selling at 99.00.

Since the price of a futures contract increases as interest rates fall, management should take a short position in futures contracts. Later, if rates increase, the bank will buy futures contracts at a lower price and offset the loss on the exposure position. Since the bank wishes to hedge the position for one month using 91-day Treasury bill futures, it sells three Treasury bill futures contracts at 99.00.

One month later interest rates have risen by two percent and Treasury bill futures contracts are selling at 98.00. The bank has incurred an extra $30,000 in interest expense on its $18 million gap position ($18 million $\times$ 0.02 $\times$ 1/12). The bank closes its futures position by purchasing three Treasury bill futures contracts at 98.00, generating a profit of $30,000 on the hedge ($2.97 million – $2.94 million). The net effect on earnings is zero.

REFERENCES

Beaver, W. H., A. A. Christie, and P. A. Griffin. 1980. The information content of SEC ASR #190. *Journal of Accounting and Economics* 2 (August): 127–57.

Benston, G., and M. Krasney. 1978. Economic consequences of financial accounting statements. *Conference on the Economic Consequences of Financial Accounting Standards* (March): 159–252.

Booth, J. R., R. L. Smith, and R. Stolz. 1984. Use of interest rate futures by financial institutions. *Journal of Bank Research* 15 (Spring): 15–20.

Breeden, D. Bank risk management. Forthcoming in *Handbook of Modern Finance*, edited by D. Logue, 2d ed. Boston: Warren Gorham & Lamont.

Collins, D. W. 1975. SEC product-line reporting and market efficiency. *Journal of Financial Economics* 4 (June): 125–64.

Conover, W. 1980. *Practical Nonparametric Statistics*. 2d ed. New York: Wiley & Sons, Inc.

Diamond, D. 1984. Financial intermediation and delegated monitoring. *Review of Economic Studies* 51 (July): 393–414.

Dukes, R. E., T. R. Dyckman, and J. A. Elliott. 1980. Accounting for research and development costs: The impact on research and development expenditures. *Journal of Accounting Research* (Supplement) 18: 1–37.

Dyckman, T. R., and A. J. Smith. 1979. Financial accounting and reporting by oil and gas producing companies: A study of information effects. *Journal of Accounting and Economics* 1 (March): 45–75.

Fabozzi, F., ed. 1988. *Handbook of Mortgage-Backed Securities*. 2d ed. Chicago: Probus.

Financial Accounting Standards Board. 1975. Statement of financial accounting standards no. 12: Accounting for certain marketable equity securities. Stamford, Conn.: FASB (December).

———. 1984. Statement of financial accounting standards no. 80: Accounting for futures contracts. Stamford, Conn.: FASB (August).

Foster, G. 1980. Accounting policy decisions and capital market research. *Journal of Accounting and Economics* 2 (March): 29–62.

Francis, J. Management anticipation of interest rates: The case of commercial banks. Forthcoming. *Journal of Business, Finance & Accounting*.

Goodman, L. S., and M. J. Langer. 1983. Accounting for interest rate futures in bank asset-liability management. *The Journal of Futures Markets* 3 (Winter): 415–28.

Hill, J. M., and T. Schneeweis. 1984. Reducing volatility with financial futures. *Financial Analysts Journal* 40 (November–December): 34–40.

Koppenhaver, G. D. 1983. A t-bill futures hedging strategy for banks. *Economic Review*, Federal Reserve Bank of Dallas (March): 15–28.

Moses, O. D. 1987. Income smoothing and incentives: Empirical tests using accounting changes. *The Accounting Review* 62 (April): 358–77.

Sinkey, J. 1986. *Commercial Bank Financial Management.* 2d ed. New York: Macmillan.

Smith, C. W., and R. M. Stulz. 1985. The determinants of firms' hedging policies. *Journal of Financial and Quantitative Analysis* 20 (December): 391–405.

CHARACTERISTICS OF HEDGING FIRMS: AN EMPIRICAL EXAMINATION

Jennifer Francis and Jens Stephan*

28

Characteristics of Hedging Firms: An Empirical Examination

I. Introduction

This paper tests several theories about why firms hedge. Smith and Stultz (1985) note that other studies investigating hedging practices focus on risk-averse producers who hedge to reduce the variability of the firm's income and the risk of the firm (e.g., Ho and Saunders (1983) and Anderson and Danthine (1980)). While this argument has merit for private and closely-held companies, it ignores the fact that investors of publicly traded corporations can diversify their portfolios and eliminate risk without the assistance of managers.[1] Consequently, there must be other explanations for the large number of publicly traded companies that hedge.

A review of the literature provides five explanations for why firms hedge: restrictive debt covenants; bankruptcy costs; political costs; taxes; and managerial incentives. This paper empirically tests these five explanations with a set of proxy variables. Because univariate procedures are unable to discriminate among competing explanations, each explanation is assessed separately using multivariate logit models. In addition to assessing the cross-sectional determinants of hedging firms, we examine whether the five explanations are consistent with time series changes in the proxy variables of hedging versus nonhedging firms.

---

*We are grateful for helpful comments provided by Doug Foster and S. Viswanathan, and two anonymous referees. Research assistance provided by Richard Grayeski is gratefully acknowledged.
[1] If managers can eliminate unsystematic risk at a lower cost than investors, then this argument has merit for publicly traded companies as well.

II. Why Firms Hedge

Smith and Stultz (1985) (hereafter SS) develop several explanations of why firms hedge. In particular, SS show that a value-maximizing firm may hedge because of financial distress costs, managerial risk aversion and taxes.[2] Another explanation of hedging behavior addresses political costs (Watts and Zimmerman 1978). Finally, Breeden and Viswanathan's (1990) hedging model posits that some managers hedge to communicate their higher ability to the market.

A. Financial Distress Costs. A firm in financial distress will typically face three decisions: debt default, bankruptcy filing, and reorganization/liquidation. Each of these decisions entails ex-post costs (such as transactions costs, legal fees, and so on) and ex-ante costs (such as managers' attempts to increase the financial well being of the firm by taking excessive risks). In this paper, we assume that the sum of ex-ante and ex-post costs is positively correlated with the probability that the firm enters into each distress stage. In the next two subsections, we describe why firms that face higher probabilities of financial distress (debt default and bankruptcy) are more likely to hedge.

A.1. Debt Covenants: In their examination of the covenants contained in debt agreements, Smith and Warner (1979) argue that these contractual arrangements may constrain managers' choices of operating, investment or financing decisions. Consequently, debt covenants may create incentives for managers to take actions aimed at reducing the restrictiveness of these constraints. For example, consider the interest coverage restriction included in many debt agreements. The interest coverage ratio specifies a minimum ratio of net income to interest expense that must be maintained by the borrower. Failure to maintain the specified level constitutes an act of technical default, and gives debtholders the right to accelerate payment of the remaining debt.[3] Further, because debt covenants are frequently defined in terms of accounting numbers, managers may have incentives to manage accounting numbers to avoid restrictive debt covenants. That is, by hedging, a firm may be able to decrease the variability of its accounting earnings and thus reduce the probability that the interest coverage ratio is binding. A direct hedging effect is also possible: a successful interest-rate hedge may reduce interest expense, thus increasing net income, and directly reduce the probability that the firm violates

---

[2] SS also argue that managers may have incentives to hedge (or not hedge) if their expected utility depends on the distribution of the firm's payoffs. This might occur, for example, if the manager's compensation included stock options or profit sharing. We do not investigate the empirical validity of this management contracting explanation because of the paucity of available data on and the appropriate valuation of the components of managers' compensation packages.

[3] In the event that shareholders are unable to pay off the remaining debt immediately, debtholders may initiate involuntary bankruptcy proceedings.

its interest coverage ratio.[4] Similar arguments apply to other debt covenants that are tied to accounting earnings, e.g., dividend payout restrictions and minimum net worth constraints which are based on the level of retained earnings. The debt covenant argument is summarized in Hypothesis 1:

> H1: Hedging firms are more likely to have binding debt restrictions than nonhedging firms.

A.2. Bankruptcy Costs: Diamond (1984), Mayers and Smith (1987), Shapiro and Titman (1985) and SS argue that transactions costs of bankruptcy may be reduced by decreasing the variability of present and future cash flows. The argument is as follows. Let D be the amount of debt of a levered firm maturing at time N. At time N, two states are possible. One, the market value of the firm (MV) may be less than or equal to D. In this case, debtholders receive MV net of transactions costs of bankruptcy, and shareholders receive nothing. Two, the market value of the firm exceeds D. In this case, debtholders receive D, and shareholders claim MV-D. Consequently, expected bankruptcy costs are inversely related to debtholders and shareholders expected payoffs. Therefore, to the extent that hedging reduces bankruptcy costs (by reducing the variability of present and future cash flows), hedging benefits claimsholders, particularly the residual claimants—shareholders.

SS also posit that small firms are more likely to hedge than large firms if: (i) hedging costs are proportional to firm size, and (ii) bankruptcy costs are less than proportional to firm size. Also, larger firms are more likely to be better diversified through varied product lines and divisions than small firms. In order to reduce risk, firms with fewer product lines may resort to hedging outside the firm. These arguments lead to the following two hypotheses:

> H2: Hedging firms have a higher probability of bankruptcy than onhedging firms.

> H3: Hedging firms are smaller than nonhedging firms.

B. Political Costs. Watts and Zimmerman (1978) claim that firms that are exposed to regulatory or investor scrutiny face higher political costs and, therefore, may take actions to reduce their visibility. If firms with volatile earnings patterns are more visible than other firms and if

---

[4] Under generally accepted accounting principles, gains and losses on futures contracts designated as hedges are deferred and amortized over the life of the hedged assets or liabilities and are included as adjustments to interest income or interest expense. Gains and losses on futures contracts which do not meet the hedge criteria are included in current income. (Statement of Financial Accounting Standards No. 80 specifies two criteria for a qualifying hedge: (1) the hedged item must expose the firm to price or interest rate risk; and (2) the futures contracts must reduce that exposure and be designated as a hedge.)

hedging reduces earnings variability, then more visible firms will hedge. Because successful hedging activity reduces the volatility of earnings, it is not possible to distinguish hedging and non-hedging firms on the basis of this visibility factor. Consequently, firm size, a common surrogate for political costs, is used as a proxy for political visibility.[5]

H4: Hedging firms are larger than nonhedging firms.

C. Taxes. SS show that the progressive nature of corporate profit taxes makes the expected value of aftertax earnings a decreasing function of the volatility of taxable income. By reducing the variability of taxable income, hedging may reduce a firm's tax liability and increase its expected aftertax value. SS argue further that the tax benefits of hedging increase as the tax function becomes more convex, e.g., with the inclusion of excess profit taxes. The firm's average tax rate is used as a proxy for the convexity of their tax function.

H5: Hedging firms have higher tax rates than nonhedging firms.

A second test of the tax explanation is that firms' propensity to hedge declines (increases) when marginal corporate tax rates decline (increase). One test of this hypothesis would examine whether firm's hedging behavior changed following implementation of the Tax Reform Act of 1986. Effective January 1, 1987, the Tax Reform Act reduced corporate tax rates from 46 percent to 34 percent; consequently, one might expect a decline in the number of firms that hedge in the post-1986 period.

D. Managerial Incentives. Breeden and Viswanathan (1990) posit that high ability managers hedge to indirectly communicate their higher ability to the market. In their model, which is couched in terms of a bank or thrift institution, bank profits depend on interest rate fluctuations and managers' loan making abilities. By hedging interest rate risk (through interest rate swaps, futures or options contracts), bank managers reduce noise in the earnings process, and thereby provide investors with a more informative measure of profits that depicts their ability. Breeden and Viswanathan show that high ability managers have incentives to hedge when they care only about their reputations or when they hold equity in the firm and reputations matter (provided that the difference in abilities between low and high ability managers is not too small). A low ability manager will not choose to hedge interest rate risk (provided that the difference in abilities is not too small) because by not hedging he/she may be mistaken for a high ability manager if future interest rate realizations are low. This model leads to the following hypothesis:

---

[5] Zimmerman (1983) examines whether larger firms have higher political costs (proxied by income tax rates) than smaller firms. He finds some evidence that larger firms have higher tax rates than smaller firms, but the relationship is not stable over time or across industries.

H6: Managers of hedging firms are of higher ability than managers of nonhedging firms.

III. Time Series Analysis

One drawback of hypotheses H1-H6 is that it is not possible to control both for managers' motivations to hedge and for the success (or lack thereof) of their hedging strategies. For example, suppose the manager of a financially distressed firm decides to hedge in order to reduce the probability of default/bankruptcy. If the hedge is successful, then the firm will not appear to be financially distressed in the year in which they hedged. Consequently, the absence of empirical evidence supporting H1-H6 may imply either that the sample firms were successful hedgers, or that the sample firms did not hedge for the motivations examined. To distinguish between these two alternatives, we compute, over time, changes in the proxy variables used to test H1-H6 for hedger and nonhedger firms. If managers hedge for the reasons noted, and if they successfully implement these hedges, then we expect to observe systematic patterns in the signed differences. For example, consider the bankruptcy motivation for hedging. If firm i hedges in 1983 to reduce their expected bankruptcy costs, then we expect that firm i's expected bankruptcy costs will decline over time. Similar arguments hold for the other hedging explanations, and are encompassed in the following hypotheses:

H7: Over time, hedging firms are more likely to experience reductions in the restrictiveness of their debt covenants, expected bankruptcy costs, and tax rates than are non-hedging firms.

H8: Over time, hedging firms are more likely to experience increases in proxies for managerial ability than are non-hedging firms.

H9: Over time, hedging firms are more likely to experience: (a) increases in size (as measured by total assets, net sales, and market value of equity) if managers hedge to reduce bankruptcy costs; or (b) reductions in size if managers hedge to avoid political costs, than are non-hedging firms.

IV. Sample and Test Design

A. Sample. The National Automated Accounting Research System (NAARS) data base was searched for the period 1983–87 to identify all firms that engaged in one or more hedging strategies. NAARS contains numeric and text information reported in firms' financial statements. To the extent that hedging activities are material, this information should be disclosed in the financial statements. Consequently, the search may not reveal firms that engaged in immaterial amounts of hedging activity. The search words/phrases (and derivatives) used were "hedge," "interest rate futures," "interest rate" or "foreign currency" "option," and "interest rate" or "foreign currency" "swap" contracts. The search revealed 2,113 firm-year observations (Table 28.1) which were similar to the following sample references (emphasis added):

> "The Corporation uses *interest rate futures* contracts to manage its overall interest rate risk exposure for asset-liability management purposes and as part of its trading account activities. Gains and losses on futures contracts used for asset-liability management purposes are deferred and amortized over the life of the hedged assets or liabilities and are included as adjustments to Interest Income or Interest Expense as appropriate. Gains and losses from the change in the market value of futures contracts used in connection with trading account activities are recognized in current income and are reported in Trading Account Profits (Losses)." (from the notes to The Chase Manhattan Corporation and Subsidiaries' 1986 annual report).

> "The Corporation . . . enters into forward rate agreements and *foreign currency options.*" (from the notes to Irving Bank Corporation's 1986 annual report).

> "In addition, during 1985 the Company entered into an *interest rate swap* agreement replacing variable short-term interest rates with a long-term fixed rate of 10.65% on $200,000,000 with a maturity of ten years." (from the notes to Borden Inc.'s 1985 annual report).

> "The Company has entered into a *currency swap* agreement, whereby the Company receives pounds sterling covering floating rate interest and principal on the Notes and makes payments in U.S. dollars covering interest on a floating rate basis and principal in an amount comparable to the Notes." (from the notes to Wells Fargo & Co.'s 1984 annual report).

Of the 2113 observations, 594 firm-year observations were eliminated because the firm was not included on Compustat (see Table 28.1 for a summary of the filter procedures and results). Of the remaining 1519 firm-year observations, 118 firm-year observations were removed because they did not actually refer to a hedging strategy.[6,7] The remaining 1401

---

[6] Most of these 118 citations related to the interest rate option category, but referred to alternative choices of interest rates for a company's debt (e.g., prime, LIBOR, fixed, etc.) rather than an option contract (the right to buy or sell interest rate futures contracts). For example, the notes to Stone Container Corporation's 1984 annual report stated that "(t)he Company has short-term bank lines of credit aggregating $175,000,000, which have multiple interest rate options."

[7] Most of the firms in the final sample stated that the futures, option and swap contracts were used to hedge rather than to speculate. It is also possible that firms that engaged in swaps did so to obtain a lower cost of funds, and not for the reasons cited in section II. Inclusion of these firms biases the results toward the null hypotheses. To assess the significance of this bias, we reran the tests excluding those firms that used swaps. The results are similar, and therefore, are not reported.

Table 28.1: Summary of Sample Selection and Filter Procedures

Key word or phrase:[a]	Number of firm-year observations	
(1) "Interest rate futures" contract	270	
(2) "Interest rate" or "foreign currency" option	213	
(3) "Currency" or "interest rate" swap	581	
(4) "Hedge"; "hedging"	1,049	
Number of observations not on Compustat.	594	
Number of observations which did not refer to hedging activity.	118	
	1,401	(representing 615 firms)
Number of observations with incomplete 1972–82 earnings data.[b]	258	
Number of observations without a comparable matched control firm.[b]	82	(representing 35 firms)
Number of observations in pooled hedger sample.	1,061	(representing 434 firms)

[a] The NAARS data base was searched for company financial statement references of these words and phrases during 1983–87.
[b] 1972–82 annual earnings per share data are required to estimate the standard deviation of earnings, $\sigma(EPS)$. This variable is used to match each hedger firm with a same-industry, similar earnings volatility, nonhedger control firm.

firm-year observations, representing 615 firms, constitute the hedger sample. The control sample includes all Compustat firms that did not disclose hedging activity and were in (at least) the same two-digit industry code as a hedging firm.[8]

Each hedger firm is matched with a same-industry nonhedger control firm based on the standard deviation of the firm's reported earnings per share computed over the 1972–82 period. This matching procedure is necessary to control for one objective of hedging which is to reduce earnings variability. Because ten years of earnings data are required, it is necessary to eliminate 146 hedger firms which do not have complete 1972–82 earnings data on Compustat. In addition, no suitable match control firm could be identified for 35 firms (82 firm-year observations). Thus, the final sample of matched hedger and control firms contains 1061 firm-year observations of hedging activity, representing 434 firms in 54 industries, matched with an observation of a nonhedging firm in the same industry, year and with similar earnings volatility. Table 28.2 reports mean, median

---

[8] About half the sample hedger firms are matched with nonhedger firms in the same four-digit industry code; about 30 percent with firms in the same three-digit SIC code; and 20% with firms in the same two-digit industry classification. SIC codes are taken from Compustat.

Table 28.2: Comparison of Hedger and Control Firms' Earnings
Variability

σ (EPS) statistic[a]	Hedger firms[b]	Control firms[b]	Difference	
Sample size	434	434	0	
Mean	1.443	1.416	0.027	(Z-stat.=1.326,[c] α-level .186)
Median	1.050	1.072	0.007	(Z-stat.=−1.016,[d] α-level .309)
Minimum	0.027	0.030	n/a	
Maximum	12.651	10.434	n/a	

[a] σ(EPS), the standard deviation of annual earnings per share during 1972–82, is used to match each hedger firm with a control firm in the same industry. The reported cross-sectional statistics are based on the paired samples of 434 firms.

[b] The pooled hedger sample consists of 1061 firm-year observations (representing 434 firms) which disclosed some form of hedging activity during 1983–87. (See Table 28.1 for a summary of the selection and filter processes.) Each hedger firm is matched with a same-industry, nonhedger firm with similar earnings variability computed over 1972–82.

[c] Z-statistic tests the average paired difference in the σ(EPS) of hedger and control firms.

[d] Z-statistic tests the median paired difference in the σ(EPS) of hedger and control firms.

and extreme statistics about the earnings volatility matching variable. Both the parametric and nonparametric Z-statistics (examining the mean and median paired differences, respectively) indicate no significant difference between the variability of hedger and control firms' 1972–82 earnings streams.

In both the univariate and multivariate analyses, the pooled time series sample is separated into subsamples for each year, where t subscripts the subsample. By comparing the results across the subsamples, this study examines whether the determinants of firms' hedging decisions change through time. As shown in Panel A, Table 28.3, the number of sample hedging firms increases from 129 (12 percent) in 1983 to 281 (26 percent) in 1986, and then falls to 238 (22 percent) in 1987. To determine whether the data filter requiring inclusion on Compustat affected the distribution of the sample, the frequency of sample observations during 1983–87 is compared with the NAARS population distribution. Panel A, Table 28.3 indicates that the time series distribution of the Compustat sample is indistinguishable from the NAARS sample population. Finally, Panel B, Table 28.3 reports the frequency that the same firm appears in the pooled sample. For example, a firm appearing five times in the

Table 28.3: Distribution of Pooled Hedger Sample[a]

Panel A: Time Series Comparison of Pooled Hedger and Original NAARS Sample Distributions

	1983	1984	1985	1986	1987	Total
Number of observations	129	178	235	281	238	1,061
(% of pooled sample)	(12.2%)	(16.8%)	(22.1%)	(26.5%)	(22.4%)	(100%)
Original NAARS sample	278	364	479	555	437	2,113
(% of NAARS sample)	(13.2%)	(17.2%)	(22.7%)	(26.3%)	(20.7%)	(100%)
% Difference	−1.0%	−0.4%	−0.6%	0.2%	1.7%	—

Panel B: Frequency of Multiple Firm Observations in Pooled Hedger Sample

	1	2	3	4	5	Total
Number of hedger firms	136	113	85	56	44	434
(% of hedger firms)	(31.4%)	(26.0%)	(19.6%)	(12.9%)	(10.1%)	(100%)

[a] The pooled hedger sample consists of 1061 firm-year observations (representing 434 firms) which disclosed some form of hedging activity during 1983–87. See Table 28.1 for a summary of the selection and filter processes.

pooled sample disclosed hedging activity in each of the 1983–87 sample years. About one third of the sample is composed of firms disclosing hedging activity in only one sample year; only 10 percent (44) of the sample firms reported hedging activity in all five sample years. The statistical implications of the dependence problems introduced by multiple observations are discussed below.

Parametric and nonparametric tests are used to compare values of the proxy variables of the matched hedger and control subsamples. The parametric statistic averages the deviations between the jth proxy variable of the matched control and hedger firm-year observation. For the pooled sample of matched control and hedger firms, it is inappropriate to simply aggregate these deviations over time because of the dependence introduced by roughly two-thirds of the firms that appear in multiple years (see Panel B, Table 28.3). To control for this dependence, the deviations of the matched pairs which appear more than once in the pooled sample are first averaged over time, and this summary average is included as a single observation in the pooled sample. This procedure yields a sample of 434 paired differences on each proxy variable. The Wilcoxon nonparametric test examines the sum of the ranks of the deviations between the jth proxy variable of the matched control and hedger firms.

B. Proxy Variables. Values of the following proxy variables are collected or computed from Compustat for all hedger and control observations:

Restrictions in Debt Covenants: Two measures of debt covenant costs are used: firm i's ratio of net income to interest expense in year t ($X1_{it}$) and firm i's ratio of total debt to the book value of equity in year t ($X2_{it}$). The interest coverage ratio $X1_{it}$, is used because hedging may be used to affect this covenant directly (by reducing interest expense via successful hedges aimed at lowering the firm's cost of funds) and indirectly (by reducing the variability of accounting earnings that define this covenant). Firm i's degree of financial leverage in year t, $X2_{it}$, is included based on the findings of two prior studies. Kelly's (1985) finding that firms with debt covenants have higher leverage ratios than firms without debt covenants suggests that leverage proxies for the existence of these constraints. Press and Weintrop's (1990) evidence of positive correlations between measures of nearness to actual debt covenant restrictions and debt-equity ratios suggests that the leverage ratio also captures the tightness of debt covenant restrictions. Since there is little public information available on the number or restrictiveness of debt covenants, particularly for privately placed debt, we view the leverage ratio as a reasonable proxy.

Bankruptcy Costs: Altman's (1983) multivariate bankruptcy prediction model is used to generate bankruptcy indices or "Z-scores" ($X3_{it}$) for all firm-year observations. Altman's (1983) model is:

$$X3_{it} = .717\ Y1_{it} + .847\ Y2_{it} + 3.10\ Y3_{it} + .420\ Y4_{it} + .998\ Y5_{it}$$

where

$X3_{it}$ = bankruptcy index (Altman assigned scores above 2.90 to nonbankrupt group and scores below 1.20 to bankrupt group; scores less than 2.90 and greater than 1.20 fall in a gray area where classification is difficult).

$Y1_{it}$ = (Current assets − current liabilities)/total assets of firm i in year t.

$Y2_{it}$ = Retained earnings/total assets of firm i in year t.

$Y3_{it}$ = Earnings before interest and taxes/total assets of firm i in year t.

$Y4_{it}$ = Book value of preferred and common equity/book value of total liabilities of firm i in year t.

$Y5_{it}$ = Net sales/total assets of firm i in year t.

Firm Size: Three measures of firm size are used: firm i's total assets in year t ($X4_{it}$), firm i's net sales in year t ($X5_{it}$), and firm i's market value of equity in year t ($X6_{it}$).

Managerial Ability: Two proxies for managerial ability are examined. The first, total common and preferred stock dividends paid by firm i in year t ($X7_{it}$), is based on Battacharya's (1979) and John and Williams' (1985) models in which firms signal their higher quality by paying dividends. The second proxy, firm i's price-earnings ratio in year t ($X8_{it}$), measures the association between the present value expected future cash flows and current reported income. If managers hedge to signal their ability, H6 posits that firms with managers of high ability will pay out more dividends and have higher price-earnings ratios than low ability managed firms.

Average Tax Rate: The average tax rate of each firm is measured as the ratio of the firm i's income tax expense to pretax earnings in year t ($X9_{it}$).

V. Results

A. Univariate Tests. The univariate tests of H1-H6 are based on student t- and Wilcoxon statistics. Mean and median values of the deviations between the proxy variables for matched hedger and control firms and the sign of the difference predicted by the appropriate underlying theory are reported in Table 28.4. The predicted sign of each *t*-statistic is given in column (3), and the calculated t- and Wilcoxon statistics are in parentheses below the mean and median values, respectively, of each subsample. The deviations expressed as a fraction of the value of the proxy variable of the control firm are also examined, but because the results are very similar to the raw difference results, they are not reported.

The pooled sample results show that, on average, the hedger firms are more highly levered than the control firms, and in almost all cases, the median difference in the ratio of debt to equity is positive. Also consistent with H1, mean and median differences in interest coverage ratios are negative for the pooled sample and most of the subsample periods.

With few exceptions, mean and median differences in bankruptcy indices of hedging and nonhedging firms are consistent with H2. In almost all cases, the deviations are negative (implying higher probabilities of bankruptcy for hedging firms), though not statistically significant at conventional levels. A second bankruptcy argument, described by H3, posits that hedging firms are likely to be smaller than nonhedging firms. An opposite prediction (H4) is derived from the political cost which argues that larger firms hedge to reduce their exposure to regulatory and investor scrutiny. For all subsamples, the t- and Wilcoxon statistics on the size variables (assets, sales and market value of equity) overwhelmingly reject H3 in favor of H4.

Mean and median test results for the managerial signalling variables support the hypothesis that managers hedge to communicate their ability to the market. In nearly every sample, the mean and median difference in dividend payment policies of hedger and control firms is significantly positive. Although the mean and median deviations in the price-earnings ra-

Table 28.4: Univariate Analysis of Hedging Decision

Variables	Theory^c	Pred. Sign	1983 Mean^a (t-stat)	1983 Median^b (Wilcoxon stat)	1984 Mean (t-stat)	1984 Median (Wilcoxon stat)	1985 Mean (t-stat)	1985 Median (Wilcoxon stat)
X1 Net income/interest expense ratio	D	−	1.224 (.506)	−.043 (−.499)	−5.278 (−1.496)	−.094 (.722)	−10.841 (−1.650)	−.096 (−1.973)*
X2 Debt/equity ratio	D	+	.890 (1.439)	.224 (1.121)	−1.250 (−.733)	.115 (1.122)	2.894 (1.520)	.462 (2.868)**
X3 Z-score	B,P	+	−.030 (−.288)	.004 (.073)	−.159 (−1.387)	−.019 (−.301)	−.128 (−1.552)	−.043 (−.628)
X4 Total assets	B / P	− / +	3805.77 (2.167)*	660.67 (5.545)**	3247.33 (2.610)**	448.98 (4.967)**	1657.34 (3.210)**	528.04 (6.439)**
X5 Net sales	B / P	− / +	880.17 (3.105)**	275.07 (4.247)**	792.03 (2.014)*	284.42 (4.118)**	604.28 (3.476)**	280.52 (5.698)**
X6 Market value of equity	B / P	− / +	−37.03 (−.092)	182.76 (5.019)**	339.82 (2.369)*	128.17 (4.141)**	673.44 (3.671)**	147.12 (5.623)**
X7 Dividends	B,S	+	11.686 (1.495)	4.748 (4.162)**	19.139 (2.107)*	4.150 (3.445)**	23.598 (3.036)**	3.565 (4.098)**
X8 Price/earnings ratio	B,S	+	−1.604 (−.116)	.344 (1.172)	13.106 (1.448)	.334 (1.760)*	−3.353 (−.201)	.392 (.277)
X9 Tax rate	TX	+	.002 (.086)	−.514 (.183)	.002 (.116)	−.005 (−.670)	−.008 (−.449)	.000 (.886)

[a] Mean paired difference between the proxy variable for the hedging firm and its matched nonhedging control firm. The t-statistic tests whether the average difference is significantly different from zero.

[b] Median paired difference between the proxy variable for the hedging firm and its matched nonhedging control firm. The t-statistic tests whether the average difference is significantly different from zero. The Wilcoxon statistic examines the sum of the ranks of differences.

[c] D stands for debt covenant hypothesis, B for bankruptcy cost hypothesis; S for signalling hypothesis; P for political cost hypothesis; TX for tax hypothesis.

* Significant at the 0.05 level; ** at the .01 level.

Table 28.4 (continued): Univariate Analysis of Hedging Decision

Variables	Theory[c]	Pred. Sign	1986		1987		All Years	
			Mean[a] (t-stat)	Median[b] (Wilcoxon stat)	Mean (t-stat)	Median (Wilcoxon stat)	Mean (t-stat)	Median (Wilcoxon stat)
X1 Net income/interest expense ratio	D	–	10.026 (.895)	-.029 (-.291)	-32.648 (-1.401)	-.001 (-1.276)	-13.951 (-.951)	-.054 (-.512)
X2 Debt/equity ratio	D	+	1.385 (1.321)	.404 (1.572)	5.799 (1.104)	.188 (.981)	2.588 (2.193)*	.254 (2.896)**
X3 Z-score	B,P	+	-.174 (-1.689)	-.052 (-.531)	.040 (.344)	-.013 (-.497)	-.148 (-1.941)	-.033 (-1.055)
X4 Total assets	B / P	– / +	1625.03 (2.086)	450.26 (6.622)	1134.31 (1.211)	391.49 (6.672)**	2013.80 (2.917)**	323.22 (7.730)
X5 Net sales	B / P	– / +	664.96 (2.048)	227.05 (5.885)**	928.93 (3.254)**	297.81 (5.661)**	1065.30 (3.234)**	234.31 (8.424)**
X6 Market value of equity	B / P	– / +	388.22 (2.039)*	163.85 (6.718)**	784.55 (3.653)**	174.54 (6.636)**	338.42 (1.853)*	150.54 (7.966)**
X7 Dividends	B,S	+	2.467 (.168)	2.748 (4.741)**	22.254 (2.389)**	4.036 (4.904)**	10.892 (1.071)	2.083 (5.752)**
X8 Price/earnings ratio	B,S	+	-1.604 (-.116)	.344 (1.172)	13.106 (1.448)	.334 (1.760)*	-3.353 (-.201)	.392 (.277)
X9 Tax rate	TX	+	.002 (.086)	-.514 (.183)	.002 (.116)	-.005 (-.670)	-.008 (-.449)	.000 (.886)

[a] Mean paired difference between the proxy variable for the hedging firm and its matched nonhedging control firm. The t-statistic tests whether the average difference is significantly different from zero.

[b] Median paired difference between the proxy variable for the hedging firm and its matched nonhedging control firm. The t-statistic tests whether the average difference is significantly different from zero. The Wilcoxon statistic examines the sum of the ranks of differences.

[c] D stands for debt covenant hypothesis, B for bankruptcy cost hypothesis; S for signalling hypothesis; P for political cost hypothesis; TX for tax hypothesis.

* Significant at the 0.05 level; ** at the .01 level.

tios of the paired sample are generally positive, the differences are insignificant.

With few exceptions, mean and median differences in the average taxrates of hedger and control firms are positive, though the differences in tax rates is small (about 1–2 percent) and not statistically significant. In 1986, however, the average deviation in taxrates increased to about 4 percent (significant at the .01 level). The distribution of hedgers by year (reported in Table 28.3) provides further empirical support for the hypothesis that the Tax Reform Act of 1986 affected firms' hedging activities: while the proportion of hedger firms in the population steadily increased in the 1983–1986 period, there is a 4 percent decline in 1987.

Table 28.5 shows the Pearson correlations among the nine proxy variables and the decision to hedge or not to hedge. As expected, many of the variables are related: in particular, total assets (X4), net sales (X5), market value of equity (X6), dividend payments (X7) and average taxrates (X9).

Table 28.5: Pearson Correlation Coefficients Between Proxy Variables

Variable	X1	X2	X3	X4	X5	X6	X7	X8	X9	X10
X1	1.000									
X2	−.007	1.000								
X3	.086*	−.095*	1.000							
X4	−.020	.116*	−.242**	1.000						
X5	−.018	.025	.013	.542**	1.000					
X6	−.016	−.015	.030	.338**	.594**	1.000				
X7	−.019	−.002	−.005	.349**	.506**	.539**	1.000			
X8	.001	−.008	.030	.016	.010	.023	.004	1.000		
X9	.036	−.020	.350**	−.041	.129*	.136*	.077*	.065*	1.000	
X10	.001	.036	−.031	.109*	.118*	.096*	.062*	.019	.034	1.000

* Significant at .05 confidence level; ** at the .01 level.

Variable definitions:

$X1_{it}$ = firm i's net income/interest expense ratio in year t.
$X2_{it}$ = firm i's debt/equity ratio in year t.
$X3_{it}$ = Altman's [1983] bankruptcy index (Z-score) for firm i in year t.
$X4_{it}$ = firm i's total assets in year t.
$X5_{it}$ = firm i's net sales in year t.
$X6_{it}$ = firm i's market value of equity in year t.
$X7_{it}$ = firm i's dividend payments in year t.
$X8_{it}$ = firm i's price-earnings ratio in year t.
$X9_{it}$ = firm i's average tax rate in year t.
$X10_{it}$ = dummy variable capturing hedging decision; $X10_{it} = 1$ if firm i hedges in year t; $X10_{it} = 0$ otherwise.

B. Multivariate Tests. Because several of the hypotheses offered to explain why firms hedge rely on the same proxy variables, it is difficult to isolate the "best" explanation from the univariate tests. For example, Zimmerman's (1983) finding that larger firms have higher tax rates than small firms makes it difficult for the univariate tests to discriminate between the political cost and tax hypotheses. In this section, the variables are examined simultaneously in a multivariate logit analysis. Four logit models are reported: each model contains one of the debt covenant and signalling variables plus the other proxy variables. (Because the size variables produce similar results, only the models that include net sales are reported.) Analyses 1 and 2 (3 and 4) use dividends to measure managerial ability (price-earnings ratio), but differ in their measurement of the restrictiveness of debt covenants—the ratio of net income to interest expense in Analyses 1 and 3 and the ratio of total debt to the book value of equity in Analyses 2 and 4.

The models are estimated using the pooled sample, where the data consist of observations on the proxy variables for each firm contained in the hedger and nonhedger samples. The variables included in each analysis, the sign of the coefficient predicted by the appropriate underlying hypothesis, and t-statistics on the estimated coefficients are reported in Panel A, Table 28.6. The explanatory power of the models is less than 2 percent; this is not surprising given the correlations between the proxy variables and the hedge decision variable documented in Table 28.5. However, the values of the log-likelihood function reject the hypothesis of no association between the explanatory and dependent variables at the .0001 level.

the results show that while leverage is of the hypothesized (positive) sign, it is not significant in either analysis 1 or 3. The coefficient on the interest coverage ratio is also insignificant in analyses 2 and 4. Coefficients on the size variables are inconsistent with the bankruptcy argument, but support H4, the political cost hypothesis. Further, after controlling for other variables, the bankruptcy index, tax and signalling variables are insignificant in explaining the hedging decision, though the signs of the coefficients are generally consistent with H2, H5 and H6, respectively.

A logit model is also estimated for each subsample period. The subsample results, reported in Panel B, Table 28.6 for Analysis 1, do not support the debt covenant, bankruptcy cost or managerial ability hypotheses. The political cost explanation is supported in 1983, 1985, and 1987, while the 1986 period shows a significant positive association between the decision to hedge and firms' average tax rates.

Overall, the multivariate analyses reveal that the most significant variable affecting the sample firms' hedging decisions is size. While hedging decisions made in 1986 support the tax hypothesis, there is little evidence from the other subperiods to support the tax, debt covenant, bankruptcy

Table 28.6: Multivariate Analysis of Hedging Decision

Panel A: Pooled Data (1983–1987) from Hedger and Nonhedger Samples

Variables	Theory	Pred. Sign	#1	#2	#3	#4
Intercept			−1.51	−1.04	−1.18	−.81
X1 Net income/interest expense ratio	D	−	n/i	.20	n/i	.14
X2 Debt/equity ratio	D	+	1.20	n/i	1.11	n/i
X3 Z-score	B,S	+	−1.49	−.69	−1.30	−.37
X4 Total assets	P	+	n/i	n/i	n/i	n/i
	B	−				
X5 Net sales	P	+	4.58**	3.14**	5.36**	5.23**
	B	−				
X6 Market value of equity	P	+	n/i	n/i	n/i	n/i
	B	−				
X7 Dividends	S	+	−.94	.36	n/i	n/i
X8 Price/earnings ratio	S	+	n/i	n/i	.77	.40
X9 Average taxrate	TX	+	1.09	.71	.69	.35
Estimated R^2			.012	.010	.012	.010
% Correctly Predicted			59.0%	59.6%	59.1%	61.7%
Model Chi Square			34.36	29.48	35.30	28.38

Panel B: Data from Hedger and Nonhedger Subsamples During 1983–1987

Variables	Theory	Pred. Sign	1983	1984	1985	1986	1987
Intercept			−.22	−.32	−.46	−.96	−1.14
X1 Net Income/interest expense ratio	D −1.34	−	.79	1.15	−1.24	.73	
X3 Z-score	B,S	+	−.79	1.15	−1.24	.73	−1.34
X5 Net sales	P	+	2.53**	0.24	2.94**	.44	1.94*
	B	−					
X7 Dividends	S	+	−1.07	1.09	−.94	.62	−.22
X9 Average taxrate	TX	+	−.24	.00	−.73	2.42**	−.22
Estimated R^2			.004	.001	.001	.001	.008
% Correctly Predicted			62.5%	59.1%	63.9%	56.9%	60.7%
Model Chi Square			9.85	6.49	14.00	10.28	11.80

n/i Variable is not included in the model.
Entry is t-statistic of the estimated coefficient of each proxy variable.
D stands for debt covenant hypothesis; B for bankruptcy cost hypothesis; S for signalling hypothesis; P for political cost hypothesis; Tx for tax hypothesis.
* Significant at .05 level; ** at .01 level.

cost or managerial ability arguments. Two points should be noted, however. First, because firm size is correlated with dividens and tax rates, it is difficult to discriminate among the political cost, signalling or tax explanations. To verify this, the logit results were rerun excluding the size variable. In each case, the coefficient on the dividend or tax rate variable is significantly positive, and the explanatory power of the model is only slightly reduced. Second, the lack of support for the alternative hedging explanations does not preclude the possibility that some firms in the sample hedge for those reasons.

C. Time Series Tests. The univariate and multivariate tests attempt to identify cross-sectional characteristics of firms that disclosed hedging behavior by comparison to a control sample of same-industry firms with similar earnings volatility. Those tests are not designed to address whether firms that hedge, say to reduce expected bankruptcy costs, are successful in this endeavor. Therefore, we examine time-series changes in the proxy variables, and compare these signed differences across hedger and control firms. If firms hedge for the reasons noted in section II, and if they successfully implement these hedges, then we expect to observe systematic patterns in the signed differences. For example, if firm i hedges in 1983 to reduce expected bankruptcy costs, then we expect that the difference in firm i's bankruptcy index between 1983 and 1984 ($X3_{i,1983} - X3_{i,1984}$) will be positive (since a higher Z-score indicates a lower probability of bankruptcy). Similar arguments hold for the other hedging explanations, and are encompassed in hypotheses H7-H9.

To test hypotheses H7-H9, first compute differences of the proxy variables for all firms with available data for each pair of sample years (t, $t+1$): (1983, 1984); (1984, 1985); (1985, 1986); (1986, 1987). The number of matched hedger firms in each of these samples was, respectively, 108, 151, 199 and 195. We also examine the cumulative five-year difference (t, $t+5$) in each proxy variable for the sample of 44 firms that hedged in all sample years.

Table 28.7 reports the frequency of predicted sign differences for each proxy variable. Chi-square statistics, which test whether the cell frequencies are independent, are also shown. Consistent with H7-H9, we find that most (33/45 or 73%) of the proportions exceed 50 percent, suggesting that the majority of hedger firms implement "successful" hedges, i.e., hedges that result in changes in the proxy variables that are consistent with the motivations for hedging. However, with the exceptions of the size variables, few of the chi-square statistics indicate significant differences in the frequency of positive and negative changes in proxy variables between hedger and control firms. While 28 of the possible 45 combinations of change years and proxy variables (five differences × nine variables), are in the posited direction (i.e., cases where the fraction of hedgers with predicted direction differences exceeds that of the fraction

Table 28.7: Analysis of Time Series Differences in Proxy Variables For Hedger Versus Control Firms[a]

Variable[b]	Pred Dir.[c]	1984–83	1985–84	Difference[d] 1986–85	1987–86	5 Yr.-Cum.
$\Delta X1$	+	51/59 (2.175)	64/59 (1.131)	57/58 (0.007)	59/51 (1.715)	61/58 (0.079)
$\Delta X2$	−	49/56 (1.596)	60/46 (7.616)**	40/51 (3.666)*	46/46 (0.013)	49/45 (0.140)
$\Delta X3$	+	46/47 (0.164)	40/35 (1.318)	24/35 4.063)**	59/63 (0.396)	29/32 (0.148)
$\Delta X4$	−/+	77/71 (1.593)	82/70 (7.424)**	81/80 (0.041)	81/78 (0.275)	88/77 (1.894)
$\Delta X5$	−/+	89/67 (5.669)*	76/65 (5.510)*	65/71 (1.125)	90/86 (0.859)	88/77 (1.894)
$\Delta X6$	−/+	46/41 (1.040)	75/58 (11.871)**	82/83 (0.064)	54/60 (0.686)	76/63 (1.722)
$\Delta X7$	+	78/74 (0.938)	76/68 (2.323)	73/83 (3.683)*	82/82 (0.003)	82/77 (0.271)
$\Delta X8$	+	38/38 (0.010)	51/48 (0.377)	74/76 (0.135)	41/48 (1.223)	51/54 (0.081)
$\Delta X9$	−	59/56 (0.231)	42/44 (0.245)	54/51 (0.226)	51/53 (0.089)	48/36 (1.429)

[a] Cell entry is (the percentage of hedger firms with differences in predicted direction) divided by (the percentage of non-hedger firms with differences in predicted direction). Chi-square statistics for independence in the frequency of positive and negative differences across hedger and control firms are in parentheses.
[b] Variable definitions are reported in Table 5. Δ indicates the change in the variable computed over the noted time periods.
[c] Predicted direction is the sign of the difference posited in hypotheses H7-H9. For X4-X6, the cell frequencies relate to the + predicted sign.
[d] Paired year difference is the difference in the value of the proxy variable for the hedger (control) firm computed over successive years (i.e., $X3_{i,t}+1 - X3_{i,t}$). 5-Year Cumulative difference is the difference in the value of the proxy variable for those firms that are included in all five sample years (i.e., $X3_{i,t}+5 - X3_{i,t}$).
* Significant at .05 level; ** at .01 level.

of non-hedgers), 15 of these combinations relate to the size variables which have both positive and negative predicted directions. Excluding the size variables, we find that about half of the differences are in the directions predicted by H7 and H8. This is precisely the percentage that one might expect to observe by chance.

Table 28.8: Analysis of Mean and Median Time Series Differences in Proxy Variables for Hedger Versus Control Firms[a]

Variable[b]	Pred. Dir.[c]	1984–83	1985–84	Difference[d] 1986–85	1987–86	5 Yr.-Cum.
$\Delta X1$	+	−1.231 (0.672)	1.571 (−.982)	0.228 (0.242)	−1.445 (0.208)	−1.254 (0.388)
$\Delta X2$	−	1.123 (2.100)**	−1.291 (−3.383)**	1.356 (1.229)	0.485 (−.395)	−1.326 (−.509)
$\Delta X3$	+	2.259** (−.253)	0.942 (1.259)	0.789 (−.782)	-0.645 (−.552)	0.856 (−.228)
$\Delta X4$	+/−	0.093 (−2.843)**	2.176** (3.813)**	2.591** (2.515)**	20.043** (2.137)**	1.695* (1.433)
$\Delta X5$	+/−	1.669* (4.727)**	0.784 (3.518)**	0.016 (0.764	2.078** (3.864)**	1.192 (2.706)**
$\Delta X6$	+/−	0.633 (.0579)	2.474** (4.136)**	2.480** (2.826)**	−.896 (−.246)	1.768* (1.768)*
$\Delta X7$	+	−0.352 (2.373)**	-0.517 (2.559)**	−0.382 (0.102)	0.161 (1.950)*	0.273 (1.621)
$\Delta X8$	+	−0.665 (0.905)	1.509 (−.920)	−1.052 (0.281)	1.456 (−.706)	−0.106 (−.750)
$\Delta X9$	−	−0.360 (−.889)	−1.422 (1.163)	−0.173 (−.030)	0.376 (0.137)	−0.936 (−1.001)

[a] Top row of cell entry is the Z-statistic for the mean difference between (the change in hedger i's value of the proxy variable over the appropriate years) minus (the change in hedger i's matched control firm's proxy variable for the same years). Wilcoxon statistics (in parentheses) test median differences between the change variables for the hedger and control firms.
[b] Variable definitions are reported in Table 5.
[c] Predicted direction is the sign of the difference posited in H7-H9.
[d] Paired year difference is the difference in the value of the proxy variable for the hedger (control) firm computed over successive years (i.e., $X3_{i,t}+1-X3_{i,t}$). 5-Year Cumulative difference is the difference in the value of the proxy variable for those firms that are included in all five sample years (i.e., $X3_{i,t}+t-X3_{i,t}$).
* Significant at .05 level; ** at .01 level.

The generally weak results reported in Table 28.7 may be due to several factors. First, the frequency tests use only the signs of the differences, not their magnitudes. Incorporating information about the magnitudes of the differences may yield stronger results. To address this concern, we compare mean and median first differences in the proxy variables for each pair of sample years and for the cumulative five-year period. Table 28.8 reports Z- and Wilcoxon statistics which test whether mean and median values of the time series changes are significantly different for hedger and nonhedger firms. Both the parametric and nonparametric tests note significant positive differences for the size variables. With some exceptions, the other comparisons are not significant. A focus on the cumulative five-year sample indicates, however, some support for H7 and H8: there is some empirical evidence that over the five-year horizon leverage and tax rates declined, and interest coverage ratios, dividend payments and Z-scores increased.

Second, the weak frequency and univariate results reported in Tables 28.7 and 28.8 may be due to sample restrictions. Specifically, in most cases, the sample time series does not include the year prior to the year in which the firm first disclosed hedging behavior. If the immediate gains (for example, in terms of reduced probability of bankruptcy or increased flexibility of debt covenant restrictions) are large relative to subsequent gains realized by hedging, then our results, which exclude the first change, are conservative.

VI. Conclusion

This study examines systematic differences in the characteristics of hedging and nonhedging firms using cross-sectional and time-series tests. Five theories about firms' hedging decisions are explored: debt covenant restrictions, bankruptcy costs, political costs, taxes and managerial incentives to communicate ability. The univariate tests support the debt covenant, political cost and signalling hypotheses, but do not provide strong evidence consistent with tax motivations to hedge or the theory that firms hedge to avoid bankruptcy costs. The multivariate tests, which assess each hypothesis separately, do not support the debt covenant or bankruptcy cost explanations, but provide strong evidence favoring the political cost explanation. Consistent with several of the explanations, the time series results show some evidence that over time hedger firms experience reductions in the restrictiveness of debt covenants, the probability of bankruptcy and tax rates; and increases in size and managerial ability. Also, the frequency and magnitude of the time series differences in the proxy variables appears to be greater for hedgers than nonhedgers, though only the size variables are statistically significant.

In summary, we find that the primary factor distinguishing hedger versus nonhedger firms is their size, and that over time, hedger firms increase their size differential. While these results support both the bankruptcy and political cost motivations, it is difficult to rule out the tax or signalling explanations because of the high degree of association between firm size and the tax and managerial ability proxy variables. Consequently, it appears that the most important variables affecting a firm's decision to hedge are its size, dividend policy and average tax rate.

REFERENCES

Altman, E. 1983. *Corporate Financial Distress*, New York: John Wiley.

Anderson, R. and J. Danthine. 1980. Hedging and joint production: Theory and illustration, *Journal of Finance* 35, 487–497.

Bhattacharya, S. 1979. Imperfect information, dividend policy and the 'bird in the hand' fallacy, *Bell Journal of Economics* 10, 259–70.

Breeden, D. and S. Viswanathan. 1990. Why do firms hedge? An asymmetric information model, Duke University working paper.

Diamond, D. 1984. Financial intermediation and delegated monitoring, *Review of Economic Studies*, 393–414.

Ho, T. and A. Saunders. 1983. Fixed rate loan commitments, take down risk, and the dynamics of hedging with futures, *Journal of Financial and Quantitative Analysis* 18, 499–516.

John, K. and J. Williams. 1984. Dividends, dilution, and taxes: A signalling equilibrium, *Journal of Finance* 40, 1053–70.

Kelly, L. 1985. Corporate management lobbying on FAS No. 8: Some Further Evidence, *Journal of Accounting Research*, Autumn, 619–32.

Mayers, D. and C. Smith. 1987. Corporate insurance and the underinvestment problem, *Journal of Risk and Insurance* 54, 45–54.

Press, E. and J. Weintrop. 1990. Accounting-based constraints in public and private debt agreements: Their association with leverage and impact on accounting choice, *Journal of Accounting and Economics* 1–3, 65–96.

Shapiro, A. and S. Titman. 1985. An integrated approach to corporate risk management, *Midland Corporate Finance Journal* 3, 41–56.

Smith, C. and R. Stultz. 1985. The determinants of firms' hedging policies, *Journal of Financial and Quantitative Analysis* 20, 391–405.

Smith, C. and J. Warner. 1979. On financial contracting: An analysis of bond covenants, *Journal of Financial Economics* 7, 117–61.

Watts, R. and J. Zimmerman. 1978. Towards a positive theory of the determination of accounting standards, *Accounting Review* 53, 112–134.

Zimmerman, J. 1983. Taxes and firm size, *Journal of Accounting and Economics* 5, 119–149.

GLOSSARY

Tanya Styblo Beder, Robert J. Schwartz and Clifford Smith, Jr.

All-or-Nothing Option: An option that provides for the payment of a fixed amount for a fixed period of time, only if the purchase or sale of an asset or index is beyond a stated level over the life of the option.

American Option: A contract that gives the holder the right to either (1) purchase from or (2) to sell to the writer of the option a specified amount of commodities or securities at a stated price. The contract is good for a specific period of time and may be exercised *at any time* up to its maturity date.

American Stock Exchange: AMEX or ASE is the second largest securities exchange in the United States. Listed stocks, bonds and options are traded on the AMEX.

American Window: An exercise period at the end of an option's life that allows the owner to exercise anytime within that window. Cheaper than an American-style option that allows exercise anytime over the life of the option.

Arbitrage: Strictly speaking, the simultaneous purchase of a commodity or security in one market and its immediate sale in another. Often used for the purchase of an underpriced security and the simultaneous sale of a security with similar characteristics with the expectation of a resumption of a more normal price relationship. Stock arbitrageurs are those who purchase a security with the expectation that it can be sold to a prospective corporate acquirer.

Asian Option: An option on an average of rates. Alternately, an option with windows of one or more American Options.

Asset Swap: Refers to (1) the application of an interest-rate swap to transform the rate of return on a given asset from fixed to floating, or vice versa; and, (2) the application of a currency swap to transform the rate of return on a given asset from one currency to a different currency.

Balloon: A payment to principal in a loan that is larger than the normal periodic payment. Typically occurs at the maturity.

Bank Basis: See Money Market Basis.

Basis Point: One one-hundredth of a percent. [1/100 of 1%]. Used to measure the yield or cost of debt instruments.

Bear Spread: An options strategy utilizing puts and calls that provides the greatest return when the price of the underlying stock bond, commodity or currency drops and experiences the greatest risk when the price rises. Contrast with bull spread.

Bid: An offer to buy a security at a specified price.

Bond: A borrowing evidenced by an obligation to repay a determinable amount at a future date.

Bull Spread: An options strategy utilizing puts and calls that provides the greatest return when the price of the underlying security rises and the maximum risk when the price drops. Contrast with bear spread.

Bullet: Repayment of principal on a loan that occurs only at maturity.

Butterfly Spread: An options strategy utilizing two calls and two puts on the same or different securities with several maturity dates.

Calendar Spread: An options strategy utilizing the purchase and sale of options on the same security with different maturities.

Call: Definition (1): A contract that gives the holder the right to purchase from the writer of the option a specified amount of commodities or securities at a stated price. This contract is good for a specific period of time. Definition (2): A contract that gives the issuer of securities (e.g., corporation, mortgagor, etc.) the right to prepay all or a portion of its borrowing obligation. This contract may be good on specific dates or during specific periods of time, for which specific redemption/refunding prices are provided.

Call Provision: An issuer's right to redeem a security at a predetermined price utilizing a set formula on or after a certain date.

Cancellable Foreign Exchange Contract: A forward foreign exchange contract where the purchaser has the unilateral right to cancel the contract after a specified date.

Cap: A contract giving the purchaser the right to receive from the seller a payment that equals the amount that a floating-rate index exceeds a stated level (the agreed-upon cap level) during a specific period of time. In addition, the contract specifies the principal amount upon which the (potential) payments are to be made.

Capital Adequacy: The concept that all on- and off-balance sheet items entail an inherent credit risk and that a minimum of capital must be available to offset potential losses.

Caption: A contract that gives the holder the right to purchase from the writer a cap on a specific floating rate-index for a stated period of time at a set price.

Ceiling: See Cap.

CTFC: The Commodities Futures Trading Commission—an independent government agency whose board is appointed by the President of the United States which has responsibility for regulating the U.S. futures exchanges.

Chicago Board of Trade: The CBOT is the United States' largest exchange for the trading of futures contracts. The CBOT trades commodity, currency and fixed income futures. Parent organization of the Chicago Board Options Exchange.

Chicago Board Options Exchange: An exchange sponsored by the Chicago Board of Trade (CBOT) and registered with appropriate regulators to trade standardized options contracts through the Options Clearing Corporation.

Chicago Mercantile Exchange: The second largest commodities exchange in the United States. Parent of the International Monetary Market.

Clean Risk: The risk in a settlement of a foreign exchange transaction that one party will fail to deliver its currency after it has received the counterparty's payment. The full amount is therefore at risk. Can be mitigated by escrow arrangements or by net payments through conversion to a common currency. Same as overnight risk.

Collateral: An obligation, security, cash or asset provided in conjunction with another obligation to secure its performance.

Collateralized Mortgage Obligation: A borrowing obligation backed by a group (or pool) of mortgages. Typically a "CMO" consists of a series of bonds (or tranches) that receive the cash flow of the mortgage pool sequentially. The payments made to investors may be in the form of fixed or floating interest rates (floating-rate tranches typically include a series of caps), plus principal repayments.

Commercial Paper: An unsecured and short-term note issued by a credit-worthy corporation or financial institution for up to a maximum of 270 days (if it is to be unregistered). Maturity and structure is negotiable.

Commodity Option: An option to buy or sell a put or a call on a specific commodity at a predetermined price and date.

Commodity (Price) Swap: An agreement between two parties specifying the exchange of future payments based on a commodity index. Typically parties exchange a fixed for a floating rate (e.g., West Texas Intermediate spot vs. a fixed price per barrel). The calculation is based on a notional amount of the commodity and the commodity is not typically delivered.

Compound Interest: Reinvestment of each interest payment at the current rate.

Compound Option: An option on an option. Example: Caption.

Contract Month: The month in which futures contracts may be satisfied by accepting or making delivery.

Conversion: As related to options, the process where a put can be changed to a call and a call to a put. In the context of the capital markets, a conversion is typically the exercise of the right to change a convertible bond to equity.

Covered: When a position with options is offset to a one-to-one basis with the underlying instrument.

Covered Writer: A call writer who owns the underlying stock or a put writer who is short the stock.

Credit Risk: A risk existing in financial transactions where there is an exposure to receiving cash flow(s) from another party. Examples: an issuer may default on its borrowing obligation, or a counterparty/option writer may not meet the payment/delivery requirements of its swap agreement, cap contract, and so on.

Currency Exchange Agreement: See Currency Swap.

Currency Swap: An agreement between two parties that specifies the exchange of future payments in one currency for future payments in another currency. The exchange of interest payments and principal payments (typically at maturity) are included in the agreement.

Cycle: The expiration date of the three groups of options: Jan/Apr/Jul/Oct, Feb/May/Aug/Nov and Mar/Jun/Sep/Dec.

Debenture: Unsecured debt, typically long term.

Debt-Equity Warrant: A contract that gives the holder the right to purchase from the issuer of the warrant a specified amount of debt or equity securities at a given price. Debt-equity warrants may be issued for stated periods of time, or on a perpetual basis.

Delivery Risk: A risk that exists in financial transactions where there is an exposure to receiving cash flows/securities in different time zones. An example is the risk that a currency swap payment may be required to be made prior to the close of business in one time zone, while the related currency swap inflow payment may not be able to be made until the opening of business in a different time zone.

Delta: The expected change in the option value given a small change in the price of the underlying asset, with all other things constant.

Derivative Product: Typically an instrument that is created (derived) through a combination of cash market instruments. Derivative Products is used to refer to swaps, options, FRAs, futures and securities with the preceding instruments imbedded within. They may be interest, currency, commodity or equity based.

Difference Option: An option that provides for the purchase or sale of the difference between two assets relative to a fixed price spread for a fixed period of time.

Discount: An instrument trading at less than its face value.

Down and Out Call: A call option that expires if the market price of the underlying instrument falls below a predetermined level.

Downside Protection: Utilizing options or other hedges, the protection against a decrease in prices in the underlying instrument.

Dual Currency Bond: A security that typically pays interest in one currency and principal in a second currency.

Dual Index Floaters: A floating rate security that pays interest based on a spread calculation on more than one floating rate index. An example would be a certificate of deposit which pays the higher of (1) 3 month LIBOR, or (2) 3 month T-Bill plus 100 basis points.

Equity Swap: An agreement between two parties specifying the exchange of future payments based on an equity index and second index. The second index can be an interest rate (e.g., LIBOR), another equity index (e.g., S&P vs. Nikkei), a single stock or series of stocks, a commodity price index, etc. The calculation is based on a notional amount of the equities and the equities are not typically exchanged.

Eurodollar: A U.S. dollar that is originated and held in a European country. Eurodollars may be created through U.S. dollar denominated bank deposits in foreign countries, or through other foreign U.S. dollar denominated transactions (e.g., loans, bankers' acceptances, bond underwritings, etc.).

European Option: A contract giving the holder the right to either (1) purchase from or (2) sell to the writer of the option a specified amount of commodities or securities at a stated price. The contract is good for a specific period of time and may be exercised *only* on its maturity date.

Exercise Price: As related to options, the price at which an option is exercisable.

Expiration Date: The date after which an option or futures contract is void.

Fair Option Value: The theoretical value of an option utilizing a probability based option valuation model.

Federal (Fed) Funds: Deposits by financial institutions at Federal Reserve Banks. Banks often lend these deposits to each other at overnight or longer Fed Funds rates.

Federal Home Loan Bank Board: Formerly the primary regulator for the savings and loan industry. Succeeded by the Office of Thrift Supervision.

Federal Home Loan Mortgage Corp: Freddie Mac, as the FHLMC is often known, provides liquidity in the secondary market for conventional mortgages.

Federal Reserve Bank: The central bank of the United States of America whose primary responsibility is to manage the money supply and financial markets and ensure the stability of the financial system.

Floor-Ceiling: For a given principal amount, a contract that gives the purchaser the right to receive from the seller a payment which equals the amount that a floating rate index exceeds a stated level (the agreed upon ceiling level) during a specific period of time. In addition, the floor-ceiling contract requires the purchaser to provide to the seller a payment which equals the amount that a floating rate index falls below a stated level (the floor level) during that same period of time.

FNMA: The Federal National Mortgage Association was established in 1938 to improve the liquidity of the mortgage market. In 1968, when the Government National Mortgage Association was formed (see "GNMA") FNMA became a government-sponsored, but privately owned corporation. Under regulation by the Secretary of Housing and Urban Development, FNMA buys and sells FHA-insured or VA-guaranteed residential mortgages. Funds for such purchases are raised via the sale of corporate obligations in the capital markets.

Forward Exchange Contract: An agreement between two or more parties to exchange payments in two or more currencies at a specified exchange rate (forward rate) on a given date (or series of dates).

Future: A contract traded on an exchange that gives the holder the right to buy or sell a specified amount of commodities or securities at a stated price and date in the future.

Gamma: The expected change in the Delta of an option given a small change in the value of the underlying asset, other things constant.

GNMA: The Government National Mortgage Association was established in 1968 as a corporation within the Department of

Housing and Urban Development (it is 100% owned by the U.S. Government). The main businesses of GNMA are (1) to buy and sell certain Federal Housing Administration (FHA) and Veteran's Administration (VA) mortgages in order to support the housing market; (2) to provide a guarantee for mortgage-backed securities which are issued against pools of FHA and VA mortgages; and, (3) to manage the operations, assets and liabilities of the Federal National Mortgage Association's (FNMA) Special Assistance and Managing and Liquidating Functions which were transferred to GNMA in 1968.

Haircut: The difference between the amount received by the borrower in a repo transaction and the higher amount (typically the market value of the repoed securities) returned by the borrower to the lender at maturity. The term also refers to the amount of the security's value which may not be used to meet a collateral requirement.

Hedging: As related to futures, the sale or purchase of a contract as a substitute for the cash instrument. More generally, the substitution of one financial instrument with one or more cash instruments or synthetics so that the effect of subsequent movements in prices of the underlying instrument are largely offset by movements in the value of the hedge.

Hi-Low Floaters: A floating rate security that, at the time of issuance, pays a higher rate of return to investors (in the form of a greater spread to the floating rate index) but caps the possible ultimate return through the inclusion of a short put option.

Hi-Low Option: An option that provides for the purchase or sale of the difference between the high and low price of two assets relative to a fixed spread for a fixed period of time.

Immunization: The process of designing a portfolio of debt securities whose value is unaffected by changes in interest rates.

Interest Rate Swap: An agreement between two parties specifying the exchange of future payments based on interest rates. Typically, parties exchange a fixed rate of interest for a floating rate of interest (or vice versa)—transactions are also done in which parties exchange *types* of floating rate interest (e.g., 3 month LIBOR for 6 month LIBOR; the Prime rate for the Commercial Paper rate, etc.). The exchange of interest payments is based on a notional principal amount; there is no exchange of principal.

Internal Rate of Return: Definition (1): The rate of return or cost of funds implied by the interest flows and principal flows of a given transaction. Definition (2): The discount rate required to make the price of a security equal the sum of the discounted interest flows and principal flows of the security.

International Swap Dealers Association: ISDA is the preeminent voice to the public and regulators of users, dealers and associated firms involved in Derivative Products. ISDA is not a self regulatory organization. Membership encompasses virtually every major financial institution worldwide and issues the most definitive market data available.

Intrinsic Option Value: The market value of the option less the strike price of the security.

Inverted Yield Curve: Occurs when short-term interest rates exceed longer-term rates. See yield curve.

Ito's Lemma: A rule by which functions of certain random variables can be differentiated. Specifically, random variables whose movement can be described as a continuous Markov process in continuous time. (Note that a Markov process depends at most on the most recent observation.) The sample path of such a process will be continuous (it can be drawn without lifting the pen from the paper).

Knock-in Options: An option that provides for the purchase of a specified asset at a fixed price but does not commence until the price moves beyond a stated level (the "knock-in" level) over the life of the option.

Knock-out Options: An option that provides for the purchase of a specified asset at a fixed price but expire if the price moves beyond a stated level (the "knock-out"level) over the life of the option.

LIBOR: (London Interbank Offered Rate); The rates specified for maturities ranging from overnight to five years, at which major banks offer to make deposits denominated in Eurodollars available to other major banks.

Line of Credit: The maximum amount a financial institution will lend to a borrower.

London International Financial Futures Exchange: The LIFFE is the London Financial Futures Exchange which provides a market for futures on currencies and equity indices.

Lookback Option: An option that provides for the purchase or sale of a specified asset at the best price / strike achieved over the life of the option. For example, at the option's maturity the owner of a lookback call on IBM stock has the right to buy IBM at the lowest price that occurred over the life of the option.

Margin: The equity required to collateralize an investment position.

Marked-To-Market: The calculation and realization of the differential, if any, between (1) an asset's current value and most recently "booked" value; (2) a liability's current value and most recently "booked" value; or, (3) a risk management tool's current value and most recently "booked" value. The realization of the differential may be in the form of a positive or negative earnings charge, margin call, or collateral call.

Market Risk: The risk that exists in financial transactions in which there is an exposure to changing market prices of a security caused by changing interest rates and/or changing currency exchange rates.

Master Swap Agreement: A contract between two parties that specifies all definitions, non-trade detail elements and laws governing any swaps between the two parties. A master swap agreement enables the parties to execute one master agreement and transact multiple swaps through brief appendices to that master agreement, rather than executing multiple complete swap agreements.

Modified American Option: Also known as Semi-American Option, a contract that gives the holder the right to either (1) purchase from or (2) sell to the writer of the option a specified amount of commodities or securities at a stated price. The contract is good for a specified period and may be exercised at certain specific dates up to its maturity date.

Money Market Basis: The calculation methodology used to determine accrued interest owed on money market securities (T-bills, Federal Funds, Commercial Paper, Certificates of Deposit, Repurchase Agreements, and Bankers' Acceptances). The calculation requires that a security's rate of interest be multiplied by the actual number of days which have elapsed, and then be divided by the number of days in the accounting year for the particular market (typically 360 in Europe, and 365 in the United States).

Naked Option Writing: The act of writing an option without an underlying position in the security.

Net Present Value: The difference between the interest flows and principal flows of a given transaction discounted at a specified interest rate, less the initial investment/proceeds.

New York Futures Exchange: The NYFE is a wholly owned subsidiary of the New York Stock Exchange and provides a market for futures on Treasury bills, notes and bonds and on *GNMA* securities.

New York Mercantile Exchange: The NYMEX or MERC is a commodities exchange located in New York City that offers a market in futures on commodities and currencies.

New York Stock Exchange: The NYSE is the largest securities exchange in the United States.

Novation: In foreign exchange, when two or more currency payments are due on the same date novation provides for the cancellation of those trades and the substitution of one net payment.

Offset: Generally the right to net liabilities against assets of the same counterparty in a default.

Open Interest: The total number of a specific future contract not offset or satisfied.

Option: The right to buy or sell a security, asset, commodity or equity index at a given price (strike price) at or before a certain date.

Outperformance Option: An option that provides for the purchase or sale of the best performing of two assets over the life of the option.

Perpetual Floaters: A floating rate security with no maturity date.

Plain Vanilla: The simplest version of the use of a derivative or the creation of a derivative product.

Premium: The price paid for an option.

Principal: The amount of debt that must be repaid.

Protected Strategy: A strategy to ensure that the value of a portfolio of instruments has minimal exposure to a change in prices. See Immunization.

Put: A contract that gives the holder the right to sell to the writer of the option a specified amount of commodities or securities at a stated price. This contract is good for a specific period of time.

Put-Call Parity Theorem: The relationship between European put and call options of the same maturity written on the same asset.

Range Forward: A forward foreign exchange contract specifying a maximum and minimum rate at which a future currency exchange will be made. If the spot two days prior to close falls within that range it becomes the contract rate. Otherwise the maximum or minimum prevail.

Rate Bet: An open position taken with a view towards profiting from an absolute movement in rates. Contrast with a hedged position.

Reinvestment Risk: The risk that the reinvestment of interim cashflows (e.g., interest payments) is exposed to changing interest rates or currency exchange rates.

Return On (Credit) Risk: A calculation that measures the performance of a financial institution or corporation in determining the income received on the credit risk incurred. Financial institutions typically determine the credit risk associated with a derivative product as a function of the notional principal amount. Credit risk is existent throughout the life of the transaction. Therefore the Return on Risk measures the performance over time.

Return On Assets: A calculation that measures the performance of a financial institution or corporation in using its assets (net of financing charges) to create earnings. Typically, the calculation is:

Return On Equity: A calculation that measures the performance of a financial institution or corporation in using its equity to create earnings. Typically, the calculation is:

Rho: The expected change in the value of an option given a small change in market interest rates, other things constant.

Safe Harbor: Financial markets and/or transactions which avoid tax or legal consequences. Also refers to the transfer of assets to less volatile sectors of the financial markets.

SEC: Securities and Exchange Commission—an independent government agency whose board is appointed by the President of the United States and with responsibility for regulation of the securities markets.

Short Sale: The sale of a security that the investor does not own and that the investor expects will fall in value.

Spot Exchange: The foreign exchange rate for immediate delivery, two days for most currencies.

Spread: Options: the purchase of one option and the sale of another on the same security. Swaps: the differential over or under the government securities curve at which the swap is executed.

Spreadlock: A forward commitment to enter into an interest rate swap at a swap spread which is specified in the contract. Although the contract sets the swap spread, it does not set the interest rate level to which the swap spread is applied. (The interest rate level is determined when the swap is entered into.)

Strike Price: See Exercise price.

Strip: Technically, a combination of two puts and one call, often used to refer to a series of futures spread over various maturities.

Stripped Mortgage Backed Security: A mortgage backed security which has been divided into two separately traded parts, (1) coupon payments, and (2) its principal portion which is traded independently from its coupon payments.

Super Floater: A floating rate security that pays a rate of return equal to a multiple of a specified floating rate index, less a fixed interest rate spread (e.g., 2 × 3 month LIBOR − 8%). These securities typically have caps (e.g., a maximum rate of 13%) and some have had floors (e.g., a minimum rate of 5%).

Swap Agreement: A contract between two parties specifying all definitions, trade detail elements and laws that will govern a particular swap between the two parties.

Swaption: A contract that gives the holder the right to either (1) purchase from or (2) sell to the writer of the swaption a specified amount and type of interest rate swaps or currency swaps at a stated price. The contract is good for a specific period of time and typically may be exercised only on its maturity date.

Synthetic Instruments: Two or more transactions that taken together have the effect of a financial instrument that may or may not exist by itself. For instance a floating rate note

(FRN) with an interest rate swap synthetically creates a fixed rate bond.

Term Structure Of Interest Rates: The relationship between the yield to maturity of similar securities of differing maturities.

Theta: The expected change in the option value given a small change in the option's term-to-expiration, other things constant.

Treasury Bills: Full faith and credit obligations of the United States government with original maturities of three months to one year.

Treasury Bond: Direct obligations of the U.S. government with an original maturity of more than ten years.

Treasury Note: Direct obligations of the U.S. government with an original maturity of more than one and less than ten years.

Uncovered Option: An option written without ownership of the underlying instrument.

Unwind: To terminate a transaction before its original end date by an exchange of payments reflecting its mark to market value.

Up And Out Put: A put option that expires if the market price of the underlying security rises above a predetermined price.

Vega: The expected change in option value given a small change in volatility, other things constant.

Volatility: A measure of the likelihood that prices, yields, returns, etc., will change over a given period. Generally, volatility is represented in the form of standard deviation of possible ending prices, yields, returns, etc.

Warrant: The right (option) to purchase a security at a given date or set of dates in the future at a predetermined price.

Yield: The return on an investment. The discount rate at which the net present value of cash flows is zero. The internal rate of return of the cash flows.

Yield Curve: A graph representing the relationship between maturity and yield for equivalent securities (e.g., a U.S. Treasury yield curve, an "AA" yield curve, an interest rate swap yield curve, etc.).

Yield Spread: Definition (1): The difference in yield between assets dissimilar in issuer or maturity. Alternatively the difference in yield between a financial institution's assets and liabilities. Definition (2): The graphical relationship between yields on similar securities of different tenors. Most readily constructed utilizing United States Treasury instruments because of the depth and breadth of the market.

Zero Coupon Bond: A debt security issued at a discount and redeemed at a par (or another stated amount) at maturity. As no periodic interest payments are made, the investor receives the rate of return represented by the difference between the issue/purchase price and the maturity/sale price.

Zero Coupon Swap: An interest rate swap in which a floating rate of interest is exchanged for a single, fixed rate payment at the maturity of the swap, or vice versa.

Zero Curve: A graph that represents the relationship between maturity and yield for equivalent zero-coupon securities (e.g., strips, zero coupon interest rate swaps, etc.).

Chapter 23 Appendix

CFTC PART 34—REGULATION OF HYBRID INSTRUMENTS
17 Code of Federal Regulations Part 34 (1993)

---

§34.1 Scope.

The provisions of this part shall apply to any hybrid instrument which may be subject to the Act, and which has been entered into on or after October 23, 1974.

§34.2 Definitions.

(a) *Hybrid instruments.* Hybrid instrument means an equity or debt security or depository instrument as defined in § 34.3(a)(1) with one or more commodity-dependent components that have payment features similar to commodity futures or commodity option contracts or combinations thereof.

(b) *Commodity-independent component.* Commodity-independent component means the component of a hybrid instrument, the payments of which do not result from indexing to, or calculation by reference to, the price of a commodity.

(c) *Commodity-independent value.* Commodity-independent value means the present value of the payments attributable to the commodity-independent component calculated as of the time of issuance of the hybrid instrument.

(d) *Commodity-dependent component.* A commodity-dependent component means a component of a hybrid instrument, the payment of which results from indexing to, or calculation by reference to, the price of a commodity.

(e) *Commodity-dependent value.* For purposes of application of Rule 34.3(a)(2), a commodity-dependent value means the value of a commodity dependent-component, which when decomposed into an option payout or payouts, is measured by the absolute net value of the put option premia with strike prices less than or equal to the reference price plus the absolute net value of the call option premia with strike prices less than or equal to the reference price plus the absolute net value of the call option premia with strike prices greater than or equal to the reference price, calculated as of the time of issuance of the hybrid instrument.

(f) *Option premium.* Option premium means the value of an option on the referenced commodity of the hybrid instrument, and calculated using the same method as that used to determine the issue price of the instrument, or where such premia are not explicitly calculated in determining the issue price of the instrument, the value of such options calculated using a commercially reasonable method appropriate to the instrument being priced.

(g) *Reference Price.* A reference price means a price nearest the current spot or forward price, whichever is used to price instrument, at which a commodity–dependent payment becomes non-zero, or, in the case where two potential reference prices exist, the price that results in the greatest commodity-dependent value.

§34.3 Hybrid instrument exemption.

(a) A hybrid instrument is exempt from all provisions of the Act and any person or class of persons offering, entering into, rendering advice or rendering other services with respect to such exempt hybrid instrument is exempt for such activity from all provisions of the Act (except in each case section 2(a)(1)(B)), provided the following terms and conditions are met:

(1) The instrument is:

(i) An equity or debt security within the meaning of section 2(1) of the Securities Act of 1933; or

(ii) A demand deposit, time deposit or transaction account within the meaning of 12 CFR 204.2 (b)(1), (c)(1) and (e), respectively, offered by an insured depository institution as defined in section 3 of the Federal Deposit Insurance Act; an insured credit union as defined in section 101 of the Federal Credit Union Act; or a Federal or State branch or agency of a foreign bank as defined in section 1 of the International Banking Act;

(2) The sum of the commodity-dependent values of the commodity-dependent components is less than the commodity-independent value of the commodity-independent component;

(3) Provided that:

(i) An issuer must receive full payment of the hybrid instrument's purchase price, and a purchaser or holder of a hybrid instrument may not be required to make additional out-of-pocket payments to the issuer during the life of the instrument or at maturity; and

(ii) The instrument is not marketed as a futures contract or a commodity option, or, except to the extent necessary to describe the functioning of the instrument or to comply with applicable disclosure requirements, as having the characteristics of a futures contract or a commodity option; and

(iii) The instrument does not provide for settlement in the form of a delivery instrument that is specified as such in the rules of a designed contract market;

(4) The instrument is initially issued or sold subject to applicable federal or state securities or banking laws to persons permitted thereunder to purchase or enter into the hybrid instrument.

INDEX